AF797649

ASCENT

CENTER FOR TECHNICAL KNOWLEDGE

Autodesk® 3ds Max® 2025 Fundamentals

Learning Guide

Mixed Units - Edition 1.0

ASCENT - Center for Technical Knowledge®
Autodesk® 3ds Max® 2025
Fundamentals

Mixed Units - Edition 1.0

Prepared and produced by:

ASCENT Center for Technical Knowledge
630 Peter Jefferson Parkway, Suite 175
Charlottesville, VA 22911

866-527-2368
www.ASCENTed.com

Lead Contributor: Renu Muthoo

ASCENT - Center for Technical Knowledge (a division of Rand Worldwide Inc.) is a leading developer of professional learning materials and knowledge products for engineering software applications. ASCENT specializes in designing targeted content that facilitates application-based learning with hands-on software experience. For over 25 years, ASCENT has helped users become more productive through tailored custom learning solutions.

We welcome any comments you may have regarding this guide, or any of our products. To contact us please email: feedback@ASCENTed.com.

AS-3DS2501-FND1MU-SG // IS-3DS2501-FND1MU-SG

Contents

Chapter 6: Materials 6-1

Preface

The *Autodesk® 3ds Max® 2025: Fundamentals* guide provides a thorough introduction to the Autodesk 3ds Max 2025 software that will help new users make the most of this sophisticated application, as well as broaden the horizons of existing, self-taught users. The guide instructs you on how to effectively use the software interface and navigate through the scenes. It explores the creation of 3D objects and how to bring in objects from other software such as Autodesk Revit, AutoCAD, and Civil 3D. Additionally, it teaches you to prepare the scenes for renderings by adding materials, lights, and cameras. Finally, the guide covers an understanding of various renderers included with the software, as well as image creation and animation techniques.

The practices in this guide are primarily geared towards real-world tasks encountered by users of the Autodesk 3ds Max software in the Architecture, Interior Design, and Civil Engineering industries. Advanced topics such as character modeling, character animation, and rigging are not covered in this guide.

Topics Covered

- Autodesk 3ds Max interface and workflow
- Assembling files by importing, linking, or merging
- 3D modeling with primitives and 2D objects
- Using modifiers to create and modify 3D objects
- Materials and maps
- Autodesk 3ds Max lighting
- Working with cameras and exposure control
- Rendering using various renderers, such as Arnold and ART
- Animation for visualization

Prerequisites

- Access to the 2025.0 version of the software, to ensure compatibility with this guide. Future software updates that are released by Autodesk may include changes that are not reflected in this guide. The practices and files included with this guide might not be compatible with prior versions (e.g., 2024).
- Experience with 3D modeling is recommended.

Note on Software Setup

This guide assumes a standard installation of the software using the default preferences during installation. Lectures and practices use the standard software templates and default options for the Content Libraries.

Note on Learning Guide Content

ASCENT's learning guides are intended to teach the technical aspects of using the software and do not focus on professional design principles and standards. The exercises aim to demonstrate the capabilities and flexibility of the software, rather than following specific design codes or standards, which can vary between regions.

Lead Contributor: Renu Muthoo

Renu is a learning content developer for Autodesk products at ASCENT. She has over 25 years of experience working with Autodesk products and specializes in AutoCAD and design visualization software.

Holding a bachelor's degree in Computer Engineering, Renu began her career as an Instructional Designer, co-authoring 3ds Max and AutoCAD books. At ASCENT, she continues her passion for instructional design by developing off the shelf and custom courseware for AutoCAD, AutoCAD Toolsets (Electrical, Mechanical, and Plant 3D), Autodesk 3ds Max, and other software products. An Autodesk Certified Professional in AutoCAD, Renu also enjoys educating users by sharing her knowledge through webcasts and blogs.

Renu Muthoo has been the Lead Contributor for *Autodesk 3ds Max: Fundamentals* since 2010.

In This Guide

The following highlights the key features of this guide.

Feature	Description
Practice Files	The Practice Files page includes a link to the practice files and instructions on how to download and install them. The practice files are required to complete the practices in this guide.
Chapters	A chapter consists of the following: Learning Objectives, Instructional Content, Practices, Chapter Review Questions, and Command Summary. • **Learning Objectives** define the skills you can acquire by learning the content provided in the chapter. • **Instructional Content**, which begins right after Learning Objectives, refers to the descriptive and procedural information related to various topics. Each main topic introduces a product feature, discusses various aspects of that feature, and provides step-by-step procedures on how to use that feature. Where relevant, examples, figures, helpful hints, and notes are provided. • **Practice** for a topic follows the instructional content. Practices enable you to use the software to perform a hands-on review of a topic. It is required that you download the practice files (using the link found on the Practice Files page) prior to starting the first practice. • **Chapter Review Questions**, located close to the end of a chapter, enable you to test your knowledge of the key concepts discussed in the chapter. • **Command Summary** concludes a chapter. It contains a list of the software commands that are used throughout the chapter and provides information on where the command can be found in the software.
Appendices	Appendices provide additional information to the main course content. It could be in the form of instructional content, practices, tables, projects, or skills assessment.

Practice Files

To download the practice files for this guide, use the following steps:

1. Type the URL *exactly as shown below* into the address bar of your Internet browser to access the Course File Download page.

   Note: If you are using the ebook, you do not have to type the URL. Instead, you can access the page by clicking the URL below.

   https://www.ascented.com/getfile/id/neotineaPF

2. On the Course File Download page, click the **DOWNLOAD NOW** button, as shown below, to download the .ZIP file that contains the practice files.

3. Once the download is complete, unzip the file and extract its contents.

   The recommended practice files folder location is:
   C:\Autodesk 3ds Max Fundamentals Practice Files

   Note: It is recommended that you do not change the location of the practice files folder. Doing so may cause errors when completing the practices.

> **Stay Informed!**
> To receive information about upcoming events, promotional offers, and complimentary webcasts, visit:
> **www.ASCENTed.com/updates**

Chapter 1

Introduction to Autodesk 3ds Max

The Autodesk® 3ds Max® software is a modeling, rendering, and animation package used for the visualization and presentation of scenes. Projects can be created and modeled in the software or files from other software packages can be linked/imported for use in the software. A solid understanding of the interface, configuration settings, and workflow used to create, render, and animate models enables you to visualize your models prior to building the final design.

Learning Objectives

- Identify the various data sources that can be imported into and then output from the Autodesk 3ds Max software.
- Understand the common workflow process to plan your visualization projects.
- Understand the various components of the interface.
- Set the preferences for the scene.
- Set the project folder to organize all of the files in the project.
- Set the path locations of reusable data files and reconfigurable items.
- Identify the display drivers available with the software.
- Identify the viewport display labels and the various options available in them.

1.1 Overview

The Autodesk® 3ds Max® software is a modeling, rendering, and animation package used for design visualization. It can be used to create high-quality 3D models, single-frame still renderings of virtually any size (including large-format presentation graphics), and desktop animations.

Input Into Autodesk 3ds Max

You can create geometry directly in the 3ds Max software or import it from multiple data sources, including the following:

- **AutoCAD® drawing files (.DWG, .DXF):** Including objects created in AutoCAD vertical applications, such as the AutoCAD® Architecture and Autodesk® Civil 3D® software.
- **Autodesk® Revit® Architecture designs:** Linked into the Autodesk 3ds Max software using .RVT files or the exported .FBX or .DWG files. The Autodesk® Revit® Structure and Autodesk® Revit® MEP software can also be imported using .DWG.
- **Autodesk® Civil 3D® (VSP3D):** Using **Autodesk Civil View**, you can import files from various civil design programs.
- **Autodesk® Inventor® files (.IPT, .IAM):** The Autodesk Inventor software must be installed on the same machine as the Autodesk 3ds Max software to import these files.
- **3D Studio Mesh format (.3DS):** A common data format used when transferring between 3D applications.
- Autodesk® Alias® .Wire files and the Autodesk® Showcase® .APF (Autodesk Packet File).
- LandXML and DEM data files.
- **Adobe® Illustrator® (.AI):** The Autodesk 3ds Max software only supports the Adobe Illustrator 88 software.

Vector Data

The input data formats are considered to be vector data. Graphics displayed from vector data formats are defined by point locations and mathematical formulas. Since their data is defined mathematically, vector graphics can be redrawn or regenerated at different scales or from different 3D viewpoints. The Autodesk 3ds Max software file format (.MAX file) is also a vector data file.

Output from Autodesk 3ds Max

The Autodesk 3ds Max software stores its data in vector-based .MAX files, used to generate raster images as final products. These images, called *renderings*, can be configured as simple illustrations or fully realized photorealistic images. The most common Autodesk 3ds Max animations are created by combining a series of individually-rendered raster images into a desktop animation file (e.g., Windows .AVI or QuickTime .MOV).

Raster Data

Raster graphics consist of a grid of colored points called pixels Pixels are viewed at a resolution at which they cannot be identified individually, and instead are permitted to present a unified image, as shown in Figure 1–1.

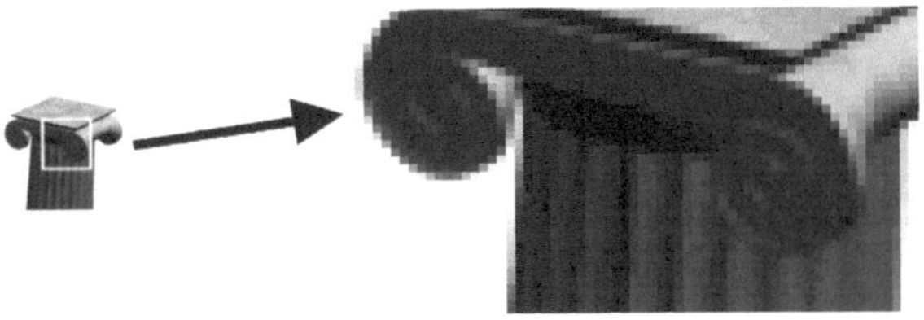

Figure 1–1

The Autodesk 3ds Max software is also used to create raster images or raster based animations (Autodesk 3ds Max renderings). Raster image renderings must be recreated (re-rendered) if the point-of-view is animated or otherwise changed. Common raster file formats include .JPEG, Windows bitmap (.BMP), and .TIFF files. They can also be used as input into the Autodesk 3ds Max software to supplement the vector geometry as follows:

- Scanned or digital photographs of a proposed construction site can be used as a background image.
- Images that illustrate material texture, such as wall coverings, wood grain, or a scratched metal surface.
- Image files created in other computer graphic applications can be used as signs, posters, or company logos.

1.2 Visualization Workflow

Each visualization project can be very different from the next, but most follow a common general workflow. A suggested approach to plan your visualization project is as follows.

1. Setting Goals and Expectations

Every project should start with a clear understanding of the deliverables and expectations.

- Determine viewpoints, animation paths, lighting conditions, etc. before modeling.
- Sketch a mock-up storyboard to agree on the content and scope of an animation.
- Incorporate resolution time in your time estimates. Simple oversights and design problems are often found during the visualization process.

2. Scene Creation and Modeling

The next step is to gather data together into scenes (.MAX files).

- Create a project folder to store all of your data and source material, such as site photos, textures, drawings, scans, in the appropriate locations.
- Import or link 2D or 3D data into one or more scene files, when it is available from other design applications.
- Merge together or externally reference scene files when a project requires multiple scene files.
- Add modeled geometry at this stage. The **Graphite Modeling** tools have many features for creating new geometry on the surfaces of imported files.

3. Material Design

Materials define how surfaces display and how light interacts with them. Often the next step is to configure the surface characteristics using the Material Editor. It is recommended that you consider the lighting and rendering as materials might need to be coordinated with renderers and lights.

- Detail materials to help simplify the geometry. For example, you do not need to model the grout along a brick wall. Material definitions, such as bump mapping, can add the appearance of depth.
- Fine-tune the material properties, as required, to make them realistic.
- Lighting and materials are often adjusted together, but it can be useful to have a first draft of your materials completed before adding lights.

4. Lighting Design

For realistic results, the 3D models need light sources to illuminate the objects.

- There are different approaches to lighting scenes in the Autodesk 3ds Max software, some are more straightforward and some are more technical.
- Most scenes might require lighting adjustments.

5. Configuring Rendered Views and Animations

Once your model, materials, and lights have been initially configured, you can focus on the final output.

- The length of any animations, their frame rate, and the required time display should be assigned first.
- Camera objects can then be positioned to set up both single-frame still renderings and animations.
- Objects are animated and animated details such as clouds blowing through the sky, pedestrians on the sidewalks, etc. can then be added.
- The rendering options should be configured at this stage.

6. Testing and Final Adjustments

Test the rendering and adjust the model, materials, and lights to achieve the required results. Note that computer processing of the renderings can be very time-consuming, especially for long animations or large still renderings.

7. Post Production

You can add details to your final renderings outside the Autodesk 3ds Max software using third-party image editing programs (Adobe® Photoshop® or Adobe® AfterEffects®) and other video post-production software (Autodesk Combustion). Usually, the finished animation segments are mixed with actual video footage, voice-over narration, background sound effects, and music in a different software (such as Apple's Final Cut Pro, or another video editing and assembly tool).

1.3 The Autodesk 3ds Max Interface

To launch the Autodesk 3ds Max software, use one of the following methods:

- Double-click on (3ds Max) on your desktop.
- Click **Start** in the Windows Task Bar and select **Autodesk>3ds Max 2025**.

Welcome Screen

When you launch the software, a Welcome screen displays, as shown in Figure 1–2. It presents a slide show moving through various pages showcasing the software and tips for navigation. On the Next steps slide, it has options for opening the help documentation and connecting you to the online community page where you can find tutorials and resources on 3ds Max. It also enables you to connect to an online page where you can download the sample files and watch 1-minute startup videos.

- To prevent the Welcome Screen from displaying every time you launch the Autodesk 3ds Max software, clear the **Show this Welcome Screen at startup** option.
- You can close the Welcome Screen by clicking .
- You can open the Welcome Screen at any time during the current session by selecting **Welcome Screen** in the Help menu.

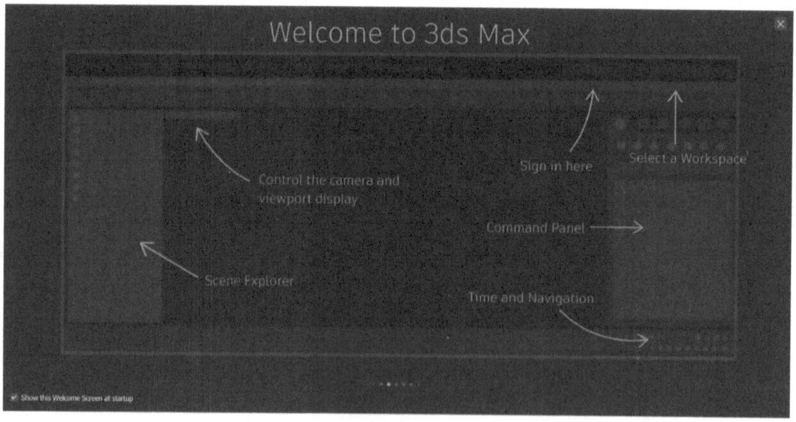

Figure 1–2

Interface

The Autodesk 3ds Max software consists of a main modeling window, called the *viewport*, which is surrounded by interface tools and panels. Figure 1–3 shows an example of a model created using various modifiers in the Command Panel, to display the different interface features.

- By default, the scene is set as one viewport/four equal viewports that display the model at different viewing angles.
- You can toggle between the four viewport displays or one maximized viewport (as shown in Figure 1–3) by clicking (Maximize Viewport), located in the Navigation toolbar along the lower right corner of the interface, or by pressing <Alt>+<W>.
- The active viewport displays a yellow border. Clicking in empty space in a viewport makes it active.

Note: *For printing purposes, the UI color scheme used in the figures is set to* ***ame-light*** *(Menu bar: Customize>Custom Defaults Switcher>User interface schemes).*

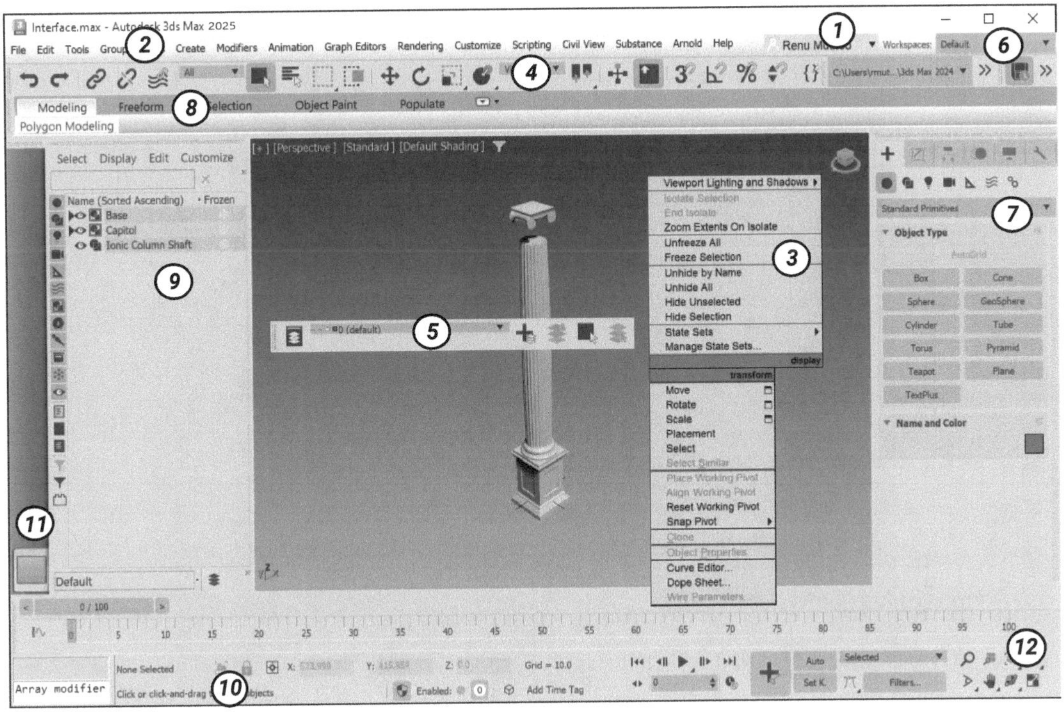

Figure 1–3

1. User Account Menu
2. Menu Bar
3. Quad Menus
4. Main Toolbar
5. Toolbars
6. Workspace Selector
7. Command Panel
8. Modeling Ribbon
9. Scene Explorer
10. Status Bar
11. Viewport Layouts Tab Bar
12. Viewport Navigation Tools

1. User Account Menu

The User Account menu can be used to sign out of your Autodesk account and manage licenses for your Autodesk products. You are required to sign in when you start the software. Once you have logged in, your sign in name displays in the User Account menu.

2. Menu Bar

The Menu Bar is located below the 3ds Max title bar and contains working commands that are grouped together in the menu titles, as shown in Figure 1–4 for **Create>Standard Primitives** menu. The software provides two menu bars: the default menu bar and the Alt menu bar.

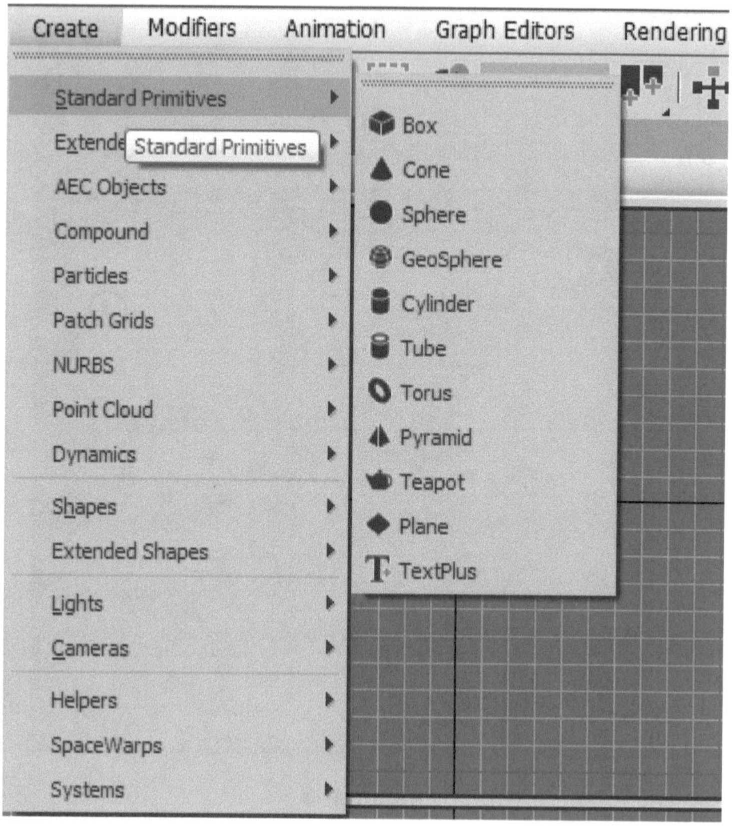

Figure 1–4

The menus in the default menu bar are described as follows:

File	Contains file management tools for opening a scene, saving your work, and setting preferences to work in the software.
Edit	Contains undo and redo functions, transform tools (Move, Scale etc.), object selection options, and delete functions.
Tools	From this menu, you can open all the various Explorers (Scene Explorer, Layer Explorer etc) that are used in the software. It also contains the **Mirror**, **Array**, **Align**, and **Measure Distance** options along with the **Snap** and **Grid** settings and options.
Group	Contains tools to create and edit Autodesk 3ds Max group objects and attach/ detach objects.
Views	Contains features, such as preset viewport views, viewport display options, and ViewCube and SteeringWheel options.
Create	Contains options that enable you to create objects, such as 3D geometry, 2D shapes, cameras, and lights. The creation tools are grouped based on the type of objects created, such as Standard primitive objects, compound objects, Light objects, camera objects, etc.
Modifiers	Contains sub-menus categorized by the available modifiers.
Animation	Contains common features used when creating animations.
Graph Editors	Contains several Track View features. Track View offers advanced controls for animations.
Rendering	Contains functions for rendering, such as setting up the scene environment, advanced lighting controls, and output image resolution.
Customize	Contains features for customizing the user interface, setting up the drawing units, and setting the overall Autodesk 3ds Max default options.
Scripting	Contains tools for working with the MAXScript programming language used by the Autodesk 3ds Max software.
Civil View	Contains features that can be used for displaying the contents of a scene created in a civil design program and to create visualizations of civil engineering projects. It offers support for various civil design programs, including the Autodesk® Civil 3D® software. If you are opening Civil View for the first time, you need to initialize it and set the system units, country resource kit, and start mode.
Substance	Contains options for Adobe Substance (software for 3D digital materials) with 3ds Max, including Substance settings and links to the Adobe Substance website.
Arnold	Contains options for Arnold renderer, which is a physically-based ray/path tracing renderer. It is intended for rendering complex scenes for animation and visual effects.
Help	The **Help** menu connects you directly to the Autodesk 3ds Max Help documentation, Tutorials, Learning Resources etc on the *autodesk.com* website.You can also link to 3ds Max Learning Channel on YouTube and 3ds Max communities such as *AREA*.

Alt Menu Bar

In the Alt Menu Bar, the commands are organized as menu items, with sub-menus containing relevant commands. The Alt Menu Bar contains various menus: **File, Edit, Objects, Modifiers, Animation, Simulate, Materials, Lighting/ Cameras, Rendering, Scene, Publish, Scripting, Customize, Arnold, Substance,** and **Help**. To display the Alt Menu Bar, select **Alt Menu and Toolbar** in the *Workspaces* drop-down list, as shown in Figure 1–5. To revert to the default menu bar, select **Default**.

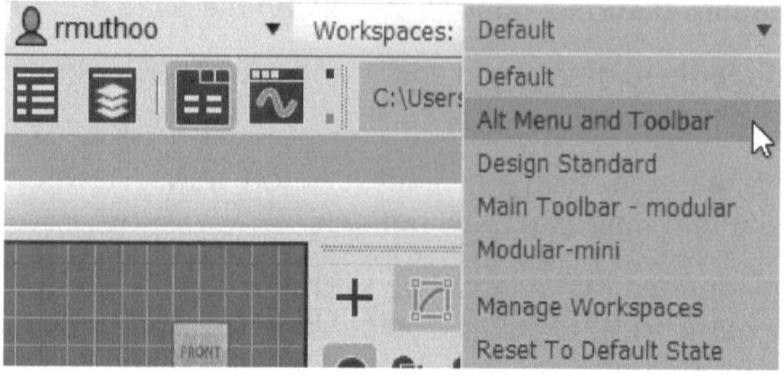

Figure 1–5

Hint: Global Menu Search

You can search for any menu command or action using the global menu search method. Press <X> to open the Search actions edit box at the cursor location and enter the name of the command or action that you want to use. As you enter the first letter of the command, a list of matching actions displays, as shown in Figure 1–6. Select an option in the list or continue entering letters to display a more specific list of actions. To clear the search action, click the **X** in the upper right corner of the *Search* edit box. To exit the search feature, click anywhere in empty space or press <Esc>.

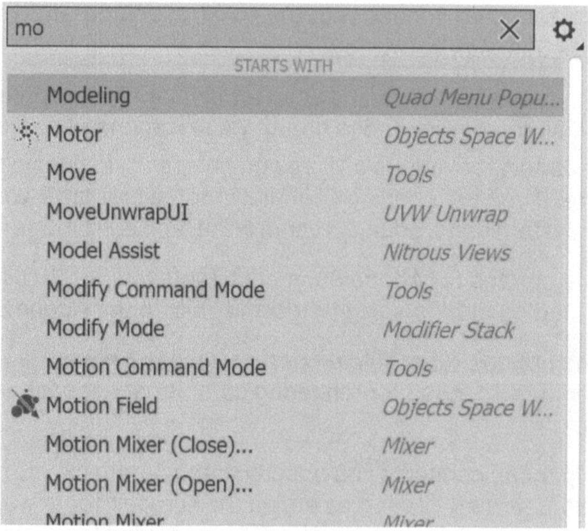

Figure 1–6

3. Quad Menus

The quad menus (shown in Figure 1–7) are a series of context-sensitive menus that open when selecting and right-clicking on one or more objects in the viewport. The commands display in different quadrant areas and each quad menu can have a maximum of four quadrant areas, as shown in Figure 1–8.

- Quad menus also display when nothing is selected.
- Different quad menus display when <Ctrl>, <Alt>, or <Shift> are combined with right-clicking.

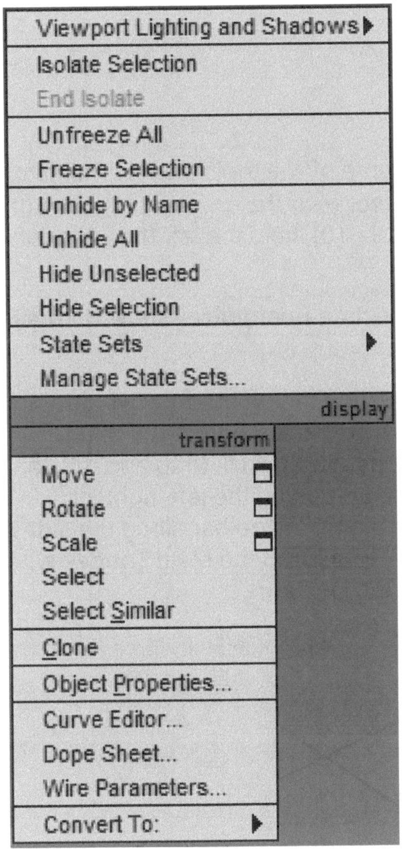

Figure 1–7

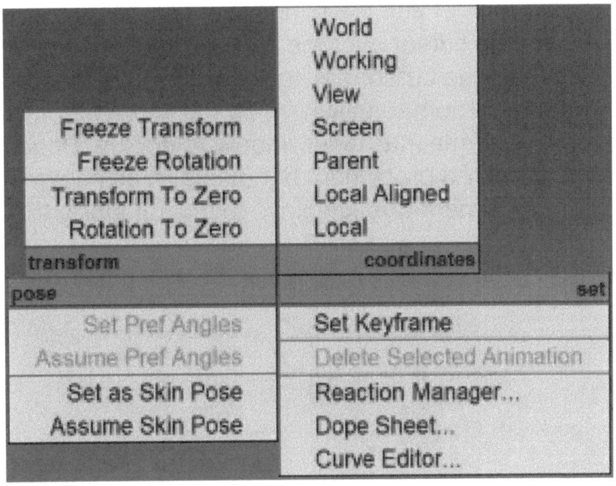

Figure 1–8

4. Main Toolbar

The Main Toolbar (shown in Figure 1–9) is visible by default and contains tools for some of the most commonly used options. These include the **Selection**, **Transforms**, **Snap**, **Rendering**, **Project** and **Autobackup** tools. When you hover the cursor over a tool, a tooltip with the name of the tool displays.

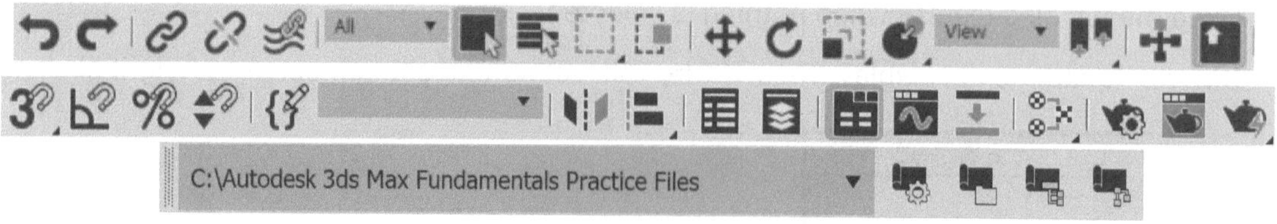

Figure 1–9

- The Main Toolbar can extend beyond the interface and some of the tools are not visible on the screen. To slide the buttons left or right, hover the cursor over the gray empty area until the cursor changes into a Pan cursor (as shown in Figure 1–10), hold the left mouse button, and drag.
- If the Main Toolbar is not visible, you can display it by selecting **Customize>Show UI>Main Toolbar**.
- You can float and dock the Main Toolbar to a different location in the interface window. Hover the cursor over the handle (double lines) located along the left end of the Main Toolbar. The cursor changes into a move icon, as shown in Figure 1–10. Drag and relocate the Main Toolbar anywhere on the screen. You can also drag it along the left, right, or bottom of the interface window to dock it. Once you drag the Main Toolbar along the side of the screen, a placement bar displays, as shown in Figure 1–10. Drop the Main Toolbar when the placement area displays to dock it along that side of the viewport.

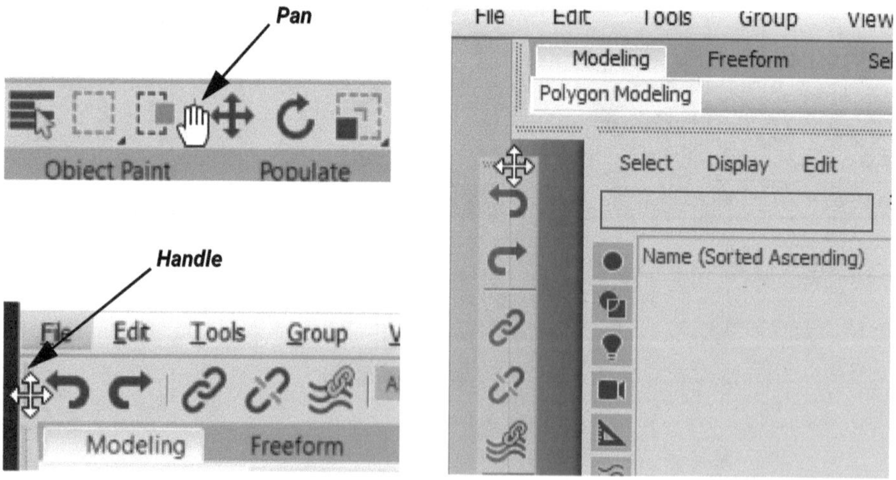

Figure 1–10

- You can also dock or float the Main Toolbar by hovering the cursor over its handle, then right-clicking and selecting either **Dock>Top/Bottom/Right/Left** or **Float** as shown in the Figure 1–11.

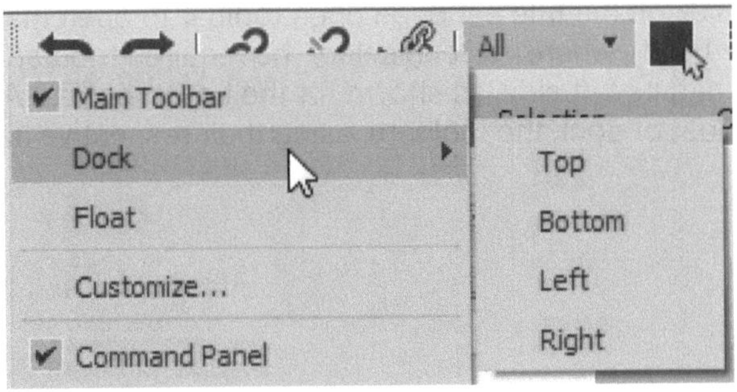

Figure 1–11

- You can break the Main Toolbar into modular pieces and then float or dock the modular groups to different locations in the interface. To make the Main Toolbar modular, in the *Workspaces selector* drop-down list, select **Main Toolbar - modular**, as shown on the left in Figure 1–12. The division lines are changed into Handles (double lines), which are located along the left side of each modular group, as shown on the right in Figure 1–12. Drag and drop to relocate or dock each module separately to different locations.

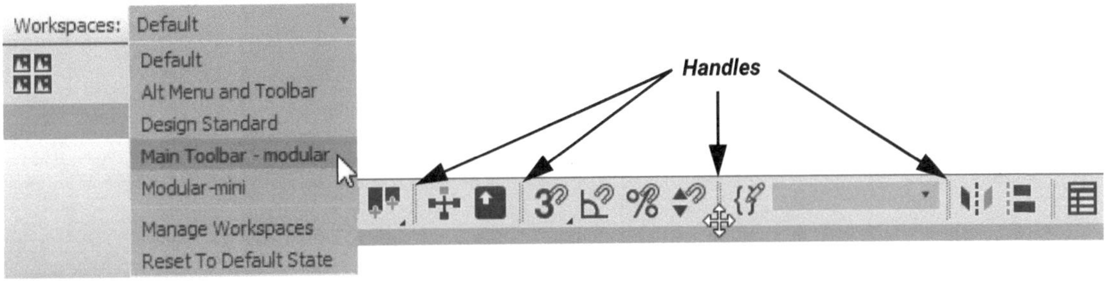

Figure 1–12

- You can revert back to the standard Main Toolbar by selecting **Default** in the *Workspace selector* drop-down list.
- Selecting **Modular-mini** in the *Workspaces selector* drop-down list, displays a smaller version of the Main Toolbar and the Menu Bar, containing the frequently used tools, as shown in Figure 1–13.

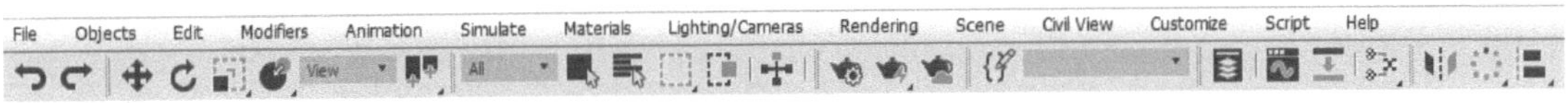

Figure 1–13

5. Toolbars

By default, the Main Toolbar, Projects, and Autobackup toolbars are displayed along the top of the viewport window. Right-click on the gray empty space of a docked toolbar including the Main Toolbar or right-click on the title bar of an open toolbar to open the **Customize Display** menu (shown in Figure 1–14), where you can select the required toolbar name to display it. The toolbar has a handle along its left side, as shown for the Layer toolbar. As with other interface components, you can float or dock the toolbars, using their respective handles.

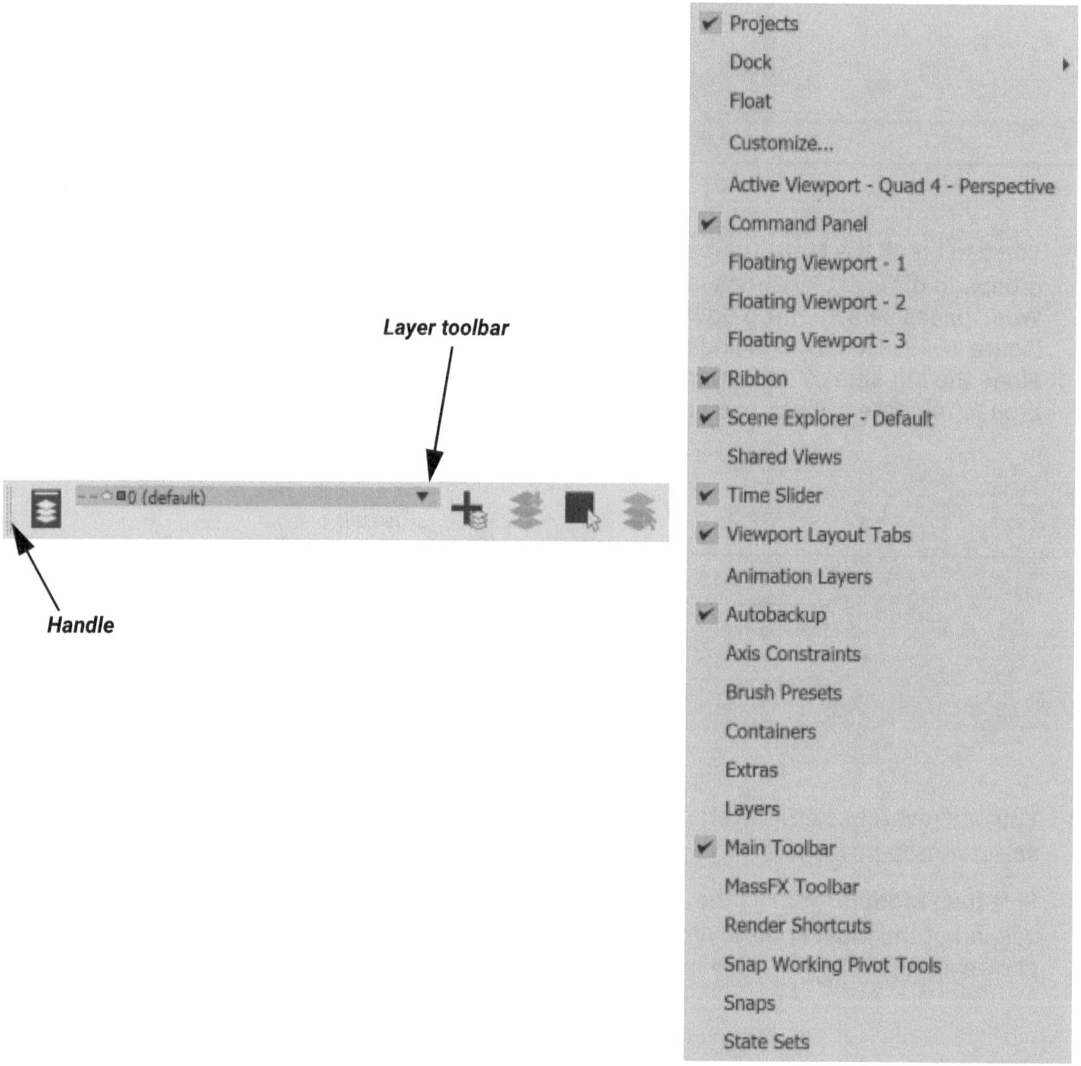

Figure 1–14

6. Workspace Selector

The Workspace selector (shown in Figure 1–15) enables you to manage and switch between different interface setups.

- You can create a custom interface setup that contains commonly used toolbars, menus, quad menus, viewport layout settings, ribbon tools, and hotkeys for commands and save them as workspaces.

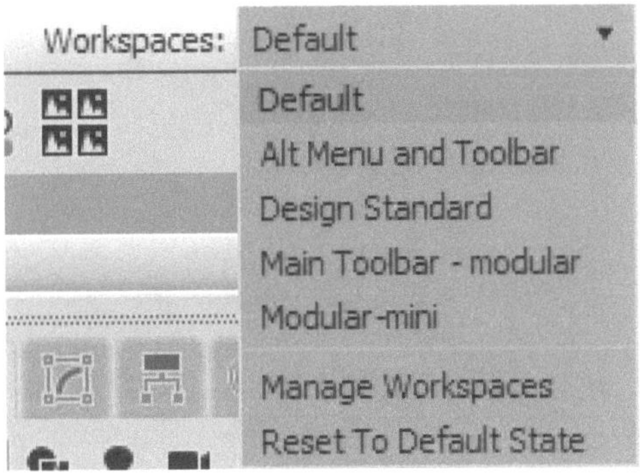

Figure 1–15

- **Manage Workspaces:** Opens the *Manage Workspaces* dialog box, in which you can add new workspaces, edit workspaces, and delete workspaces.
- **Alt Menu and Toolbar:** Displays an alternate menu in the menu bar with Scene Explorer docked under the Command Panel.
- **Design Standard:** Displays an alternate ribbon containing commonly used features along with help and other learning resources in the ribbon.
- **Main Toolbar - modular:** Displays the Main Toolbar in the modular form which can be broken into smaller groups.
- **Modular - mini:** Displays an alternate Main Toolbar containing a limited number of commonly used tools.
- **Default:** Reverts back to the standard menu bar.

7. Command Panel

The Command Panel enables you to efficiently create, edit, and manage the settings of 3D objects. It contains six different panels or tabs, each with a different appearance and function.

Figure 1–16 shows the *Object Type* rollout in the *Create* panel (+).

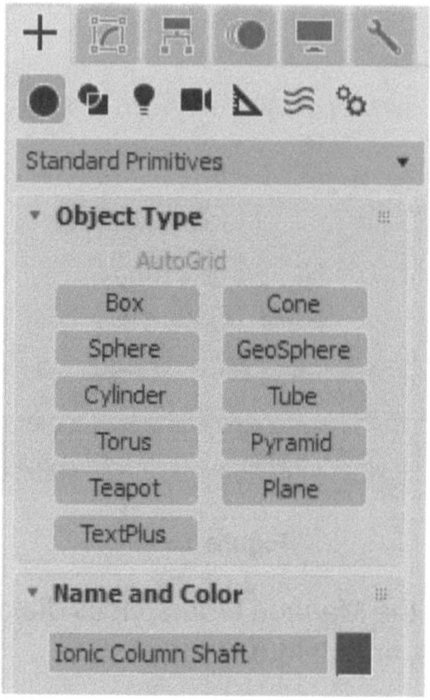

Figure 1–16

- The options in the lower portion of each panel are grouped into rollouts. You can expand and collapse the rollouts by clicking on the title bar of the rollout or the downward/sideward facing arrows (or the **+/-** signs).
- If the list of rollouts are extensive and extend beyond the bottom of the interface, pan the list up and down by holding and dragging the mouse button in the Command Panel.
- By default, the Command Panel is docked along the right side of the viewport window. You can dock or float the Command Panel by hovering the cursor over the top handle (edge) of the Command Panel, then right-clicking and selecting either **Dock>Right**, **Dock>Left**, or **Float** as shown in the Figure 1–17.

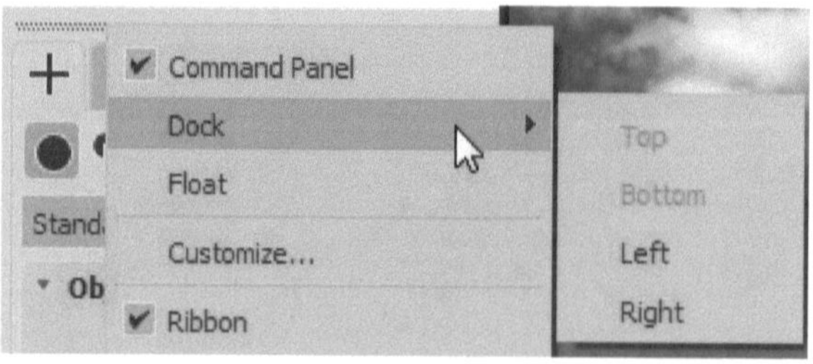

Figure 1–17

- You can also use the Command Panel handle to drag and drop it to dock or float it.

Create Panel

The *Create* panel enables you to interactively create objects in the Autodesk 3ds Max software and contains the following categories of object types:

- **Geometry** is 3D objects.
- **Shapes** are 2D objects.
- **Lights** are used to illuminate the scene.
- **Cameras** are objects that provide scene views.
- **Helpers** are non-rendering tools that help with layout or work with other objects, such as a distance measuring tape object.
- **Space warps** are non-renderable objects that deform or otherwise influence the geometry of other objects. They are used to create ripples and waves, using forces such as wind and gravity.
- **Systems** contains the Sunlight and Daylight Systems, Biped, and the controls for some 3rd party plug-ins.

Modify Panel

The *Modify* panel shows the selected object's parameter values, a list of modifiers added to an object, and the parameters that apply to them.

- Modifiers are geometric modifications and additional property controls that can be added to objects, as required.
- Object and modifier parameters can be changed at any time after the object's creation, if the Modifier Stack remains intact.
- The *Modifier List* drop-down list contains all of the modifiers that can be applied to the current selection.

- The *Modifier Stack* lists the modifiers that have been applied to an object. Figure 1–18 shows the *Modifier Stack* of a circle that was edited, extruded, and tapered into a 3D column shaft.
- The *Modify* panel is blank if no object is selected or if more than one object is selected.

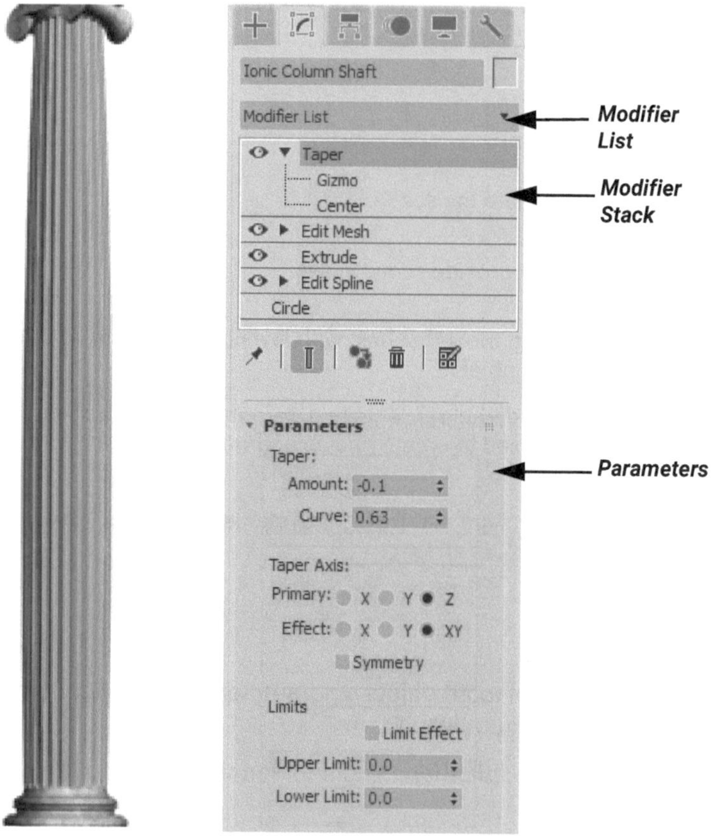

Figure 1–18

Hierarchy Panel

The *Hierarchy* panel contains controls for objects that are linked together into hierarchies, such as for mechanical equipment with interconnected parts.

Motion Panel

The *Motion* panel contains sophisticated motion controls for animating.

Display Panel

The *Display* panel contains object-level visibility controls, enabling you to hide or unhide objects individually or by category, independent of the layer settings.

Utilities Panel

The *Utilities* panel contains a number of miscellaneous utilities as follows:

Perspective Match Utility	Helps match the position and field of view of the camera in your 3D scene to the perspective photographic background image.
Collapse Utility	Removes the modifiers from an object's stack, turning the object into an editable mesh or poly.
Color Clipboard Utility	Stores color swatches for copying from one map or material to another.
Measure Utility	Lists the surface area and volume of objects.
Motion Capture Utility	Enables you to animate virtual objects with the real-time movement of the mouse or they input device.
Reset XForm Utility	Removes rotation and scale values of an object, applying them to the XForm modifier gizmo.
MAXScript	Accesses a scripting language that can be used to automate repetitive functions or build new tools and interfaces.
Flight Studio Utility	Enables you to open and manage the open Flight models.
More...	Provides access to a complete list of Utilities, including the controls for many 3rd party plug-in applications.

8. Modeling Ribbon

The Modeling ribbon (shown in Figure 1–19) provides easy access to polygon modeling tools, including the editing and modification tools used at sub-object level. The ribbon contains most of the commonly used tools that are also found in the Command Panel's *Modify* panel (at the Edit Poly sub-object level).

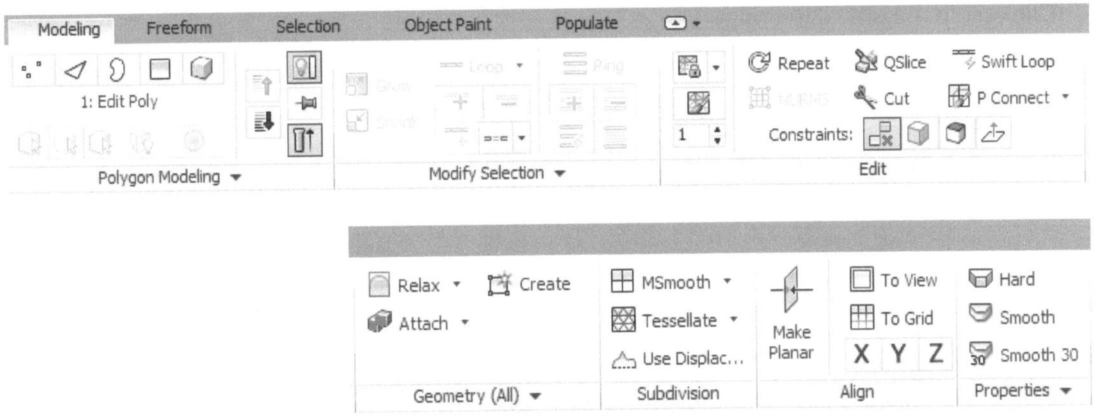

Figure 1–19

The ribbon contains five tabs: *Modeling*, *Freeform*, *Selection*, *Object Paint*, and *Populate* that are further subdivided into various panels that are context dependent. All of the tools are grouped based on context and are placed in separate panels.

- For example, the *Modeling* tab contains the tools used for modeling and are grouped in the *Polygon Modeling* panel, *Modify Selection* panel, *Edit* panel, etc. Each of the panels has a set of related tools and commands present for easy access. For example, the *Polygon Modeling* panel contains tools used for **Edit Poly** modifier, as shown in Figure 1–20.

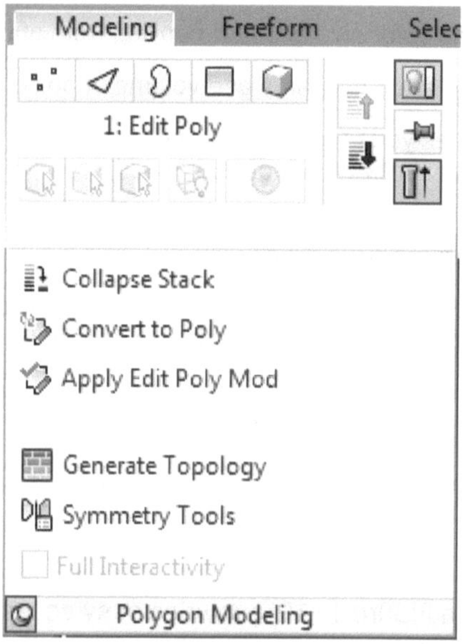

Figure 1–20

- The ribbon is docked under the Main Toolbar and might be minimized to the panel tiles. Click the icon to maximize the ribbon.
- The display of the tabs and panels can be controlled by right-clicking on the ribbon and select the options in the menu, as shown in Figure 1–21.

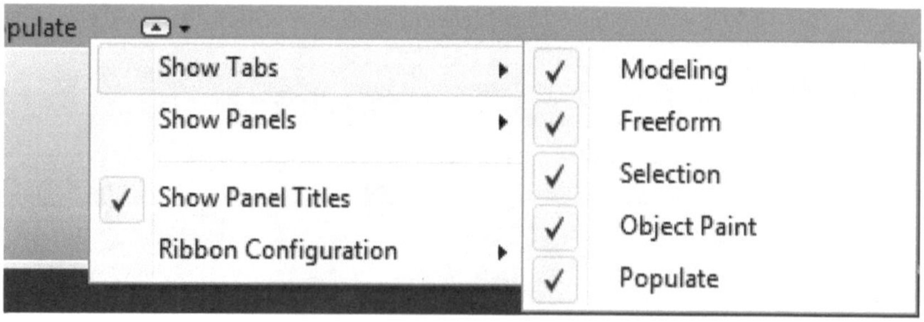

Figure 1–21

- If you are continuously using the options from a panel, you can click in the expanded panel to lock it.
- If the ribbon is not displayed, in the menu bar, select **Customize>Show UI>Ribbon**. You can also click (Toggle Ribbon) in the Main Toolbar or select **Ribbon** in the Customize Display shortcut menu.

Hint: Design Workspace

The Design Workspace ribbon contains the commonly used 3ds Max commands and features grouped together in tabs, as shown in Figure 1–22. It can be started by selecting **Design Standard** in the *Workspaces selector* drop-down list.

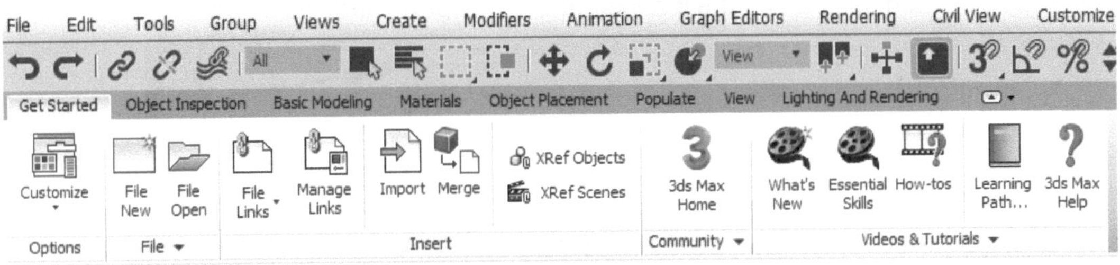

Figure 1–22

The various tabs included are:

- **Get Started**: Commands for starting a new scene, opening an already saved scene, and linking geometry and files from other 3D data software. It also contains commands for customizing the software and accessing to learning resources.
- **Object Inspection**: Commands used to control the display of objects in viewports and also explore the geometry in the scene.
- **Basic Modeling**: Tools for creating new geometry in the scene.
- **Materials**: Tools for creating, managing, and editing the materials.
- **Object Placement**: Tools for moving, placing and editing geometry. You can also open Civil View from this tab.
- **Populate**: Tools for adding animated or idle people to a scene.
- **View**: Commands to add cameras and control the viewport display.
- **Lighting and Rendering**: Tools for adding lights and creating renderings of the scene.

9. Scene Explorer

The Scene Explorer (shown in Figure 1–23) lists all of the objects that are present in a scene in the form of a tree structure, along with each object's properties displayed in a tabular form.

- By default, the Scene Explorer is docked along the left side of the viewport. You can float it or dock it to top, bottom, left, or right by right-clicking on its handle and selecting the required option.
- You can also drag and drop the Scene Explorer by its handle to float or dock it.
- It is a modeless dialog box that can remains open while you are working in the scene.
- The display of Scene Explorer might be dependent on your display monitor. If the Scene Explorer is not displayed, expand **Tools** in the menu bar and select **Scene Explorer** to open it. You can then dock it along the left side of the viewport window.

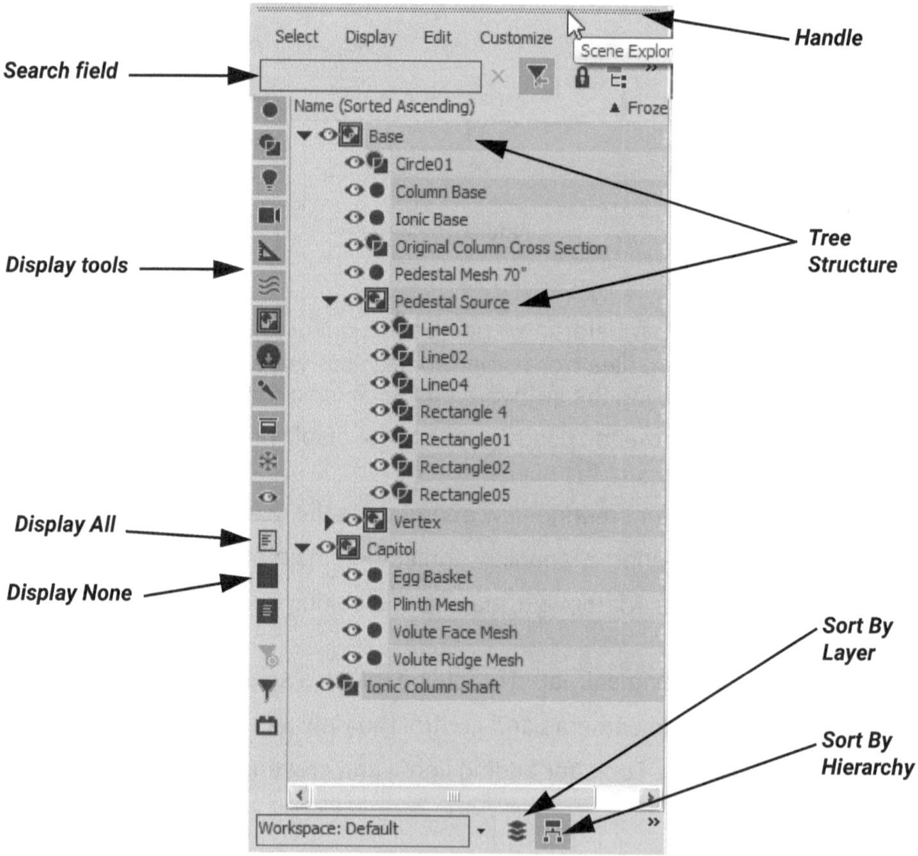

Figure 1–23

- A default Scene Explorer is included for each workspace and can be saved with a specific name with that workspace.

- The objects can be toggled to be displayed either as hierarchies ( ) or as layers ( ).
- Objects and layers can be nested to any depth. Use the arrow next to the name to expand or collapse the group.
- You can perform actions and modifications such as sorting, filtering, selecting, renaming, hiding, and freezing objects, directly in the Scene Explorer.
- You can drag and drop objects and layers to reorganize the groups.
- A toolbar is provided along the left edge of the Scene Explorer that enables you to list only those objects that belong to a particular category. There are tools for various categories such as (Display Geometry), (Display Cameras), (Display Lights), etc. When the tool for a category is active (i.e., displays with a blue background), the objects belonging to that category are listed. The (Display All) tool lists all of the different categories of objects. To only list the objects belonging to the category that you need, use (Display None) to clear any existing selections, and then select the required display category.
- To easily find and select an item, use the *Search* field.

10. Status Bar

The Status Bar (shown in Figure 1–24), found along the bottom left and center of the interface, contains the following elements:

Figure 1–24

MAXScript Mini-Listener	Enables you to enter commands and receive feedback (MaxScript commands).
Status Line	Identifies the number of objects selected.
Prompt Line	Prompts for the next action or input that is required.
(Isolate Selection Toggle)	Zooms the current selection in the active viewport while temporarily hiding unselected objects in all viewports (except the **Camera** viewport). This enables you to work on the required object without the other objects getting in your way. You can also access this command by selecting Tools>Isolate Selection or pressing <Alt>+<Q>.
(Selection Lock Toggle)	Toggles a lock to prevent you from changing your current selection between options. Pressing the space bar toggles this on or off.

or (Absolute/Offset Transform Mode Toggle)	Enables you to toggle between Absolute mode (which sets the coordinates in the world space) and the Offset transform mode (which transforms the objects relative to its coordinates).
Transform Type-In	Enables you to review and adjust transform values for the X, Y, and Z coordinates.
Grid Setting Display	Controls the distance between grid lines. Select *Tools>Grids and Snaps>Grid and Snap Settings* to open the dialog box. Use the *Home Grid* tab to adjust the spacing. To toggle the Grid on or off, press <G>.
(Security Shield)	Displays that the Safe Scene Script Execution is enabled (by default), and the counter displays the number of commands that have been blocked in the embedded scripts. You can disable it from the *Security* tab in the *Preference Settings* dialog box.
(Adaptive Degradation Toggle)	Enables you to toggle adaptive degradation on or off. Right-click to open the *Viewport Configuration* dialog box in the *Display Performance* tab (the *Adaptive Degradation* tab is for legacy drivers). You can improve the viewport quality progressively and set the resolution for the texture display (for nitrous drivers). It also contains options for controlling adaptive degradation.
Time Tag	Enables you to add or edit time tags, which are labels describing specific points of an animation.

11. Viewport Layouts Tab Bar

The *Viewport Layouts* tab bar is a vertically, expandable bar containing a list of viewport layouts that can be selected to quickly change the layout of the viewports, as shown in Figure 1–25.

- For a new scene, only one layout tab is available. Once you have saved additional viewport layouts, they are listed along with the default one. In Figure 1–25, the *Viewport Layouts* tab bar displays the default layout and three additional viewport layouts that were saved.

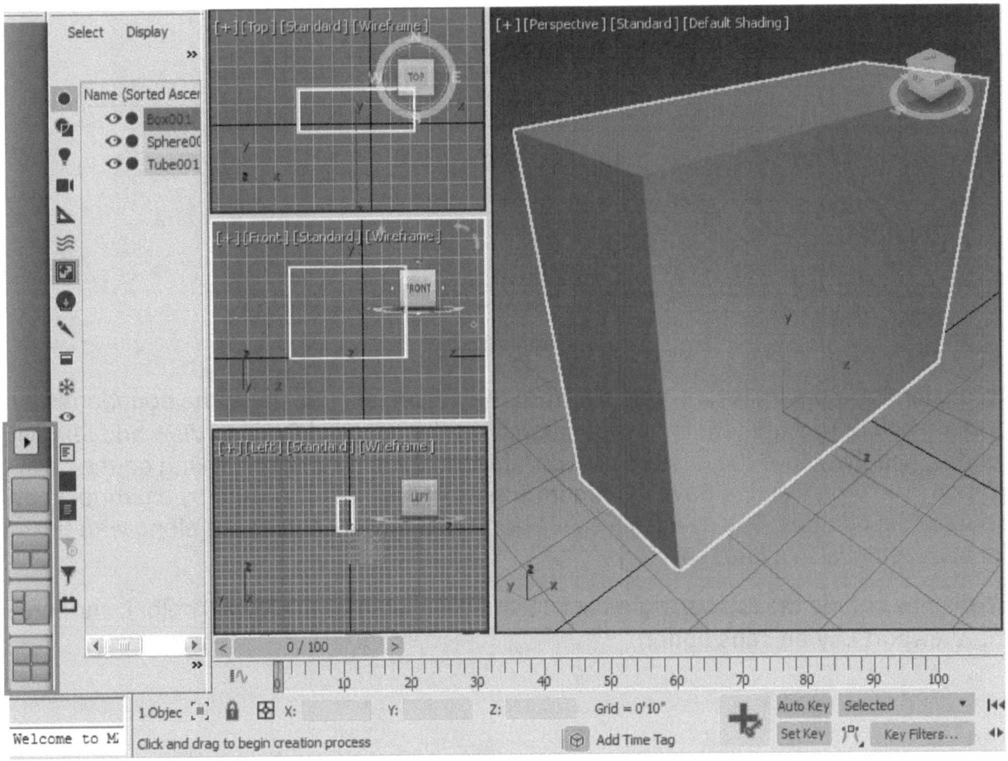

Figure 1–25

- Click  (as shown in Figure 1–26), to open the available standard viewport layouts for selection and customization. Once you have selected a layout, it is listed in the tab bar with any previously saved layouts. The viewports display as the new layout.

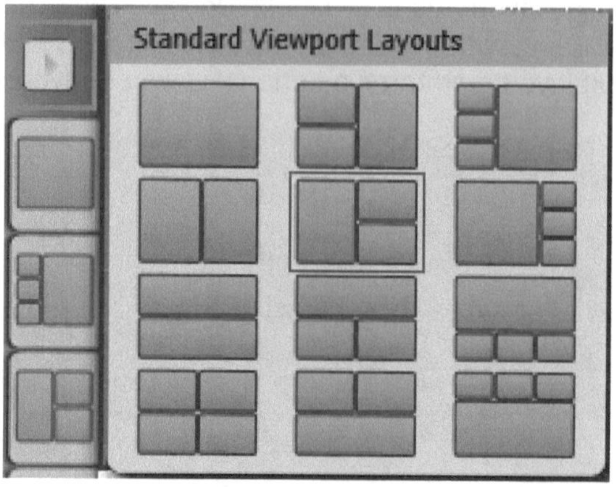

Figure 1–26

- To customize a preset layout, select it from the preset layouts, move the boundaries by clicking and dragging them to new positions, set the required *Point of View* and *Shading* modes, and then save the custom viewport layout. Save it by right-clicking on the new custom tab and selecting **Save Configuration as Preset**. Set its name by entering a new name in the edit box. The newly saved viewport configuration is saved along with the scene for easy retrieval in a later session.
- To display or hide the tab bar, right-click in an empty area of the Main Toolbar, and toggle the **Viewport Layout Tabs** option.

Hint: Interface Item Customize Menu

The interface items that can be docked/floated (Main Toolbar, Command Panel, ribbon, Scene Explorer, Time Slider, and *Viewport Layout* tabs bar) contain a shortcut menu that can be used to display or hide these interface elements. To display the menu, right-click on the handle of the interface item, as shown for Command Panel in Figure 1–27. A checkmark next to an item indicates that it displays in the interface.

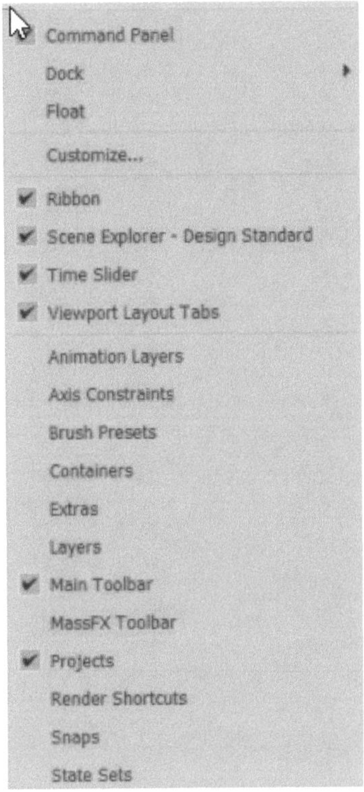

Figure 1–27

12. Viewport Navigation Tools

The navigation tools (shown in Figure 1–28), are located in the lower right corner of the interface and contain tools for navigating and displaying objects in the viewports. The tools are dependent on the active viewport.

Figure 1–28

***Note:** The navigation tools are discussed in detail later in this guide.*

1.4 File Commands

The **File** menu provides access to the file commands used for saving, opening, or creating new scenes, import/ export options, and preferences, as shown in Figure 1–29. Some of the commands have sub-menus that contain additional options, as shown for the **New** command in Figure 1–30.

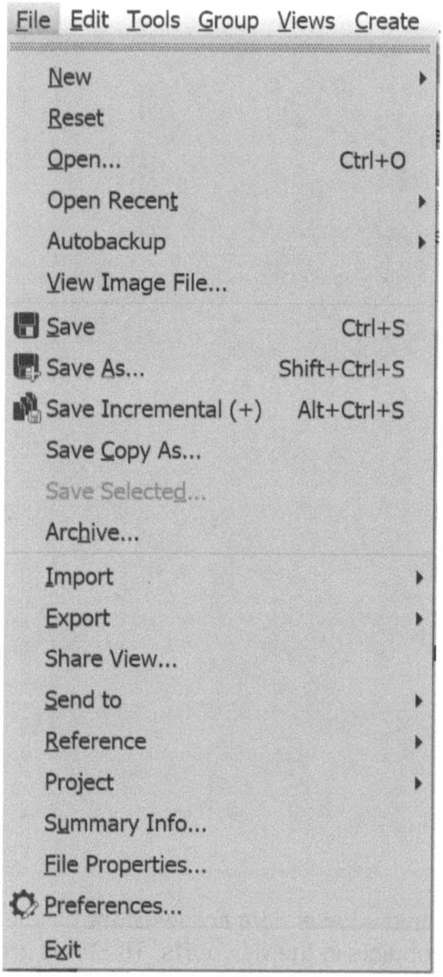

Figure 1–29

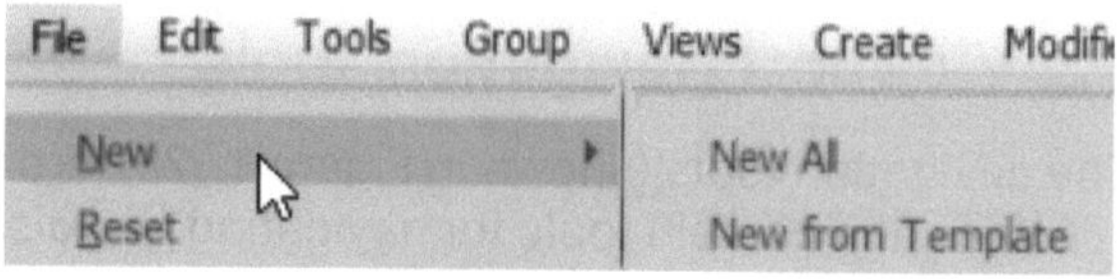

Figure 1–30

Create New Scenes

The commands in the **File>New** menu (shown above in Figure 1–30) are described as follows:

- **New All:** Opens a new empty scene from scratch. If there are unsaved objects drawn on the screen, the software prompts you to save or discard the changes first and then opens a new scene.
- **New from Template:** Opens the *Create New Scene* dialog box, which contains five standard start-up templates for creating a new empty scene, as shown in Figure 1–31. These templates contain built-in settings (rendering, environment, lighting, units, etc.) optimum for that particular type of scene. The **Open Template Manager** option enables you to create new templates or modify the existing ones.

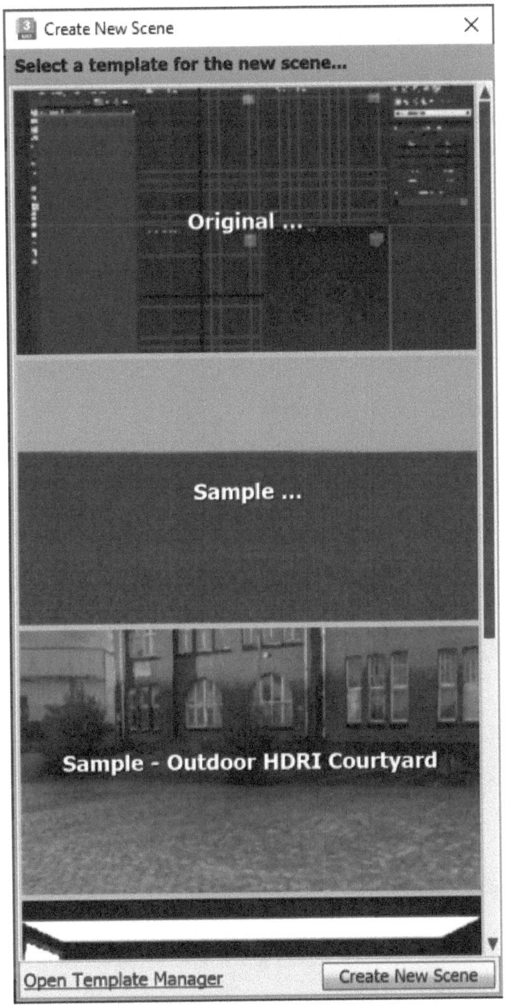

Figure 1–31

Open and Save Files

You can open and save scenes using various commands in the **File** menu.

- The **Open** command opens an already saved .MAX file and the **Open Recent** option opens a file from the list of recently opened files.
- The **Reset** option enables you to clear all data from the already opened file.
- Use **Save** to save a scene as a .MAX file and it overwrites the currently open file. If you are using the **Save** command to save an unnamed file for the first time, the option works as **Save As**.
- The **Save As** opens a *Save File As* dialog box, where you can save the file as a .MAX (current software version or three previous versions) or .CHR file in the required location. If you save it under a different name, the newly saved file remains open.
- The **Save Copy As** option enables you to save the current open file with a different file name and save a separate copy of it without overwriting the last saved version of the file. The currently open file remains open.

Preferences

The *Preference Settings* dialog box (shown in Figure 1–32) contains tabs that control the display and operational settings at the program level. To open the dialog box, select **File>Preferences** or **Customize>Preferences**.

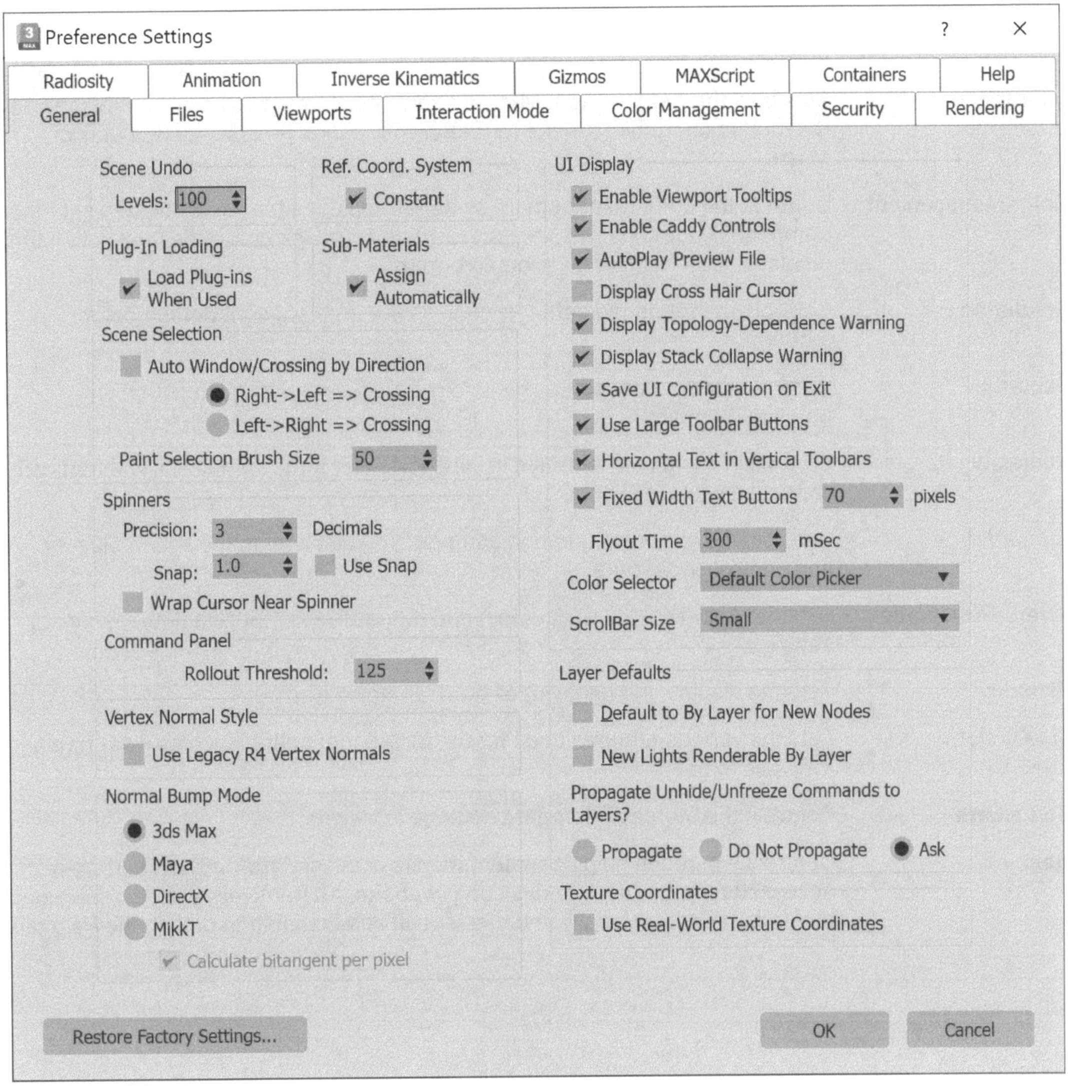

Figure 1–32

The following tabs are available:

General	Controls the interface settings, such as Number of Scene Undo steps (levels) that are saved, settings for the transform center, user interface display options, etc.
Files	Contains options for file handling, such as Automatic backup save settings.
Viewports	Contains options for viewport settings, highlighting options for selection and preview, and setting the display drivers.
Interaction Mode	Sets how the mouse and keyboard shortcuts are going to behave. You can set the mouse shortcut behavior to match with earlier releases of 3ds Max or Maya.
Color Management	Controls the color management system to be used for the scene and sets the compatibility options with respect to other Autodesk programs for a consistent display of colors among various programs.
Rendering	Controls the rendering settings, such as the ambient light default color settings.
Security	Controls the security settings, such as Safe Scene Script Execution and Malware Removal.
Radiosity	Controls the radiosity settings in viewports and if the light levels with radiosity are saved with a file or not.
Animation	Controls the various animation settings. You can assign the sound plug-ins and controller defaults.
Inverse Kinematics	Sets the Applied IK (for accuracy) and Interactive IK (for real-time response) settings.
Gizmos	Sets the display and behavior of the Transform gizmos.
MAXScript	Sets the various features used for the MAXScript editor, such as what font and font size to use.
Containers	Controls the Status and Update settings in viewports.
Help	Controls where the help documentation is accessed from. By default, help is accessed through the Autodesk.com website. Alternatively, you can download the documentation locally and then specify its installation path in the *Help* tab.

Security Settings

Security has been considerably improved over the years and a new *Security* tab has been added to the *Preference Settings* dialog box, as shown in Figure 1–33.

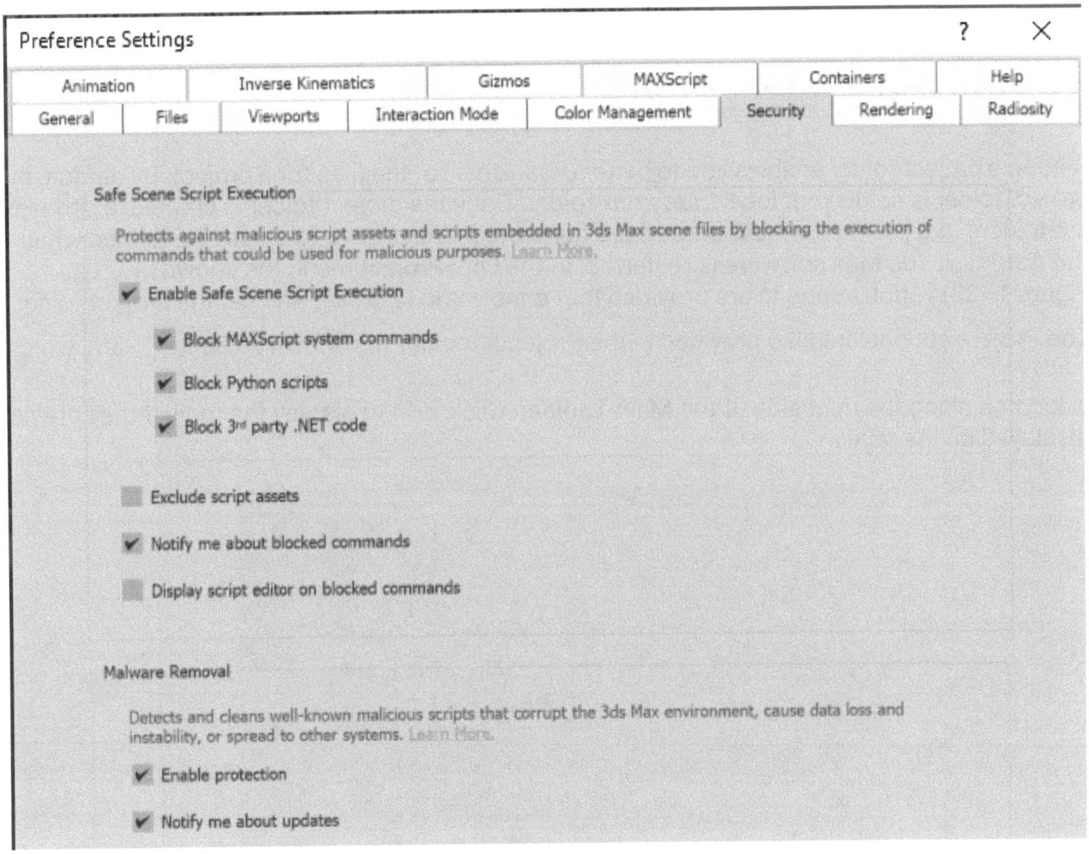

Figure 1–33

The security options are as follows:

- **Safe Scene Script Execution:** The options in this area scan the embedded scripts and block potentially unsafe commands from execution. The commands that are not meant to act on just the scene/scene assets but can perform actions on something else (such as accessing the operating system) are considered unsafe. By default, Safe Scene Script Execution is enabled, and the security shield icon displays "Enabled" and is green in the Status Bar, as shown in Figure 1–34. When disabled, the security shield icon says "Disabled" and turns red.

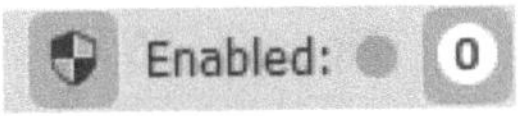

Figure 1–34

- **Malware Removal:** The options in this area detect and remove malicious scripts. It looks for malicious scripts in the scene files and script directories that are accessed during startup. If you open a scene with a known malicious script, this option enables you to either remove the script or disregard the warning and continue to open the scene. There is also an option which notifies you about any updates that are available in the Autodesk App Store.

Setting the Project Folder

Setting a project folder enables you to better organize all of the files for a project. By default, the project folder is set to your local *../3dsmax* folder. Once the project folder is created, a series of subfolders (e.g., scenes, render output) are generated. The project folder is maintained when the Autodesk 3ds Max software is restarted. In the **File>Project** menu (as shown in Figure 1–35) various options are provided that enable you to create and set the project folder.

The Project options are also provided in the Projects toolbar (as shown in Figure 1–35), which is located along the right side of the Main Toolbar. Click  to display the tools if they are not displayed on the screen.

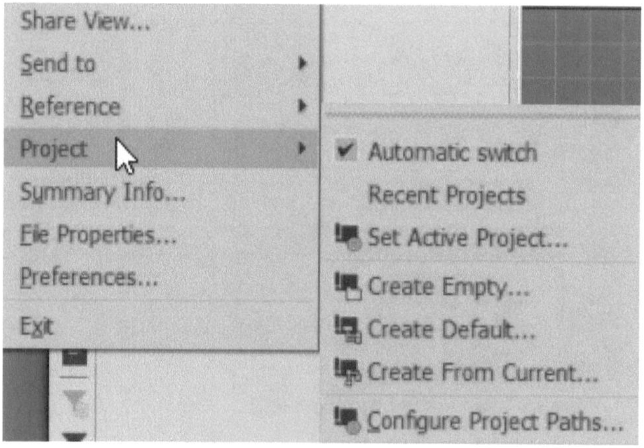

Project tools in File menu

Projects toolbar

Figure 1–35

- The file path of the current project folder displays in the **Project** toolbar. It also lists all of the different Project Folders that were created.

- **Set Active Project:** This opens the *Set Active Project* dialog box, which displays the system drives and folders. Select a folder to use as the root for the current project.
- **Create Empty:** Opens the *Choose a folder* dialog box, where you can create a new project folder without a folder structure.
- **Create Default:** Creates a new project folder with a default folder structure using the *Choose a folder* dialog box.
- **Create from Current**: Creates a new project folder based on the folder structure that you select in the *Choose a folder* dialog box.
- The **Recent Projects** option lists the previously opened projects and you can select one to make it current.

1.5 Configure Paths

Projects can use external files such as fonts, image maps for materials, IES (Illuminating Engineering Society) data files for lights, etc. The locations of these and other required data files are identified in the *Configure Project Paths and Configure User and System Paths* dialog boxes. These dialog boxes can be opened by selecting **Customize>Configure Project Paths/ Configure User and System Paths**.

Configure User and System Paths

The *Configure User and System Paths* dialog box (shown in Figure 1–36) stores paths to data files and contains the following tabs:

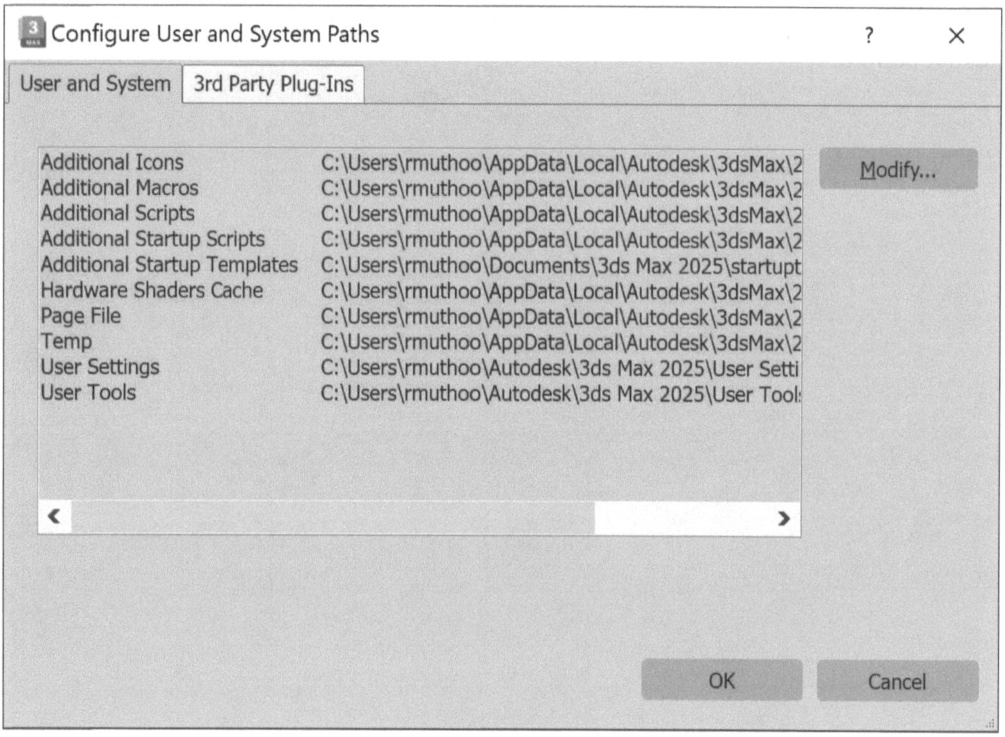

Figure 1–36

User and System	Paths used for additional buttons, macros, scripts and startup scripts, and temp files.
3rd Party Plug-Ins	Default paths to search for add-on application data (some standard functions and 3rd party products).

Configure Project Paths

The *Configure Project Paths* dialog box (shown in Figure 1–37) stores items that might be reconfigured for different users or for different projects. The Project path settings are saved as a path configuration (.MXP) file. The dialog box has the following tabs:

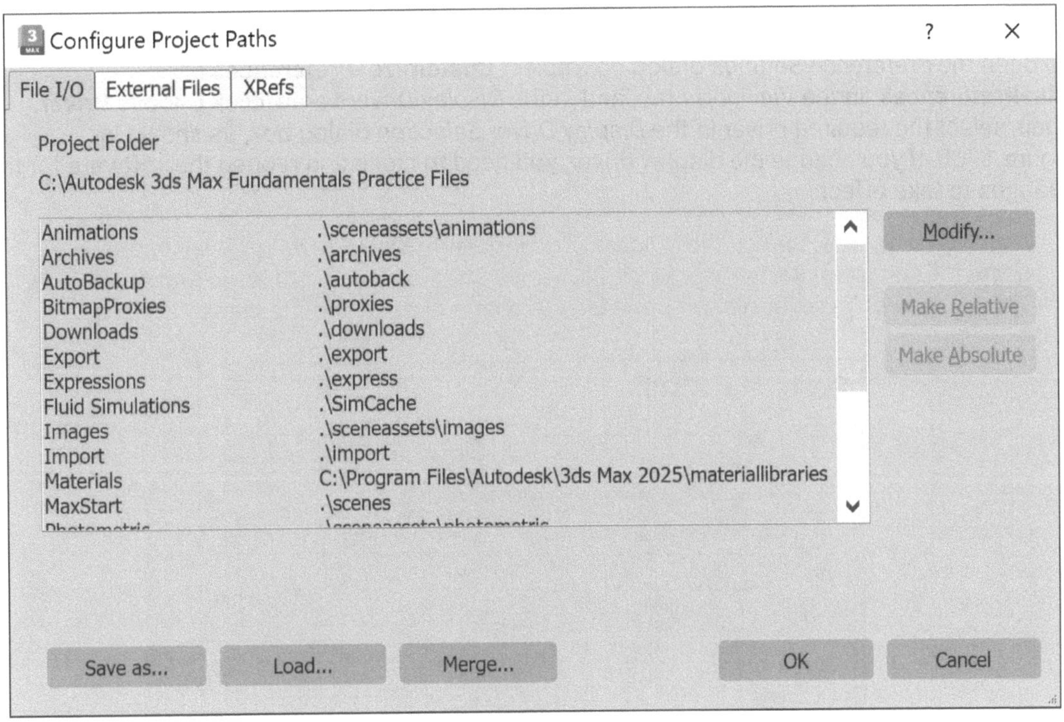

Figure 1–37

File I/O	Paths used to locate files for options such as open, save, export, etc.
External Files	Paths to external data files such as image maps, IES files, etc.
XRefs	Paths that are searched to find externally referenced objects and scene files.

- Since multiple workstations often make use of the same data files, it is often helpful to create shared network locations for these files (especially when network rendering).
- Relative paths are used to help prevent *missing external files* problems when sharing or moving files from one location to another. In the Configure Project Paths, all of the File I/O paths are preceded with a dot and backslash (.\) indicating that they are relative paths.
- There are certain paths which are hard-coded absolute paths. You can use the *Configure Project Paths* dialog box to change hard-coded absolute paths from earlier versions to Relative paths. Select the path and click **Make Relative**.

1.6 Display Drivers

The Nitrous Direct3D 11 driver is the default and recommended display driver, but you can change to the other Nitrous drivers or legacy drivers. Nitrous Direct3D 9 is set as the default driver if the graphics card or operating system on your system does not support Nitrous Direct3D 11.

To open the *Preference Settings* dialog box, select **Customize>Preferences** or **File>Preferences**. In the *Viewports* tab, and in the *Display Drivers* area, click **Choose Driver**. Then, select the required driver in the *Display Driver Selection* dialog box, as shown in Figure 1–38. If you change the display driver, you need to close and reopen the software for the changes to take effect.

> ***Note:*** *You can also change the graphics driver outside the software (if it is not open) using the Windows Start menu. Select Windows* ***Start>Autodesk>Change Graphics Mode****. This launches the software and provides the option of selecting the display driver.*

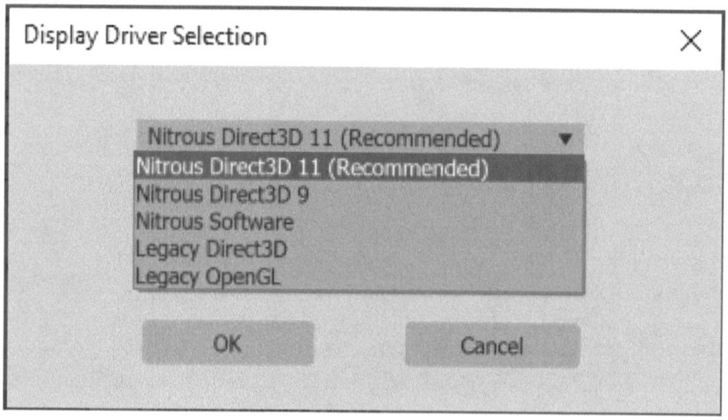

Figure 1–38

The following display drivers are available:

- **Nitrous Direct3D 11:** The Nitrous Direct 3D 11 driver requires Direct 3D 11.0. This driver takes advantage of video card features (when available), and provides high quality realistic viewport display options and faster rendering times. The visual display is render quality and supports unlimited lights, shadows, tone mapping, etc. The Nitrous driver also enables you to display your scenes in stylized images (pencil, acrylic, ink, etc.) in the viewports.
- **Nitrous Direct3D 9:** The Nitrous Direct 3D 9 driver requires Direct3D 9.0. It works in the same way as the Direct3D 11 driver.
- **Nitrous Software:** The Nitrous Software driver has similar capabilities to the other nitrous drivers, but the hardware support is not required and it might be slower during rendering.
- **Legacy Direct3D:** The Direct3D driver supports data culling and works well for the high-color displays.

- **Legacy OpenGL:** The OpenGL driver works well for hardware acceleration, including geometry acceleration and rasterization acceleration. You cannot display shadows or ambient occlusion in viewports while using this driver.

  Note: *The* ***OpenGL*** *and* ***Direct3D*** *options are useful if your system supports those forms of hardware acceleration. Experiment with these options to determine the best option for your workstation.*

1.7 Viewport Display and Labels

Geometry opens in the software through one or more viewports, which can be configured to show objects from different viewing angles and with different viewport shading modes.

The *Viewport* label menus (shown in Figure 1–39) display in the upper left corner of each viewport. Note that the four labels are only available for the Nitrous displays, while the legacy driver display shows only three labels.

Figure 1–39

General Viewport

Click on **[+]** to open the *General Viewport* label menu, as shown in Figure 1–40. It includes the ability to display grids, the ViewCube, and the SteeringWheels. It also contains tools for the **xView** functionality, which enables you to show statistics and diagnose problems in polygonal geometry such as overlapping faces, unwelded vertices, or face normal orientation issues.

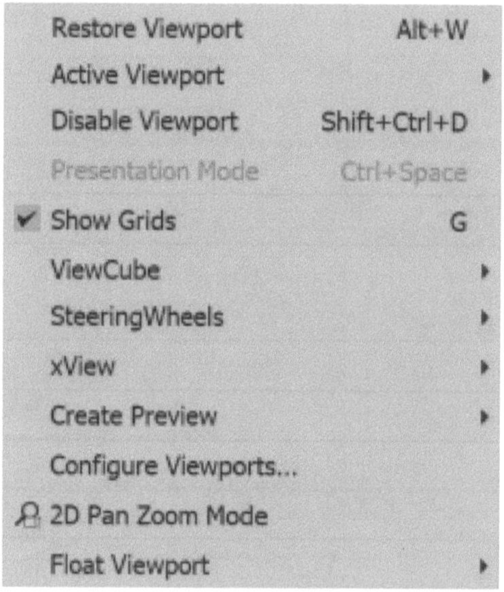

Figure 1–40

Point of View

The *Point of View* label displays the name of the view projection (i.e., Perspective, Orthographic) that is being shown in the viewport. Clicking on this *Viewport* label opens the *Point of View* label menu (shown in Figure 1–41), which enables you to change the view type. You can also change the view using the shortcut keys that are listed next to the type in the label menu (e.g., <T> for **Top**, <B> for **Bottom**, etc.).

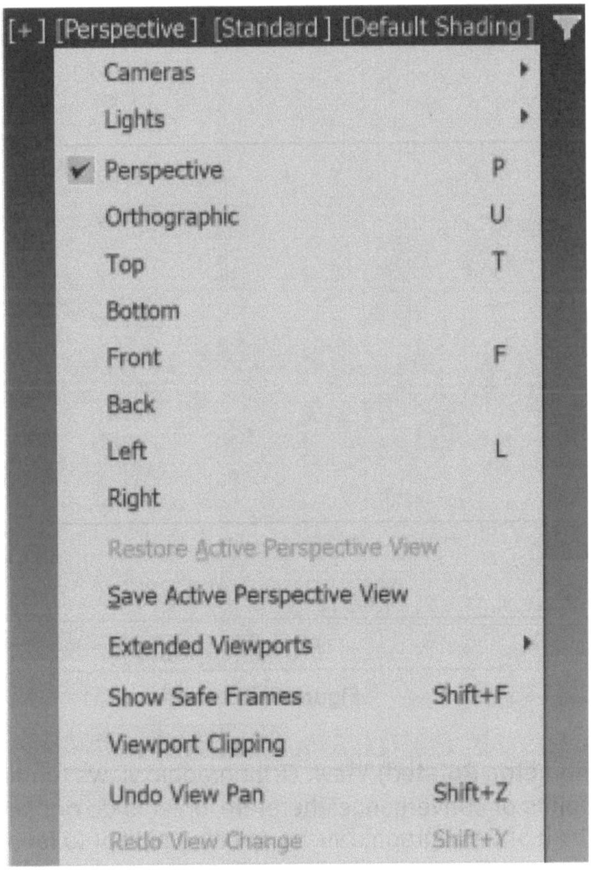

Figure 1–41

The three most common view types are:

- **Perspective View:** This view displays what is seen with human vision and uses vanishing points to make distant objects appear to recede from view. The most realistic output is shown through perspective views or the camera view, as shown in Figure 1–42.

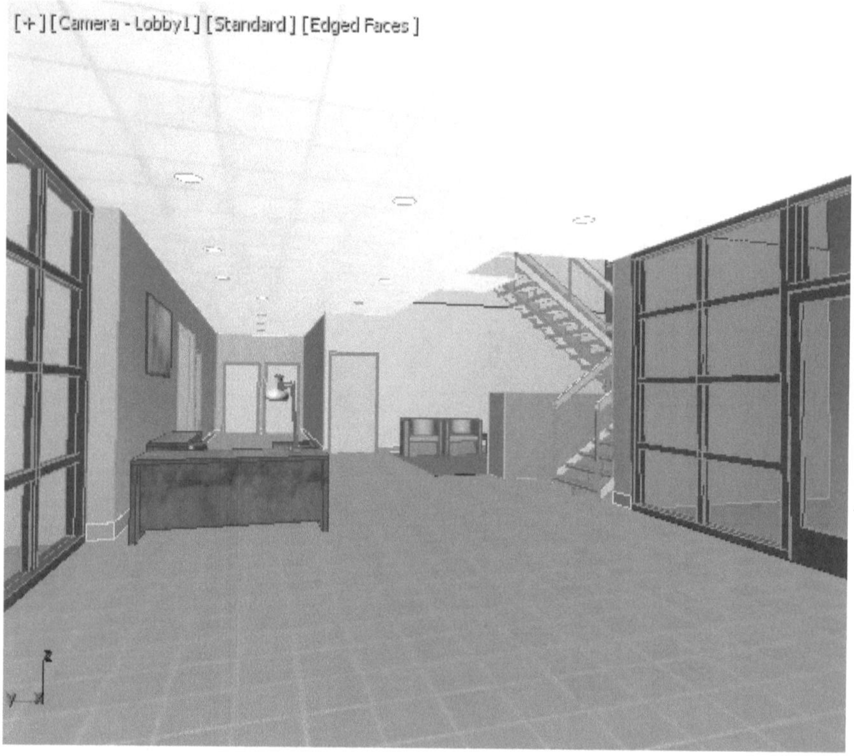

Figure 1–42

- **Orthographic (Axonometric Rotated) View:** Orthographic views (shown in Figure 1–43) do not use vanishing points or convergence; therefore, objects do not seem to recede over distance. You can think of Orthographic views as being similar to Isometric views (Isometric views are special cases of Axonometric views where the axes are equally inclined to the screen).

  Note: *You might find Orthographic views easier to navigate (especially when zooming with a mouse wheel), but the rendered output often does not display as realistic as from a perspective view.*

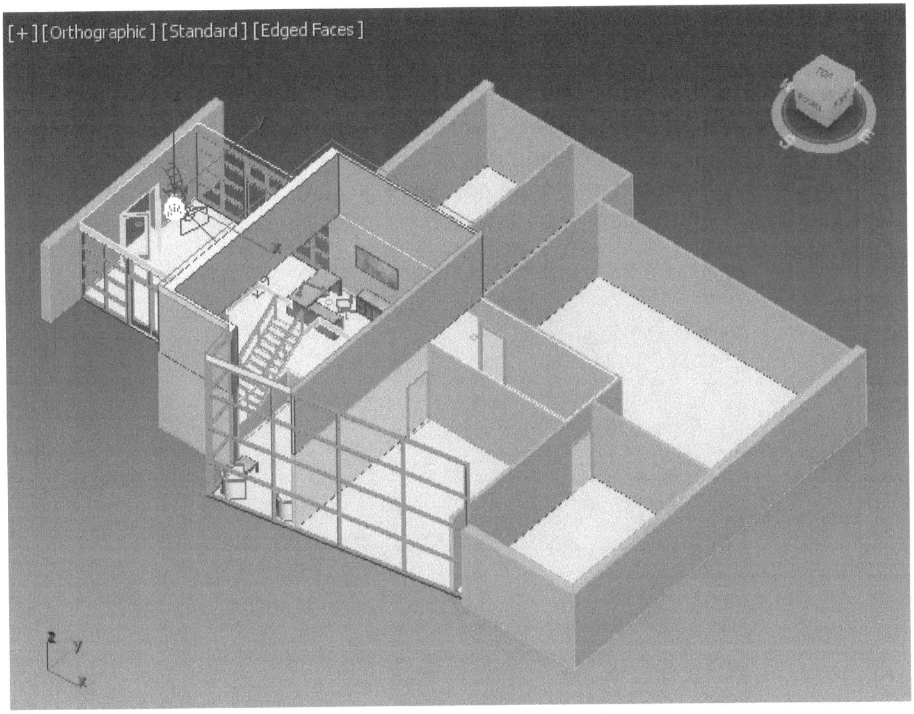

Figure 1–43

- **Other Views:** The **Left**, **Right**, **Top**, **Bottom**, **Front**, and **Back** views are all types of predefined views, which show a 2D projection of the model.

Shading Viewport

The *Shading Viewport* label provides options to change the shading display methods used in the viewport, such as **High Quality**, **Standard**, **Performance**, and **DX Mode** (as shown in Figure 1–44). In addition to shading, this menu contains tools for the **Lighting and Shadows** and display of materials with textures and maps.

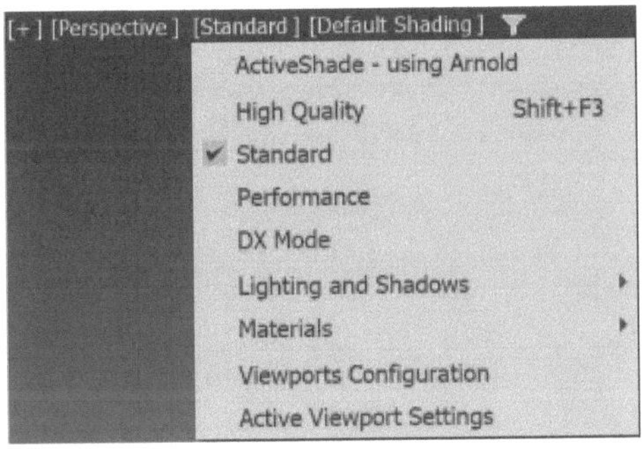

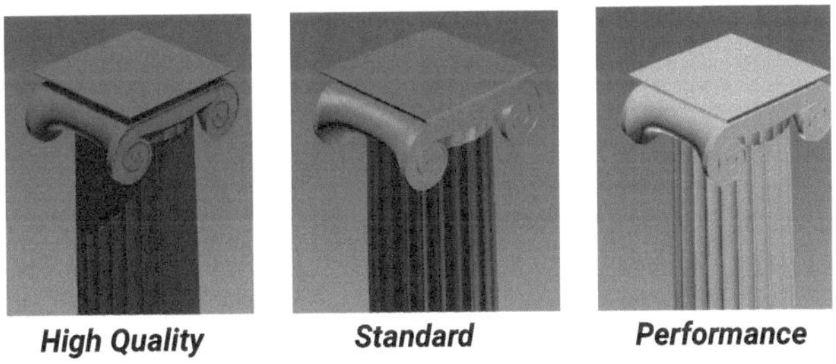

Figure 1–44

Per-View Preference

The *Per-View Preference* label menu (shown in Figure 1–45) displays the visual style methods for a view, such as **Default Shading, Facets, Bounding Box, Clay**, etc. You can select different edge modes and with the selected shading method. This menu also contains tools for various **Stylized** options, **Display Selected**, and **Viewport Background**. You can use the **Display Selected** options to control the display of selected geometry in shaded viewports.

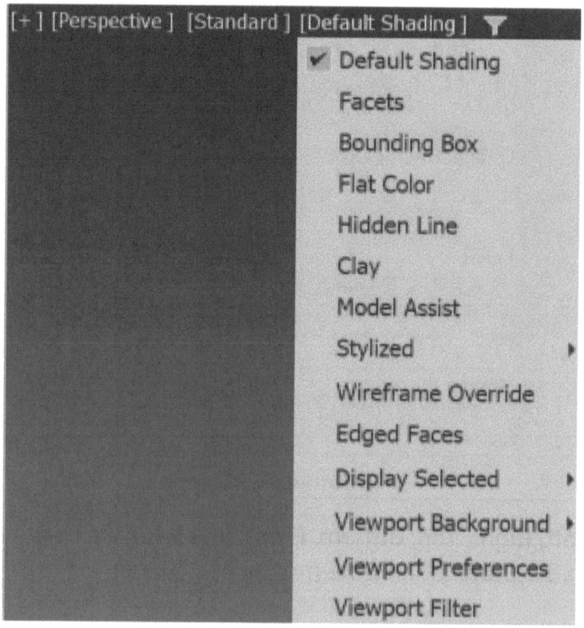

Figure 1–45

Some of the visual style modes (using the Standard shading viewport display) are shown in Figure 1–46.

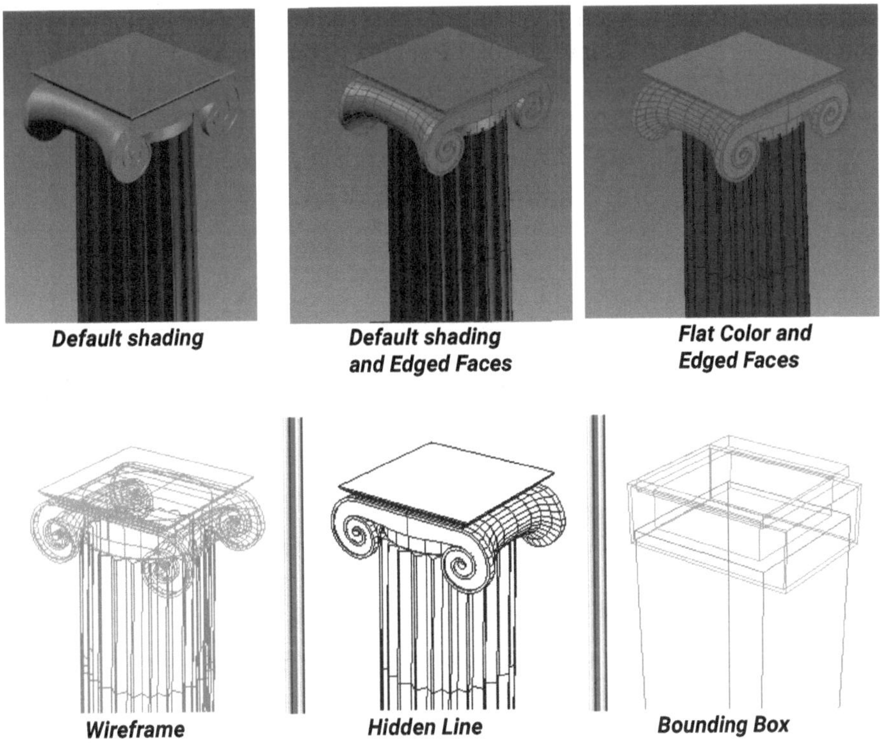

Figure 1–46

- The **Default Shading** mode displays the object as smooth with Phong shading being applied to it.
- The **Facets** option always displays the geometry as faceted even if the **Smooth** modifier or Smoothing have been applied to the object. This enables you to precisely locate the edges in the model and makes it easier to work with the geometry.
- The **Bounding Box** option is useful when scenes are extremely complex and software performance is an issue. Alternatively, in this situation, individual objects can be set to view as bounding boxes through Object Properties.
- In the **Flat Color** mode, lighting effects are disabled and the object displays with just the color.
- The **Hidden Line** option improves the Wireframe display by hiding the lines that are on the backside of the objects.
- The **Edged Faces** option overlays a wireframe over any other visual style, such as Default shading, Facets, Clay, and others.
- The **Clay** option displays the geometry in a terracotta color without any material or texture color.

- The **Stylized** menu options enable you to display objects with a variety of effects that are non-photorealistic, such as **Graphite**, **Color Pencil**, **Pastel**, etc., as shown in Figure 1–47.

Figure 1–47

Hint: Legacy Driver Display Labels

When you set your display driver as one of the legacy drivers, such as the **OpenGL** or **Direct3D** options, the driver display shows only three labels:

- The *General Viewport* label and the *Point of View* label contain the same menu options as for the nitrous drivers.
- The *Shading Viewport* label has menu options pertaining to the legacy drivers, as shown in Figure 1–48.

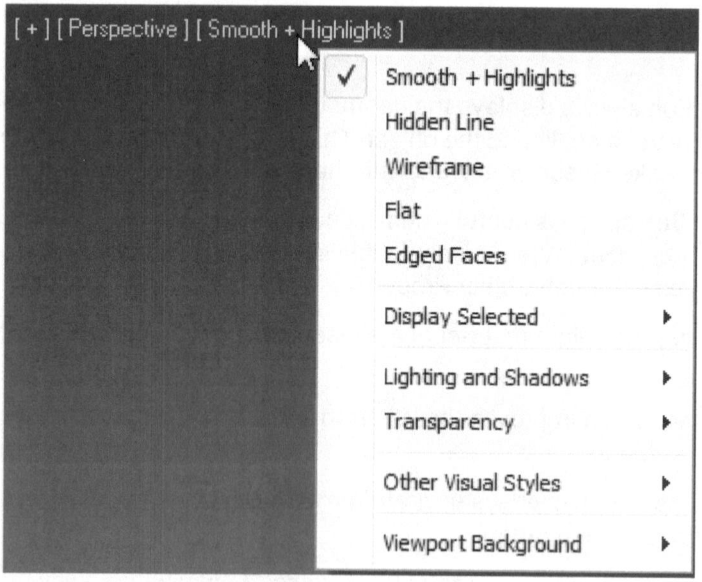

Figure 1–48

Practice 1a
Organize Folders and Work with the Interface

Practice Objectives

- Set the project folder and configure the paths.
- Create viewport layouts and navigate the graphic user interface.
- Modify an object using the Command Panel and using the Scene Explorer.

In this practice, you will work with the Autodesk 3ds Max software by setting the project folder to organize the files in the project. You will also configure the paths to set the folders. You will then create different viewport layouts by changing the viewing angles and different shading modes. You will also navigate the graphic user interface. To complete the practice, you will open a file and modify the objects using different interface components.

For printing purposes, the UI color scheme used for the practices has been set to **ame-light** (Menu bar: **Customize>Custom Defaults Switcher>ame-light** in *UI schemes* list).

Task 1: Set the project folder.

1. Download the practice files and ensure that the files are located in the *C:\Autodesk 3ds Max Fundamentals Practice Files* folder.
2. Launch the Autodesk 3ds Max 2025 software.
   - If a Welcome Screen displays, clear the **Show this Welcome Screen at startup** option and close the Welcome Screen.
   - If a *Security Message* dialog box displays, indicating that a new update to the **Malware Removal** is available, click **Close**, and install the update at a later time.
   - If you are already in the Autodesk 3ds Max 2025 screen, reset the program by selecting **Reset** in the **File** menu. This closes the current file and opens a new blank file. If an unsaved scene is open, you might be required to save or discard the changes to the scene. Click **Don't Save**. Click **Yes** to reset the file.
3. Along the right end of the Main Toolbar, in the **Project** toolbar, note the folder path. It is the current project folder based on your local settings.
4. In the Project toolbar, if it is not fully displayed, click » to display the tools and click (Create from Current), or in the **File** menu, expand **Project** and select **Create from Current**.

   ***Note:** Instructions to select from the menu bar will be styled as "**File>Project>Create from Current**" in the rest of this guide.*

5. In the *Choose a folder* dialog box, navigate to C: and select the *Autodesk 3ds Max Fundamentals Practice Files* folder.
   - This is the path to the location where you have saved the practice files that are provided with this learning guide.
6. Click **Select Folder**.
7. In the Project toolbar, note that **C:\Autodesk 3ds Max Fundamentals Practice Files** displays, as shown in Figure 1–49.

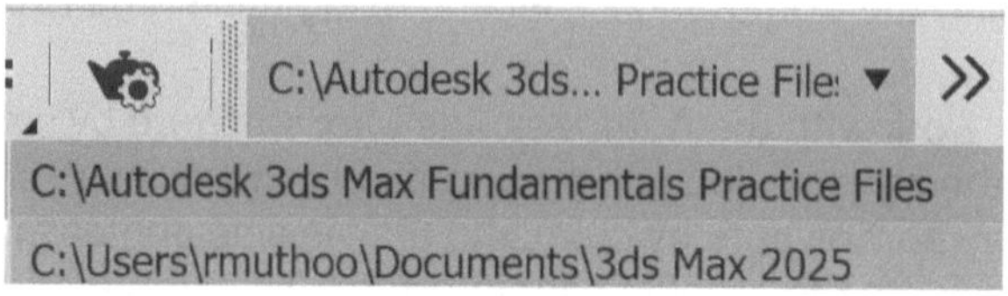

Figure 1–49

Task 2: Set preferences.

1. In the menu bar, select **File>Preferences** or **Customize>Preferences**. The *Preference Settings* dialog box opens.
2. In the *General* tab, in the *Ref. Coord. System* area, select **Constant**, as shown in Figure 1–50. This enables the Transform types to use the same Reference Coordinate System.

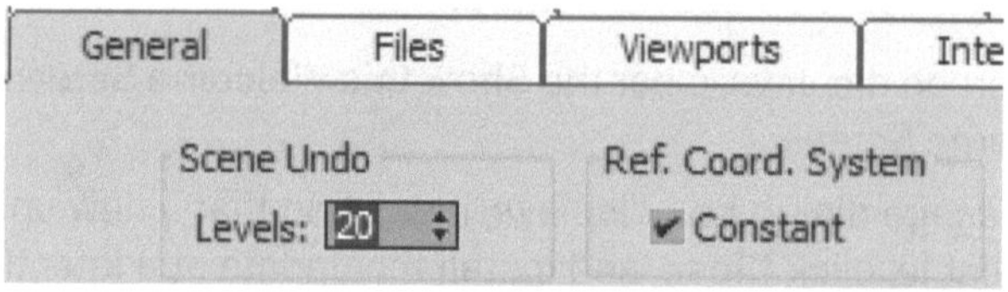

Figure 1–50

3. In the *Layer Defaults* area, verify that **Default to By Layer for New Nodes** is cleared, as shown in Figure 1–51.

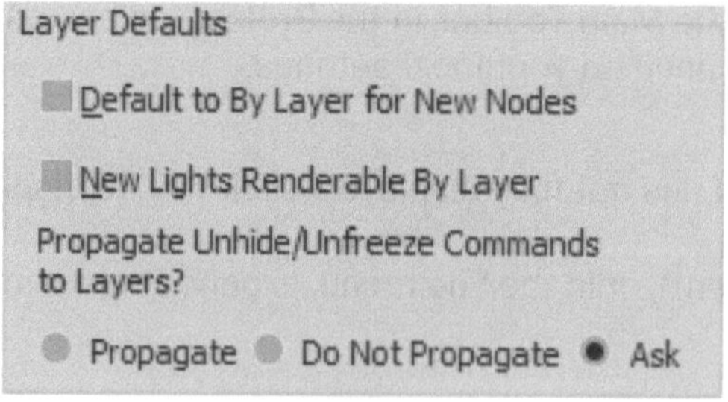

Figure 1–51

4. Select the *Security* tab, and verify that the **Safe Scene Script Execution** options are checked (excluding **Exclude script assets** and **Display script editor on blocked commands**, which should be cleared). Verify that both the **Malware Removal** options are checked, indicating that all the security options are in place. Also note that in the Status Bar, the security shield icon says "Enabled" and is green, as shown in Figure 1–52.

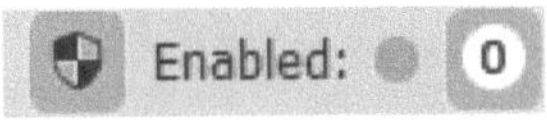

Figure 1–52

5. Click **OK** to close the *Preference Settings* dialog box.

Task 3: Configure the project paths.

1. Select **Customize>Configure Project Paths** to open the *Configure Project Paths* dialog box. Note that the Project Folder is set to the current active folder (*C:\Autodesk 3ds Max Fundamentals Practice Files*).
2. Verify that the *File I/O* tab is selected. In the list, select **Materials** and click **Modify.** In the *Choose Directory for Materials* dialog box, browse to *C:\Program Files\Autodesk\3ds Max 2025\materiallibraries*. Click **Use Path** (you might have to click **Use Path** again until you are back in the *Configure Project Paths* dialog box). The path displays as shown in Figure 1–53.

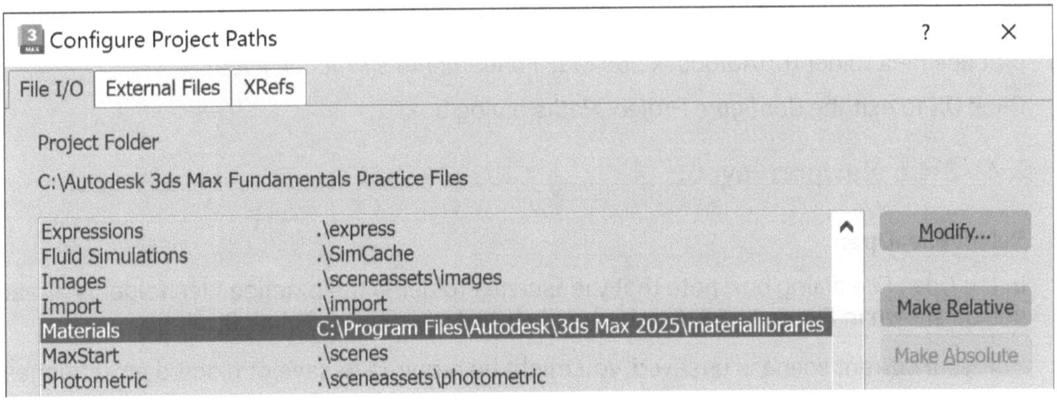

Figure 1–53

3. In the *Configure Project Paths* dialog box, select the *External Files* tab and click **Add**.
4. In the *Choose New External Files Path* dialog box, navigate to *C:\Autodesk 3ds Max Fundamentals Practice Files* and double-click on the folder. (Or you can just select it and click **Use Path**). Double-click on the *Maps* folder and click **Use Path**. Verify that you have returned to the *Configure Project Paths* dialog box. This enables all of the folders under the main folder to be searched for missing external files.

5. In the *Configure Project Paths* dialog box, verify that the new *Maps* path is still selected and click **Move Up**. Continue clicking **Move Up** until the new path is at the top of the list, as shown in Figure 1–54.
   - The paths are searched in order from top to bottom, so moving a custom path to the top saves time when searching for files.

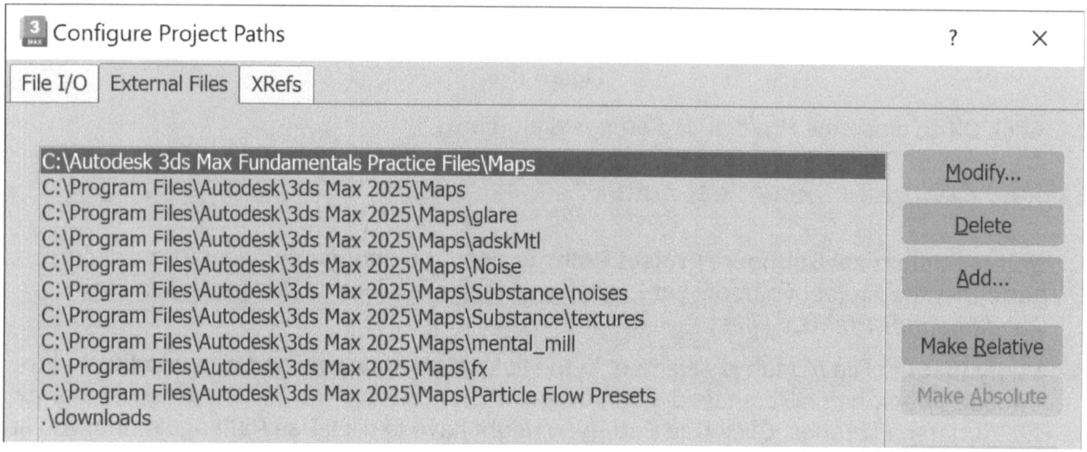

Figure 1–54

6. Select the *XRefs* tab and verify that the ...*\scenes* folder displays, which is pointing to the practice files folder (*C:\Autodesk 3ds Max Fundamentals Practice Files*).
7. Click **OK** to exit the *Configure Project Paths* dialog box.

Task 4: Set a viewport layout.

1. Select **File>Open**.
2. In the *Open File* dialog box, note that the *\scenes* folder in the practice files folder is already set, as shown in Figure 1–55. Select the file **Interface.max** and click **Open**.
   - If your current scene is unsaved, you might be required to save or discard any changes.

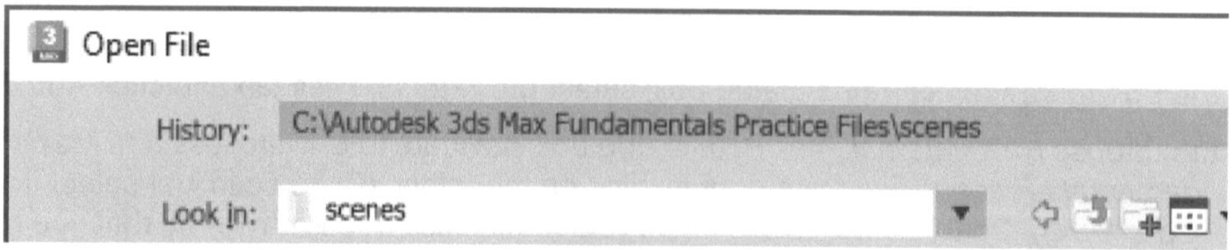

Figure 1–55

3. The model should display similar to that shown in Figure 1–56. Note that it opens in one maximized viewport layout, which was previously saved with the scene.
   - If the ribbon is covering the top portion of your model, use your middle mouse button to zoom out.
4. Verify that the *Viewport Layouts* tab bar and the Scene Explorer are displayed and docked along the left side of the viewport, as shown in Figure 1–56.
   - If the Scene Explorer is not displayed, select **Tools>Scene Explorer** and then dock it along the left side of the viewport window. The display of Scene Explorer might be dependent on your display monitor.
5. Verify that in the InfoCenter, the *Workspaces* is set to **Default**.
6. In the *Scene Explorer* toolbar, click (Display None) to clear all the categories. Note that the object list is empty.
7. Click (Display All) to activate all the different categories of objects. All of the selected tools have a blue background, indicating that they are active. Note the three main objects that make up the model are listed, as shown in Figure 1–56.

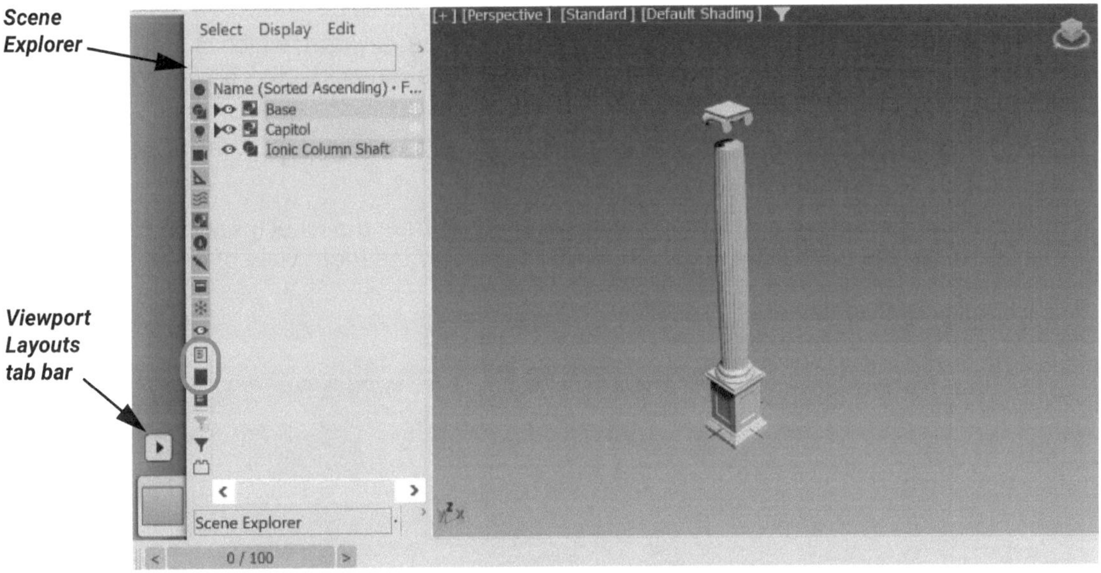

Figure 1–56

- The file can be zoomed in/out by rolling the middle mouse button. Display the complete model in the viewport. Click and hold the middle mouse button to pan the model such that it is centered in the viewport.

8. In the *Viewport Layouts* tab bar, click ▶ to expand the *Standard Viewport Layouts* panel. Select the layout, as shown in Figure 1–57 (second row, second column).
   - Note that the model displays in three viewport layouts and the newly selected layout is added to the tabs list, as shown in Figure 1–58.

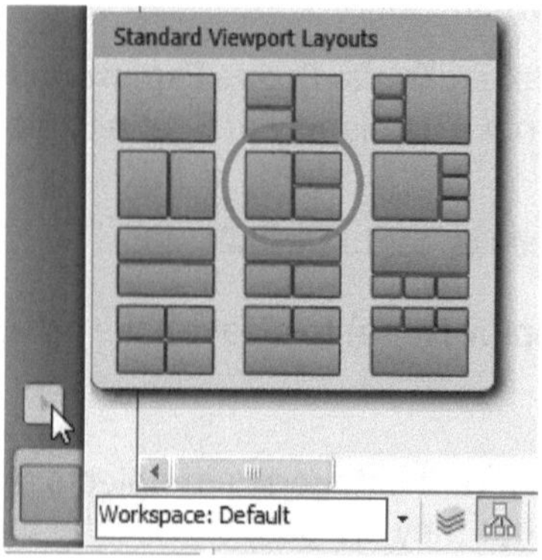

Figure 1–57

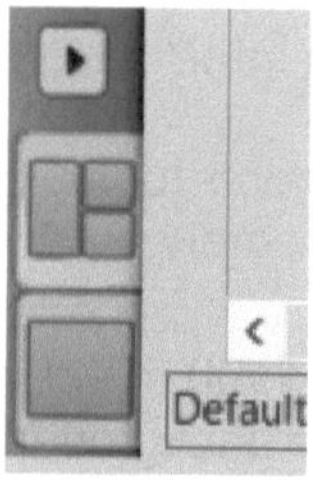

Figure 1–58

9. Note that a yellow border displays around the left single viewport, which is the **Top** viewport, indicating that it is the active viewport. In this viewport, click on the **[Wireframe]** *Per-View Preference* label to display the label menu.
10. Select **Stylized>Graphite**, as shown in Figure 1–59. Note the change in the display of objects in this view only.
11. Click on the **[Top]** *Point of View* label and select **Right** from the label menu, as shown in Figure 1–60. Alternatively, you can press <R> to display the **Right** view of the object.

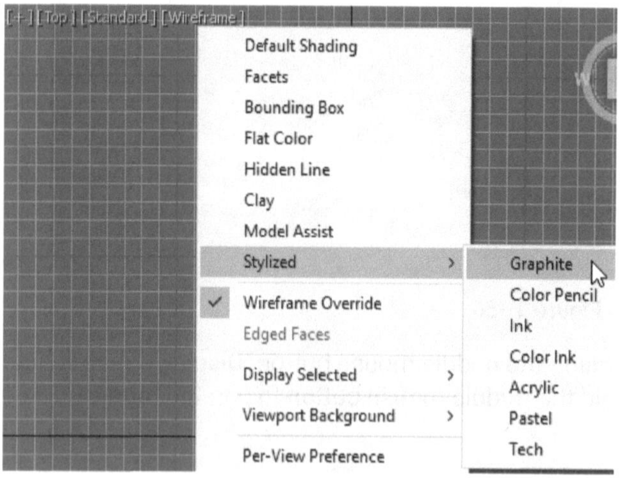

Figure 1–59

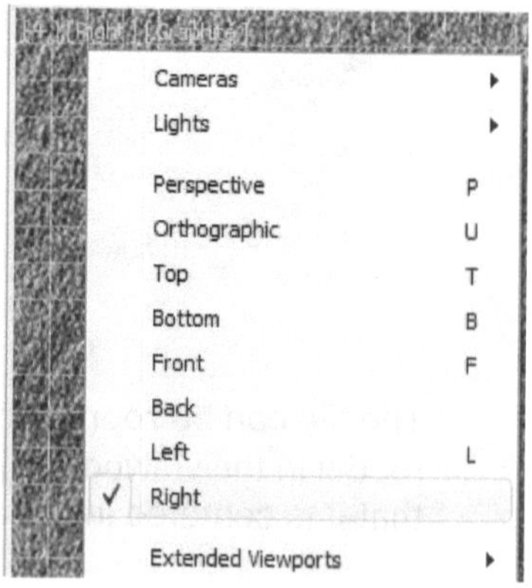

Figure 1–60

12. Use the mouse wheel to zoom out so that the complete model displays in this viewport. While holding the middle mouse button, drag the cursor to pan the objects so that they are centered in the viewport.
13. Click in empty space in the lower right viewport (**Left** view). Note that the yellow border now displays around this viewport, indicating that it is the active viewport.
14. Set the following by clicking the respective labels and selecting the required option from each label menu:
    - **[Left]** *Point of View* label: **Perspective**
    - **[Wireframe]** *Per-View Preference* label: **Default Shading**

    Note: *Instructions for clicking on the* ***[Left]*** *Point of View label and selecting* ***Perspective*** *in the label menu will be styled as "click the* ***[Left]*** *Point of View label and select* ***Perspective****" in the rest of this guide.*
15. Press <Z> to zoom in to the objects in this viewport.
16. Activate the top right viewport by clicking in empty space. Ensure that the *Point of View* label is set to **Front**. Click the **[Wireframe]** *Per-View Preference* label and select **Clay**.
17. Use the middle mouse button to pan and zoom to display the objects in this view.
    - The objects and the viewport layout should look similar to those in Figure 1–61.

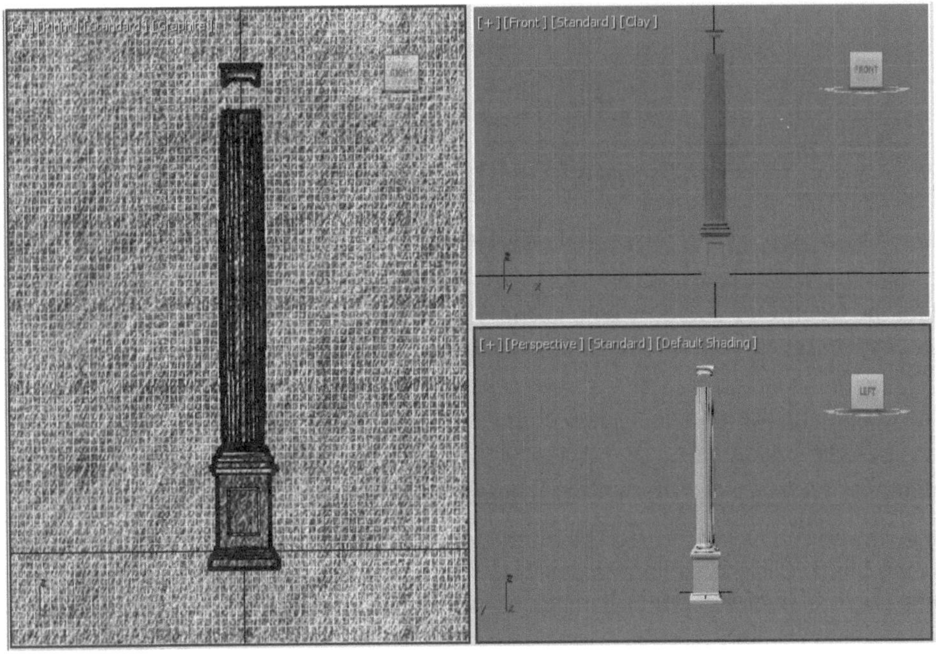

Figure 1–61

Task 5: Modify the objects using the Command Panel.

1. In the *Viewport Layouts* tab bar, select the initial layout (single viewport) that existed with the scene, as shown in Figure 1–62. The objects display in a single viewport in the **Perspective** view with the **Default Shading** visual style.

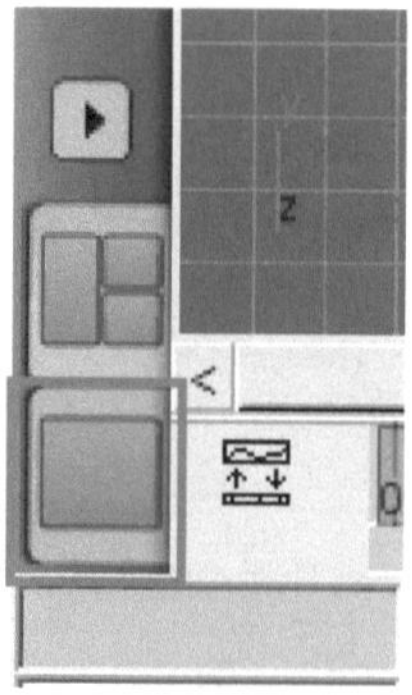

Figure 1–62

2. In the Command Panel, select the *Create* panel (), if required (active by default), as shown in Figure 1–63.

Figure 1–63

3. Select the **Geometry** category by clicking  (Geometry), if required (active by default). The different types of geometry that you can create are listed here.

4. In the Command Panel, select the *Modify* panel (). The panel is empty as no objects are currently selected.
5. In the Main Toolbar, click  (Select Object), if required.
6. In the viewport, hover the cursor over the cyan (blue) object to display its name, **Ionic Column Shaft**. Click the object to select it. The **Ionic Column Shaft** is highlighted in the Scene Explorer, indicating that it is selected. The name and modifiers that have been applied display in the Command Panel. The Status Line at the bottom of the viewport, displays **1 Object Selected**, as shown in Figure 1–64.

   Note: *Names display in the tooltip when the cursor is hovered over an unselected object. Once the object has been selected, its name displays in the Modifier Stack.*

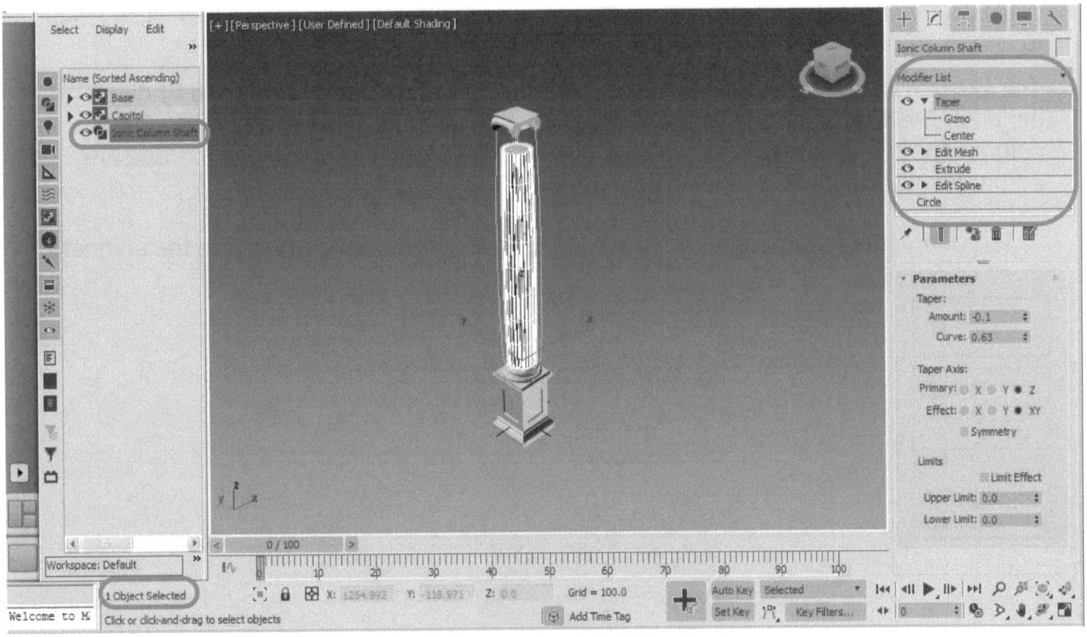

Figure 1–64

7. In the Command Panel, next to the object name **Ionic Column Shaft**, select the color swatch. Select a different color and click **OK** to change the color of the column shaft.
8. In the *Modifier Stack*, the list of modifiers that have been used on the column shaft display, as shown in Figure 1–65. Click (eye) next to the **Taper** modifier to toggle the taper off and then on again and note the effect on the object. Leave it on.

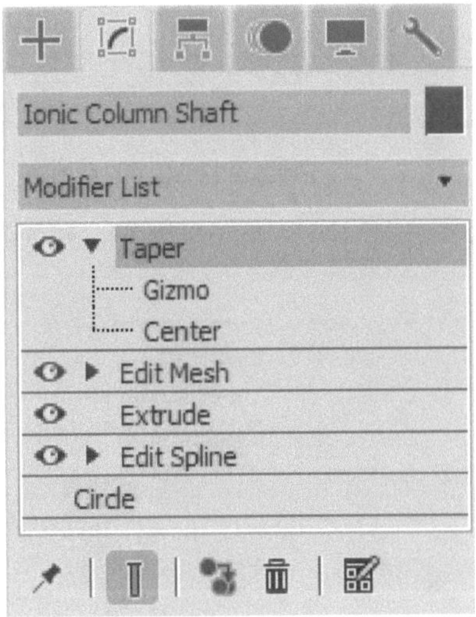

Figure 1–65

9. In the *Modifier Stack*, select the **Extrude** modifier. In the *Warning* dialog box, click **Hold/Yes** to continue.
10. The **Extrude** parameters display in the rollouts. Note that the *Amount* (400.0) displays the height of the shaft. Change it to **440.0** (as shown in Figure 1–66) and press <Enter>. The column shaft is extended and touches the top. The modifiers above the extrude are automatically reapplied to the object with its new height.
    - To change the parameter, enter the value in the *Amount* edit box or use the spinners.

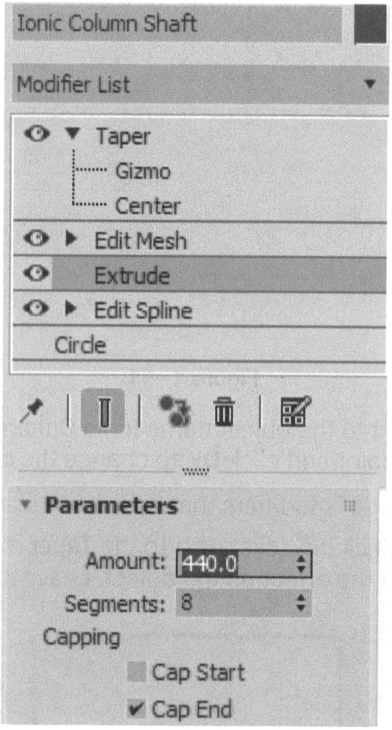

Figure 1–66

Note: *You can adjust parameters at any level of the Modifier Stack.*

Task 6: Use the Scene Explorer.

1. In the Scene Explorer, note an arrow besides the objects **Capitol** and **Base,** indicating that each has a group of objects inside it. Click on the arrow besides **Capitol** to expand the group and note the different objects sorted in a hierarchical fashion, as shown in Figure 1–67.

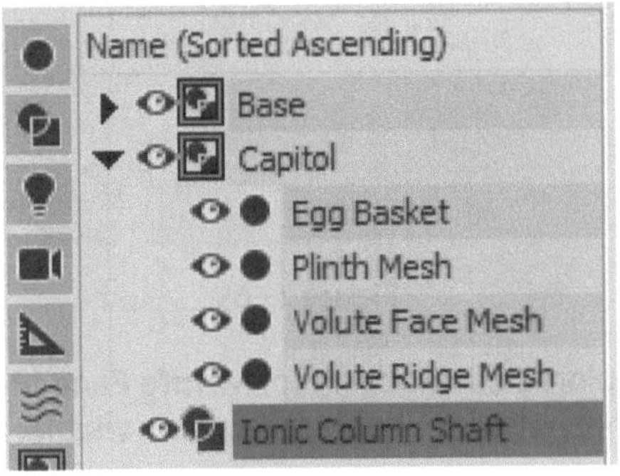

Figure 1–67

2. Click in empty space in the viewport to clear the selection. Note that the Command Panel is empty as there are no objects currently selected. Also note that nothing is highlighted in the Scene Explorer.
3. In the viewport, hover the cursor over the top gray square portion of the object. It displays the name as **[Capitol] Plinth Mesh**, as shown in Figure 1–68.

Figure 1–68

4. As the  (Select Object) is already active, click on **[Capitol] Plinth Mesh** in the viewport to select it. The complete object is selected although, the Plinth Mesh is just the top square portion.
5. Click in empty space in the viewport to clear the selection.

6. In the Scene Explorer, click on (eye icon) for **Plinth Mesh** and note that only the topmost square object of the Capitol is hidden in the viewport, as shown in Figure 1–69.

Figure 1–69

7. Similarly, in the Scene Explorer, click on (eye icon) for **Volute Face Mesh** and **Volute Ridge Mesh** and note that only the inner cylindrical object remains visible, as shown in Figure 1–70.

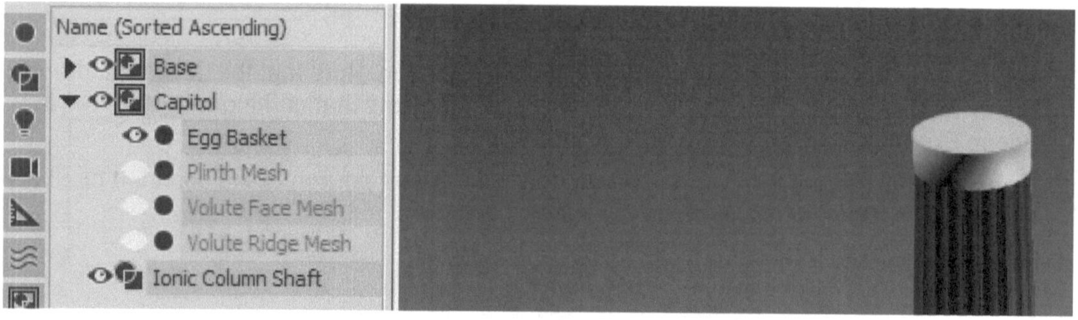

Figure 1–70

8. In the Scene Explorer, click on (grayed out eye) for the three hidden sub objects to make them visible again.
9. Select **File>Save As** and save your work as **MyInterface.max**.
   - When you save a file, note that it is being saved to the practice files ...*scenes* folder.

End of practice

Practice 1b
Autodesk 3ds Max Quickstart

Practice Objective

- Create primitive objects and apply basic animation to a primitive object.

In this practice, you will model and animate a teapot driving through a city of pyramids. This practice will introduce you to the Autodesk 3ds Max interface and workflow fundamentals. Many of the commands used in this practice are discussed later in the guide.

Many of you will probably never need to animate a teapot driving through a city of pyramids. This practice is designed to introduce you to interactive 3D modeling and animation and working with the interface.

Task 1: Create primitive objects.

1. Select **File>Reset** to start a new file. Click **Yes** in the confirmation dialog box.
   - If an unsaved scene is open, you might be required to save or discard any changes to the scene.
2. In the Command Panel, verify that the *Create* panel ( ) and (Geometry) are selected (active by default). Also, ensure that the **Standard Primitives** sub-category displays.
3. Click inside the **Perspective** viewport to activate it (yellow border). Maximize it (single viewport) by clicking (Maximize Viewport) in the Navigation toolbar, found in the lower right corner of the interface. Alternatively, you can press <Alt>+<W>.
4. In the *Object Type* rollout, click **Pyramid** to activate it, as shown in Figure 1–71.

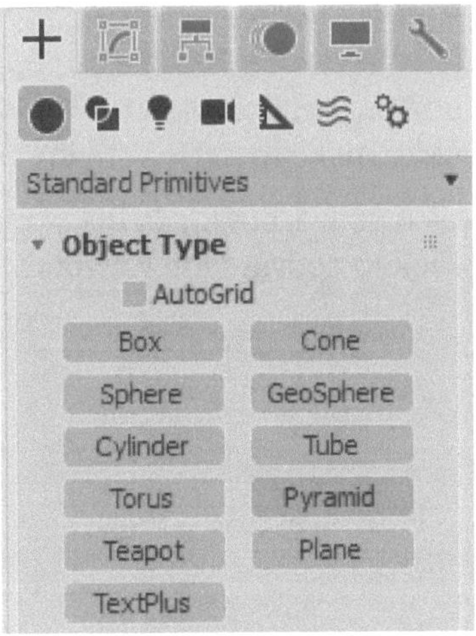

Figure 1–71

5. Near the center of the grid, click, hold, and drag to create the base for a pyramid, as shown in Figure 1–72 (eyeball the size of the pyramid). Release the mouse button and continue to move the cursor up to set the height of the pyramid. When your pyramid displays correctly (similar to that shown in Figure 1–73), click to end the creation process. In the Scene Explorer, note that a highlighted geometry is listed with the name **Pyramid001**, indicating that it is selected.

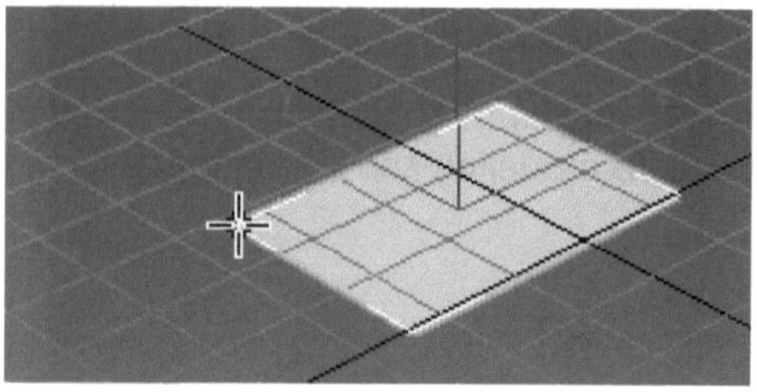

Figure 1–72

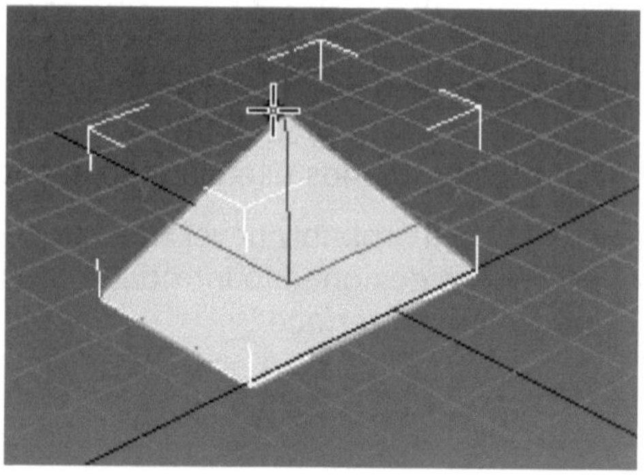

Figure 1–73

6. In the Command Panel, in the *Name and Color* rollout, click the **Color** swatch to the right of the pyramid name (**Pyramid001),** select a different color in the *Object Color* dialog box and verify that **Assign Random Colors** is selected. This enables you to create objects with different colors automatically. Click **OK**. Note that the swatch color changes and the pyramid color changes in the viewport.
    - Your objects will be of different colors than those shown in the figures.
7. In the Navigation toolbar, click (Maximize Viewport) or use <Alt>+<W>. Note that the pyramid displays in four equal viewports with different viewing angles.
8. You will need to move the pyramid to the upper left quadrant of the home grid. Verify that the pyramid is selected. In the Main Toolbar, click (Select and Move). In the **Top** view (upper left viewport), right-click to make it active with the object still selected.
    - Clicking in a viewport makes it active, but loses the selection of objects. To maintain the selection of objects, right-click to activate the viewport.

9. Click and hold the yellow square (anywhere along the two outer edges when the cursor displays as a move cursor) of the Transform gizmo, as shown in Figure 1–74. While holding the object, drag it to the new location (upper left quadrant). Leave the gizmo once the object is at the correct location.

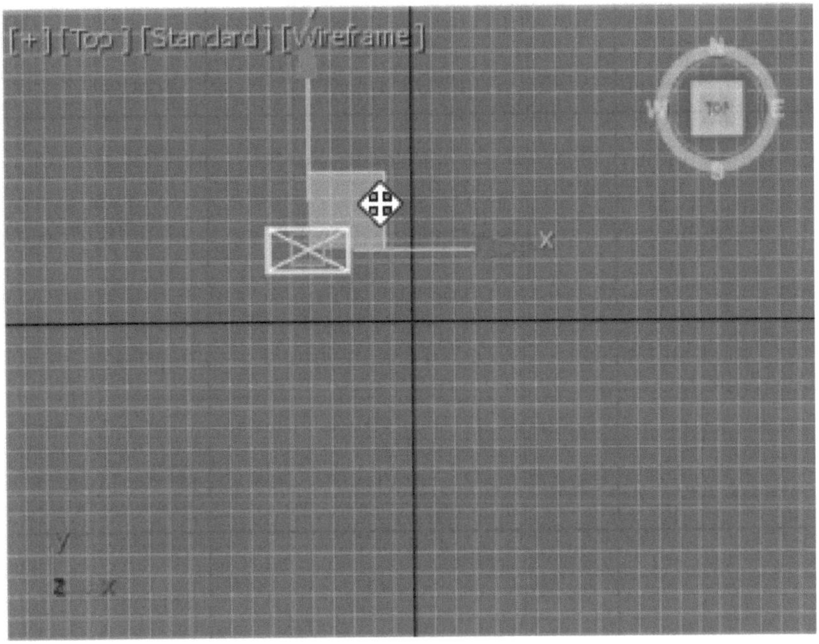

Figure 1–74

Note: *The transform tools are discussed in detail later in this guide.*

10. In the Command Panel, in the *Object Type* rollout, click **Pyramid** again. In the **Top** viewport, click, hold, and drag to create the base for another pyramid on the lower side of the main grid line, opposite to the first one. Release the mouse button and continue to move the cursor up to set the height of the pyramid. Because you are in the **Top** viewport, the height of the pyramid is not displayed. You can visually note the height in other three viewports in which the height displays. Once the pyramid displays as required, click to complete the command.

Note: *You can create objects in any viewport, but the orientation of the objects depends on the viewport created. Note that their creation is displayed interactively in all the viewports.*

11. In the Top viewport, create a number of pyramids on the home grid. Create a row of pyramids in one direction and a few others to create a street corner in the pyramid city, as shown in Figure 1–75. Try to keep all of the pyramids in the grid visible in the **Perspective** viewport. Use (Select and Move) tool to place the pyramids similar to that shown in Figure 1–75.
    - To display all of the pyramids in a viewport, use the middle mouse wheel to zoom in and out and press, hold, and drag it to pan.
12. Once the required number of pyramids have been created, right-click in empty space or press <Esc> to exit the **Pyramid** command.
13. You can organize them as shown in Figure 1–75 by moving them in the **Top** viewport using (Select and Move) in the Main Toolbar. Once you have moved the objects, click (Select Object) in the Main Toolbar to exit the **Move** command and avoid moving the objects accidentally.

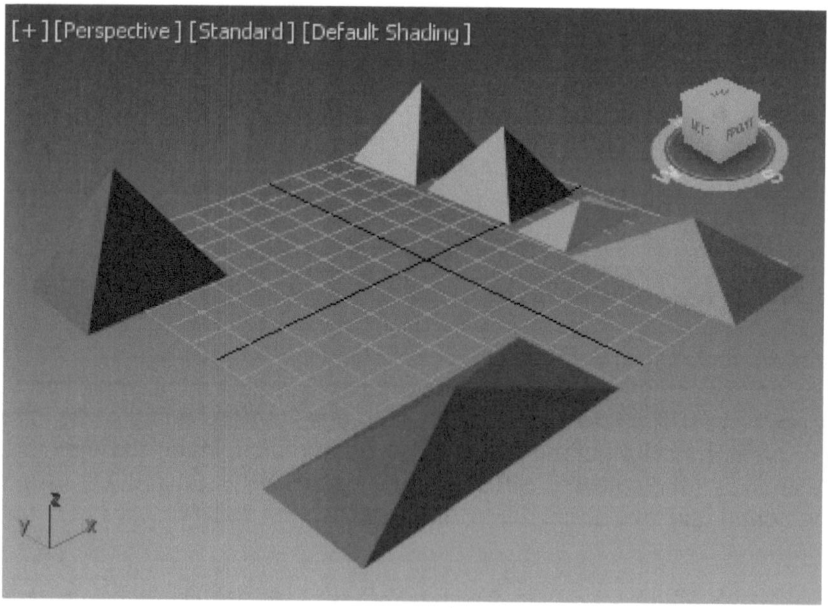

Figure 1–75

14. Make the **Perspective** viewport active and maximize the viewport by clicking (Maximize Viewport) or use <Alt>+<W>. You can click anywhere in empty space to clear a selected object and activate the viewport.
15. In the *Create* panel (+)> (Geometry), in the *Object Type* rollout, click **Teapot** to activate it.

16. In the lower left area of the **Perspective** viewport, click and drag to create a teapot, as shown in Figure 1–76. Using  (Select and Move), move it toward the left of the quadrant grid line.
    - If the selection brackets bounding box is not displayed with the teapot, click the **[Default Shading]** *Per-View Preference* label and select **Viewport Preferences**. In the dialog box, select **Selection Brackets** and close it.

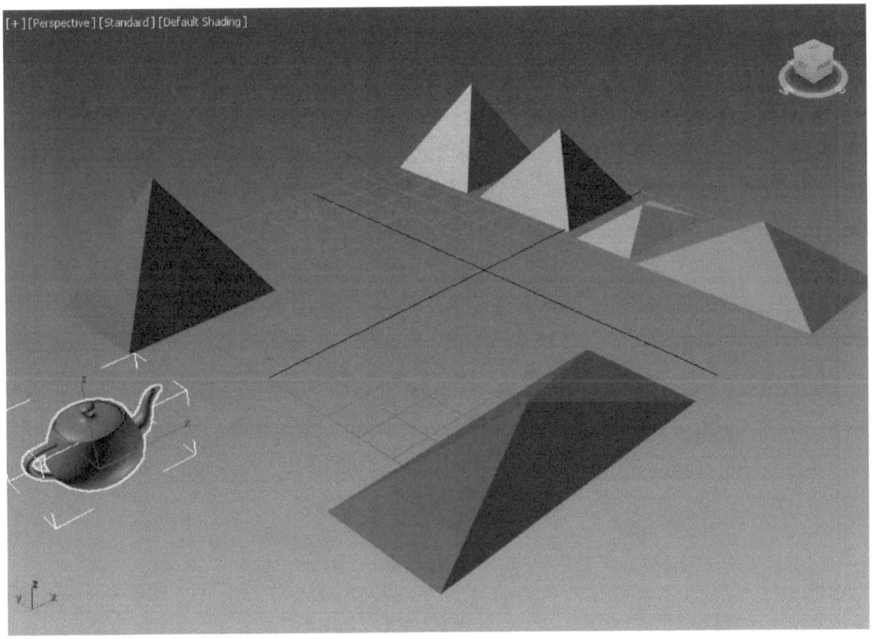

Figure 1–76

Task 2: Add basic animation.

1. The Animation controls are located on the left of the Navigation tools at the bottom right of the screen. Click the **Auto** button, as shown in Figure 1–77. Once you click it, the Auto key button, time slider bar, and border around the active viewport (**Perspective** viewport) are highlighted in red.

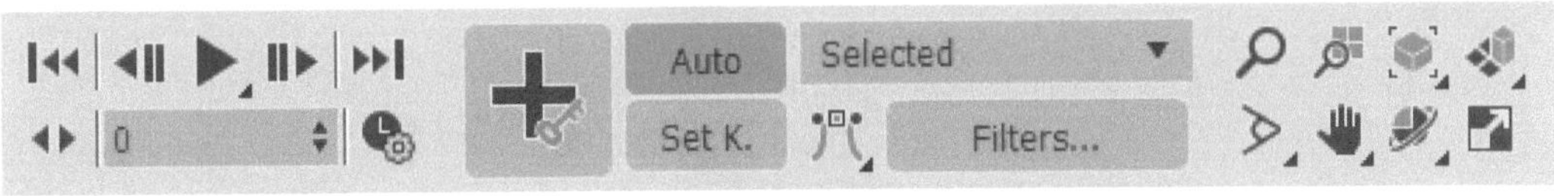

Figure 1–77

Note: *Animation controls are discussed in detail later in this guide.*

2. Along the bottom of the viewport, click and hold the time slider (0/100 button). Drag the time slider button in the red slider bar until the frame indicator displays **30/100** () and the blue marker is on 30 in the track bar, as shown in Figure 1–78.

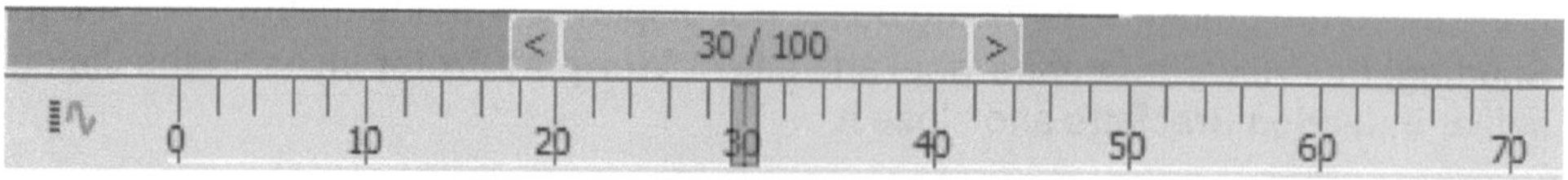

Figure 1–78

3. Click on the teapot, if not already selected. Verify that  (Select and Move) is still highlighted (blue background), If not, right-click and select **Move** in the **quad** menu, as shown in Figure 1–79, or simply click it in the Main Toolbar.
   - A selected object has a blue boundary and the cursor gizmo attached with it.

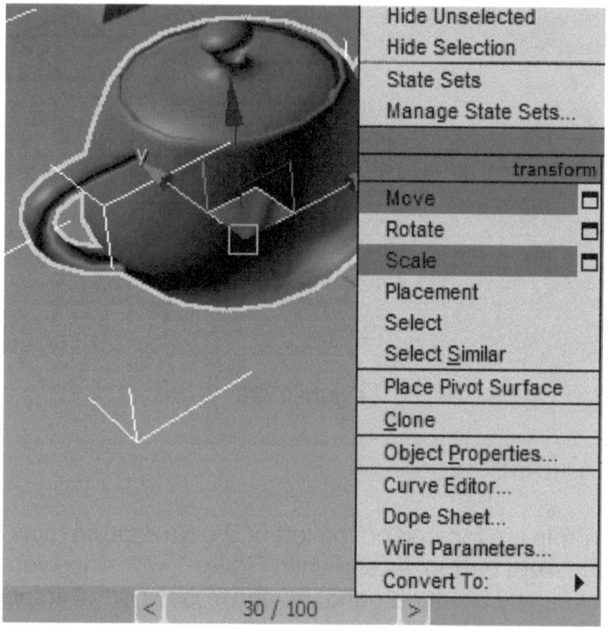

Figure 1–79

4. Hover the cursor over the X-axis (red arrow) of the Move gizmo so that only the X arrow displays in yellow. Hold and drag to move the teapot in the X-direction, as shown in Figure 1–80. Move it to approximate midway between the original position and the intersection of the home grid.

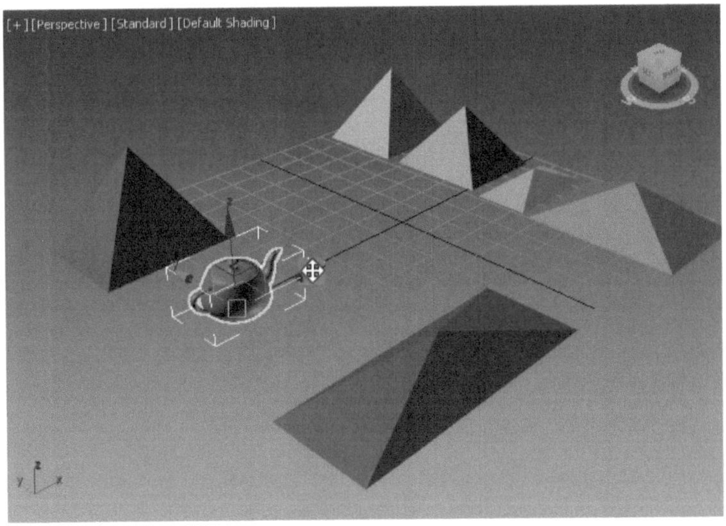

Figure 1–80

5. Click and drag the time slider again to read **60/100**.
6. Move the teapot in the X-direction till it reaches the intersection of the horizontal street, as shown in Figure 1–81.

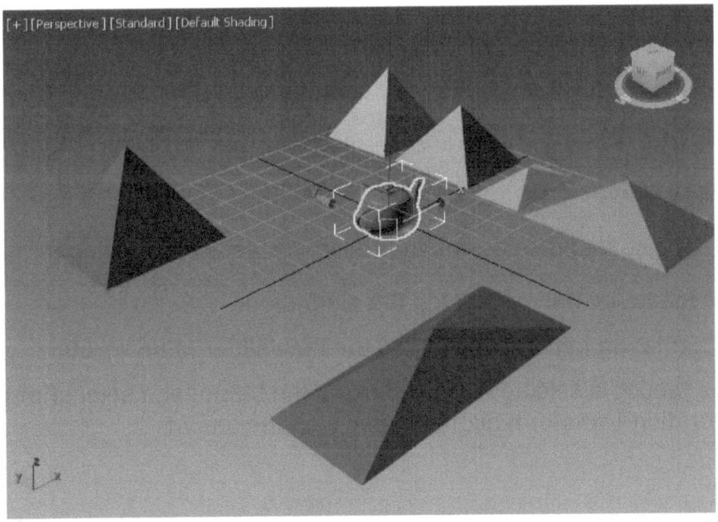

Figure 1–81

7. Click and drag the time slider to read **90/100**. Hover the cursor over the Y-axis (left, green arrow) of the Move gizmo. Click and drag to move the teapot in the Y-direction until it reaches the end of the horizontal street, as shown in Figure 1–82.

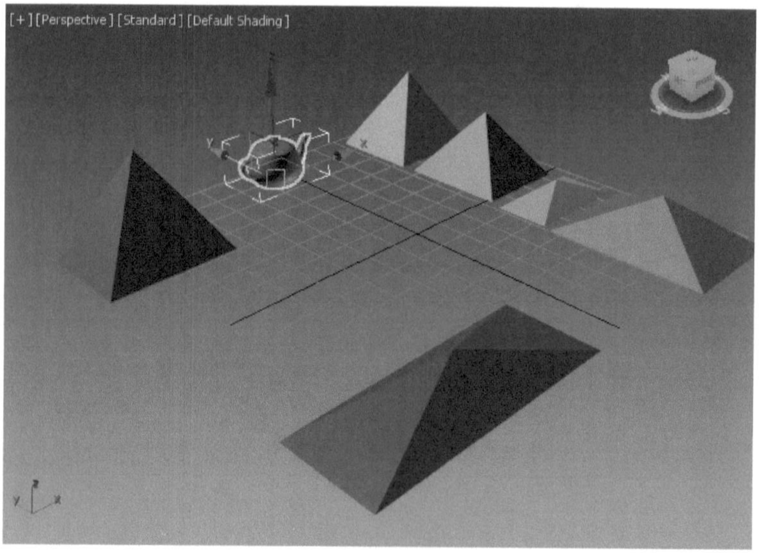

Figure 1–82

8. Note that the track bar below the time slider now has four red boxes (as shown in Figure 1–83), indicating that the keyframes have been set at frames 0, 30, 60, and 90.

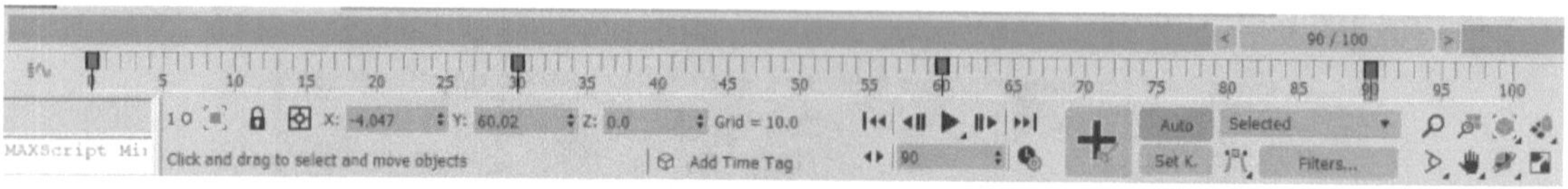

Figure 1–83

9. In the Animation Controls () located near the bottom right of the screen, click  (Play). The teapot is now animated in the viewport, moving through the pyramid city. Click  (Stop Animation) to stop the animation.
10. You can add a rotation to the teapot. Drag the time slider to frame **60**.
11. Verify that the teapot is selected. Right-click on the teapot and select **Rotate** in the quad menu. The Rotation Transform gizmo displays on the teapot.

12. In the Status Bar, along the left of the animation controls, in the **Z** *Transform Type-in* field, enter **90.0** and press <Enter>, as shown in Figure 1–84. The teapot is rotated and the spout is pointing to the left.

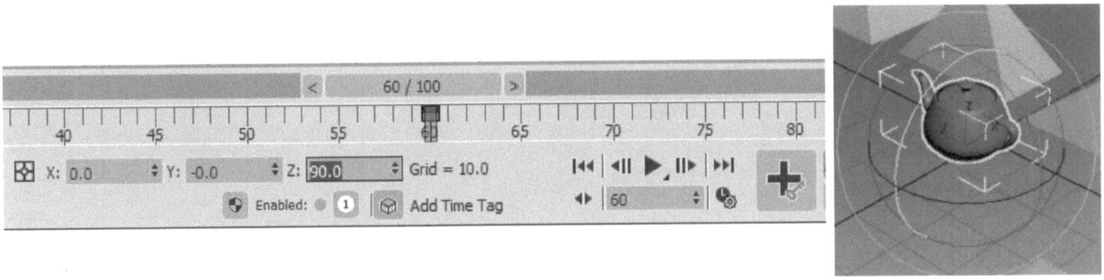

Figure 1–84

- At frame 60, the time slider now displays a red and green marker, indicating both rotation and position keys.

13. Play the animation using (Play). Click (Stop) to stop the animation. You can also view the animation by dragging the time slider back and forth. This is called *scrubbing* the time slider.
14. To only rotate the teapot after frame 45, add a keyframe rotation of **0** at frame 45 by moving the time slider to 45 and entering 0 in the **Z** *Transform Type-in* field. Play the animation to view the changes.
15. Stop the animation. Toggle off Auto key mode by clicking the red **Auto** button to complete the animation of the teapot.
16. Click in empty space to clear the object selection.
17. Select **File>Save As** and save your work as **MyPyramidCity.max**. Verify that it is being saved in the ...*scenes* folder.
    - You can also open **Pyramidcity.max** from the practices files folder to compare with a similar type file. You can play the animation and select the teapot to check the various keys.

End of practice

Chapter Review Questions

1. Which of the Autodesk 3ds Max interface components contains (Selection Lock)?
   a. Modeling Ribbon
   b. Status Bar
   c. InfoCenter
   d. Command Panel

2. Which menu or drop-down list enables you to break the Main Toolbar into modular pieces?
   a. Workspace selector drop-down list
   b. Quad menu (shortcut menu)
   c. Customize menu
   d. *General Viewport* label menu

3. Which of the following tabs are part of the Modeling ribbon? (Select all that apply.)
   a. Freeform
   b. Display
   c. Utilities
   d. Modeling

4. In the *Configure Project Paths* dialog box, which tab stores the location of the files for open, save, export, etc.?
   a. *XRefs* tab
   b. *System* tab
   c. *External Files* tab
   d. *File I/O* tab

5. Which display driver does not require hardware support?
    a. Nitrous Direct3D 11
    b. Nitrous Direct3D 9
    c. Nitrous Software

6. Which of the following is NOT a **Stylized** menu option?
    a. Color Pencil
    b. Graphite
    c. Shading
    d. Pastel

Command Summary

Button	Command	Location
	**Create Default**	• **Project Toolbar** • **Menu Bar:** File>Project
	**Create Empty**	• **Project Toolbar** • **Menu Bar:** File>Project
	**Create from Current**	• **Project Toolbar** • **Menu Bar:** File>Project
	**Create panel**	• **Command Panel**
N/A	**New**	• **Menu Bar:** File>New>New All
N/A	**Open**	• **Menu Bar:** File>Open
N/A	**Preferences**	• **Menu Bar:** File>Preferences
	**Ribbon**	• **Main Toolbar** • **Customize:** Show UI>Show Ribbon
N/A	**Save**	• **Menu Bar:** File>Save
N/A	**Save As**	• **Menu Bar:** File>Save As
N/A	**Scene Explorer**	• **Menu Bar:** Tools>Scene Explorer
	**Set Active Project**	• **Project Toolbar** • **Menu Bar:** File>Project

Chapter 2

Autodesk 3ds Max Configuration

The Autodesk® 3ds Max® software layout is unique compared to other Autodesk products. Becoming familiar with its navigation tools, how to view the model in the viewport, and how to work with the model in the interface is an important step to efficiently creating a visualization project.

Learning Objectives

- Move around in a scene using the various navigation tools.
- Set the layout and viewport configuration settings.
- Select objects using the object selection tools.
- Assign and change units in a scene.
- Group similar objects together in a layer and adjust layer properties.
- Modify the display settings of layers and objects.

2.1 Viewport Navigation

Navigation tools are used to change the point of view in viewports. Perspective, User, and Orthographic views (non-camera views such as Top, Front, etc.) share common viewport controls. The navigation tools are different in the non-camera and camera views.

- You can scroll the middle mouse wheel to zoom in and zoom out of the objects in the modeling window.
- Press, hold, and drag the middle mouse wheel to pan.
- Zooming with the mouse wheel in a perspective view might not work in all scenes due to roundoff issues. If you are unable to zoom using the mouse wheel, click  (Zoom Extents) and use  (Zoom) in the navigation toolbar.

Viewport Navigation Toolbar

The navigation tools (shown in Figure 2–1) are available in the lower right corner of the interface.

Figure 2–1

- When selected, the tool button is highlighted. Press <Esc> or select another tool to toggle a selected tool off.
- Several buttons contain an arrow symbol in the lower right corner, which you can hold to expand a flyout.

	**Zoom:** When this tool is active, click, hold, and drag the cursor to zoom in or out of the active viewport.
	**Zoom All:** Activate and then click and drag to zoom in or out simultaneously in all viewports.
	**Zoom Extents/Zoom Extents Selected:** Zooms to the extents of all visible objects/ selected objects only in the active viewport.
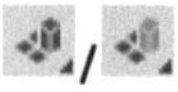	**Zoom Extents All/Zoom Extents All Selected:** Zoom to the extents of all visible objects/ selected objects only in all viewports.
	**Zoom Region** (zoom window) in the active viewport.

	**Field of View**: This is a flyout option in Zoom Region, available only in **Perspective** or **Camera** view. It adjusts the perspective of the view, similar to changing the focal length of a camera. Even small changes to the Field of View setting can cause large distortions. To reset, enter a default field of view value of **45 degrees** in the *Viewport Configuration* dialog box.
	**Pan View:** Hold in a viewport and drag to pan your objects. You can also hold and drag the middle mouse wheel to pan.
	**2D Pan Zoom mode:** A flyout option in Pan View, available in **Perspective** and **Camera** views only. It enables you to zoom/pan on objects in a viewport that are not located in the rendering frame. The camera remains unchanged when you are panning and zooming in the **Camera** viewport.
	**Walk Through:** A flyout option in Pan View, available in **Perspective** and **Camera** views only. Click and hold while moving the cursor to change where you are looking. Use the arrow keys to walk forward, back, and to the side. Move up or down by pressing <Shift>+<Up> or <Down>. To speed up a movement hold <]> (right bracket) while moving, and slow down movement by pressing <[> (left bracket).
	**Orbit**, **Orbit Selected,** and **Orbit SubObject**: Enables you to rotate the view by clicking and dragging inside or outside a trackball. Dragging inside the trackball causes the view to rotate around the scene, while dragging outside causes the view to twist in place. Click and drag on the boxes that display along the trackball to constrain the rotation to a single axis.
	**Orbit Point of Interest**: The point of interest is set as the point of rotation around which the view is rotated.
	**Maximize Viewport:** Toggles between the display of multiple viewports and the display of a single maximized viewport. Keyboard shortcut is <Alt>+<W>.

Hint: Switching Maximized Viewports

When you maximize to a single viewport from a multi-viewport layout, you can switch to any other available viewport while in the current maximized viewport display. In the maximized viewport display, hold <Win> (the Windows logo key, which might also be the <Start> key) and then press <Shift> (do not hold <Shift>). An overlay opens displaying all of the available viewports and the currently maximized viewport highlighted with a yellow border, as shown in Figure 2–2. While holding <Win>, press <Shift> repeatedly to highlight the next viewport option and release <Win> to maximize the highlighted viewport.

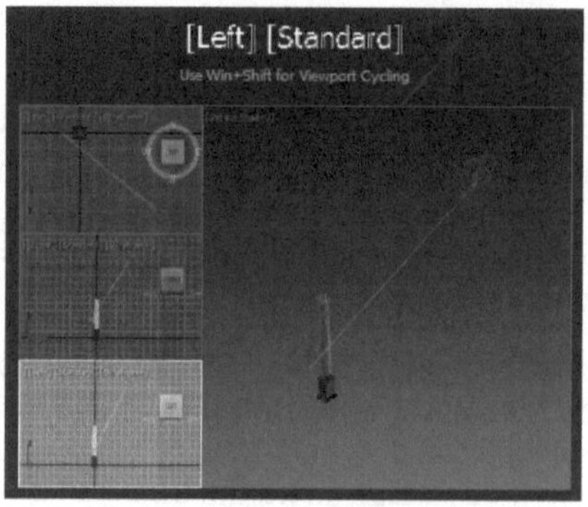

Figure 2–2

Viewport Navigation Toolbar (Camera Viewport)

Camera viewports show what is visible to the camera object based on its Field of View. Similar to other viewports, camera viewports can be directly navigated, but some of the controls are slightly different, as shown in Figure 2–3.

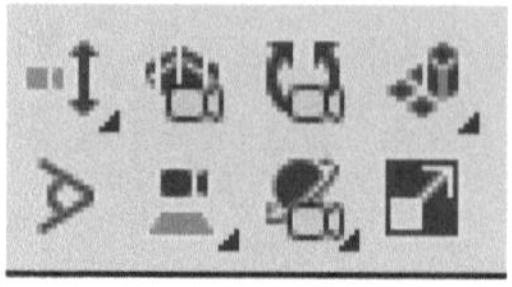

Figure 2–3

- Note that most of these controls actually move the camera or target object.

	**Dolly Camera** is similar to **Zoom**. The flyout contains options to dolly (move) the camera, the target, or both along the camera's directional axis.
	**Perspective** is a combination of **Field of View** and **Dolly** that attempts to maintain the same scene composition while changing the camera's Field of View.
	**Roll Camera** rotates a camera along the axis of its view.

	**Orbit Camera** rotates a camera around the target position similar to **Orbit**. The flyout option (**Pan Camera**) rotates the target around the camera instead.
	**Truck Camera** is similar to Pan when used in a **Camera** view.

Viewport Navigation Using the ViewCube

The ViewCube (shown in Figure 2–4) is a navigation tool and by default, it displays in the top right corner of each viewport indicating the orientation of the scene. The ViewCube is activated by hovering the cursor over it in the active viewport.

- Selecting any of the ViewCube faces or edges, causes the viewport to immediately swing around to that view. You can also select the ViewCube and drag the mouse to quickly rotate the Viewport.
- When the ViewCube is active, the **Home** icon becomes visible near the top left corner. Clicking the **Home** icon resets the viewport.

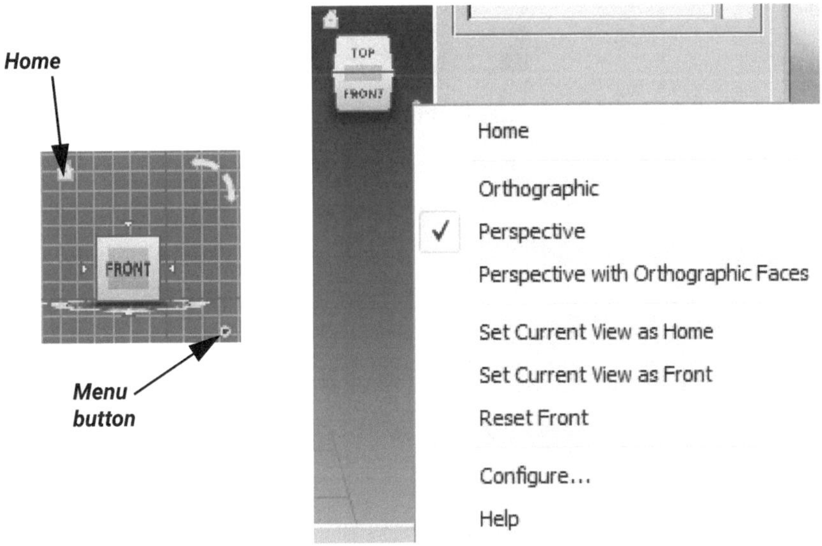

Figure 2–4

- Clicking on the menu button or right-clicking on the ViewCube provides you with additional options (shown in Figure 2–4) that enable you to set the current view as Home, Orthographic, Configure etc. The ViewCube tool options can also be accessed in the **Views** menu.
- Selecting the **Configure** option, opens the *Viewport Configuration* dialog box in the *ViewCube* tab. It contains options to show/hide the ViewCube, control its size and display, control what happens when dragging on the ViewCube, and displaying the compass below the ViewCube.

Viewport Navigation Using the SteeringWheel

The SteeringWheel (shown in Figure 2–5) is another navigation tool and it can be toggled on by pressing <Shift>+<W> or **Views>SteeringWheels>Toggle SteeringWheels**. When toggled on, it gets attached to the cursor.

- It provides instant access to zoom/pan, orbit, etc. The **Rewind** feature is unique to this tool and provides a thumbnail of all of your previous views. It also enables you to visually select any of them to return to that view. Press <Shift>+<W> to toggle the SteeringWheel on and off. You can also press <Esc> to hide its display.
- The Steering wheel tool options can also be accessed in the **Views** menu.

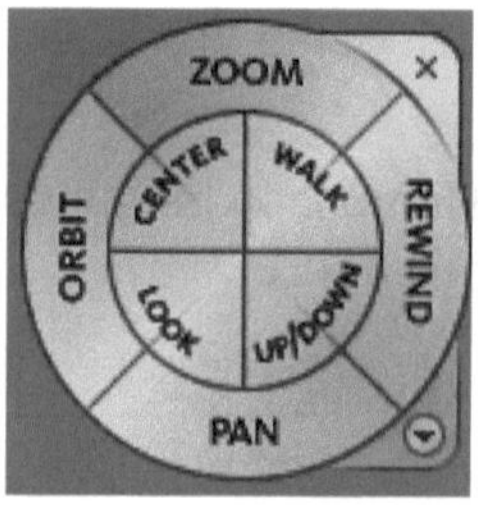

Figure 2–5

2.2 Viewport Configuration and Settings

Viewport Configuration

The layout and display settings of your viewports can be set through the *Viewport Configuration* dialog box. In the *Viewport* labels, click the **[+]** *General* label to display the label menu and select **Configure Viewports**, as shown in Figure 2–6.

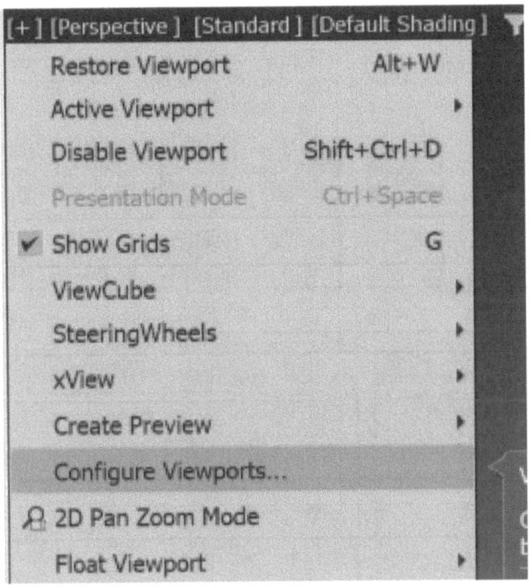

Figure 2–6

The *Viewport Configuration* dialog box opens and contains tabs which differ based on the selected display driver. By default, the *Viewport Configuration* dialog box opens with the *Display Performance* tab active. Some of the tabs that are available in the *Viewport Configuration* dialog box are described in the following section. The remaining tabs are discussed throughout this guide, as required.

Layout Tab

The *Layout* tab in the *Viewport Configuration* dialog box (shown in Figure 2–7) enables you to set the size and shape of viewports and its view type. Select one of the preset viewport layouts to select a view type.

- You can also set up multiple viewport layouts and switch between them by selecting the saved tabs in the *Viewport Layouts* tab bar.

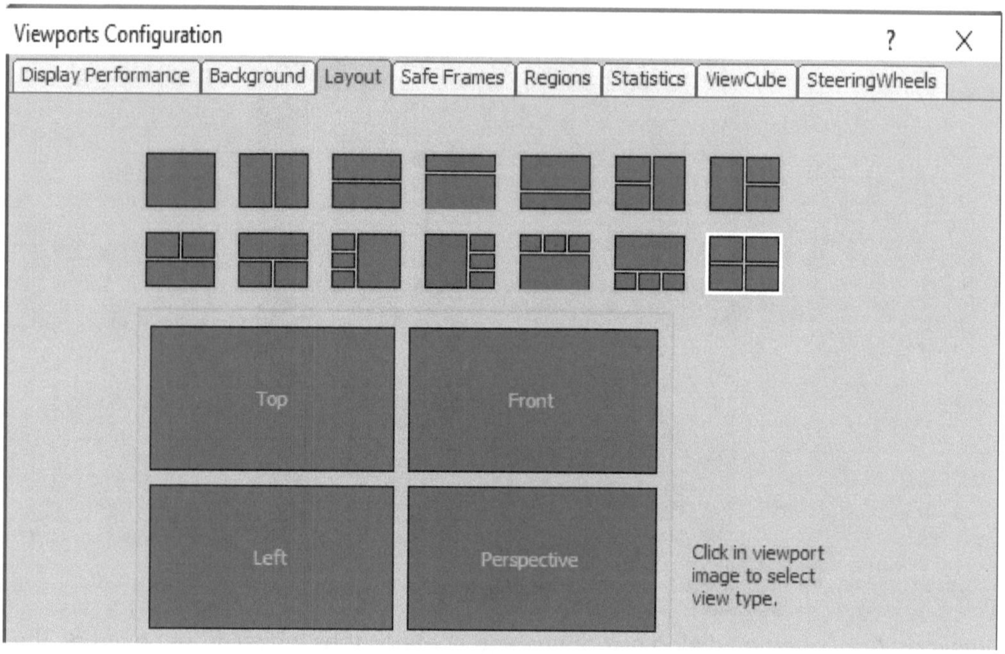

Figure 2–7

SteeringWheels Tab

The *SteeringWheels* tab (shown in Figure 2–8) enables you control the properties of the Steering Wheel such as displaying them as Big or Mini Wheels and setting their respective sizes and opacity. You can also set the options for tools, such as the **Zoom** tool and the **Orbit** tool.

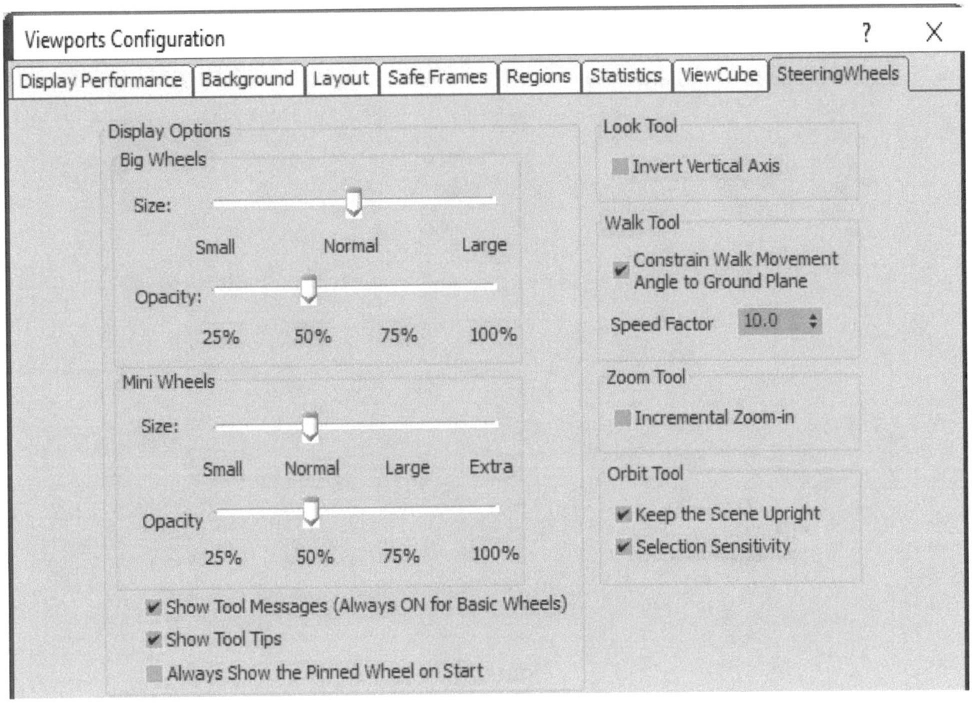

Figure 2–8

ViewCube Tab

Similar to the *SteeringWheels* tab, the *ViewCube* tab has options for controlling the display of the ViewCube. You can control its size, what it displays when selected, and the position of the compass.

Statistics Tab

The *Statistics* tab enables you to customize the display of various statistics for the selected geometry or the complete scene. In the viewports, you can display the number of polygons in a scene, number of triangular faces, number of edges, number of vertices, etc. The statistics can be displayed on the screen, near the left hand corner of the active viewport by selecting **Show Statistics in Active View** in the dialog box. You can also display statistics by selecting **Show Statistics** in the *General Viewport* label menu>**xView** or by pressing <7>.

Background Tab

The *Background* tab (shown in Figure 2–9) enables you to set an image, environment map, or animation as the background of your active viewport or all viewports.

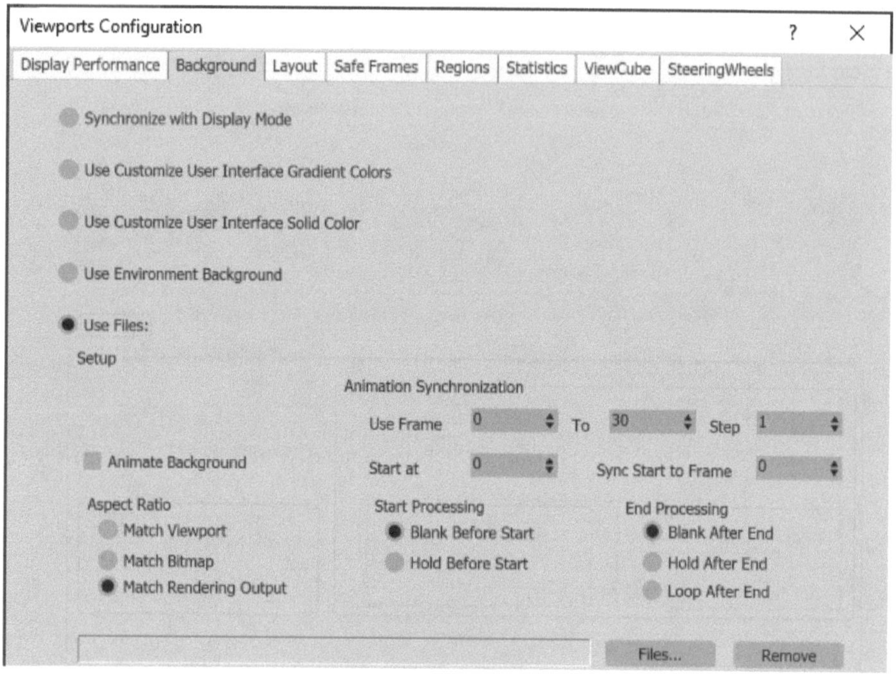

Figure 2–9

Active Viewport Settings

You can control the viewport display of the models in the *Viewport Settings* dialog box. To open the dialog box, in the viewport, click the *Shading Viewport* label and select **Active Viewport Settings**, as shown in Figure 2–10. Alternatively, click the *Per-View Preference* label and select **Viewport Preferences**.

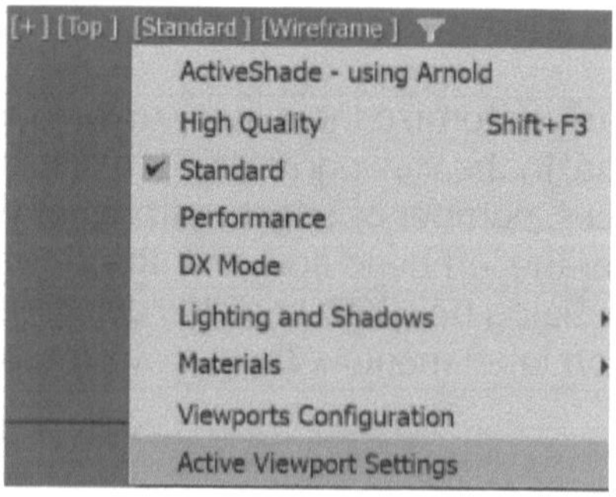

Figure 2–10

The *Active Viewport* dialog box contains three tabs: *Settings, Preferences, and Filter.* The *Settings* tab (shown in Figure 2–11) has the following options:

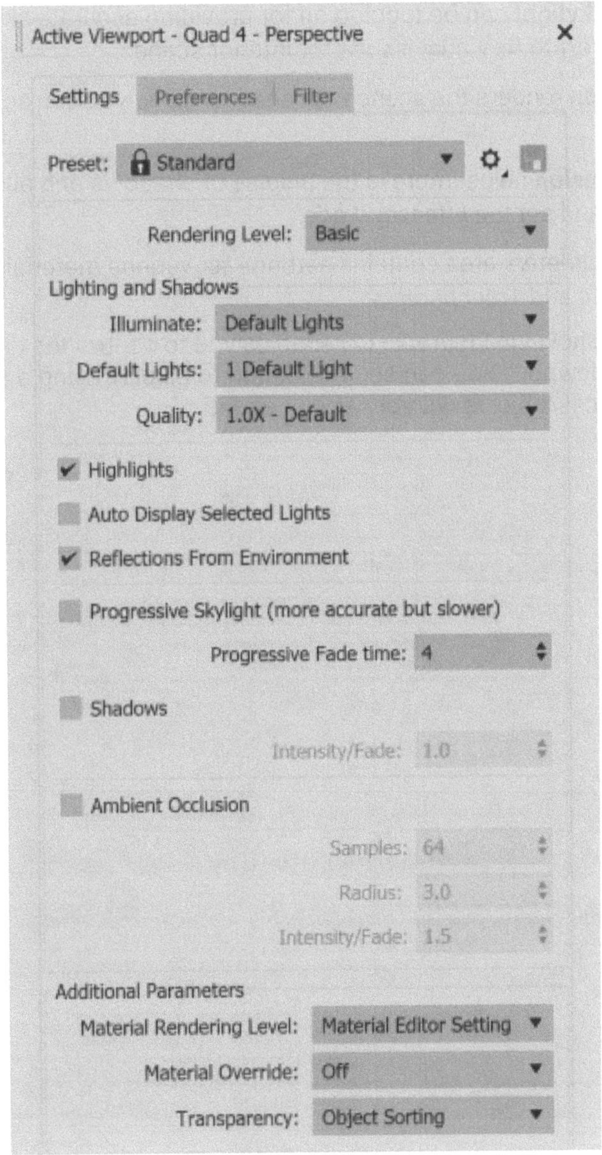

Figure 2–11

- You can create and add a user-defined view setting preset to the list of choices. Note, however, that you can have only one user-defined view setting, and you cannot change the four existing presets (i.e., High Quality, Standard, Performance, or DX mode).

- The **Default Lights** are used to illuminate the viewports, providing even illumination. You can select **1 Default Light** or **2 Default Lights**.
- The **Progressive Skylight** can be toggled on for providing accurate skylight shadows. It should be toggled off to fix visual issues for interior scenes.
- The **Shadows** option renders the scene with shadows, and you can set the *Intensity/Fade* of the shadows.
- The **Ambient Occlusion** helps improve the display of shadows and allows you to set an *Occlusion Radius* and set the *Intensity/Fade*.
- The *Additional Parameters* area contains settings for various material-related options, such as *Material Override* and *Transparency*.

The *Preferences* tab (shown in Figure 2–12) enables you to control the display of selected objects in a specific viewport. You can set a selection to display using a selection bracket, or shade the selected faces/objects with or without edges.

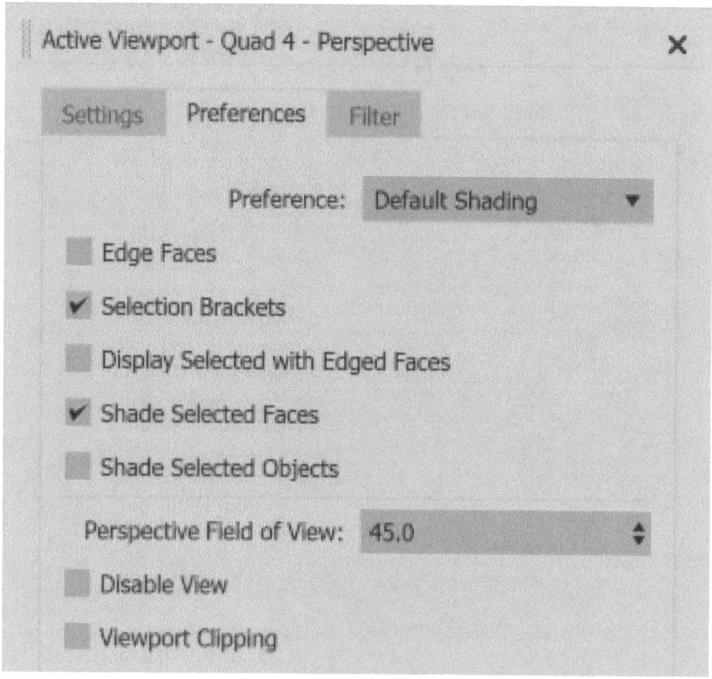

Figure 2–12

Practice 2a
Viewport Configuration and Navigation

Practice Objectives

- Set the configuration of the viewport.
- Move around a scene using different navigation tools.

In this practice, you will set various configuration option for an exiting viewport layout. You will then move around a scene and experiment with changing the camera position by using navigations tools such as **Zoom, Orbit, Pan View, and other SE Camera options.**

1. Select **File>Open** to open the *Open File* dialog box. If you were working in the software, you might be prompted to save or discard any changes to the scene.
    - In the *Open File* dialog box, note that the *C:\Autodesk 3ds Max Fundamentals Practice Files\scenes* folder is set, because you have already set the Project Folder. If you did not set the path to the practice files folder, return to Chapter 1 and complete Task 1 to Task 3 in *Practice 1a: Organize Folders and Work with the Interface*. You are required to set the project folder only once.
2. In the *Open File* dialog box, select **Navigation.max** and click **Open**.
    - The file opens the objects in four equal sized viewports. Along the left edge of the interface, in the *Viewport Layouts* tab bar, note that the file has been saved with two different viewport layout configurations.
3. To create another layout, in the *Viewport Layouts* tab bar, click  to expand the *Standard Viewport Layouts* panel. Select the layout (top, right layout) shown in Figure 2–13.

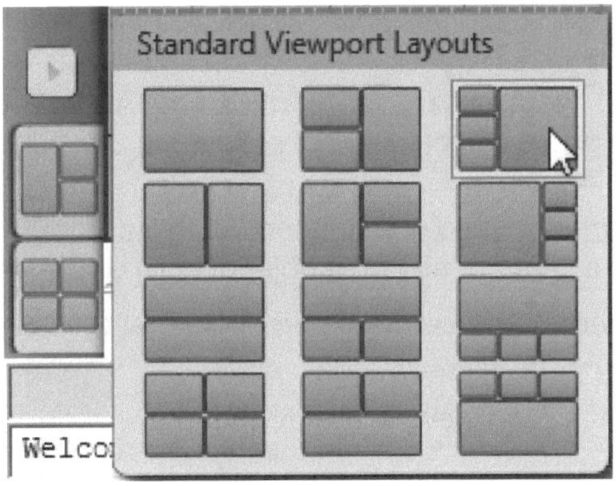

Figure 2–13

- The pillar objects display in the **3 X 1** viewport layout and another layout tab is added to the *Layouts* tab bar.

4. Note that the **Top** viewport is the active viewport (it displays a yellow border). In the Navigation toolbar, note the available navigation tools are for the **Orthographic** view, as shown in Figure 2–14.

Figure 2–14

5. The complete objects are not displayed in the viewports. In the Navigation toolbar, click and hold **Zoom Extents All** to open the flyout. Click (Zoom Extents All) to zoom to the extents of all of the objects in all of the viewports. The file contains a pillar object and a camera object.
6. Click on empty space in the **Front** viewport to activate it.
7. In the Scene Explorer, select **Base** to select the base objects in all the viewports, as shown in Figure 2–15.
   - If the Scene Explorer is not displayed, select **Tools>Scene Explorer** and then dock it.

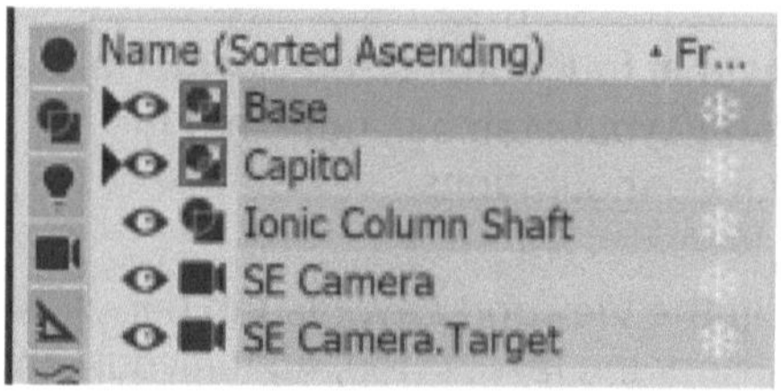

Figure 2–15

8. In the Zoom Extents All flyout, click (Zoom Extents All Selected). Note that you are zoomed to the extents of the selected objects (Base) in all of the viewports.
9. With the **Base** still selected, in the Zoom Extents All flyout, click (Zoom Extents All). The viewports zoom to the extents of all of the objects in all of the viewports.
10. Right-click in empty space in the **Left** viewport. Note that the **Left** viewport becomes active and the base object remains selected.
11. Click in empty space in the **Top** viewport. Note that the viewport becomes active, but the selection is cleared.
12. Hover the cursor over the left edge of the **Perspective** viewport. The cursor displays as a two-sided arrow. Click and drag the arrow horizontally to the right to resize the viewports, as shown in Figure 2–16.

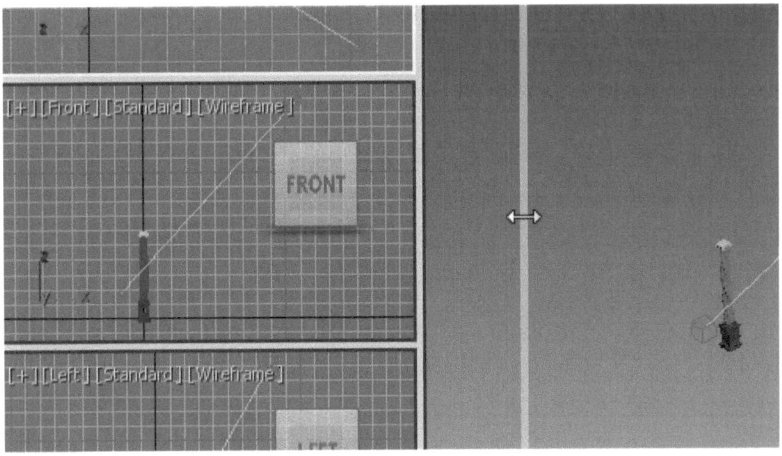

Figure 2–16

13. Click in the **Perspective** viewport to make it active. In the Viewport navigation tools, click  (Maximize Viewport Toggle) to maximize the active viewport. Select the toggle again to return to the four viewport arrangement. Alternatively, press <Alt>+<W> to toggle between the maximized single viewport and multiple viewports. Leave the **Perspective** viewport maximized.
14. Hold <Win> (windows logo or the <Start> key) continuously and press <Shift> once. An overlay displays all of the available viewports in the layout, as shown in Figure 2–17. With <Win> still pressed, press <Shift> repeatedly to cycle through all of the viewports. When [Left] [Standard] is highlighted (as shown in Figure 2–17), release <Win> to maximize the Left viewport.

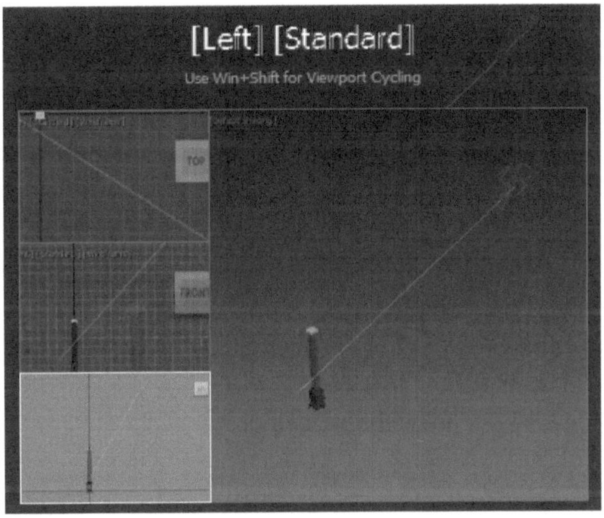

Figure 2–17

15. Click the **[Left]** *Point of View* label and select **Cameras>SE Camera**, as shown in Figure 2–18, to display the **Camera** view.
    - A Camera was added to the file to create a camera view.

Figure 2–18

    - Note that the navigation tools are different in the camera viewport, as shown in Figure 2–19.

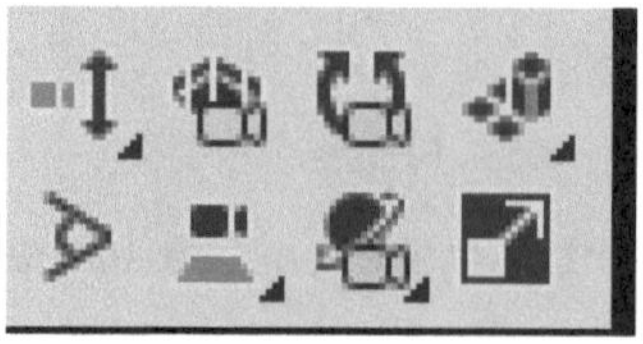

Figure 2–19

16. Click  (Maximize Viewport Toggle) to toggle to the four viewport display.
17. Click  (Zoom Extents All). Note that the **SE Camera** (lower left viewport) does not change because the non-camera navigation tools do not affect the camera views.
18. Click in the **Perspective** view to make it active and note how the navigation tools change.
19. Click in the **SE Camera** viewport to make it active.
20. Click  (Orbit Camera) and use it in the **SE Camera** viewport to orbit the camera. In the other viewports, note that only the camera object is moving simultaneously as the pillar object moves in the camera viewport.
21. Experiment with changing the camera position using  (Roll Camera) and  (Dolly Camera).
22. In the **Perspective** viewport, practice navigating with the **Zoom**, **Zoom All**, **Orbit**, and **Pan View** options.
    - You can use the mouse wheel to zoom in and out in a viewport and hold and drag the middle mouse button to pan.
23. Use **File>Reset** and close the file without saving.

End of practice

2.3 Object Selection Methods

Working with modifiers and other functions requires you to select objects accurately, using various methods. The recommended method is to click on the required geometry in one of the viewports to select it. It uses the  (Select Object) tool in the Main Toolbar which is active by default.

Selection Preview

In the Nitrous viewports, hovering the cursor over an object displays a yellow outline for that object. This enables you to easily determine the object that is going to be selected. Once you click on an object a cyan outline displays indicating the selection, as shown in Figure 2–20.

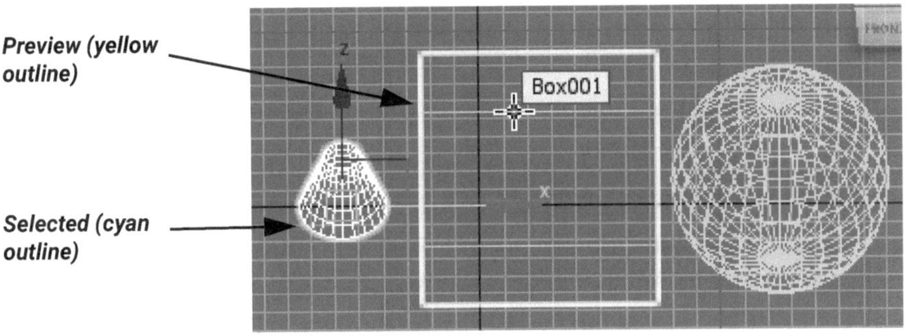

Figure 2–20

The highlighting can be controlled in the *Preference Settings* dialog box>*Viewports* tab, as shown in Figure 2–21.

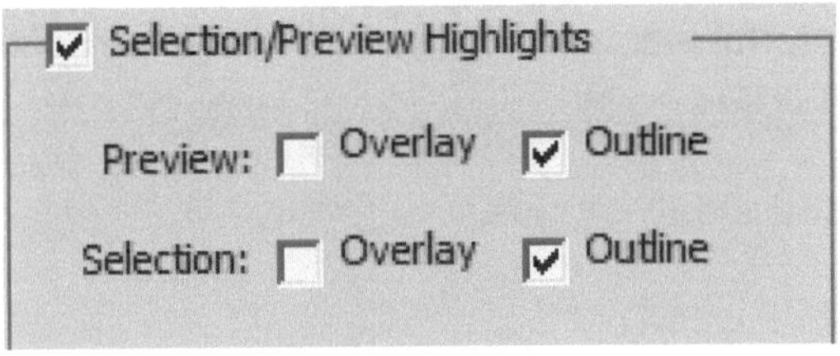

Figure 2–21

Scene Explorer

The Scene Explorer can be used to easily select objects. If you know the name of the object, locate it in the tree list and select it, as shown in Figure 2–22. It gets selected in the viewports interactively. Use <Ctrl> to click on multiple objects in the list to select them together.

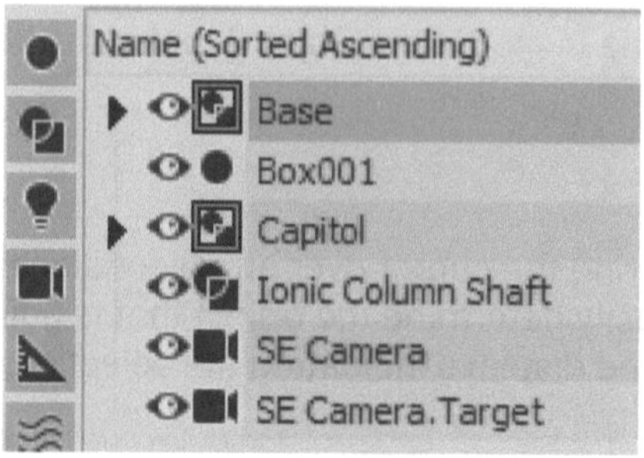

Figure 2–22

You can use the Scene Explorer toolbar to list only those objects that belong to the particular type and then select it. Use  (Display None) first to clear all the selected categories, and then select the tools for the required categories to list only the objects belonging to that category.

To easily find and select an item you can use the *Find* field in the Scene Explorer. Enter the initial letters to select only the objects that begin with the entered letters.

In the Scene Explorer menu bar, in the **Display** menu, verify that **Display Children**, **Display Influences**, and **Display Dependants** are cleared to display all the objects in the list.

- If the Scene Explorer is not displayed, click  (Scene Explorer) in the Main Toolbar or select **Tools>Scene Explorer**. Dock the Scene Explorer.
- Being a modeless interface component, you can have the Scene Explorer open while working in the viewports.

Main Toolbar - Selection Tools

A variety of selection tools are provided in the Main Toolbar, as shown in Figure 2–23.

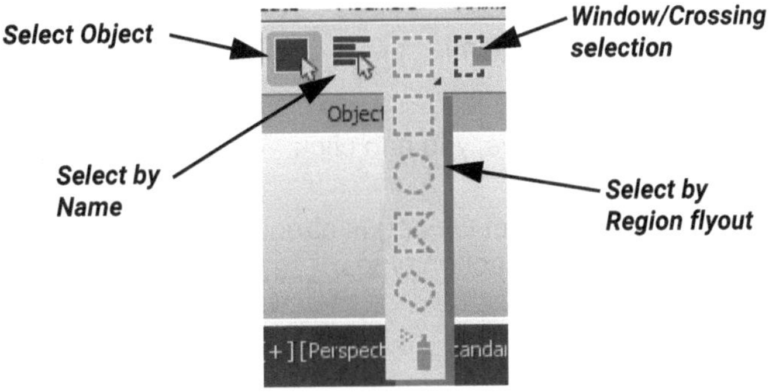

Figure 2–23

Select by Name Tool

 (Select by Name) opens the *Select From Scene* dialog box (shown in Figure 2–24), which enables you to select one or more objects. It is a modal version of the Scene Explorer, and therefore works the same way as the Scene Explorer. However, the only difference is that after selecting objects in the list of the dialog box, you must click **OK** to close the dialog box in order to continue working with the selection.

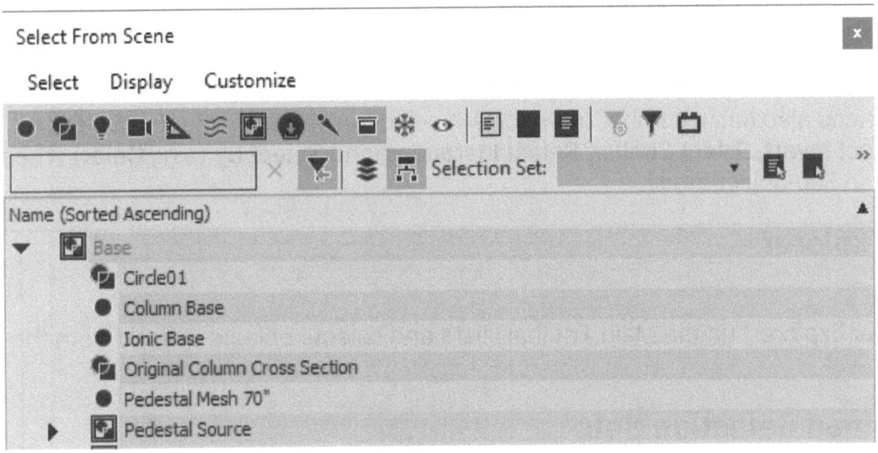

Figure 2–24

Select Object Tool

 (Select Object) enables you to select objects and to drag selection regions inside your viewports depending on the selected Region selection type.

- You can add to your current selection if you select or drag a region while holding <Ctrl>. You can remove items from the selection with <Alt>.
- You can also select with the **Move, Rotate, Scale**, and **Place** tools.
- You can access **Select** in the **quad** menu.
- If one of the **Transform** tools is active, you can click  (Select Object) or press <Q> to activate select objects. If  (Select Object) is already active, press <Q> repeatedly to cycle through the various Region selection types.

Rectangular Selection Region

 (Rectangular Selection Region) in the Main Toolbar enables you to draw the shape of your selection region. The default is a rectangular region. There are also flyout options for **Lasso**, **Paint**, **Circular**, and **Fence** selections, as shown previously in Figure 2–23. Paint selection is particularly useful when you have thousands of objects or vertices that need selecting.

Window/Crossing

/ (Window/Crossing) enables you to define the *Window Selection Region* (only objects completely within the region are selected), or the *Crossing Region* (objects within or crossing the boundary are selected) as the selection toggle.

Edit Menu

The **Edit** menu also has a number of important selection options including **Select All**, **Select None**, **Select Invert**, **Select Similar**, **Select Instances**, and **Select By** (e.g., **Color**). These options also work in Sub-object mode.

Layer Explorer

 (Layer Explorer) (in the Main Toolbar) lists and selects objects directly from the Layer Explorer.

Edit Named Selection Sets

 (Edit Named Selection Sets) (in the Main Toolbar) enables you to create and edit named selection sets. Named Selection Sets are different than layers, in that an object can be in many different named selections. An object can only be on one layer, making Named Selection Sets more flexible.

Practice 2b
Selection Methods

Practice Objective

- Select objects using various selection tools.

In this practice, you will select objects in a scene using the Window and Crossing selection tools. You will also use the Scene Explorer and the *Select from Scene* dialog box to select objects.

You must set the paths to locate the External files used in the practice. If you have not done this already, return to Chapter 1 and complete Task 1 to Task 3 in *Practice 1a: Organize Folders and Work with the Interface*. You only have to set the paths once.

1. Select **File>Open** to open the *Open File* dialog box. If you were working in the software, you might be prompted to save or discard any changes to the scene. Open **Selection Methods.max**.
2. Click anywhere in the **Perspective** viewport to make it active.
3. Maximize the **Perspective** viewport by clicking  (Maximize Viewport Toggle) or by pressing <Alt>+<W>.
4. In the viewport, click on the leftmost parking lot light pole. Note that it is selected, as a cyan outline encloses the object and all the face edges of the geometry are highlighted as white, with white bounding brackets enclosing the geometry.
    - If selecting an object is difficult, you can change the viewport shading to **Wireframe Override**.

5. Hover the cursor on the other parking lot light pole and note that it is highlighted with a yellow outline indicating the selection preview, as shown in Figure 2–25.

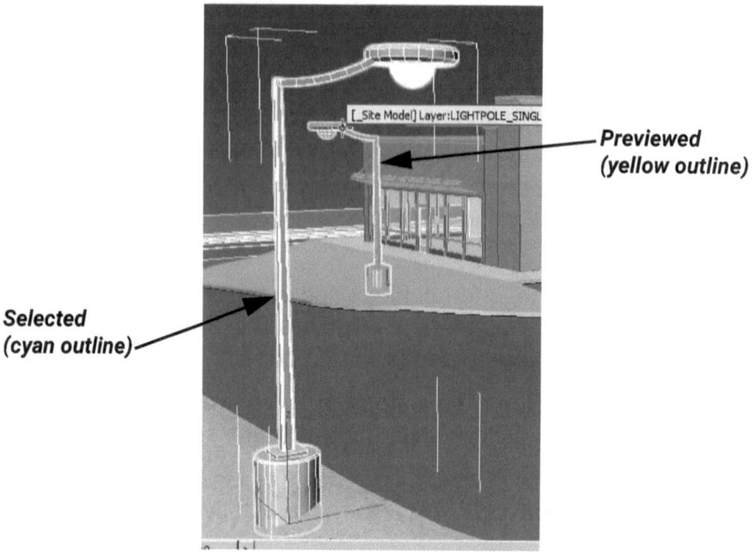

Figure 2–25

6. Click the **[Edged Faces]** *Per-View Preference* label and select **Viewport Preferences**. The *Active Viewport* dialog box>*Preferences* tab opens. Select **Display Selected with Edged Faces** and clear all of the other options, as shown in Figure 2–26. Close the dialog box.

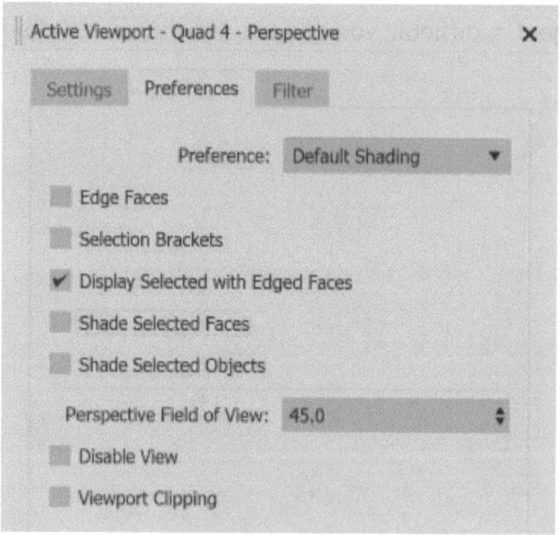

Figure 2–26

- In the viewport, note how the white bounding brackets are no longer displayed.

7. Open the *Active Viewport* dialog box again. In the *Preferences* tab, select **Selection Brackets** and **Edge Faces**. Close the dialog box. The selection brackets and edged faces display.
8. Click in empty space to clear your selection.
   - You can also select **Edit>Select None** in the Menu bar.
9. In the Main Toolbar, verify that the *Window/Crossing* toggle is set to (Crossing), the *Selection Region* is set to (Rectangular), and (Select Object) is selected. Starting in a blank area, near the top left corner of the farther parking lot light, click, hold, and drag the cursor diagonally down to create a rectangular crossing region around the light pole, as shown in Figure 2–27. Once you let go, the crossing window will select the light pole and several other objects in the background.
   - In the Status Bar, near the bottom left of the screen, note the number of entities selected.

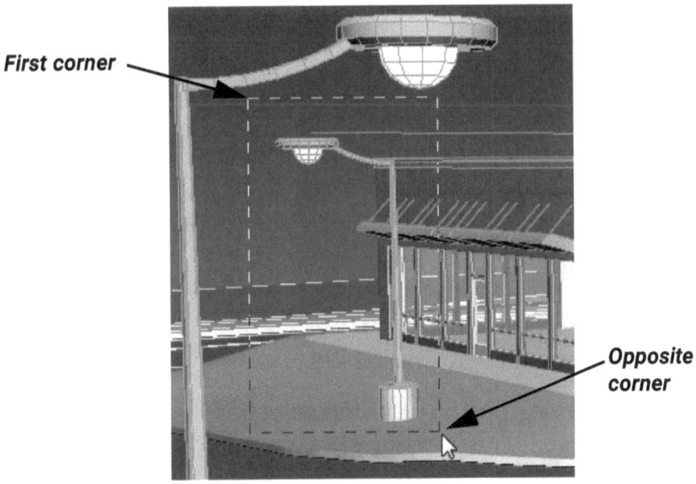

Figure 2–27

10. Click in empty space to clear the selection.
11. Toggle the **Selection/Crossing** toggle from (Crossing) to (Window). Click, hold, and drag the selection region around the same area of the light pole.
    - In the Status Bar, note that you selected fewer entities than before, but some additional objects are still selected.
12. In the Scene Explorer toolbar, click (Display None). Note that the list is empty.
    - If the Scene Explorer is not displayed, click (Scene Explorer) in the Main Toolbar or select **Tools>Scene Explorer**.

13. In the Scene Explorer toolbar, click (Display All). Note that the list of objects is very long as all the different categories of objects are listed.

14. In the Scene Explorer toolbar, click (Display None) and then click (Display Geometry) to display all of the geometry objects in the scene. Note that some objects are highlighted (as shown in Figure 2–28), indicating that they are selected in the viewport.

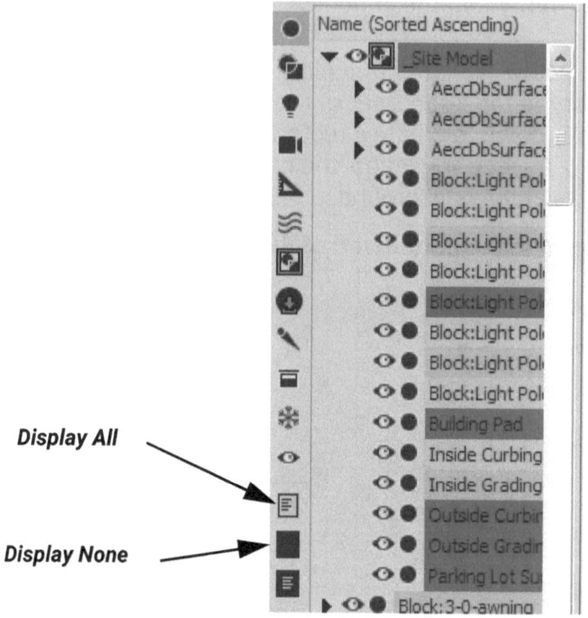

Figure 2–28

15. Click in empty space in the viewport to clear the selection.

16. In the Main Toolbar, click (Select by Name) to open the *Select From Scene* dialog box.

17. The objects listed depend on the selection tools that are toggled on in the dialog box toolbar. In the toolbar, click (Display None) to clear any selection group. Verify that (Sort by Hierarchy) is selected, as shown in Figure 2–29.

Figure 2–29

18. In the *Select From Scene* dialog box, click (Display Shapes), as shown in Figure 2–30. This enables you to filter the number of items listed in the dialog box so that you can easily select the required items.

Figure 2–30

19. Using <Ctrl> or <Shift>, select all of the **Block:Light Pole - Single** shapes (six objects). Click **OK** to close the dialog box. Note that the two single lights are selected in the viewport.
20. Click in an empty space in the viewport to clear the selection.
21. In the Scene Explorer toolbar, click (Display None) and click (Display Shapes). If required, expand the tree list by clicking on the arrow left of the Site Model, as shown in Figure 2–31.

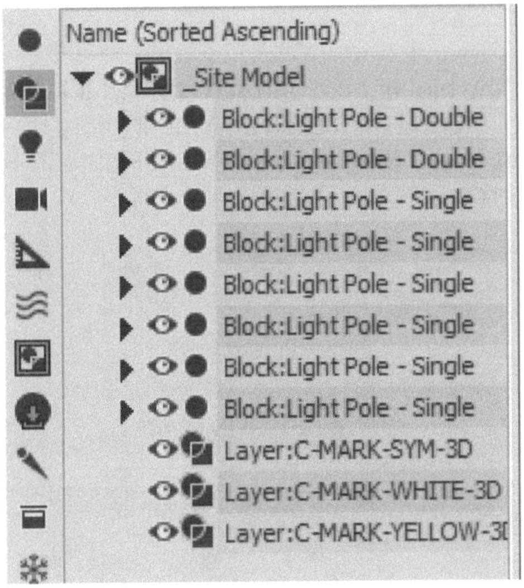

Figure 2–31

22. Select the first **Block:Light Pole - Single**. Note that this light pole is not visible in the viewport.

23. Select the second **Block:Light Pole - Single** and continue selecting from the list. The third **Block:Light Pole - Single** selects the light pole in the view, as shown in Figure 2–32.

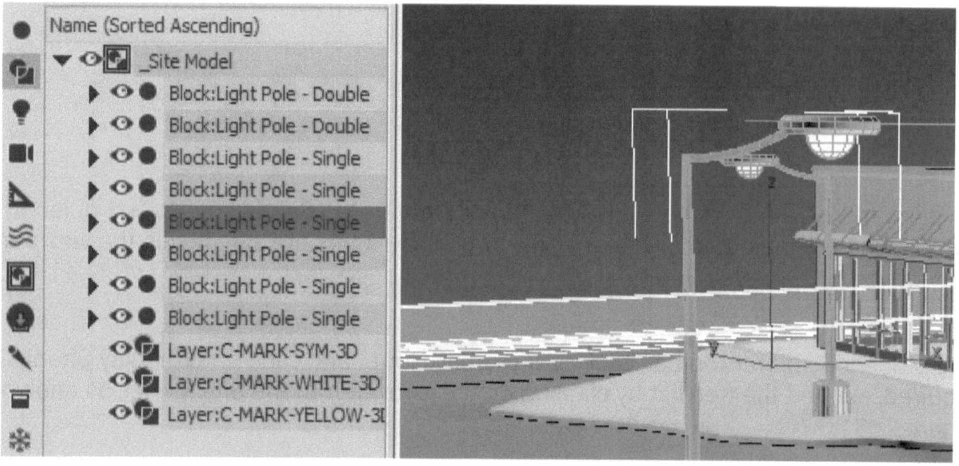

Figure 2–32

24. In the list, click again on the highlighted entry to convert it into an edit box and rename it to **Block:Light Pole - Front Left** and then click anywhere. Note that the newly-named entry moves above **Block:Light Pole - Single**, as shown in Figure 2–33, as the list is sorted in ascending alphabetical order.

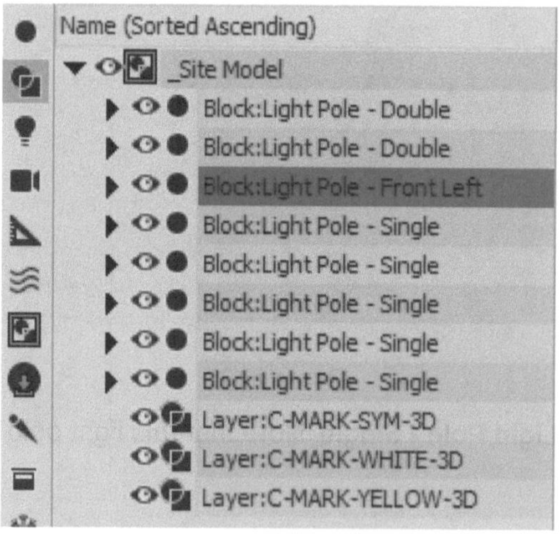

Figure 2–33

25. Select **File>Reset**. Click **Don't Save** and click **Yes** to close the current file without saving it.

End of practice

2.4 Units Setup

Each scene file is based on a unit of measurement called the System Unit Scale. You can change and assign the units settings using the *Units Setup* dialog box. Select **Customize> Units Setup** to open the *Units Setup* dialog box, as shown in Figure 2–34. In the dialog box, click **System Unit Setup** to open the *System Unit Setup* dialog box, as shown in Figure 2–35.

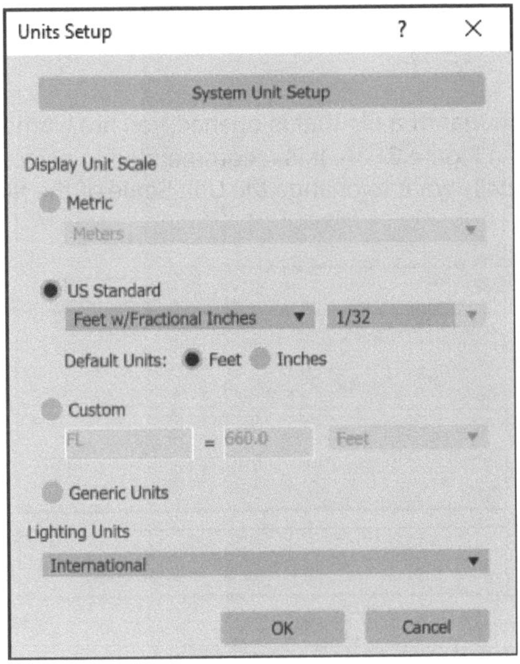

Figure 2–34

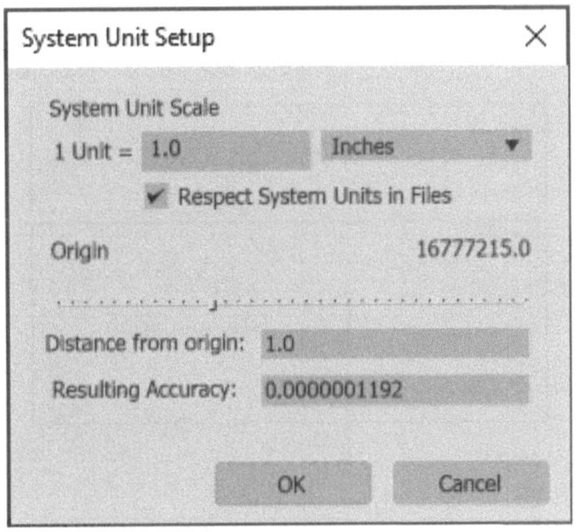

Figure 2–35

- For efficient viewport rendering, the Autodesk 3ds Max software might incur round off errors to very large and very small numerical values, as displayed by the slider bar in the *System Unit Setup* dialog box. These round off errors become problematic when the geometry is located further away from the center of the virtual universe.
- The Autodesk 3ds Max Help recommends that you center scene geometry close to the origin and not have any significant details smaller than one system unit. (For example, a unit scale of meters might not be appropriate for architectural work. Instead, you might consider using a **System Unit Scale** of inches, millimeters, or centimeters.) It is recommended not to make changes to the System Unit Scale unless there is a viewport problem due to very small or large models.
- Assign the unit scale before adding any geometry to the scene. Changing the System Unit Scale later does not rescale the existing objects. (To rescale objects, use the **Rescale World Units** utility in the Command Panel's *Utilities* panel ().

- Selecting **Respect System Units in Files** enables individual scene files that have different Unit Scales assigned to them to be scaled when merging them together.
- The *Display Unit Scale* area defines the units to be displayed by the interface when measuring coordinates and distances.
- The *Display Unit Scale* does not need to match the *System Unit Scale*.
- When the *Display Unit Scale* is set to **Feet w/Fractional Inches** or **Feet w/Decimal Inches,** the **Default Units** option identifies how a distance is read if a value is entered without a unit designation (' or ").
- If the current *System Unit Scale* does not match that of a file that is opened, you are warned with the *Units Mismatch* dialog box, as shown in Figure 2–36. It is recommended to select **Adopt the File's Unit Scale**, unless you specifically want to change the Unit Scale of the file being opened.

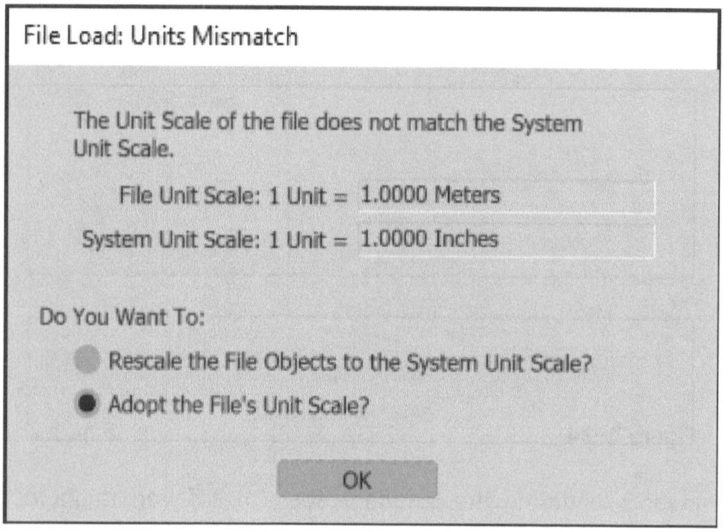

Figure 2–36

Practice 2c
Work with Units Setup

Practice Objective

- Assign and set up units in a scene.

In this practice, you will set up units for the projects.

1. In the Menu Bar, select **File>Reset** and click **Yes** in the confirmation dialog box.
   - If an unsaved scene is open, you might be required to save or discard the changes to the scene.
2. Select **Customize>Units Setup** to open the *Units Setup* dialog box. Click **System Unit Setup**.
3. In the *System Unit Setup* dialog box, in the *System Unit Scale* area, verify that *1 Unit =* is set to **1.0** and to **Inches**. Click **OK**.
4. You are returned to *Units Setup* dialog box. In the *Display Unit Scale* area, select **US Standard**, and then select **Feet w/Fractional Inches** and **1/8** in the respective drop-down lists, as shown in Figure 2–37.
5. Further set the following, as shown in Figure 2–37:
   - *Default Units:* **Inches**
   - *Lighting Units*: **American**

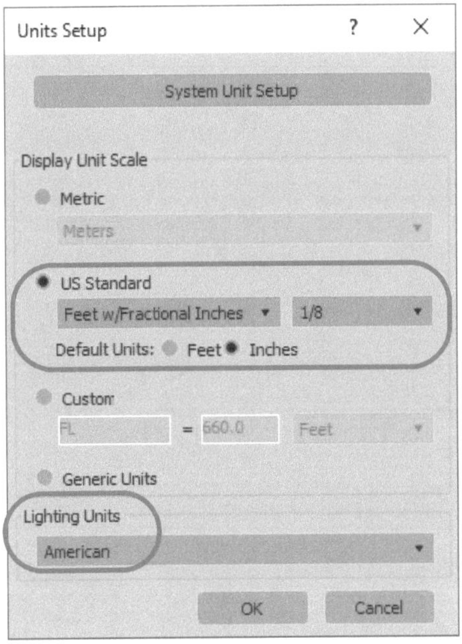

Figure 2–37

6. Click **OK** to close the *Units Setup* dialog box.
7. Select **File>Save As** to save your work as **MyUnits Setup.max**. Verify that it is being saved in the ...*scenes* folder.

End of practice

2.5 Layer and Object Properties

It is convenient to group similar objects into layers to modify these objects' properties and control their visibility together.

Layers Toolbar

By default, the Layers toolbar does not display. You can display it by selecting **Layers** from the Interface Item customize menu, which displays by right-clicking on the handle of any interface item, such as the Main Toolbar or Scene Explorer. The Layers toolbar (shown in Figure 2–38) enables you to set an active layer by selecting it from the drop-down list. Additionally, it contains various layer-specific tools.

Figure 2–38

	Opens the Layer Explorer.
	Creates a new layer.
	Adds selected objects to the current layer.
	Selects all objects in the current layer.
	Sets the current layer to the layer of a selected object.

Layer Explorer

In the Scene Explorer, click  (Sort by Layer) to display it as a Layer Explorer. If you want to display both the Scene Explorer and the Layer Explorer, click  (Layer Explorer) either in the Main Toolbar or in the Layers toolbar, or select **Tools>Layer Explorer**. Using the Layer Explorer handle, you can pull the Layer Explorer and float it as a separate window.

This version of Scene Explorer has tools and functions specific to layers, as shown in Figure 2–39.

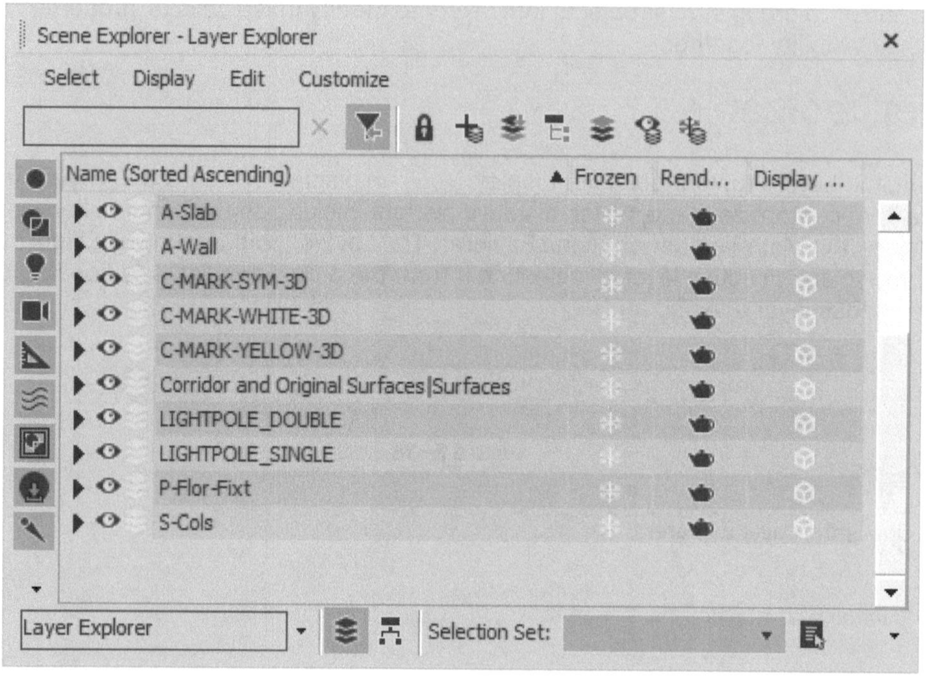

Figure 2–39

- View all of the objects on a layer by expanding the layer and clicking the arrow beside it. Right-clicking on an object in the list enables you to select and/or change its **Object Properties**.
- Click (gray layer icon) next to a layer to make the layer active. An active layer displays the (blue layer icon).

Tools in the Layer Explorer

You can create and adjust layers using the tools in the Layer Explorer toolbar.

	Creates a new layer and makes it the active layer. Using this button in the Layer Explorer automatically moves selected objects to a new layer. If no objects are selected, an empty layer is created.
	Moves selected objects to the active layer.
	Selects all of the objects in the selected layer.

	Activates the selected layer.
	Hides or Unhides all of the layers. Hiding a layer makes those objects invisible in the viewports and in renderings.
	Freezes or Thaws all of the layers. You can freeze or thaw an individual object or layer by clicking (Freeze) in the *Frozen* column. Freezing a layer (or individual object) displays those objects, but makes them unselectable. Frozen objects display as gray in the viewports, but render normally.

- The **Layers** quad menu (shown in Figure 2–40) opens by right-clicking on the name of the layer in the Layer Explorer and enables you to view and adjust other layer properties.

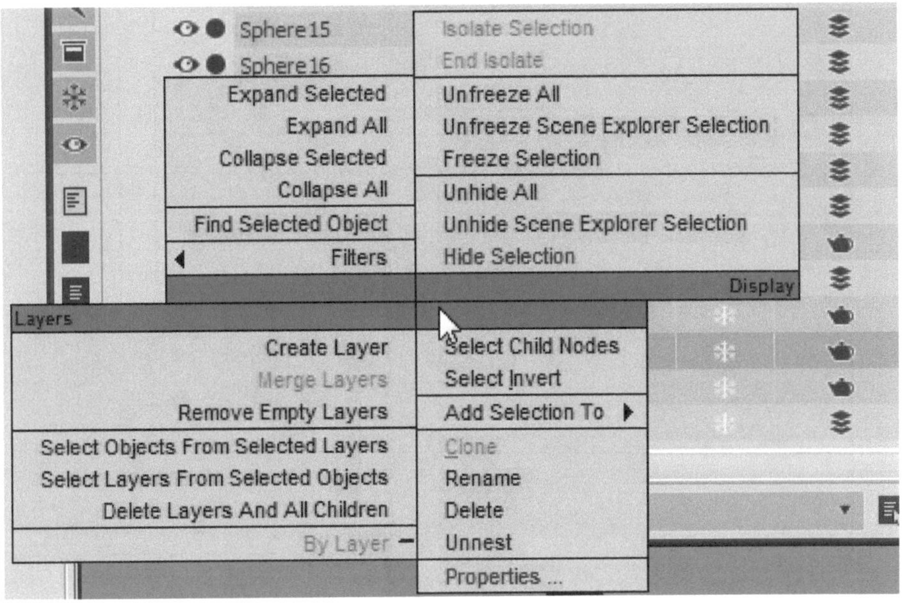

Figure 2–40

- You can also modify the display settings of one or more layers using the *Layer Properties* dialog box, that can be opened by selecting **Properties** in the **Layers** quad menu. Layer properties apply to all objects on that layer that do not have overrides set in their Object Properties.

Layer Properties

The *Layer Properties* dialog box (shown in Figure 2–41) contains two tabs:

- *General* tab: Used to set the display properties, hide and freeze options, or the rendering options of the layer.
- *Adv. Lighting* tab: Used to set the radiosity properties such as whether the layer objects can cast shadows and receive illumination.

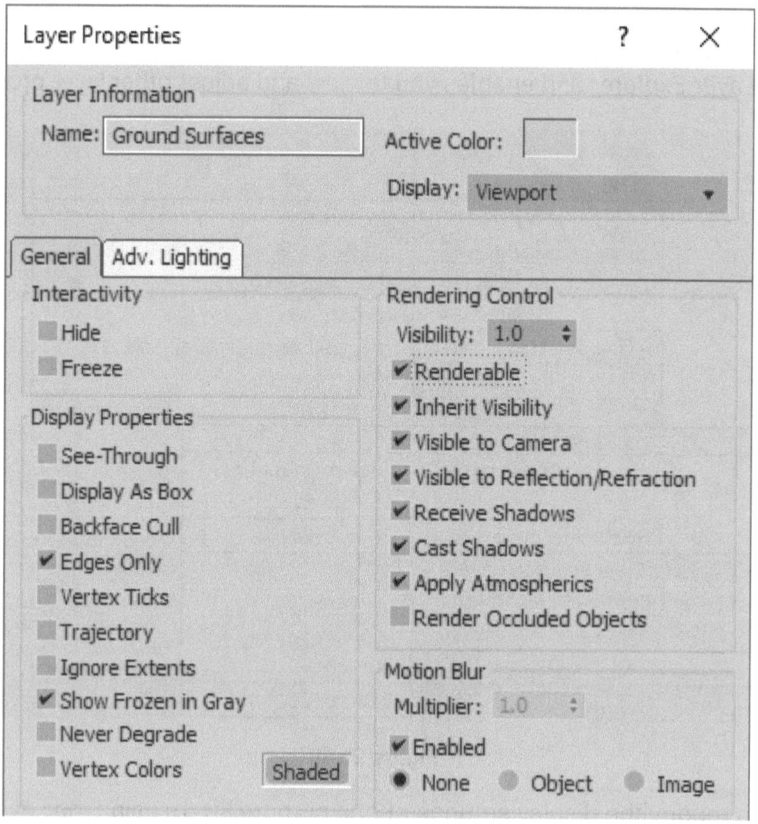

Figure 2–41

Object Properties

Right-clicking on an object in the Scene Explorer or Layer Explorer opens the quad menu for the object, as shown in Figure 2–42. In this menu, you can quickly edit or modify the properties of an object. Using the menu to edit the Display Properties is shown in Figure 2–42.

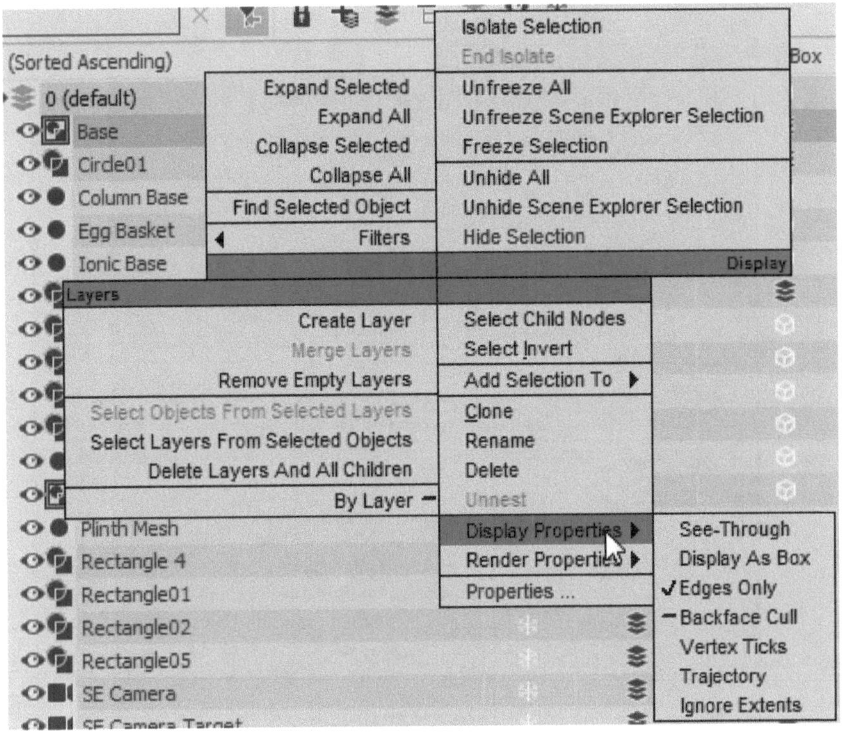

Figure 2–42

You can modify the detailed properties of an object in the *Object Properties* dialog box, as shown in Figure 2–43. The *Object Properties* dialog box is opened by selecting **Properties** in the quad menu. Alternatively, you can right-click on an object in a viewport and select **Object Properties**.

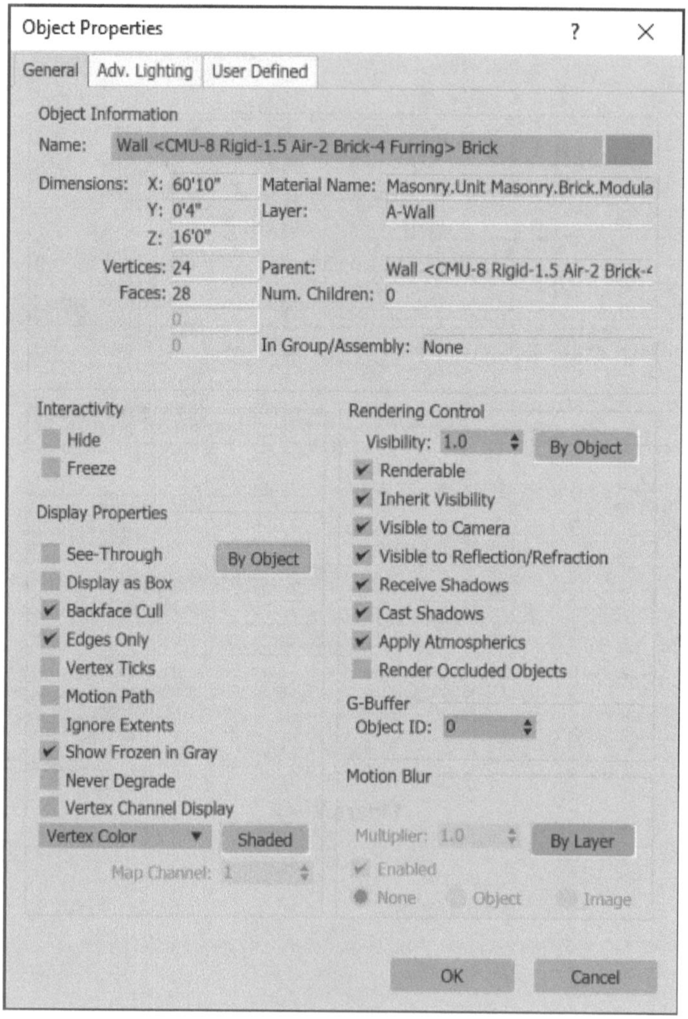

Figure 2–43

- It lists important information about an object, such as the name of the object, how many faces it consists of, the material assigned to it, whether its properties are controlled by layer or by object, etc.
- Changes made in the *Object Properties* dialog box override any layer settings for that object. The *Rendering Control* area in the *Object Properties* dialog box enables you to change setting for casting shadows on individual objects in a layer. This is useful when you do not want an object to cast shadows, while keeping the display of the other objects.

- To override the layer properties for an object, click the appropriate **By Layer** so that it changes to **By Object**.

Display Panel and Display Floater

The Command Panel's *Display* panel ( ) contains controls for hiding and freezing objects, as shown on the left in Figure 2–44.

A Display Floater (shown on the right in Figure 2–44), where you can **Hide**, **Unhide**, **Freeze**, and **Unfreeze** objects, is available in the **Tools** menu.

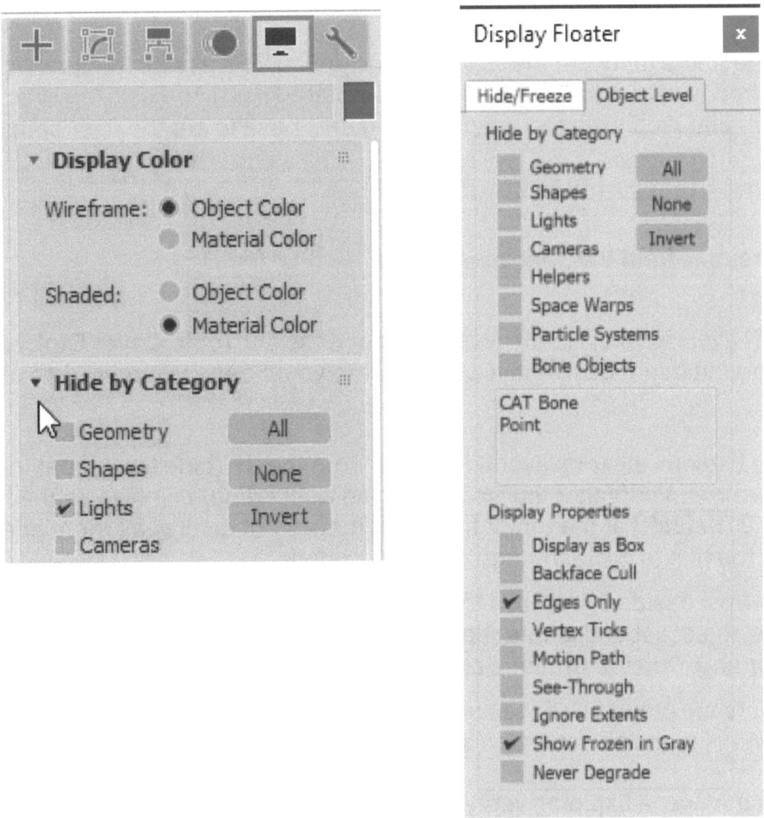

Figure 2–44

The *Display* panel and Display Floater enable you to:

- Hide all objects by category (all lights, all geometry, etc.).
- Hide or freeze objects individually or by selecting them first.
- Unhide or unfreeze all objects, or do so by object name. You can also freeze or hide by hit.

Practice 2d
Layer and Object Properties

Practice Objectives

- Create a new layer and move objects into a layer.
- Adjust properties of the layer and objects in the layer.

In this practice, you will create a new layer and move several objects into it. You will also set and modify the properties of the layer and of an individual object using Layer Properties and Object Properties respectively.

You must set the paths to locate the External files and XREFs used in the practice. If you have not done this already, return to Chapter 1 and complete Task 1 to Task 3 in *Practice 1a: Organize Folders and Work with the Interface*. You only have to set the user paths once.

Task 1: Practice layer management.

1. Open **Layers.max** from the ...*scenes* folder.
2. Click (Layer Explorer) in the Main Toolbar or select **Tools>Layer Explorer** to open the Layer Explorer. It might be displayed adjacent to your Scene Explorer or as a separate dialog box.
3. In the Layer Explorer, next to layer **0 (default)** note the (blue layer icon) indicating that it is the active layer. Verify that the **Name (Sorted Ascending)** displays as the title heading to display the **0 (default)** at the top of the list. If it does not display as mentioned, keep on clicking on the title to cycle through different options.
4. Select the arrow beside **0 (default)** to expand it and list all of the objects on this layer. Scroll down in the object list and locate the objects **Building Pad, Inside Curbing**, **Inside Grading**, **Outside Curbing**, **Outside Grading**, and **Parking Lot Surface**.
5. These objects are ground surfaces and part of a group called **Site XREF**. You can verify it by selecting one of these objects such as the **Building Pad** (shown in Figure 2–45) in the Layer Explorer. In the Scene Explorer, verify that (Sort by Hierarchy) is selected. Note that **Site XREF** is highlighted and all of the objects in the group are highlighted as well, as shown in Figure 2–46.

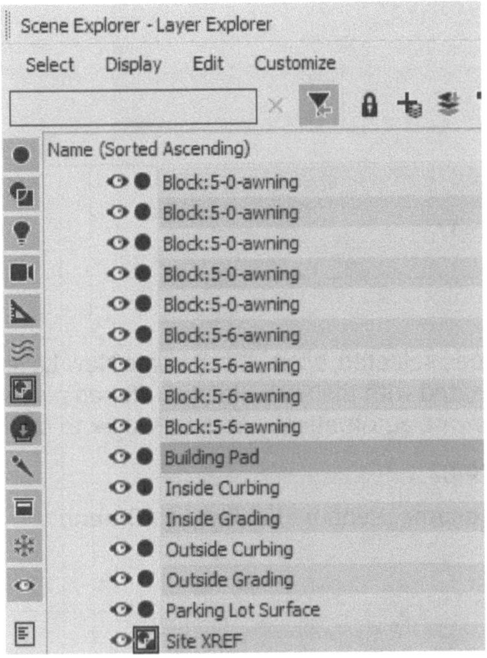

Figure 2–45

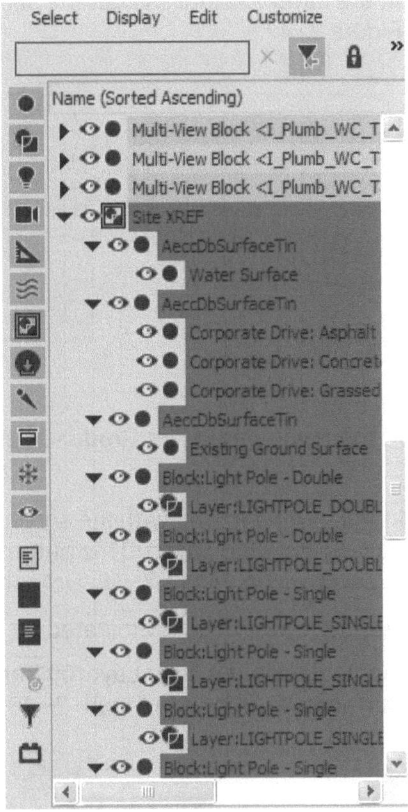

Figure 2–46

6. Zoom out in the viewport so that all the objects are visible.

   Note: *If you already have objects selected, click in empty space in the viewport to clear selection.*

7. In the Layer Explorer, in layer **0 (default)**, select **Site XREF.** Note that a number of objects are selected in the viewport and **1 Group Selected** displays in the Status Bar.
8. With **Site XREF** selected, in the Menu bar, select **Group>Open**. The Site XREF group is now open. Note that nothing is selected now.
   - To verify this, in the Layer Explorer, select **Building Pad**. Note that only **Building Pad** is selected in the Scene Explorer and that a single object is highlighted in the viewport. Also, **1 Object Selected** displays in the Status Bar.

9. In the Layer Explorer, select the six ground surfaces by using <Shift> or <Ctrl>, as shown in Figure 2–47.

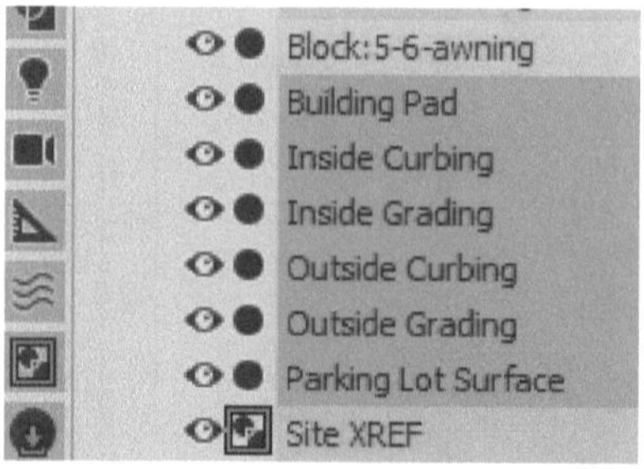

Figure 2–47

10. In the menu bar, select **Group>Detach**.

11. In the Layer Explorer with the six ground surfaces selected, click  (Create New Layer). A new layer called **Layer001** is automatically created with the six building surfaces placed in it, as shown in Figure 2–48. Note that the software automatically sets this layer to be the current layer, which is indicated by  (blue icon).

12. Right-click on the layer **Layer001** and select **Rename**. Rename the layer as **Ground Surfaces**, as shown in Figure 2–49.

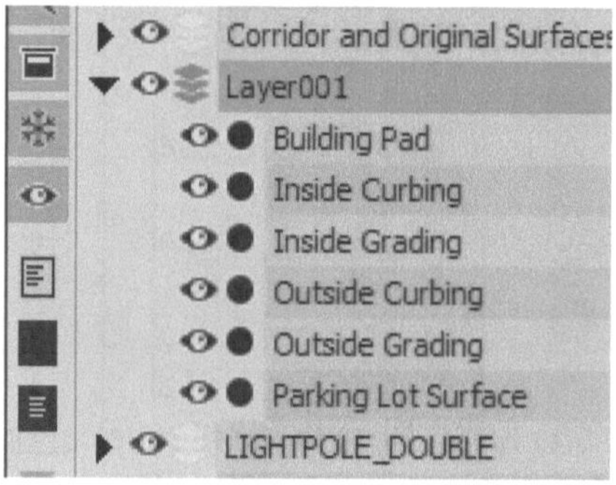

Figure 2–48

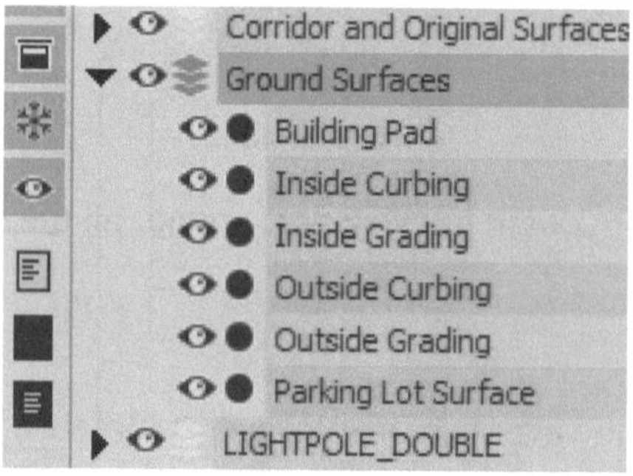

Figure 2–49

13. Expand layer **Corridor and Original Surfaces|Surfaces** and note that there are eight ground surfaces in it. Right-click on this layer to open the menu and note that **Delete** is unavailable (grayed out), because the layer contains objects.

14. With the **Corridor and Original Surfaces|Surfaces** layer selected, in the Layer Explorer toolbar, click  (Select Children). This selects all of the objects in this layer.
    - You can also select **Select Child Nodes** in the right-click quad menu.

15. In the Layer Explorer toolbar, click (Add to Active Layer). The eight objects from the **Corridor and Original Surfaces|Surface** layer are moved to the **Ground Surfaces** layer (which is the active layer), as shown in Figure 2–50.

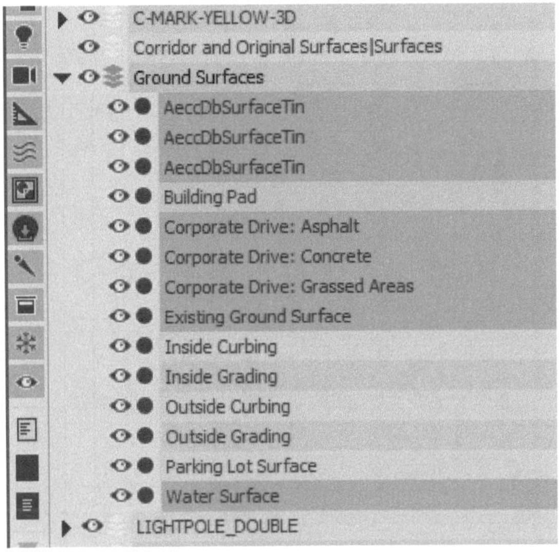

Figure 2–50

16. Right-click on **Corridor and Original Surfaces|Surfaces** and note that **Delete** is now available because the layer is empty. Select **Delete** to remove **Corridor and Original Surfaces|Surfaces**.

17. Select (gray layer icon) next to layer **0 (default)** to make the layer active. Selecting it toggles the icon to (blue layer icon).

Task 2: Set layer and object properties.

Set the ground surfaces so that it does not cast shadows although they will still receive shadows. This simplification can save rendering time without significantly affecting the final output when using relatively flat ground surfaces.

1. In the Layer Explorer, select and right-click on the layer **Ground Surfaces**, and then select **Properties**.

2. In the *Layer Properties* dialog box, in the *Rendering Control* area, toggle off **Cast Shadows** (as shown in Figure 2–51) and click **OK.**

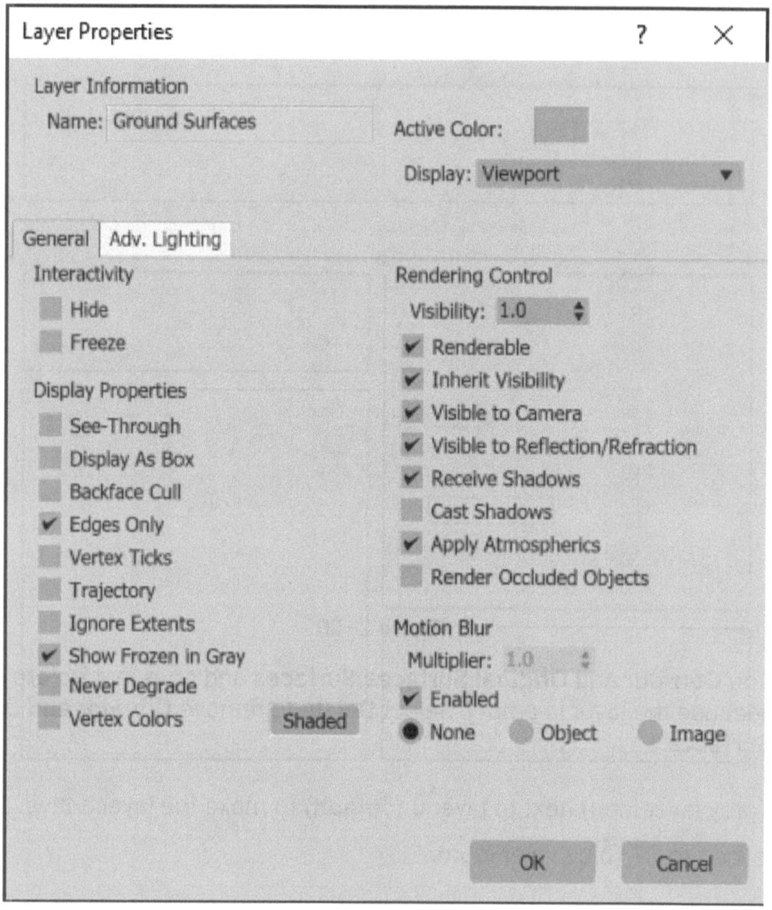

Figure 2–51

3. You can override this setting for one of the ground surfaces. In the Layer Explorer, in the layer **Ground Surfaces**, select and right-click on **Outside Grading**. Select **Properties** to open the *Object Properties* dialog box.
4. In the *Object Properties* dialog box, in the *Rendering Control* area, click **By Layer** so that it changes to **By Object**. Verify that **Cast Shadows** for this object is enabled and click **OK**.
5. Close the Layer Explorer by toggling  (Layer Explorer) off in the Main Toolbar.
6. Select **File>Save As**, and save your work as **MyLayers.max**.

End of practice

Chapter Review Questions

1. Which tool can be used to zoom to the extents of all visible objects in all viewports?

   a.  (Zoom Extents)

   b.  (Zoom All)

   c.  (Zoom Extents All)

   d.  (Zoom Region)

2. After selecting a number of objects, which key do you press to remove items from the selection?

   a. <Shift>

   b. <Ctrl>

   c. <Alt>

   d. <Esc>

3. In the maximized viewport display, along with holding <Win>, which key do you need to press to open the viewport overlay where you can switch to a different viewport?

   a. <Shift>

   b. <Ctrl>

   c. <Alt>

   d. <Tab>

4. You should assign the unit scale before adding any geometry to the scene. Changing the **System Unit Scale** later does not rescale objects that are already present.

   a. True

   b. False

5. In the Layer Explorer, which option makes objects unselectable, but leaves them visible in the viewport and renders them normally?
    a. Hide
    b. Freeze
    c. Render
    d. Radiosity

6. In the Layer Explorer, selecting a few objects and then clicking  (Create New Layer) creates:
    a. A new inactive layer that is empty.
    b. A new active layer that is empty.
    c. A new inactive layer that contains the selected objects.
    d. A new active layer that contains the selected objects.

Command Summary

Button	Command	Location
Layers		
	**Add Selection to Current Layer**	• **Layers Toolbar**
	**Add to Active Layer**	• **Layers Toolbar** • **Layer Explorer Toolbar**
	**Create New Layers**	• **Layers Toolbar** • **Layer Explorer Toolbar**
	**Layer Explorer**	• **Main Toolbar** • **Layers Toolbar**
	**Select Objects in Current Layer**	• **Layers Toolbar**
	**Set Current Layer to Selection's Layer**	• **Layers Toolbar**
Object Selection		
	**Crossing**	• **Main Toolbar:** Window/Crossing Toggle
	**Rectangular Selection Region**	• **Main Toolbar**
	**Select Object**	• **Main Toolbar**
	**Select by Name**	• **Main Toolbar**
	**Window**	• **Main Toolbar:** Window/Crossing Toggle
Viewport Navigation		
	**Dolly Camera**	• **Viewport Navigation Toolbar (Camera Views):** *Dolly Camera* flyout
	**Field-of-View**	• **Viewport Navigation Toolbar:** *Zoom Region* flyout in Perspective and Camera views
	**Maximize Viewport Toggle**	• **Viewport Navigation Toolbar**

Button	Command	Location
	**Orbit Camera**	• **Viewport Navigation Toolbar (Camera Views)**
	**Orbit**	• **Viewport Navigation Toolbar (Non-Camera Views):** Orbit flyout
	**Orbit Point of View**	• **Viewport Navigation Toolbar (Non-Camera Views):** Orbit flyout
	**Pan View**	• **Viewport Navigation Toolbar**
	**Perspective**	• **Viewport Navigation Toolbar (Camera Views)**
	**Roll Camera**	• **Viewport Navigation Toolbar (Camera Views)**
	**Truck Camera**	• **Viewport Navigation Toolbar (Camera Views)**
	**Walk Through**	• **Viewport Navigation Toolbar:** *Pan View* flyout in Perspective and Camera views
	**Zoom**	• **Viewport Navigation Toolbar (Non-Camera Views)**
	**Zoom All**	• **Viewport Navigation Toolbar (Non-Camera Views)**
	**Zoom Extents**	• **Viewport Navigation Toolbar (Non-Camera Views):** *Zoom Extents* flyout
	**Zoom Extents Selected**	• **Viewport Navigation Toolbar (Non-Camera Views):** *Zoom Extents* flyout
	**Zoom Extents All**	• **Viewport Navigation Toolbar:** *Zoom Extents All* flyout
	**Zoom Extents All Selected**	• **Viewport Navigation Toolbar:** *Zoom Extents All* flyout
	**Zoom Region**	• **Viewport Navigation Toolbar (Non-Camera Views)**

Chapter 3

Assembling Project Files

The files used in the Autodesk® 3ds Max® software can be modeled directly in the software, referenced by linking, or directly imported from another source. Linking files enables you to incorporate objects or other scene files into the current scene by externally referencing them. Once referenced, the connection between the two files can be maintained. If files are imported, they are merged with the project and no link is established. Understanding the benefits and drawbacks of using external data helps you decide how to best reference it in a project.

Learning Objectives

- Understand the difference between file linking and file importing, and edit the linked data files.
- Combine entities from .DWG, .DXF, .FBX, and .RVT files into an active Autodesk 3ds Max scene.
- Understand how to link AutoCAD® .DWG, .DXF, generic .FBX files, and Autodesk® Revit® .RVT/.FBX files.
- Create and modify presets.
- Incorporate objects or other scene files into the current scene by externally referencing them.
- Manage data using the asset tracking systems.

3.1 Data Linking and Importing

Although the Autodesk 3ds Max software has a robust 2D and 3D modeling system, it might be efficient to link or import some or all of the design data from other Autodesk software, such as AutoCAD®, Autodesk® Revit® Architecture, AutoCAD® Architecture, or Autodesk® Inventor®.

Linking vs. Importing

You can link or import files using the **File Link** and **Import** tools. You can link files such as .DWG, .DXF, .FBX, and .RVT, and import files such as Autodesk® Inventor® (.IPT, .IAM), Autodesk® Alias® .Wire, LandXML and DEM data files, and Adobe® Illustrator® (.AI).

- Linked geometry differs from imported geometry in that it remains connected to the source file. If the source file is edited, the Autodesk 3ds Max Scene can be updated to show those changes. Imported geometry maintains no connection to the source file.
- If a source .DWG, .DXF, .FBX, or .RVT file is likely to change (or you would prefer to make changes in the .DWG, .DXF, .FBX, or .RVT directly), then using **File Linking** might be the best way to incorporate this data into the Autodesk 3ds Max software.
- **Importing** can be used as a faster alternative to linking to bring large amounts of data into the software. Complex geometry might be faster to reimport than to update through a file link.
- File links and imports are launched from the **File>Import** in the Menu bar, as shown in Figure 3–1.

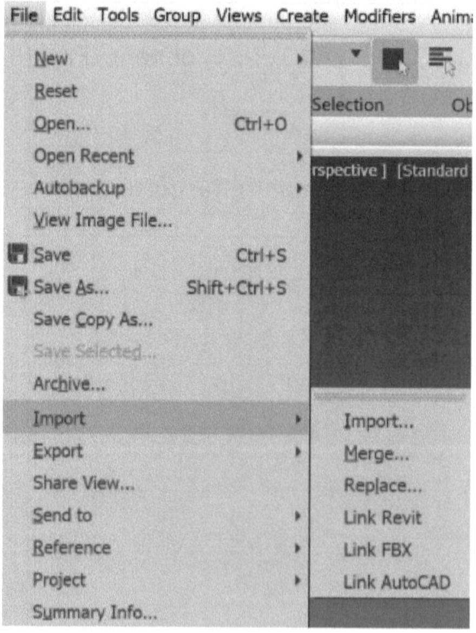

Figure 3–1

Editing Linked Data

- Linked geometry can be edited but not directly deleted from a scene file. Alternatively, the layer on which the objects are placed might be ignored during a reload, or set to **Hide** in the Layer Explorer.
- Edits applied to linked geometry (such as through modifiers) are reapplied after a link is updated. Some complex modifications might not apply as expected, so you should always review your geometry carefully after a link is updated.
- Links to drawing files are not bi-directional, so that changes you make to the data in the Autodesk 3ds Max software do not update the original .DWG, .FBX, .DXF, or .RVT file.
- In linked files that are bound, the geometry stays in the scene file as-is, but the connection to the source file is dropped.

Importing

You can export an .FBX file from the Autodesk Revit software and import it in Autodesk 3ds Max software. The FBX importer is an independent plug-in that is frequently updated. In the *FBX Import* dialog box, use **Web Update** to check for web updates, download the latest updates, and install them. Close 3ds Max when you do the install.

Merging Autodesk 3ds Max Scene Files

Objects already saved in Autodesk 3ds Max scenes (.MAX files) are imported into the current scene using the **Merge** option (**File>Import>Merge**). Merging files is a one-directional transfer that does not maintain any connection between the two files. Using the **Merge** option, you can either load a few objects from a scene or you can load a complete scene into the current one.

Civil View

Civil View enables you to import 3D geometry from Civil/Survey products, such as Autodesk Civil 3D, Land Desktop, and other formats such as BentleyMX files.

Initializing Civil View

To use Civil View the first time, you are required to initialize it by selecting **Civil View>Initialize Civil View**. In the *Initialize Autodesk Civil View* dialog box that opens (as shown in Figure 3–2), you can set the *System Units* and the *Country Resource Kit* based on the civil project that you will be opening. After initializing the Civil View, you are required to exit and restart the Autodesk 3ds Max software. Note that you only have to initialize Civil View once.

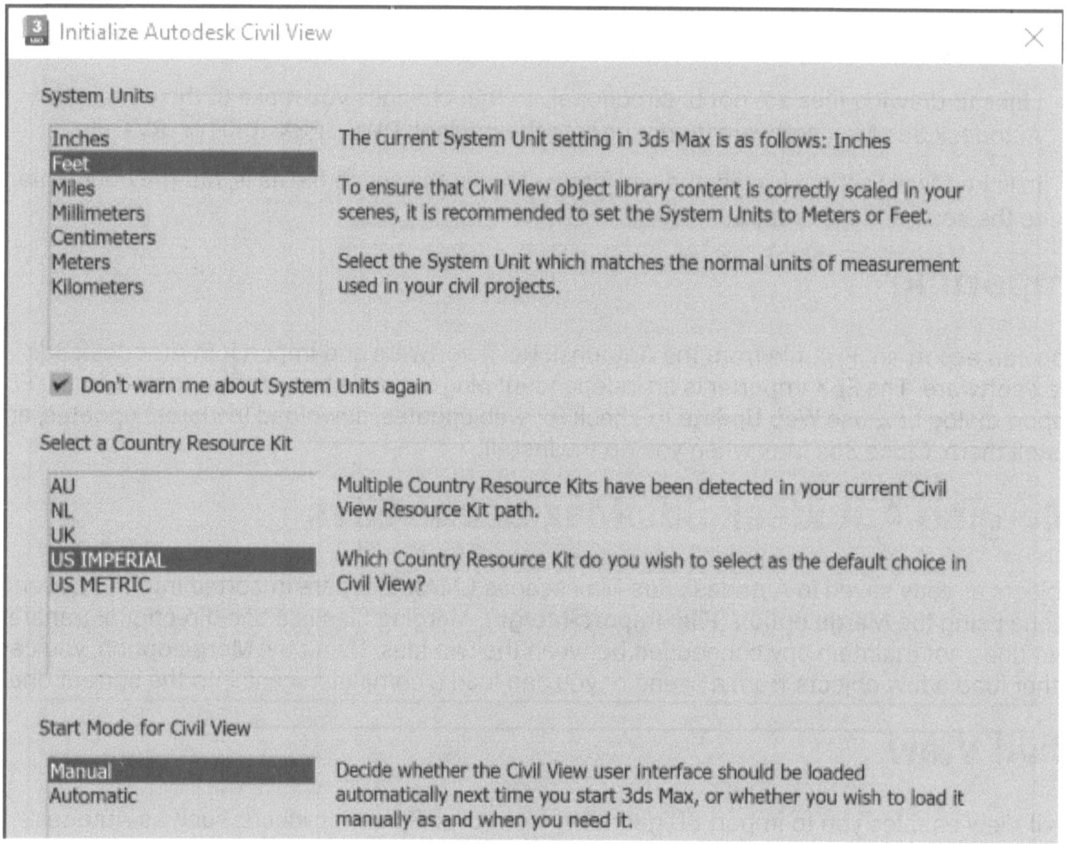

Figure 3–2

Although Civil View is initialized, if the *Start Mode for Civil View* is set to **Manual**, next time you launch the Autodesk 3ds Max software, you are required to start Civil View. You can change this setting in the *Civil View Preferences* dialog box, which can be accessed by selecting **Civil View>Civil View> Preferences**, in the *General* tab of the dialog box, selecting **Automatically start Civil View?,** as shown in Figure 3–3.

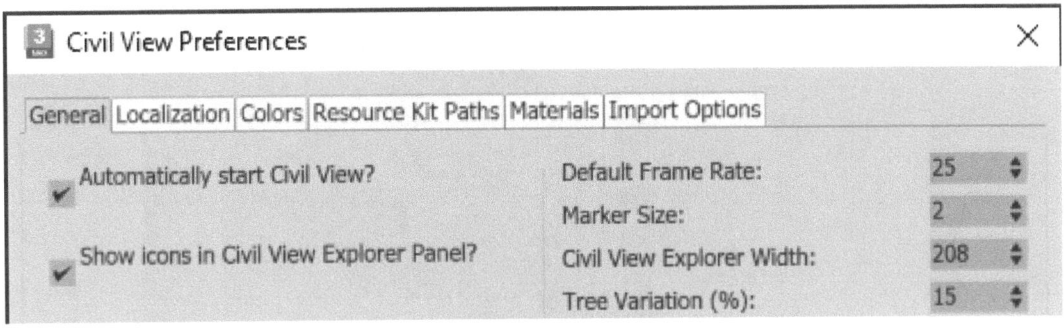

Figure 3–3

Using Civil View

- You can start the interface from the Menu bar by selecting **Civil View>Initialize Civil View**.
- Once Civil View is started, menu options are displayed in the Civil View menu bar. Here you can import the required geometry by selecting **Civil View>Geometry Import**, as shown in Figure 3–4.

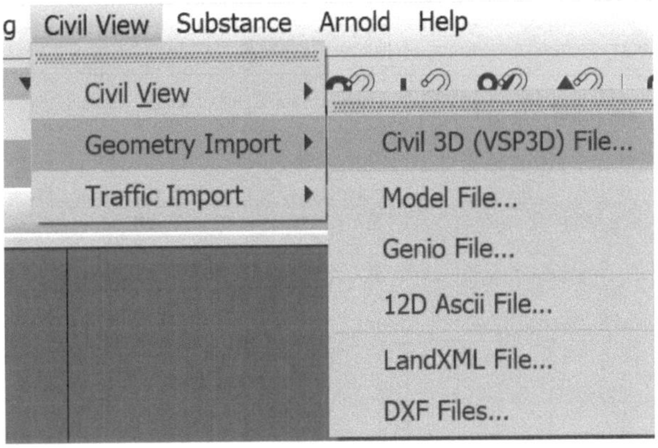

Figure 3–4

Civil View Explorer

You can use the Civil View Explorer (shown in Figure 3–5) to access the visualization aspects of the objects in the scene. It also contains all the editing commands for the selected objects. The objects that are imported retain a link to the original source file. The Civil View visualization model retains a link to the original source file and updates the model whenever a design changes.

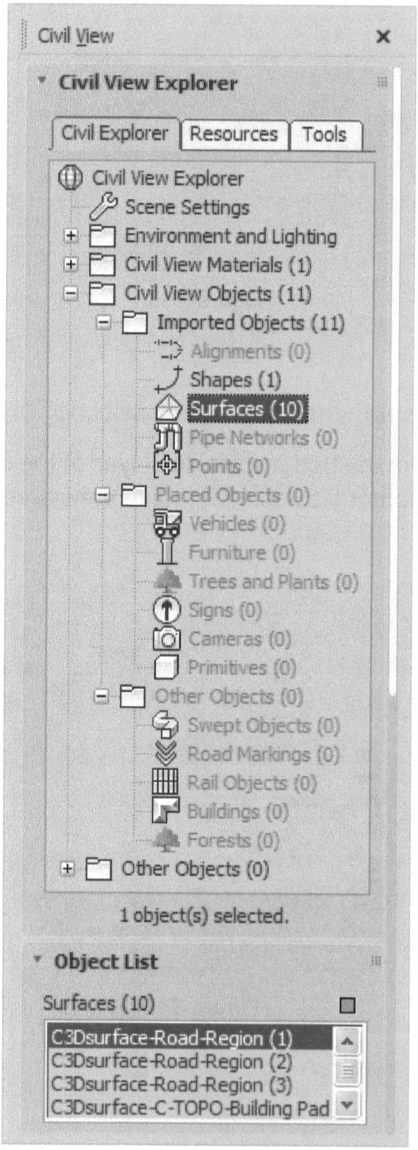

Figure 3–5

Practice 3a
Ground Surfaces Using Civil View

Practice Objective

- Open a Civil 3D data file in a scene file.

In this practice, you will open a .VSP3D file for importing ground surfaces using Civil View. You will then modify the material assignment for various ground surfaces using the Civil View Explorer.

You must set the paths to locate the External files and XREFs used in the practice. If you have not done this already, return to Chapter 1 and complete Task 1 to Task 3 in *Practice 1a: Organize Folders and Work with the Interface*. You only have to set the user paths once.

Task 1: Initialize Civil View.

It is recommended that you import 3D ground surfaces from Civil/Survey products, such as Autodesk Civil 3D or Land Desktop using the vsp3d data format.

1. In the menu bar, select **Civil View>Initialize Civil View**. You only have to initialize Civil View once. If you have already initialized Civil View, go to Step 5.
2. In the *Initialize Autodesk Civil View* dialog box, set the *System Units* to **Feet** because the civil project that you will be opening uses Feet as its unit of measurement. Verify that **Don't warn me about System Units again** is selected.
3. In the *Select a Country Resource Kit* area, select **US IMPERIAL** and verify that *Start Mode for Civil View* is set to **Manual**. Click **OK**. In the *Civil View Information* dialog box, click **OK**.
4. Exit and then restart the Autodesk 3ds Max software.
5. Select **Civil View>Initialize Civil View** to start Civil View.

Task 2: Open a Civil 3D file.

1. Open **Civil Base XRef.max** from the ...*\scenes* folder. If a *Mismatch* dialog box opens, click **OK** to accept the default values. This is an empty scene in which the System Unit Scale has been set to **1 Unit=1.0 Feet**.
2. In the menu bar, select **Civil View>Geometry Import>Civil 3D (VSP3D) File**, as shown in Figure 3–6.

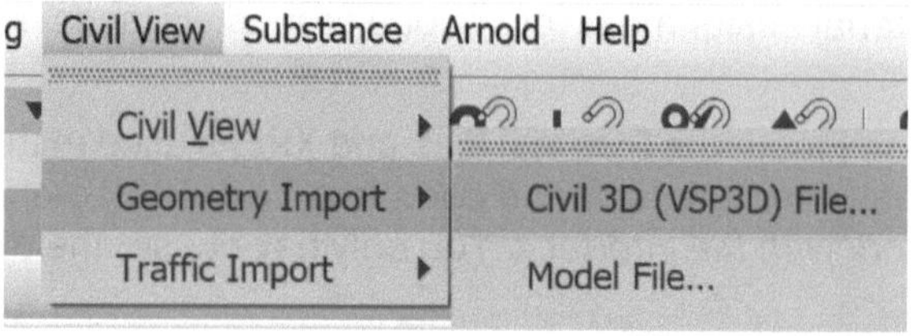

Figure 3–6

3. In the *Civil 3D Import Panel* dialog box, click **Open**. In the *Select a VSP3D File* dialog box, browse to the ...*\import* folder in the practice files folder and open **Civil surfaces.vsp3d**.
4. In the *Civil 3D Import Panel* dialog box, a list of objects that are in the Autodesk Civil 3D file are listed. The objects listed include surfaces, site/grading objects, corridors (surfaces, baselines, featurelines, etc.), and point groups.
5. In the left pane, select **Surfaces [9]** to display all of the surfaces in the right pane. Select **Building Pad**, hold <Shift>, and select **Parking Lot Surface** to highlight the first seven surfaces. Select the checkbox for **Building Pad** to select all seven highlighted surfaces, as shown in Figure 3–7. You can select them individually as well.

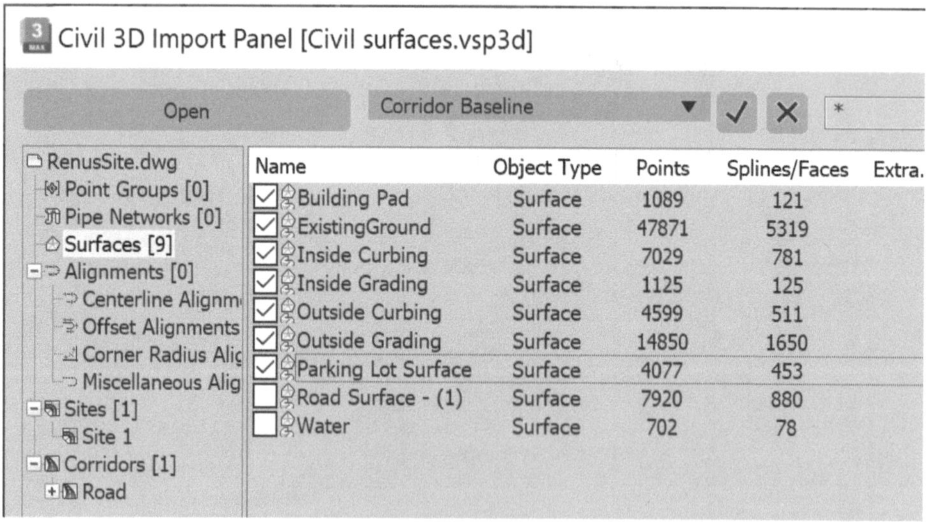

Figure 3–7

6. You will select the corridor surfaces and the baseline. In the left pane, select **Corridors [1]** and in the right pane, click in the checkboxes for **PrimaryAccess**, **Region(1)**, **Region(2)**, and **Region(3)**, as shown in Figure 3–8.

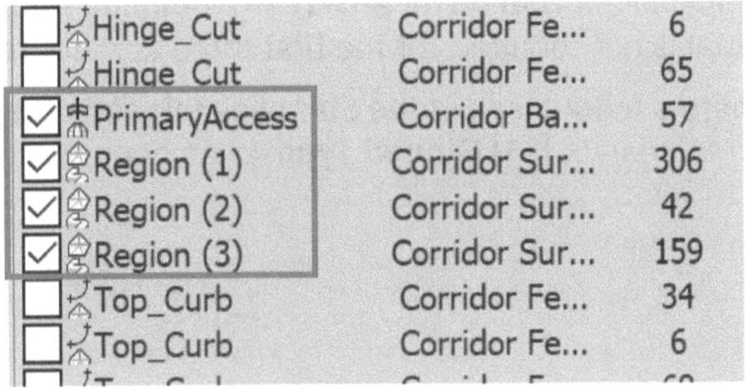

Figure 3–8

7. Click **OK**. In the Civil View Information, click **Yes** to accept the global shift values.
8. Click **Yes** to proceed without a feature interpretation style.
9. If a *Material Library File Save* Warning dialog box opens, click **OK**. Click **OK** again.
10. It might take a few seconds to load the file. The ground surfaces, building pad, corridor, and parking lot display in all the viewports. If they are not, click  (Zoom Extents All). In the Perspective viewport, note that only the corridor displays the right surface material but the rest of the surfaces display a checkerboard material.
11. In the menu bar, select **Civil View>Civil View>Civil View Explorer** to open the Civil View Explorer. Right-click on the title bar and select **Dock>Left**. Keep it open along the left side of the screen.

Task 3: Modify material assignment.

1. Verify that the *Civil Explorer* tab is selected. Expand **Civil View Objects>Imported Objects**, if not already expanded. Select **Surfaces** and note that the left portion of the corridor is selected in the viewports. In the Civil View Explorer, the *Object List* rollout opens with all of the surfaces listed, as shown in Figure 3–9.

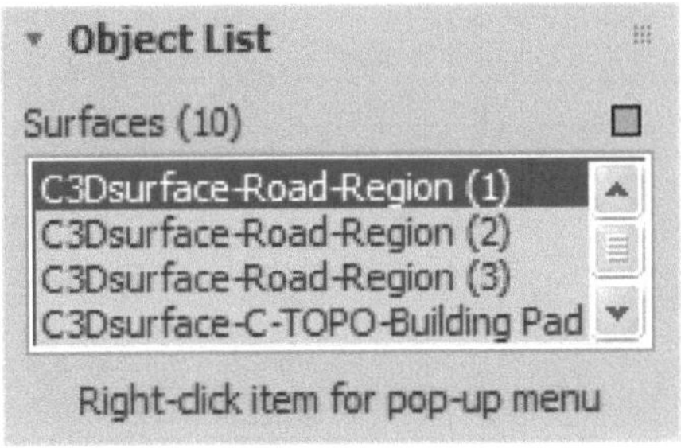

Figure 3–9

2. The complete list might not be visible in the Explorer. Hover the cursor in the empty space in the information area until it displays as a Pan (hand) cursor, as shown in Figure 3–10. Scroll or pan down to display the rest of the parameters in the *Object List* rollout.
3. In the *Object List* rollout, select **C3Dsurface-C-TOPO-Building Pad**, as shown in Figure 3–11. A material is not required for the first three corridor regions.
4. In the *Surface Parameters* rollout, select the *Statistics* tab and note that in the *Face Selection Sets*, in *By Material ID*, **[31] Ground Type 4** has been assigned, as shown in Figure 3–11.

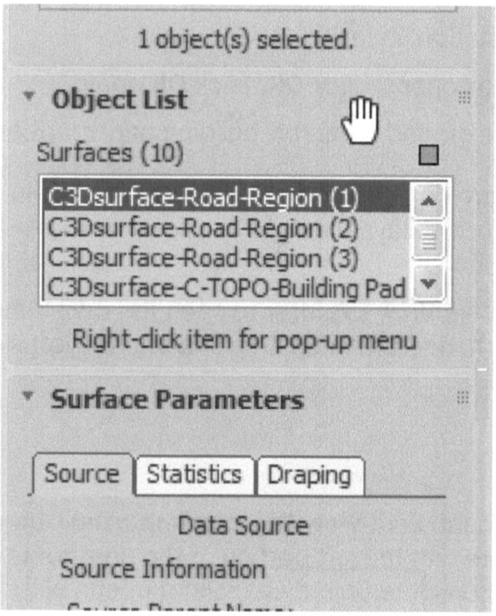

Figure 3–10

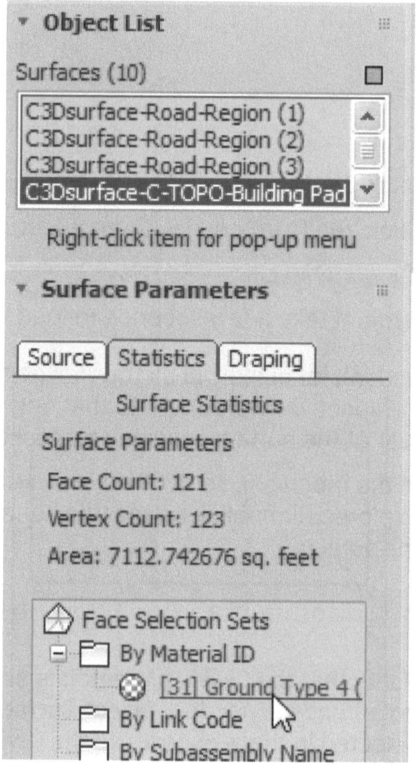

Figure 3–11

5. Right-click on **[31] Ground Type 4** and select **Modify Material ID Assignment**, as shown in Figure 3–12.

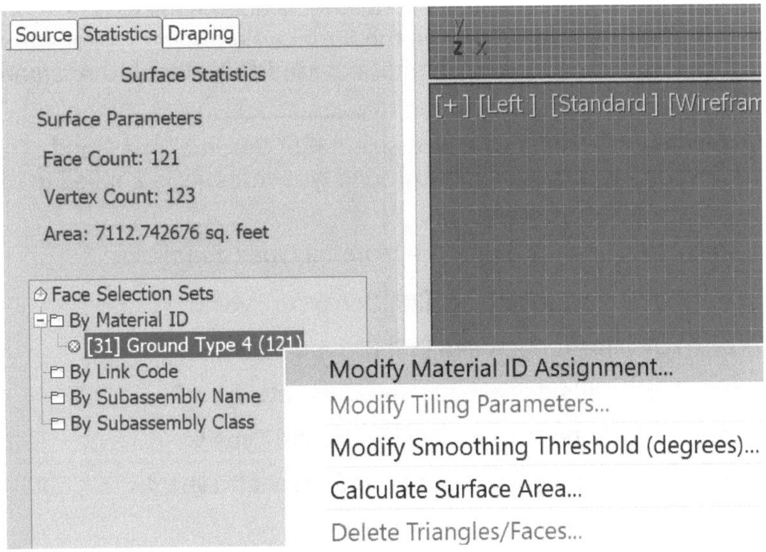

Figure 3–12

6. Click **Yes** in the Warning dialog box.
7. In the *Modify material channel* dialog box, select **[22] Concrete Type 1**, as shown in Figure 3–13. Click **OK**.

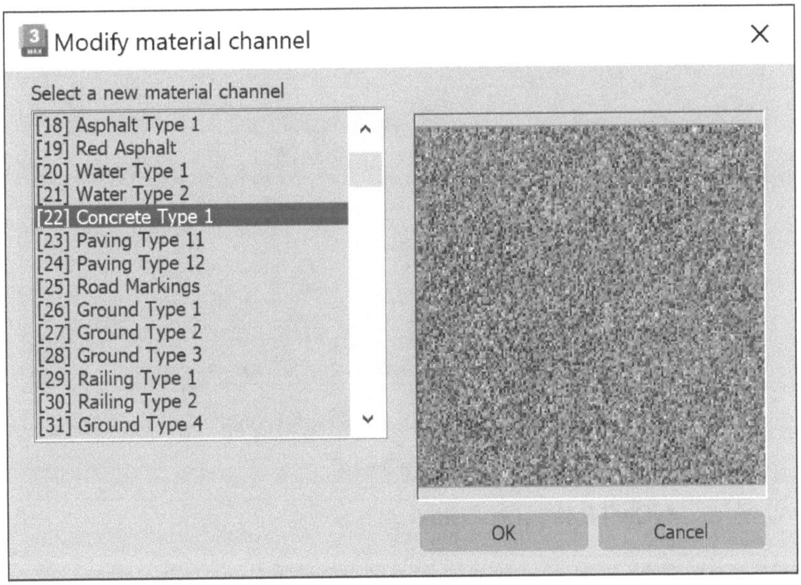

Figure 3–13

8. In the **Perspective** viewport, use **Zoom** and **Pan** to zoom in to the building pad. Note how the new material is applied.
9. In the Civil View Explorer, in the *Object List* rollout, select the next surface, which is **C3Dsurface-C-TOPO-Existing Ground**. In the *Surface Parameters* rollout, in the *Statistics* tab, right-click on **[31] Ground Type 4**, and select **Modify Material ID Assignment**. In the Warning dialog box, click **Yes**.
10. In the *Modify material channel* dialog box, select **[35] Ground Type 6** and click **OK**. In the **Perspective** viewport, note that the new ground type material is applied to the ground surface.
11. Similarly, for the other surfaces, apply the material types as follows:
    - C3Dsurface-C-TOPO-Inside Curbing: **[38] Concrete Type 3**
    - C3Dsurface-C-TOPO-Inside Grading: **[35] Ground Type 6**
    - C3Dsurface-C-TOPO-Outside Curbing: **[38] Concrete Type 3**
    - C3Dsurface-C-TOPO-Outside Grading: **[35] Ground Type 6**
    - C3Dsurface-C-TOPO-Parking Lot Surface: **[39] Asphalt Type 4**
12. Close the Civil View Explorer.
13. Click  (Zoom Extents All). In the **Perspective** view, the scene displays with all the required materials, as shown in Figure 3–14.

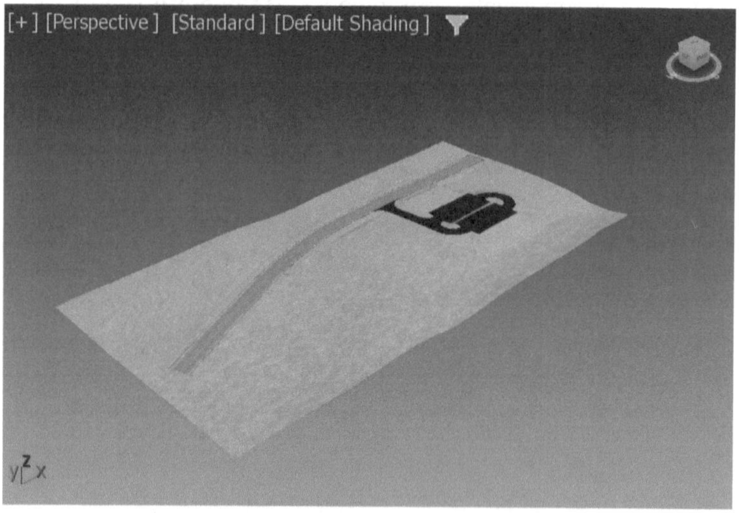

Figure 3–14

14. Save your work as **MyCivil Base XRef.max**.

End of practice

3.2 Linking Files

File Linking is used to incorporate data from other Autodesk software such as Autodesk Revit and AutoCAD into the Autodesk 3ds Max scene. If the incorporated data is changed in the originating software, the file link enables you to update those changes in the 3ds Max scene. File linking is useful when you are working on a visualization project and know that all design decisions have not yet been made. You can link files using the *Manage Links* dialog box that can be opened as follows:

- **File>Import>Link Revit**: Links the .RVT files from the Autodesk Revit Architecture software.
- **File>Import>Link FBX**: Links the .FBX files that can be created in the Autodesk Revit, Autodesk MotionBuilder, Autodesk Maya, and Autodesk Mudbox software.
- **File>Import>Link AutoCAD**: Links the .DWG and .DXF files from the AutoCAD software.
- You can also open the *Manage Links* dialog box outside of the Link commands (**File>Reference> Manage Links**) and modify the Link settings.

Linking DWG Files

In CAD data files it is common to have large numbers of objects. When linking or importing AutoCAD .DWG or .DXF files, it is efficient to combine multiple, related objects together into a single Autodesk 3ds Max object to control their display and visibility.

- When multiple entities are combined into compound Autodesk 3ds Max shapes (2D objects) and meshes (3D objects), you can still access and adjust the original geometry using the Sub-object level modifiers, such as **Edit Spline**, **Edit Mesh**, and **Edit Poly**.
- Once multiple entities are combined, you can detach objects or portions of an objects to form new ones for individual editing control.

Linking FBX and RVT Files

The Autodesk Revit and Autodesk 3ds Max software share the Autodesk Material Library materials.

- The .RVT and .FBX file format supports the import of photometric lights, both interior artificial lights and exterior daylight systems.
- Detailed .RVT and .FBX file formats can become very large in size and importing them as single files cannot be accomplished. In such cases, use a section box in the **3D View** in the Autodesk Revit software to limit the amount of the scene you are exporting.

Manage Links Options

The *Manage Links* dialog box (shown in Figure 3–15) contains the following tabs:

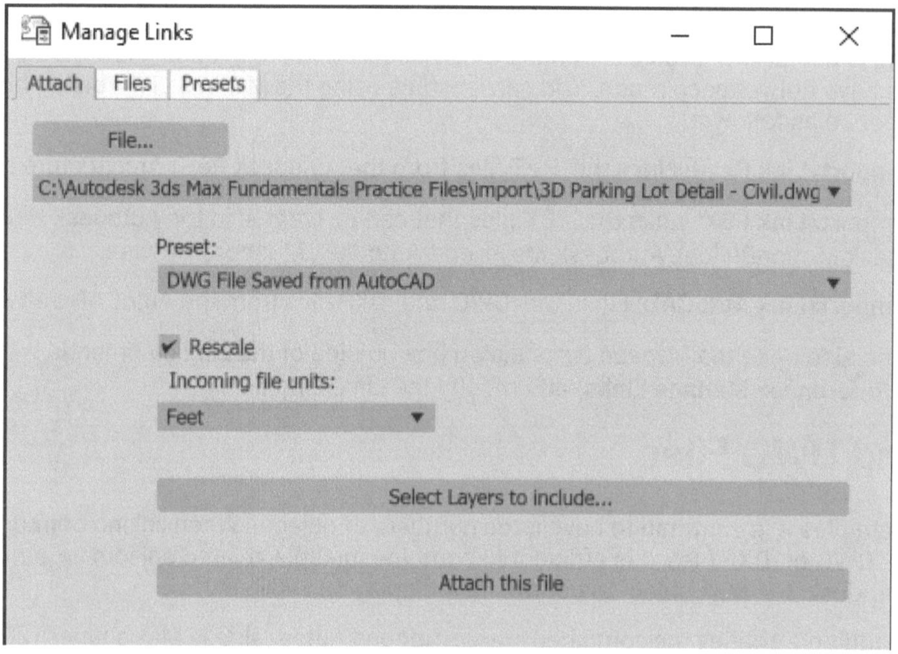

Figure 3–15

Attach Tab

The options available in the *Attach* tab are described as follows:

- **File... enables y**ou to open a file (.DWG, .DXF, .FBX, or .RVT) for linking. The selected filename and its path display in the *File* drop-down list. If the file that you selected is a .RVT file with more than one camera view, you are prompted to select a camera view.
- The *Preset* drop-down list enables you to select the preset settings. The Presets listed here can be created or modified using the *Presets* tab. You can set the units by selecting them in the Incoming file units drop-down list.
- **Select Layers to include** is only available with .DWG and .DXF file formats and enables you to select the layers that you want included with the drawing file.
- **Attach this file** links the selected file with the specified preset settings to the current Autodesk 3ds Max scene.

Files Tab

The *Files* tab displays a list of files that are linked to the current scene with a specific status icon.

- If the linked file has been modified, displays with the linked filename.
- indicates that the linked file is unchanged and does not have any errors.
- When a file is highlighted, the following options are available:

Reload...	When the original file has been changed, it displays the changes in the current scene. Use **Reload...** to update the file in the scene.
Detach...	Use when you want to remove the link with the original file. This option removes all geometry associated with the linked file.
Bind...	Removes the link with the original file, but the geometry stays in the current scene, although the link between the original file is broken. Changes made to the original linked file cannot be reloaded.

Presets Tab

Many options are available before files are linked to your current scene. These options are configured and saved as **Presets** and can be used when linking files at a later stage. Many of these options require trial and error to find the most appropriate settings. You can link a file and then reload (or detach and relink) with different settings until you achieve the required results.

The *Presets* tab lists all existing presets and contains options for creating new presets, modifying existing presets, copying existing ones, renaming and deleting them. You need to select a preset for the **Modify**, **Copy**, **Rename**, and **Delete** options to be available, as shown in Figure 3–16. If no preset is selected, **Copy** is replaced by **New** and is the only available option.

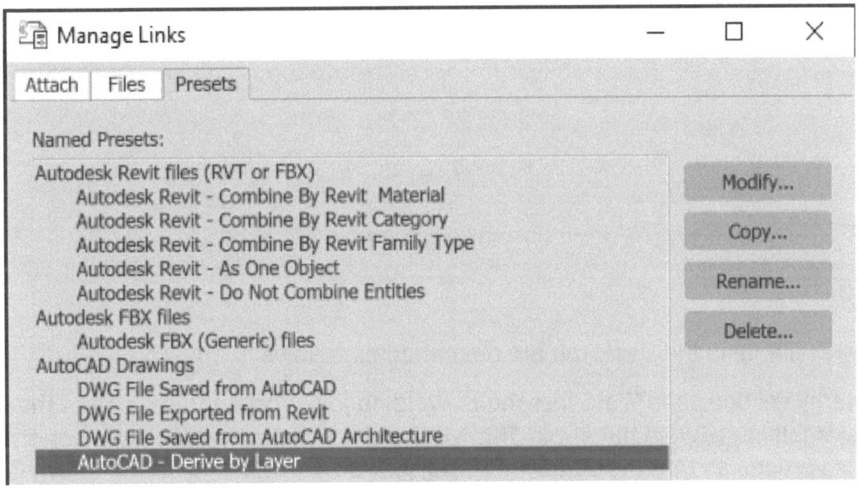

Figure 3–16

Depending on the type of preset selected (.RVT, .FBX, or .DWG), clicking **Modify...** opens a specific *File Link Settings* dialog box, which enables you to define the way you want the geometry to be linked, what portions of the file are to be modified on **Reload**, and how the geometry is combined.

File Link Settings: DWG Files

In the *Manage Links* dialog box, in the *Presets* tab, selecting an AutoCAD DWG file preset and clicking **Modify...** opens the *File Link Settings: DWG Files* dialog box, as shown in Figure 3–17.

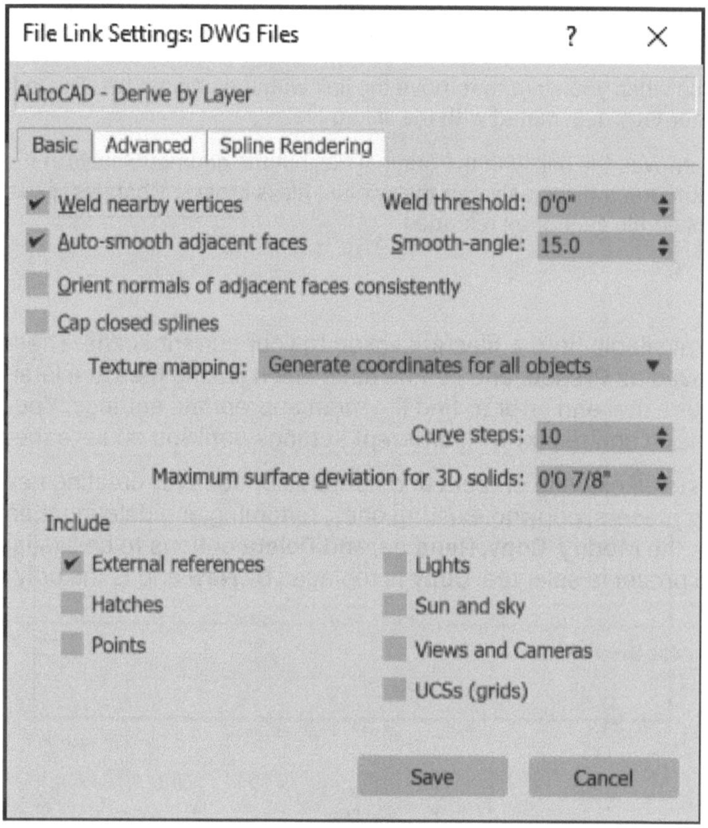

Figure 3–17

Basic Tab

The options available in the *Basic* tab are described as follows:

- **Weld nearby vertices** and **Weld threshold:** Welding joins together vertices of the same object that fall in the weld threshold. If the objects are joined by layer, this option removes duplicate vertices so that the adjacent 2D objects on the same layer are automatically combined into splines. Adjacent 3D objects that are welded become faces in a single mesh that share common vertices.

- **Auto-smooth adjacent face** and **Smooth-angle:** Auto-smooth enables adjacent faces in the same 3D mesh to display smooth if the angles of separation between their face normals (a directional vector perpendicular to the face) is equal to or less than the Smooth-angle. Otherwise, the adjacent faces have a faceted edge between them. This is the same smoothing process used in the Edit Mesh and Edit Poly modifiers.
- **Orient normals of adjacent faces consistently:** This option coordinates the face normals of linked objects. This option should be left off by default unless some faces of your 3D objects are missing after the link.
- **Cap closed splines:** It assigns an Extrude modifier to all closed 2D geometry (e.g., circles and closed polylines).
- **Texture mapping:** Texture mapping is used to locate texture maps on objects. Two options are available:

Generate coordinates on-demand	• Links objects without adding any texture mapping. • Adds the mapping when it is first called for by the software. • Enables a faster link but might cause some discrepancies.
Generate coordinates for all objects	• Adds texture mapping to all objects at the time of the link, matching any that might have existed in the original drawing file.

- **Curve steps:** This setting defines the number of segments to subdivide each 2D curve segment into if they are later extruded in the Autodesk 3ds Max software. This setting applies to circles, arcs, polyline curves, spines, and similar curved objects.
- **Maximum surface deviation for 3D solids:** This setting defines the allowed deviation distance from a parametric AutoCAD 3D curve (such as a curved AutoCAD extrusion) and the resulting Autodesk 3ds Max mesh. The lower the value, the more a 3D curve is subdivided. This value can be set as low as 0.01. In the Autodesk 3ds Max software, all 3D curves must be segmented.
- **Include area options:** These options enable you to select the type of objects to be brought into the scene. Note that the **Lights** option only brings in Lights from AutoCAD drawings pre-2007. If you have Sun and Sky checked, a daylight system is created based on the information in the incoming DWG file from the Autodesk Revit 2009 software.

Advanced Tab

The *Advanced* tab (shown in Figure 3–18) controls the import of AutoCAD primitives and the effect of scene materials while importing.

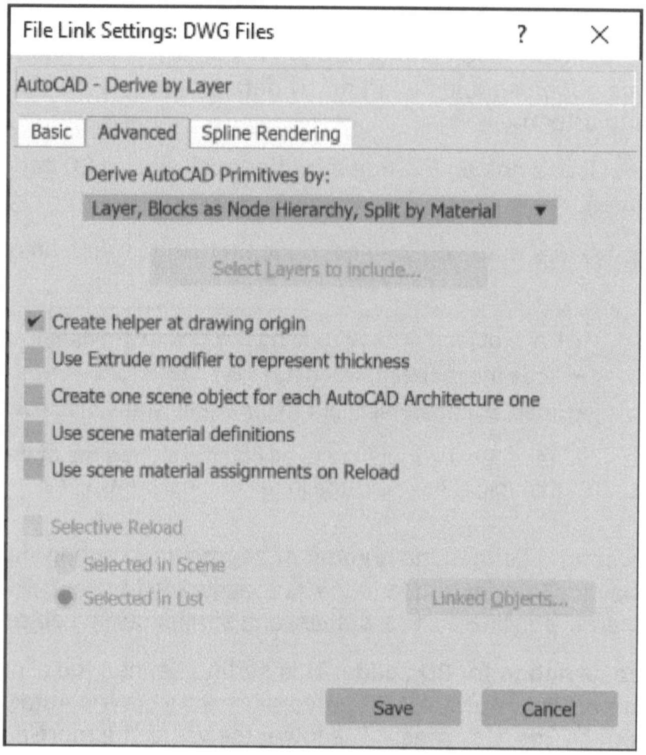

Figure 3–18

The options available in the *Advanced* tab are described as follows:

- **Derive AutoCAD Primitives by:** Controls how AutoCAD objects are combined when linked.

Layer	Creates one object for each AutoCAD layer. Each AutoCAD block links as a single object called a VIZBlock.
Layer, Blocks as Node Hierarchy	This option preserves material assignments in linked AutoCAD blocks. It structures each as a hierarchy of objects rather than single objects.
Layer, Blocks as Node Hierarchy, Split by Material	This option works similarly to the one above but takes into account drawings that have more than one material applied to objects on the same layer. Separate hierarchies are created for each material type on each layer.
Entity, Blocks as Node Hierarchy	This option includes all non-blocks as separate, individual objects. Blocks are preserved as hierarchies, however, organized by layer.
Color	Combines AutoCAD objects by color. All objects of one color are joined in as a single object, regardless of layer.

Entity	Does not combine AutoCAD objects at all. Instead, each AutoCAD object becomes an individual object.
One Object	This option combines all AutoCAD objects into a single object.

- **Create helper at drawing origin:** Adds an origin point helper at the origin of the current coordinate system. All of the linked geometry is part of a hierarchy parented by this helper, so all of the linked objects can be repositioned as one by transforming the helper.
- **Use Extrude modifier to represent thickness: When disabled,** linking 2D AutoCAD objects with a non-zero thickness value translates the objects into the Autodesk 3ds Max software as a 3D mesh. When enabled, objects translate as 2D objects with a parametric extrude modifier. The resulting geometry is the same but when this option is enabled, the extrusion properties (such as height) can be modified after the link or imported using the modifier stack.
- **Create one scene object for each AutoCAD Architecture one:** When unchecked, AutoCAD Architecture and AutoCAD MEP objects are subdivided into separate objects by material.
- **Use scene material definitions:** When unchecked, the Autodesk 3ds Max software includes the current state of any material applied to the linked objects in the AutoCAD software. If selected and the current scene has a material with the same exact name as the AutoCAD material, the scene material is used instead.
- **Use scene material assignments on Reload:** When unchecked, the Autodesk 3ds Max software re-loads the current state of any AutoCAD materials present in the drawing file when the link is updated. When enabled, the Autodesk 3ds Max software maintains the current state of any materials in the scene file after a link is updated. Select this option if you intend to adjust linked materials in the Autodesk 3ds Max software or leave it unchecked if you intend to adjust them the AutoCAD software.
- **Selective Reload:** Enables you to reload a subset of the original file. You can select objects to reload by selecting them in the scene or by selecting them from a list. If you select **Selected in List**, and click **Linked Objects** a list opens.

Hint: Hierarchies and File Linking

Autodesk 3ds Max Hierarchies are collections of objects linked together into parent/child relationships where transform applied to a parent are automatically passed on to its children. Connecting multiple objects in a hierarchical chain can enable sophisticated animations in the Autodesk 3ds Max software, such as the motion of jointed robotic arms.

In the case of the **hierarchy** file link options, incoming AutoCAD blocks are brought into the Autodesk 3ds Max software as multiple objects so that they can maintain multiple material assignments from the AutoCAD software. The parent object itself does not have any geometry and does not render. Most modifiers (such as **Substitute**) must be applied to the objects in the hierarchy rather than the parent.

Spline Rendering Tab

The options available in the *Spline Rendering* tab (shown in Figure 3–19) enable linear objects (2D and 3D lines, polylines, etc.) to display as extruded 3D objects in the viewports or rendering. Normally, splines cannot be rendered because they do not have surface area to interact with scene lighting. These options enable splines to link into the Autodesk 3ds Max software as 3D linear objects with a cross-sectional radius or a rectangular length and width. This provides the surface area for rendering.

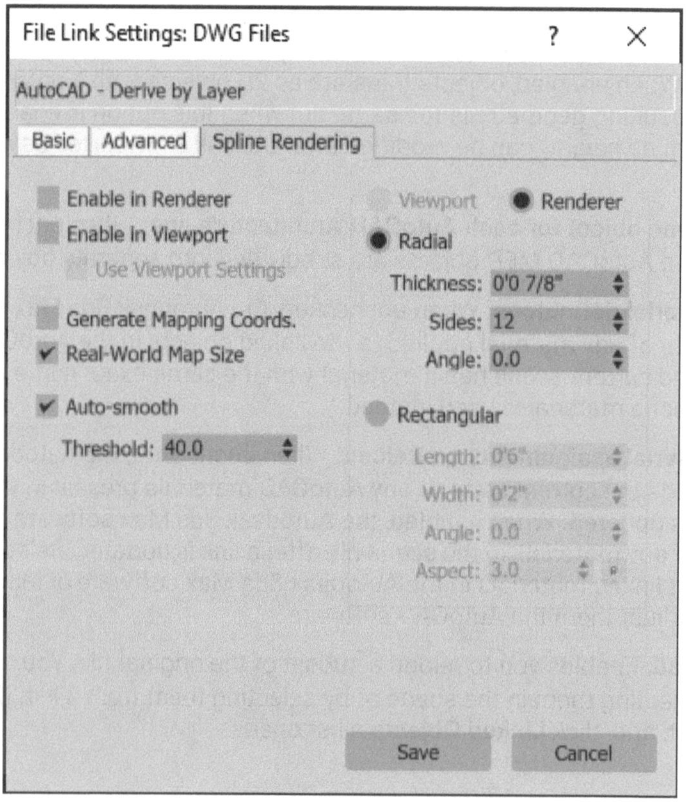

Figure 3–19

- If splines are to be rendered with materials then options such as smoothing, mapping coordinates, and/or real-world map size are often important.
- When enabled, all of the splines linked with this setting are renderable, and all have the same cross-section geometry.
- To make only certain 2D objects renderable (or want some to render differently than others) you could apply a Renderable Spline modifier directly to those objects after linking.

File Link Settings: Revit Files (RVT or FBX)

In the *Manage Links* dialog box, in the *Presets* tab, selecting an Autodesk Revit file and clicking **Modify...** opens the *File Link Settings: Revit Files (RVT or FBX)* dialog box, as shown in Figure 3–20. Additionally, you can also select the Autodesk FBX (Generic) file preset and click **Modify....**This opens the *File Link Settings: FBX Files* dialog box. This dialog box is similar to the Autodesk Revit Files (.RVT and .FBX) but without a *Geometry* area for controlling the segments and smoothing the linked geometry.

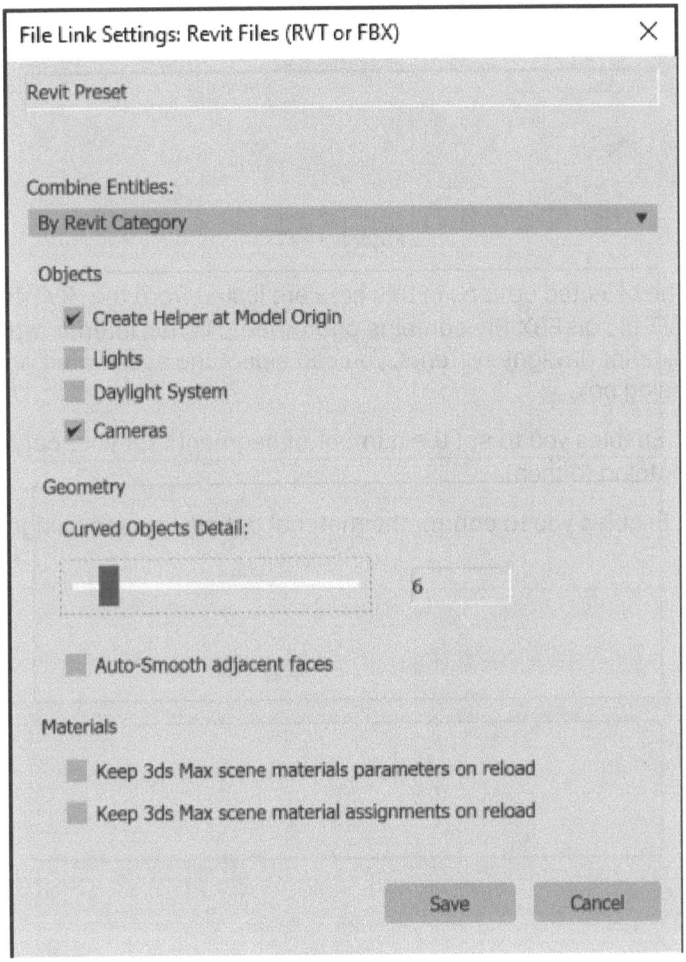

Figure 3–20

The options available in the *File Link Settings: Revit Files (RVT or FBX)* dialog box are described as follows:

- **Combine Entities** list: Enables you to select the Autodesk Revit entities that you want to combine, as shown in Figure 3–21. For example, if you select **By Revit Material**, all of the entities that have the same material are linked in the current Autodesk 3ds Max scene as a single object. It is a good practice to combine entities to reduce the number of objects.

Figure 3–21

- ***Objects* area:** The selected options in this area are linked from the .RVT file to your current scene. If the .RVT file or .FBX file contains photometric lights, interior artificial lights, cameras, and exterior daylight systems, you can select the associated options in the File Link Settings dialog box.
- ***Geometry* area:** Enables you to set the number of segments for your curved entities and apply auto-smoothing to them.
- ***Materials* area:** Enables you to control the material definitions and assignment settings.

Practice 3b
Link an AutoCAD DWG

Practice Objectives

- Create a preset to link an AutoCAD .DWG file and reposition it.
- Revise the link settings and reload the linked file.

In this practice, you will link AutoCAD geometry to represent the parking lot details, such as pavement markings and other details. You will reposition this file using the Helper object, and will create 3D markings by projecting 2D lines to the elevation of a terrain model.

You must set the paths to locate the External files and XREFs used in the practice. If you have not done this already, return to Chapter 1 and complete Task 1 to Task 3 in *Practice 1a: Organize Folders and Work with the Interface*. You only have to set the user paths once.

Task 1: Link an AutoCAD .DWG file.

1. Open **Civil Base.max** from the ...*scenes* folder. It has the building pad, parking lot, corridor, and ground surfaces.
2. Select **File>Import>Link AutoCAD**. In the *Open* dialog box, browse and open the ...*import* folder in the practice files folder. Select **3D Parking Lot Detail-Civil.dwg** and click **Open**. The *Manage Links* dialog box opens and displays the full path of the file, as shown in Figure 3–22. The full path must display for the import to work correctly.

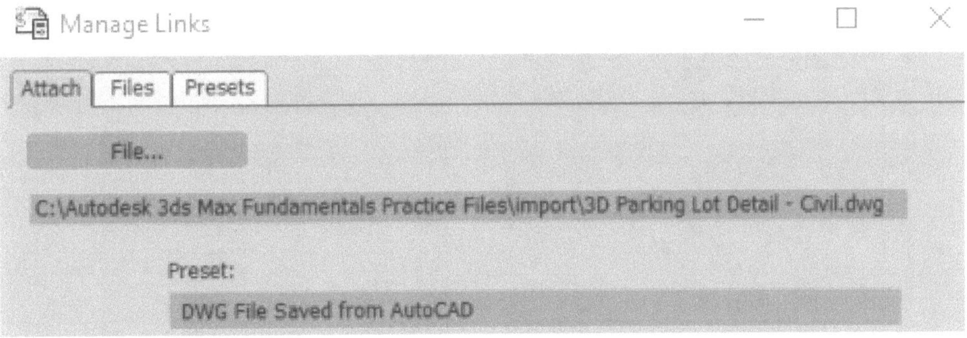

Figure 3–22

3. Select the *Presets* tab and click **New...** to create a new link preset.
   - If no preset is selected, only **New...** is available.
4. In the *New Settings Preset* dialog box, set *New Name* as **AutoCAD – Derive by Layer**. Note that the *Format* is selected as **AutoCAD Drawings**. Click **OK**.

5. In the *Manage Links* dialog box, select the new **AutoCAD – Derive by Layer** preset, as shown in Figure 3–23. Click **Modify...**.

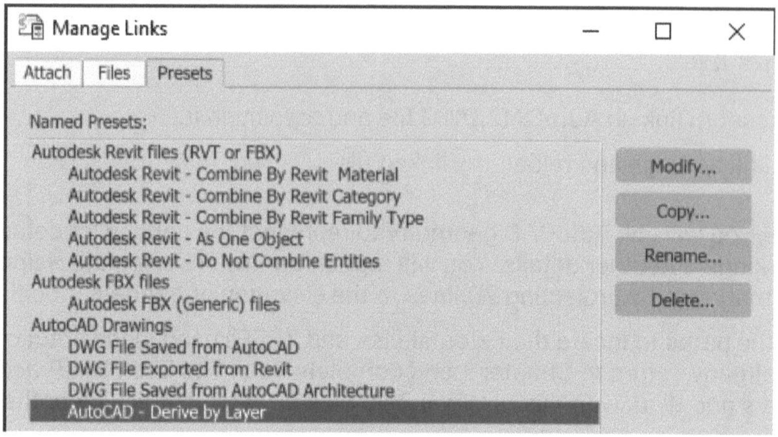

Figure 3–23

6. In the *File Link Settings: DWG Files* dialog box, in the *Basic* tab, set the link options, as shown in Figure 3–24. Select the *Advanced* tab and select **Create helper at drawing origin,** as shown in Figure 3–25. Leave all other options as defaults (clear).

   - The **Create Helper at drawing origin** option adds a helper object at the origin of the linked file.

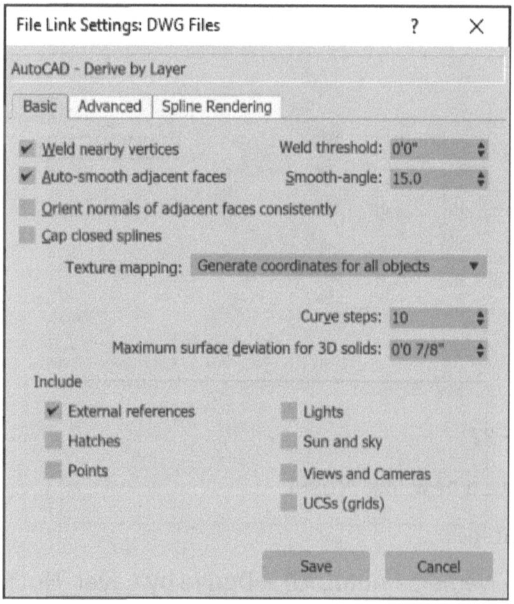

Figure 3–24

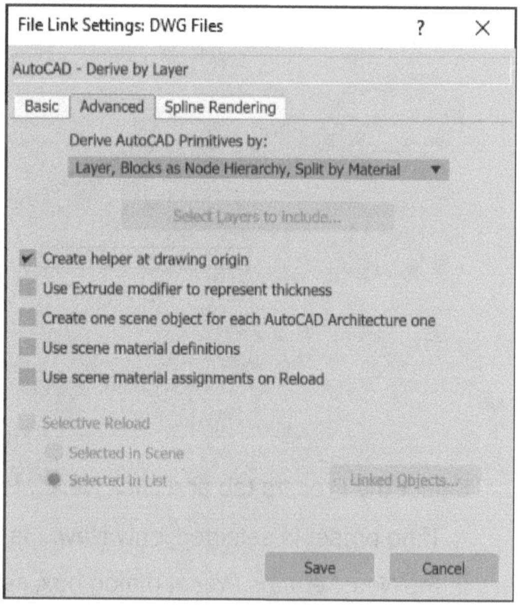

Figure 3–25

7. Select the *Spline Rendering* tab and verify that the link options are set to the defaults, as shown in Figure 3–26.

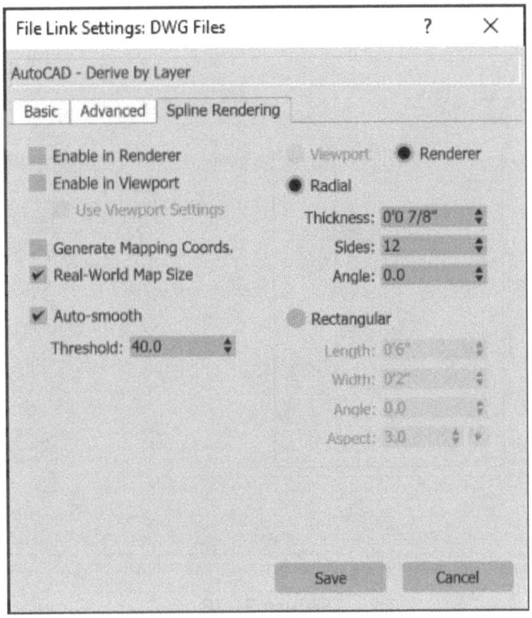

Figure 3–26

8. Click **Save**.
9. In the *Manage Links* dialog box, select the *Attach* tab. Set *Preset* to **AutoCAD – Derive by Layer**, as shown in Figure 3–27. Click **Select Layers to include...**.

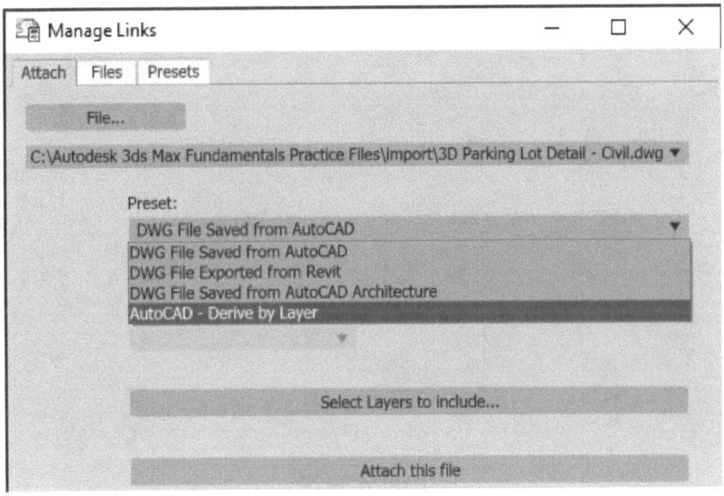

Figure 3–27

10. In the *Select Layers* dialog box, select **Select from list**. Clear **0** and **DEFPOINTS** and leave all other layers as selected, as shown in Figure 3–28. Click **OK**.

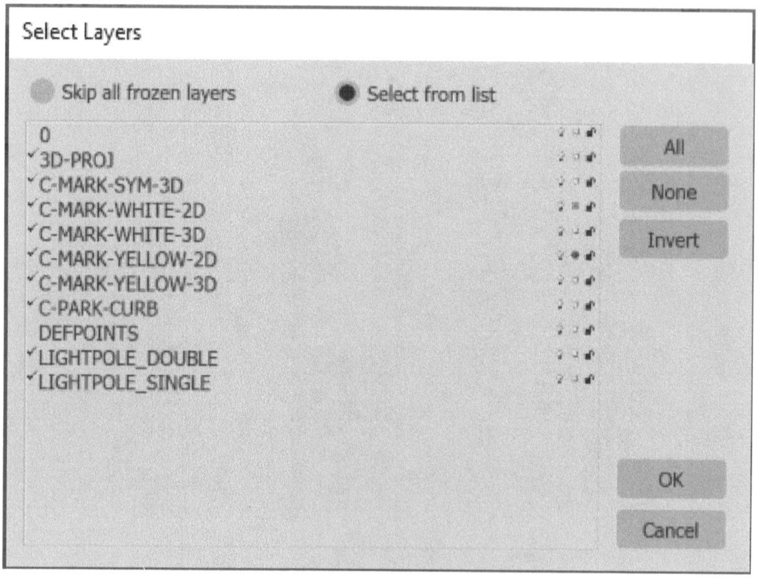

Figure 3–28

11. In the *Manage Links* dialog box, click **Attach this file**. Close the *Manage Links* dialog box. Note that the parking lot details have been added to the scene, but are located far away from the origin, as shown in the **Top** viewport in Figure 3–29.

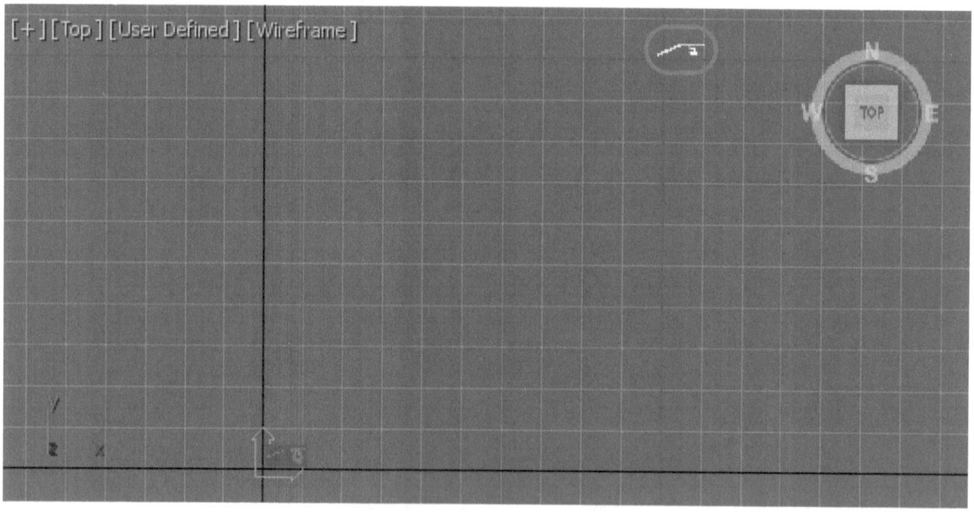

Figure 3–29

Task 2: Relocate the linked geometry.

1. You need to move the parking lot details by the global shift values in Civil View. In the menu bar, select **Civil View>Civil View>Civil View Explorer**.
   - If required, you might need to start Civil View.
2. In the Civil View Explorer, select **Scene Settings**, as shown in Figure 3–30. In the *Scene Settings* rollout, note the *Global Import Shift* values for *X Shift* and *Y Shift (-9901)*, as shown in Figure 3–31. Close the Civil View Explorer.

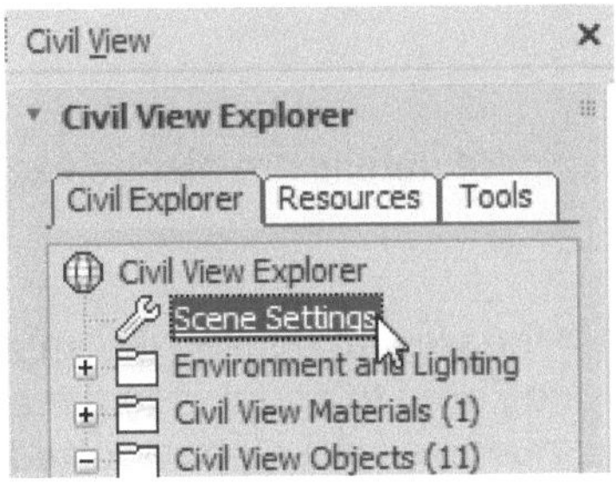

Figure 3–30

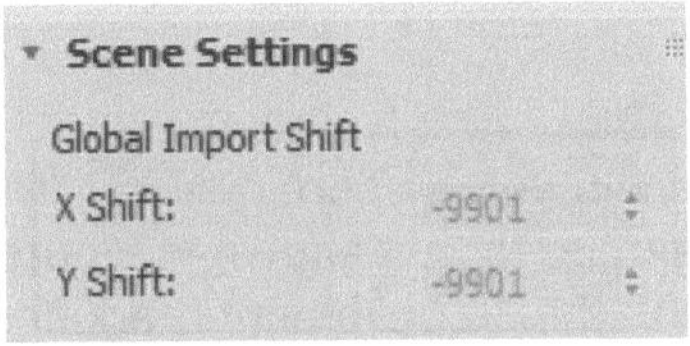

Figure 3–31

3. In the Main Toolbar, click  (Select and Move).
4. In the Scene Explorer, click ( (Display None) and  (Display Helpers)), and then select the helper object **3D Parking Lot Detail - Civil.dwg,** as shown in Figure 3–32. Note that the **User Coordinate System** icon (located at the origin) is selected, as shown in Figure 3–33.

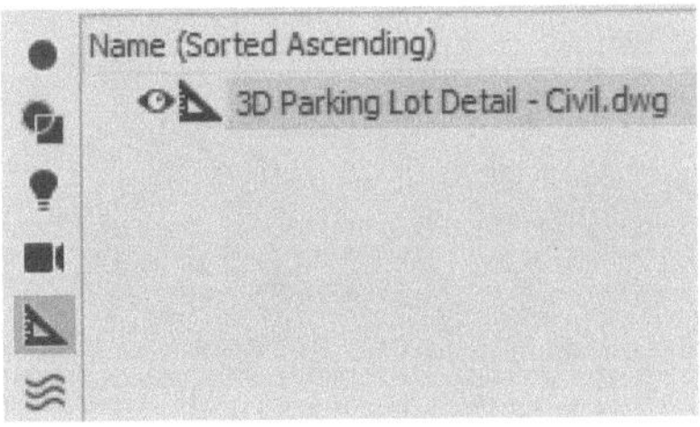

Figure 3–32

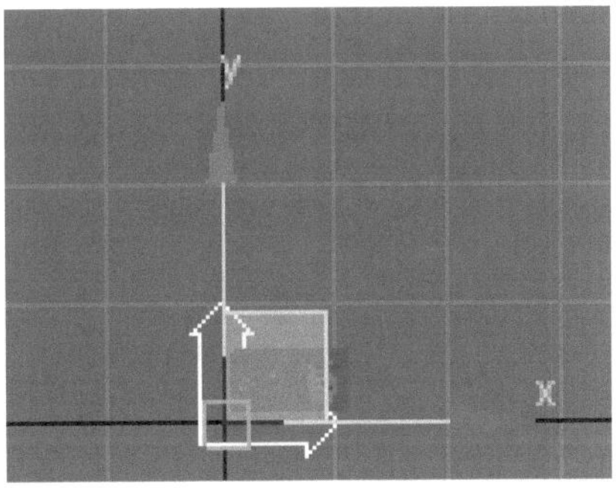

Figure 3–33

5. In the Status Bar, ensure that (Absolute Mode Transform) displays. Set the following (ensuring that the foot symbol is added with the values), as shown in Figure 3–34:
   - *X* edit box: **-9901'0"**
   - *Y* edit box: **-9901'0"**

Figure 3–34

6. Press <Enter>.

7. Click (Zoom Extents All). Note how the parking lot details are placed exactly on the parking lot surface.

8. In the **Perspective** viewport, use (Orbit) to tilt the view to display the area below the surfaces, similar to that shown in Figure 3–35. Use **Zoom** to zoom in to the area. Note that in addition to the 3D pavement markings, 2D line markings are also imported through the link.

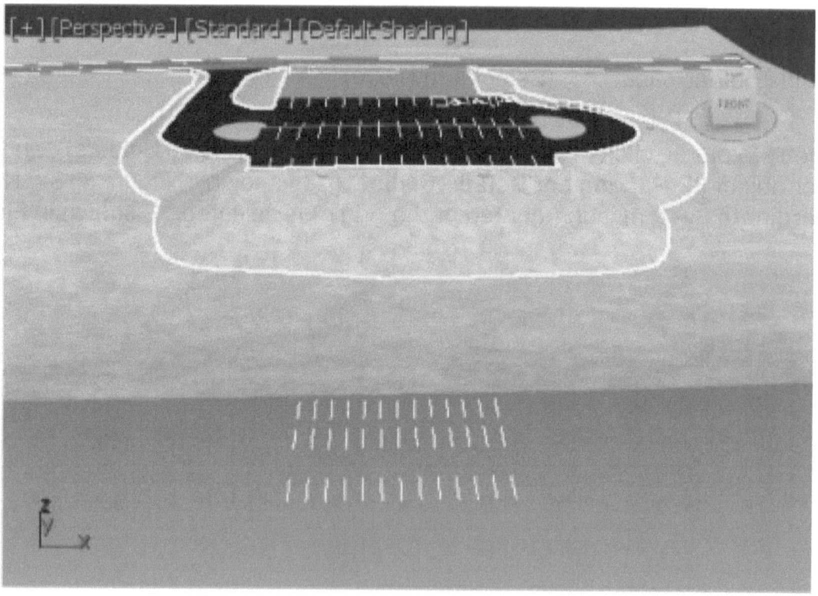

Figure 3–35

Task 3: Revise the link settings.

1. Click **File>Reference>Manage Links** to open the *Manage Links* dialog box.

2. In the *Manage Links* dialog box, select the *Files* tab and note that the linked file displays (icon), indicating that the file has not changed. Although the linked file has not changed, you can use **Reload...** to open the *File Link Settings* dialog box, where you can modify and revise the link settings. Verify that **Show Reload options** is selected. Select the file and click **Reload...**.

   Note: *You can use* **Reload...** *to update the file in the scene,* **Detach...** *to remove a linked drawing from the scene, or* **Bind...** *to insert the drawing as is and remove the connection.*

3. In the *File Link Settings: DWG Files* dialog box, in the *Advanced* tab, click **Select Layers to include...**. In the *Select Layers* dialog box, clear the 2D layers (**C-MARK-WHITE-2D** and **C-MARK-YELLOW- 2D**), and the two **LIGHTPOLE** layers, as shown in Figure 3–36.

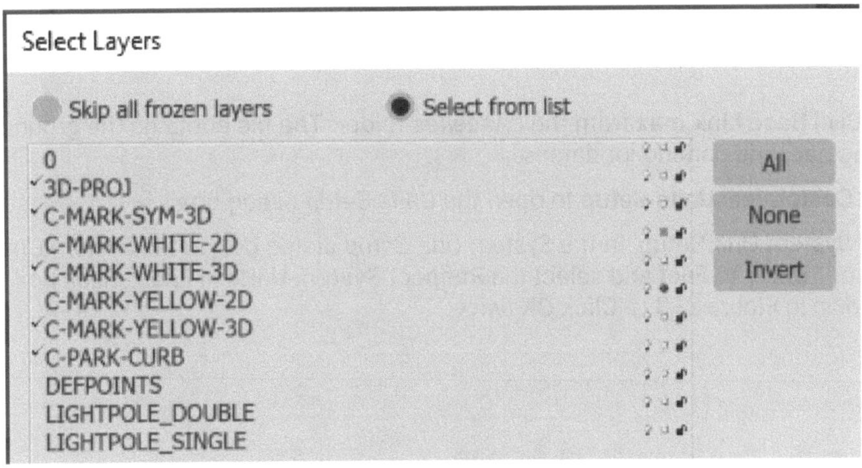

Figure 3–36

4. Click **OK** twice to close both dialog boxes.
5. Close the *Manage Links* dialog box. In the **Perspective** viewport, note that the 2D line markings do not display any longer.
6. Save your work as **MyCivil Base.max**.

End of practice

Practice 3c
Link and Reload an Autodesk Revit File

Practice Objectives

- Link and reposition an Autodesk Revit file to the current scene.
- Reload a modified .RVT file.

In this practice, you will link a .RVT file into a 3ds Max scene. You will reposition the Revit file using the Helper object. You will then reload a modified version of the .RVT linked file to incorporate the changes made to the original Autodesk Revit file using **Reload**.

You must set the paths to locate the External files and XREFs used in the practice. If you have not done this already, return to Chapter 1 and complete Task 1 to Task 3 in *Practice 1a: Organize Folders and Work with the Interface*. You only have to set the user paths once.

Task 1: Link an Autodesk Revit (.RVT) file.

1. Open **Civil Base Link.max** from the ...*\scenes* folder. The file contains the ground surfaces, building pad, and parking lot details.
2. Select **Customize>Units Setup** to open the *Units Setup* dialog box.
3. Select **System Unit Setup**. In the *System Unit Setup* dialog box, in the *System Unit Scale* area, set *1 Unit =* to **Feet** and select the **Respect System Units in Files** check box, if required (as shown in Figure 3–37). Click **OK** twice.

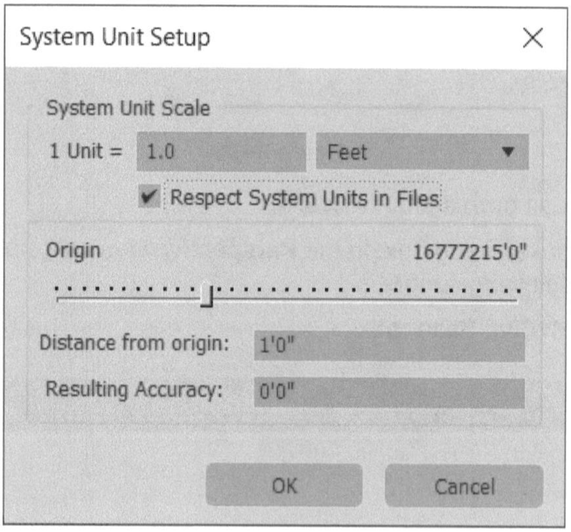

Figure 3–37

4. Select **File>Import>Link Revit**.

5. In the *Open* dialog box, in the ...*import* folder of your practice files folder, select **Revit Building-1.rvt** and click **Open**.
6. In the Status Bar, the Loading file bar is displayed, indicating the progress of the file as it loads. Once loaded, the *Select Revit View...* dialog box opens, as shown in Figure 3–38.

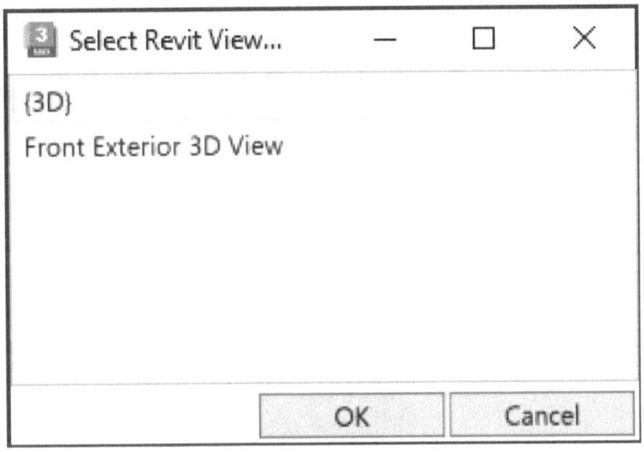

Figure 3–38

7. Select **Front Exterior 3D View** and click **OK**.
8. In the *Manage Links* dialog box, select the *Presets* tab. Click **New...** to create a new preset. In the New Settings Preset dialog box, set the following:
   - *New Name*: **Revit Preset**
   - *Format*: Select **Autodesk Revit (*.rvt,*.fbx)**
9. Click **OK**.
10. In the *Manage Links* dialog box, select **Revit Preset** and click **Modify**.

11. In the *File Link Settings* dialog box, do the following, as shown in Figure 3–39:
    - In the *Combine Entities* drop-down list, select **By Revit Category**.
    - In the *Objects* area, clear the **Lights** and **Daylight System** options.
    - In the *Objects* area, select **Create Helper at Model Origin** and **Cameras**.
    - In the *Geometry* area, set *Curved Objects Detail* to **6**.
    - In the *Materials* area, verify that **Keep 3ds Max scene materials parameters on reload** and **Keep 3ds Max scene material assignments on reload** are cleared.

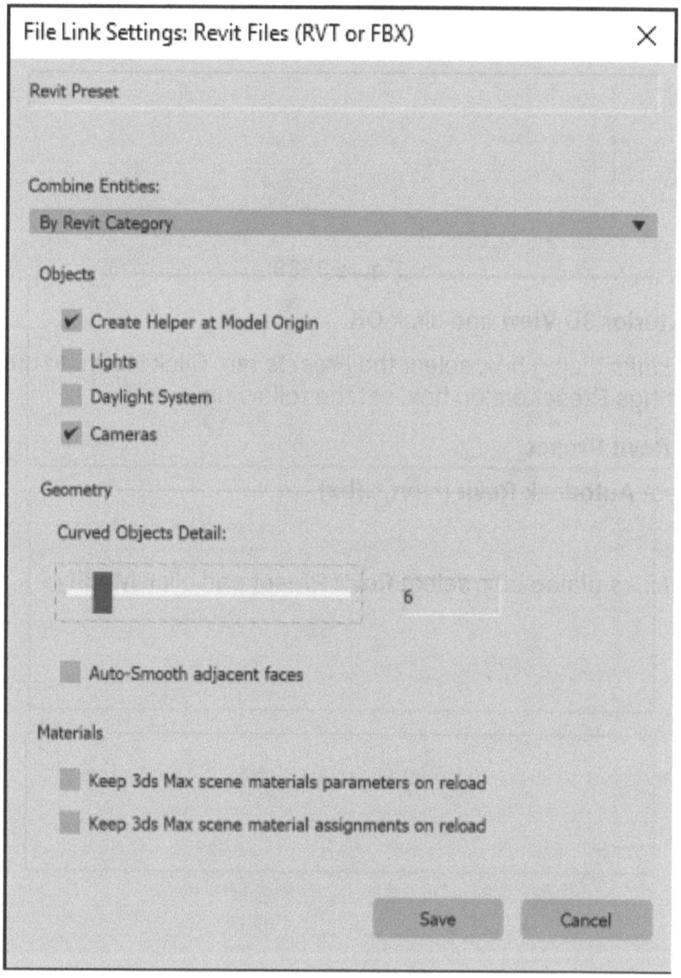

Figure 3–39

Note: *The* ***Create Helper at Model Origin*** *option adds a helper object at the origin of the linked file. Selecting and applying transforms (move, rotate, or scale) to the helper object applies the transforms to the linked geometry together.*

12. Click **Save**.
13. Select the *Attach* tab. Expand the *Preset* drop-down list and select **Revit Preset**.
14. Click **Attach this file**. Note that the Autodesk Revit building and camera are loaded at the 0,0,0 location in the viewports.
15. Close the *Manage Links* dialog box.
16. In the Scene Explorer, click (Display None) and (Display Helpers), if required, and then select the helper object **Revit Building-1.rvt,** as shown in Figure 3–40.

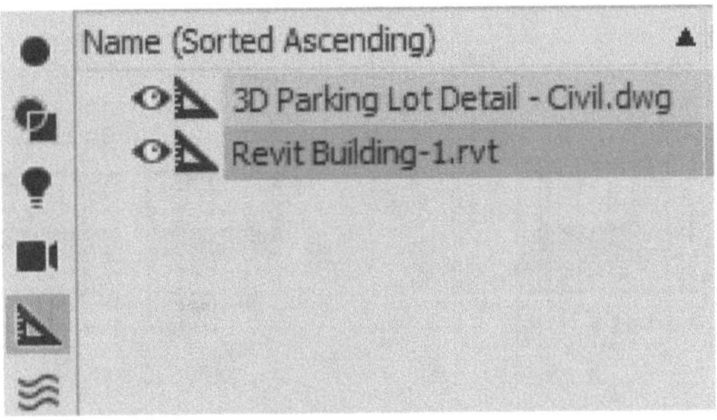

Figure 3–40

17. Right-click on the **Top** viewport to make it active and to maintain the selection. In the Main Toolbar, click (Select and Move). The Transform gizmo displays at the helper location, which is the origin of the linked Autodesk Revit file.
18. The position of the building pad from the origin has previously been calculated. In the Status Bar, verify that (Absolute Mode Transform) displays. Set the following, as shown in Figure 3–41:
    - *X* edit box: **800'0"**
    - *Y* edit box: **382'0"**
    - *Z* edit box: **154'6"**

Figure 3–41

19. Press <Enter>.
20. Click (Zoom Extents All). Note how the building is placed on top of the building pad.

21. In the **Front** viewport, use (Zoom Region) and create a rectangular window around the building to zoom in to the building. Verify that the **Standard** shading label displays. Click the **[Wireframe]** *Per-View Preference* label and select **Default Shading**. Then, select **Default Shading** again and select **Edged Faces** to define the windows and doors. Press <G> to hide the grid. In the Main Toolbar, use (Select Object) to exit any command. The building should display similar to that shown in Figure 3–42.

Figure 3–42

22. In the **Left** viewport, click the **[Wireframe]** *Per-View Preference* label and select **Default Shading** and then **Edged Faces**. Press <G> to hide the grid.
23. Click the **[Left]** *Point of View* label and select **Cameras>Views: Front Exterior 3D View**, as shown in Figure 3–43.

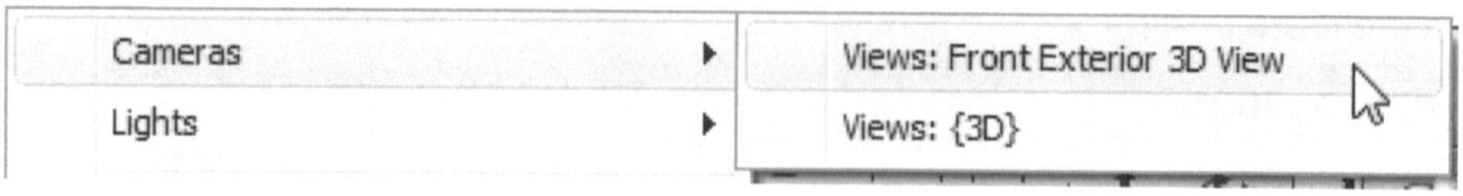

Figure 3–43

24. Use (Orbit Camera) and (Field-of-View) to display the complete building in the **Left** viewport, similar to that shown in Figure 3–44.

25. In the **Perspective** viewport, use (Zoom), (Orbit) and **Pan** to zoom in to the building and parking lot area such that the display is similar to that shown in Figure 3–44. Select **Edged Faces** for the Perspective view as well.

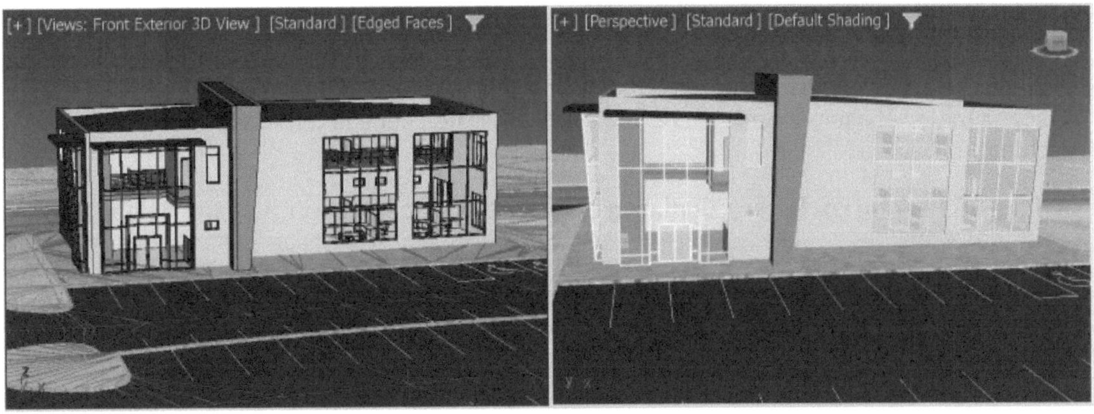

Figure 3–44

Task 2: Reload the variation of the .RVT file.

A variation to the .RVT linked file (where additional windows have been added) has been included in the ...*import* folder.

1. In Windows Explorer, open the ...*import* folder in the practice files folder.
2. Right-click on **Revit Building-1.rvt** and select **Rename**. Rename the file as **Revit Building-1_ORIGINAL.rvt**.
3. Right-click on **Revit Building-2.rvt**, and select **Copy**. Paste a copy of this file into the same directory. Right-click on the copied file, select **Rename**, and rename the file as **Revit Building-1.rvt**. This must be the same name as the original file that was linked to indicate that the original linked file has changed.
4. Return to the Autodesk 3ds Max software. Select **File>Reference>Manage Links** to open the *Manage Links* dialog box.
5. In the *Manage Links* dialog box, select the *Files* tab. Note that (icon) displays in front of the .RVT filename (as shown in Figure 3–45), indicating that changes have been made to the original linked file.

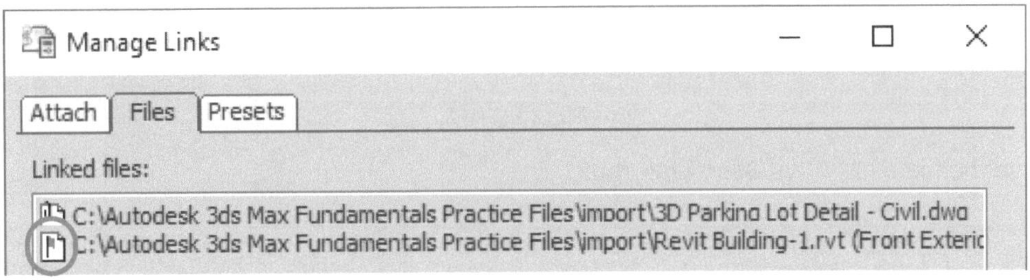

Figure 3–45

6. Select **Revit Building -1.rvt** and click **Reload...**. The Upgrading file bar displays the progress.
7. In the *File Link Settings* dialog box that opens, in the *Materials* area, select **Keep 3ds Max scene material assignments on reload**. Click **OK**. The scene is refreshed with the new changes.
8. If the **3D Parking Lot Detail - Civil.dwg** displays the icon in front, use the **Reload** option for it as well.
9. In the *Manage Links* dialog box, in the *Files* tab, the icons should display as , as shown in Figure 3–46. This indicates that there are no differences between the original file and the linked file.

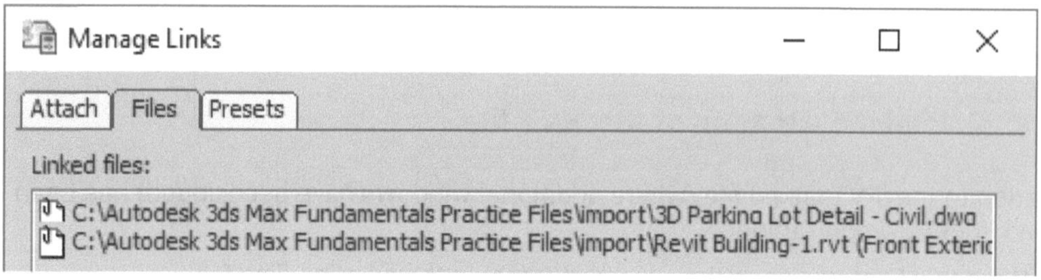

Figure 3–46

10. Close the *Manage Links* dialog box.
11. In the viewports, the modified building displays. More windows are added to the building, as shown in Figure 3–47.

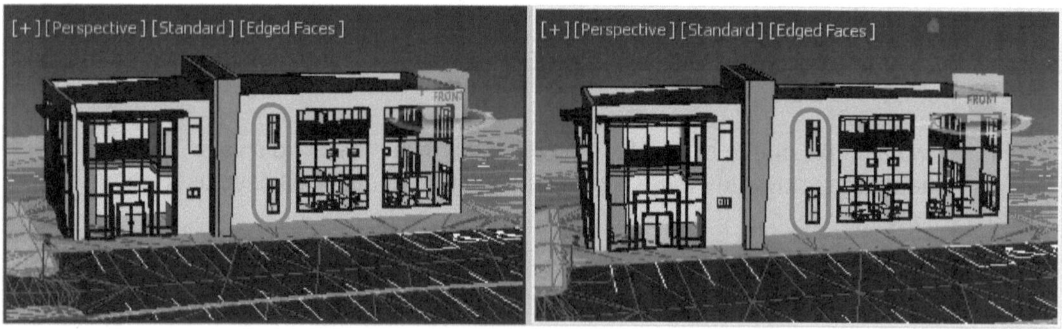

Figure 3–47

12. Save the file as **MyCivil Base Link.max**.

End of practice

3.3 References

External References (XREF)

Autodesk 3ds Max Scene files can reference data from other .MAX scene files by expanding **File>Reference>XRef Objects or XRef Scene.** The XREF data remains linked to the source (.MAX) scene file so that changes in the source file can be reflected in any scene that contains the XREF.

- External References are useful to break up large projects into more manageable pieces, permit more than one person to work on the same project at the same time in separate files, and to enable the same core scene geometry to be used in multiple files.
- **XRef Scenes** bring in the entire scene. All of the XREF objects are non-selectable and cannot be modified.
- **XRef Objects** enable you to select individual objects (or all) from an XREF scene. These objects remain selectable and modifiable in the XREF scene file.
- You can snap to XREF and use XREF objects with AutoGrid. You can also use XREF objects as alignment targets and you can select an XREF object's coordinate system for object transformation. XREF support parameter wiring and you can XREF the controllers.
- Objects in scenes (.MAX) are imported into other . MAX scenes using the **Merge** option.

Data Management and Asset Tracking

The Autodesk 3ds Max software enables you to manage your data through Data Management (DM) solutions, referred to as Asset Tracking Systems (ATSs).

- DM solutions such as the Autodesk® Vault software enables you to store scene files and any supporting data (such as material maps) in a single database repository.
- These systems can be accessed simultaneously by multiple users with different rights assigned based on their project responsibilities. Data can be checked out for editing by one individual at a time while still being referenced by other users. Users can see who is editing which portion of the project at any time.
- By centralizing the files in a DM system it is much easier to adjust paths for external files such as image maps.
- Data files can be versioned through DM solutions, so that the older versions can be readily accessed, if required.
- For more information see *Asset Tracking* in the Autodesk 3ds Max Help files. Asset Tracking is available through the **File>Reference>Asset Tracking Toggle**.

Practice 3d
XREF and Merge Objects

Practice Objective

- Link an AutoCAD .DWG file and incorporate objects from another scene file into the current scene.

In this practice, you will create a new scene file that will contain linked AutoCAD objects and XREF objects from the Civil Base scene. You will then merge objects into the current scene file.

You must set the paths to locate the External files and XREFs used in the practice. If you have not done this already, return to Chapter 1 and complete Task 1 to Task 3 in *Practice 1a: Organize Folders and Work with the Interface*. You only have to set the user paths once.

Task 1: Assemble the data.

1. Click **File>Reset** and click **Yes** to reset the scene.
2. For this scene, set the *System Unit Scale* to **Inches**. Select **Customize>Units Setup**. In the dialog box, verify that the following is set:
    - *Display Unit Scale:* **US Standard, Feet w/ Fractional Inches**
    - *Default Units*: **Inches**
    - *Lighting Units*: **American**
3. Click **System Unit Setup**. In the *System Unit Setup* dialog box, set *System Unit Scale* to **Inches**. Click **OK** in both the dialog boxes.
4. Expand **File>Reference** and select **Manage Links**.
5. In the *Manage Links* dialog box, in the *Attach* tab, click **File...**. In the ...*import* folder, select **Exterior AutoCAD Architectural Model.dwg**. Click **Open**.
6. In the *Preset* drop-down list, select **AutoCAD – Derive by Layer** and click **Attach this file**. Once the file has been loaded, close the *Manage Links* dialog box.
    - The **AutoCAD – Derive by Layer** preset was created in the *Linking an AutoCAD DWG* practice. Complete this practice to create the preset if you have not already done so.
    - The AutoCAD objects were not joined together by layer. Each was subdivided by material type into different objects. Materials previously assigned in AutoCAD were preserved on these separate objects.
7. Click  (Zoom Extents All) to display all of the objects in all of the viewports.

8. Click **File>Reference>XRef Objects**. In the *XRef Objects* dialog box, click (Create XRef Record from File) as shown in Figure 3–48.

Figure 3–48

Note: *You select objects to XREF rather than the entire scene because XREF scene objects cannot be individually selected or modified.*

9. In the *Open File* dialog box, select **Parking Lot Detail.max** (from the ...*import* folder) and click **Open**.
10. In the *Units Mismatch* dialog box, click **OK**. This rescales the XREF objects to the system units.
11. The *Duplicate Material Name* dialog box opens prompting you that there is an incoming material with the same name as an existing scene material. Select **Apply to All Duplicates** to keep both materials, as shown in Figure 3–49. Click **Auto-Rename Merged Material**.

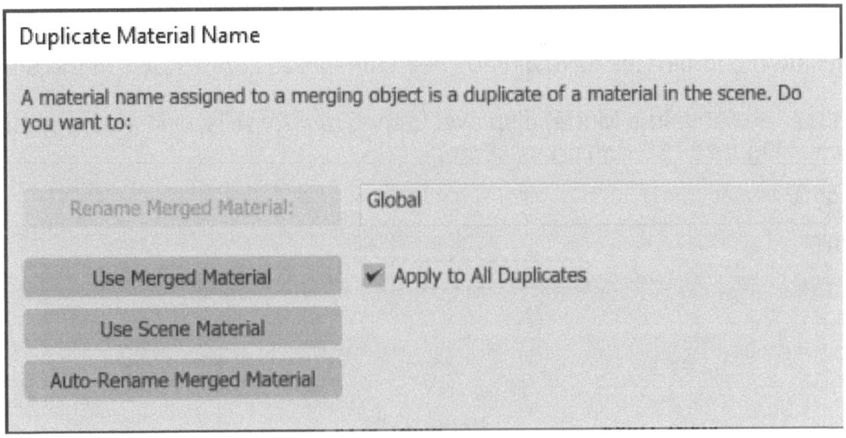

Figure 3–49

12. In the *XRef Objects* dialog box, note that the **Parking Lot Detail.max** filename displays. Close the dialog box.
13. Click (Zoom Extents All). Note that the Civil Base objects are located far from the origin. This is a coordinate system discrepancy and not a scale issue. The AutoCAD drawing is based in a different coordinate system and scale than the accompanying Civil drawing.

Task 2: Coordinate the data.

In this task, you will relocate the Civil Base in the Architectural Data. To line up the data accurately, you will need the exact coordinate translation and rotation. You can measure ahead of time in programs such as AutoCAD by comparing the coordinates of points common to both files.

1. Clear any object selection by clicking in any viewport. In the Scene Explorer, click (Display None) and (Display Object XRefs). Select all of the XREF objects in the list (select the first object, press and hold <Shift>, and then select the last object).
2. With these XREF objects selected, select **Group>Group** in the menu bar.
3. In the *Group* dialog box, set the *Group name* to **Site XRef** and click **OK**.
4. In the Main Toolbar, click (Select and Move). In the Reference Coordinate System, select **World**, as shown in Figure 3–50. Click (Use Transform Coordinate Center).

Figure 3–50

5. The translation coordinates have already been measured in AutoCAD. In the Status Bar, ensure that (Absolute Mode) displays. In the *Transform Type-in* area, set the following, as shown in Figure 3–51, and press <Enter>:
   - *X:* **-197'4"**
   - *Y:* **-30'0"**
   - *Z:* **-4'11"**

Figure 3–51

6. In the Main Toolbar, click (Select Object) to exit the **Move** transform operation.
7. Click (Zoom Extents All).

8. In the **Perspective** viewport, use  (Orbit Point of Interest) and click to place a point on the building and then orbit around that point. Using **Pan** and **Zoom**, zoom in to the parking lot and building area (similar to that shown in Figure 3–52), and verify that the building is located on the building pad. Although the XREF had a different Unit Scale (feet), it scaled correctly to the active scene (in inches).

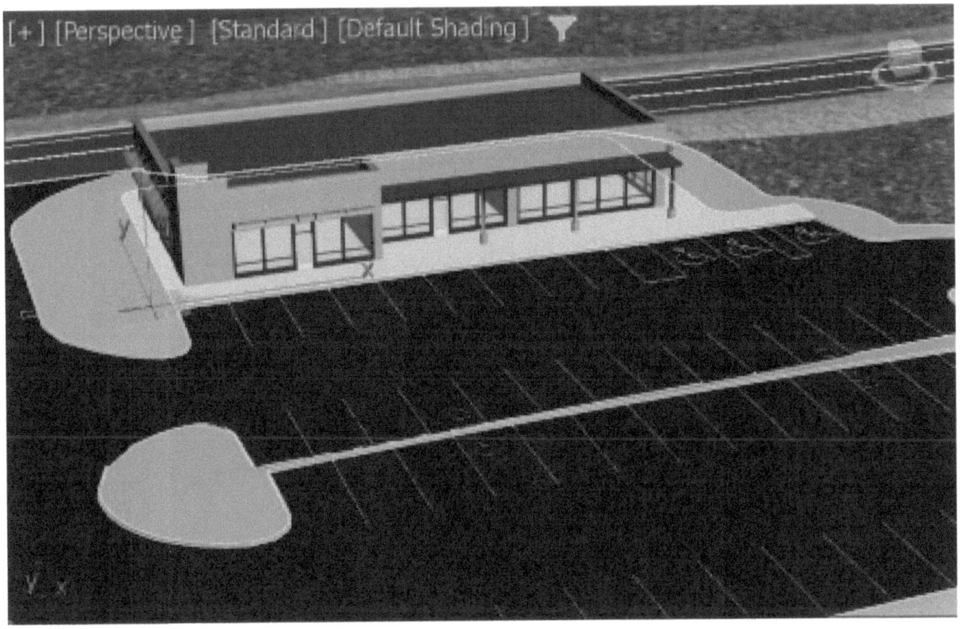

Figure 3–52

9. Save your work as **MyArchitectural Scene.max**.

Task 3: Merge objects.

1. Select **File>Import>Merge**. In the Merge File dialog box, select **Light Poles for Project1.max** from the ...*\scenes* folder. Click **Open**.

2. In the *Merge* dialog box, click **All**, as shown in Figure 3–53. Click **OK**.

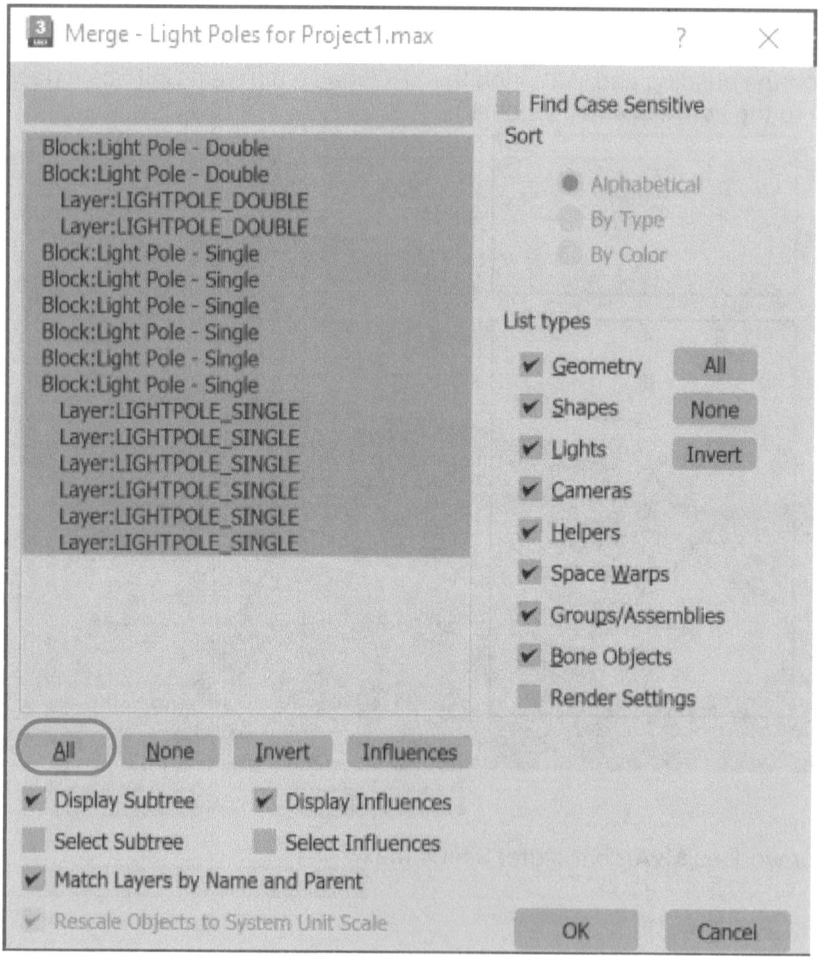

Figure 3–53

3. The *Duplicate Name* dialog box opens, prompting you that an object with the same name already exists in the scene. Select **Apply to all Duplicates** and click **Auto-Rename**.

   Note: Merge *enables both objects to have the same name,* ***Skip*** *ignores the incoming object, and* ***Delete Old*** *removes the original object.*

4. If the *Scene Converter* dialog box displays, click **Convert Scene** and close the dialog box. The light poles display in the scene, as shown in Figure 3–54.

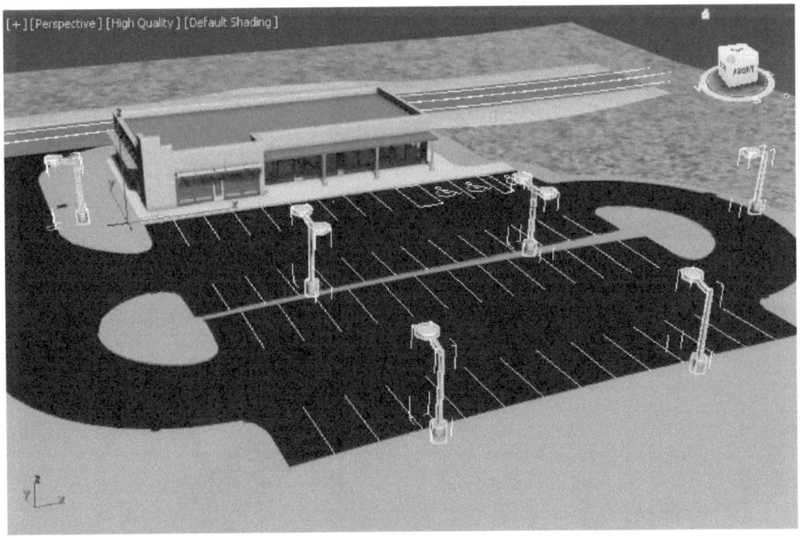

Figure 3–54

5. Save your work.

End of practice

Chapter Review Questions

1. Which of the following file formats can be linked to the current Autodesk 3ds Max scene?
   a. .DWG, .OBJ, .APF, .FBX
   b. .DWG, .DXF, .FBX, .RVT
   c. .DWG, .DXF, .OBJ, .RVT
   d. .DWG, .OBJ, .FBX, .RVT

2. In the *Manage Links* dialog box, in the *Files* tab, which of the following options do you use to remove the link with the original linked file but maintain its geometry in the current scene?
   a. Reload...
   b. Detach...
   c. Bind...

3. Which command do you use to combine objects from a saved Autodesk 3ds Max scene (.MAX file) into your current .MAX scene?
   a. Import
   b. Link
   c. Open
   d. Merge

4. While linking Autodesk Revit files in the current Autodesk 3ds Max scene, which of the following options are provided in the Combine Entities List? (Select all that apply.)
   a. By Revit Material
   b. By Revit Layer
   c. As One Object
   d. By Revit Camera

5. When an entire .MAX scene is brought into the current scene using **XRef Scene**, the XREF objects are selectable but cannot be modified.
   a. True
   b. False

Command Summary

Button	Command	Location
	**Absolute Mode**	• **Status Bar**
N/A	**Civil View**	• **Menu Bar:** Civil View
N/A	**Asset Tracking**	• **Menu Bar:** File>Reference
N/A	**Import**	• **Menu Bar:** File>Import
N/A	**Link AutoCAD**	• **Menu Bar:** File>Import
N/A	**Link FBX**	• **Menu Bar:** File>Import
N/A	**Link Revit**	• **Menu Bar:** File>Import
N/A	**Manage Links**	• **Menu Bar:** File>Reference
N/A	**Merge**	• **Menu Bar:** File>Import
	**Select by Name**	• **Main Toolbar**
	**Select Object**	• **Main Toolbar**
	**Use Transform Coordinate Center**	• **Main Toolbar**
N/A	**XRef Objects**	• **Menu Bar:** File>Reference
N/A	**XRef Scene**	• **Menu Bar:** File>Reference

Chapter

4

Basic Modeling Techniques

Autodesk® 3ds Max® is a rendering and animation software that allows for objects to be directly modeled in the software. Modeling can be accomplished using primitive objects or Polygon Modeling tools that are further manipulated using modifiers and transforms to move, rotate, and scale them. Additionally, sub-object modes can be used to further modify and control the resulting objects.

Learning Objectives

- Identify the various primitive objects provided with the software.
- Apply changes to the model geometry using modifiers.
- Move, rotate, scale, and place objects, and constrain the movement of the **Transform** tools.
- Modify objects at a sub-object level.
- Work with various coordinate systems and transform systems.
- Create copies of the same object using various **Clone** options and create a single unit by grouping multiple objects together.
- Create and modify objects using the **Polygon Modeling** tools.
- Review the status of the overall model and display information about the scene, such as polygon count, number of vertices, etc.

4.1 Modeling with Primitives

The Autodesk 3ds Max software enables you to create and adjust 3D geometry by creating a complex model from simple 3D objects called primitives, as shown in Figure 4–1.

Figure 4–1

- All various types of already built objects (e.g., Standard Primitives, Extended Primitives, Compound Objects, etc.) are listed in the Command Panel>*Create* panel (+)> (Geometry), as shown in Figure 4–2. Each of these categories consists of a group of objects that can be modeled and modified to create simple or complex objects.

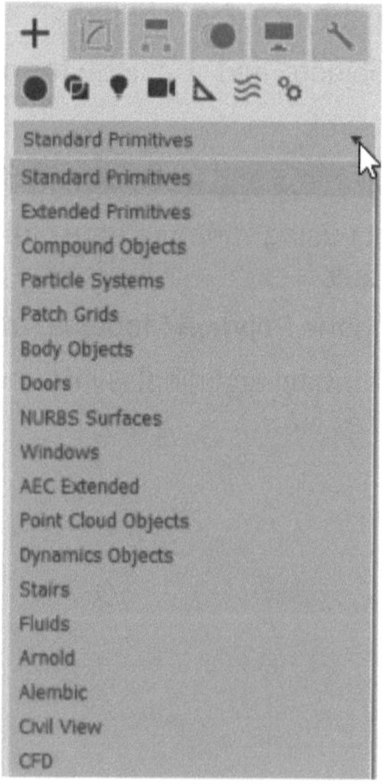

Figure 4–2

- You can model the selected 3D object directly in the viewport by using the mouse to locate and specify the starting point and then dragging the mouse to pick the other locations (length, height, etc.).
- You can also enter the precise values in the edit boxes of the *Keyboard Entry* rollout in the Command Panel (as shown in Figure 4–3), and then click **Create**. You can either enter the values or use the spinner arrows to increase or decrease the values. After entering a value in a field, click in another field or press <Enter> to assign the values to the object.
- To modify a created object, use the *Parameters* rollout in the *Modify* panel (), as shown in Figure 4–4. Using the *Keyboard Entry* rollout to enter different values creates another object and does not modify the existing one.

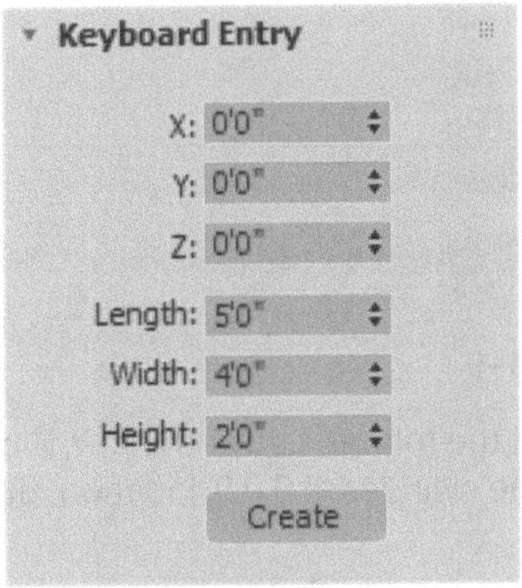

Create objects

Figure 4–3

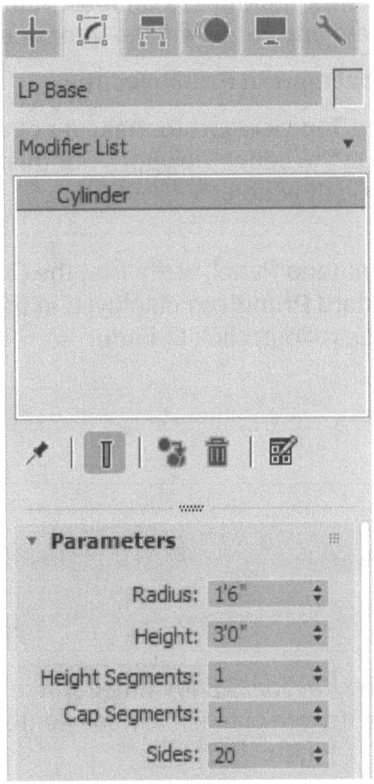

Modify objects

Figure 4–4

- You can also create geometry by modeling with modifiers, creating loft compound objects, or creating a 3D terrain from 2D contour objects.

Practice 4a
Model with Primitives

Practice Objective

- Create primitive objects by using standard primitives and the modify the object.

In this practice, you will model the base for the parking lot light fixtures by modeling the object using a standard primitive and then modifying its parameters using the *Modify* panel in the Command Panel.

You must set the paths to locate the External files and XREFs used in the practice. If you have not done this already, return to Chapter 1 and complete Task 1 to Task 3 in *Practice 1a: Organize Folders and Work with the Interface.* You only have to set the user paths once.

1. Open **Modeling with Primitives.max**. It is a blank base scene file.
2. Click in the **Top** viewport to make it active. The orientation of the object being created depends on the active viewport. For this practice, you will create the cylinder with its height in the Z-axis direction.
3. In the Command Panel, verify that the *Create* panel () and  (Geometry) are selected with **Standard Primitives** displayed in the drop-down list, as shown in Figure 4–5. In the *Object Type* rollout, click **Cylinder**.

Figure 4–5

4. Click on the *Keyboard Entry* title bar to expand the rollout. Leave the X, Y, Z coordinates at **0'0"**. The software places the base center of the cylinder at 0,0,0, location. Set the following, as shown in Figure 4–6:
   - *Radius*: **1'0"**
   - *Height*: **3'0"**

   You can enter the values in their respective fields or use the spinner arrows to increase or decrease the values. After entering a value in a field, click in another edit field or press <Enter> to assign the values to the object.

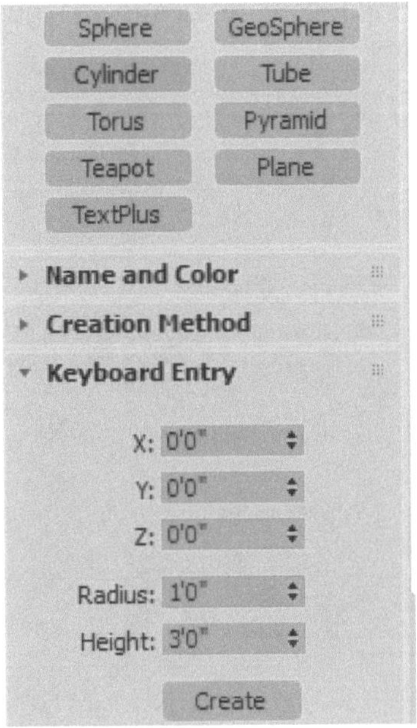

Figure 4–6

Note: *The 0,0,0 location corresponds to the default axes (center of the active grid) of the construction plane. Any value entered for X,Y, and Z offsets the object by that number in the specified direction.*

5. Click **Create**. Note that a cylinder is created and is displayed in all viewports.

   Note: *The object colors are random and your objects can be a different color than what is shown in Figure 4–8.*

Hint: Creating Objects

After creating an object, you cannot change the parameters in the *Keyboard Entry* rollout. Changing the parameters in the *Keyboard Entry* rollout and clicking **Create** adds a second object. If you created another object, in the Main Toolbar, click  once to undo the creation of the second object. Use the *Modify* panel () to change the parameters.

6. In the *Zoom Extents All* flyout, click  (Zoom Extents All) to display the base more clearly. Note that it zooms into the cylinder in all of the viewports.

7. With the cylinder still selected, in the Command Panel, select the *Modify* panel (). At the top of the modifier list, in the *Name* field, rename the object from *Cylinder001* to **LP Base**.

8. In the *Parameters* rollout, set the following, as shown Figure 4–7. Note the effect on the geometry as you set each value.
   - *Radius*: **1'6"**
   - *Height Segments:* **1**
   - *Cap Segments:* **1**
   - *Sides*: **20**

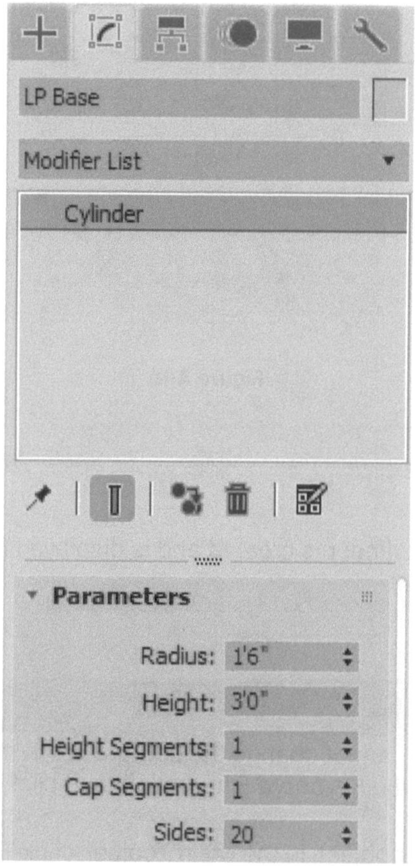

Figure 4–7

9. Select the *Create* panel (+) and in the *Object Type* rollout, click **Box** to create the anchor base plate. In the *Keyboard Entry* rollout, set the following, as shown in Figure 4–8:

    - *X:* **0'0"**
    - *Y:* **0'0"**
    - *Z:* **3'0"**
    - *Length:* **1'4"**
    - *Width:* **1'4"**
    - *Height*: **0'2"**

    The **X, Y, Z** values create the center of the base of the box at the 0,0,3 location, which is the top of the cylinder (it offsets the box by 3'0" in the Z-direction).

10. Click **Create**. A box is created on top of the **LP Base** cylinder, as shown in Figure 4–8.

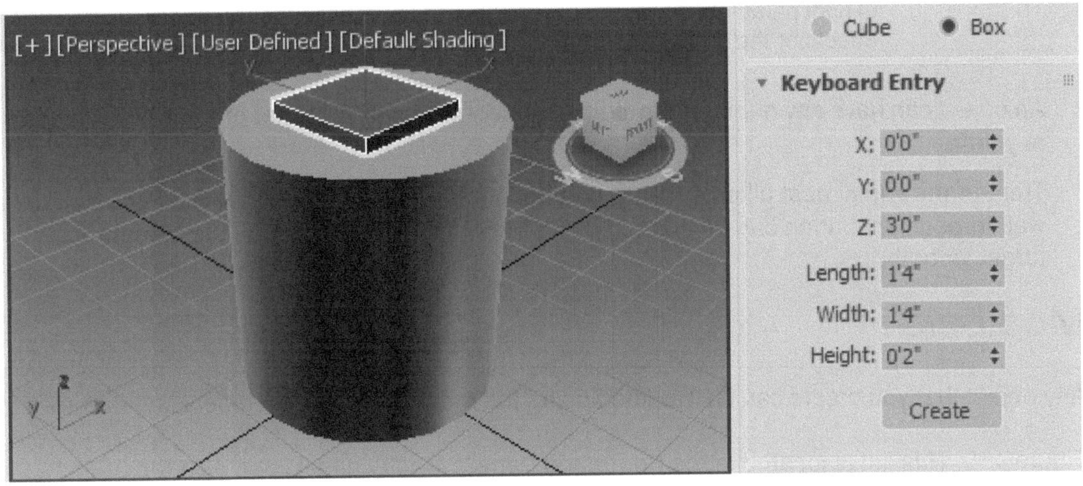

Figure 4–8

11. With the box still selected, select the *Modify* panel ( ) and rename the *Box001* as **LP Anchor Base**.

12. Save your work as **MyLight Pole.max**.

End of practice

4.2 Modifiers and Transforms

The Autodesk 3ds Max software includes various modifiers and transforms that enable you to modify your geometry. They are described as follows:

Modifiers	• Adds geometric and property alterations to objects such as Extrude, Taper etc. • Listed in the Modifier Stack and their parameter values are available for adjustment afterwards.
Transforms	• Transforms are used to translate and scale objects in the scene. • Initiated by selecting the required buttons in the Main Toolbar or by using the Transform modes in the right-click quad menu. • Conducted by accessing a transform mode and entering new values, or graphically transforming objects on the screen. • Applied to objects after basic parameters and modifiers have been taken into account (except world-space modifiers). For example, if you scale a box, the **Length** parameter shown in the Modifier Stack does not take into account the effects of the scale transform.

- An object can have any number of modifiers, but only has a single set of transform values at any time.
- Transforms and almost all object and modifier parameters can be animated. For example, a walkthrough animation can be created using **Move Transform** to move the camera, its target, or both.

Modifiers

Any object that you create can be modified using the modifiers in the *Modifier List*, as shown in Figure 4–9. This list is located in the Command Panel's *Modify* panel () on top of the *Modifier Stack*.

- Click the down arrow to display the list and use the scroll bar to navigate through the complete list of modifiers.
- The modifiers in the *Modifier* drop-down list are placed in groups and then listed alphabetically.
- If you know the name of the modifier, you can enter the first letter to bring the modifiers starting with that letter to the top of the selection list.

- Once a modifier is applied, it displays in the *Modifier Stack* as shown in Figure 4–10.
- The *Modifier Stack* lists modifiers in reverse historical order. In Figure 4–10, *Taper* modifier is applied after the *Extrude* modifier.
- The parameters of the objects and modifiers are always accessible through the *Modifier Stack*, irrespective of their position in the stack.

Figure 4–9

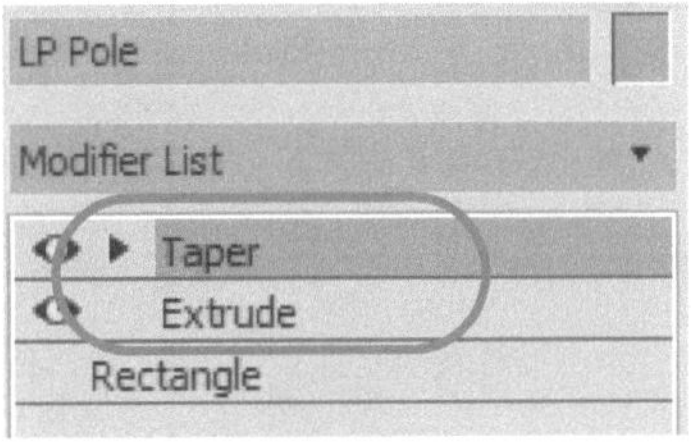

Figure 4–10

Transform Tools

The Transform tools are available in the Main Toolbar, as shown in Figure 4–11.

Figure 4–11

The available Transform tools are described as follows:

Select and Move

Select and Rotate

Select and Scale: Scaling has three flyout options: (Uniform), (Non-uniform), and (Squash).

- **Non-uniform:** Enables you to scale one or two axes independently.
- **Squash:** Enables you to do the same, but scaling one or two axes applies a simultaneous opposite scaling to the other(s). The Scale Transform gizmo also has the tools for Non-uniform scaling.

Select and Place / Select and Rotate: Enables you to locate and position/locate and rotate an object with respect to the surface of another object.

Right-click on **Select and Place** and use the *Placement Settings* dialog box (as shown in the image below) to customize how the objects are aligned. Right-clicking on **Select and Rotate** opens the same dialog box with the Rotate option selected.

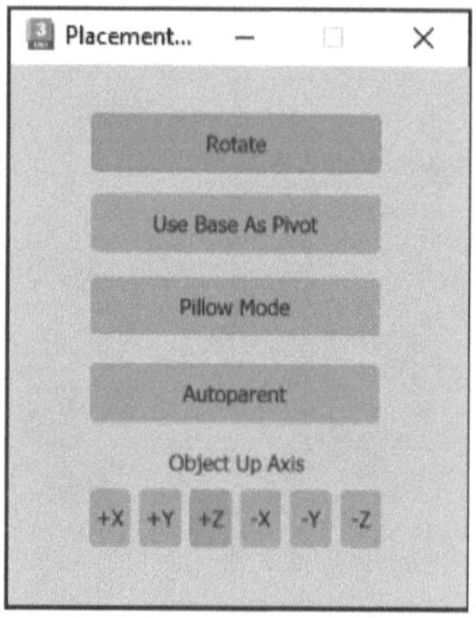

- **Rotate:** Enables you to click and drag an object to rotate around the local axis that is specified with the object Up Axis.
- **Use Base As Pivot:** Constrains the base of the object as the contact point with the surface of another object. By default, the pivot point of the object is used as the contact point.
- **Pillow Mode:** Enables you to move the objects around each other, but restricts them from intersecting. Useful when moving the object over uneven surfaces.
- **Autoparent:** Automatically links the object that is being placed as a child of the object it is being placed on, creating a hierarchical relationship.
- **Object Up Axis:** The selected up axis is used as the local axis on the object that is being moved.

Hint: XForm Modifier with Scale

To avoid problems in animation, it is recommended that you do not to use the Scale transform directly on objects. Instead, apply an XForm modifier to the objects and then **Scale** the XForm gizmo.

- Transforms can be constrained to one or two axes by selecting one of the buttons in the Axis Constraints toolbar, as shown in Figure 4–12. However, it is more common to use the gizmos or the keyboard shortcuts to constrain the transforms. This toolbar is hidden by default and can be displayed by right-clicking on any interface handle and selecting it from the menu.
- When a transform mode is active, a Transform gizmo displays (as shown in Figure 4–13) on the selected object on the screen.

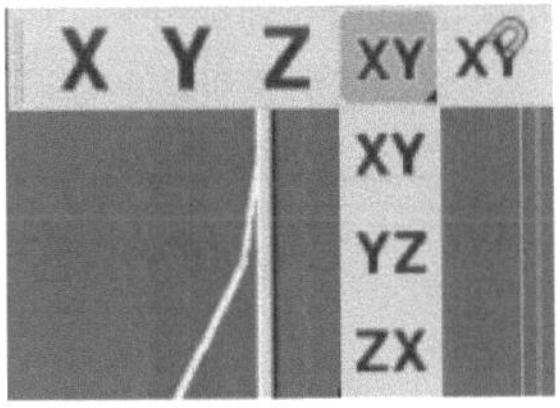

Figure 4–12

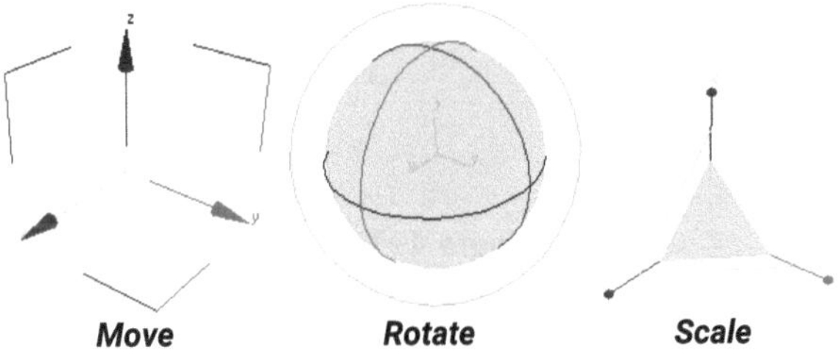

Figure 4–13

- Clicking and dragging over the gizmo enables you to perform the transform interactively on the screen. You can also constrain the transform by highlighting an axis handle on the gizmo before clicking and dragging.
- You can change the display size of the transform gizmo interactively in the viewport. Pressing <-> decreases its display size while as pressing <=> increases its display size.
- You can apply a transform accurately by entering (or using spinners) the required transform values in the *Transform Type-In* area, in the Status Bar, as shown in Figure 4–14.

Figure 4–14

- In the Main Toolbar, right-click on a **Transform** (Move, Rotate, Scale) to open its *Transform Type-In* dialog box, as shown in Figure 4–15 for the Move transform. The *Transform Type-In* dialog box can be also be accessed by clicking (Settings) in the right-click quad menu, as shown in Figure 4–16.

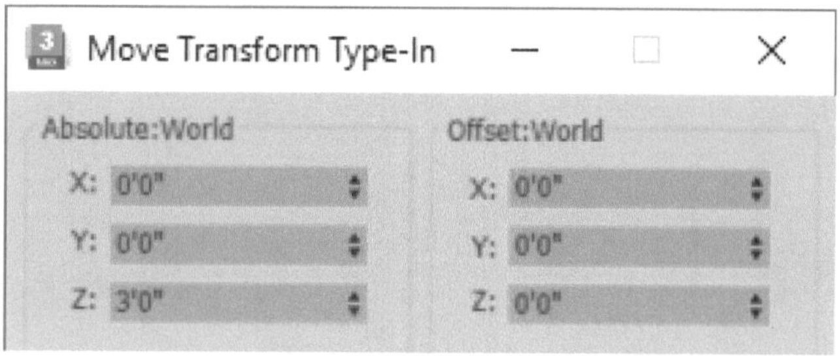

Figure 4–15

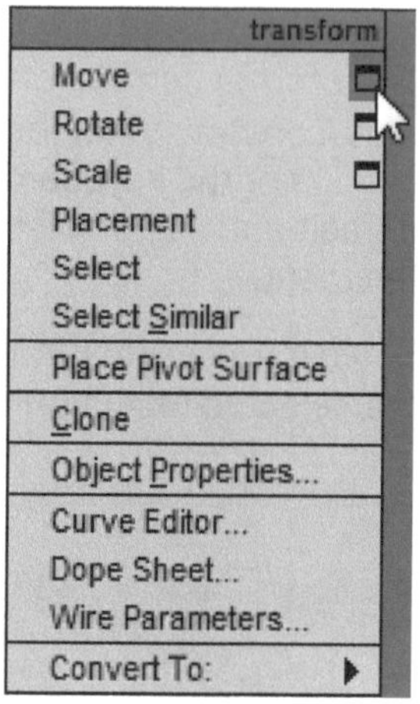

Figure 4–16

- Transform modes remain active until they are canceled by either clicking (Select Object) in the Main Toolbar or by pressing <Q>.

- Click (Select Object) after you have finished a transform to avoid accidentally moving, rotating, or scaling objects while making selections.

Practice 4b
Model with Modifiers and Transforms

Practice Objectives

- Create a 2D shape and then extrude it into a 3D object.
- Create primitive solids dynamically and modify objects.
- Transform objects to place them at the right location.

In this practice, you will refine the parking lot lighting fixture by creating a 2D shape and then extruding it to create a 3D object. You will create primitive objects dynamically in the viewport and then modify the objects using various modifiers in the Command Panel. You will also use Transforms (**Move**, **Rotate**, and **Place**) to place the created objects in the correct scene positions.

You must set the paths to locate the External files and XREFs used in the practice. If you have not done this already, return to Chapter 1 and complete Task 1 to Task 3 in *Practice 1a: Organize Folders and Work with the Interface*. You only have to set the user paths once.

Task 1: Extrude and adjust the light pole.

To create the rectangular light pole, create a 2D cross-section shape and then extrude it into a 3D object. This approach is another way to create 3D geometry.

1. Open **Modeling with Modifiers and Transforms.max**.
2. Make the **Top** viewport active. In the *Create* panel (+), click (Shapes) to create 2D objects. Verify that *Splines* displays in the drop-down list and click **Rectangle**, as shown in Figure 4–17.

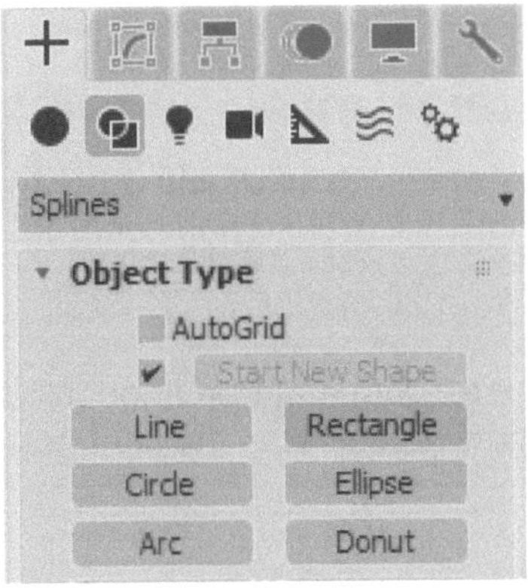

Figure 4–17

3. In the Command Panel, expand the *Keyboard Entry* rollout and set the following:
    - *X*: **0'0"**
    - *Y*: **0'0"**
    - *Z*: **3'2"**
    - *Length*: **0'6"**
    - *Width*: **0'6"**
    - *Corner Radius*: **0'1"** (this fillets the corners of the rectangle)
4. Click **Create**. A 2D rectangle is created on top of the base plate.
5. With the rectangle still selected, select the *Modify* panel (). Expand the *Modifier List* (click down arrow) and select **Extrude** in the *OBJECT-SPACE MODIFIERS* category. Note that **Extrude** is listed in the *Modifier Stack* above the **Rectangle** entry, as shown in Figure 4–18.

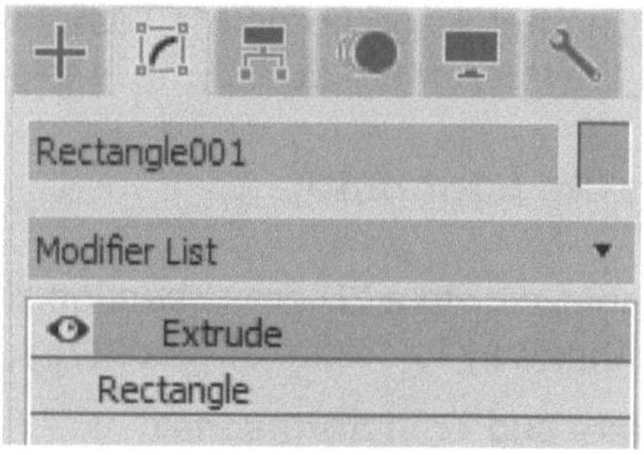

Figure 4–18

Note: *The modifiers in the Modifier drop-down list are placed in groups and then listed alphabetically. Use the scroll bar to navigate through the list or type the first letter of your modifier name in the Search box to bring the modifiers starting with that letter to the top of the selection list.*

6. Rename the object *Rectangle001* as **LP Pole**.
7. In the *Parameters* rollout, set *Amount* to **15'0"** and leave the other parameters as the defaults. Note that the rectangle is extruded and becomes a rectangular-shaped pole.

Note: *Modeling 3D geometry from 2D shapes is discussed in detail later in this guide.*

8. In the **Perspective** viewport, use **Zoom** and **Pan** to get a closer look at the light pole, as shown in Figure 4–19. Note how much detail the light pole's fillet adds to the model.

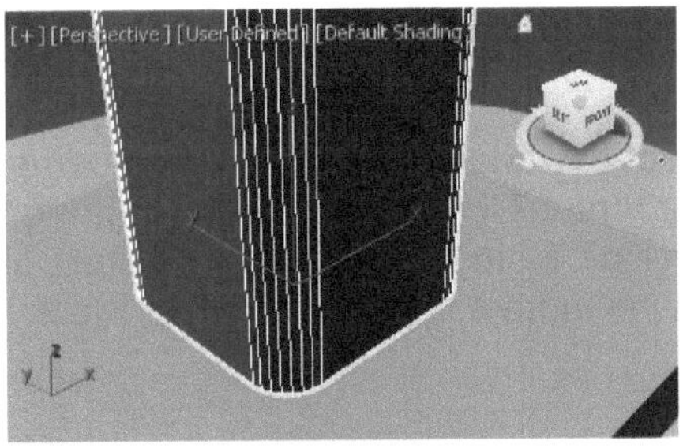

Figure 4–19

Hint: Simple Models

If the object is to be used only as a background item, you should remove any unnecessary detail. Keeping models simple reduces the file size and speeds up software performance and rendering times.

9. Although the **Extrude** modifier is listed directly above the **Rectangle** object in the Modifier Stack, the rectangle's parameters are still accessible and can be changed anytime. With the **LP Pole selected**, in the *Modify* panel (), in the *Modifier Stack*, select **Rectangle**. It is highlighted in blue. In the *Interpolation* rollout, change *Steps* to **2**, as shown in Figure 4–20, and press <Enter>. The fillet divisions are reduced, as shown in Figure 4–21.

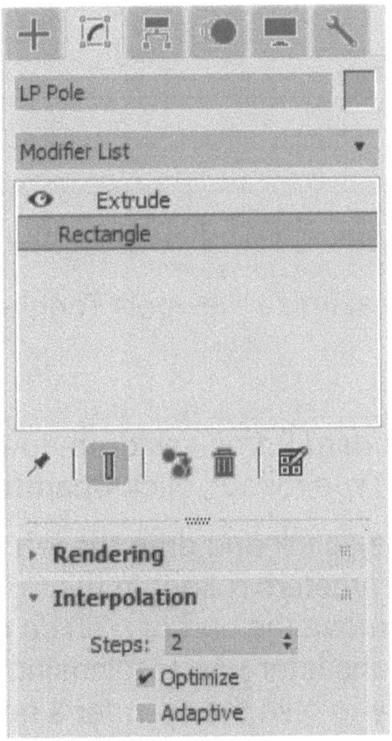

Figure 4–20

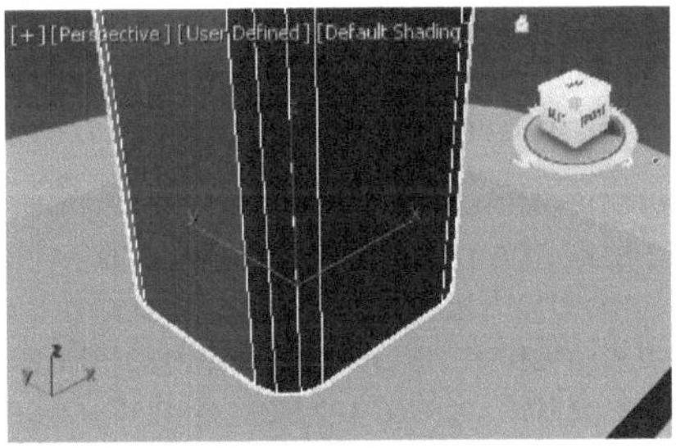

Figure 4–21

10. Save your work as **MyLightPole01.max**.

Task 2: Taper the light pole.

1. In the Modifier Stack, select **Extrude** (so that the next modifier is applied after it). In the Modifier List, select **Taper** (enter **T** in the Search box to bring the modifiers starting with T to the top of the selection list). Note that the *Taper* displays above the *Extrude* in the Modifier Stack, as shown in Figure 4–22. The Modifier Stack lists modifiers in reverse historical order.

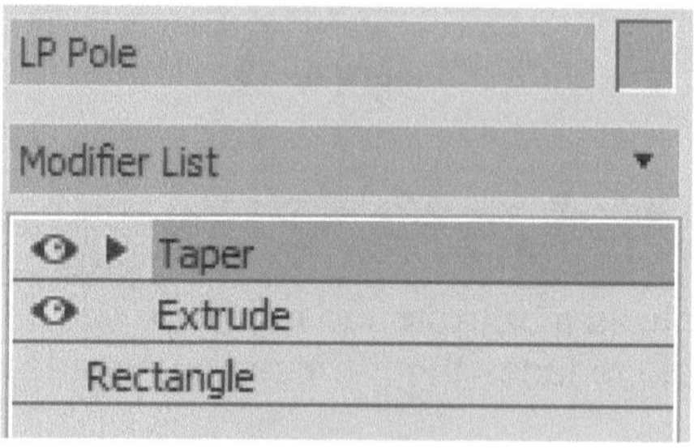

Figure 4–22

2. With **Taper** selected, in the *Parameters* rollout, set *Amount* to **-0.5** and press <Enter>. You can still adjust the original **Rectangle** and **Extrude** parameters by selecting them in the Modifier Stack.
3. Click (Zoom Extents All) to see all of the objects in the viewports. Note the taper on the pole towards the top.
4. Save your work incrementally as **MyLightPole02.max**.

Task 3: Create the fixture housing and globe.

1. In the **Perspective** viewport, zoom in so that the LP Base object displays. Additionally, maximize the **Perspective** viewport by clicking (Maximize Viewport Toggle) or pressing <Alt>+<W>.
2. In the *Create* panel ( )> (Geometry), in the *Standard Primitives* drop-down list, select **Extended Primitives** as a sub-category. In the *Object Type* rollout, click **ChamferCyl**.
3. In the **Perspective** viewport, next to the base (LP Base), click and drag the left mouse button to size the radius to roughly **2'0"**. (Note the *Parameters* rollout in the Command Panel where the Radius changes interactively as you move the cursor. You do not have to use exact dimensions as you will modify the dimensions later.) After releasing the mouse button, move the cursor upwards in the screen slightly to give the cylinder a height of approximately **1'0"**. Click a second time to set the cylinder height and complete the object creation process. The object should display as shown in Figure 4–23.

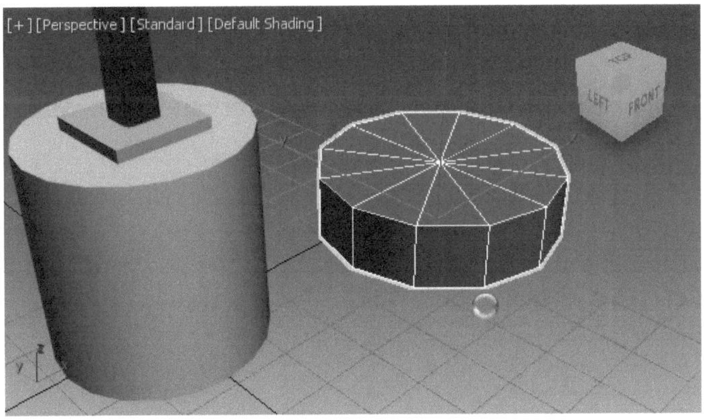

Figure 4–23

4. With the **ChamferCyl** object still selected, in the Command Panel, select the *Modify* panel ( ). Name the object **LP Fixture Housing** and modify the parameters, as shown in Figure 4–24.

5. In the *Create* panel ( ), verify that (Geometry) is selected. In the drop-down list, select **Standard Primitives.** In the *Object Type* rollout, click **Sphere** to create the fixture's globe. Click and drag anywhere on the screen to size a sphere of approximately **1'0"** in radius. Select the *Modify* panel ( ) and assign the parameters, as shown in Figure 4–25.
   - A value of **0.5** for the hemisphere creates half a sphere.

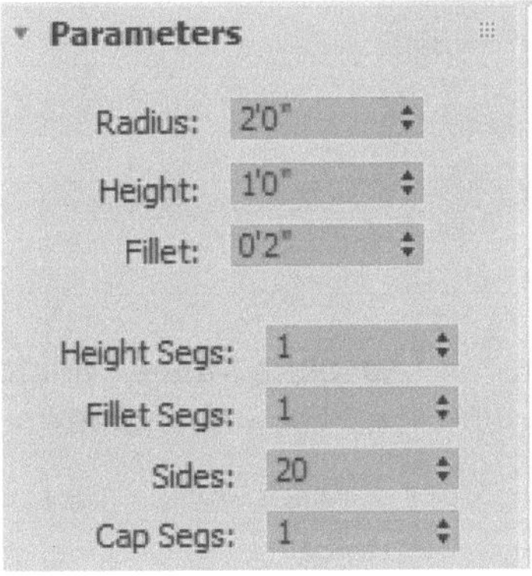

Figure 4–24

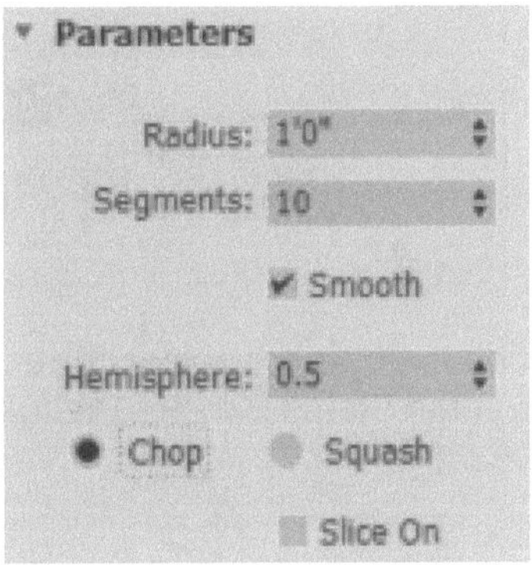

Figure 4–25

6. In the parameters for the hemisphere, select **Squash**. This option generates more faces and creates a smoother appearance.
7. Rename the hemisphere **LP Fixture Globe**.
8. Save your work incrementally as **MyLightPole03.max**.

Task 4: Use transforms to position objects.

1. Select the **LP Fixture Housing** (the chamfered cylinder) and in the Main Toolbar, click (Select and Move).

2. In the Main Toolbar, set the *Reference Coordinate System* to **World** and click (Use Pivot Point Center), as shown in Figure 4–26.

Figure 4–26

3. The Move gizmo displays for the object, as shown in Figure 4–27. Move the fixture housing by clicking and dragging the gizmo's axis handles and plane handles. By default, the gizmo displays at the object's pivot point, located at the bottom center for this object.

Figure 4–27

4. To position the cylinder object correctly, verify that (Absolute Mode Transform Type-In) displays in the Status Bar. Set the following in the type in edit boxes, as shown in Figure 4–28:

   - *X*: **0'0"**
   - *Y*: **-6'0"**
   - *Z*: **19'0"**

Figure 4–28

*Note: The  (Absolute Mode) toggles with  (Offset Mode). If the values are entered in **Offset Mode**, they are added to the current coordinates. This option is useful if you want to move an object a certain distance from the current position.*

5. Toggle  (Maximize Viewport Toggle) or press <Alt>+<W> to open the four viewport view.

   Click  (Zoom Extents All) to display all of the objects in the viewports. In the **Left** viewport, note that the **LP Fixture Housing** (the chamfered cylinder) has now moved to the top right side of the light pole assembly.
6. As the **Move** transform and **Absolute Mode** are already active, select **LP Fixture Globe** (hemisphere) and enter the same X, Y, Z coordinates as you did for LP Fixture Housing (*X*: **0'0"**, *Y*: **-6'0"**, *Z*: **19'0")**. The half globe moves inside the fixture housing.
7. With the half globe still selected, in the Main Toolbar, click  (Select and Rotate).
8. In the Status Bar, note that the *X, Y, Z Transform Type-In* fields display the current rotations of **0.0**. Set *X* to **180** and note the position of the globe is inverted. The objects display as shown in Figure 4–29 in the **Left** viewport.

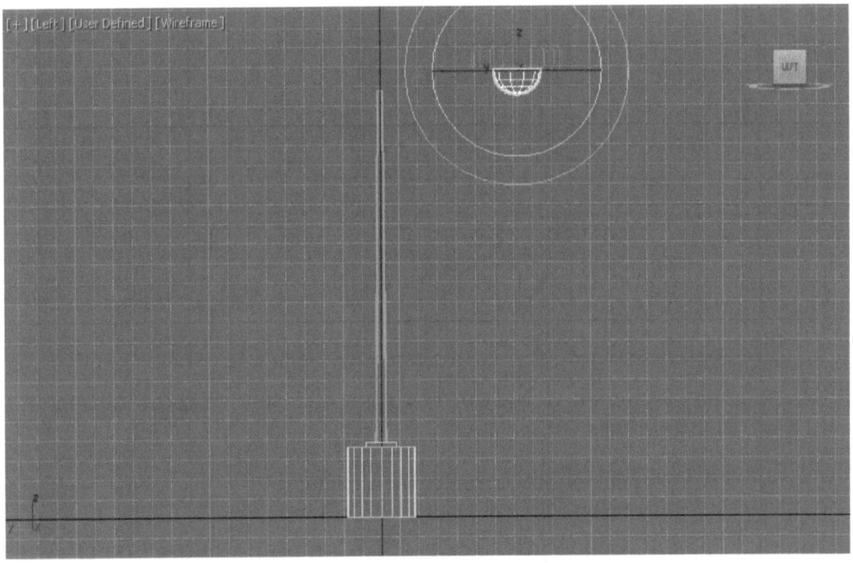

Figure 4–29

9. Click  (Select Object) or press <Q> to end the **Rotate** transform to avoid rotating objects accidentally.
10. Save your work incrementally as **MyLightPole04.max**.

Task 5: Use additional transforms to place objects.

You will create a nut and bolt group and place it on the top surface of the anchor plate.

1. In the **Perspective** viewport, zoom in to LP Base (base cylinder).
2. In the *Create* panel ( ), ensure that (Geometry) and **Standard Primitives** as a sub-category are selected. In the *Object Type* rollout, click **Cylinder**.
3. In the **Perspective** viewport, click and create a cylinder relatively much smaller than the base object.
4. With the new cylinder selected, select the *Modify* panel ( ). Rename the new cylinder as **LP Nut** and assign the parameters (*Radius:* **0'1 4/8"**, *Height:* **0'1"**, *Height Segments:* **3**, *Cap Segments:* **1**, *Sides:* **6**) shown in Figure 4–30.

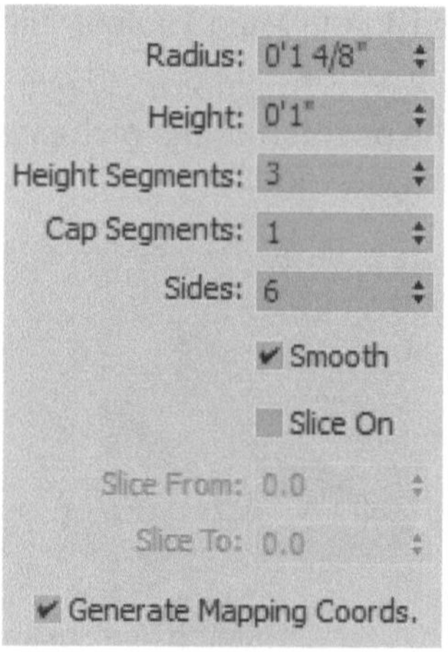

Figure 4–30

5. With **LP Nut** still selected, click (Zoom Extents All Selected) so that only the nut object is zoomed in all the viewports.
6. Click in the **Top** viewport to activate it and clear the selection.
7. In the Command Panel>*Create* panel ( )> (Geometry), in the *Object Type* rollout, click **Cylinder**, and in the **Top** viewport create a small cylinder next to LP Nut.
8. With the new cylinder selected, select the *Modify* panel ( ). Rename the new cylinder as **LP Bolt** and assign the parameters (*Radius:* **0'0 6/8"**, *Height:* **0'0 3/8"**, *Height Segments:* **2**, *Cap Segments:* **1**, *Sides:* **20**), as shown in Figure 4–31. The bolt displays as shown in Figure 4–32.

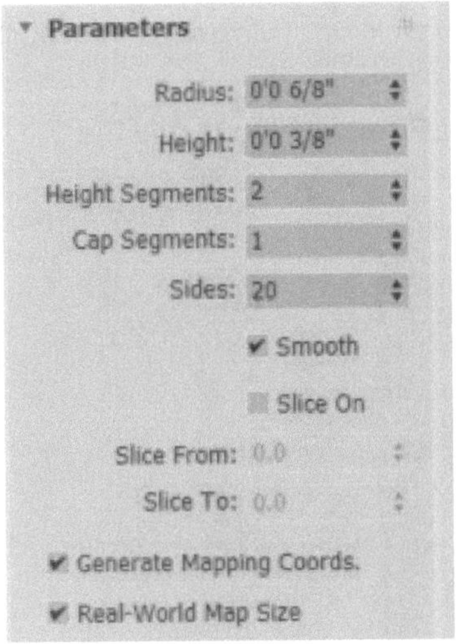

Figure 4–31

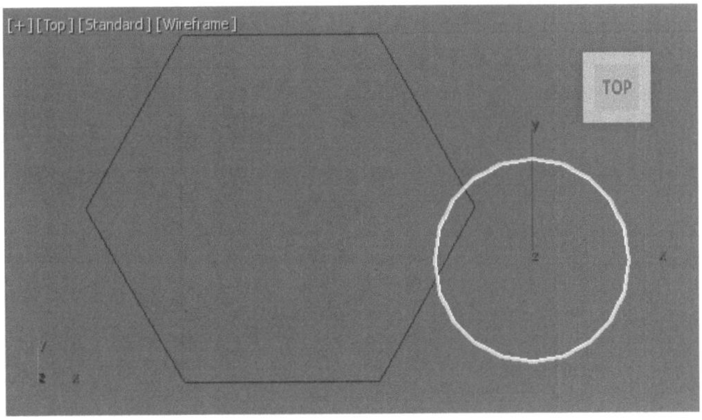

Figure 4–32

9. With **LP Bolt** selected, in the Main Toolbar, click (Select and Place).

10. In the **Perspective** viewport, click and hold over the selected **LP Bolt** object. While holding, drag it over the **LP Nut** object. Note that when you move the **LP Bolt** object along the sides of the **LP Nut** object, it automatically flips on its side, as shown in Figure 4–33. Drag the selected **LP Bolt** object along the top surface of the **LP Nut** object and note how it flips so that its base touches the top surface. Place the **LP Bolt** object at the approximate center of the **LP Nut** object (keep looking in the Top viewport for the approximate center), as shown in Figure 4–34.

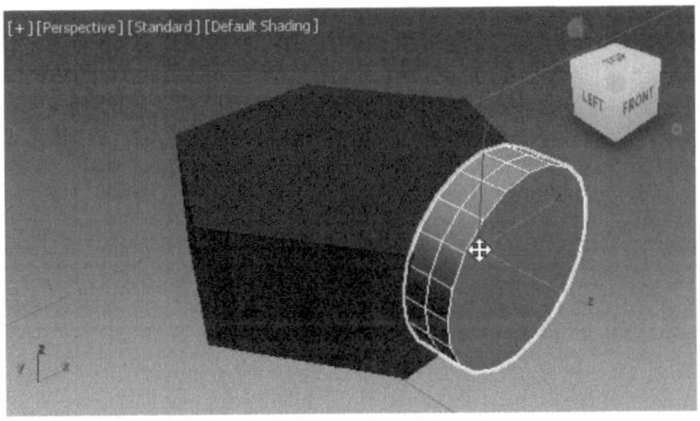

Figure 4–33

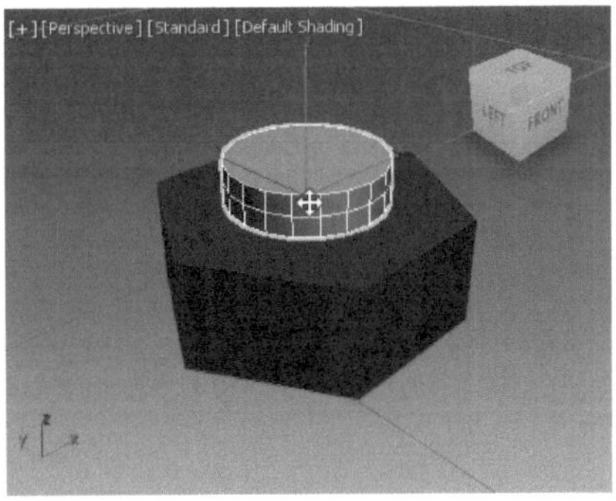

Figure 4–34

11. Click (Select Object) in the Main Toolbar to exit the Placement command.

12. Select both the **LP Nut** and the **LP Bolt** objects (<Ctrl>) and select **Group>Group**. In the *Group* dialog box, name the grouped object as **LP Anchor** and click **OK**.

13. Activate the **Perspective** viewport (if not already active) and click  (Maximize Viewport Toggle), or use <Alt>+<W> to maximize the viewport.

14. Zoom, pan, and orbit around so that you can clearly see the **LP Anchor** group and the **LP Anchor Base**, as shown in Figure 4–35.

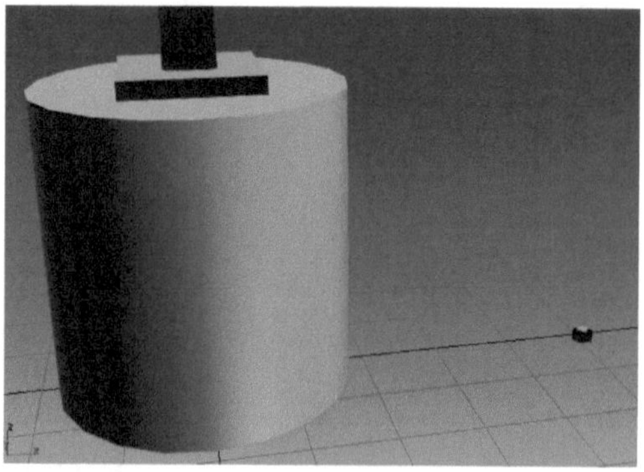

Figure 4–35

15. In the Main Toolbar, click  (Select and Place). Click and hold on the **LP Anchor** group and then drag it on top of the LP Anchor Base plate object. Place the **LP Anchor** group near one of the corners of the plate, as shown in Figure 4–36.

    - Note that the group object is placed halfway inside the LP Anchor Base object.as shown in Figure 4–37.

Figure 4–36

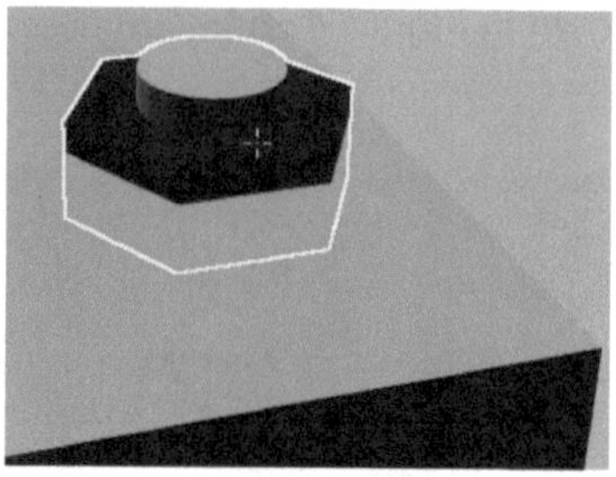

Figure 4–37

16. In the Main Toolbar, select and then right-click on  (Select and Place). In the *Placement Settings* dialog box, select **Pillow Mode** to activate it.

17. Click on the **LP Anchor** group object and slightly move it. Note how its base now touches the top surface of the anchor plate. Place it in one of the corners, as shown in Figure 4–38. Close the *Placement Settings* dialog box.

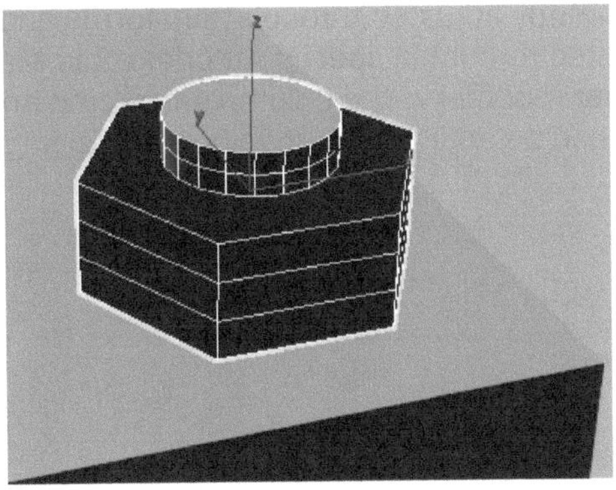

Figure 4–38

18. Maximize to four viewports and activate the Top viewport. Select the **LP Anchor** group object and click  (Select and Move). Hold <Shift> and then click and drag a copy of the **LP Anchor** group object to place it near the next corner of the plate. Click **OK** in the *Clone Options* dialog box.
19. While still holding <Shift>, place two more copies of the objects at the other corners of the plate. A total of four **LP Anchor** group objects should now be placed at the four corners of the anchor plate, as shown in Figure 4–39.

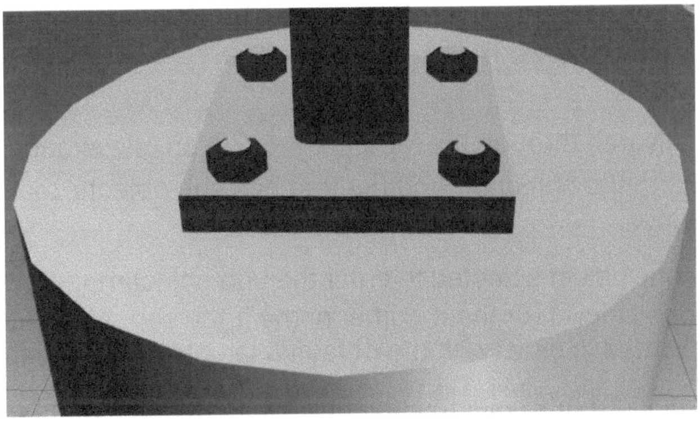

Figure 4–39

20. Save your work incrementally as **MyLightPole05.max**.

End of practice

4.3 Sub-object Mode

Many of the objects and modifiers available in the Autodesk 3ds Max software contain sub-objects that can be independently adjusted through transforms and special modifier controls. These sub-objects are adjusted through a special Autodesk 3ds Max state called Sub-object mode. For example, the **Taper** modifier in the column has Gizmo and Center sub-objects (as shown in Figure 4–40) that can be adjusted to position the Taper.

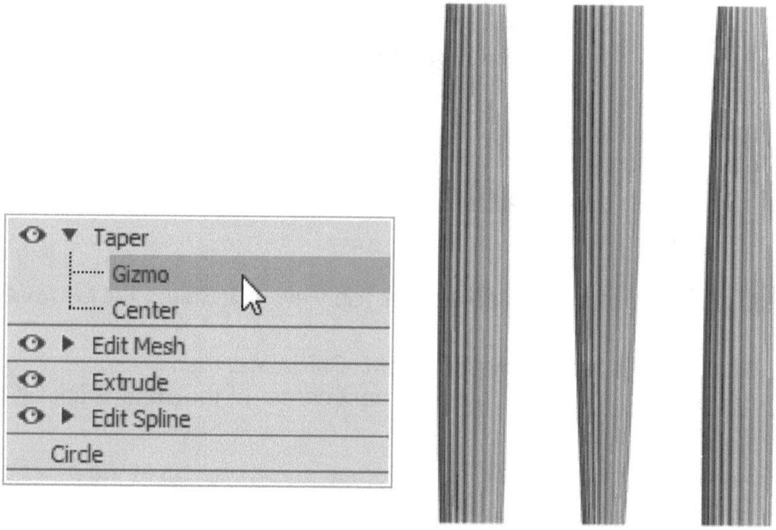

Figure 4–40

Working in Sub-object Mode

Sub-object mode is activated through the Modifier Stack. You can expand the modifier by clicking ► (arrow) next to the object or modifier that has sub-objects, then clicking the sub-object level to be adjusted.

- You can only have one object selected to enter the Sub-object mode. When Sub-object mode is active, the sub-object level (or the modifier name if the sub-object list has not been expanded) is highlighted in blue (with the default user interface settings).
- You cannot clear the currently selected object while in Sub-object mode. Therefore, to edit another object you must first exit Sub-object mode. To do so, click the level of the Modifier Stack presently highlighted to toggle it off.

Geometric Edits Through Sub-objects

A whole range of explicit geometric changes can be made through Sub-object mode.

- Objects imported into the Autodesk 3ds Max software often take the shape of **Editable Splines** or **Editable Meshes**. These have sub-object controls that can be edited directly. For example, a group of vertices in an Editable Mesh can be selected, moved, or deleted separate to the rest of the geometry.
- Many Autodesk 3ds Max objects can also have the controls applied to them through an **Edit Spline** modifier (for 2D objects) or an **Edit Mesh** or **Edit Poly** modifier (for 3D objects). This includes geometry linked to AutoCAD drawings that list only as *Linked Geometry* in the *Modify* panel.
- Figure 4–41 shows an example of a Box that is being edited geometrically by lowering two of its vertices with the **Move** transform.

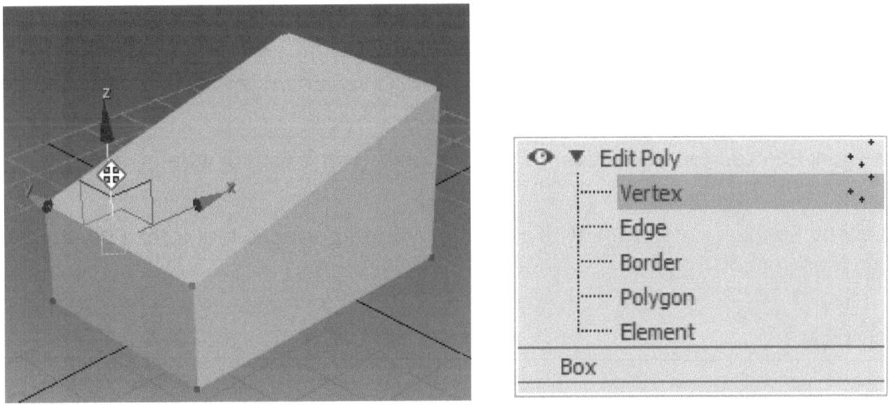

Figure 4–41

- The **Edit Mesh** modifier is best for objects based on a triangular mesh, such as triangulated terrain models.
- The **Edit Poly** modifier is best for objects with faces of more than three vertices, such as rectangular objects.
- To easily review and make changes, it is recommended to adjust objects through their core parameters (such as the length, width, and height of a primitive) and standard modifiers. When required, you can use Spline, Mesh, and Poly for editing.
- A single hotkey can be used to easily and quickly toggle between the various sub-object levels. This speeds up your overall modeling workflow. To use this, to hover the cursor over the required sub-object level and press the hotkey.
- You can also use the **Polygon Modeling** tools in the ribbon to perform modeling and use modifiers with the **Edit Poly** technique.

Geometric Sub-objects

The Editable Spline, Editable Mesh, and Editable Poly objects (and any other object with an Edit Spline, Edit Mesh, or Edit Poly Modifier applied to it) share a number of common Sub-object modes. These are described as follows:

	Vertex: The individual 3D points that define an object (Edit Spline, Edit Mesh, or Edit Poly).
	Segment: A single line or curve segment of an Editable Spline.
	Spline: A series of one or more connected Editable Spline segments. Segments are considered connected if they share a common vertex.
	Edge: The linear segments connecting vertices with Edit Mesh or Edit Poly. Three edges are shown in the button.
	Face: The triangular surface area defined by three edges (Edit Mesh only).
	Border: A series of edges that define an opening in an Editable Poly (Edit Poly only).
	Polygon: Enables you to work with coplanar faces (Edit Mesh) or a defined polygon (Edit Poly).
	Element: Enables you to work with all of the faces or polygons that form a contiguous whole (Edit Mesh or Edit Poly).

Smoothing

One of the most important properties controlled at the face or polygon sub-object level is smoothing. Figure 4–42 shows the same geometry without and with smoothing applied.

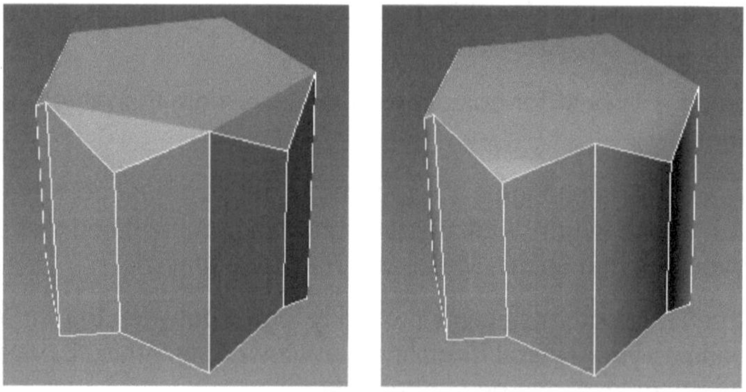

Figure 4–42

- The Autodesk 3ds Max software can have two adjacent faces appear to be smooth or faceted. When smoothed, faces display smooth but the software does not adjust the actual geometry.
- Smoothing is controlled by smoothing groups. Each face or polygon can be a member of up to 32 smoothing groups. If two adjacent faces share a common smoothing group, the software attempts to blend the surfaces together to disguise the edge that separates them.
- Figure 4–43 show an example of the smoothing groups for the selected faces that controls polygon smoothing groups (in Edit Mesh and Edit Poly). When some but not all selected faces fall into a particular smoothing group, that group's box is shown without a number.

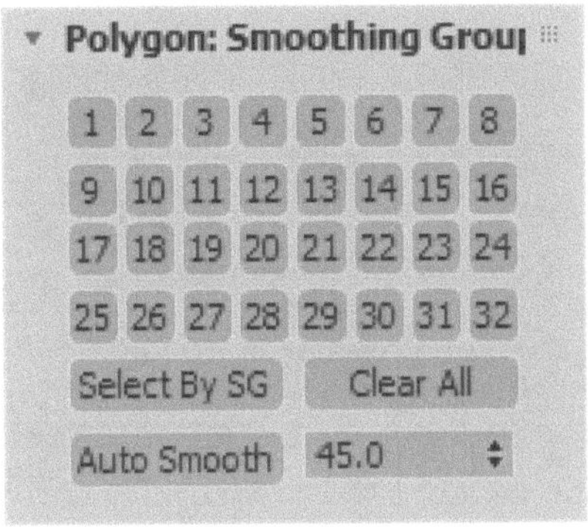

Figure 4–43

- Alternatively, the **Auto Smooth** feature automatically places adjacent selected faces into smoothing groups if their normal vectors have an angle of separation equal to or less than the Auto Smooth angle.

Caddy Display for Edit Poly Modifier

The caddy display (shown in Figure 4–44) enables you to enter values on the screen for various modifiers at the Edit Poly sub-object level. The modifications are dynamically updated and reflected in the model.

- To dynamically view and update the changes, you can type the values in the edit boxes or you can hold and drag the spinner arrows.
- Click ✓ to accept the change or + to accept the change and continue in the same modifier.

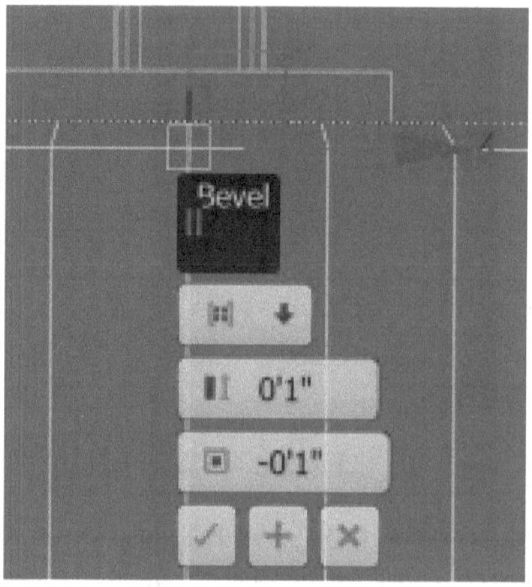

Figure 4–44

- The caddy interface can be accessed through:
  - **Modeling ribbon**: Hold <Shift> and select the sub-object level modifier tool or click the down arrow next to the modifier and select the required setting, as shown for the Bevel modifier in Figure 4–45.

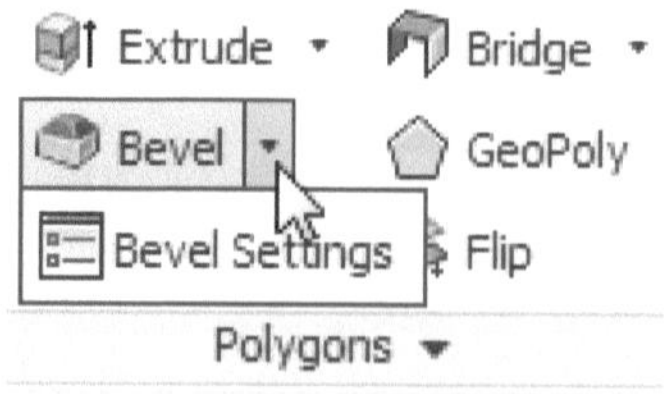

Figure 4–45

  - **Command Panel**: Click (Settings) next to the sub-object level modifier option. This enables you to enter the values while performing the operation.

- The caddy interface display is controlled by the **Enable Caddy Controls** option in the *Preference Settings* dialog box>*General* tab>*UI Display* area, as shown in Figure 4–46. By default, this option is selected.

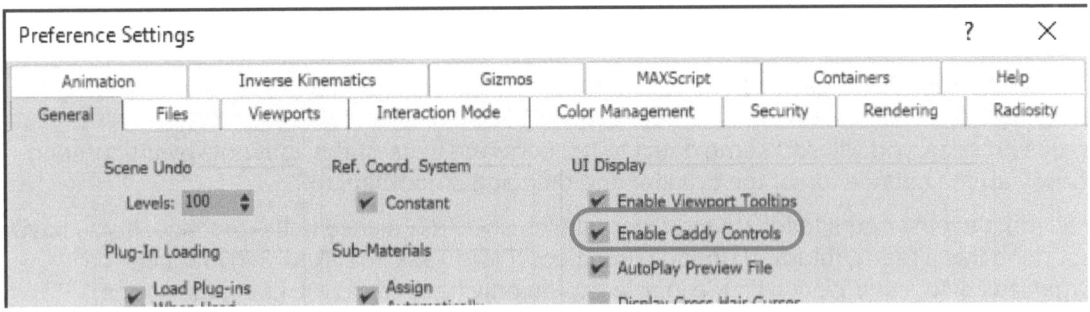

Figure 4–46

Practice 4c
Model with Edit Poly in Sub-object Mode

Practice Objective

- Modify objects at a sub-object level.

In this practice, you will add some detail to the concrete base of the light pole by chamfering (beveling) the outside top of the cylinder and then add smoothing to it.

You must set the paths to locate the External files and XREFs used in the practice. If you have not done this already, return to Chapter 1 and complete Task 1 to Task 3 in *Practice 1a: Organize Folders and Work with the Interface*. You only have to set the user paths once.

1. Open **Edit Poly in Sub-Object Mode.max**.

2. In the **Perspective** viewport, select **LP Base** and click (Zoom Extents Selected). Use (Zoom) and (Orbit) to display the base object similar to that shown in Figure 4–47.

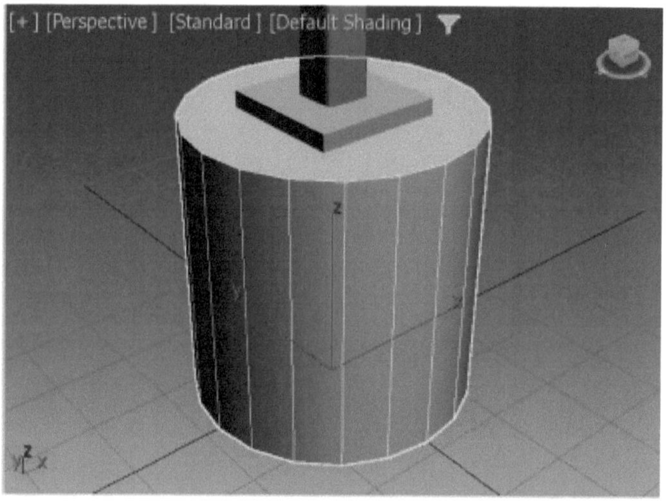

Figure 4–47

3. In the *Modify* panel ( ), select **Edit Poly** from the *Modifier List*. Click (arrow sign) for Edit Poly to display its Sub-object modes. Select **Polygon** to activate the Sub-object mode at the Polygon level. The highlighting in the *Modifier Stack* indicates that you are in the Polygon Sub-object mode, as shown in Figure 4–48.

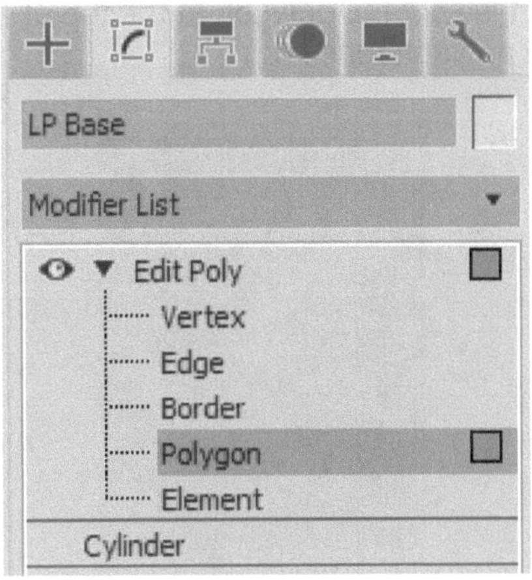

Figure 4–48

Hint: Using Modeling Tools in the Ribbon

You can also perform all of the commands using the **Polygon Modeling** tools in the Modeling ribbon. With the object selected, select the *Polygon Modeling* tab in the *Modeling* tab, in the ribbon. In the drop-down list, select **Apply Edit Poly Mod**, as shown in Figure 4–49.

Click for **Polygon** sub-object level. Note that the selections that you make in the ribbon are reflected in the Command Panel and vice-versa.

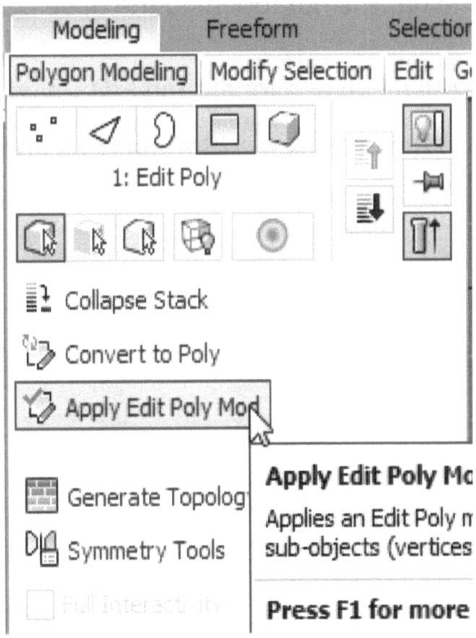

Figure 4–49

4. In the Perspective viewport, select the polygon at the top of the cylinder, as shown in Figure 4–50. The selected polygon tuns red.

Figure 4–50

5. Creating a 1" bevel will raise the cylinder top by 1". In preparation, you will first lower the top of the cylinder by that same 1". In the Main Toolbar, click  (Select and Move). Note that the Move gizmo only displays for the selected polygon.

6. In the Status Bar, click  (Absolute Mode Transform) to toggle it to  (Offset Mode Transform) and set *Z* to **-0'1".** Press <Enter>. The cylinder geometry is adjusted by moving the polygon down.

7. Right-click in the **Left** viewport to activate it (keeping the polygon selected) and zoom in to the base area. Note that the base is not touching the base plate anymore, as shown in Figure 4–51.

8. In the Command Panel, scroll down and locate the *Edit Polygons* rollout. Expand the *Edit Polygons* rollout and next to **Bevel**, click  (Settings), as shown in Figure 4–52.

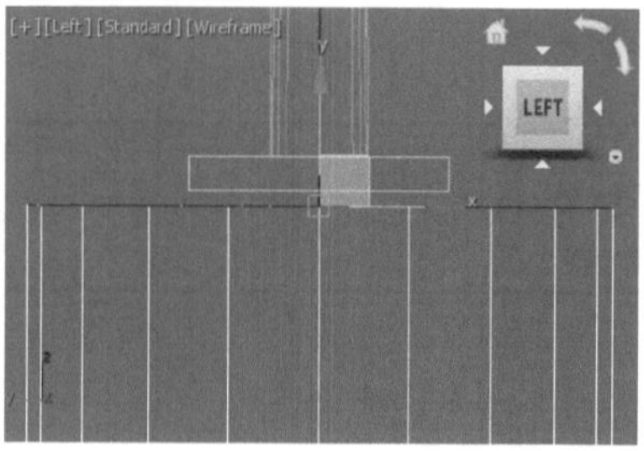

Figure 4–51

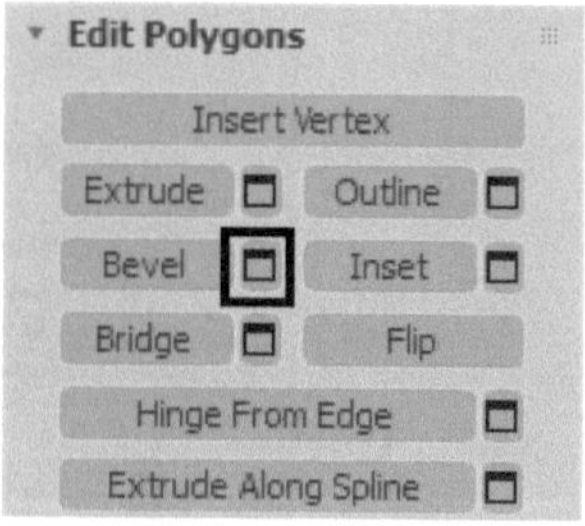

Figure 4–52

Note: *The rollouts in the Command Panel might extend below the display window. To scroll, hover the cursor over an empty gray area until it displays as a* ***Hand*** *icon, then hold and drag the cursor up or down to locate the required rollout.*

9. The caddy display opens on the screen, in the **Left** viewport. In the caddy display, hover the cursor over the *Height* edit box. Its icon changes to display as a spinner and the edit name **Height** displays in addition to the modifier name, **Bevel**, at the top. Enter a value of **0'1"**. Similarly, click on the *Outline* edit box and set its value to **-0'1"**, as shown in Figure 4–53. Click . Verify that the caddy display closes and the base is beveled, as shown in Figure 4–54.

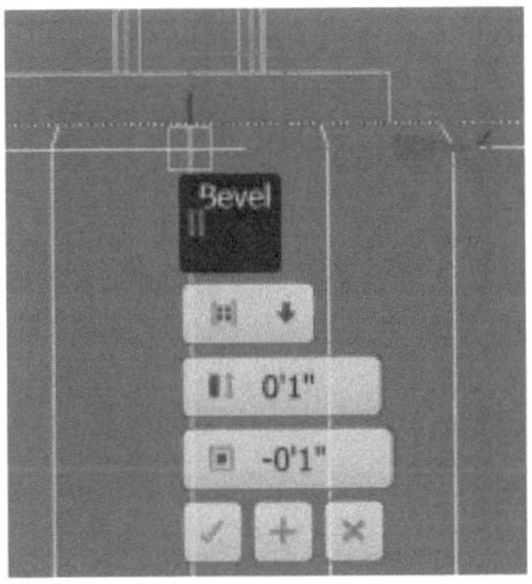

Figure 4–53

Figure 4–54

10. To make the newly created faces smooth, you will adjust the smoothing groups. While still in Polygon Sub-object mode, in the menu bar, expand **Edit** and select **Select All** to select all of the polygons in the base object.
11. In the Command Panel, scroll down and locate the *Polygon: Smoothing Groups* rollout. Click **Clear All** to remove the existing smoothing. Set the *Auto Smooth* angle to **30**, as shown in Figure 4–55, and click **Auto Smooth**.

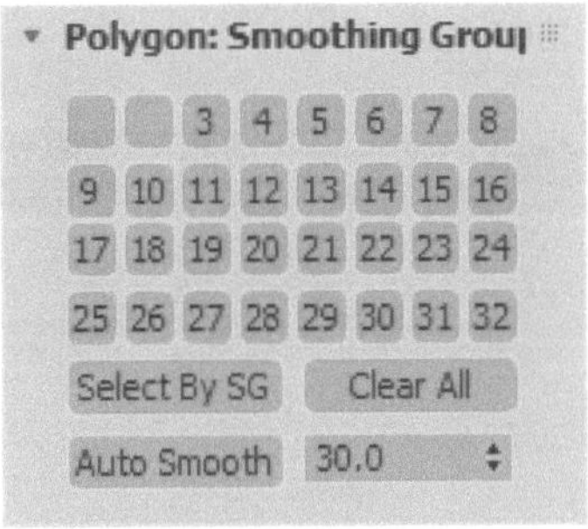

Figure 4–55

12. To end Sub-object mode, in the Command Panel>*Modifier Stack,* click the **Polygon** highlighted in blue to clear the selection.

13. To display the effect of the smoothing change, in the **Perspective** viewport, clear the object selection by clicking anywhere in empty space. The 30 degrees angle enabled the newly created faces to smooth across each other, but the faces are not smoothed with the top of the cylinder, as shown in Figure 4–56. This is the chamfered appearance that was originally intended. A larger smoothing angle enables the chamfered faces between the top and sides to smooth out.

Figure 4–56

14. In the Main Toolbar, click  (Select Object) to end the Move Transform mode as a precaution to avoid moving objects accidentally while making further selections.
15. Save your work as **MyLightPole06.max**.

End of practice

4.4 Reference Coordinate Systems and Transform Centers

All geometry in the Autodesk 3ds Max software is referenced to a base coordinate system called the Home Grid.

- You can create your own coordinate systems by creating and locating grid objects, available in the **Helpers** category in the *Create* panel.
- You can also create objects in the Auto-grid mode, which creates a temporary 3D Grid aligned to the object directly under the crosshairs. The **AutoGrid** option can be found in the *Create* panel, in the *Object Type* rollout, as shown Figure 4–57. If you hold <Alt>, the AutoGrid remains available for future use. If you use AutoGrid without any key pressed, the grid disappears after object creation.

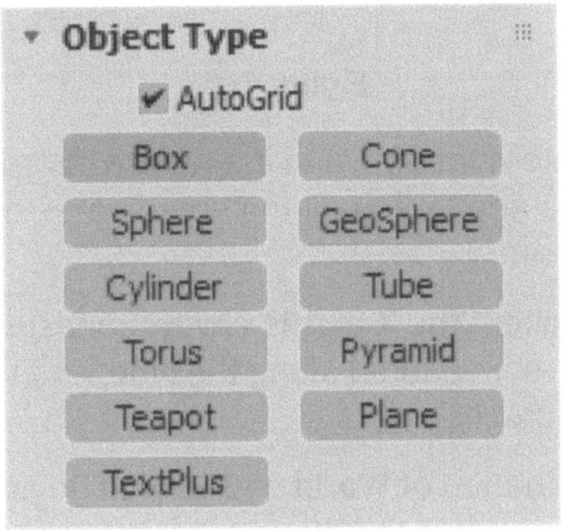

Figure 4–57

Reference Coordinate Systems

The current Reference Coordinate System might differ depending on which view you are in and which transform is active. It is recommended that new users stay in the **World** system to avoid confusion from changing axis labels. By default, the Reference Coordinate system is set to **View**.

- In the Main Toolbar, the options listed in the *Reference Coordinate System* drop-down list (shown Figure 4–58) control how transform values are read. Note that a single grid is active at any one time.

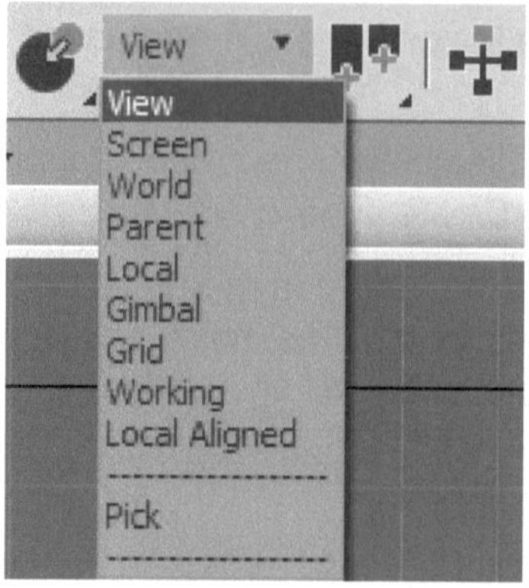

Figure 4–58

- In the **World** coordinate system the X, Y, and Z axes are interpreted based on the Home Grid, even if a user-defined grid is active. To use the coordinates of the active user-defined grid instead, select the **Grid** option.
- In the **Screen** coordinate system the X-axis is always measured along the bottom of the viewport, the Y-axis is always measured along the side, and the Z-axis is measured perpendicularly out of the screen.
- The **View** system is a combination of **World** and **Screen**. In an orthographic view, the **Screen** system is used, while in other views the **World** system is used.
- The **Local** system considers the coordinate system of the selected object. Note that only the Z-axis of the object is considered, which can cause unpredictable changes along the X- and Y-axis.
- The **Grid** system is based on the currently active grid and uses its coordinate system.
- The **Working** option enables you to use the Working Pivot. It is a temporary modeling pivot tool you create from the *Hierarchy* panel's *Pivot* tab. Generally you need to assign a hotkey to **Use Working Pivot** and **Edit Working Pivot** to make them functional tools.
- The **Local Aligned** option is used with sub-objects in an editable mesh or poly. It calculates all three (X,Y,Z) axes by using the coordinate system of the selected object. It can be used when multiple sub-objects need to be adjusted at the same time.
- The **Pick** option enables you to pick any object in the viewport or from a list and use the reference coordinate system of that object as the reference for transforms. You can use XREF objects with the **Pick** option.

Transform Centers

Transforms are applied through a Transform Center point indicated by the Transform gizmo. The Transform Center options are available in the Main Toolbar, in the Transform Center flyout, as shown Figure 4–59.

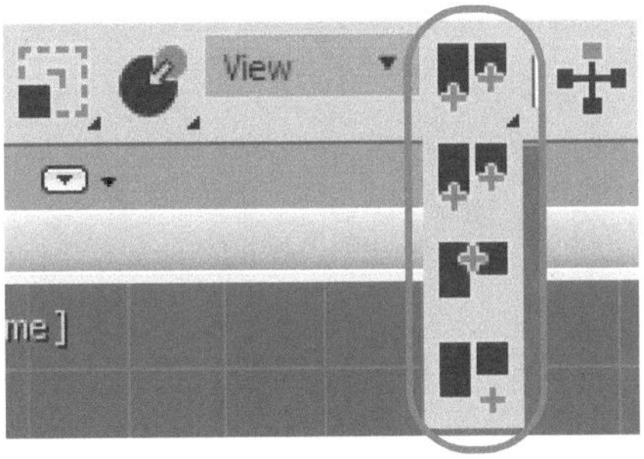

Figure 4–59

	**Pivot Point Center:** Transforms are applied through each selected object's pivot point. Pivots often default to the bottom center or geometric center of objects. Pivot points can be adjusted through controls in the *Hierarchy* panel. Select this option if you want to rotate many objects, each around its own center.
	**Selection Center:** Transforms are applied through the geometric center of all selected objects.
	**Transform Coordinate Center:** Transforms are applied through the origin point of the current Reference Coordinate System. For example, if you wanted to rotate objects around their individual pivot points about the World Z-axis, you would select the World Coordinate System and Pivot Point Transform Center. Alternatively, to rotate all of the objects around the origin, you would do the same with the Transform Coordinate Center.

- The Transform Center might automatically change depending on whether one or multiple objects are selected, and on the active transform.

- The Reference Coordinate System and Transform Center can be held using **Constant** in the *Preference Settings* dialog box, in the *General* tab, as shown in Figure 4–60.

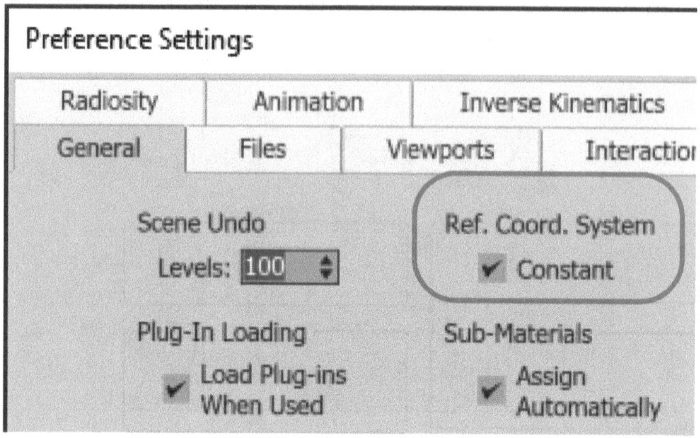

Figure 4–60

4.5 Cloning and Grouping

Cloning

In Autodesk 3ds Max, objects can be duplicated using the **Clone** option (**Edit>Clone**), which opens the *Clone Options* dialog box, as shown in Figure 4–61.

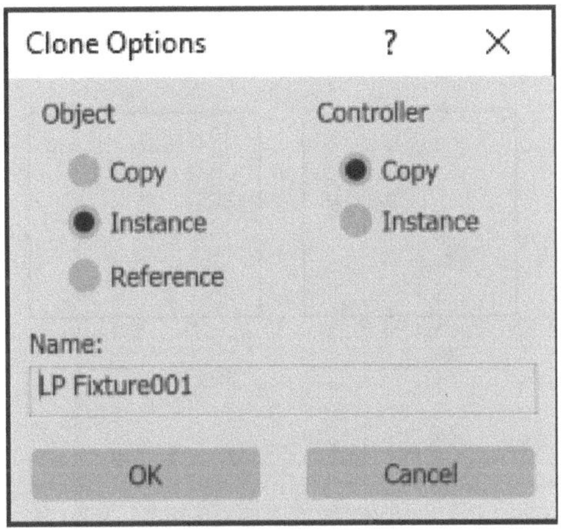

Figure 4–61

Copy	Makes an independent copy without a dynamic link to the source object.
Instance	Makes the duplicate and original Instances of each other. Changes made to any Instance automatically update all Instances, including changes to Modifiers, property changes, and material assignments (except for Transforms).
Reference	A one-directional link where changes made to the original object affect the duplicate. You can apply Modifiers to the Reference without affecting the Source object.

- To access the **Clone** command, an object should be selected first, otherwise it remains grayed out.
- You can also clone an object by holding <Shift> while transforming through a click and drag on the Transform gizmo. In this procedure, you have an additional option for specifying the number of copies you want to make, which are arrayed at the same Transform value.
- The *Controller* area in the *Clone Options* dialog box applies to objects in a group or hierarchy.
- Objects that are instanced or referenced display with the Modifier Stack text in bold type. Instancing or referencing can be disabled by right-clicking on the item in the *Modifier Stack* and selecting **Make Unique**.

Grouping

Grouping enables multiple objects to be treated as a single unit, for selection and transforms. The various grouping options are available in the **Group** menu, as shown in Figure 4–62.

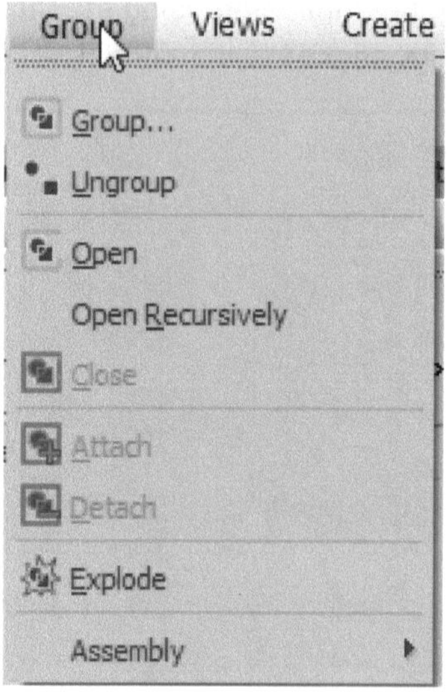

Figure 4–62

Group	Creates a group out of all of the currently selected objects. Groups can have other groups inside them (nested groups).
Ungroup	Dissolves any selected groups back into their constituent objects.
Open/Close	Enables you to select, modify, and transform individual group members as if they were not in a group. The group is still defined; however, it can be Closed to treat the objects as a single unit again.
Open Recursively	Enables you to select, modify, and transform individual members at any level in a group. The group is still defined. Use the **Close** command to restore the original group.
Attach	Enables you to add another object to a group. First select the objects to be attached, then select the **Attach** option in the **Group** menu. When prompted, select a closed group to which to add the objects.
Detach	Enables you to remove selected objects from a group. You must first open the group to select the objects to be detached.
Explode	Dissolves the selected groups and any groups nested inside them.
Assembly	Special case object grouping that are intended for creation of lighting assemblies called luminaires, and for character assemblies.

- Groups are located in the Command Panel's *Modify* panel, with group name in bold type, and a blank *Modifier Stack*. The *Modifier Stack* of individual group members displays if it is opened.
- Groups can be copied, instanced, and referenced.
- It is recommended not to use grouping on objects that are linked into a hierarchy and then animated.

Practice 4d
Model with Coordinate Systems

Practice Objective

- Create an object and modify the parameters.

In this practice, you will add the Light Pole Mounting Arm to the Light Pole model by creating the model and modifying the parameters.

You must set the paths to locate the External files and XREFs used in the practice. If you have not done this already, return to Chapter 1 and complete Task 1 to Task 3 in *Practice 1a: Organize Folders and Work with the Interface*. You only have to set the user paths once.

1. Open **Modeling with Coordinate Systems.max**.
2. Activate the **Front** viewport.
3. Use a combination of **Zoom** and **Pan** to zoom in to the top portion, as shown in Figure 4–63. If the Grid is showing in the **Front** view, in the *Viewport* labels, click the **[+]** *General Viewport* label and select **Show Grids** to clear it. Alternatively, you can press <G> to toggle the grid on or off.
4. In the *Create* panel ()> (Geometry), click **Box**. Use the cursor to create a small box near the top of the light pole with approximate dimensions for *Length*, *Width*, and *Height*, as shown in Figure 4–64.

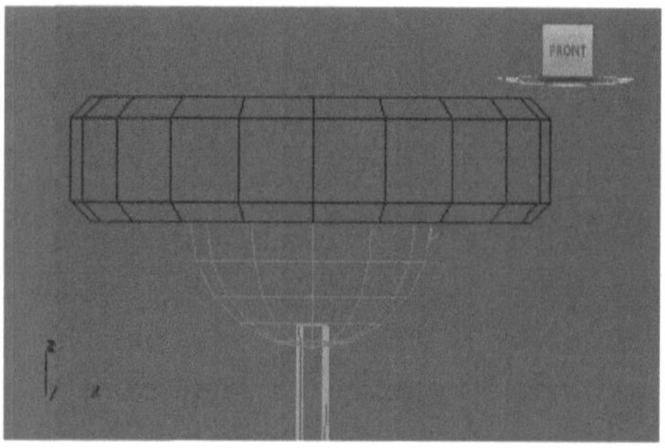

Figure 4–63

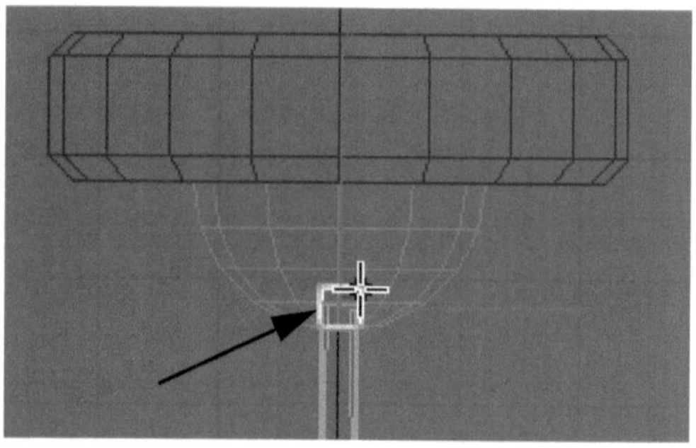

Figure 4–64

5. With this box still selected, in the *Modify* panel ( ), in the *Parameters* rollout, set the following, as shown in Figure 4–65:
   - *Name:* **LP Mounting Arm**
   - *Length*: **0'3"**
   - *Width:* **0'3"**
   - *Height:* **4'6"**
   - *Height Segs*: **6**
6. In the **Perspective** view, use a combination of **Zoom**, **Pan**, and **Orbit** to zoom in to the **LP Mounting Arm**, as shown in Figure 4–65. Since you created the box in the **Front** viewport, the height of the box is measured perpendicular to the view, in this case along the world Y-axis.

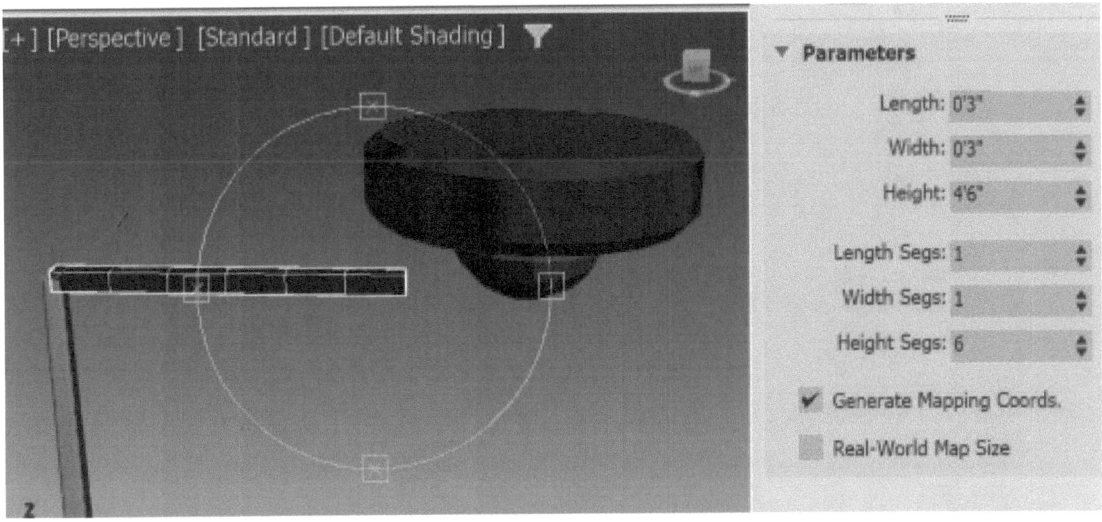

Figure 4–65

7. With the LP Mounting Arm selected, click (Select and Move). In the Status Bar, set the transform mode to (Absolute mode) and set the location of the mounting arm with the Z value at **18'0"**, as shown in Figure 4–66.

Figure 4–66

8. In the Modifier List, select **Bend** to curve the arm to the housing. In the Parameters, set the following:
    - *Bend Angle*: **30** degrees
    - *Direction:* **-90** degrees

    Note that the arm is bent.
9. Save your work as **MyLightPole07.max**.

End of practice

Practice 4e
Clone and Group

Practice Objectives

- Create a single unit of multiple objects.
- Clone an instance of the group and modify it.

In this practice, you will complete the model of the light pole using Cloning and Groups. You will first create a single unit by grouping multiple objects. You will then clone an instance of a group and modify the instance so that the original object is modified as well.

You must set the paths to locate the External files and XREFs used in the practice. If you have not done this already, return to Chapter 1 and complete Task 1 to Task 3 in *Practice 1a: Organize Folders and Work with the Interface*. You only have to set the user paths once.

1. Open **Cloning and Grouping.max**.
2. In the Scene Explorer, ((Display None) and (Display Geometry) to display the scene geometry only. Select **LP Fixture Globe**, **LP Fixture Housing**, and **LP Mounting Arm** (use <Ctrl> to select multiple items), as shown in Figure 4–67. Note that the three items are selected in the viewports.
3. In the menu bar, select **Group>Group** to combine the three objects together into a single, selectable unit. In the *Group* dialog box, name the group **LP Fixture**, as shown in Figure 4–67. Click **OK**.

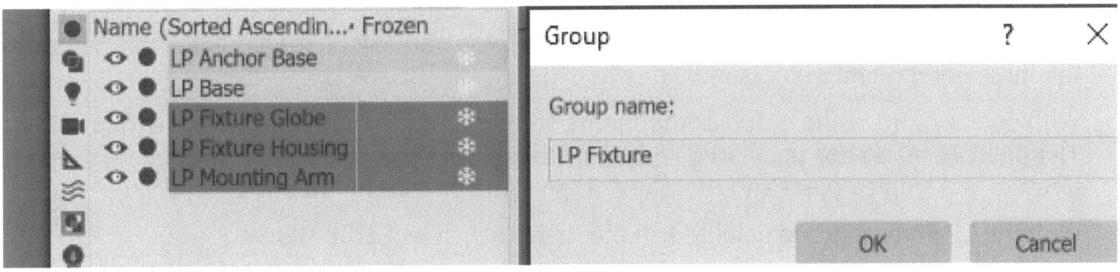

Figure 4–67

4. In the Scene Explorer, note that the group name is identified with the [group icon] symbol and the geometry objects are displayed under it, as shown in Figure 4–68. In the Scene Explorer, select the group **LP Fixture** and note that all the three objects are selected in the viewport. Similarly, select **LP Fixture Globe** in the Scene Explorer and note that the three objects are still selected in the viewports, as shown in Figure 4–68.

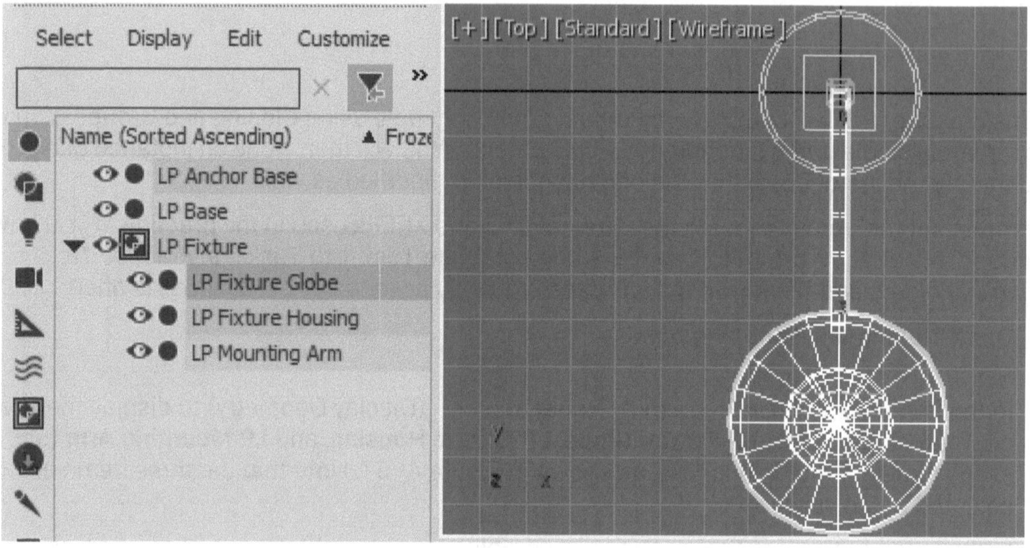

Figure 4–68

5. In the Scene Explorer, select the group **LP Fixture** and then in the menu bar, select **Group>Open**. The group remains intact with a pink bounding box enclosing the group objects, indicating that it is an open group. Here, you can select, manipulate, and transform the three component objects individually.
6. With one or more of the group components selected, in the menu bar, select **Group>Close**. The pink bounding box is cleared with all of the group objects selected, indicating that it is treated as a single object and that the components cannot be modified separately.
7. With the **LP Fixture** group selected, in the menu bar, select **Edit>Clone**.

8. In the *Clone Options* dialog box, in the *Object* area, select **Instance** (if required) leaving all other options at their default values, as shown in Figure 4–69. Click **OK**.
   - The original and the copy now directly overlay each other. Note that in the Scene Explorer, another group with the name **LP Fixture001** is created.

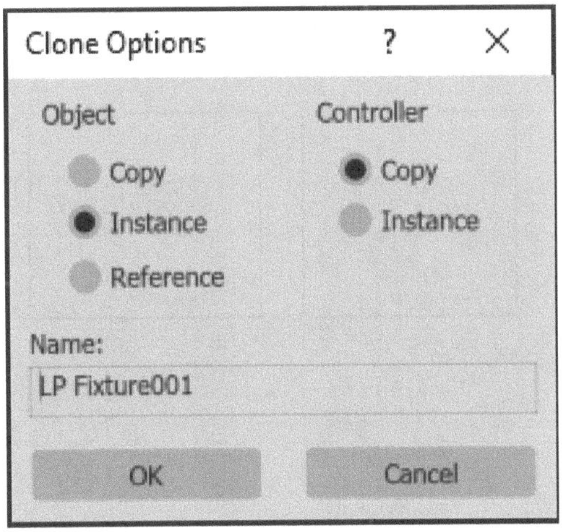

Figure 4–69

9. In the Scene Explorer, select **LP Fixture001**.
10. In the Main Toolbar, click  (Select and Rotate).
11. The position of the Transform gizmo is dependent on the Reference Coordinate System and the active **Use Transform**. In the Main Toolbar, in the Reference Coordinate System, select **Parent**, as shown in Figure 4–70.

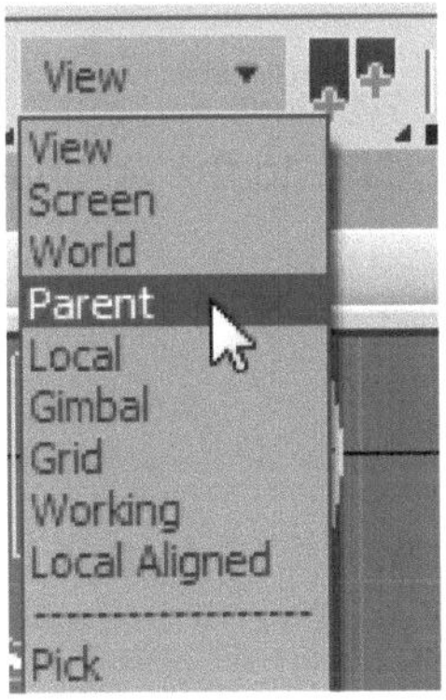

Figure 4–70

12. In the *Use Transform* flyout, click  (Use Pivot Point Center). Note in the **Top** viewport that the Rotate transform gizmo is in the center of the group, as shown in Figure 4–71. This rotation will not place **LP Fixture001** in the correct position.

13. In the *Use Transform* flyout, click  (Use Transform Coordinate Center). In the **Top** viewport, note that the Rotation gizmo moves to the base of the selected group, as shown in Figure 4–72.

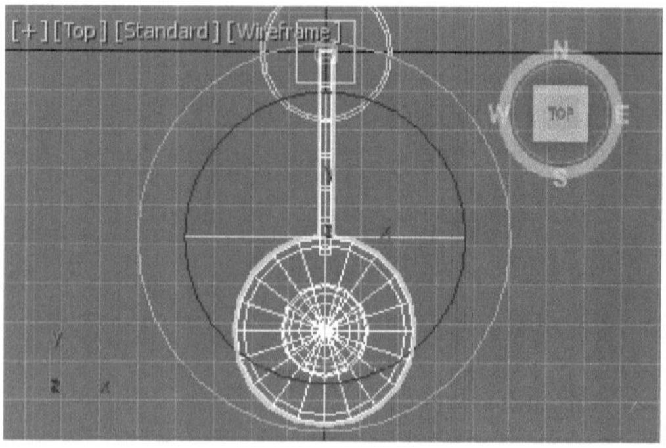

Figure 4–71

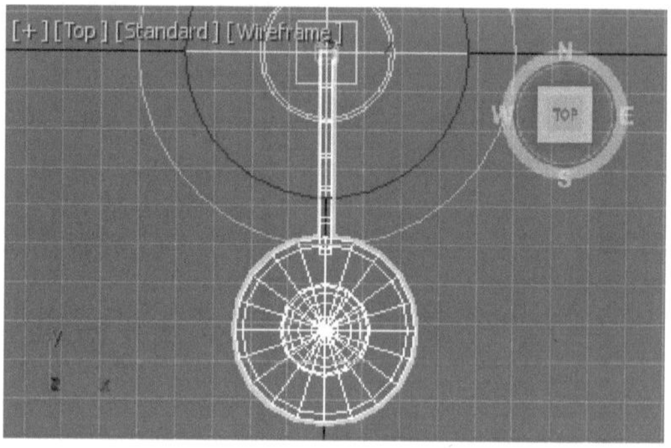

Figure 4–72

14. Right-click in the **Front** viewport to activate it and keep the selection of **LP Fixture001** intact.
15. In the Status Bar, in the *Transform Type-In* area, set *Z* to **180.0** (as shown in Figure 4–73) to rotate **LP Fixture001** by **180°** about the Z-axis. Press <Enter>.

Figure 4–73

- The cloned group is moved opposite to the original group, as shown in the Left viewport in Figure 4–74.

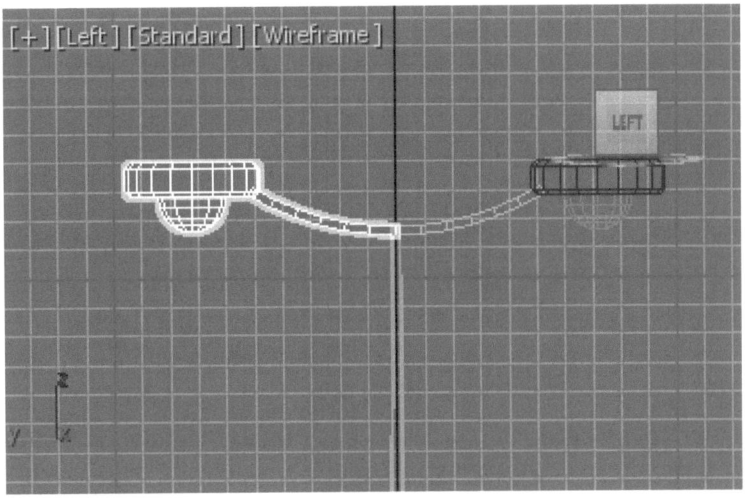

Figure 4–74

16. Click  (Select Object) to end the Rotate transform mode.
17. To verify that the groups are instanced, with **LP Fixture001** selected, select **Group>Open**. A pink bounding box displays around the group.
18. In the Scene Explorer, select **LP Fixture Housing001**.
19. In the *Modify* panel (), in the *Parameters* rollout, reduce the *Height* from *1'0"* to **0'8"**. Both Fixture Housings update and have reduced height as shown in Figure 4–75.

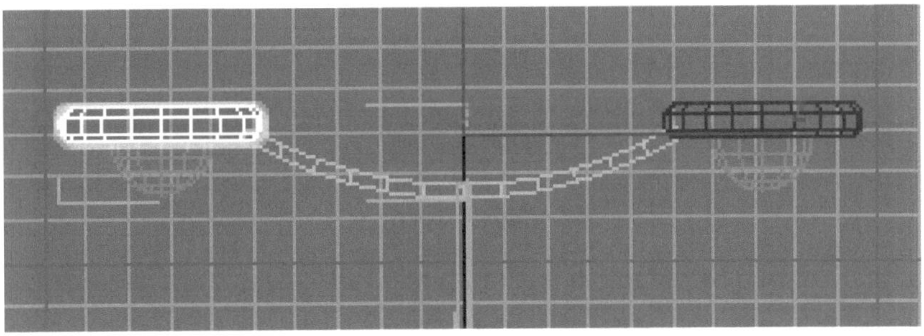

Figure 4–75

20. Select **Group>Close** to close **LP Fixture001**.
21. Save your work as **MyLightPole08.max**.

End of practice

4.6 Polygon Modeling Tools in the Ribbon

The Autodesk 3ds Max software is a powerful environment for creating a variety of 3D models. The box modeling technique, also called polygon modeling or mesh modeling, is an interactive method for creating vertices, edges, faces, and surfaces in a free form way.

- Box modeling can be performed using either the **Edit Mesh** or **Edit Poly** modifiers, or be converted to an **Editable Mesh** or **Editable Poly** object. Any of these methods give you the access to the sub-object levels required to do this type of modeling.
- The **Edit Poly** modifier is a commonly used modeling technique, although you can convert the object to an editable mesh or editable poly object and discard the modifier. You can also use the **Edit Mesh** modifier which is the most stable.
- The Modeling ribbon (*Modeling* tab) provides easy access to polygon modeling tools, including the editing and modification tools used at sub-object level. The ribbon contains many of the commonly used tools that are present in the Command Panel's *Modify* panel, at the Edit Poly sub-object level. In the *Modeling* tab, the polygon modeling and modifying tools are organized into panels.
- By default, the ribbon can be minimized to the panel tiles by clicking and can be docked under the Main Toolbar. By default, **Minimize to Panel Titles** is set in the drop-down list, as shown in Figure 4–76. Click to maximize the ribbon. You can also set the ribbon to be minimized to tabs or Panel Buttons by selecting the respective option in the drop-down list.

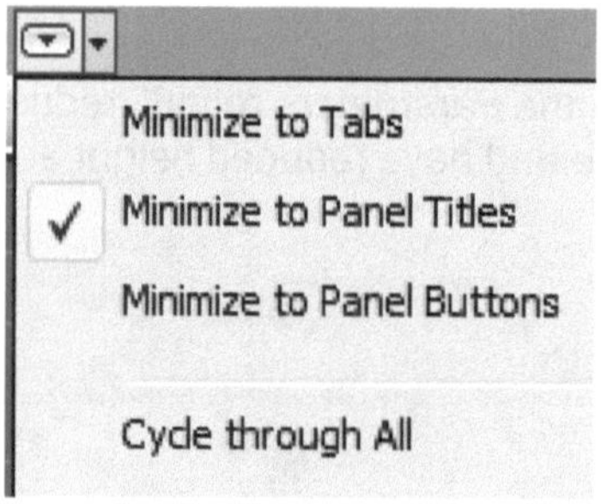

Figure 4–76

- The ribbon is displayed by default. If it is not displayed, select **Customize>Show UI>Show Ribbon** in the Menu Bar, click (Toggle Ribbon) in the Main Toolbar, or select **Ribbon** in the Interface Item menu to display the ribbon.

Practice 4f
(Optional) Poly Modeling Using the Ribbon

Practice Objective

- Create and modify a model using the box modeling technique.

In this practice, you will learn to create a model using some of the tools and techniques of box modeling. You will also use the **Edit Poly** modifier and the modifier tools available in the ribbon.

Task 1: Model the armchair.

1. Start an empty file by selecting **File>Reset**.
2. In the *Create* panel ()> (Geometry), click **Box** in the *Object Type* rollout to activate the **Box** tool.
3. In the **Perspective** viewport, near the center of the grid, create a box of any size by clicking and dragging to define the length and width of the rectangle. Click and continue moving the mouse upwards to define the height.
4. Use the *Modify* panel () to edit the values. Set the following:
    - *Length*: **4'2"**
    - *Width*: **2'9"**
    - *Height*: **0'10"**

    Press <Enter>. In the **Perspective** viewport, the box should look similar to that shown in Figure 4–77.

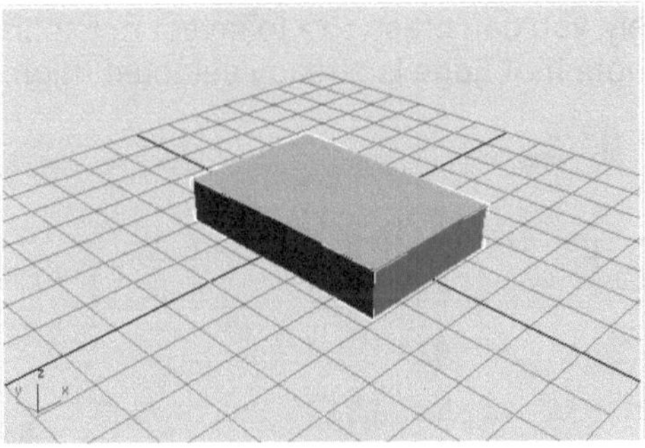

Figure 4–77

5. In the *Modify* panel (), name the box **armchair**.
6. To display the edges more clearly, change the display mode to wireframe by clicking the *Per-View Preference* label and selecting **Wireframe Override**.

7. Press <G> to hide the grid.
8. If the Modeling ribbon is only displaying Panel titles, click (Show Full Ribbon).
9. Verify that the *Modeling* tab is active. Ensure that the armchair model is selected. Expand the *Polygon Modeling* panel and select **Apply Edit Poly Mod**, as shown in Figure 4–78. This adds an **Edit Poly** modifier to the armchair model. This is also displayed in the Command Panel. Note that the *Modify* panel ( ) is already open and that the *Modifier Stack* displays the **Edit Poly** modifier, as shown in Figure 4–79.

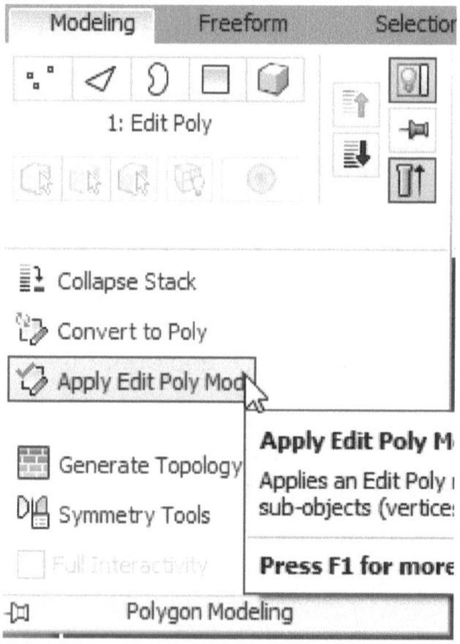

Figure 4–78

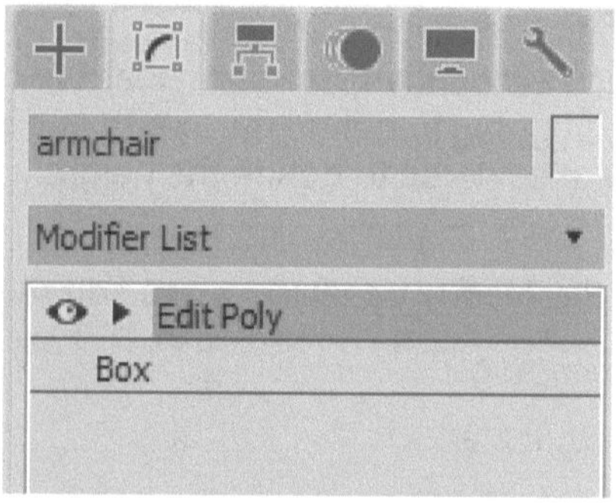

Figure 4–79

10. In the *Modeling* panel of the ribbon, click (Edge) to activate Edge Selection, as shown in Figure 4–80. Alternatively, you can press <2> to select it. Expand the **Edit Poly** modifier in the *Modifier Stack* and note that **Edge** is already selected (highlighted in blue).

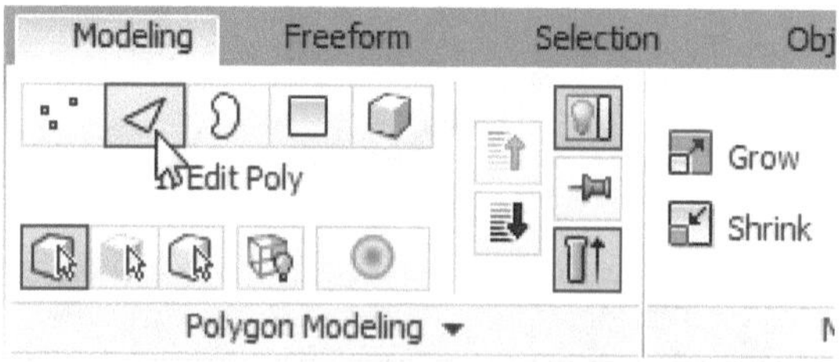

Figure 4–80

11. In the Navigation toolbar, click (Zoom Extents All Selected) and using **Pan** and **Zoom** fill the viewport with the box. Maximize the **Perspective** viewport.

12. Hold <Ctrl> and select the upper two long edges, as shown in Figure 4–81. The selected edges display in red.

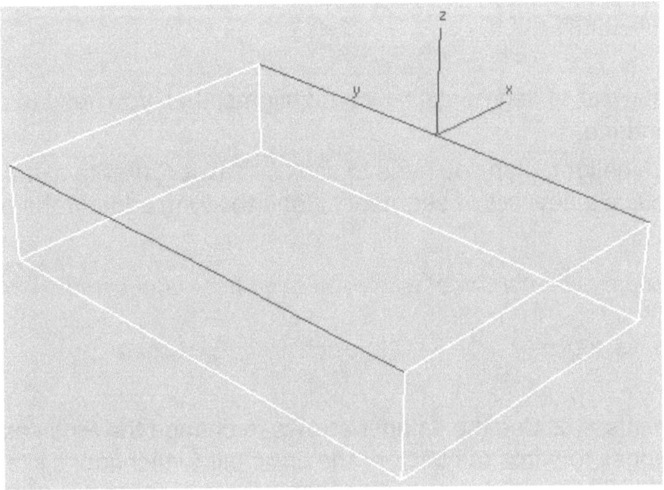

Figure 4–81

13. Hold <Shift>, and in the ribbon, in the *Loops* panel, click (Connect) to open the **Connect Edges** caddy display.
14. In the Connect Edges caddy display, set *Segments* to **2** and *Pinch* to **70.** Press <Enter> (leaving *Slide* as **0**). Note that two new edges are created along the two short edges, as shown in Figure 4–82.

   Note: *In the caddy display, hover the cursor over the edit box to display the option in its title.*

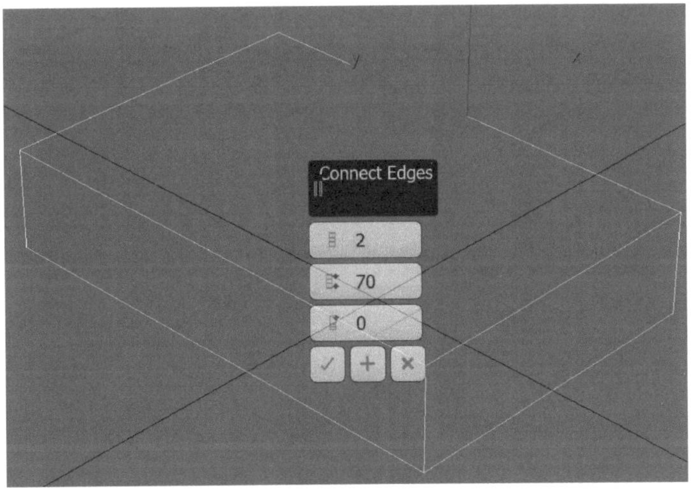

Figure 4–82

15. If your *Pinch* edit box is still highlighted (white) with the cursor in the edit box, you are required to exit it first. Press (Apply and continue) and note that two more edges are created along the longer edge.

   - To create a new set of segments, if highlights, then you need to click once to apply and continue.
   - If it does not highlight, then you need to click twice, first to exit the *Pinch* edit box and then to place a new set of segments along the long edge of the box.

   Note: *Use (Apply and continue) when you need to continue in the same tool. If you want to use another tool, use (OK) to exit the caddy display.*

16. Leave the *Segments* at **2**. Use the spinner arrows to change the *Pinch* and *Slide* values and move the new edges towards the back of the armchair (which looks like a rectangle), as shown in Figure 4–83. You can drag their slider arrows in either direction viewing the changes dynamically. The values of *Pinch* and *Slide* are approximately **-30** and **-180** respectively. Press <Enter> each time if you enter a new value in the edit box, to see how it affects the lines. Click (OK) to accept the changes and exit the caddy display.

   - *Pinch* moves the lines in opposite directions, while *Slide* moves both of them in the X-direction.

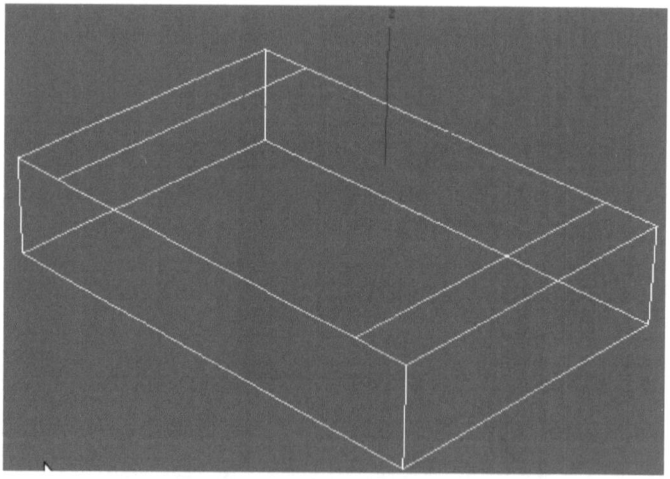

Figure 4–83

17. In the *Modeling* panel, click (Polygon), or press <4> to change the sub-object selection level from *Edge* to **Polygon**. Alternatively, select **Polygon** in the **Edit Poly** modifier in the *Modifier Stack*. Note that **Polygon** is highlighted in the *Edit Poly* modifier stack. Hold <Ctrl> and select the two polygons along the shorter side of the box, as shown in Figure 4–84.

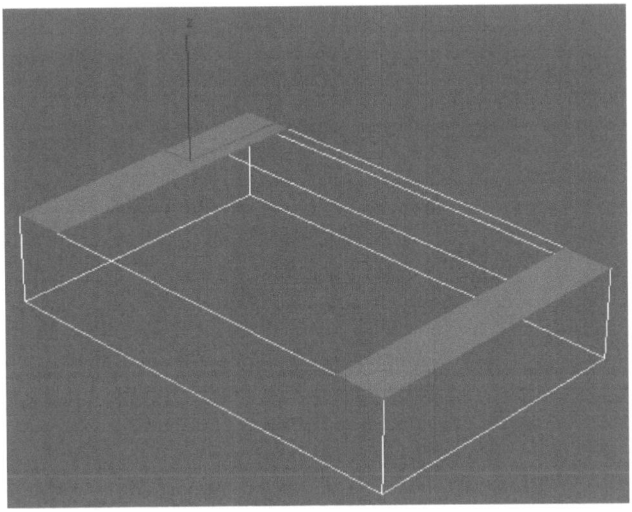

Figure 4–84

18. In the Modeling ribbon>*Polygons* panel, hold <Shift> and click (Extrude) to open the **Extrude Polygons** caddy display. Set *Height* to **0'2",** as shown in Figure 4–85. Then, click to apply the change and exit the caddy display.

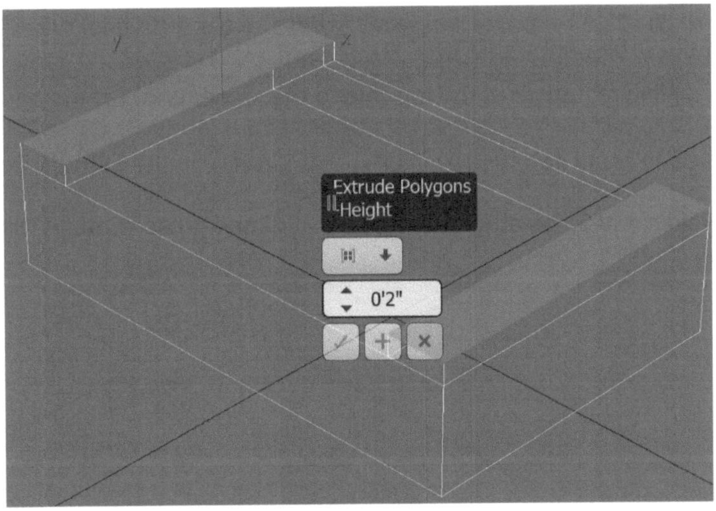

Figure 4–85

19. In the *Polygons* panel, hold <Shift> and click (Bevel) to open the **Bevel** caddy display. Set the following, as shown in Figure 4–86:
    - *Height*: **0'1"**
    - *Outline*: **-0'1"**

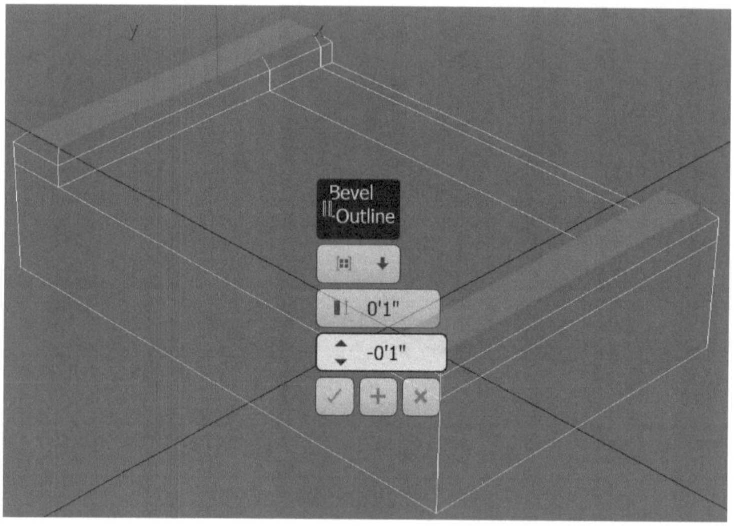

Figure 4–86

20. Click to apply and accept the changes.
21. In the Navigation toolbar, click (Orbit) or use <Alt> + middle mouse button to orbit in the **Perspective** viewport so that you can see the back of the armchair. Right-click in an empty space to exit the **Orbit** command.
22. Select the long, thin rectangle at the top (along the longer end) for the back of the chair. In the *Polygons* panel, hold <Shift> and click (Extrude). In the **Extrude Polygons** caddy display, set *Height* to **0'5"** (as shown in Figure 4–87) and press <Enter>. Click to exit the caddy display.

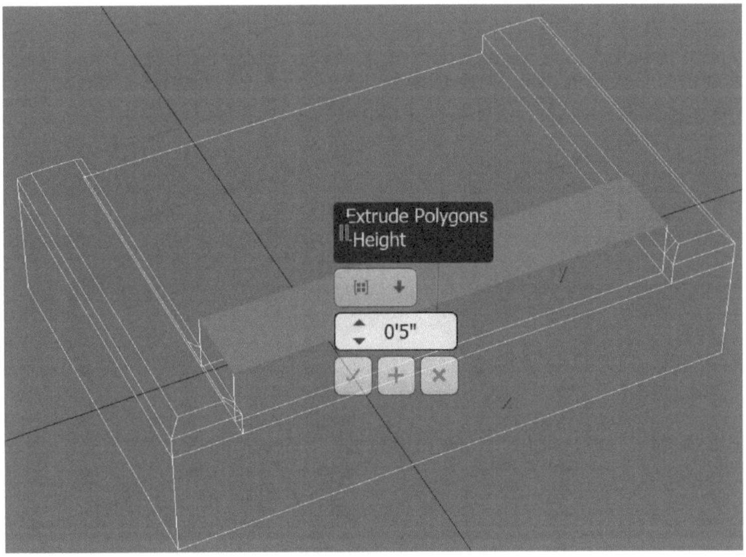

Figure 4–87

23. With the polygon still selected, in the *Polygons* panel, hold <Shift> and click  (Bevel) to access the Bevel caddy display. Bevel up the back of the chair, as shown in Figure 4–88. Do not to bevel too much or the edges will overlap. The values are approximately **0'7"** for *Height* and **-0'2"** for *Outline*. Click  to exit the caddy display.

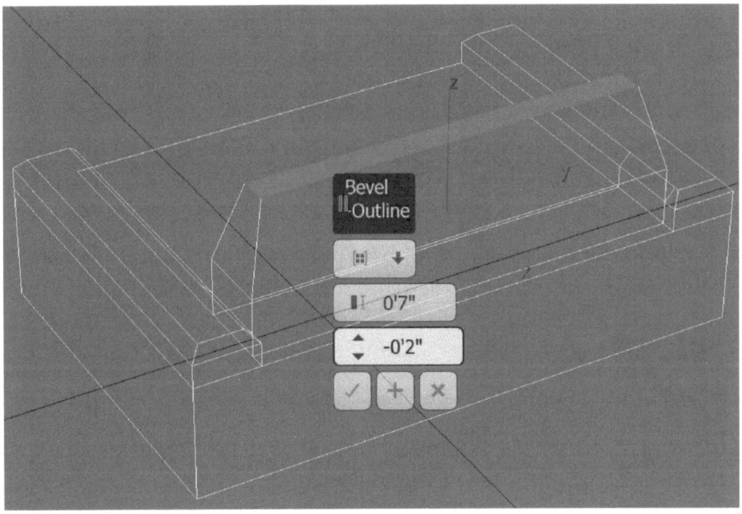

Figure 4–88

24. In the Main Toolbar, click (Select and Move) and move the selected polygon backwards along the X-axis, as shown in Figure 4–89 (It might be easier to move the polygon in the **Top** viewport). Orbit the viewport to view the design.

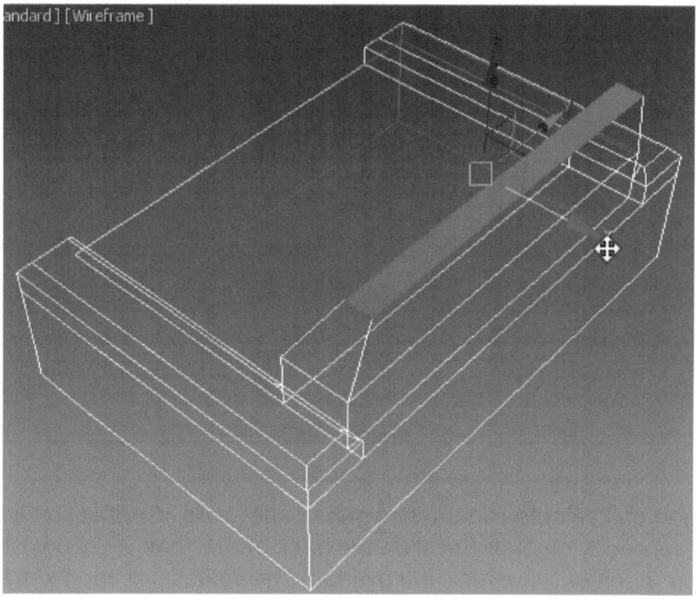

Figure 4–89

25. Press <2> to change to the **Edge** selection level. Alternatively, click (Edge) in the *Modeling* panel or select **Edge** in the *Modifier Stack*. If some edge(s) have already been selected, click in an empty area in the viewport to clear the selection.

26. In the *Modify Selection* panel, click (Ring Mode) at the bottom of the panel (Ensure that you select **Ring Mode** and not **Ring**). This enables to select a ring of edges when a single edge is selected.

27. Select one of the long edges at the top of the chair back. Because the **Ring Mode** is toggled on, all of the other edges along the first edge are selected and display in red.

28. In the *Modify Selection* panel, click (Ring Mode) again to toggle it off.

29. Orbit in the **Perspective** viewport for easy access for clicking the edges. In the *Modify Selection* panel, click (Shrink Ring) to clear one edge on either side of the ring. Alternatively, you can hold <Alt> and select one edge in front and one edge in the back to remove them from the selection. Only six edges should be selected, as shown in Figure 4–90.

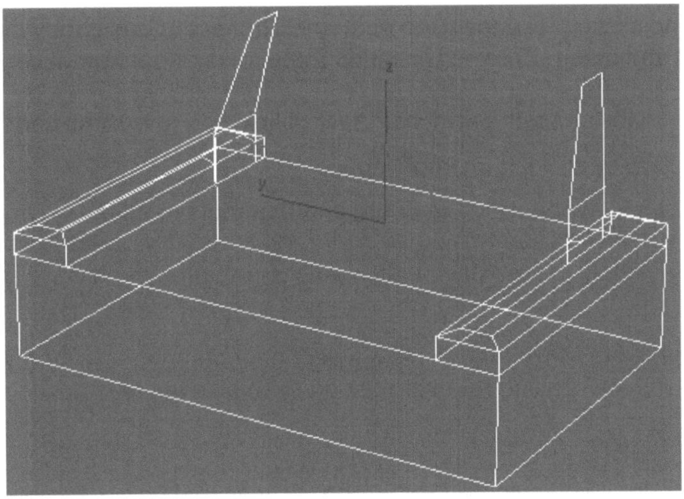

Figure 4–90

30. In the *Loops* panel, hold <Shift> and click (Connect). In the **Connect Edges** caddy display, reset the Pinch and Slide to 0, set the segments to **21** and press <Enter>. This adds 21 vertical segments, as shown in Figure 4–91. Click (OK) to exit the caddy display.

    Note: *Sometimes clicking does not work correctly when you need to continue in the same modifier. You can use and then reopen the modifier.*

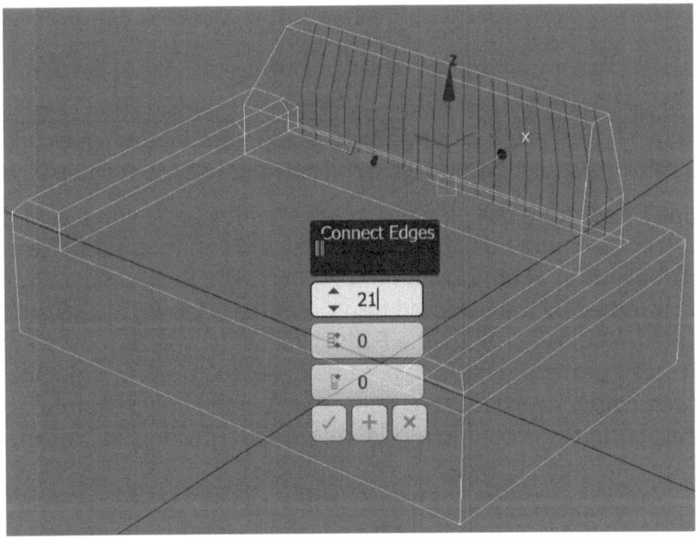

Figure 4–91

31. Hold <Shift> and click (Connect) to open the **Connect Edges** caddy display. Change the *Segments* to **3** and press <Enter>. This adds three rows of horizontal segments between two horizontal edges along the armchair back. Click to exit the caddy display.
32. Clear the selection by clicking in empty space.
33. Maximize the **Left** viewport. Use the **Zoom** and **Pan** tools to fill the viewport with the model.
34. In the Modeling ribbon, in the *Polygon Modeling* panel, click (Vertex) or press <1>.
35. Click (Select and Move) and using a selection rectangle, select only the middle vertices in the top row leaving four vertices on each side unselected, as shown in Figure 4–92.
    - Click (Undo) if you selected the wrong vertices and select again.

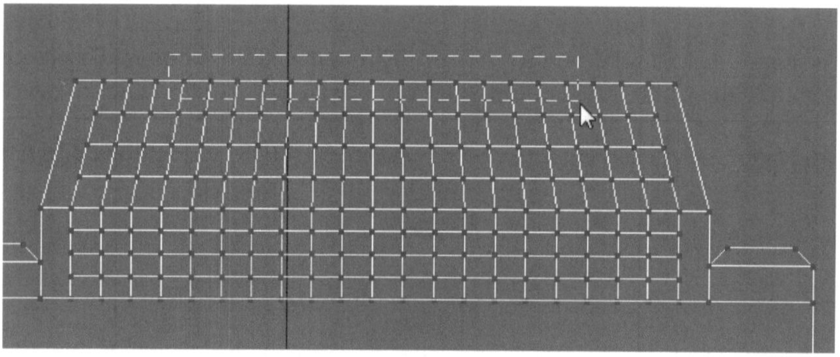

Figure 4–92

    - The row of vertices selected display in red.
36. Maximize to display all of the four viewports. In the **Perspective** view, orbit around and verify that you have selected the correct row (only the top most row) of vertices.
37. In the Command Panel, note that you are in the *Modify* panel with the *Modifier Stack* indicating that you are at the **Edit Poly>Vertex** level. Expand the *Soft Selection* rollout and select **Use Soft Selection**. A rainbow color displays. The Red/Yellow/Orange/Green vertices will be affected by the selected transform (e.g., **Move**), while the Dark Blue vertices remain unaffected. You can change the Falloff values to add or remove vertices from the affected/unaffected group. Using the spinners in *Falloff,* note that decreasing the falloff changes the cyan colored vertices to a dark blue. Set the *Falloff* similar to that shown in Figure 4–93. Note that the resulting model might differ from that shown.

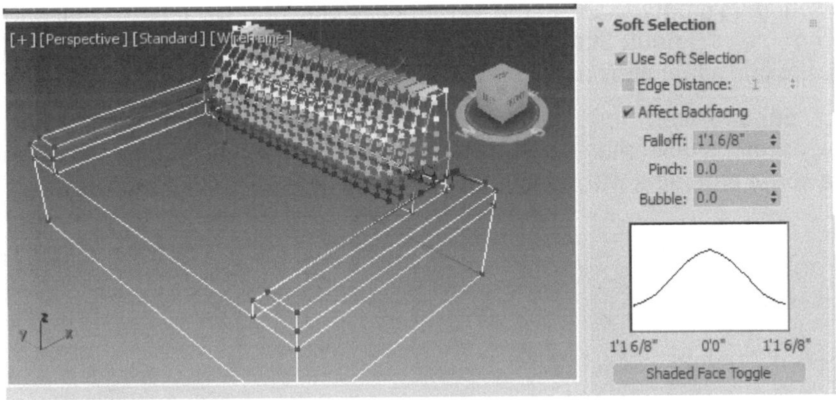

Figure 4–93

38. Use  (Select and Move) and move the vertices up by moving the gizmo along the Z-axis, to create the curved chair back, similar to that shown in Figure 4–94. Note that while moving the vertices, the dark blue vertices remain unaffected.

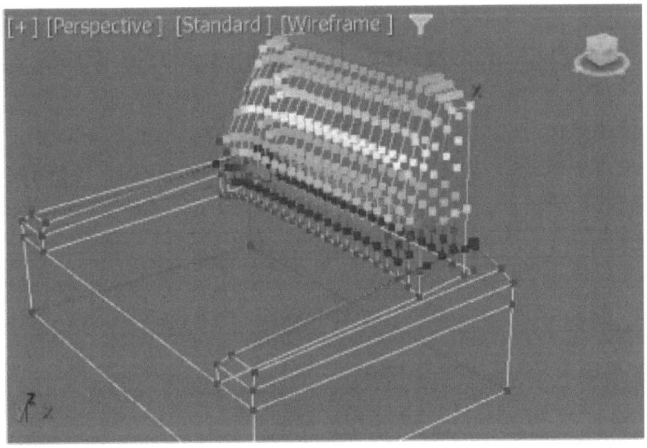

Figure 4–94

Note: *You can change the size of the Transform gizmo using <-> (hyphen) and <=> (equal sign).*

Hint: Assign Hotkey

You can assign a hotkey to interactively adjust the Soft selection falloff and pinch in the viewport. To do this, assign a hotkey to **Edit Soft Selection Mode**. Refer to **To edit a soft selection** in the Autodesk 3ds Max Help.

39. In the *Modifier Stack*, select **Edit Poly** to toggle off the sub-object selection.

40. Click anywhere in empty space in the **Perspective** viewport to clear the selection. Toggle from *Wireframe* to **Default Shading** mode and toggle on **Edged Faces** as well. The model displays similar to that shown in Figure 4–95.

41. Toggle off **Edged Faces** mode and display the model using the **Default Shading** mode. In the *Display Method* label menu, select **High Quality**, as shown in Figure 4–96. Note that there are some problems with smoothing and that the chair looks faceted.

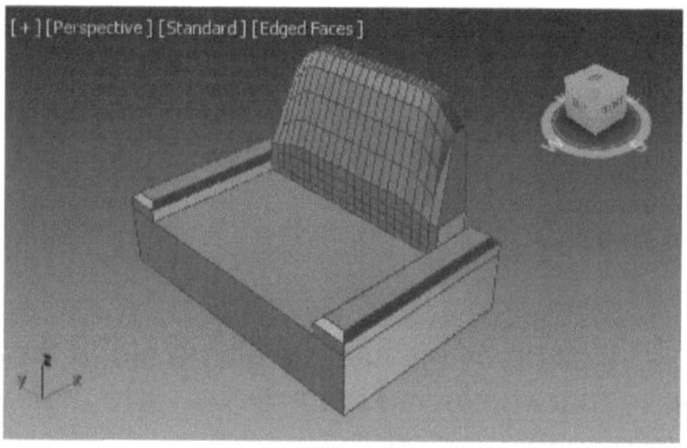

Figure 4–95

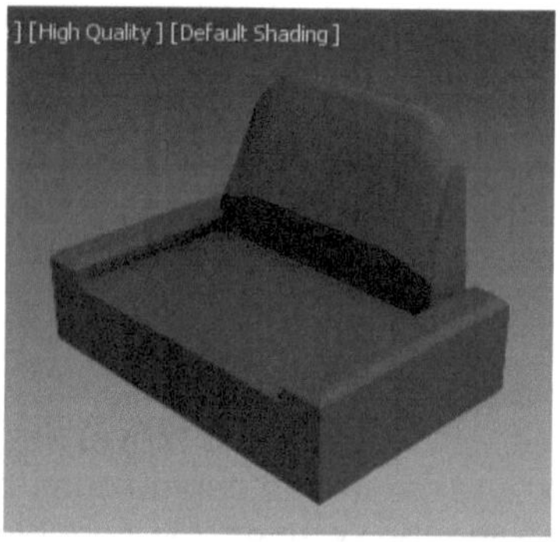

Figure 4–96

42. Select the chair and in the Modifier Stack or ribbon, select **Polygon** or press <4> to access the **Polygon** sub-object level.

43. In the Command Panel, scroll down and expand the *Polygon: Smoothing Groups* rollout. Press <Ctrl>+<A> to select all of the polygons, and click **Auto Smooth** in the rollout, as shown in Figure 4–97.

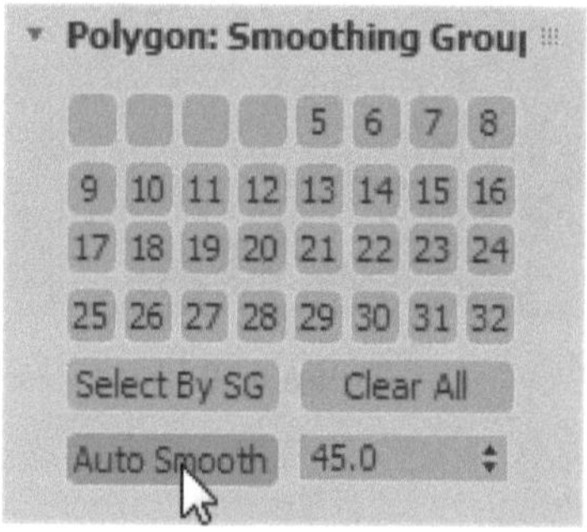

Figure 4–97

44. Click in empty space in the viewport to clear all of the selections. Note that the faceted problem has been fixed, as shown in Figure 4–98. Select Edit Poly to exit the Polygon selection mode.

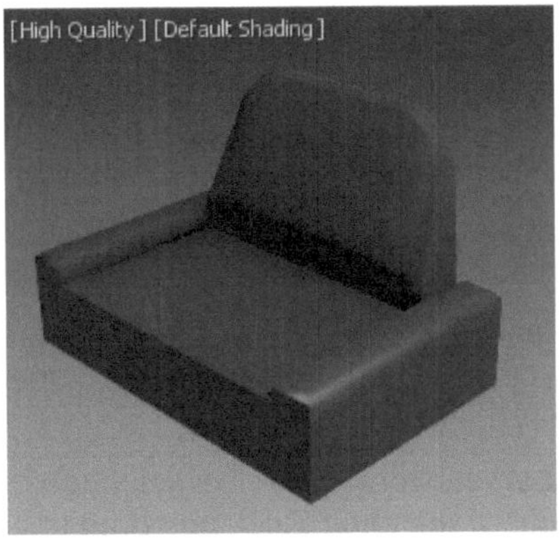

Figure 4–98

Task 2: Apply geometry smoothing.

In this task, you will add geometry smoothing using the **MSmooth** operation.

1. In the **Perspective** view, select the chair, if not already selected. In the Modeling ribbon, in the *Polygon Modeling* panel, click  (Polygon), or press <4>.
2. Press <Ctrl>+<A> to select all of the polygons. If they are completely displayed in red, press <F2> to only display the faces in a red outline (edges).
3. In the Modeling ribbon, in the *Subdivision* panel, hold <Shift> and click  (MSmooth). **Msmooth** changes the geometry by adding density to the mesh.

   Note: *You can add divisions to the seat portion of the chair for the* ***MSmooth*** *modifier to have a smoother effect. Use the* ***Slice*** *modifier to add divisions.*

4. Click  to exit the caddy display, and then save the file as **My Armchair.max**.

Task 3: (Optional) Use Freeform tools.

If you have time, you can soften the model using the **Freeform** tools.

1. In the *Polygon Modeling* tab, click  (Polygon), if it is not selected. Press <Ctrl>+<A> to select all of the polygons.

2. Select the *Freeform* tab, as shown in Figure 4–99.

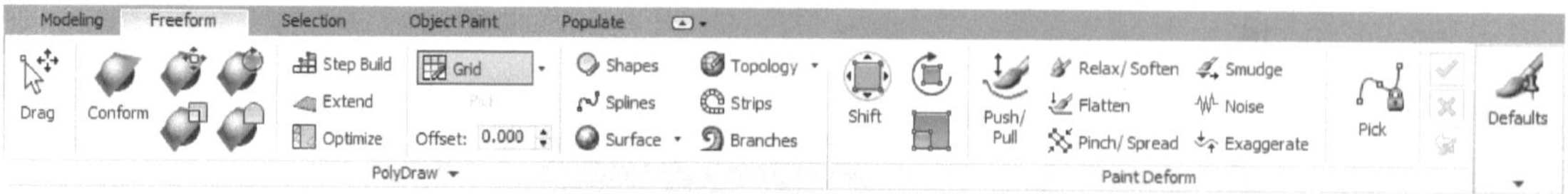

Figure 4–99

3. In the *Paint Deform* panel, click  (Shift).
4. When you start this command, a *Shift Options* panel displays on the screen. Also note that the cursor displays as two circles in the active viewport, specifying the brush size. Set the values shown in Figure 4–100.
5. Right-click to activate the **Left** viewport (with the selection on) and hover the cursor (two circles) near the back middle of the chair. Click and drag the cursor (2 circles) to stretch the back upward, as shown in Figure 4–101.

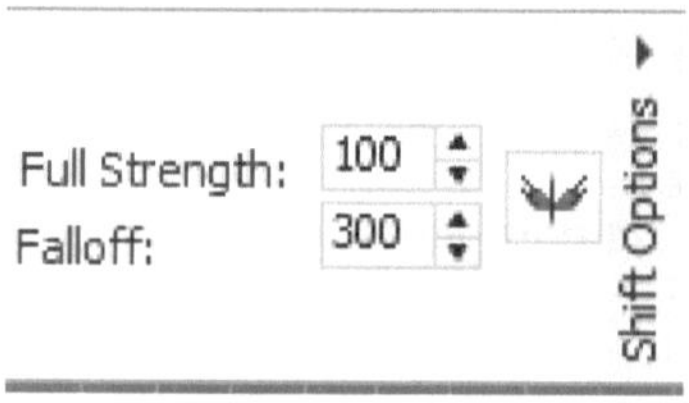

Figure 4–100

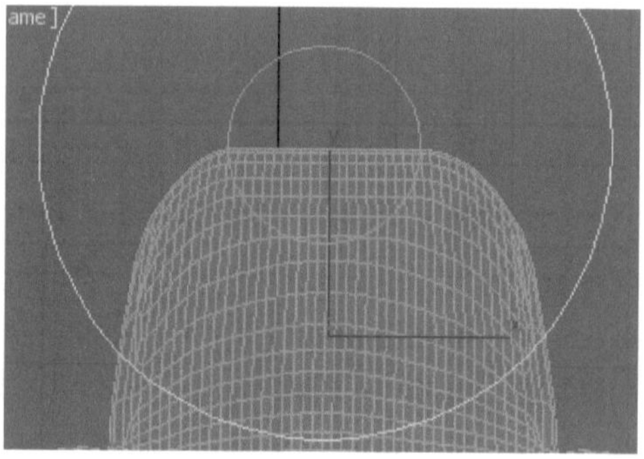

Figure 4–101

- In the Main Toolbar, click  (Undo) if you moved the wrong vertices.

Task 4: Optimize the mesh.

The shape of the chair has been softened. Now you need to reduce the polycount so the file can be used efficiently. The **ProOptimizer** modifier will achieve this.

1. Select the **Edit Poly** modifier in the stack to disable Sub-object mode. In the *Modifier* drop-down list, select **ProOptimizer**, as shown in Figure 4–102.
2. In the Command Panel, in the *Optimization Level* rollout, click **Calculate**. Change the *Vertex %* to **22**. Use the spinner to move it up or down as shown in Figure 4–103. Keep watching the viewport. The statistics display in the rollout.

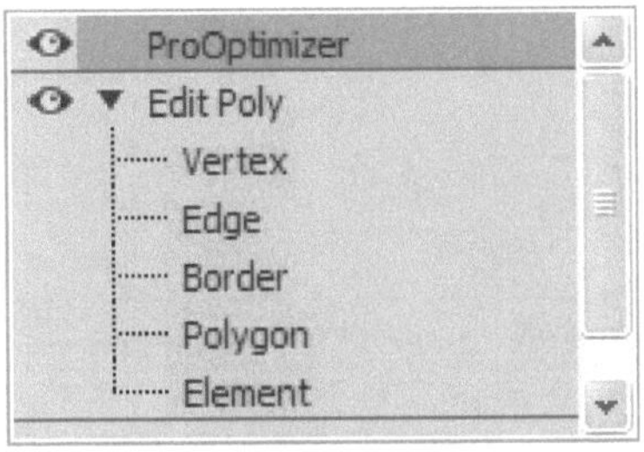

Figure 4–102

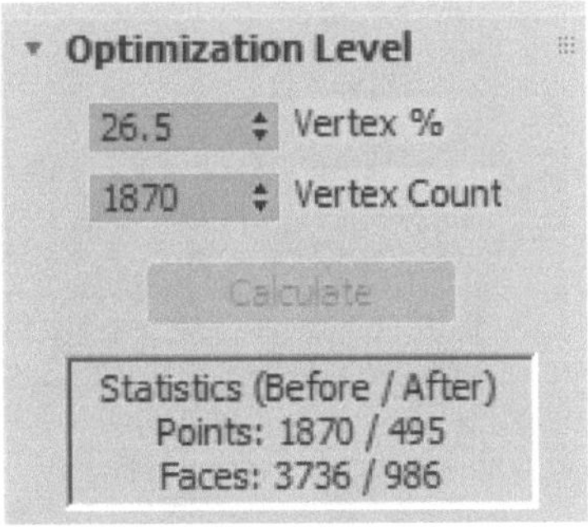

Figure 4–103

3. Save your work as **Myarmchair_softened.max**.

Hint: Using Optimize and MultiRes Modifiers

The **Optimize** and **MultiRes** modifiers are both accessed from the Modifier List. They can be used to reduce the number of vertices and polygons.

- **Optimize:** Reduces the model geometry, but does not critically change the appearance of the model.
- **MultiRes**: Reduces the model geometry and enables you to specify the exact vertex count to be used for reduction. This modifier should be used if you have to export the models to other 3D applications because it maintains the map channels.

End of practice

4.7 Statistics in Viewport

While Box modeling it is recommended to frequently review the status of your model. You can expand **File>Summary Info** to get details about the file. You can also **Show Statistics** directly in the viewport by, clicking **[+]>xView>Show Statistics**. The total number of polygons, vertices, and Frames Per Second display in the viewport (as shown in Figure 4–104) and are dependent on the options selected in the *Viewport Configuration* dialog box. Alternatively, press <7> to toggle the statistics display in the viewport on and off, in the active viewport.

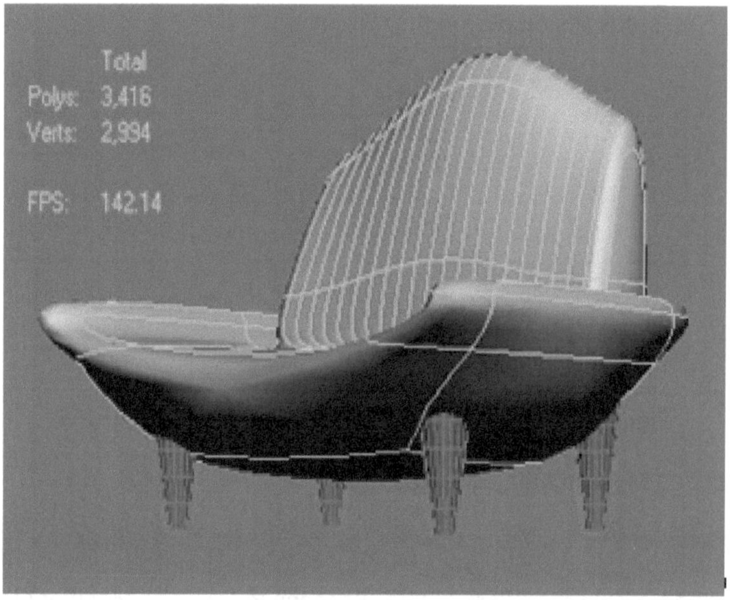

Figure 4–104

The statistics options can be controlled by selecting **Views>Viewport Configuration** and in the *Statistics* tab of the *Viewport Configuration* dialog box, as shown in Figure 4–105. Here, you can customize the display (e.g., **Polygon Count**, **Triangle Count**, **Edge Count**, **Vertex Count**, etc.).

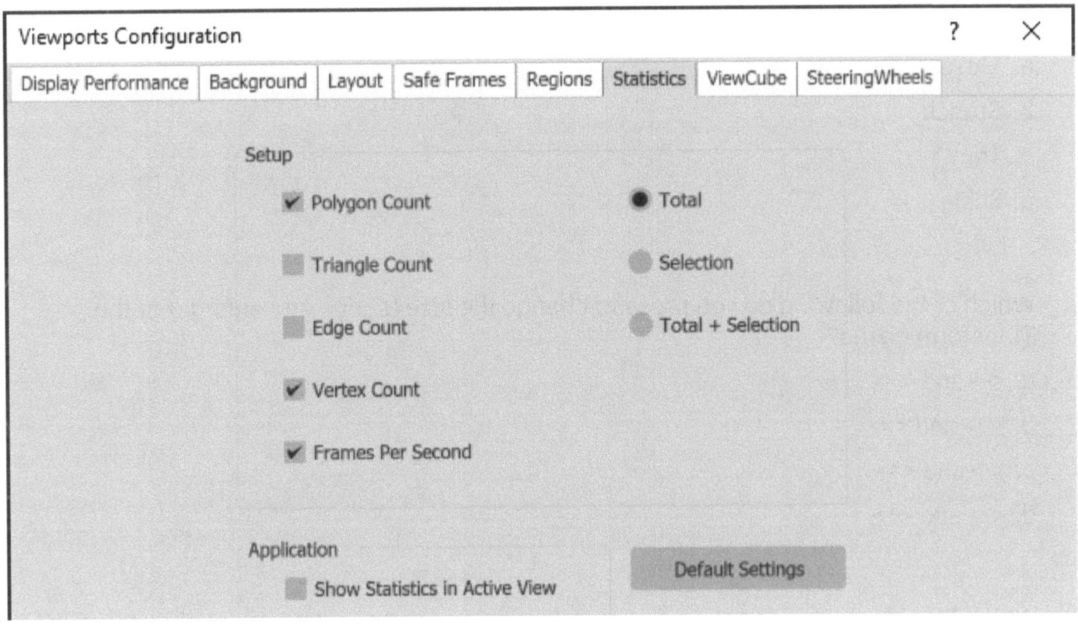

Figure 4–105

- You can toggle the view of the statistics on and off, as required.

Hint: Low Polygon Count

When designing, it is recommended to keep the **Polygon Count** or **Triangle Count** as low as possible to speed up rendering and viewport performance. If you are creating real time models, this impacts the interactive viewport navigation and playback speed.

Hint: Use Summary Info

Sometimes **Show Statistics** does not give correct results. To check the information, expand **File>Summary Info** and then compare the Vertex/Face/Poly count displayed there.

Chapter Review Questions

1. Which of the following are the **Transform** tools in the Autodesk 3ds Max software? (Select all that apply.)
   a. Move
   b. Stretch
   c. Trim
   d. Scale

2. Which of the following do you press to change the size (shrink and enlarge) of the Transform gizmo?
   a. <-> and <+>
   b. <+> and <=>
   c. <-> and <=>
   d. </> and <+>

3. Which **Transform center** option do you select if you want to rotate many objects, each around its own center?
   a.  (Pivot Point Center)
   b.  (Selection Center)
   c.  (Transform Coordinate Center)

4. Which clone option creates a one-directional link in which changes made to the original object affect the duplicate, but the modifiers applied to the duplicate do not affect the source object?
   a. Copy
   b. Instance
   c. Reference

5. In addition to the **Polygon Modeling** tools, the *Modeling* tab in the ribbon contains the commonly used tools from which panel of the Command Panel?

   a. Modify panel ()

   b. Hierarchy panel ()

   c. Display panel ()

   d. Utilities panel ()

6. Which key on the keyboard can be used as a shortcut to toggle the statistics display in the viewport on and off?

   a. <1>

   b. <3>

   c. <5>

   d. <7>

Command Summary

Button	Command	Location
	**Ribbon (Graphite Modeling Tools)**	• **Main Toolbar** • **Customize**>Show UI>Show Ribbon • **Interface Item Menu**: Ribbon
	**Select and Move**	• **Main Toolbar** • **Edit**>Move
	**Select and Place**	• **Main Toolbar** • **Edit**>Placement
	**Select and Rotate**	• **Main Toolbar** • **Edit**>Rotate
	**Select and Uniform Scale**	• **Main Toolbar:** *Scale* flyout • **Edit>**Scale
	**Select and Non-uniform Scale**	• **Main Toolbar:** *Scale* flyout
	**Select and Squash**	• **Main Toolbar:** *Scale* flyout
	**Use Pivot Point Center**	• **Main Toolbar:** *Transform Center* flyout
	**Use Selection Center**	• **Main Toolbar:** *Transform Center* flyout
	**Use Transform Coordinate Center**	• **Main Toolbar:** *Transform Center* flyout

Chapter 5

Modeling from 2D Objects

In addition to primitive objects or Polygon Modeling tools, models in the Autodesk® 3ds Max® software can also be created using 2D shapes that are subsequently used to generate 3D geometry. Tools such as Lathe, Extrude, and Sweep modifiers enable you to create 3D geometry from a 2D shape.

Learning Objectives

- Create 2D shapes, such as lines and closed shape objects.
- Revolve a profile around an axis using the Lathe modifier.
- Add and subtract shapes using the 2D Boolean operations.
- Add depth to a 2D shape to create 3D geometry using the Extrude modifier.
- Combine two or more 3D objects to generate a third 3D object by performing Boolean operations on their geometry.
- Modify shapes and geometry with precision using various snap modes.
- Create 3D geometry based on a 2D section that follows a series of spline segment paths using the Sweep modifier.

5.1 3D Modeling from 2D Objects

The Autodesk 3ds Max software enables you to create 2D shapes in the form of splines and NURBS, and using various modifiers, to create organic smooth curved surfaces from the shapes. Shapes can be created using  (Shapes) in the Command Panel's *Create* panel (), as shown in Figure 5–1. The splines consist of:

- Basic shapes (Splines): **Line**, **Rectangle**, **Ellipse**, etc.
- Extended Splines: **WRectangle**, **Channel**, **Angle**, etc.

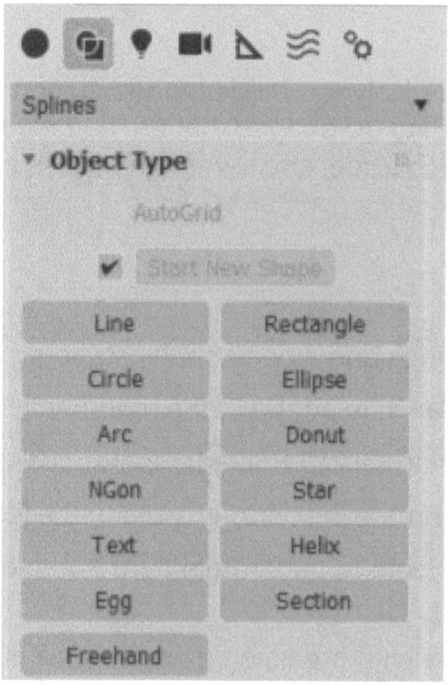

Figure 5–1

The software enables you to draw lines and curves in a freeform interactive manner by clicking points in the viewport.

- Lines can be drawn to create three kinds of shapes: open, closed, and self-intersecting. You cannot draw a 2D line that forks or branches.
- Closed shapes can also be created using other shape object types, such as Rectangle, Ellipse, Ngon, or Text.
- Closed shapes and open shapes are both used in creating 3D objects. Modifiers, such as **Extrude**, **Lathe**, and **Surface**, can be used to build 3D surfaces based on 2D shapes.
- Open shapes and self-intersecting shapes can be extruded to create 3D objects, but these objects have mixed face normals. Some faces do not render and might not be visible in the viewport.

- The **Edit Spline** modifier: Enables you to apply edits such as trim, extend, fillet, and chamfer to 2D objects.
- The **Extrude** modifier: Enables you to create 3D objects by extruding closed shapes. The outside of these objects is visible and renderable from all sides. All face normals point away from the center of the object.
- The **Lathe** modifier: Enables you to create 3D objects by using on open shapes where a profile is revolved.
- Transform Type-In: Enables you to achieve precision using snaps and vertices, which can be shifted after placement.

The **Line** tool has two basic drawing techniques:

Method 1

You can draw straight line segments by clicking and moving the cursor repeatedly. This method does not create any curves at first. All of the vertices created are Corner type. After clicking to set the vertices, you select the line vertices individually or in sets and then change their type from Corner to **Bezier** or **Smooth** to create curves.

Hint: Preventing Self-intersecting Shapes

If you draw too quickly when drawing using Method 1, the program might translate your motions into press and drag, and self-intersecting shapes can be inadvertently drawn. To prevent this, in the *Create* panel's *Creation Method* rollout, change the drag type to **Corner**. In doing so, you are not able to drag curves interactively.

Method 2

Draw curves directly by clicking, holding, and dragging to create **Bezier** vertices rather than **Corner** vertices. This is a faster method but harder to control, since you are defining the curve on both sides of the vertex in a single move. Holding <Alt> while dragging enables you to define the curve on the leading side of the vertex, introducing an angle between the vertex handles. If both the *Initial Type* and *Drag Type* have been set to **Corner** in the Creation Method rollout, in the **Line** tool, you cannot create **Bezier** vertices by clicking, holding, and dragging.

- Using either method, these curved segments are created out of smaller straight line segments. Increasing the segments makes the curve smoother. The *Steps* value in the *Interpolation* rollout sets the number of segments.
- Drawing while holding <Shift> also draws straight lines and perpendicular lines.
- Press <Backspace> to undo the last drawn vertex in a line.

Practice 5a
Draw Lines

Practice Objectives

- Create an open and closed 2D shape.
- Move the location of a vertex and change the shape of a curve.

In this practice, you will create, open, and close 2D shapes using the **Line** command. You will then move the location of a vertex and change the shape of a curve using the Bezier handles. Finally, you will create a candlestick model using the 2D shapes drawn.

You must set the paths to locate the External files and XREFs used in the practice. If you have not done this already, return to Chapter 1 and complete Task 1 to Task 3 in *Practice 1a: Organize Folders and Work with the Interface*. You only have to set the user paths once.

Task 1: Draw 2D lines.

1. Reset the scene.
2. Maximize the **Front** viewport from the layout overlay using <Shift> and <Win>, if you are already in another maximized viewport. If you are maximizing from the four viewport screen, use  (Maximize Viewport) or press <Alt>+<W>.
3. Press <G> to hide the grid, if required.
4. In the Command Panel>*Create* panel (), click  (Shapes). Note that **Splines** is set by default in the list, as shown in Figure 5–2.

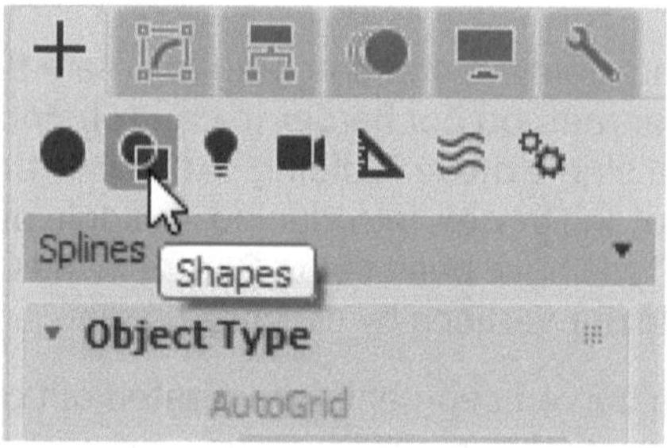

Figure 5–2

5. In the *Object Type* rollout, click **Line**.

6. In the **Front** viewport, draw a saw-tooth pattern line, as shown in Figure 5–3. Click to set the first point, move the cursor to the next location of the point and click to place the second point. The first line displays. Continue the pattern. Right-click to end, once you have placed the last line. An open shape is created.

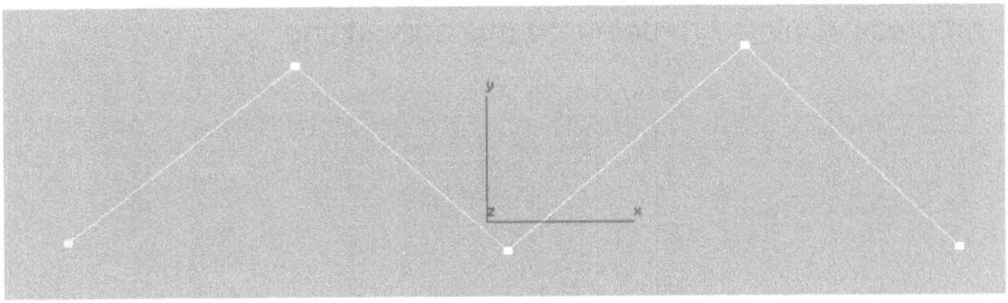

Figure 5–3

7. With the line still selected, press <Delete> to delete the saw-tooth pattern line.
8. Still in the **Line** command, repeat the drawing process to create a closed shape, similar to that shown in Figure 5–4. Click to set each point and for the last point, click on the starting point (yellow vertex) to close the shape. In the *Spline* dialog box, click **Yes** to close the shape. Right-click in the empty space to exit the command. Do not delete this shape.

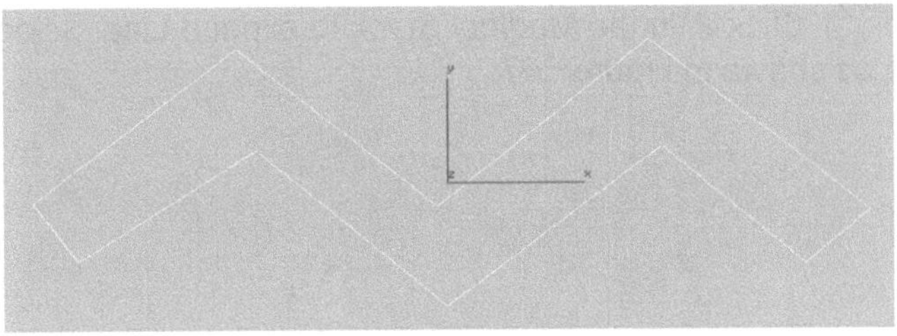

Figure 5–4

9. To draw curved lines, in the *Object Type* rollout, click **Line** again. In the *Creation Method* rollout, set the *Drag Type* to **Bezier**, as shown in Figure 5–5.

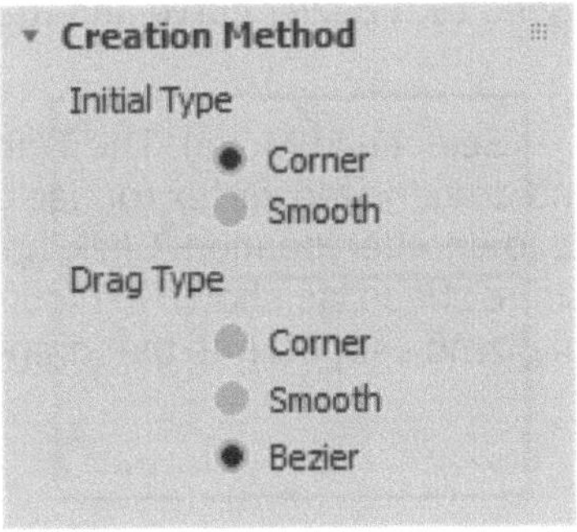

Figure 5–5

10. Click to set the first point. Move the cursor to the location of the second point, then click, hold, and drag to create a Bezier curve running through the second point. Each time you click, hold, and drag, the curve extends through the new point. This draws a curve, but it is difficult to control, since dragging affects the curve on both sides of the point at the same time. Draw a curved line similar to the one shown in Figure 5–6. Right-click to exit the command and press <Delete> to delete to this curved line.

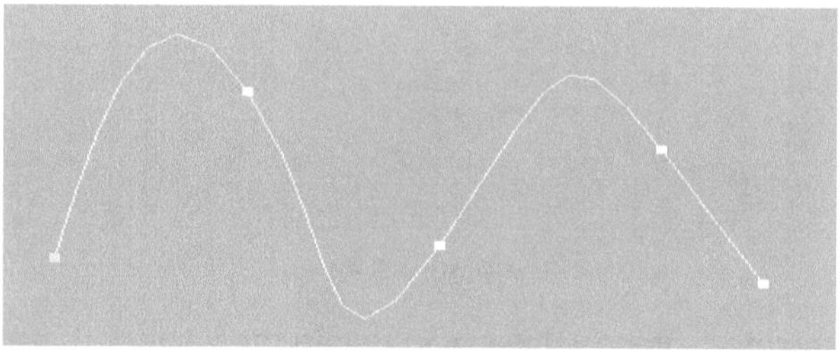

Figure 5–6

11. Right-click in empty space to exit the **Line** command.
12. Select the closed shape that was previously created. In the Command Panel, select the *Modify* panel ( ). Click ▶ in the *Modifier Stack* to expand **Line**. Select **Vertex** at the sub-object level, as shown in Figure 5–7.

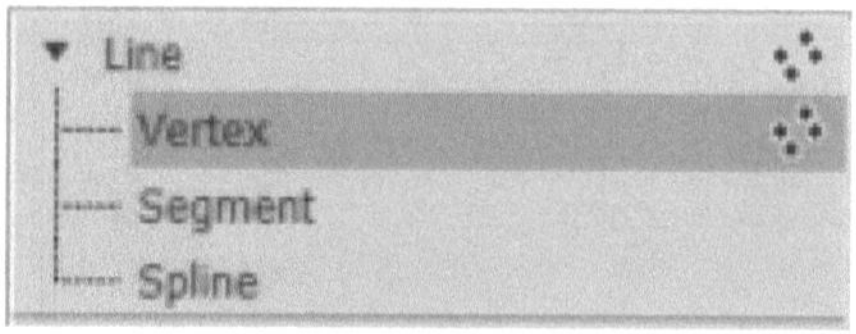

Figure 5–7

13. In the viewport, select the vertex at the top left of the saw tooth pattern. The selected vertex displays in red. Right-click and select **Bezier** in the tools 1 quadrant of the quad menu. Note that the vertex corner is replaced by a Bezier curve and that the Bezier handles display.
14. In the Main Toolbar, click (Select and Move). The Transform gizmo displays with the bezier handles. Click, hold, and drag the red vertex (or use the yellow plane on the interior of the gizmo) to move the curve to another location. Click, hold, and drag either handle end (green point) to modify the curve shape, as shown in Figure 5–8. The handle movement is constrained by the Transform gizmo usage. Note that dragging one handle moves the other handle simultaneously.

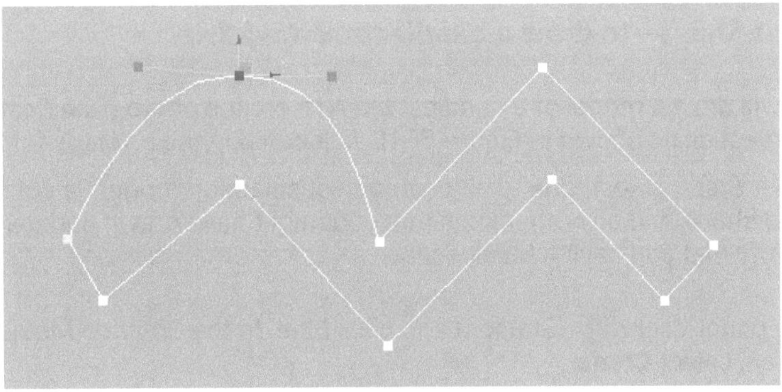

Figure 5–8

Hint: Transform Gizmo Size

You can press <-> (hyphen) and <=> (equal sign) to decrease or increase the size of the Transform gizmo. If the Transform gizmo handles extend beyond the vertex handles, you might have trouble moving the vertex handles.

15. Right-click on the red vertex and select **Bezier Corner**. This enables you to break the continuity of the curve to manipulate the handles on one side of the curve separately from the other, as shown in Figure 5–9. Right-click on the red vertex and select **Reset Tangents** to return the original curve shape. To return to **Bezier**, right-click on the red vertex and select **Bezier** again in the quad menu.
    - In the Bezier Corner option, moving the Transform gizmo in one axis constrains the movement of the bezier handles to that axis. To have the handles move freely, select the yellow square of the gizmo to have movement in the X and Y axes. This can also be controlled using the Axis Constraints toolbar.

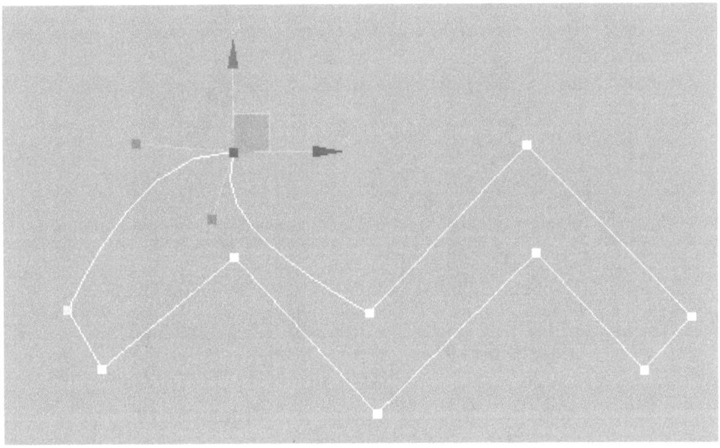

Figure 5–9

Task 2: Use 2D Shapes to draw a candlestick model.

In this task, you will draw a model of a candlestick. A reference photo (**Candlestick_pewter.jpg**) of an actual candlestick as shown in Figure 5–10, is located in the ...*Maps* folder.

1. In the *Modifier Stack*, select **Line** to exit sub-object selection mode. Select the previously drawn closed shape and any other lines that you might have drawn and delete them using <Delete>. Verify that you have a blank scene.
2. In the *Create* panel, click  (Shapes) and click **Line**. In the *Creation Method* rollout, in the *Drag Type* area, select **Corner**.
3. Start at the bottom right (the yellow vertex indicates the start point) and click to place the first line vertex, as shown in Figure 5–11. Hold <Shift>, move the cursor left, and click to draw the base of the candlestick of approximate length, similar to that shown in Figure 5–11. (Holding <Shift> creates straight lines.) Still holding <Shift>, move the cursor up to draw the long straight vertical line segment, and then click to place the vertex. Release <Shift> and continue clicking and drawing in a clockwise direction.
4. Continue to place approximately 16 points and close the shape by clicking over the first point. Click **Yes** and then right-click to exit the **Line** command. The shape should look similar to the one shown in Figure 5–11. Press <Backspace> to undo the points if you make a mistake.

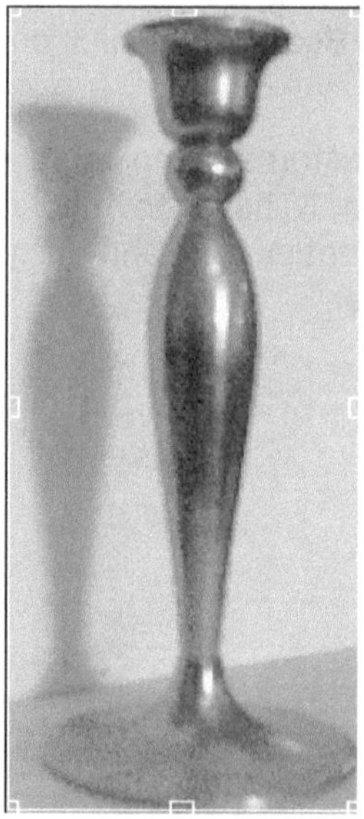

Figure 5–10

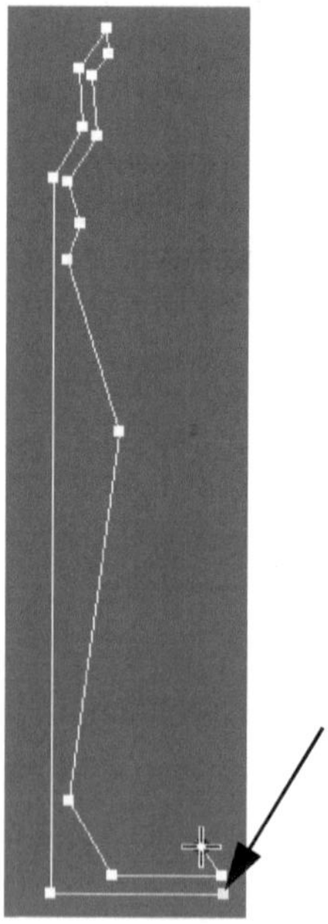

Figure 5–11

5. With the shape selected, in the *Modify* panel (), in the *Modifier Stack*, expand **Line** and select the **Vertex** sub-object level. Hold <Ctrl> and select the four vertices, as shown in Figure 5–12. Note that the vertices turn red once you select them.

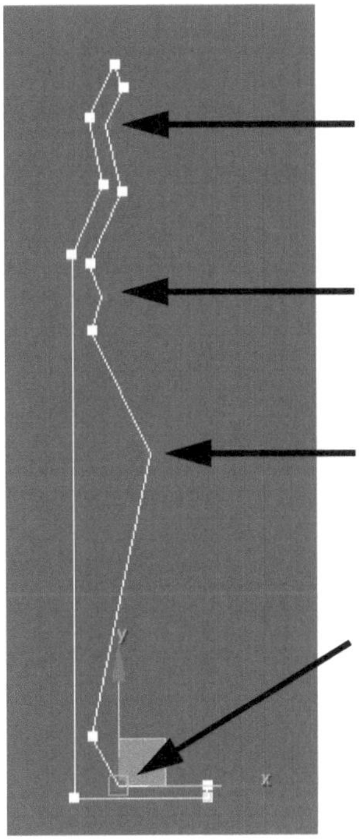

Figure 5–12

6. Right-click and select **Bezier** in the quad menu. This changes all the four vertices to **Bezier** vertices with handles.

7. Adjust the handles of each vertex using  (Select and Move) to obtain a shape similar to that shown in Figure 5–13. Move the vertices and handles individually to get a shape similar to that shown in Figure 5–14.

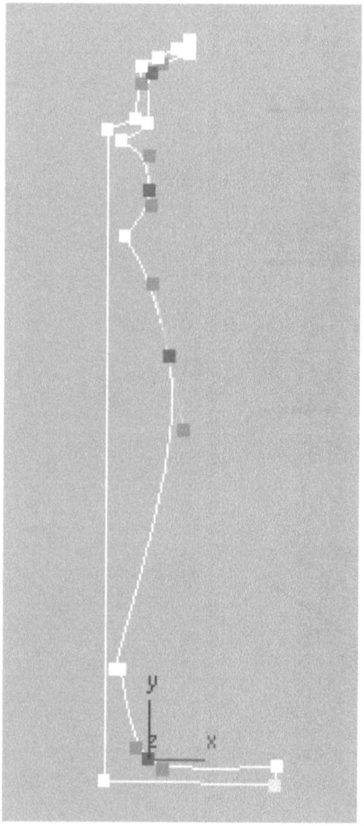

Figure 5–13

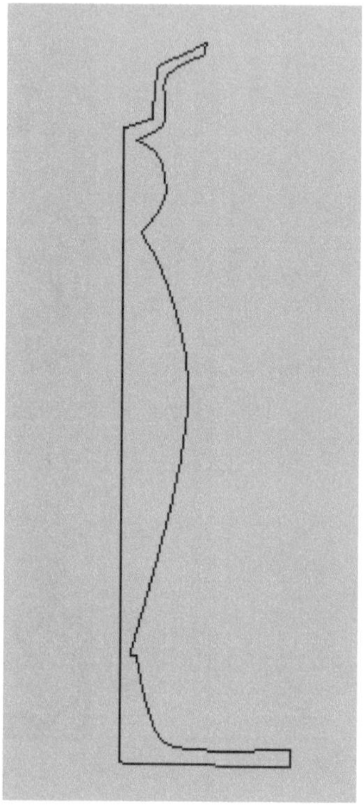

Figure 5–14

8. After completing the shape, click on **Line** in the *Modifier Stack* to exit the sub-object level and click anywhere in the viewport to clear the selection.
9. Save your work as **MyCandlestickProfile.max**.

End of practice

5.2 The Lathe Modifier

The **Lathe** modifier enables you to create a 3D object by revolving a profile (2D shape) around an axis. It can be accessed in the *Modifier List*, in the *Modify* panel () in the Command Panel.

How To: Create a 3D Object Using the Lathe Modifier

1. Select a profile (usually a line object).
2. Apply a **Lathe** Modifier.
3. Adjust the axis of revolution.
4. Adjust the alignment of the axis with the profile.

Practice 5b
Create a Candlestick

Practice Objective

- Revolve a 2D shape around its axis.

In this practice, you will resolve a 2D shape around its axis, using the **Lathe** modifier to create the solid geometry for the candlestick.

You must set the paths to locate the External files and XREFs used in the practice. If you have not done this already, return to Chapter 1 and complete Task 1 to Task 3 in *Practice 1a: Organize Folders and Work with the Interface*. You only have to set the user paths once.

1. Open **Candlestick_Profile.max.** A line profile of the candlestick holder is displayed in the viewports.
2. Maximize the **Front** viewport.
3. Select the line profile. In the *Modify* panel (), in the *Modifier Stack*, verify that the **Line** is highlighted and no sub-object level is highlighted.
4. In the *Modifier List*, select **Lathe**. The profile revolves around a center point, but the alignment is off, as shown in Figure 5–15.
    - Sometimes, lathed objects display inside-out. If something looks wrong with your candlestick, use the **Flip Normals** option in the Parameters rollout.
5. In the *Parameters* rollout, in the *Align* area, click **Min**. The candlestick should now display as shown in Figure 5–16.

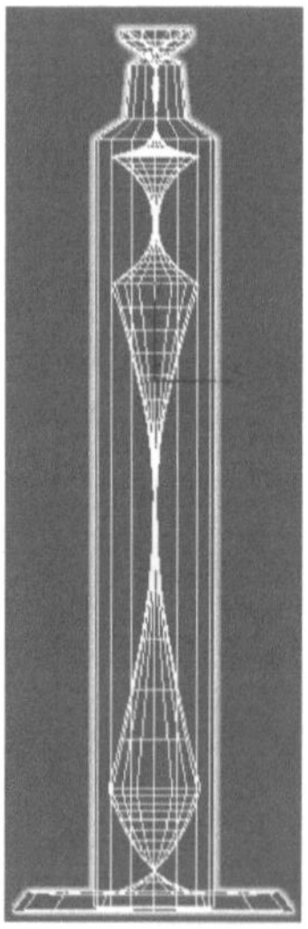

Figure 5–15

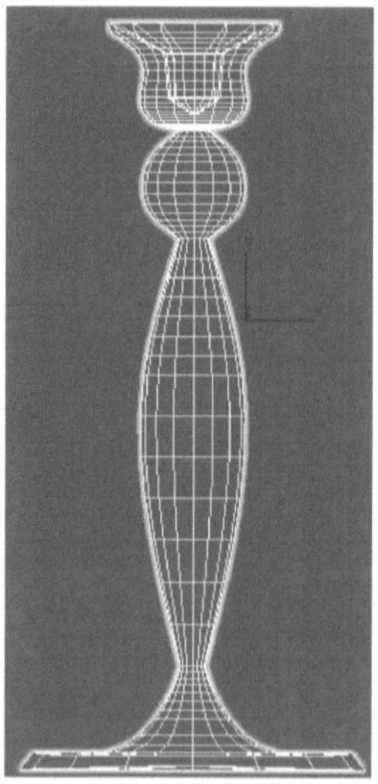

Figure 5–16

6. In the *Modifier Stack*, expand **Lathe** and select **Axis**. Using (Select and Move), move the X-axis to display the candlestick in various positions.

7. In the Main Toolbar, click (Undo) or press <Ctrl>+<Z> to undo the axis moves.

8. Select **Lathe** (highlighted) to exit the Sub-object mode. Maximize the viewport to display the four viewports.

9. Assign a color to the geometry by selecting the candlestick first, selecting the color swatch next to the **Line** name (Line06), and selecting a color in the *Object Color* dialog box.

10. In the **Perspective** viewport, use (Orbit) and examine the geometry, as shown in Figure 5–17.

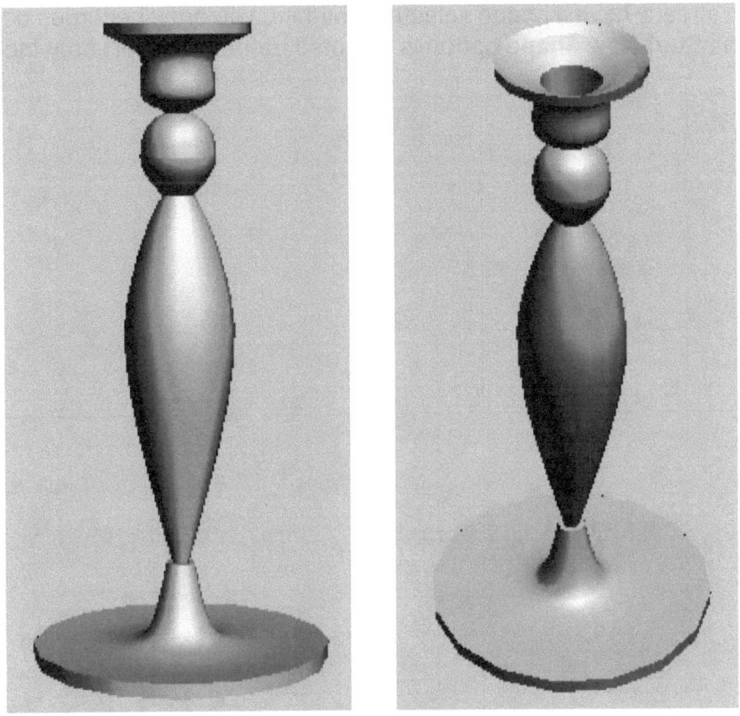

Figure 5–17

11. Save your work as **MyCandlestick.max**.

End of practice

5.3 2D Booleans

2D Boolean operations enable you to create shapes by combining drawn lines and shapes. Using the **Edit Spline** modifier, you can add or subtract shapes at the sub-object level. The **Edit Spline** modifier enables you to convert a shape to an editable spline

- 2D Boolean operations (Union, Subtraction, Intersection) are available in the **Spline** sub-object level, in the *Geometry parameters* rollout, as shown in Figure 5–18.
- Before using a boolean operation, all shapes that are to be combined must be part of a single shape. The **Attach** and **Attach Mult.** options (Spline sub-object level, *Geometry parameters* rollout) enable you to combine multiple shapes into a single shape.
- When drawing shapes, if you clear the **Start New Shape** option in the *Object Type* rollout (as shown in Figure 5–19), all of the subsequent shapes that you create become part of a single shape. If you already have a shape selected, anything you draw becomes part of that shape. By default, the **Start New Shape** option is selected before you start drawing any shapes.

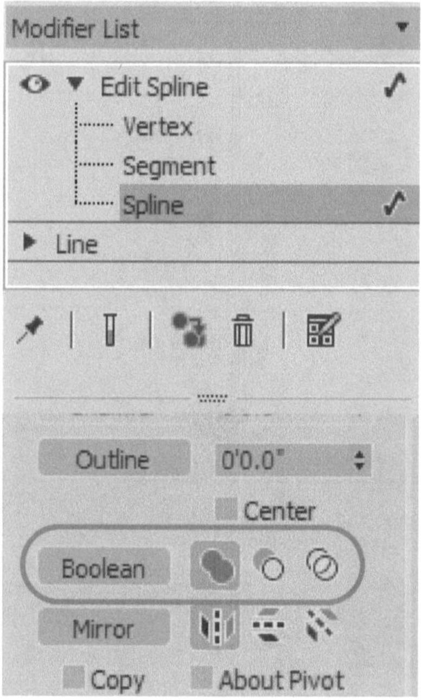

Figure 5–18

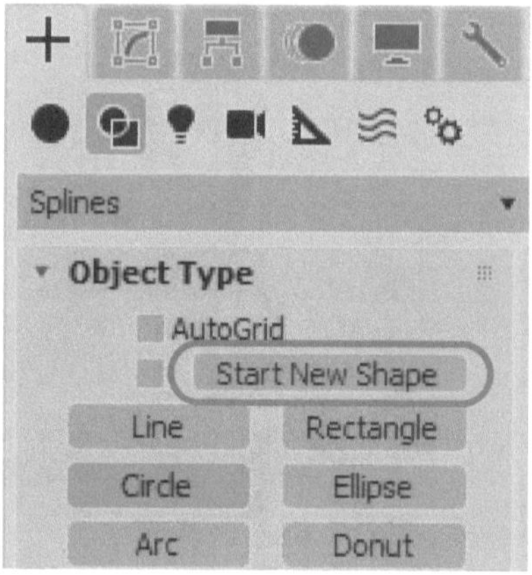

Figure 5–19

- No history is associated with 2D Boolean operations and you are not able to retrieve the various Boolean components after saving.

Practice 5c
2D Booleans

Practice Objective

- Modify a shape using 2D Booleans.

In this practice, you will add and subtract rectangles using 2D Booleans to change the shape of the profile for the candlestick.

You must set the paths to locate the External files and XREFs used in the practice. If you have not done this already, return to Chapter 1 and complete Task 1 to Task 3 in *Practice 1a: Organize Folders and Work with the Interface*. You only have to set the user paths once.

Task 1: Create and attach shapes.

1. Open **Candlestick.max**.
2. Maximize the **Front** viewport and zoom to the extents of the objects.
3. Select the candlestick. In the *Modify* panel ( ), in the *Modifier Stack*, click (eye) next to the **Lathe** to toggle the **Lathe** modifier off. The line profile and the **Lathe** axis displays in the viewport.
4. In the *Create* panel ( ), click (Shapes).
5. Click **Rectangle**. Draw four small rectangles intersecting the right edge of the profile, similar to that shown in Figure 5–20.

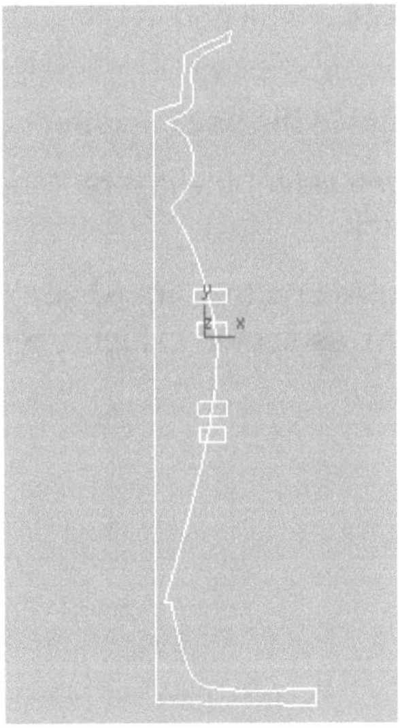

Figure 5–20

6. Right-click to cancel the command and click anywhere in the blank space to clear the selection.
7. Select the candlestick profile. Open the *Modify* panel ( ), and in the *Modifier Stack*, select **Line**.
8. Scroll down and in the *Geometry* rollout, click **Attach Mult**.
9. In the *Attach Multiple* dialog box, click (Display Shapes) to activate it, if not already active. Select all of the four rectangles (using <Ctrl>) and click **Attach**. The dialog box closes and all of the rectangles become part of the candlestick profile spline object.

Task 2: Apply Boolean operations.

1. In the *Modifier Stack*, select the **Spline** sub-object in the **Line** object and select the candlestick profile in the viewport. The selected profile displays in red and the rectangles remain white (unselected).
2. In the *Geometry* rollout, scroll down and click **Boolean** to activate it. Verify that (Union) has a blue background, indicating that it is already active (by default).
3. In the viewport, hover the cursor over the topmost rectangle, and note that the cursor displays as a Union cursor ( ). Select the topmost rectangle and then select the second rectangle. Note that in each case, the profile is extended to the right to include part of the rectangle, and the inner part of the rectangle is discarded. Also note that the parts of both the rectangles turn red, indicating that they are part of the profile.
4. In the Command Panel, with **Boolean** still active, click (Subtraction) to activate it. Hover the cursor over the third rectangle to display the cursor as a Subtraction cursor ( ).
5. Select the third rectangle and then select the last rectangle. For these shapes, the rectangle is subtracted from the candlestick.
   - Note that the top two rectangles create a rim (Union), and the bottom two create an inscribed groove (Subtraction), as shown in Figure 5–21.

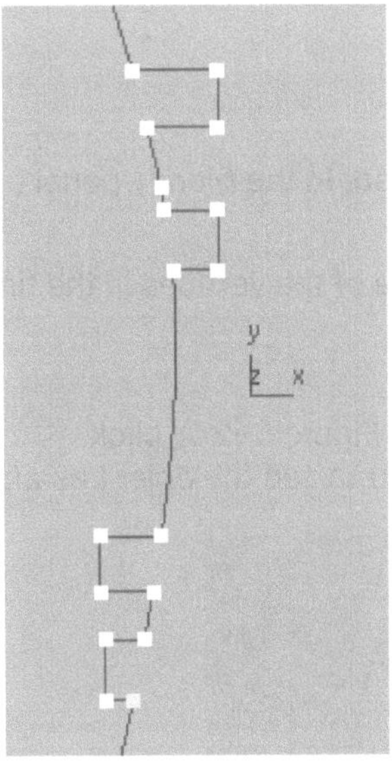

Figure 5–21

6. In the Modifier Stack, select **Lathe**, and then click (grayed out eye) next to **Lathe** to toggle it on.
7. Press <Alt>+<W> to return to four viewports. Activate the **Perspective** viewport and review the results in **Default Shading** display mode. The two rims and two grooves are created in the candle stick, as shown in Figure 5–22.

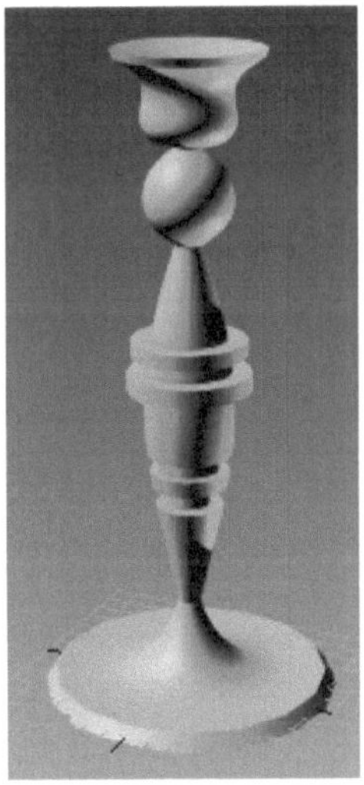

Figure 5–22

8. Save your work as **MyCandlestick01.max**.

Task 3: Modify shapes.

1. Select the candlestick, if required. In the *Modify* panel ( ), select **Line** and **Vertex** sub-objects.
2. In the **Front** viewport, select one of the vertices in the first rim that you created, as shown in Figure 5–23.
3. In the *Modifier Stack* (shown in Figure 5–24), click (Show end result on/off toggle) to activate it. This tool enables you to see the object as an end product.

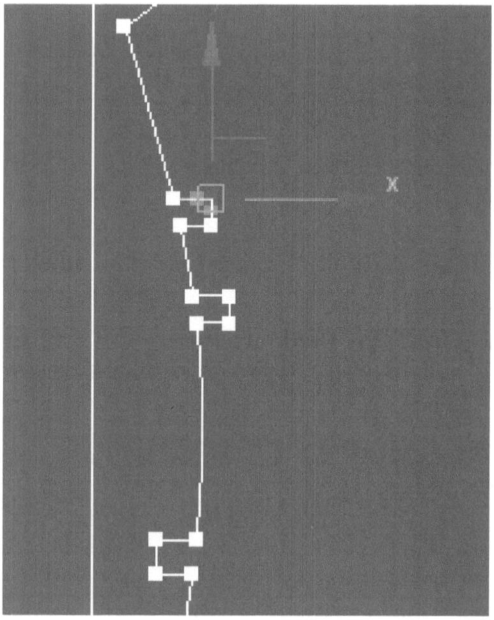

Figure 5–23

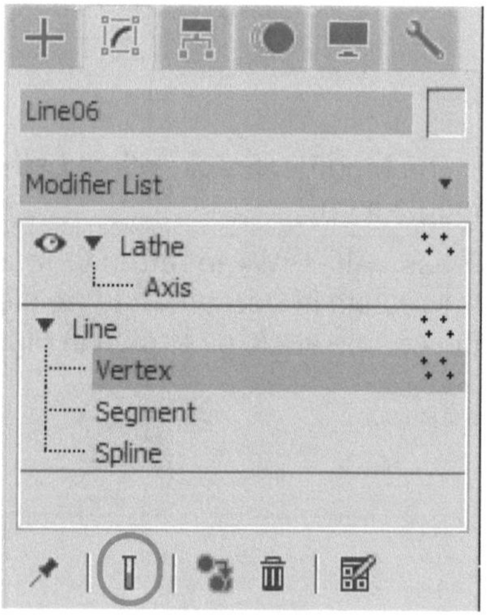

Figure 5–24

4. Move the selected vertex in the **Front** viewport and note the change in the **Perspective** viewport. You are now sculpting the candlestick in real time, as shown in Figure 5–25.

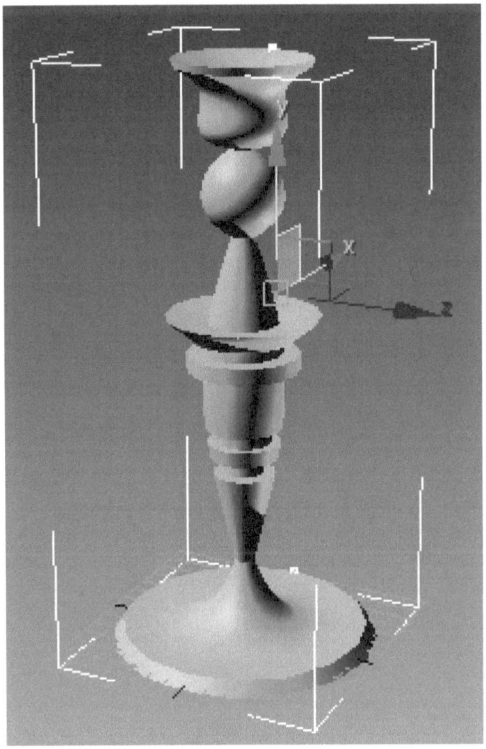

Figure 5–25

5. In the *Modifier Stack*, select **Line** to exit the sub-object level.
6. Save your work as **MyCandlestick01.max**.

End of practice

5.4 The Extrude Modifier

The **Extrude** modifier enables you to add depth to a 2D shape to create 3D geometry. As with other modifiers, the **Extrude** modifier is available in the *Modifier List*, in the Command Panel's *Modify* panel (), as shown in Figure 5–26.

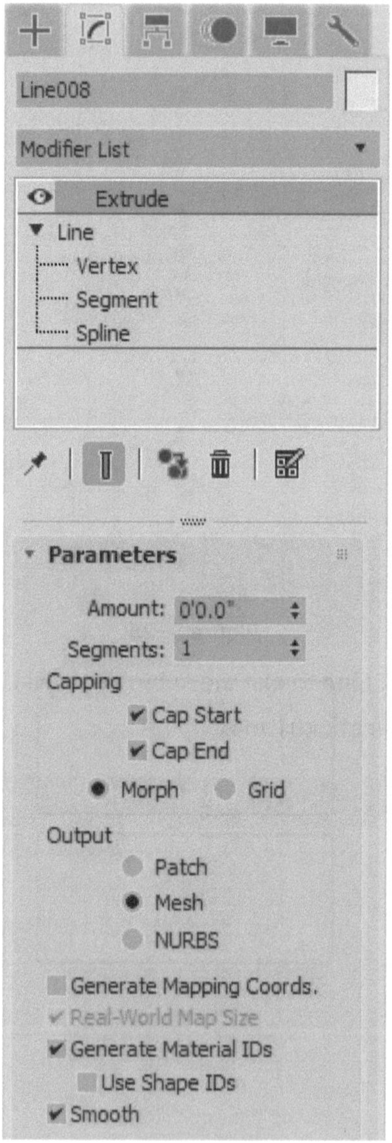

Figure 5–26

Capping Area

The capping options are located in the *Parameters* rollout, in the *Capping* area, as shown in Figure 5–26.

- Capping only applies to closed extruded shapes. Open shapes can be extruded but they cannot be capped.
- Closed shapes often do not cap if they cross themselves or if they have more than one vertex at the same location.
- You can also extrude with a height of **0** to create a flat surface. In this situation, only the start or end cap is required.
- Figure 5–27 shows **various** capping options.

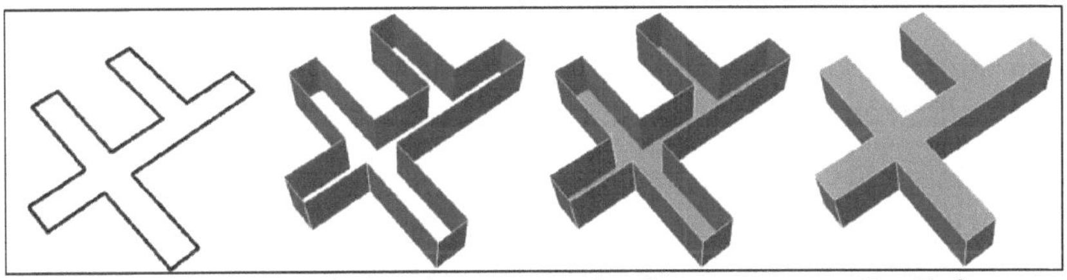

Original Shape ***No Capping*** ***Cap Start*** ***Cap End***

Figure 5–27

- **Morph** capping type linearly interpolates across the vertices to create the cap, as shown in Figure 5–28. This option creates less geometry and is the default setting.
- **Grid** capping type breaks down the cap into a repeating grid of vertices, in square shapes, as shown in Figure 5–29. The grid method enables more complex modeling on the surface of the cap, but adds a great deal of geometry.

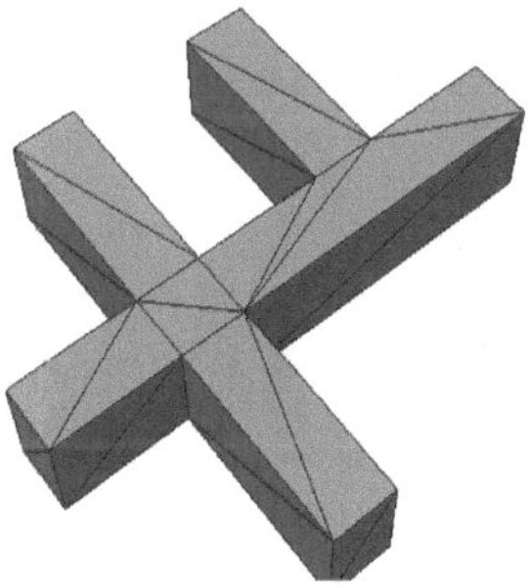

Figure 5–28

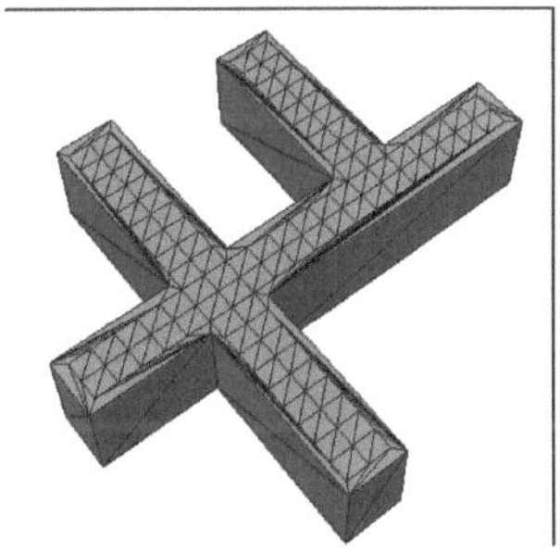

Figure 5–29

Output Area

The *Output* area options controls the kind of object that is derived if you simplify (collapse) the object. It is recommended to select the default **Mesh** option. **Patch** and **NURBS** options are used to create complex curved geometry.

Mapping Coordinates

The options for mapping coordinates and real-world map sizing are described with materials.

- For surfaces that have tiled, repeating textures of a specific size (e.g., carpeting, wall surfaces, metal, etc.) select **Generate Mapping Coords** and **Real-World Map Size**.
- For surfaces meant to show textures that are scaled explicitly (e.g., signs, labels, company logos, paintings, computer screens, etc.) you might use **Generate Mapping Coords option,** but the **Real-World Map Size** option can be cleared.
- Select **Generate Material IDs** to apply a different material to the sides, start, and end cap through a Multi/Sub-object material.
- Selecting **Use Shape IDs** assigns material IDs that have been applied to the segments of the spline that you extruded.

Extruding Nested Splines

When linked or imported geometry is merged together (such as by layer with the weld option) or, when 2D objects become attached to form complex splines, these objects are called **nested splines**. When extruding a nested spline (as shown in Figure 5–30), the enclosed areas form solid masses and can be used for modeling wall systems and similar geometry.

Figure 5–30

5.5 3D Boolean Operations

Boolean operations enable you to graphically bring together two 3D objects to generate a third 3D object. This is an intuitive way to create complex geometry from simple 3D primitives and extruded 2D shapes.

The Boolean objects are available in the *Create* panel (+) by clicking (Geometry) and selecting **Compound Objects** in the drop-down list. You can select the required Boolean object in the *Object Type* rollout, as shown in Figure 5–31.

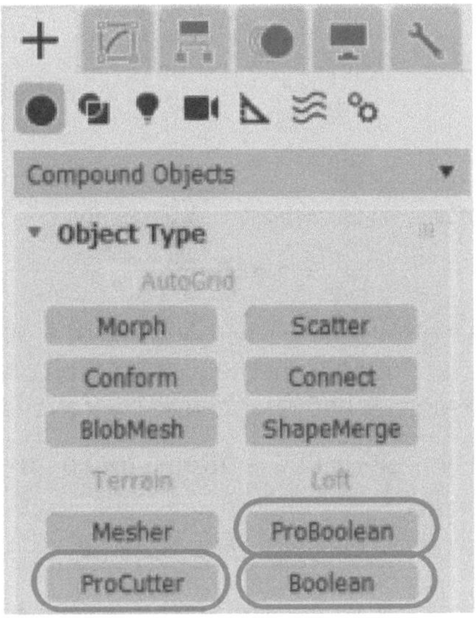

Figure 5–31

The three types of Boolean objects that can be created are as follows:

Boolean compound object	Combines two 3D objects to generate a third 3D object by applying a logical operation. The Boolean compound object offers improved stability.
ProBoolean compound object	Similar to the Boolean compound object, this option has more advanced functionality and alternate workflow.
ProCutter compound object	Enables you to separate objects into pieces so that you can use them in dynamic simulations.

Boolean Operations

The original objects are referred to as **Operands** and the final result is a **Boolean** object. The operands can be combined in three ways, as shown in Figure 5–32:

- By subtraction of one from the other.
- By finding the intersection where their geometries overlap.
- By the union of the two together.

Figure 5–32

- Boolean operations can be nested where the results of one operation can be used as input to the next. **ProBooleans** offer superior methodology when creating objects with multiple operands. It enables you to reorder and change the operations interactively.
- Boolean operations can be animated, this is often a technique used to reveal or hide geometry in a presentation.

Boolean Explorer

The Boolean Explorer can help you to keep track of the various operands that are being used, as shown in Figure 5–33. The Boolean Explorer is only available with the Boolean compound object.

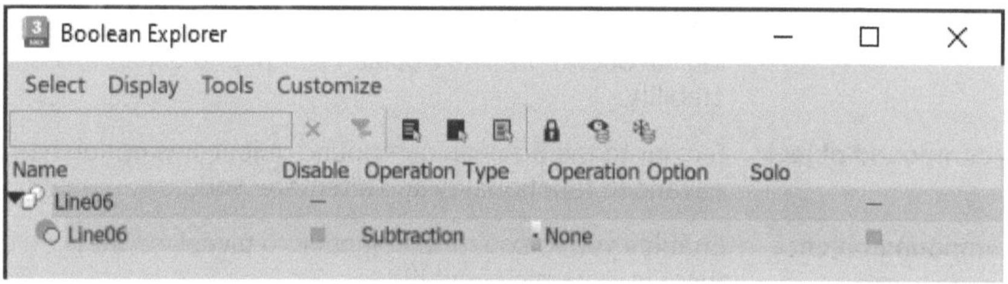

Figure 5–33

- To open the Boolean Explorer, in the *Boolean Parameters* rollout, click **Open Boolean Explorer**.
- Whenever you add an operand, it displays in the Boolean Explorer.
- If you change the order of the operands, the change is reflected in the Boolean Explorer.

Adjusting Boolean Results

The results of a Boolean operation can be adjusted dynamically by making changes to the operands' parameters or modifier stack. This dynamic update requires that operands be identified as a reference or instance on creation (or an extracted operand is selected to be an instance).

- The original operands can be maintained for editing after the fact or they can be reconstituted (extracted) from the Boolean result later on.
- The practical application of adjusting Boolean results is best left for Intermediate course material.

Best Practices

Boolean operations are known to produce unexpected results if the operand geometries had certain issues such as: gaps, irregular face normals, did not overlap each other, etc. It is recommended to avoid the following issues whenever possible:

- Avoid coplanar operands, whenever possible, to minimize Boolean complexity.
- Boolean operations expect water-tight geometry. If the geometry does not cleanly define a volume, the Boolean might not work, as shown in Figure 5–34.

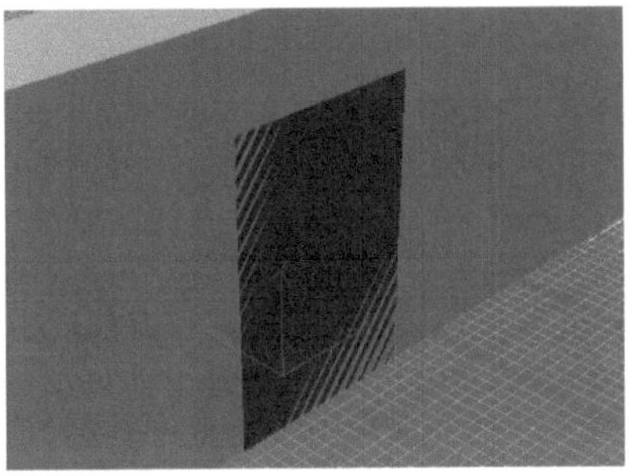

Figure 5–34

Collapsing Booleans

When an object has been sufficiently modeled with Boolean operations you can leave the result as a Boolean object or simplify (collapse) it to a mesh.

- To collapse a Boolean object to an editable mesh, in the Modifier Stack, right-click on the Boolean and select **Convert to: Editable Mesh** or **Convert to: Editable Poly**.
- If you are using a Boolean result as an operand for another Boolean operation and are not getting the expected results, it might help to convert the original Boolean object to an editable mesh before the second operation. It is recommended to use ProBooleans if you have multiple operands.
- Boolean objects that originate from linked AutoCAD geometry might react unpredictably after an updated DWG link.

- Many other kinds of 3D objects besides Booleans can be collapsed to a mesh to simplify them.
- Once an object is converted to a mesh, it loses all of its parametric controls. Therefore, converted Boolean objects cannot be updated by editing instanced operands or a file link update.

Hint: Controlling Edge Line Visibility

After a Boolean or other complex operation, there might be missing or unnecessary edge lines in a wireframe or default shading viewport rendering mode. To easily read the geometry on the screen, only certain edges across your 3D object are visible.

To display the edges, right-click on the object and select **Object Properties**. In the *Display Properties* area, clear the **Edges Only** option. The **Edges Only** option is available in the **By Object** mode, as shown in Figure 5–35. Then, click **By Layer** to toggle it to **By Object**.

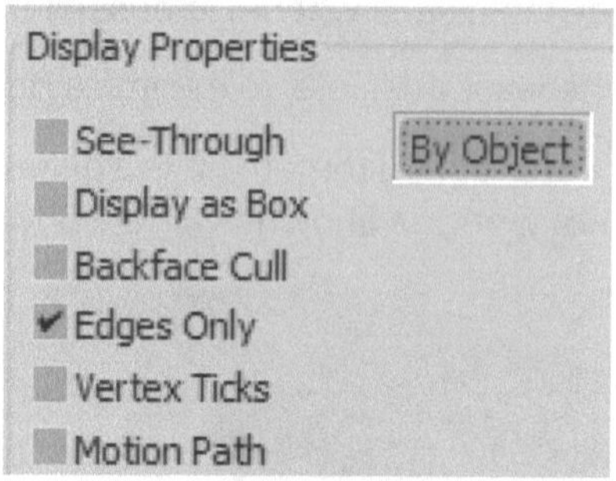

Figure 5–35

Alternatively, in the *Modify* panel, add an **Edit Mesh** modifier to your object and select **Edge** Sub-object mode. In the **Edit** menu, select **Select All**. In the *Surface Properties* rollout, click **Invisible** to make all edges invisible. Click **Auto Edge** to only show the edges with 24°+ separation. To get required results on curved objects (including curved walls), you might have to enter different separation angles.

Practice 5d
Extrude Walls and Create Wall Openings

Practice Objective

- Add depth to a 2D spline to create 3D walls and openings in 3D walls.

In this practice, you will extrude walls from a spline to create 3D walls. You will then refine the walls by creating openings for a corridor and doors, using the **Extrude** modifier. Additionally, you will use **ProBoolean** objects to graphically subtract two objects from the walls.

You must set the paths to locate the External files and XREFs used in the practice. If you have not done this already, return to Chapter 1 and complete Task 1 to Task 3 in *Practice 1a: Organize Folders and Work with the Interface*. You only have to set the user paths once.

Task 1: Extrude the walls.

1. Open **Spline Walls Bound.max**. The scene contains various line shapes.
2. In the Scene Explorer toolbar, click (Display None) and click (Display Shapes). Select **Layer:VIZ-1-Walls** and note that the 2D lines for the walls (cyan colored shapes) are selected in the viewport.
3. In the Command Panel, select the *Modify* panel ( ). The name **Layer:VIZ-1-Walls** displays in the Command Panel and it is an **Editable Spline**.

4. In the *Modifier List*, select **Extrude**. In the *Parameters* rollout, set *Amount* to **11'0"** (the height of the first floor walls), as shown in Figure 5–36. Press <Enter>.

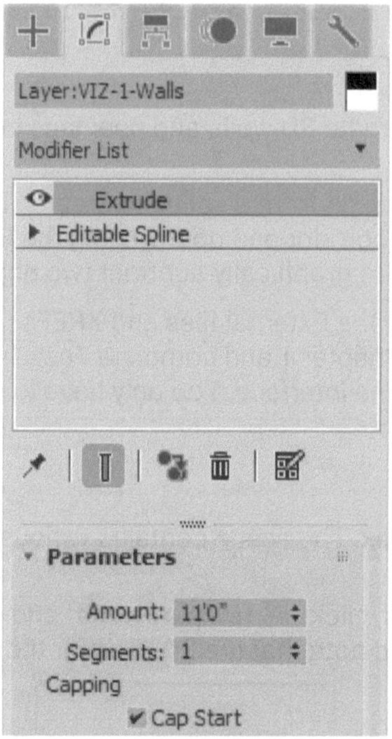

Figure 5–36

5. Click  (Zoom Extents All). Only the areas enclosed by the wall linework are extruded, as shown in Figure 5–37.
   - The missing wall sections are meant for curtain walls.

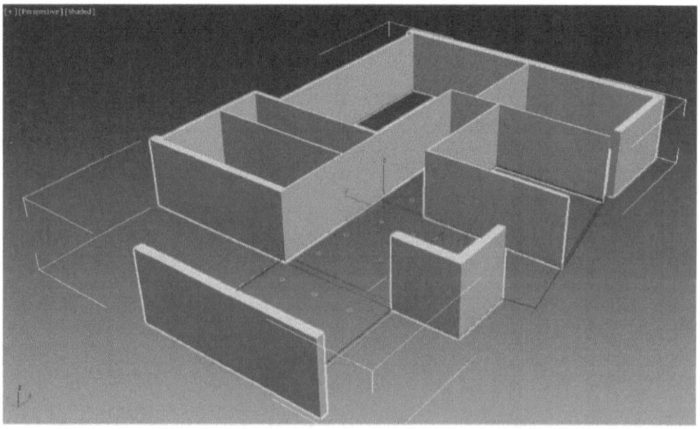

Figure 5–37

Task 2: Create the subtraction operands.

1. In the Main Toolbar, click  (Layer Explorer). In the Layer Explorer, select the two layers **VIZ-1-Booleans-Doors** and **VIZ-1-Boolean-Soffit**. Right-click on any of the selected layer and click **Select Child Nodes**, as shown in Figure 5–38. These layers contain closed polylines that define the openings to be created. Note that these polylines are selected.

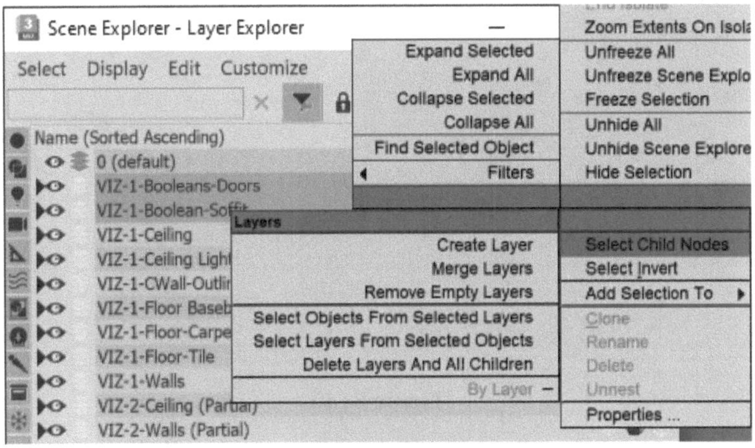

Figure 5–38

2. To avoid a coplanar face along the floor, first move these objects below the floor level. In the Main Toolbar, click  (Select and Move). Set coordinate system to **World** and click  (Use Transform Coordinate Center), as shown in Figure 5–39.

Figure 5–39

3. In the Status Bar, in the *Transform Type-In* area, activate  (Offset Mode Transform), enter **-1'0"** in the *Z* field, and press <Enter>.
4. In the Main Toolbar, click  (Select Object).
5. Click anywhere in empty space to clear the selection. In the Layer Explorer, highlight only **VIZ-1-Boolean-Soffit**. Right-click on the selected layer and click **Select Child Nodes**. This layer contains a single polyline defining an opening in one of the walls.
6. In the Command Panel>*Modify* panel (), verify that the name **Layer:VIZ-1-Boolean-Soffit** displays in the panel.

7. In the *Modifier List*, select **Extrude**. In the *Parameters* rollout, set *Amount* to **9'0"** and press <Enter> (this is **8'** + the **1'** that was just used to lower the object). The first subtraction operand (8'0") is created, as shown in Figure 5–40.

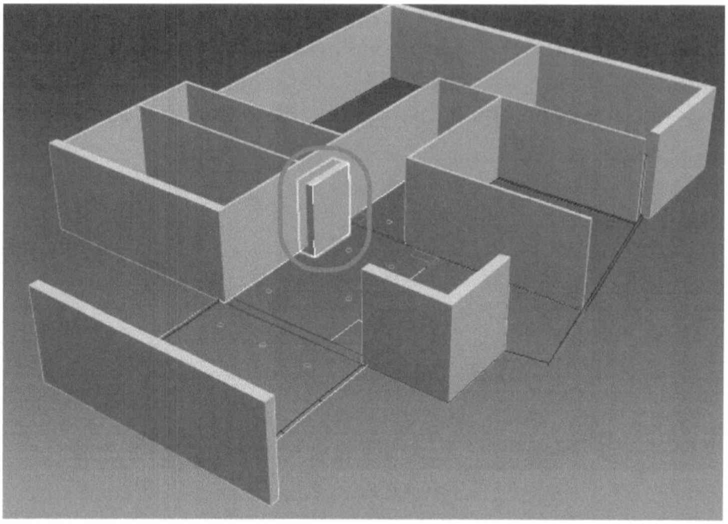

Figure 5–40

8. Repeat Steps 5 to 7 for **VIZ-1-Booleans-Doors**. Select the child layer of **VIZ-1-Booleans-Doors** and extrude it with an *Amount* of **8'0"**. The four 7'0" subtraction operands are created, as shown in Figure 5–41.

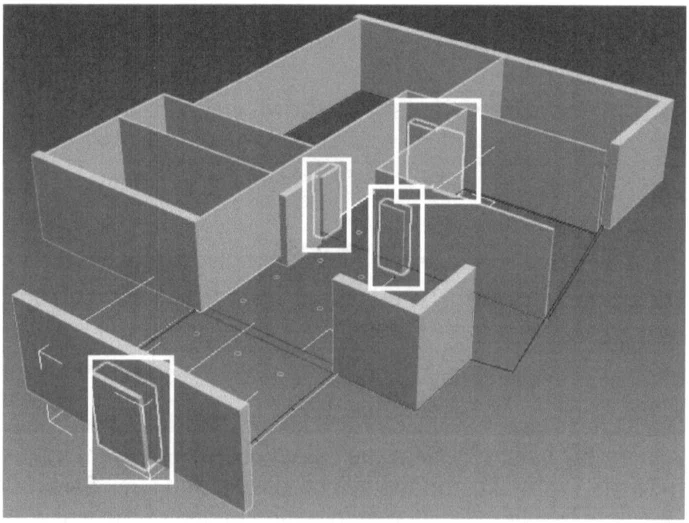

Figure 5–41

Task 3: Create the wall openings.

1. In the Layer Explorer, select **VIZ-1-Walls.** Right-click on the selected layer and click **Select Child Nodes**.

2. In the *Create* panel ( )> (Geometry), select **Compound Objects** in the drop-down list, as shown in Figure 5–42. Click **ProBoolean** to convert the wall system into a Boolean object. The selected walls (**VIZ-1-Walls**) are now your Operand A.
3. In the *Pick Boolean* rollout, verify that **Move** is selected and click **Start Picking**.
4. In the *Parameters* rollout, in the *Operation* area, verify that **Subtraction** is selected, as shown in Figure 5–43. This subtracts **Operand B** (the soffit opening) from **Operand A** (the walls).

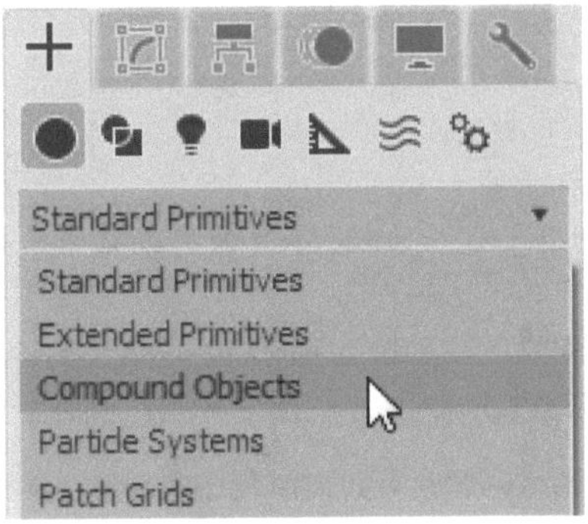

Figure 5–42

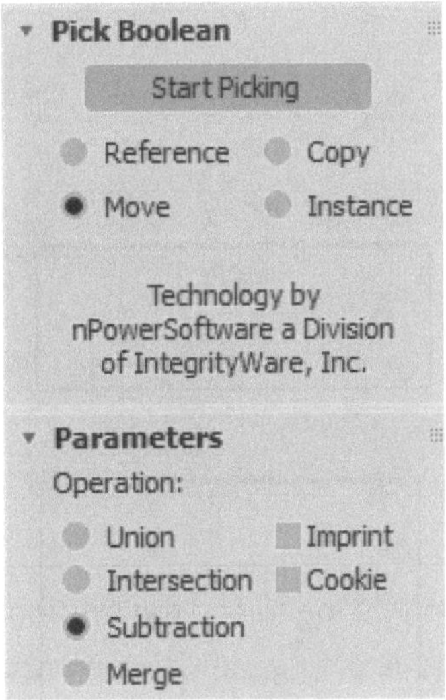

Figure 5–43

5. In the viewport, select the Boolean Soffit extrusion (**VIZ -1-Boolean Soffit**, the 9'0" operand that was created first). The volume contained by the Soffit object is removed from the walls, as shown in Figure 5–44.
6. Click any of the **VIZ-1-Boolean-Doors** objects to complete the second ProBoolean subtraction operation. The volume contained by the Doors object is also removed from the walls, as shown in Figure 5–44.

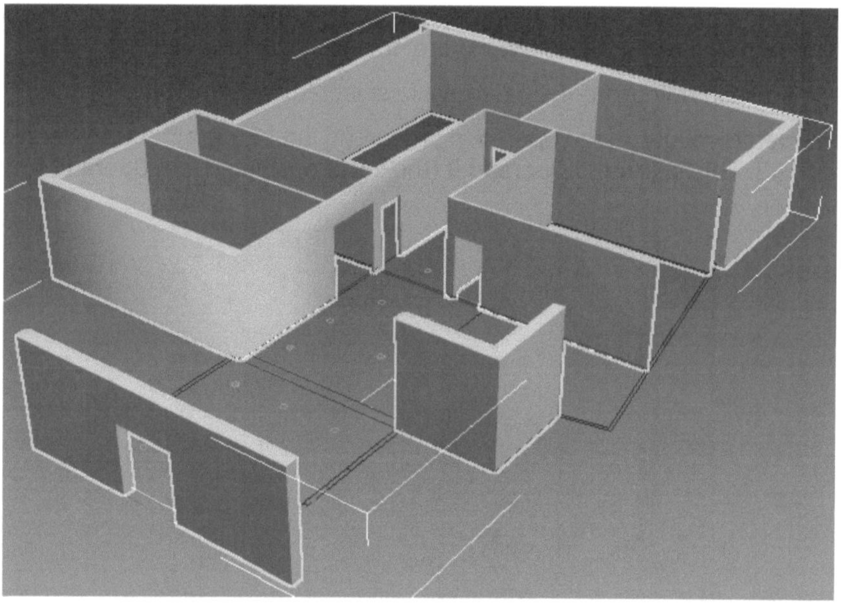

Figure 5–44

7. Click **Start Picking** to end the ProBoolean operation.
8. The ProBoolean operation has the ability to change the way the faces are built in the object using the Quadrilateral Tessellation function. In the Layer Explorer, with the **VIZ-1-Walls** highlighted, right-click on **VIZ-1-Walls** and select **Properties**. In the *Object Properties* dialog box, verify that the *Name* displays as **Layer:VIZ-1-Walls**. In the *Display Properties* area, click **By Layer** to toggle it to **By Object**. Clear **Edges Only** and click **OK**.
9. Press <F4> to display the edges of the newly created faces, as shown in Figure 5–45. Note the way long triangular faces are created on some of the walls.

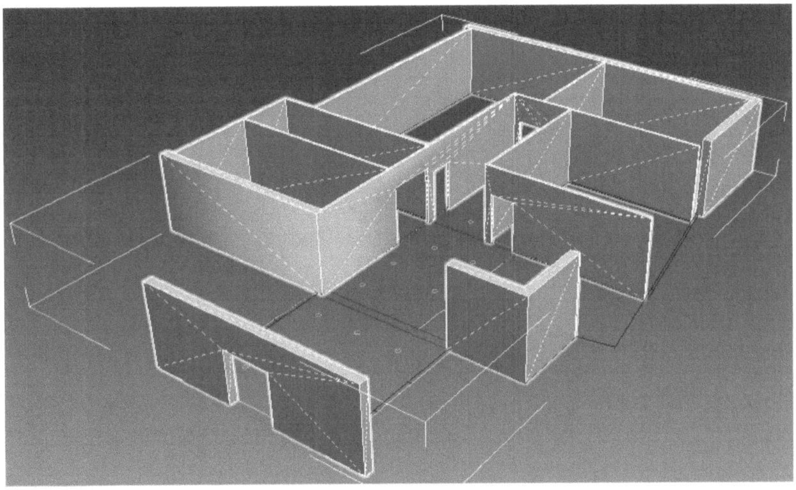

Figure 5–45

10. In the Command Panel>*Modify* panel (), note that the **ProBoolean** displays in the *Modifier Stack*. Expand the *Advanced Options* rollout. (It is located at the bottom of the rollouts.) In the *Quadrilateral Tessellation* area, select **Make Quadrilaterals**, as shown in Figure 5–46. Note how the geometry changes. There are no long triangular faces, as shown on the right in Figure 5–47.

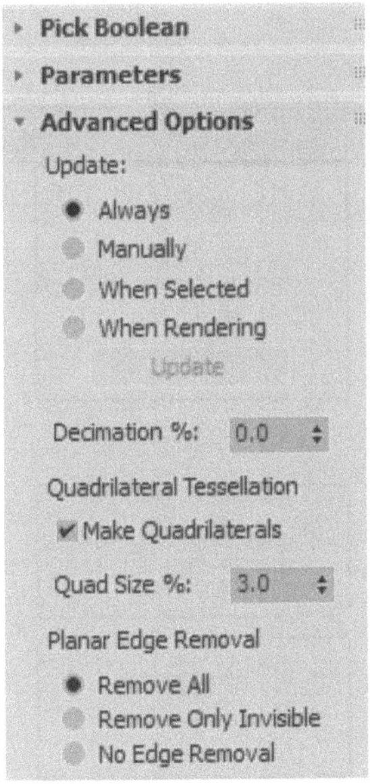

Figure 5–46

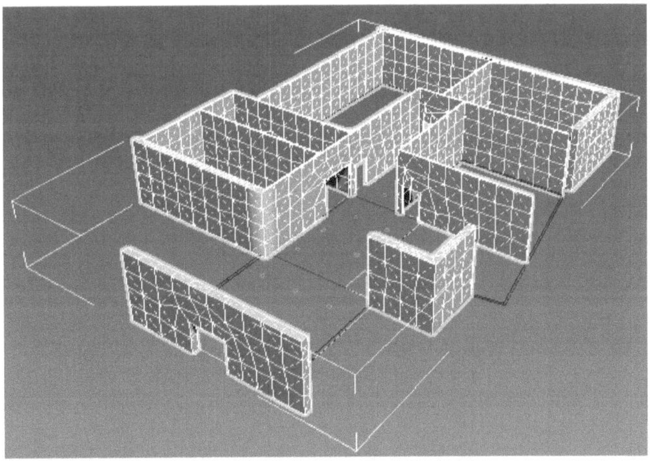

Figure 5–47

11. Increase the *Quad Size %* to **10.0**. This modifies the geometry so that the polygons are bigger, as shown in Figure 5–48.

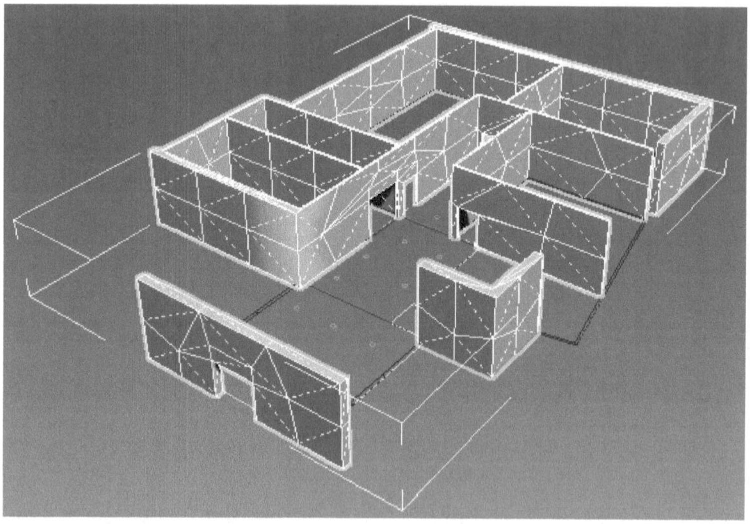

Figure 5–48

12. You can collapse the **ProBoolean** to a simple mesh. In the *Modifier Stack*, right-click on **ProBoolean** and select **Editable Poly**.
13. Click in an empty space to clear the selection and close the Layer Explorer.
14. Save your work as **MySpline Walls Bound.max**.

End of practice

5.6 Using Snaps for Precision

Snaps enable you to create, move, rotate, and scale objects with precision and are activated using the buttons in the Main Toolbar, as shown in Figure 5–49. Press <S> to toggle Snaps on and off while drawing lines, creating primitives, or transforming objects.

Figure 5–49

The available Toggle options are described as follows:

	**3D Snap:** This mode snaps to objects in 3D. It is the default option.
	**2.5D Snap:** This mode snaps to a projection of the selected point at elevation 0 on the current grid.
	**2D Snap:** This mode enables you to snap to points at elevation 0 on the current grid.
	**Angle Snap:** This mode enables you to set rotational values (such as a Rotate Transform amount) in angle increments.
	**Percent Snap:** This mode enables percentile-based values (such as a Scale Transform amount) in percent increments (5%, 10%, etc.).
	**Spinner Snap:** This mode causes all spinner controls to increment at a set value with a single click. Transform and a host of parameter values can be adjusted by spinners (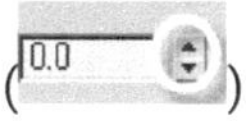).

- Snap settings, such as the increment values for angle and percent snap, can be set in the *Options* tab of the *Grid and Snap Settings* dialog box, as shown in Figure 5–50. You can access the dialog box by right-clicking on **2D, 2.5D, 3D, Angle**, or **Percent Snap**, from **Tools>Grids and Snaps> Grid and Snap Settings**, or by holding <Shift> and right-clicking anywhere in the viewport and selecting **Grid and Snap Settings** in the quad menu.
- The active snaps are selected in the *Snaps* tab of the *Grid and Snap Settings* dialog box, as shown in Figure 5–51.

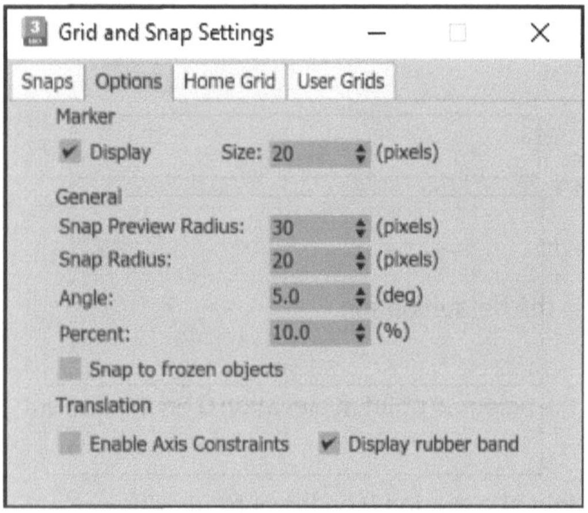

Figure 5–50

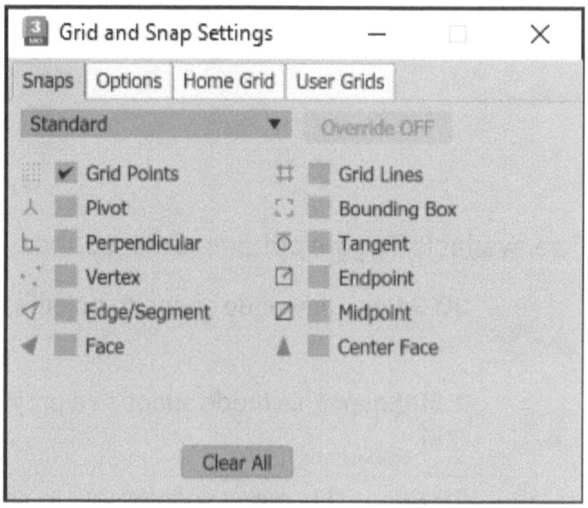

Figure 5–51

- You can activate snaps by selecting buttons in the Snaps toolbar (hidden by default), as shown in Figure 5–52. Right-click on the heading bar of any interface item and select **Snaps** in the menu to open the Snaps toolbar.

Figure 5–52

- You can also activate snaps in the **Snaps** quad menu. Hold <Shift>, right-click anywhere in the viewport, and select **Standard,** as shown in Figure 5–53.

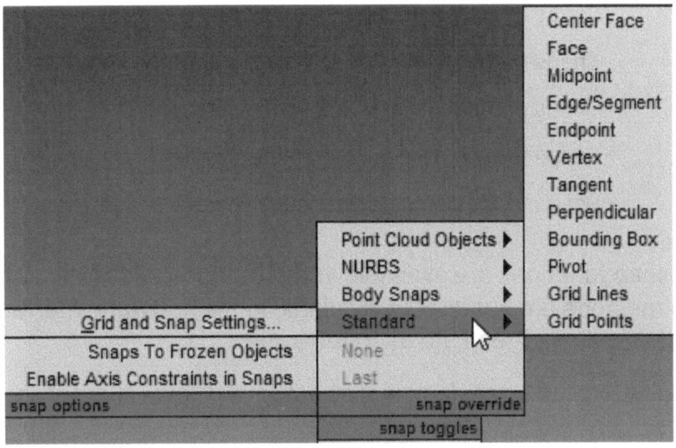

Figure 5–53

- The toolbar contains buttons for the most common snap settings. These are as follows:

	**Grid Points:** Snaps to grid intersections.
	**Pivot:** Snaps to the pivot point of an object.
	**Vertex:** Snaps to vertices on splines, meshes, or similar geometry.
	**Endpoint:** Snaps to the vertices at the end of a spline segment, mesh edge, or similar geometry. Similar to Vertex except that not all vertices are at the endpoints of spline segments and mesh edges.
	**Midpoint:** Snaps to the middle of spline segments, mesh edges, or similar geometry.
	**Edge/Segment:** Snaps to anywhere along spline segments, mesh edges, or similar geometry.
	**Face:** Snaps anywhere on the surface of a face.
	**Snap to Frozen Objects:** Enables other snaps to reference frozen objects.
	**Snaps Use Axis Constraints:** Forces result along the selected axis constraints set in the Axis Constraints toolbar.

- The following additional snaps are available in the *Snap and Grid Settings* dialog box and the **Snaps** quad menu.

Grid Lines	Snaps to anywhere along a grid line.
Bounding Box	Snaps to the corners of an object's bounding box.
Perpendicular	Snaps perpendicularly to a spline segment.
Tangent	Snaps tangent to a curved spline segment.
Center Face	Snaps to the center of triangular faces.

- Two additional snap functions are available in the Autodesk 3ds Max software. By default, these snapping methods are not directly available in the software interface and are required to be added to the toolbar. These are as follows:

	**Ortho Snapping:** Forces a transform in the horizontal or vertical directions based on the active grid.
	**Polar Snapping:** Forces results to the angle increment set in the *Grid and Snap Settings* dialog box.

- You can snap to XREF objects just like any other object.

Practice 5e
Create a Door with Snaps

Practice Objective

- Create doors at precise locations using snaps.

In this practice, you will add a door to an opening, using snaps to position it precisely.

You must set the paths to locate the External files and XREFs used in the practice. If you have not done this already, return to Chapter 1 and complete Task 1 to Task 3 in *Practice 1a: Organize Folders and Work with the Interface*. You only have to set the user paths once.

1. Reset the scene and open **Creating a Door.max**.
    - The scene contains extruded walls with openings and extruded carpet and tile areas. A camera has also been added.
2. Maximize the **Perspective** viewport.
3. In a **Perspective** viewport, use  (Zoom),  (Pan), and  (Orbit) to display the west side of the model (where the space for the front outer door is located), similar to that shown in Figure 5–54. Verify that the **Perspective** viewport is set as **Default Shading** and **Edged Faces**.

Figure 5–54

4. Using (Zoom) and (Pan), zoom in to the front doorway opening (as shown in Figure 5–55) to easily identify the points for snapping.

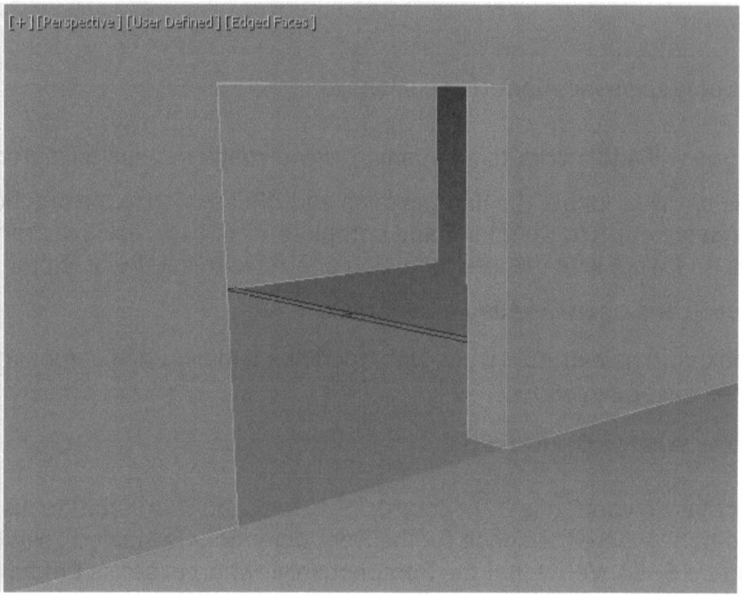

Figure 5–55

5. In the Main Toolbar, click (3D Snaps) to activate it. In the Command Panel, verify that *Create* panel ( )> (Geometry) is open. Expand the *Standard Primitives* drop-down list and select **Doors**.

Hint: Create Window and Door Objects

By default, Autodesk 3ds Max Doors and Windows are created using one of the following methods:

- **Clicking and dragging:** To define the width of the door/window.
- **Releasing and picking:** A point to define the depth of the wall opening.
- **Releasing and picking:** A point to define the height of the opening.

6. In the *Object Type* rollout, click **Pivot** to start the door creation process, as shown in Figure 5–56.
7. Right-click on any interface item menu to open the **Item** menu and select **Snaps** to open the Snaps toolbar. Click  (Snap to Endpoint Toggle), as shown in Figure 5–57, or press <Shift> and right-click to open the **Snaps** quad menu and select **Standard>Endpoint**.

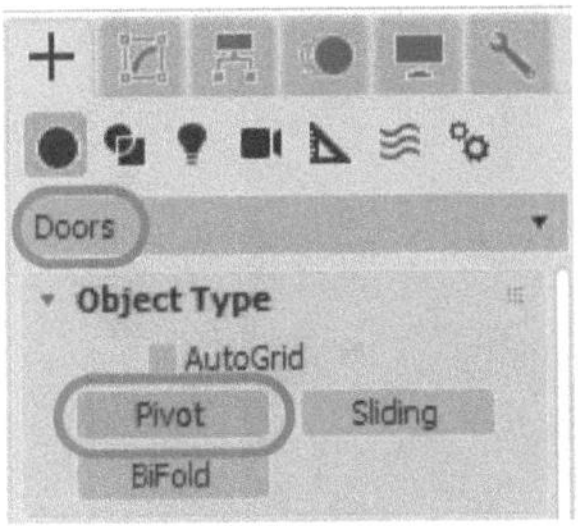

Figure 5–56

Figure 5–57

8. Hover the cursor at the bottom left corner of the door opening. Note that when the cursor hovers over the endpoint (corner), it snaps to that point and a small yellow square (endpoint marker) displays, as shown in Figure 5–58.

Figure 5–58

9. Click and hold at this point and then while still holding, drag the cursor over to the lower right corner. Once it snaps to the lower right corner (as shown in Figure 5–59), release the mouse button to define the width of the door.
   - If you have difficulty with this, you might want to change to Wireframe display.

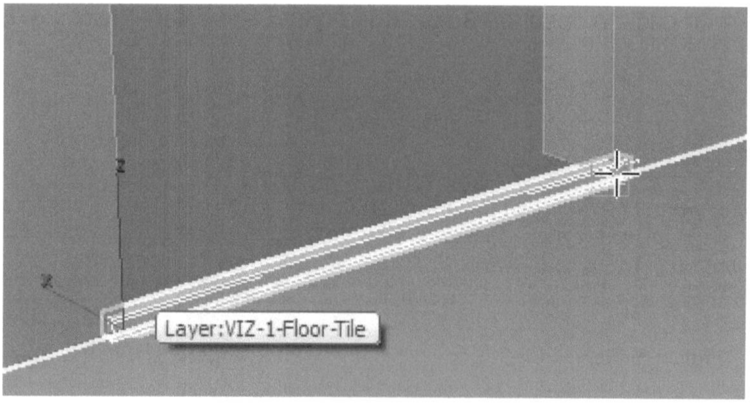

Figure 5–59

10. Move the cursor to the back corner of the door opening and click (not click and drag) to define the depth of the opening, as shown in Figure 5–60.

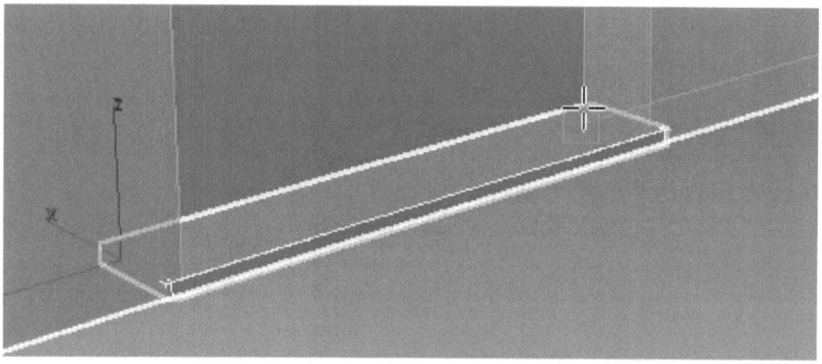

Figure 5–60

11. Move the cursor to the upper right corner of the door opening and click (not click and drag) to define the height, as shown in Figure 5–61. Sometimes this is difficult to do, depending on the angle of your view. You can toggle off the Snap by pressing <S>, then adjust the height (7'0") using the *Parameters* rollout.

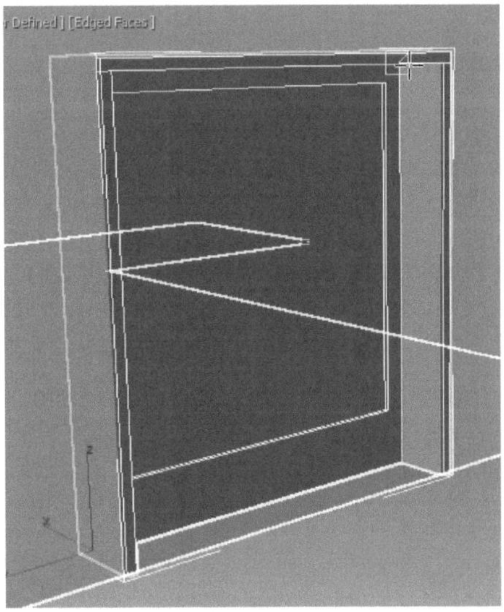

Figure 5–61

12. Select (Display Geometry) in the Scene Explorer and verify that the **PivotDoor** object is still selected. In the Command Panel, select the *Modify* panel ( ). In the *Parameters* rollout, select **Double Doors**. Set the *Open* angle to **45**, as shown in Figure 5–62. In the *Leaf Parameters* rollout, in the *Panels* area, select **Beveled**. Note that in the viewport, the door will change to double doors with beveled panels and will be open at a **45°** angle, as shown in Figure 5–62.

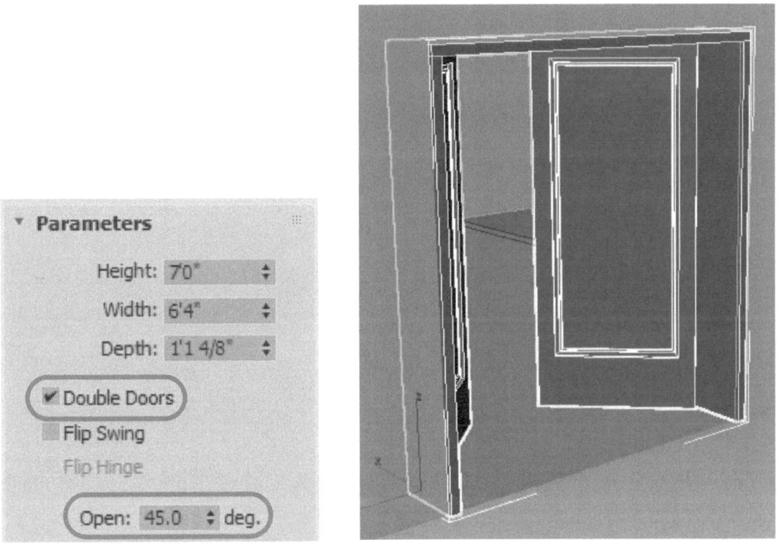

Figure 5–62

13. Set the *Open* angle to **0°** to display the panels as closed.
14. Save your work as **MyCreating a Door.max**.

Hint: Holes in Walls Using Window and Door Objects

When you use Autodesk 3ds Max Wall objects combined with Window or Door objects, you can automatically create holes for the doors and windows using snaps to align them in place. If you create the door or window away from the wall, you can move it so it intersects with the wall. Use **Select and Link** to link the door or window to the wall to automatically create the hole. You can use Edge snap to align the doors with the walls.

The advantage is that if you move the door or window, the hole moves with it. However, this functionality only works when you create Autodesk 3ds Max wall objects and it is not available when you are extruding linked geometry.

End of practice

5.7 The Sweep Modifier

The **Sweep** modifier is a simple and effective option to create 3D geometry based on a 2D section that follows a series of spline segment paths.

- This modifier can create 3D pipe networks, curbing, moldings, and similar types of geometry, very quickly.
- Sweeps are created by adding the **Sweep** modifier to the path, followed by adjusting cross-section settings and other parameters in the *Modify* panel.
- You can select a predefined cross-section shape such as, boxes, pipes, tees, and angles, or you can use a custom shape.
- Although this functionality is also available through the **Loft** compound object, the **Sweep** modifier is easier to configure.

To use the **Sweep** modifier, select a spline and then in the Modify panel (), select **Sweep** from the *Modifier List*. Figure 5–63 shows an example of a wall baseboard created using the **Sweep** modifier.

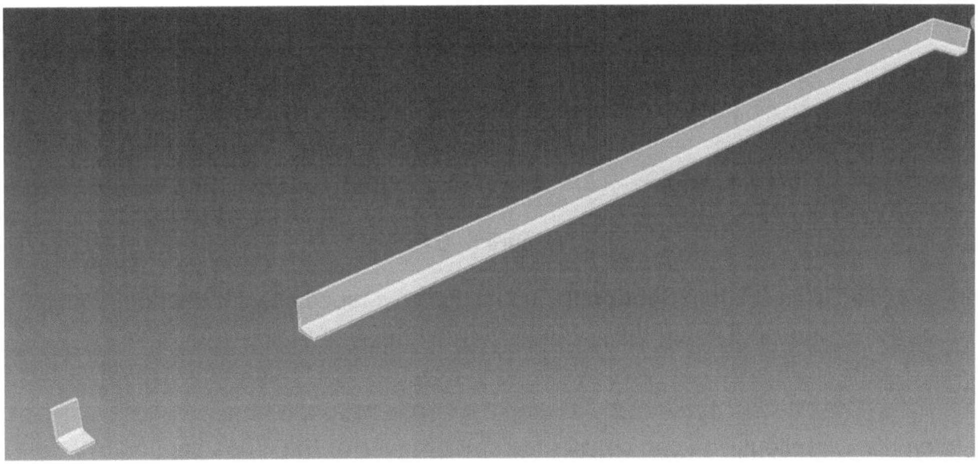

Figure 5–63

Sweep Parameters

Section Type

In the *Section Type* rollout, you can select the type of profile that you want to sweep along the spline segments.

- If you selected **Use Built-In Section**, a list of precreated cross-sections is available as your profile, as shown in Figure 5–64. The **Angle** is the default cross-section.

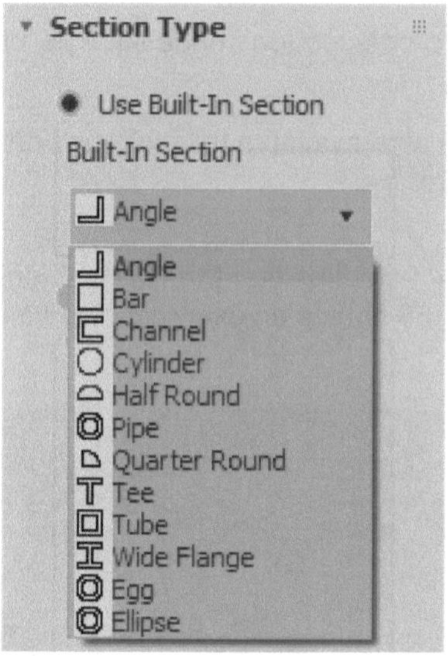

Figure 5–64

- You can select **Use Custom Section** to use a custom shapes as your section. You can either create your section in the current scene or obtain it from another .MAX file.

Interpolation

In the *Interpolation* rollout, you can control the smoothness of the cross-section by adding or removing vertices.

- Steps can be set to **0** for cross-section shapes that have sharp edges (no curves). Otherwise this value should be kept low to reduce complexity. The two options available are as follows:

Optimize	Groups the supplemented vertices closer to the corners rather than evenly along the shape.
Adaptive	Tessellates (break into segments) curves in the section shape. Select Adaptive results in a wireframe rendering mode to reduce complexity

Parameters

In the *Parameters* rollout, you can control the size and shape of the predefined cross-sections.

Sweep Parameters

In the *Sweep Parameters* rollout, you can control the placement and orientation of the cross-section shape along the path object.

- If a sweep result is backwards or upside down, use the two mirroring options to correct it. The options available are as follows:

Offset	This option enables you to shift the horizontal and vertical position of the sweep geometry away from the spline path
Angle	This options rotates the section relative to the plane. The spline path is drawn as defined by its pivot point.
Smooth Section/ Smooth Path	Selecting these options enables you to make the object smooth, even if the path object or shape are not smooth. In the case of the swept wall baseboard, the section is smoothed to make the cross-section display as filleted, not because the baseboard follows the angled corners of the wall.
Pivot Alignment	This options enables you to anchor the cross-section shape to the path based on the shape's pivot point.
Banking	This option rotates a cross-section shape assigned to a 3D path, similar to an airplane rolling during a turn.

Practice 5f
Sweep the Wall Baseboard

Practice Objective

- Create a wall baseboard by extruding a precreated cross-section along a selected spline.

In this practice, you will create a vinyl baseboard object around the walls using the **Sweep** modifier.

You must set the paths to locate the External files and XREFs used in the practice. If you have not done this already, return to Chapter 1 and complete Task 1 to Task 3 in *Practice 1a: Organize Folders and Work with the Interface*. You only have to set the user paths once.

Task 1: Sweep the path.

1. Reset the scene and open **Sweep Modifier.max.**
   - The scene contains the extruded walls and main door in a closed position. A camera has also been added.

2. Open the Layer Explorer (Main Toolbar> (Layer Explorer). Select and right-click on **VIZ-1-Floor Baseboard Path**. In the quad menu, select **Select Child Nodes.** This layer contains a series of lines and polylines that define the base of the wall with gaps at the openings. Close the Layer Explorer. The **VIZ-1-Floor Baseboard Path** is still selected.

3. In the Status Bar, click the (Isolate Selection) toggle or right-click in the viewport and select **Isolate Selection** in the quad menu. This displays only the selected sweep path (2D line). Click anywhere in the **Perspective** viewport to clear the selection. Zoom in so that the path (lines) display as shown in Figure 5–65.

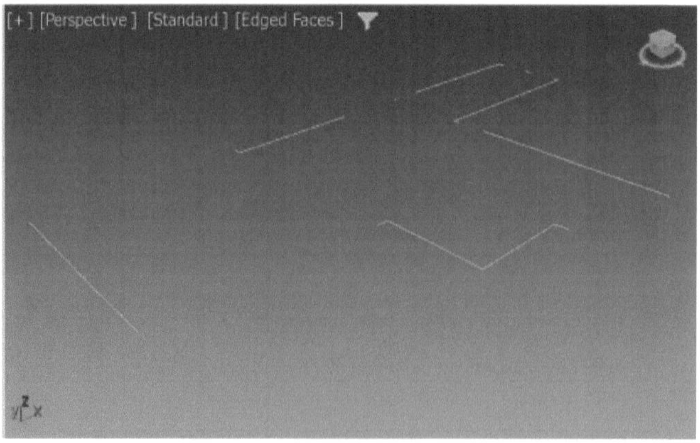

Figure 5–65

4. Maximize the **Perspective** viewport and click on any portion of the 2D line to select it.

5. In the Command Panel, select the *Modify* panel (). The name **VIZ-1-Floor Baseboard Path** displays. In the *Modifier List*, select **Sweep**. The **Sweep** modifier displays in the *Modifier Stack*. In the **Perspective** viewport, zoom in on the left side baseboard. Note that the lines have extruded along an angled cross-section, as shown in Figure 5–66. The shape of the extrusion depends on the selected *Built In Selection* in the *Section Type* rollout. The **Angle** type is the default selection, as shown in Figure 5–67.

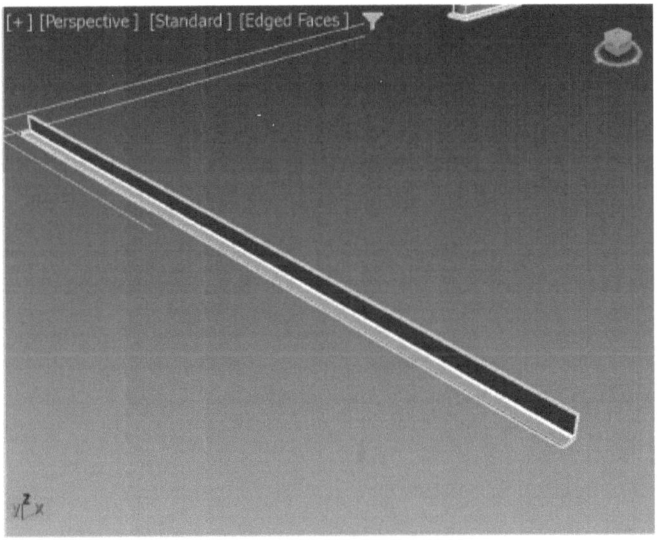

Figure 5–66

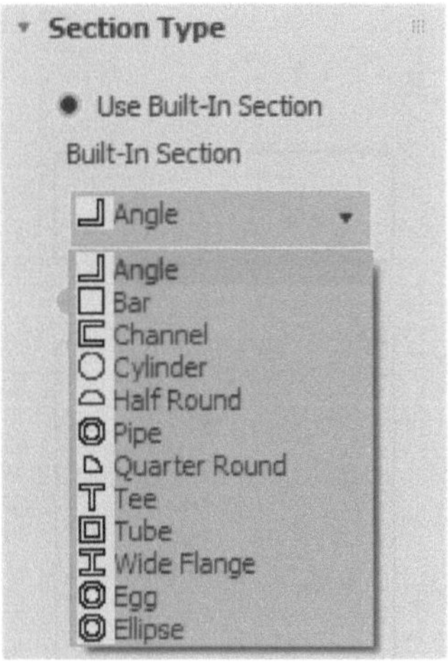

Figure 5–67

6. In the *Interpolation* rollout, set *Steps* to **0**. (Since all of the wall corners are square, there are no curves required to interpolate along the path.)

7. In the *Parameters* rollout, set the values shown in Figure 5–68. This shape is meant to create a baseboard with minimal detail. In the viewport, note how the baseboard detail changes.
8. The angle is still facing outward (in the wrong direction). In the *Sweep Parameters* rollout, select **Mirror on XZ Plane** to reverse the angle face. Clear **Smooth Path** (all of the corners are square and should not display as rounded). Anchor the **Pivot Alignment** option by clicking in the lower right corner. This option creates the 3D geometry object by sweeping the lower left corner of the baseboard cross-section along the baseboard path. Select **Gen. Mapping Coords.** and **Real-World Map Size**, as shown in Figure 5–69.

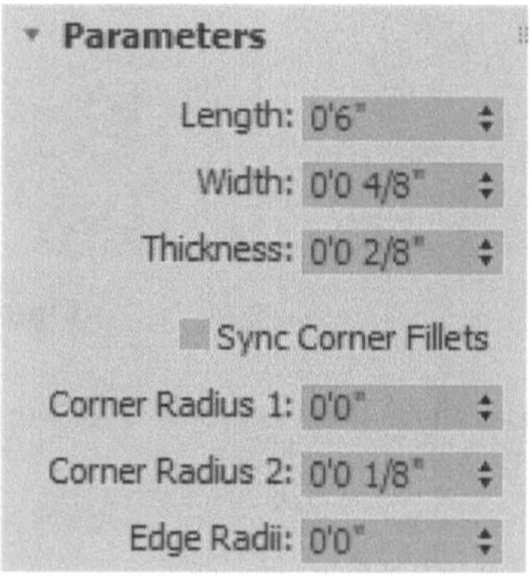

Figure 5–68

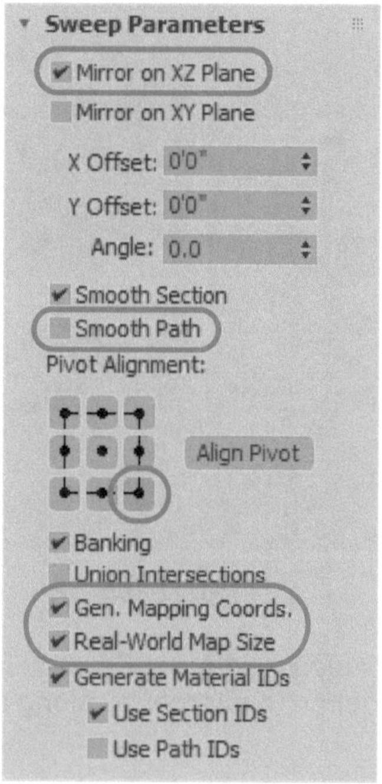

Figure 5–69

9. In the Status Bar, click the (Isolate Selection) toggle again to clear it. The walls and other geometry are now displayed.
10. Click **Maximize** to switch to four viewports display.

11. In the **Front** viewport, click the **[Front]** *Point of View* label and select **Cameras>Camera002-Door**. This displays the door from the inside. Click the *Per-View Preference* label and select **Default Shading** and **Edged Faces**. Also select **Standard** as the *Shading Viewport* label option (if Standard is set, select **Standard** again to clear the shadows). Note that the baseboard runs along the entire wall, including across the door, as shown in Figure 5–70.

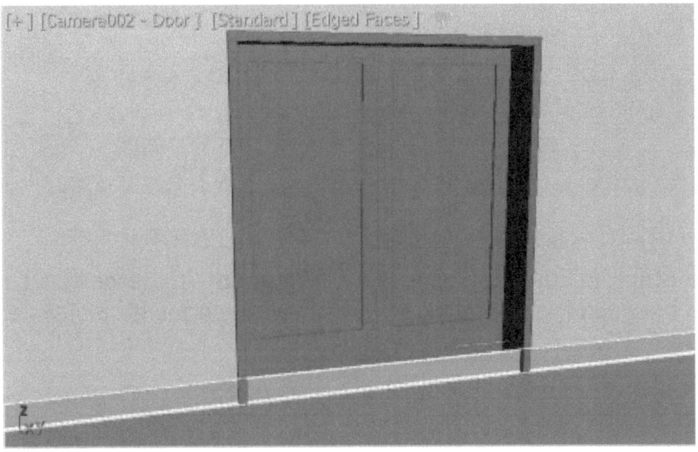

Figure 5–70

Task 2: Modify the path.

1. Maximize the **Camera002-Door** viewport.

2. Click anywhere on the baseboard to select it. In the *Modify* panel (), verify that *Name* displays **Layer:VIZ-1-Floor Baseboard Path**.

3. In the *Modifier Stack*, in *Editable Spline*, select **Vertex**. In the viewport, note that the baseboard is not displayed because you have selected an option before the **Sweep** modifier.

4. In the *Geometry* rollout, click **Refine**.

5. In the Main Toolbar, clear  (3D Snaps). In the viewport, click on the spline to place a vertex on either side and outside of the door frame, as shown in Figure 5–71. Once the two vertices have been placed, click **Refine** again to clear it.

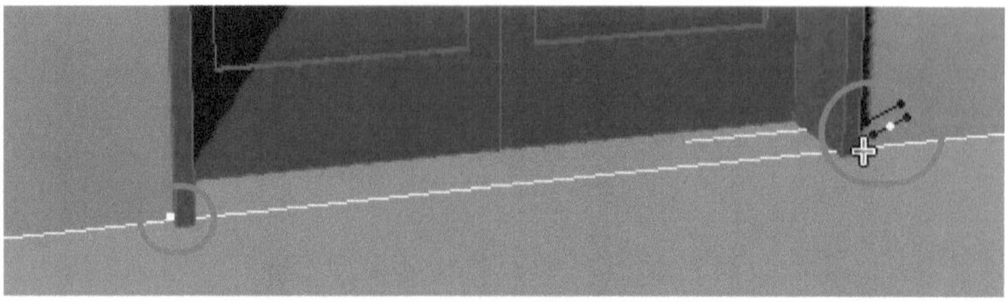

Figure 5–71

6. In the Modifier Stack, in Editable Spline, select **Segment**. In the viewport, click on the segment (line) between the two vertices, in front of the door. It displays as a red line, as shown in Figure 5–72.

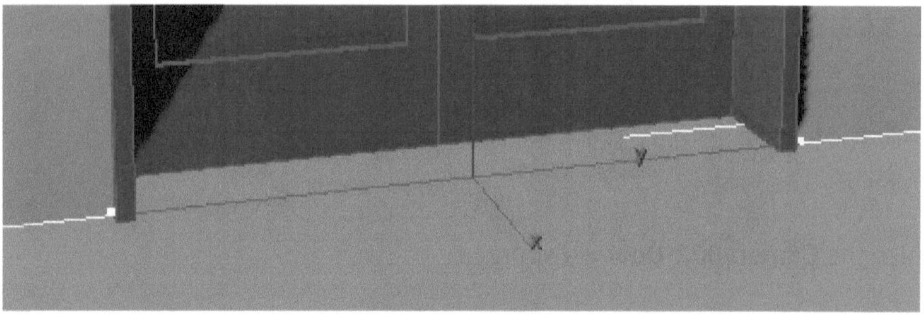

Figure 5–72

7. With the segment selected, press <Delete> to remove the segment.
8. In the Modifier Stack, select **Sweep**. In the viewport, note that the baseboard has been modified and does not pass in front of the door, as shown in Figure 5–73.

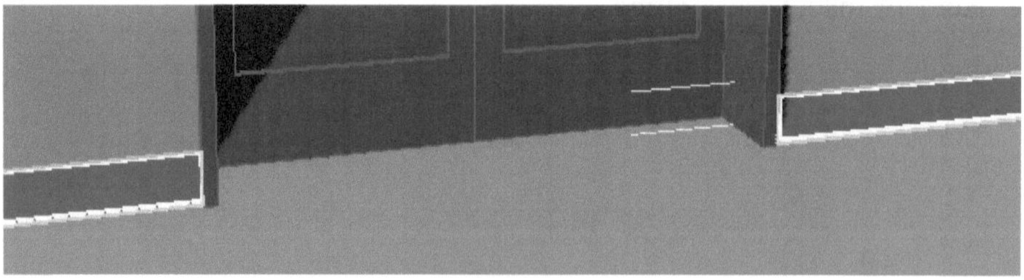

Figure 5–73

9. Click **Maximize** to switch to four viewports display.

Task 3: Merge objects.

1. Select **File>Import>Merge**. In the *Merge File* dialog box, select **Interior Furnishings and Detail.max.** Click **Open**. In the *Merge* dialog box, click **All** at the bottom left to select all of the objects and click **OK**.
2. In the **Perspective** viewport, click the **[Perspective]** *Point of View* label and select **Cameras>Camera001 – Lobby1**. This changes the display to look through the newly merged **Camera – Lobby1**. Set the *Shading Viewport* label to **Standard** and clear **Edged Faces**.
3. Clear any selections by selecting **Edit>Select None**. The scene should display similar to that shown in Figure 5–74.
    - Note that the desk, chairs, and other furnishings are AutoCAD 3D blocks. The curtain walls, stairs, and doors are examples of architectural objects that can be created.

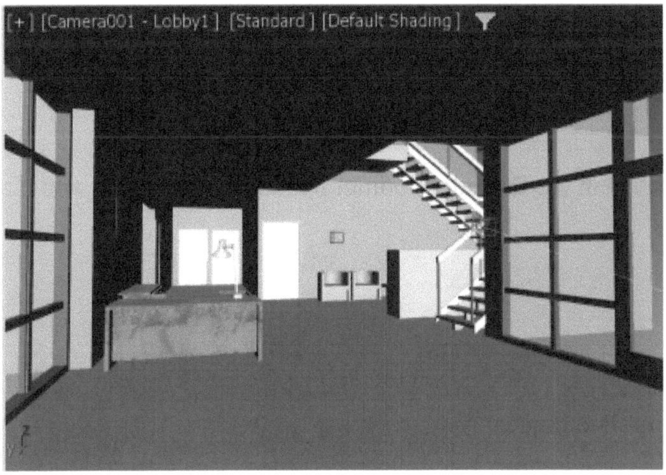

Figure 5–74

4. Save your work as **MySweep Modifier.max**.

Hint: Precreated Objects

Instead of modeling all of your scene content from scratch, look for royalty-free or low-cost objects posted on the Internet. Consider 3D blocks from other software, such as AutoCAD, Autodesk Revit, Autodesk Civil 3D, or directly from manufacturer's web sites.

End of practice

Chapter Review Questions

1. While editing a spline at the vertex sub-object level, which tool enables you to manipulate the handles on one side of the curve separately from the other handle?
    a. Bezier
    b. Bezier Corner
    c. Smooth
    d. Smooth Corner

2. To combine shapes using the 2D Boolean operations, which sub-object level in the **Edit Spline** modifier should be selected?
    a. Vertex
    b. Segment
    c. Spline

3. The **Capping** option in the **Extrude** modifier applies to both open and closed shapes.
    a. True
    b. False

4. The Boolean Explorer is available with which type of 3D Boolean object?
    a. Boolean compound object
    b. ProBoolean compound object
    c. Procutter compound object

5. Which **Sweep** modifier option in the *Sweep Parameters* rollout rotates a cross-section shape assigned to a 3D path?
    a. Offset
    b. Angle
    c. Banking
    d. Pivot Alignment

6. Which of the following Snap mode enables you to snap to points at elevation **0** on the current grid?

    a.  (Angle Snap)

    b.  (3D Snap)

    c.  (2.5D Snap)

    d.  (2D Snap)

Command Summary

Button	Command	Location
	**3D Snap**	• **Main Toolbar:** Snaps flyout
	**2.5D Snap**	• **Main Toolbar:** Snaps flyout
	**2D Snap**	• **Main Toolbar:** Snaps flyout
	**Angle Snap**	• **Main Toolbar**
	**Isolate Selection**	• **Status Bar** • **Quad Menu**
	**Layer Explorer**	• **Main Toolbar** • **Layers Toolbar**
N/A	**Merge**	• **Menu Bar:** File>Import>Merge
	**Offset Mode**	• **Status Bar**
	**Percent Snap**	• **Main Toolbar**
	**Shapes**	• **Command Panel:** *Create* panel • **Menu Bar:** Create>Shapes
	**Snap to Edge/ Segment**	• **Snaps Toolbar**
	**Snap to Endpoint**	• **Snaps Toolbar**
	**Snap to Face**	• **Snaps Toolbar**
	**Snap to Frozen Objects**	• **Snaps Toolbar**
	**Snap to Grid Point**	• **Snaps Toolbar**
	**Snap to Midpoint**	• **Snaps Toolbar**

Button	Command	Location
	**Snap to Pivot**	• **Snaps Toolbar**
	**Snap to Vertex**	• **Snaps Toolbar**
	**Snaps use Axis Constraints**	• **Snaps Toolbar**

Chapter 6

Materials

To create a realistic visualization, materials are used to more accurately represent the model as a realistic real-world design. The Autodesk® 3ds Max® software provides material libraries that can be used to assign materials to objects in a scene or to create and customize materials. Materials control such attributes as color, texture, transparency, and a host of other physical properties that you can adjust to create a realistic representation of the model.

Learning Objectives

- Understand the role of materials and maps in visualization.Display and manage all of the materials used in a scene using the Slate Material Explorer.
- Work with Arnold materials and modify the Standard Surface material to create different types of materials from it.
- Assign bitmaps or procedural maps to replace the shader parameters in materials.
- Assign Physical materials and apply the various presets provided with the material.
- Create a Multi/Sub-Object material and assign different materials to specific faces of a single object.
- Learn to use the Material Explorer and the Scene Converter.

6.1 Understanding Materials and Maps

Introduction to Materials

Materials can be used to create believable visualizations and to dress up geometry so that it resembles objects in the real world. Materials control how light interacts with surfaces in 3D models. If an object is shiny it reflects the light; however, if transparency is applied, the light passes through the object.

- Materials use Maps to paint the surfaces with all types of textures to resemble the actual construction materials for your design.
- Different material types use different material shaders to generate their work. Shaders are algorithms that create the image. Each shader has its own set of parameters.

Materials and Renderers in the Autodesk 3ds Max Software

Materials are deeply interconnected with the renderers. Regardless of which renderer is used, the rendering process is similar for all material types. In the 3D visualization process, to create an image in the viewport or in a image file, a *renderer* is employed. The viewport display uses an interactive viewport renderer, however the image is created using an *image* (production) renderer. The renderer determines what the pixel's RGB (red, green, blue) values are in the image based on the material assignments.

- In the Autodesk 3ds Max software, you can use the Scanline, Quicksilver, VUE File, ART renderer, or Arnold as image renderers. You can set the appropriate renderer in the *Render Setup* dialog box. in the Main Toolbar, click  (Render Setup) and select the required renderer in the *Renderer* list.
- Depending on the selected image renderer, the materials displayed in the material list vary.
- To create an image render of a view, use  (Render Production) in the Main Toolbar. You are required to use  (Render Production) throughout the practices in this chapter.
- The viewport renderer can use Nitrous Direct 3D 11 (default), Nitrous Direct3D 9, Nitrous Software, Legacy Direct3D, or Legacy OpenGL graphics drivers to create the real-time interactive display.
- The viewport provides a frame around the image and the output resolution determines the number of pixels to be created in that frame. The renderer then examines the geometry in the scene, first looking at the face normals, removing the faces whose normals face away from the camera (face normals are directional vectors perpendicular to the surface of the face). The remaining faces are z-sorted, the faces in front covering up the ones further away.

- Once the faces are determined, the color, transparency, shininess, texture, reflection, bumpiness, and other values are defined based on the material type, shaders, and map channels.
- The visible faces are calculated using the UVW mapping coordinates and the scene illumination. This determines RGB values, which are applied to the pixels in the image.

Material Components

Materials have several fundamental components. Materials have channels that determine the color applied in the calculation based on the lighting interaction. The components available are described as follows:

- The *Base* color represents those faces that are receiving illumination.
- The *Specular* channel determines color based on shininess and lighting information.
- The Shininess is controlled by various parameters, such as **Metalness** and **Roughness**. Shininess also plays a part in reflection and refraction.
- A Transmission quality is determined by *opacity* values.
- Materials are defined by maps and other physical properties.

Maps

Maps are the key components when working with materials. Maps are based on either 2D image files (bitmaps) or are formula-based, computer-generated images called procedural maps. Some maps can be configured as composites or adjustments to other maps.

- Materials can include multiple maps to serve different purposes.
- Map also serve in other roles, such as an environment background or a lighting projection.

- Maps cannot be applied directly to objects in a scene; instead, they are assigned to materials. These materials containing maps are then directly applied to objects, as shown in Figure 6–1.
- When a material containing a map is applied to an object, mapping coordinates are required for the software to render it correctly.

Figure 6–1

- Two of the most commonly used maps types are **diffuse color** and **bump**.

Diffuse Color	Defines the color of objects under normal lighting. • Digital or scanned photographs can be used as diffuse color maps. • The figure below is a brick image map (left) and a rendering of an object with a brick material that uses it (right). 

Bump	Make objects appear to have texture without modifying object geometry. • Bump maps are used to describe indentations, relief, and roughness. • In bump maps the lighter-colored areas display projected away from the surface while the darker areas display recessed. • The figure below displays a brick bump map (left) and a rendering of an object with a brick material that uses it (right). • You can apply both the diffuse and bump map to a single object. 

- In addition to these two map types, the Autodesk 3ds Max software can use maps to control many different material parameters that might vary across a surface, including shininess, transparency, and more.

6.2 Managing Materials

Materials are managed through the Material Editor (Slate or Compact). The *Slate Material Editor* has the *Material/Map Browser* included with it whereas the *Compact Material Editor* has an option for accessing the *Material/Map Browser*.

- Use the *Slate Material Editor* to design and build materials.
- Use the *Compact Material Editor* to apply existing materials.

Slate Material Editor Interface

The *Slate Material Editor* is a graphical interface for listing, creating, modifying, and assigning different kinds of materials. It enables you to graphically create and modify complex materials by wiring the maps and materials to different channels of the parent material. It also enables you to edit and modify the parameters of already created materials.

- In the Main Toolbar, in the *Material* flyout, use  (Slate Material Editor) to open the *Slate Material Editor*, as shown in Figure 6–2.
- You can also select **Rendering>Material Editor>Slate Material Editor**. Pressing <M> opens the last material editor that was used.

Figure 6–2

The interface of the *Slate Material Editor* has the following main areas:

- Material/Map Browser
- Active View
- Navigator Window
- Parameter Editor
- Toolbar
- Menu Bar

Material/Map Browser

The *Material/Map Browser* area (shown in Figure 6–3) contains an extensive list of predefined materials and maps. You can use the predefined materials directly or as a base for modifying them to get the required material effect.

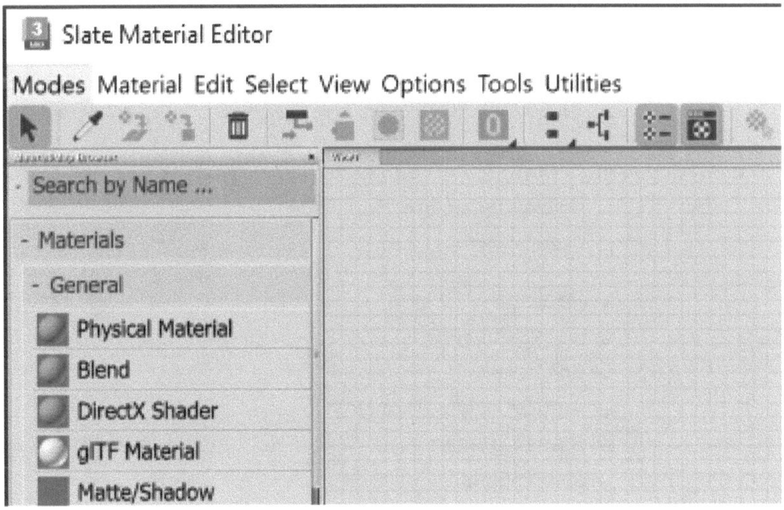

Figure 6–3

- The Browser displays by default, but you can temporarily close it by clicking x in the title bar. You can open it by selecting **Tools>Material/Map Browser** in the *Slate Material Editor's* menu bar (as shown in Figure 6–4) or by pressing <O> when the *Slate Material Editor* is the active window.

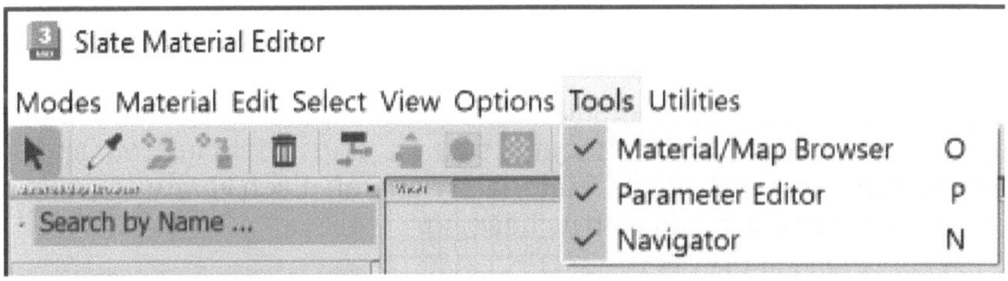

Figure 6–4

- You can also open the *Material/Map Browser* independent of the Material Editor by selecting **Rendering>Material/Map Browser** in the menu bar.

- At the top of the *Material/Map Browser*, click  to open the drop-down list (options menu), as shown in Figure 6–5. It contains options that enable you to control the display of the libraries, materials, maps, and other groups of materials. It also enables you to create and manage new custom libraries and groups.

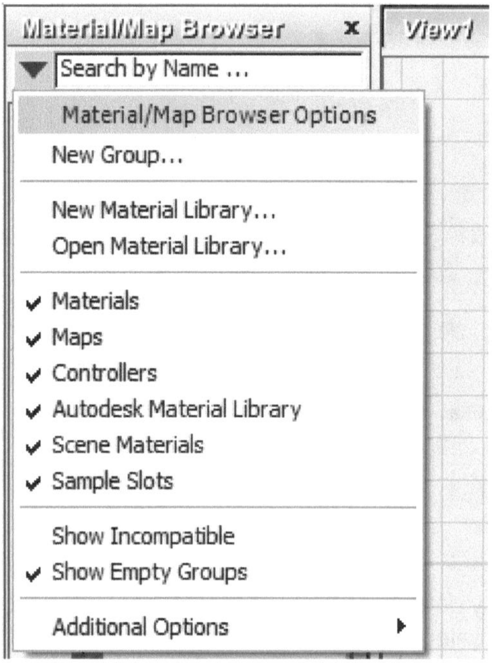

Figure 6–5

- The *Search by Name* box enables you to enter the first few characters of the material/map name to display the list of materials/maps that you want to use.
- The materials in the Browser are organized in the form of libraries and groups. The groups are organized on the basis of their attributes such as Maps, Materials, etc and are further divided into subgroups (For example, **Materials>General**). Each library or group has a +/- sign, to expand or contract, along with its heading.
- The *Materials* and *Maps* groups contain the type of materials and maps that can be used as templates for creating custom materials and maps.
- The *Controller* group contains the animation controllers that can be used for material animation.
- The materials and maps listed in the *Material/Map Browser* are dependent on the active image renderer.

- The Autodesk Material Library contains Autodesk materials, which are shared between various Autodesk applications, such as AutoCAD, Inventor, and Revit. The library displays when the active production renderer is set to the **ART** renderer or **Quicksilver Hardware** renderer.
- All of the materials used in the scene are listed in the *Scene Materials* group. A solid wedge shaped red band displayed with a scene material name indicates that the **Show Shaded Material In Viewport** option has been selected.
- The materials listed in the Browser are dependent on the type of renderer currently in use. To see all of the materials independent of the renderer, select **Show Incompatible** option in the *Material/Map Browser* drop-down list (click ▼ to open the options menu).

Active View

The Active View is an area in the *Slate Material Editor* that displays the expanded view of materials with all its elements shown as nodes, as shown in Figure 6–6. You can graphically create and modify complex materials by wiring their nodes together, and further edit their parameters through this view.

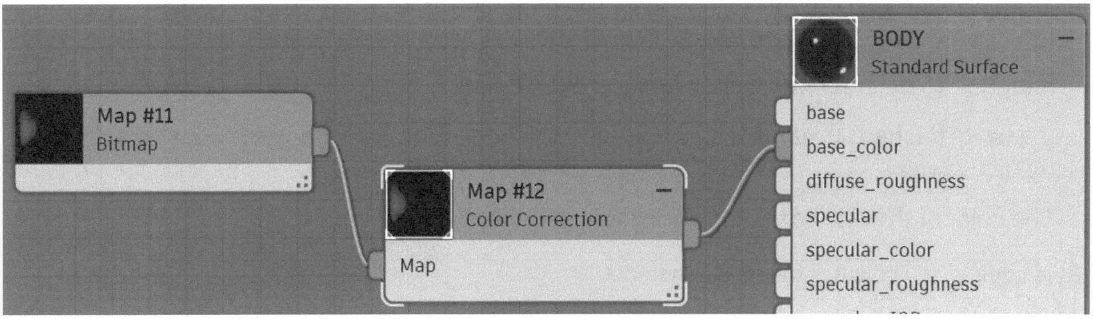

Figure 6–6

- To display a material in the active view (*View1*, by default), drag the material from the Map/ Material Browser and then drop it on the *View1* sheet. These are called nodes.
- You can also double-click on the material in the *Material/Map Browser* to automatically place it on the *View1* sheet.
- Once the material node is loaded on the active view, the title bar with a preview icon is displayed and the list of various channel slots are listed, as shown in Figure 6–6. You can wire each of these slots to another map or material. On the left side, each node has a number of input sockets for each slot. On the right side of each node is a single output socket. These can be wired to the sockets of other material. If a map or material is wired to a channel, the slot displays in green. This material, with its input sockets wired, becomes the parent material and the materials and maps that are wired to the slots become the children. You can further wire the children to other materials to create complex material trees.

- You can also right-click in an empty area of the active view to open a menu containing options for selecting any material/map/controller listed in the *Material/Map Browser*.
- The main material node has a blank output socket on the right side that can be used to assign this material to geometry in the viewport. Click and hold the output socket and drag the cursor on to the object. A temporary wire displays indicating that you are assigning the material. Assigning material in this way ignores already selected objects or geometry in the viewport.
- You can use the scroll wheel to zoom in or zoom out on the nodes in the *View1* sheet. Hold the scroll wheel to pan around in the sheet.
- If you cannot find a material node in the *View1* sheet, you can use the  (Search) button to open the **Search Bar**. Enter the material node name (as shown in Figure 6–7) to display the material node in the *View1* sheet.

Figure 6–7

- You can also delete wires to cut the connection between the parent material and the child material. To delete a wire, select it and press <Delete>.
- If a white dashed line displays as a border around a node, its Parameter Editor displays in the active view.
- The color of the title bar of the node indicates the type of material.

Blue node	Indicates that it is a material.
Green node	Indicates that it is a map.
Yellow node	Indicates that it is a controller

- Right-clicking on a title bar of a node displays a specific shortcut menu containing the options for managing that material or map. The options enable you to control the display and how you want the preview to be displayed on the active sheet. It also enables you to organize the material nodes and their children more efficiently.
- You can select multiple material/map nodes together, then right-click to open the combined menu and use the options for all of the nodes at the same time.
- You can toggle between a large and small material preview icon by double-clicking on the icon in the node title bar.

- The outline of a preview icon indicates whether the material is assigned or not (hot or cold) to objects in the viewport.

	No white boundary around the icon indicates that the material is not used in the scene and is cold.
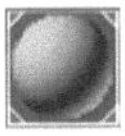	Outlined white triangles at the four corners indicate the material is hot and is being used in the scene. Modifying this material interactively displays the modifications in the scene.
	Solid white triangles at the four corners indicate the material is applied to the currently selected object on the scene.

- Additional sheets can be added to the View area by right-clicking on the default *View1* tab and selecting **Create New View**. Using this menu, you can also rename and delete your views. Once multiple sheets exist, you can select the appropriate tab to active it.

Hint: Active View

To organize your working space, it is recommended that you delete any unused materials from the active view. Deleting a material from the active view does not delete the material from the *Scene materials* list. You can drag and drop (or double-click) the material back to the active view.

- After you have created and applied materials to a scene, the *View* sheets are saved with the .MAX file. When you open the file again, the sheets display the saved material nodes.

Navigator Window

The Navigator window, which displays by default, provides a quick layout of the nodes in the active sheet, as shown in Figure 6–8. It can be used to pan around in the active view by dragging the active box. The colored nodes indicate the same concepts as that of a sheet.

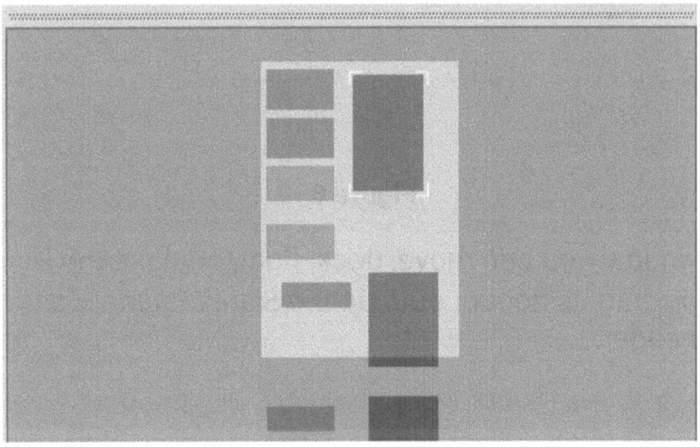

Figure 6–8

Parameter Editor

You can modify a material or a map by adjusting their parameters. Click on the material's title bar heading to display the Parameters, as shown in Figure 6–9. A white line border displays around the node indicating that its Parameter Editor is displayed. The parameters are grouped in rollouts and you can click the arrow on the rollout name bar to expand the rollout and access its parameters. You can rename the material by entering a new name in the *Name* field of the Parameter Editor.

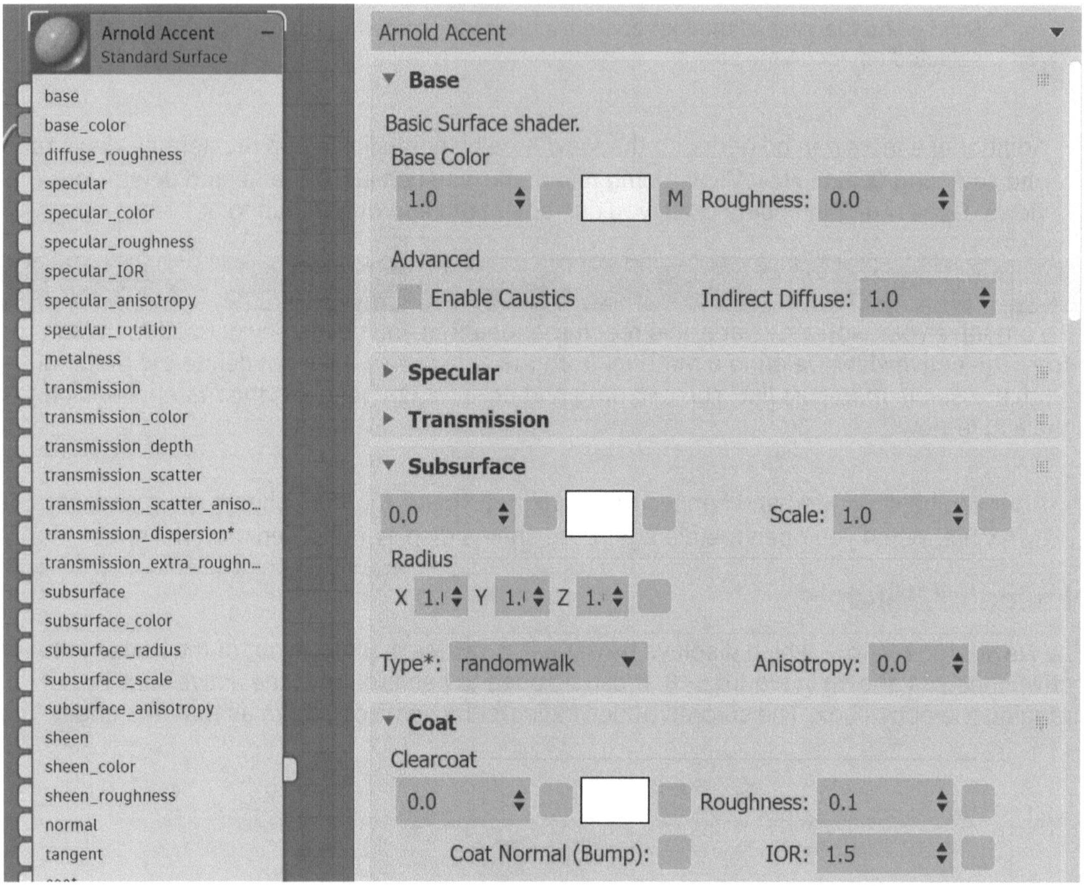

Figure 6–9

- As with any other window, you can move, dock, float, or close the Parameter Editor. To float the Parameter Editor, drag its header outside the *Slate Material Editor*. To dock it again, double-click on its header.

  Note: *Floating the Parameter Editor and hiding the Navigator can help reduce the footprint of the Slate Material Editor on the screen.*

Toolbar

The *Slate Material Editor* includes a toolbar (shown in Figure 6–10) at the top left corner of the window and contains the following tools.

Figure 6–10

(Select Tool)	Enables you to select a material node in the Active View. It is the tool that is selected by default.
(Pick Material from Object)	Enables you to pick a material that is assigned to an object in the scene and display it in the active view.
(Put Material to Scene)	Enables you to update objects having an older material whose copy has been edited after it was applied.
(Assign Material to Selection)	Enables you to assign a selected material to selected objects in the viewport.
(Move Children)	Enables you to move the complete material tree when you move the parent material node in the Active View. Clearing this tool, moves the Parent individually and extends the wires as you move the parent
(Show Shaded Material in Viewport)	Enables you to display the maps for the active material. This is helpful when you are modifying the map in the *View* sheet, you can see the changes interactively in the viewport. You do not have to render to see the map changes.
/ (Lay Out All-Vertical/ Horizontal)	Enables you to organize all of the material nodes and their children in the *View* sheet either vertically or horizontally.
(Lay Out Children)	Enables you to lay out the children of the currently selected node without changing the position of the parent node.
(Material/Map Browser) (Parameter Editor)	Enable you to control the display of these tools in the *Slate Material Editor*.
(Select by Material)	Enables you to select objects based on the active material.

Menu Bar

The *Slate Material Editor* displays a menu bar along the top of the window (shown in Figure 6–11) that contains commands for various actions related to materials.

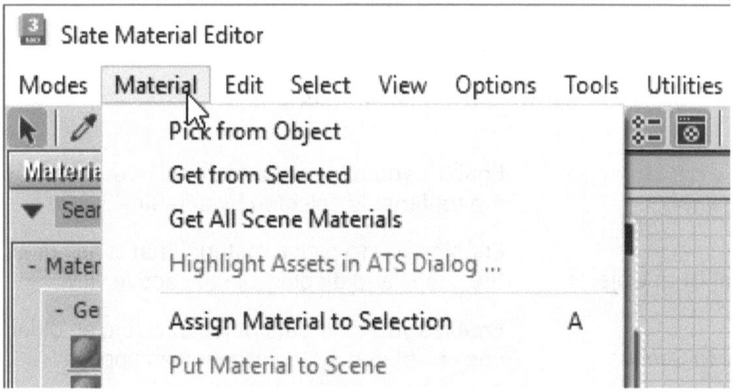

Figure 6–11

Modes	Enables you to toggle between the two editors (Slate and Compact).
Material	Enable you to select a material by picking it from the object in the viewport, by selecting an object in the viewport, or selecting all of the materials used in the scene. You also have the options for assigning materials.
Edit	Enables you to edit the active view and update the preview windows.
Select	Provides different selection options that can be used in the active view.
View	Provides different zoom and pan options and contains options for the layout of the nodes in the active view.
Options	Enables you to further manage the *Slate Material Editor*.
Tools	Controls the display of the *Material/Map Browser*, Parameter Editor, and Navigator.
Utilities	Provides the render and object selection options and contains options for managing the materials.

6.3 Arnold Materials

Arnold renderer offers high quality production rendering capabilities. Along with the renderer, a shader library is also provided. Once you set **Arnold** as the current renderer, the Arnold specific components become available for use.

In the *Slate Material Editor*, the **Arnold** category (shown in Figure 6–12) contains materials that are meant to be used specifically with the Arnold renderer.

> ***Note:*** *For the **Arnold** material category to be displayed, **Arnold** must be selected as the production renderer in the Render Setup dialog box.*

The materials are grouped into different categories (as shown in Figure 6–13) and can be used directly in your scene.

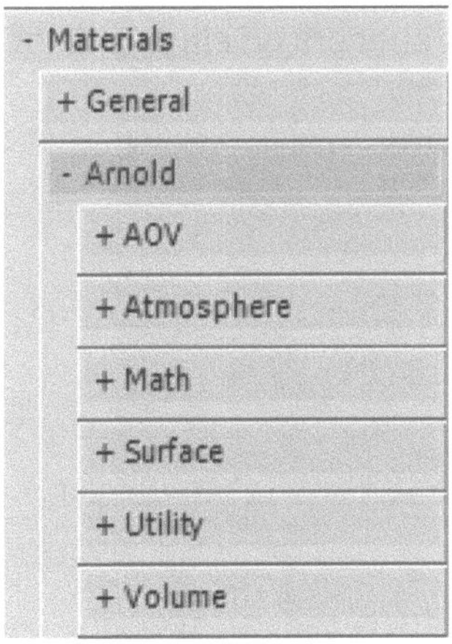

Figure 6–12

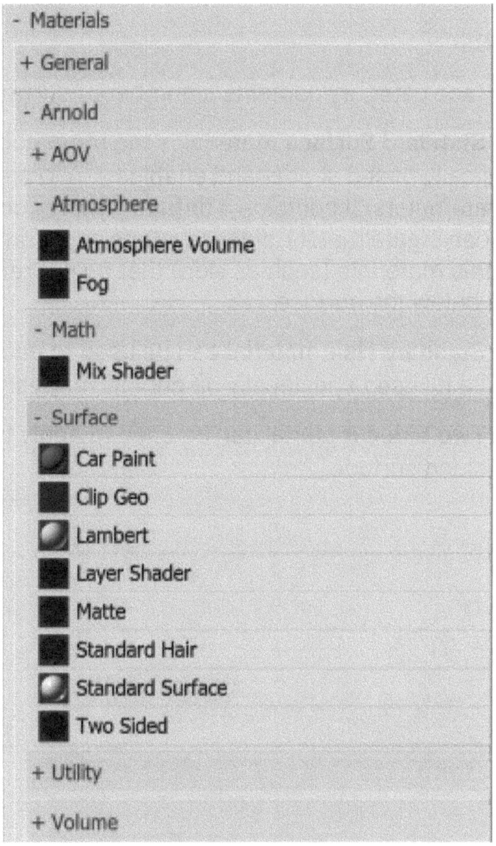

Figure 6–13

AOV

The **AOV** (Arbitrary Output Variables) category enables you to render a scene using different shading components and features and then combine them at a later time. It contains **AOV Write Float**, **AOV Write Int**, and **AOV Write RGB**.

- A new AOV file has to be created before writing an AOV. A custom AOV can be added in the *Render Setup* dialog box>*AOV Settings* tab when the current renderer is **Arnold**.

Atmosphere

The **Atmosphere** category contains **Atmosphere Volume** and **Fog**. You can use **Atmosphere Volume** when you want to simulate shafts of lights and shadows that are cast from geometric objects. The **Fog** shader causes the far off objects to display dimmer with subdued colors simulating the effects of fog.

Surface

The **Surface** category contains a number of surface shaders, as shown in Figure 6–14.

- The **Standard Surface** material is the most commonly used shader with Arnold. It is a physically-based shader and enables you to create different types of materials by modifying its parameters. It contains a diffuse layer for color and then using other group of parameters you can create metals, plastics, stone, etc. You can use the *Subsurface* parameters to create organic materials (such as skin) that do not reflect light at the surface but scatter or absorb light below the surface.
- The **Standard Hair** material can be used to easily create realistic looking hair and fur. It should be used specifically on curved shapes.
- The **Two Sided** material can be used to apply two different shaders on either side of a two-sided surface.

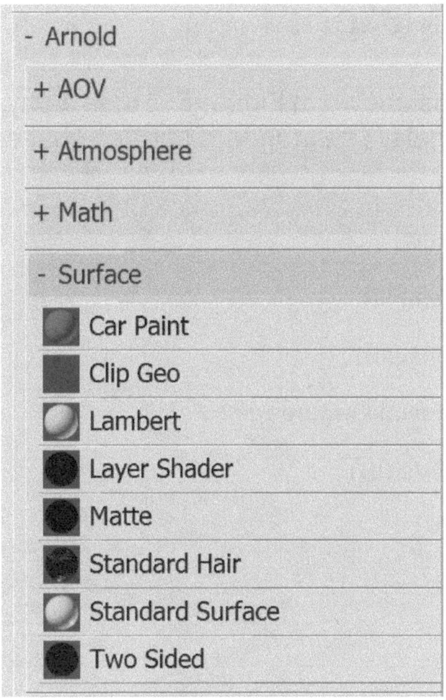

Figure 6–14

Utility

The **Utility** category contains the **Maps to Material** option that enables you to use the Maps directly on the objects in the scene. The map/input shader must be connected to the input slot of *Texture Map*, as shown in Figure 6–15.

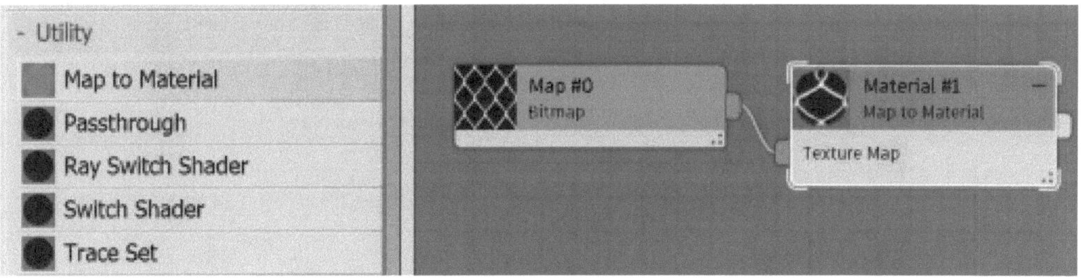

Figure 6–15

Standard Surface Material

The standard surface shader (as shown in Figure 6–16) is a physically based shader that can produce various types of materials. The standard surface shader includes the following parameters:

- Base
- Specular
- Transmission
- Subsurface
- Coat
- Sheen
- Thin Film
- Emission
- Special Features
- AOVs (ID)

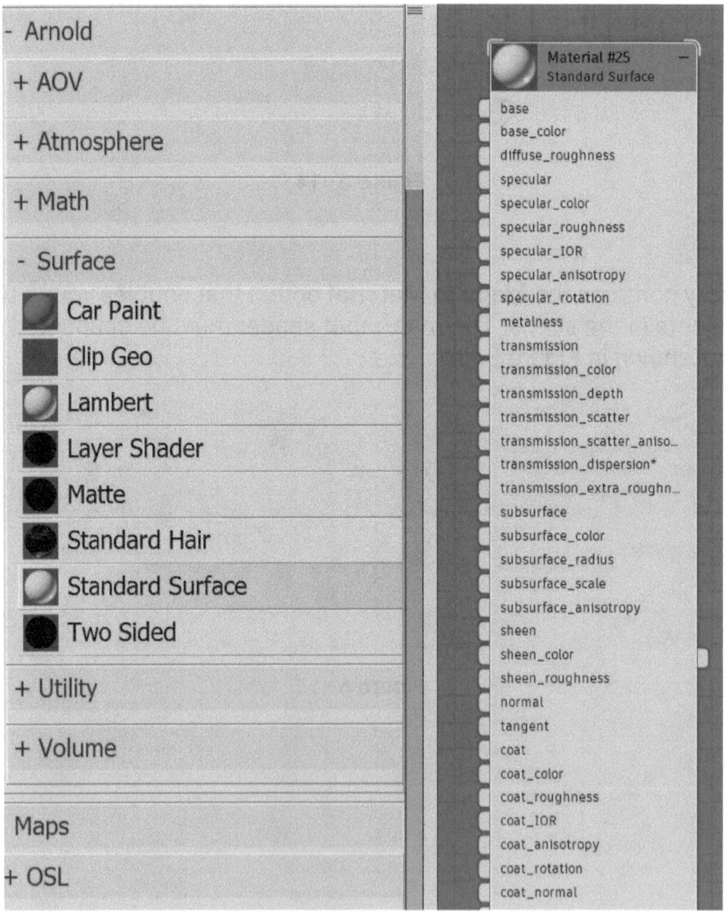

Figure 6–16

Base

The *Base* rollout has the following controls, as shown in Figure 6–17:

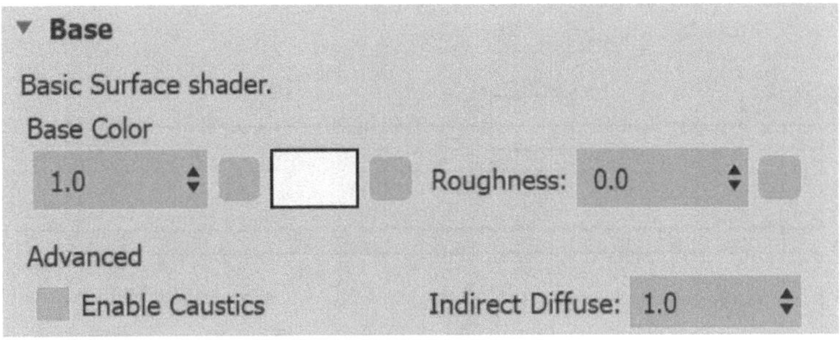

Figure 6–17

Base Color:

- *Base color:* Creates the diffuse component. The value ranges from **0.0** to **1.0**. (The default value is **1.0**.)
- *Roughness: Using* an Oren-Nayar diffuse shading system, the base component reflects the roughness of the surface. The value ranges from **0.0** to **1.0**. While a value of **0.0** produces a reflection comparable to a Lambert, higher values produce reflections that are suited for rougher surface materials such as concrete, plaster, sand, or concrete.

Advanced:

- *Enable Caustics:* Specifies whether indirect diffuse rays will produce direct specular and indirect specular light components, as well as reflection and refraction. Because caustics can create noise, this option is disabled by default.
- *Indirect Diffuse:* Uses the indirect diffuse component. The value ranges from **0.0** to **1.0**. (The default value is **1.0**.)

Specular

The *Specular* rollout has the following controls, as shown in Figure 6–18:

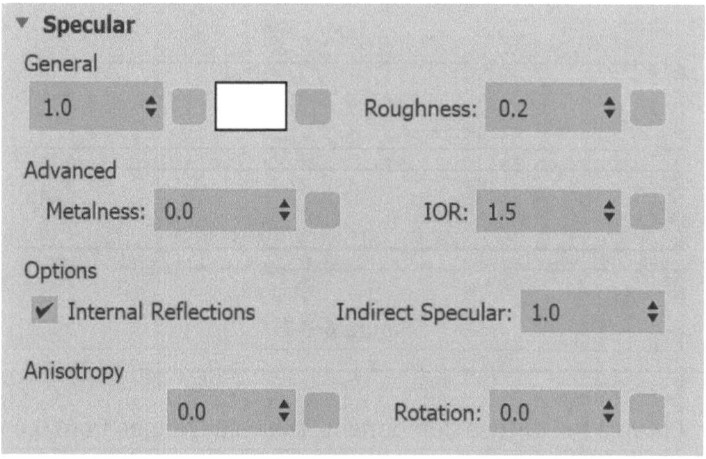

Figure 6–18

General:

- *General:* The brightness of the specular highlight is influenced by the weight. The value ranges from **0.0** to **1.0**. (The default value is **1.0**.)
- *Roughness:* You can define the roughness to specify how blurry/glossy the specular reflections are. The value ranges from **0.0** to **1.0**. The lower the value, the sharper the reflection. While **0** will produce a perfectly sharp mirror reflection, **1.0** will produce reflections that are close to diffuse shading.

Advanced:

- *Metalness:* The value ranges from **0.0** to **1.0** (The default value is **1.0**.). When metalness is **1.0**, the surface behaves like a true metal, fully utilizing the specular reflection and complex Fresnel.
- *IOR:* This attribute defines the balance between reflections on surfaces facing the viewer and on surface edges. The reflection intensity remains unchanged, but the reflection intensity on the front side changes a lot. The default value is **1.5**.

Options:

- *Internal Reflections:* When disabled, this will prevent indirect specular and mirror perfect reflection computations when ray refraction depth is greater than **0** and if there is at least one refraction ray traced in the current ray tree.
- *Indirect Specular:* The indirect specular component is adjusted. The value ranges from **0.0** to **1.0**. (The default value is **1.0**.)

Anisotropy:

- *Anisotropy:* Transmits and contrasts light with a directional bias and causes materials to appear rougher or glossier in certain directions. The default value is **0** indicating 'Isotropic'. As you move the control towards **1.0**, the surface becomes more anisotropic in the U axis.
- *Rotation:* The rotation value alters the orientation of the anisotropic reflectance in UV space. At **0.0**, there will be no rotation, while at **1.0** it will rotate by 180°. For a surface with brushed metal, this determines the angle of the material being brushed. For metallic surfaces, the anisotropic highlight should be positioned in a direction perpendicular to the brushing direction.

Transmission

The *Transmission* rollout has the following controls, as shown in Figure 6–19:

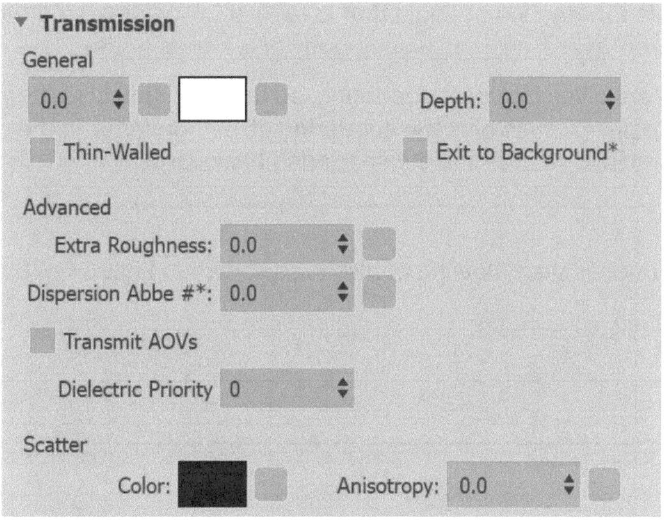

Figure 6–19

General:

- *General:* Allows light to penetrate the surface, for translucent materials such as glass or water. The value ranges from **0.0** to **1.0**.
- *Depth:* The volume at which the transmission color is obtained.
- *Thin-Walled:* The effect of a translucent object being reflected from behind. It is recommended that this only be used with thin objects (single sided geometry) as objects with a thickness may not render correctly.
- *Exit to Background*:* Used to define the environment color for reflection rays where there was inadequate ray depth. (No GPU Support)

Advanced:

- *Extra Roughness:* Extra refraction blurriness.
- *Dispersion Abbe #*:* Abbe number of the material, which indicates how much the index of refraction varies across wavelengths. (No GPU Support).
- *Transmit AOVs:* When enabled, Transmission will be able to transmit through AOVs. When the background is transparent, then the transmission surface will become transparent so that it can be incorporated into another background.
- *Dielectric Priority:* Determine how to resolve overlapping dielectrics into a well-defined medium, so that higher priority (higher number) dielectrics override lower priority ones that are effectively eliminated. This is used to create cases with adjacent dielectric media such as a glass of water with ice.

Scatter:

- *Color:* Suitable for any kind of liquid that is fairly thick or where there is enough of it for scattering to be visible, such as a deep body of water of honey.
- *Anisotropy:* Zero gives isotropic scattering, so that the light is scattered evenly in all directions. Positive values bias the scattering effect forwards, in the direction of the light, while negative values bias the scattering backwards.

Subsurface

The *Subsurface* rollout has the following controls, as shown in Figure 6–20:

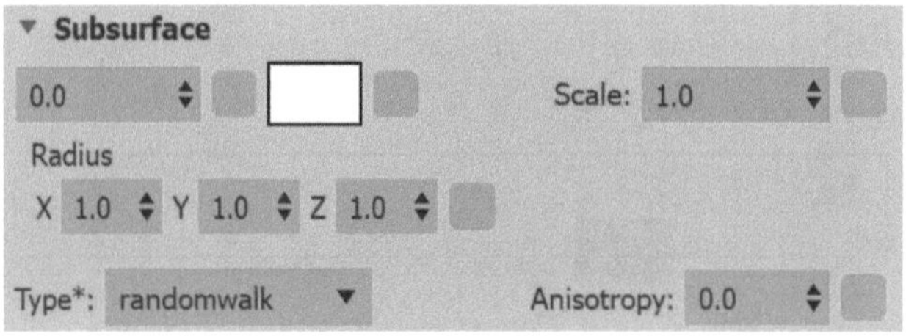

Figure 6–20

Subsurface:

- *Subsurface:* The amount of sub-surface scattering (SSS) simulates the impact of light entering an object and scattering beneath its surface. Multiplies SSS Color.
- *Scale:* The SSS component is scaled.

Radius:

- *Radius:* The radius of each sample affects the area. The higher values of the subsurface scattering are smooth. The results will vary depending on the scale of your object in the scene.

Type:

- *Randomwalk (default):* Traces below the surface with a real random walk and does not make any assumptions about the geometry being locally flat.
- *Diffusion:* Can capture both surface detail and deep scattering with a single layer,.
- Randomwalk v2: Scatters more accurately and deeply through extremely transparent/ optically-thin objects.

Anisotropy:

- When a property varies according to direction, the material is Anisotropy. Factor between **-1** (full back-scatter) and **1** (full forward-scatter). When a property is the same in all directions, the material is isotropic. The default is **0** for an isotropic medium, giving a uniform effect.

Coat

The *Coat* rollout has the following controls, as shown in Figure 6–21:

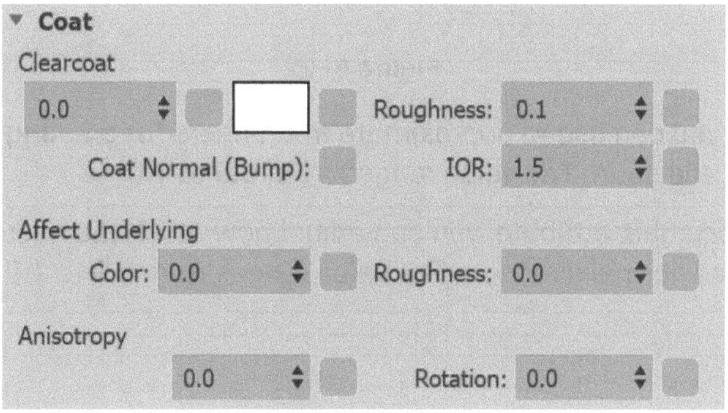

Figure 6–21

Clearcoat:

- Layer on top of all other shading properties. The value ranges from **0.0** to **1.0**.
- *Roughness:* Controls the sheen of the specular reflections. Lower values will produce sharper reflections. A value of **0** will result in a perfectly sharp mirror reflection, while **1.0** will result reflections are a diffuse reflection, 0.1(default). The value ranges from **0.0** to **1.0**.

Affect Underlying

- *Color:* In the real world, when a material is coated, there is an amount of internal reflections on the inside of the coating. This causes light to bounce onto the surface multiple times before escaping, allowing the material to have an enhanced effect. An example of this is varnished wood. The value ranges from **0.0** to **1.0**.

- *Roughness:* Causes roughness to the coating's to have an effect on the underlying layer's roughness, simulating the blurring effect of being seen through the top layer. The value ranges from **0.0** to **1.0**.

Anisotropy

- *Anisotropy:* Reflects and transmits light with a directional bias and causes materials to appear rougher or glossier in different directions. The default value for anisotropy is **0**, which means 'isotropic.' As the value changes towards **1.0**, the surface becomes more anisotropic in the U axis.
- *Rotation:* Changes the rotation of the coat.

Sheen

The *Sheen* rollout has the following controls, as shown in Figure 6–22:

Figure 6–22

- *Sheen:* A layer you can use to approximate microfibers for creating cloth-like surfaces such as velvet and satin. The value ranges from **0.0** to **1.0**.
- *Roughness:* Using this attribute, you can adjust how much the microfiber would differ from the surface normal direction. The value ranges from **0.0** to **1.0**. (The default value is **0.3**.)

Thin Film

The effect of thin film interference on a surface can be used for materials such as multitone car paint, burnt chrome, or the reflective coating on an object. The *Thin Film* rollout has the following controls, as shown in Figure 6–23:

Figure 6–23

- *Thickness:* The actual thickness of the film between the specified min and max thickness. The value ranges from **0.0** to **2000** (soft min/max).
- *IOR:* Refractive index of the material surrounding it. Typically, this is set to **1.0** for air. (The default value is **1.5**.)

Emission

An attribute, which indicates that the material is emitting incandescent lights.

The *Emission* rollout has the following controls, as shown in Figure 6–24.

Figure 6–24

- *Emission:* Using this attribute, you can control the amount of light that is emitted from the surface. The value ranges from **0.0** to **1.0**.
- Using the color swatch, you can select the color of the light that is emitted.

Special Features

The *Special Features* rollout has the following controls, as shown in Figure 6–25:

Figure 6–25

- *Opacity (Cutout):* Color and map for opacity. Set the Opacity (Cutout) to a dark color (completely black will be invisible).
- *Normal (Bump):* A shader that perturbs the normal for bump mapping.
- *Tangents:* Together with the normal shading, it defines the tangent coordinate system that the input vector applies to.

The AOVs (as shown in Figure 6–26) are suitable for creating mattes for compositing or connecting arbitrary channels (e.g. noise shaders).

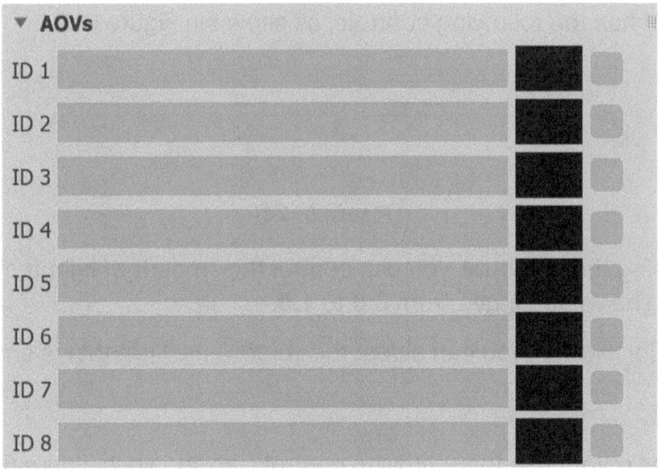

Figure 6–26

Practice 6a
Introduction to Materials

Practice Objectives

- Load a material library in the *Slate Material Editor*.
- Create and edit a new material and assign it to objects in the scene.

In this practice, you will assign previously created materials to different objects on the scene. You will then create, edit, and assign new materials to objects in the scene using the *Parameter Editor* of the *Slate Material Editor*.

You must set the paths to locate the External files and XREFs used in the practice. If you have not done this already, return to Chapter 1 and complete Task 1 to Task 3 in *Practice 1a: Organize Folders and Work with the Interface*. You only have to set the user paths once.

Task 1: Assign materials in the Slate Material Editor.

1. Open **Intro to Materials and Rendering.max.**
   - The Light pole model displays in the viewport.
2. In the Main Toolbar, in the *Material* flyout, click 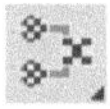 (Slate Material Editor) to open the *Slate Material Editor*. Alternatively, you can select **Rendering>Material Editor>Slate Material Editor**.

   Note: *If you start a new scene file, no materials are listed in the View1 sheet.*

3. In the *Slate Material Editor*, in the *View1* sheet, the material nodes display, as shown in Figure 6–27.
   - A blue node indicates that it is a material, a green node indicates that it is a map, and a yellow node indicates that it is a controller.

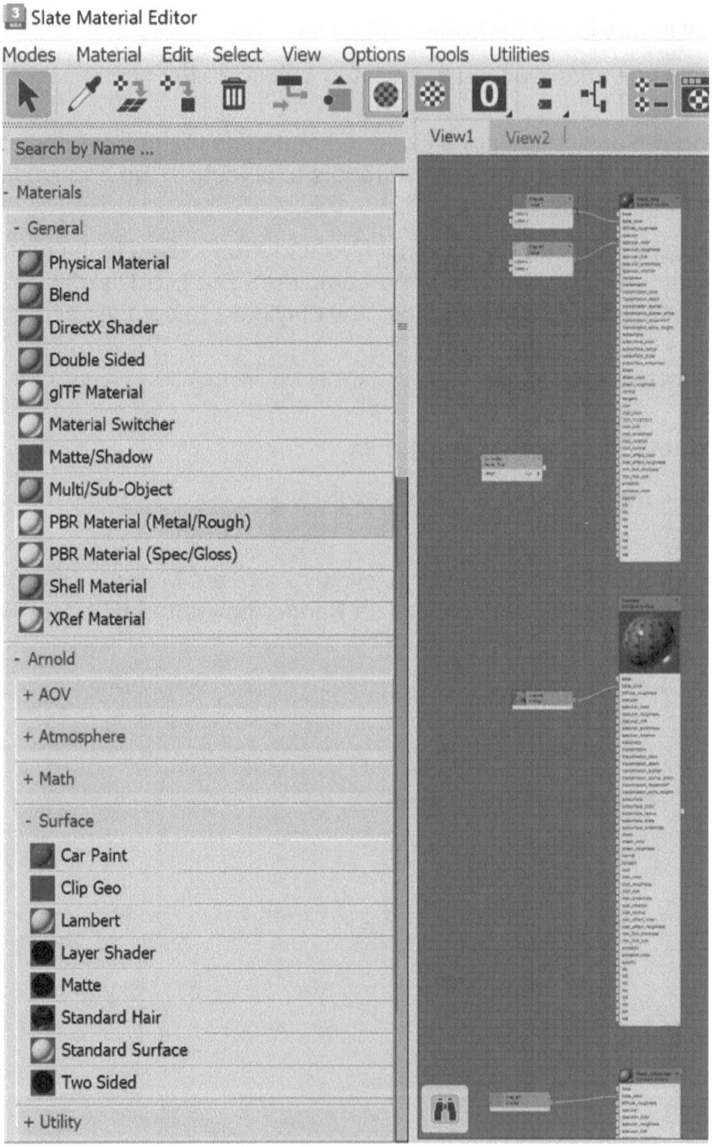

Figure 6–27

4. Click in an empty space in the *View1* sheet, and using the scroll wheel on your mouse, zoom in to the nodes. Hold the scroll wheel to pan around to see the details of each node.

5. Using Zoom and Pan locate the **Concrete** material (second material node from the top).

   Note: *You can close the Navigator and Parameter Editor to create more space for displaying the nodes in the active sheet. You can float them and then close the floating windows.*

6. Move and size the *Slate Material Editor* in the *Drawing* window so that you can see both the *Material Editor* and the model in the viewport window side by side.
7. In the **Concrete** material, click and hold the material output socket on the right side. Drag and drop the **Concrete** material from the *View1* sheet directly to the LP Base object in the viewport window, as shown in Figure 6–28. A temporary wire displays in *View1* indicating that you are assigning the material (Dragging in this way ignores which objects or geometry are currently selected in the model.). The material is assigned to the object and displays in the viewport.

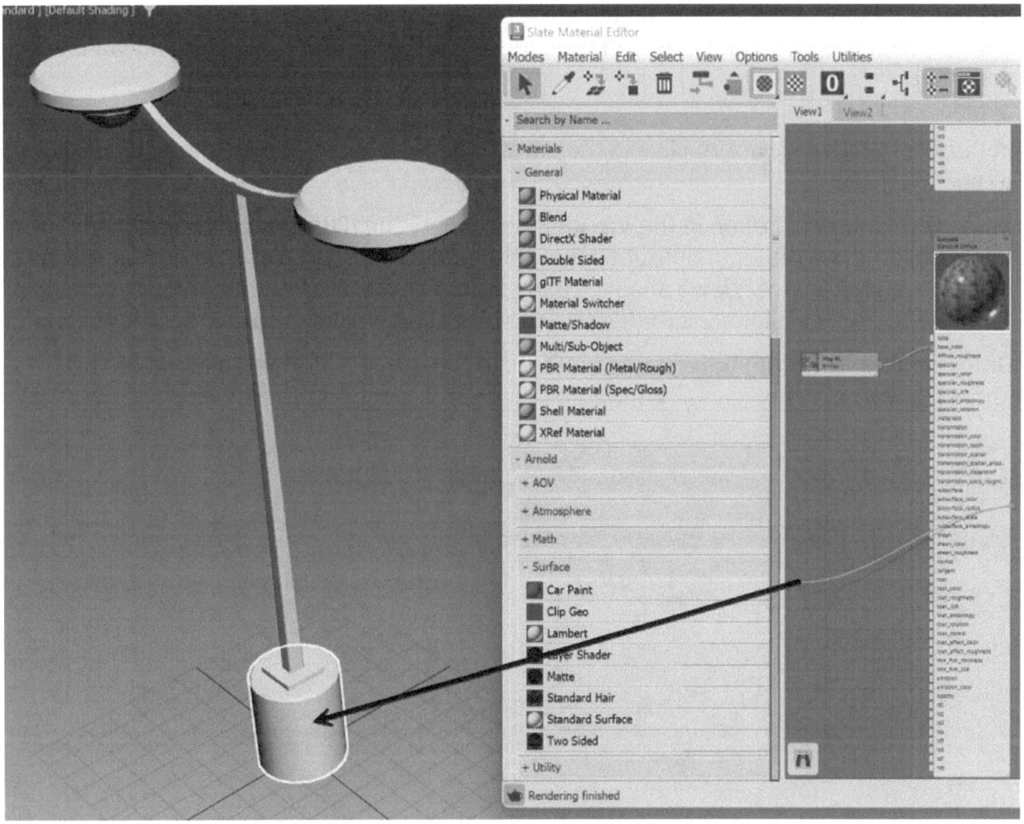

Figure 6–28

Note: *Dragging materials in highly complex scenes can be challenging. Instead, you can select objects, select the material, and use*  *(Assign Material to Selection) or select* ***Assign Material to Selection*** *in the right-click menu.*

8. Verify that the *Shading Viewport* label is set to **Standard**.
9. Using the Scene Explorer, select the groups **LP Fixture** and **LP Fixture01** (each group contains housing, globe, and mounting arm). You can also select them directly in the viewport.
10. In the *Slate Material Editor*, in the *View1* sheet, locate **Metal_Grey** material node (the first material node). Click on the title bar of the material. Note that a white line border displays around the node, and the name of the node along with its parameters is displayed in the Parameter Editor. Right-click on the title bar of the material and select **Assign Material to Selection** or use  (Assign Material to Selection) in the *Slate Material Editor* toolbar. The material is applied to all of the objects in the two **LP Fixture** groups.

Hint: Group Objects

To assign a material to individual objects in a group, select the group, select **Group>Open**, and then select the individual object in the group. Then, assign materials to individual parts in the group.

11. In the **Perspective** viewport, click in the empty space to clear the selection and orbit around to see the globes.
12. In the *Slate Material Editor,* in the *View1* sheet, locate the **Illuminated Lens** material node. Click and hold the material output socket on the right side. Drag and drop the **Illuminated Lens** material from the *View1* sheet directly onto one of the LP Globe objects in the model. This method only assigns the material to the object on which you are dropping the material.
13. Drag and drop the **Illuminated Lens** material to the other LP Globe object in the model, as shown in Figure 6–29.

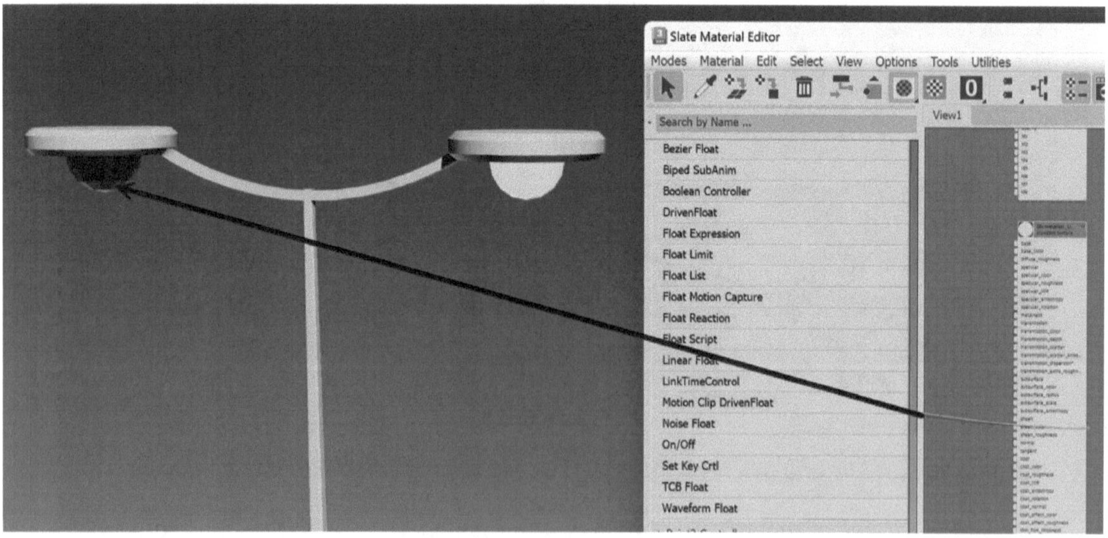

Figure 6–29

14. Assign the **Metal_Grey** material to the LP Base Plate and LP Pole objects using any of the assigning materials method.
15. Orbit and zoom in to all objects in the viewport. In the Main Toolbar, click  (Render Production) to render the scene. The scene is rendered, as shown in Figure 6–30. Close the Arnold RenderView Window.
    - A lighter background was added for visual clarity. It can be changed using **Background>Color** in the *Environment and Effects* dialog box (Rendering> Environment).
    - The globe material was made to look as if it is illuminated, but it does not actually add any light to the scene.

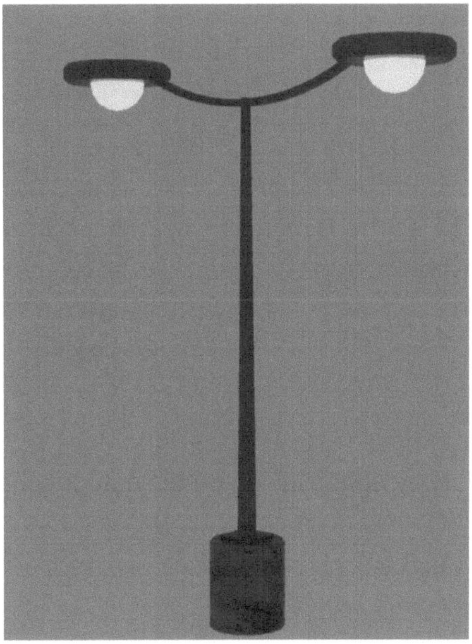

Figure 6–30

16. Save the file as **MyLightPoleMaterials.max**.

Task 2: Work with materials.

When you are starting a new scene or working in an existing scene you will have to create new materials or edit existing materials. In this task, you will be able to use the *Slate Material Editor* to create and work with materials.

1. The *Material/Map Browser* of the *Slate Material Editor* contains an extensive list of predefined materials that you can use directly or use them as a base for creating your custom materials. You can also import your own material library. Scroll through the list of materials that are available in the list.

2. At the top of the *Material/Map Browser*, click  to open the **Materials/Map Browser Options** menu.
3. In the *Materials/Map Browser Options* menu, select **Open Material Library**. The *Import Material Library* dialog box opens in the *materiallibraries* subdirectory. If required, browse to the path under the root installation (usually *C:\Program Files\Autodesk\3ds Max 2025*) and open the *\materiallibraries* subdirectory.
4. Select and open **AecTemplates.mat**, as shown in Figure 6–31.
   - In the *Material/Map Browser*, note that a list of materials is added to the top with **AecTemplates.mat** listed as the title, as shown in Figure 6–32.

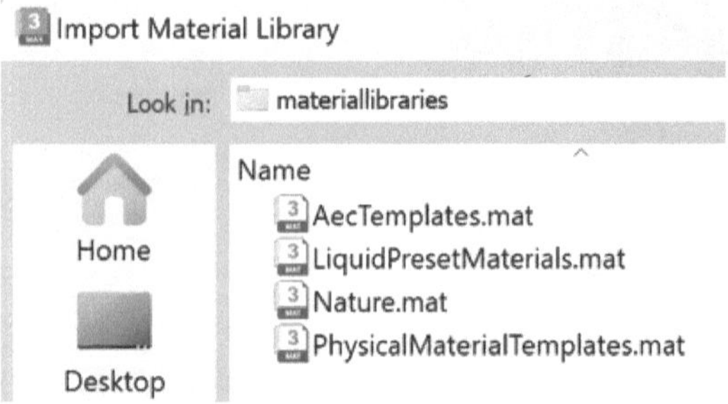

Figure 6–31

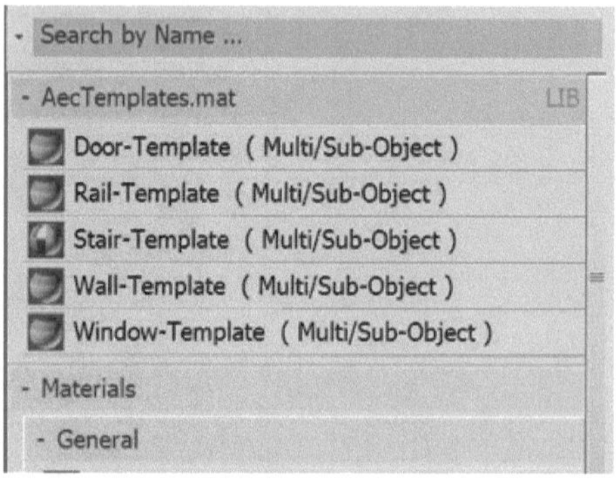

Figure 6–32

   - You can remove a library by right-clicking on the category heading and selecting **Close Material Library**.

   ***Note:** If the material libraries were not installed, there will be no files in the project folder in the \materiallibraries subdirectory.*

5. In the *Material/Map Browser*, expand the **Materials>General** category. A list of materials displays. Right-click on the **General** category and select **Display Group (and Subgroups) As>Medium Icons**. All of the materials in the **General** category now display as thumbnail images. Right-click on the **General** category again and select **Display Group (and Subgroups) As>Icons and Text** to display the materials in the icons and name format.
6. The *View1* sheet already displays the materials used in the scene. To create a new view, right-click on the *View1* label and select **Create New View**, as shown in Figure 6–33.

Figure 6–33

7. Accept the default name of **View2** and click **OK**. A new empty sheet named **View2** is added.
8. In the *Material/Map Browser*, expand the **Materials>Arnold** category. Expand **Surface** and double-click on the material **Standard Surface**. The material displays as a node in the View2 sheet. Right-click on the title bar heading of the node, select **Rename**, and change the material name to **Metal Galvanized** as shown in Figure 6–34. You can also rename in the Parameter Editor.

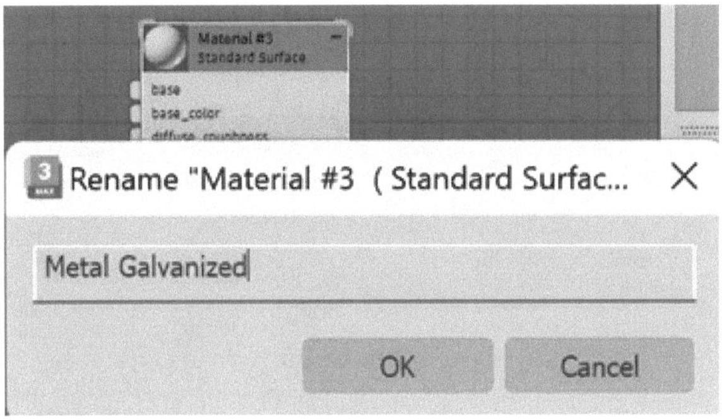

Figure 6–34

9. Verify that the new material is selected and has a white border around it. This indicates that its Parameter Editor is displayed. In the *Base* rollout, in **Base Color**, click **to pick a map** (**or drop a map**) icon, as shown in Figure 6–35. A separate *Material/Map Browser opens.*

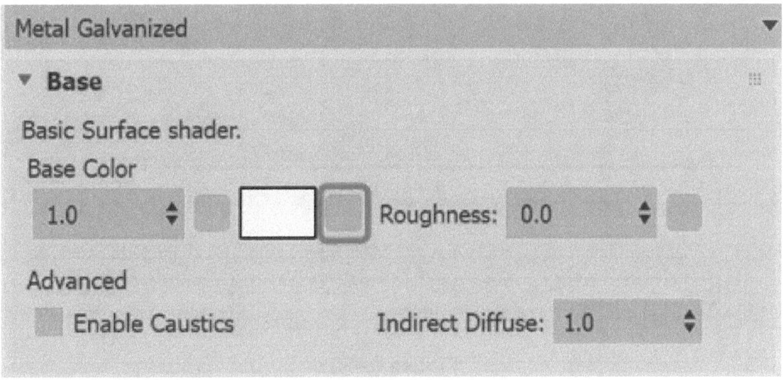

Figure 6–35

10. In the separate *Material/Map Browser*, in **Maps>General** categories, click **Bitmap**, as shown in Figure 6–36.

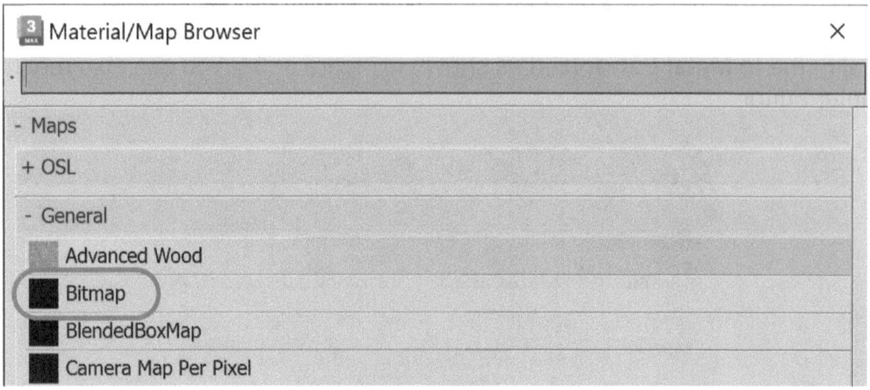

Figure 6–36

11. In the *Select Bitmap Image File* dialog box, browse to the ...*Maps* folder in the practice files folder. Select **Metals.Ornamental Metals.Galvanized.jpg** and click **Open**. A new node for Bitmap is added to the *View2* sheet and its output socket is connected to the base_color input socket of the **Metal Galvanized** material node, as shown in Figure 6–37.

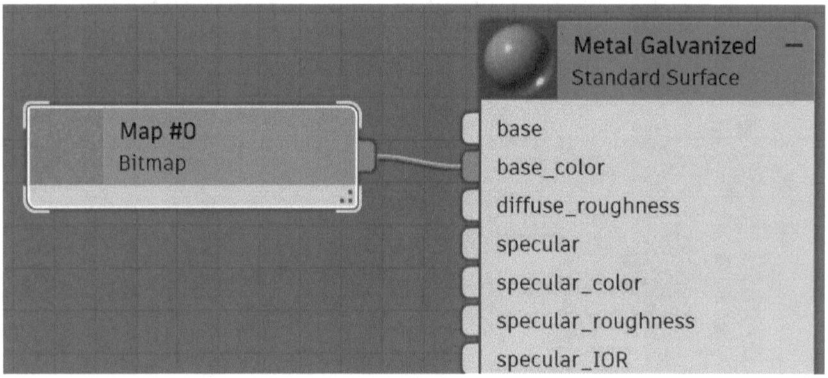

Figure 6–37

Hint: Add Materials to Sheets

Double-clicking on a material in the *Material/Map Browser* displays the material in the view sheet, where you can customize the material, as required. Add materials to view sheets if you want to modify them. If they are simply going to be assigned to an object in the scene, select and drag them directly from the *Material Browser* list onto the objects.

12. Using the drag and drop method from the output socket, assign the **Metal Galvanized** material to the **LP Fixture Housings** (the chamfer cylinders) and **LP Mounting Arms** (the arms holding the fixtures to the post). This method enables you to assign different materials to individual objects in the group.
13. In the **Perspective** viewport, select the **LP Base Plate** and **LP Pole** and in the *Slate Material Editor* toolbar, use  (Assign Material to Selection) to assign the **Metal Galvanized** material.
14. Click in an empty space in the viewport to clear the object selection. Review the preview icon for the material. Note that there is now a white outline around the thumbnail, as shown in Figure 6–38. This indicates that the material has been assigned to an object in the scene.
    - Note that this new material is also added to the *Scene Materials* list in the *Material Map Browser*, as shown in Figure 6–39.

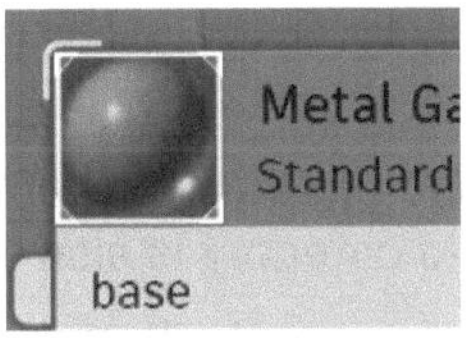

Figure 6–38

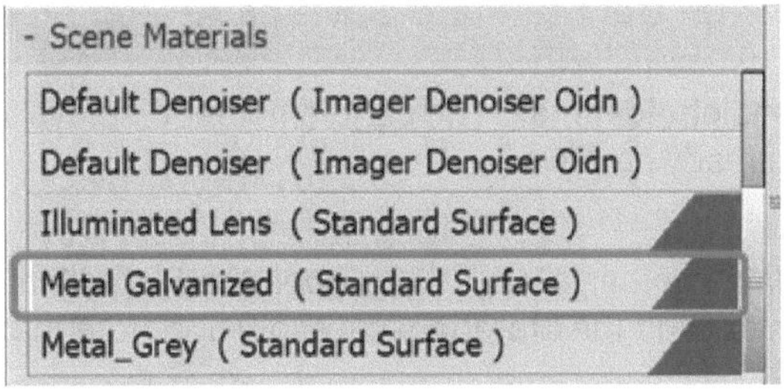

Figure 6–39

15. In the viewport, select **LP Pole**. Review the preview icon for the material and note that there is now a white outline with solid white corners around the thumbnail, as shown in Figure 6–40. This indicates that the material is assigned to a selected object in the scene.

Figure 6–40

16. Click anywhere in the viewport to clear the selection and close the *Slate Material Editor*.
17. Save the file as **My Intro to Materials**.

End of practice

Practice 6b
Work with Arnold Materials

Practice Objective

- Assign and modify Arnold material.

In this practice, you will explore the Arnold shaders. You will modify the Arnold Standard Surface shader to create different materials.

You must set the paths to locate the External files and XREFs used in the practice. If you have not done this already, return to Chapter 1 and complete Task 1 to Task 3 in *Practice 1a: Organize Folders and Work with the Interface*. You only have to set the user paths once.

Task 1: Assign the Standard Surface Arnold shader.

1. Open **candleholder.max**. The candle holder displays in the four viewports layout. A **camera** view is already created.

2. In the Main Toolbar, click 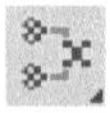 to open the *Slate Material Editor*. In the *Material/Map Browser,* expand the **Materials** category and note that **Arnold** category is also listed.

3. In the *Slate Material Editor*, expand the **Scene Materials** category at the bottom of the *Material/Map Browser*. Note that four **Standard Surface** materials are used in the scene, as shown in Figure 6–41.

    - The **Standard Surface** material is an Arnold-specific material and is similar to Physical Materials.

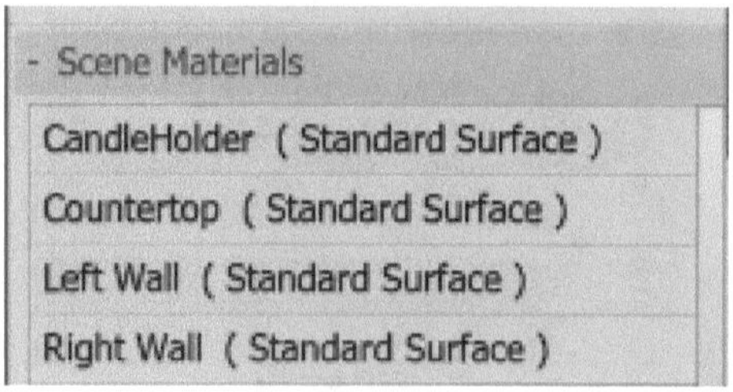

Figure 6–41

4. Double-click on each of the Scene Materials (**CandleHolder, Countertop, Left Wall,** and **Right Wall**) to place them on the *View1* sheet. They are placed on top of each other. In the *Material Editor* toolbar, click  (Layout Horizontal) to display the four materials horizontally in the *View1* sheet.

5. To change the color on each of these scene materials, click on a material node to open its Parameter Editor. In the *Base* rollout, select the color swatch for *Base Color* and select a color in the *Scene Color Selector*, as shown for the **Right Wall** in Figure 6–42. Change the color of all the four objects, using the colors as indicated: **Countertop** - dark pink, **Right Wall** - cyan, **CandleHolder** - dark blue, and **Left Wall** - green).

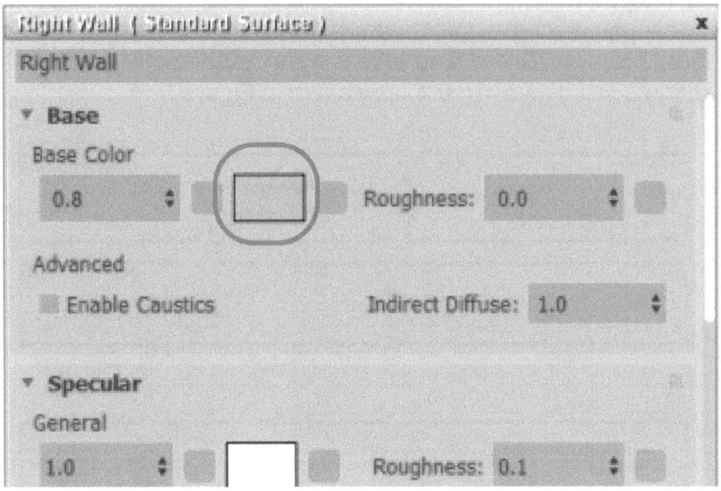

Figure 6–42

6. Verify that the **Camera01** viewport is active (yellow border) and in the Main Toolbar, click  (Render Production) or press <F9> to render the scene, as shown in Figure 6–43. Note the shadow cast by the candleholder.
   - There are two Arnold lights set up for the scene. Both are illuminating the scene, but only one of them is casting a shadow as shown in Figure 6–43. Leave the Render Window open.

Figure 6–43

Task 2: Modify the Standard Surface Arnold shader.

1. In the *Slate Material Editor*, click on the **CandleHolder** shader title bar to open its Parameter Editor. In the *Base* rollout, select the color swatch for *Base Color*, and enter the *Scene* values as **0.926, 0.721, 0.504** for the *Red*, *Green* and *Blue* values to get a beige color.
2. In the *Specular* rollout, select the color swatch for *General* and enter the *Scene* values as **0.996, 0.957, 0.823** for *Red*, *Green*, and *Blue* values. Additionally, change the *Specular Metalness* to **0.8** and *Roughness* to **0.4**. as shown in Figure 6–44.

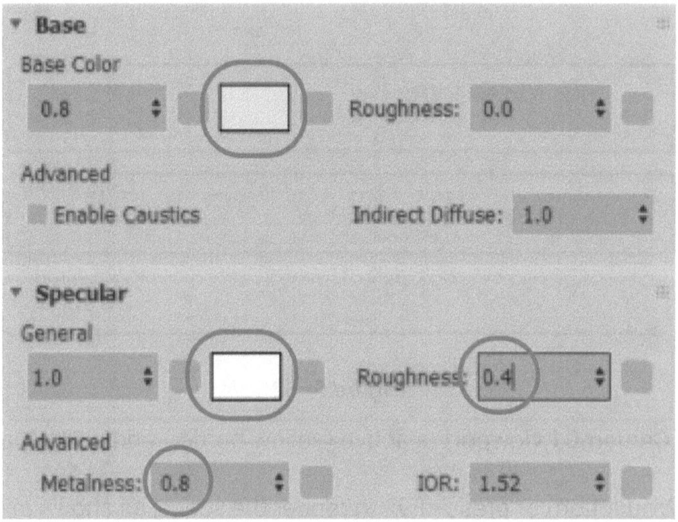

Figure 6–44

3. Click **Render** in the Render Window, or click  (Render Production) if the Render Window was closed, to render the **Camera01** viewport, as shown in Figure 6–45. A brushed metal shader has been created and it reflects the colors of the counter top around it.
   - Verify that the **Camera01** viewport is active before rendering the view.

Figure 6–45

4. In the *Slate Material Editor*, verify that the Parameters of the **CandleHolder** shader display. Then, set the following using the *Scene* values in the *Scene Color Selector* dialog box:
    - In the *Base* rollout, select the color swatch for *Base Color* and set it to **white**.
    - In the *Specular* rollout, select the color swatch for *General* and set it to **white** as well.
    - In the *Specular* rollout, increase the *Metalness* to **1.0** and lower the *Roughness* to **0.2**.

    Note: *To get a metal-looking shader, increase the* ***Metalness*** *in the Specular rollout. Increasing the* ***Roughness*** *creates a brushed-metal look.*

5. Render the **Camera** viewport. A highly reflective chrome-looking metal displays, as shown in Figure 6–46.
    - Longer rendering time might be required due to the calculations for reflections.

Figure 6–46

6. To create a glass looking shader for the **CandleHolder**, set the following, as shown in Figure 6–47 (on the right):
   - In the *Base* rollout, select the color swatch for *Base Color* and set it to **black**.
   - In the *Specular* rollout, set the *Metalness* to **0.2** and the *Roughness* to **0.1**.
   - In the *Transmission* rollout, set the *General* value to **1.0** (maximum).
7. Render the **Camera** viewport. A glass candle holder is created, as shown in Figure 6–47 (on the left). Note that the shadow on the wall has become lighter.

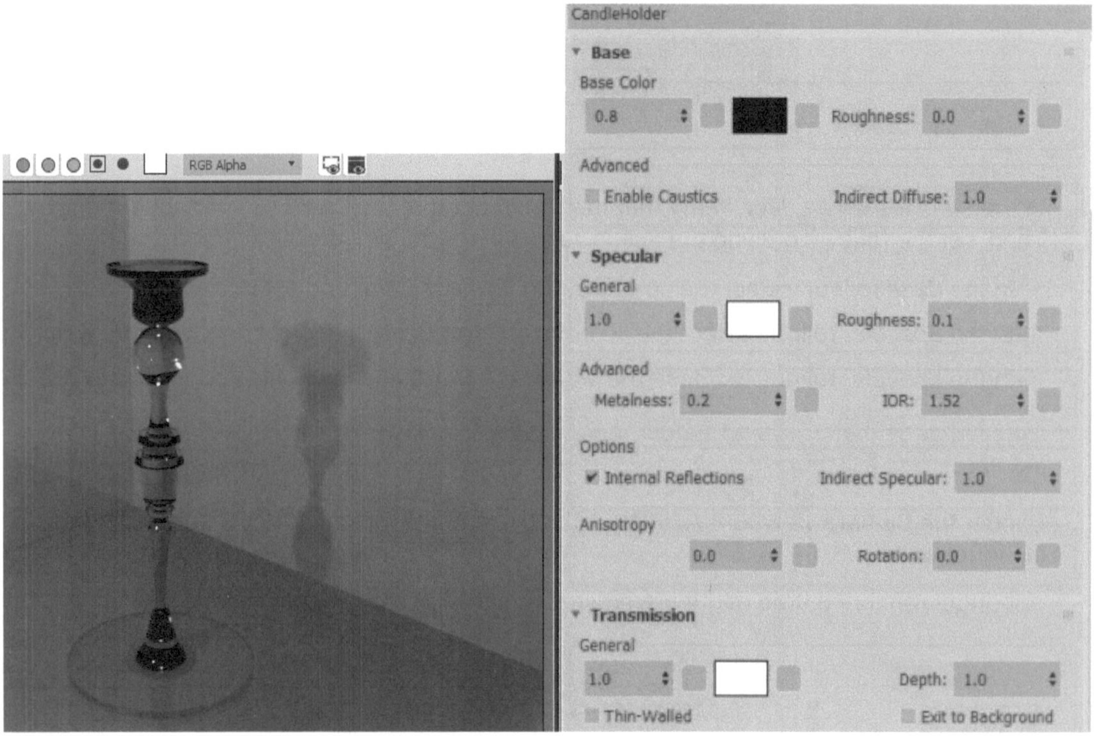

Figure 6–47

8. In the *Material/Map Browser*, expand the **Maps>General** categories and double-click on **Bitmap** to open the *Select Bitmap Image File* dialog box.
9. Open the **Finishes.Flooring.Tile.Square.Terra Cotta.jpg** file from the ...*Maps* folder in the practice files folder.

10. Wire the output socket of the bitmap to the input socket of Countertop shaders **base-color**, as shown on the left in Figure 6–48.
11. Render the **Camera** viewport again and note how the countertop has the tile image on it, as shown on the right in Figure 6–48.

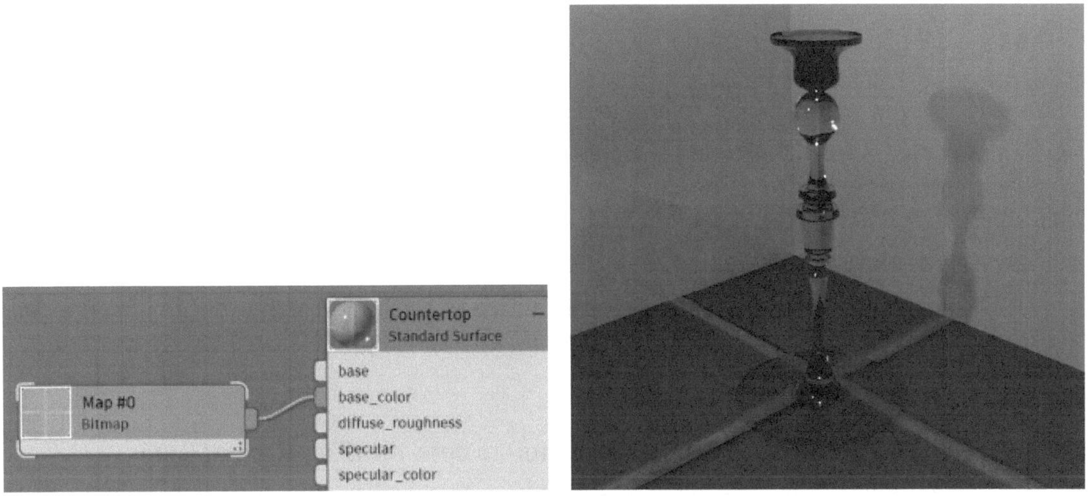

Figure 6–48

12. In the *Slate Material Editor*, click on the **Tile Bitmap** to open its Parameter Editor. In the *Coordinates* rollout, select **Use Real-World Scale**. For *Width* and *Height*, in the *Size* column, enter **0.4** in each edit box.
13. Click on the **Countertop** title heading to open its Parameter Editor. In the *Coat* rollout, set *Clearcoat* to **1.0**.
14. Render the **Camera** viewport and note how the countertop tiles are smaller and shinier.
15. Save your work as **MyCandleholder.max**.

End of practice

Practice 6c
Materials That Create Lighting

Practice Objective

- Create a self-illuminating material.

In this practice, you will learn how to create a self-illuminating material from an Arnold material.

You must set the paths to locate the External files and XREFs used in the practice. If you have not done this already, return to Chapter 1 and complete Task 1 to Task 3 in *Practice 1a: Organize Folders and Work with the Interface*. You only have to set the user paths once.

1. Open **LightPole-SelfIllumination.max**.
2. Verify that the **PhysCamera001** viewport is active. In the Main Toolbar, click (Render Production) and note the rendered image with all gray materials. Leave the Render Frame Window open and minimize it.
3. In the Main Toolbar, click (Material Editor) to open the *Slate Material Editor*.
4. In the *Material/Map Browser*, in the **Scene Materials** category, note the two materials. Both of the materials in the scene are **Standard Surface** Arnold materials, as shown in Figure 6–49.

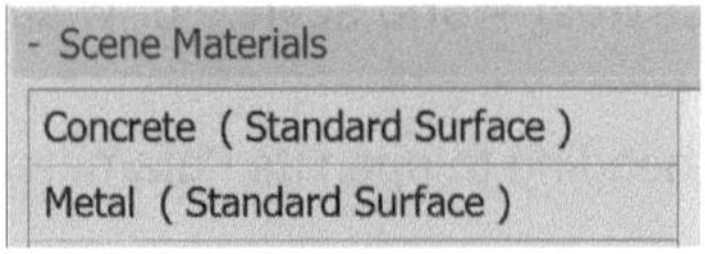

Figure 6–49

5. In the *Material/Map Browser*, expand the **Materials>Arnold>Surface** categories. Double-click on the **Standard Surface** material to place it on the *View1* sheet.
6. Click on the title bar heading of the new node to open its Parameter Editor and set its name to **Illumination**. Minimize the *Slate Material Editor*.
7. In any viewport, select one of the globes and in the menu bar, select **Group>Ungroup** to ungroup the objects. Similarly, ungroup the second globe group.
8. In the **PhysCamera001** viewport, use <Ctrl> to select the two globes (inverted hemispheres). In the *Slate Material Editor*, verify that a white border surrounds the **Illumination** material. Click (Assign Material to Selection) to apply the **Illumination** material to the globes.
9. In the Render Frame Window, click **Render** or in the Main Toolbar, click (Render Production) to render the **PhysCamera001** viewport. Note that the globes have a white material, but they are not glowing.

10. In the *Slate Material Editor*, verify that the **Illumination** materials Parameter Editor is open. Scroll down and in the *Emission* rollout, change the value to **0.5**, as shown in Figure 6–50.
11. Render the **PhysCamera001** viewport again. The globes are glowing, as shown in Figure 6–51.

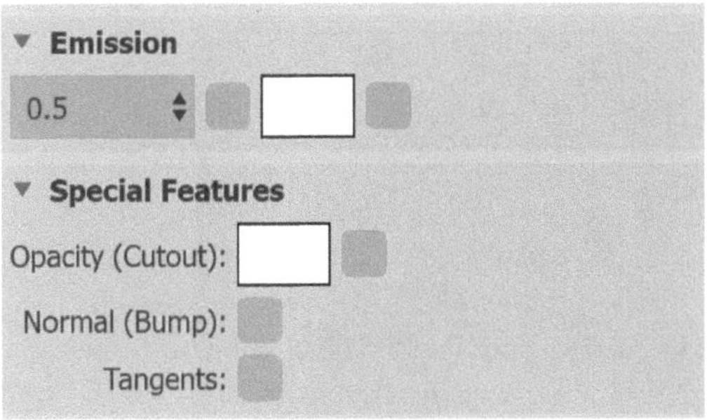

Figure 6–50

Figure 6–51

12. In the *Slate Material Editor*, in the Parameter Editor, change the *Emission* value to **1.0**. Click on the color swatch in the *Emission* rollout. In the *Scene Color Selector*, change the color to medium pink (similar to that shown in Figure 6–52) or any other color. Scroll up to the *Base* rollout and set the *Base Color* value to **0.0**.
13. Render the **PhysCamera001** viewport again. The globes have a pink glow, as shown in Figure 6–53.

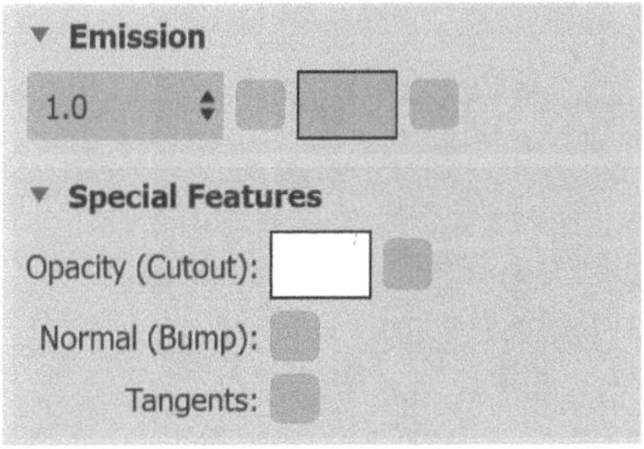

Figure 6–52

Figure 6–53

14. Close the Render Window and the *Slate Material Editor*.
15. Save your work as **MyIlluminatedMaterials.max**.

End of practice

6.4 Assigning Maps to Materials

Maps are often assigned to replace the shader parameters, especially Base Color. Maps can be assigned to various materials through the *Maps* rollout. Figure 6–54 shows the *Special Maps* and *Generic Maps* rollout for Physical Materials. Maps include Base Color, Bump map, Cutout etc.

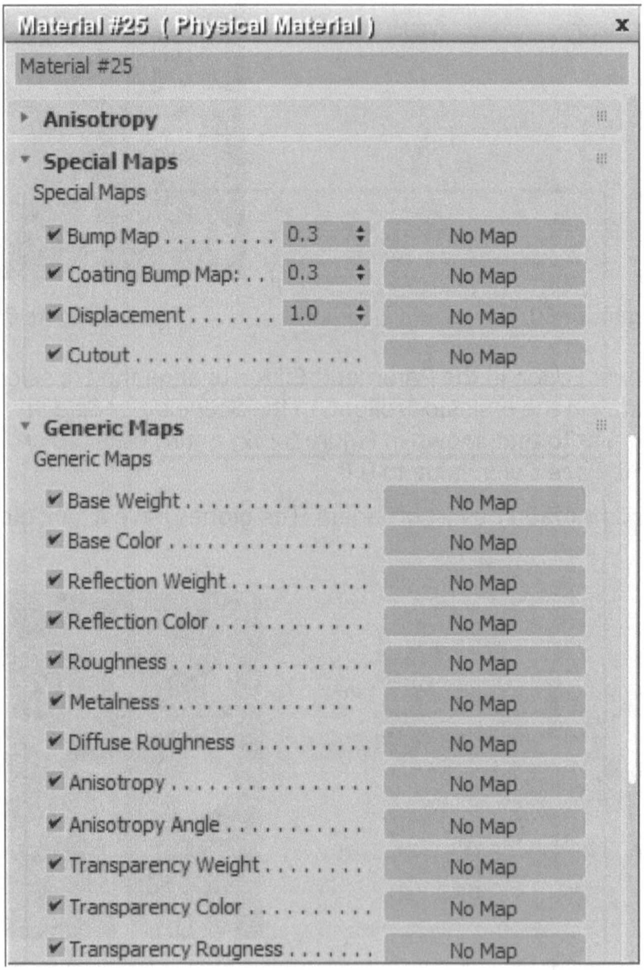

Figure 6–54

Clicking **No Map** next to a channel opens the *Material/Map Browser* (shown in Figure 6–55), where you can select a map and assign it, or change a map and its settings.

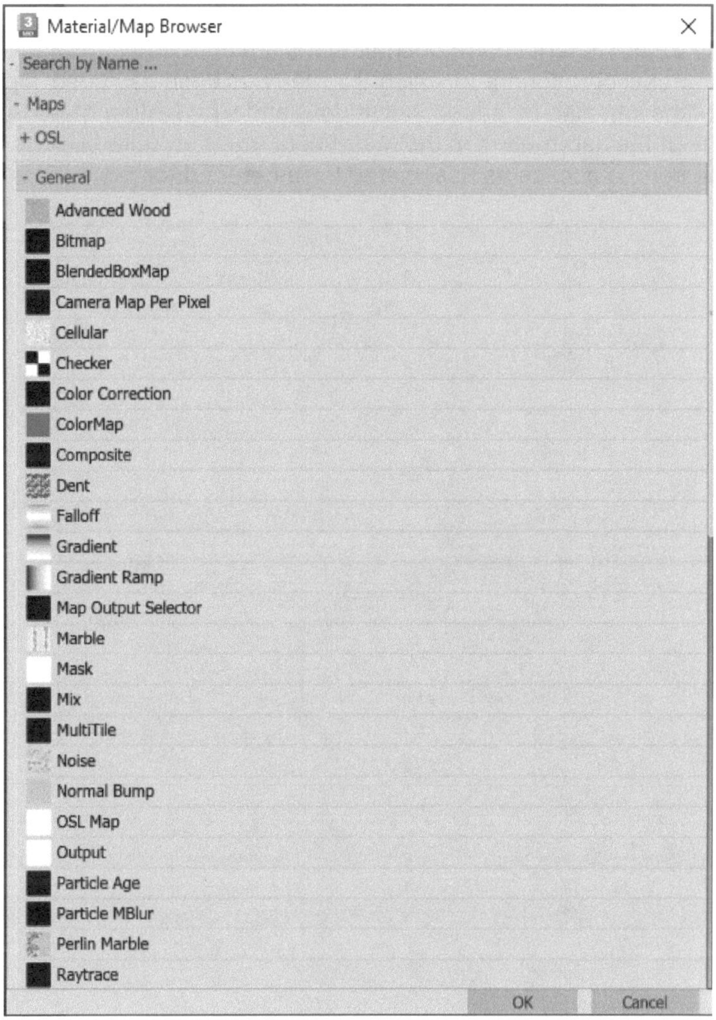

Figure 6–55

- **Bitmap:** Enables you to assign an external image as a map. Different types of image formats can be used as maps including Windows Bitmaps, JPEGs, PNGs, Targas, TIFFs, and more.
- **Color Map:** Enables you to make an instance of a solid color swatch. This helps you be consistent in the solid colors that you use in your models. You can also assign a color bitmap instead of creating a color swatch.
- **MutiTile:** Enables you to assign more than one texture maps into a *UV* editor. The map is designed so that high resolution textures can be opened and displayed. This map type supports patterns created using Mudbox, Zbrush, and Mari.

- The remainder map types are Autodesk 3ds Max **Procedural** maps, which are automatically generated mathematically rather than from image files.
- When you assign (or edit) a map to a material, individual nodes are created and display the maps assigned to the material components. Wires are created automatically between the map and the material component to which the map has been assigned, as shown in Figure 6–56. Maps can also be added individually and wired into a material to establish a link. To edit any of the parameters in the material or maps, double-click on the title bar heading for the item to access its associated Parameter Editor.

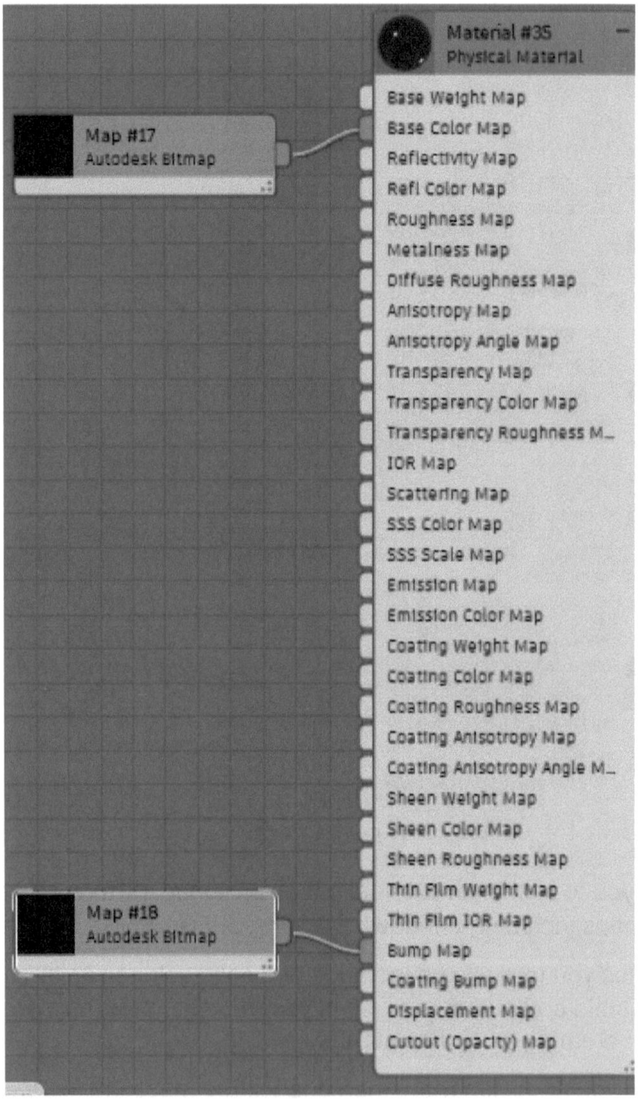

Figure 6–56

Practice 6d
Work with Arnold Materials and Maps

Practice Objectives

- Assign an Arnold material and modify it.
- Apply an image file and a procedural map to the Base Color of the material.

In this practice, you will assign an Arnold material to an object and apply parameter changes to it. You will then apply an image file and a procedural map to an object.

You must set the paths to locate the External files and XREFs used in the practice. If you have not done this already, return to Chapter 1 and complete Task 1 to Task 3 in *Practice 1a: Organize Folders and Work with the Interface*. You only have to set the user paths once.

Task 1: Load materials into the Material Editor.

1. Open **Arnold Materials.max.** A model of a guitar displays in the **Camera** viewport.
2. In the Main Toolbar, click  to open the *Slate Material Editor*.
3. In the *Slate Material Editor*, in the *Material/Map Browser*, expand the **Scene Materials** category. The materials available in this scene are listed here. Each material name is followed by its material type, in parentheses ( ), as shown in Figure 6–57.

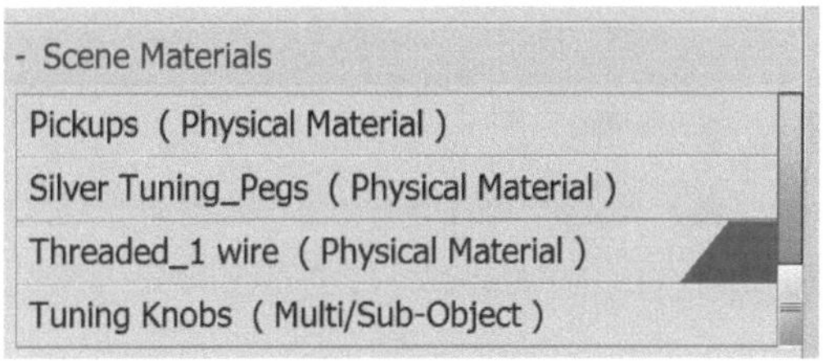

Figure 6–57

4. Note that all of these materials are also displayed in the *View1* sheet and are overlapping each other, as shown in Figure 6–58. In the *Slate Material Editor* toolbar, click (Lay Out All -Vertical) to display the materials vertically in the *View1* sheet.

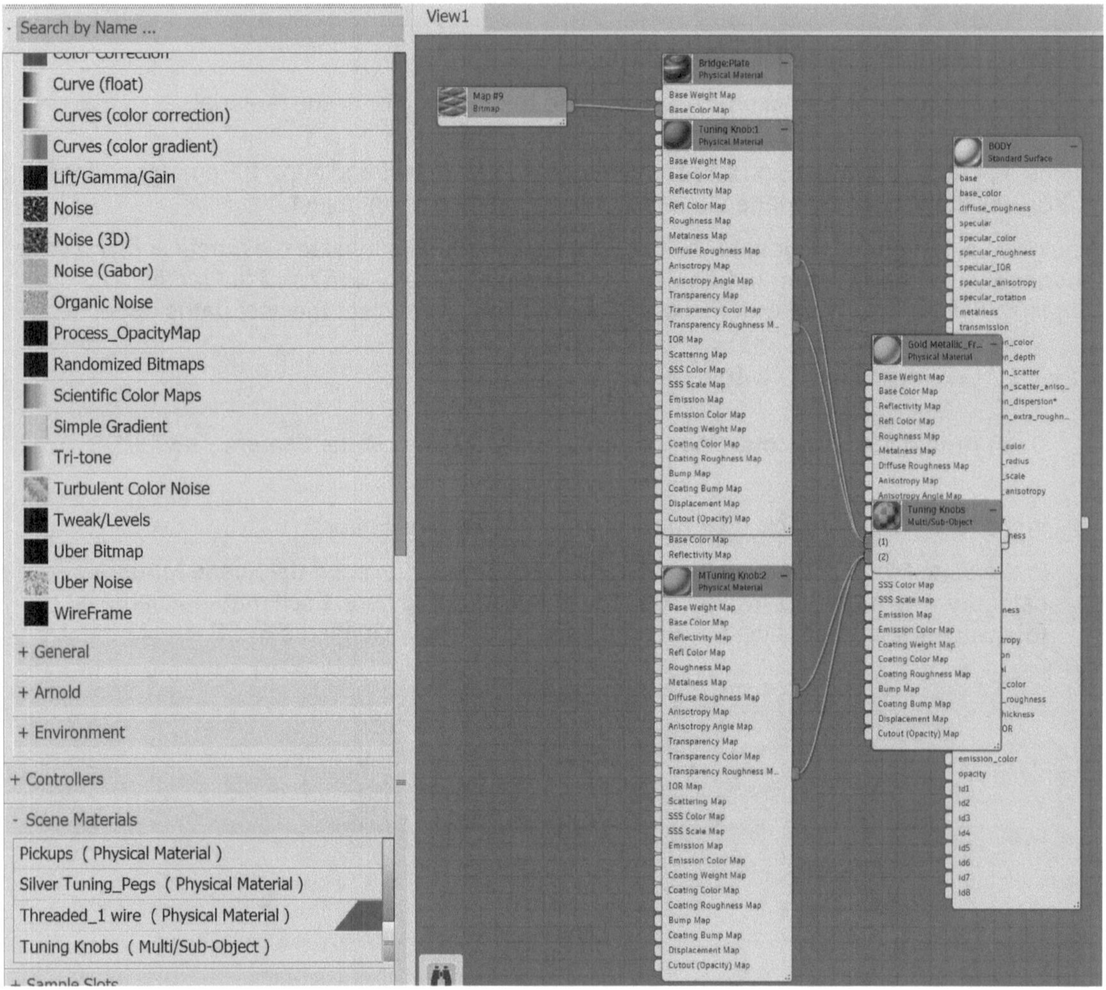

Figure 6–58

Task 2: Change the material parameters.

1. In the *View1* sheet, using pan and zoom, locate the **BODY Standard Surface** node.
2. Click on the title bar heading to open its Parameter Editor, as shown in Figure 6–59. Note that a white border displays around the node in the *View1* sheet.

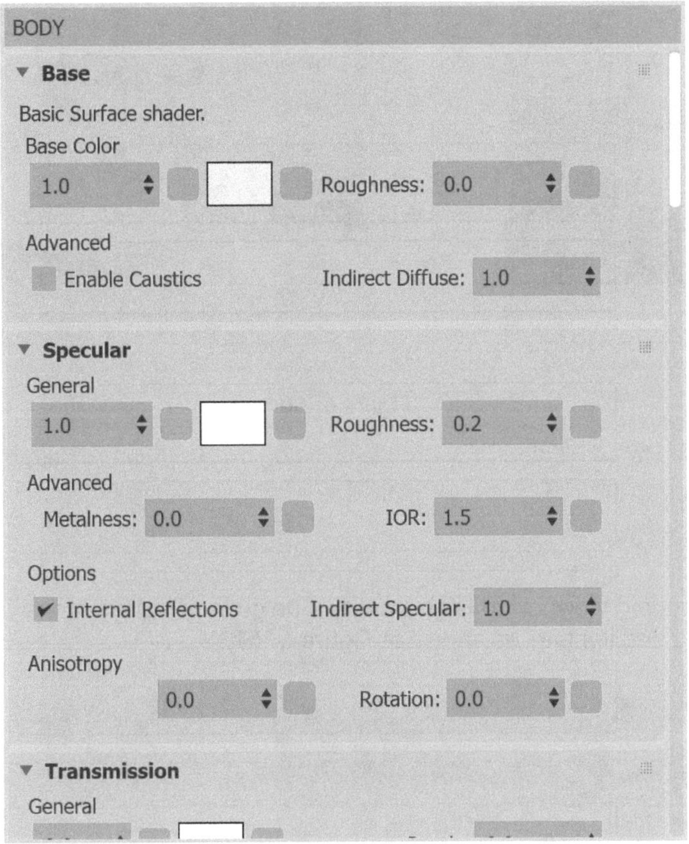

Figure 6–59

3. Note that the **Body** material is a Standard Surface material that uses the Basic Surface shader. In the *Base* rollout, select the *Base Color* swatch to open the *Scene Color Selector* dialog box.

4. In the *Scene Color Selector* dialog box, you can select a color from the chart or set RGB (red-green-blue) or HSV (hue-saturation-value) levels. Experiment with different colors for the guitar body and select a color similar to that shown in Figure 6–60. Click **OK**.

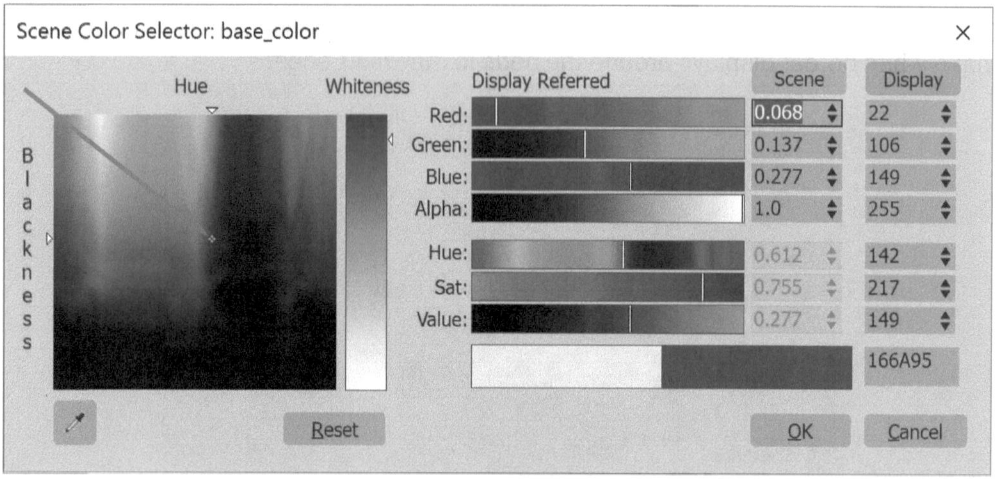

Figure 6–60

Note: *The Slate Material Editor is a modeless dialog box that can remain open when you are working in the viewport or performing other operations that do not pertain to the dialog box. You can minimize it to get more space in the viewport and maximize it when you want to work in it.*

5. Change the *Shading Viewport* to **High Quality**. The guitar displays in the viewport with high quality shading and lighting, as shown in Figure 6–61.

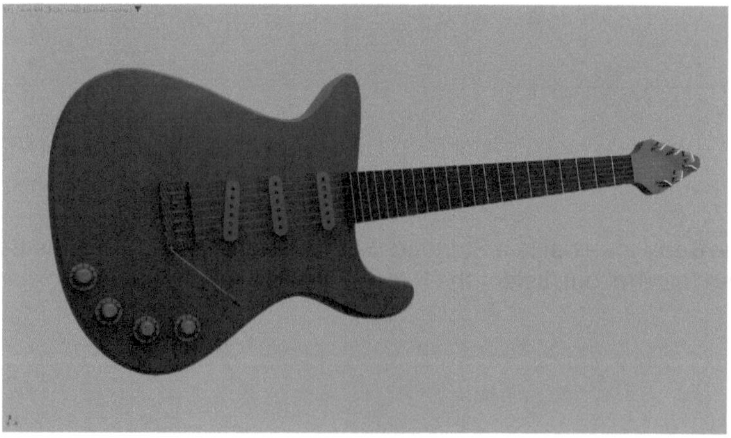

Figure 6–61

6. In the Parameters Editor, in the *Coat* area, set the material's *Clearcoat Level* to **1** as shown in Figure 6–62, which is appropriate for a material that is not too shiny.

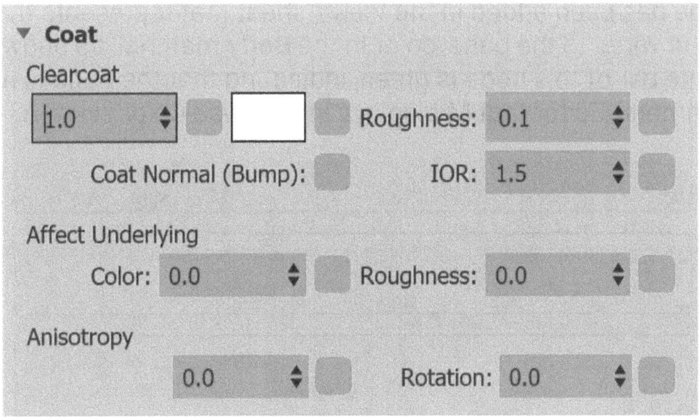

Figure 6–62

7. Click  (Render Production) in the Main Toolbar to display a rendered image in the Arnold RenderView window. Along the bottom of the render window, note the progress bar that displays the percentage of the render completed. When the render is complete, note how the render displays and then closes the Arnold RenderView window.
   - The current renderer has been set to **Arnold**.

Task 3: Apply a procedural map and image file.

1. To replace the *Diffuse Color* with a procedural map that represents a wood grain, verify that the Body material has a white boundary around it, indicating that its parameters are displayed. In the Parameter Editor, expand the *Base* rollout, as shown in Figure 6–63. Next to the **Base Color** option, click **to pick a map** (**or drop a map**) icon.

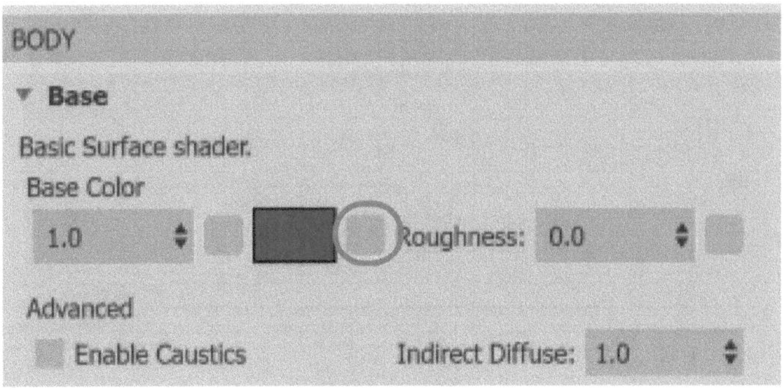

Figure 6–63

2. In the separate *Material/Map Browser* that opens, expand the **Maps>General** categories and select **Advanced Wood**. (**Advanced Wood** is a procedural map and is defined by parameters and formulas, not by an image file. Such maps should be used where the texture should not repeat in a tiled pattern.) Click **OK** to assign it as a map to the **BODY** Standard Surface material.

3. A new **Map** node has been added in the *View1* sheet that represents the **Advanced Wood** map. The node is wired to the base_color in the **Body** material, as shown in Figure 6–64. Note that the title bar of this node is green, indicating that the node is a **Map** node. Also note in the Parameter Editor that **M** displays in the *Base Color* swatch.

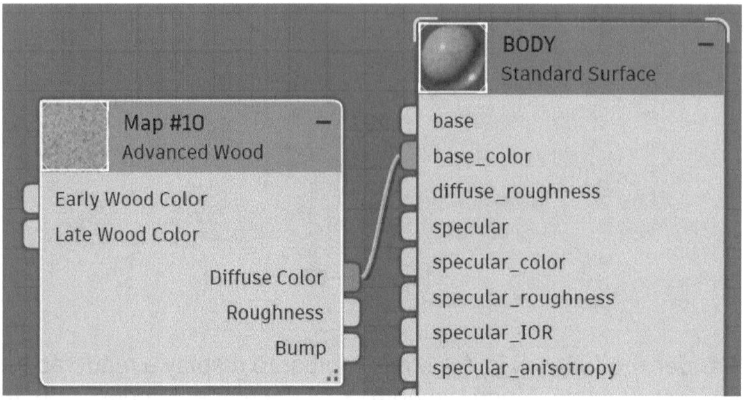

Figure 6–64

4. Click on the title bar heading for the **Advanced Wood** map. Note that a white border surrounds the **Advanced Wood** map node, indicating that its parameters display in the Parameter Editor. In the *Presets* rollout, select **3D Ash-Semigloss** in the *Presets* list. In the *General* rollout, set *Scale* to **6.00** and change the *Axis* to **X**, as shown in Figure 6–65.

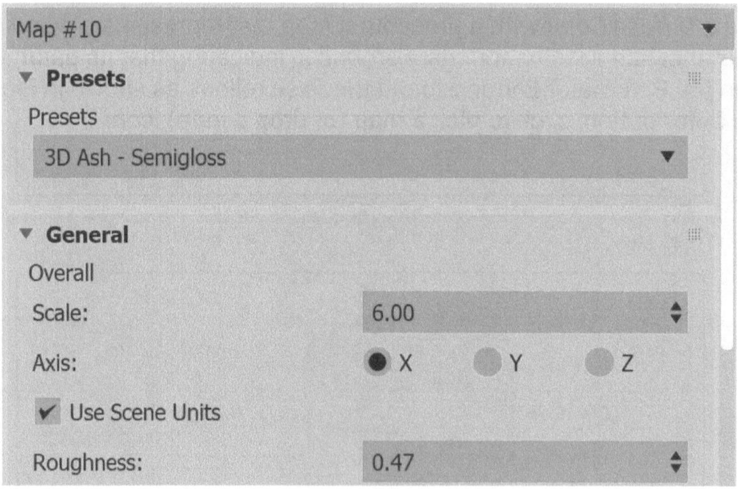

Figure 6–65

5. With the *Shading Viewport* set to **High Quality**, the wood grain might not display in the viewport. If the wood grain does not display, click the *Shading Viewport* label and select **Materials>Shaded Materials with Map**, as shown in Figure 6–66.

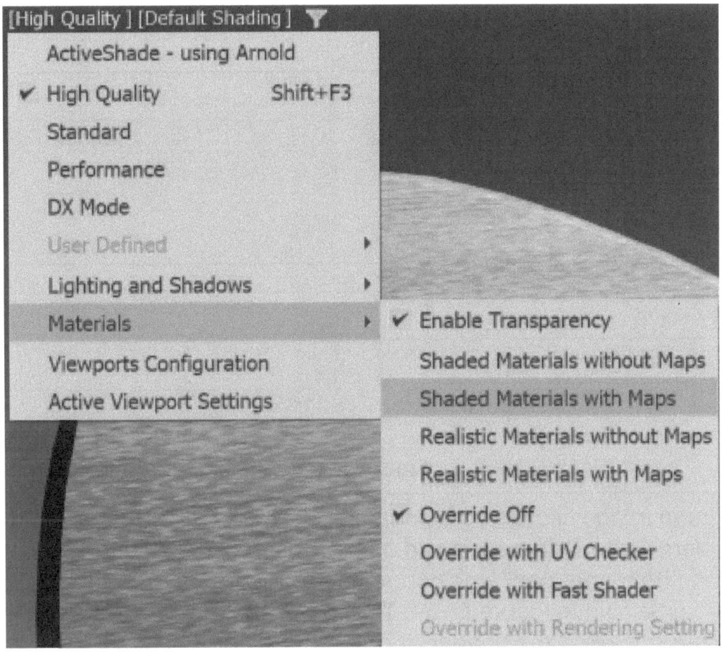

Figure 6–66

6. In the Main Toolbar, click  (Render Production) to render. The wood map displays on the body of the guitar, as shown in Figure 6–67.

Figure 6–67

7. To replace the **Advanced Wood** map with an image file, in the *View1* sheet, click on the title bar heading for the **BODY** material to open its Parameter Editor.
8. Expand the *Maps* rollout, right-click on **Map Output Selector** (for Base Color in Map), and select **Clear**. Alternatively, you can drag any **No Map** slot on top of it.

9. In the *View1* sheet, note that the wiring between the **BODY** material node and the **Advanced Wood** map node has been deleted, and the guitar in the viewport has the color finish.
10. Click **No Map** next to the **Base Color** to open its *Material/Map Browser*.
11. In the *Material/Map Browser*, double-click on **Bitmap** in the **Maps>General** categories, as shown in Figure 6–68.

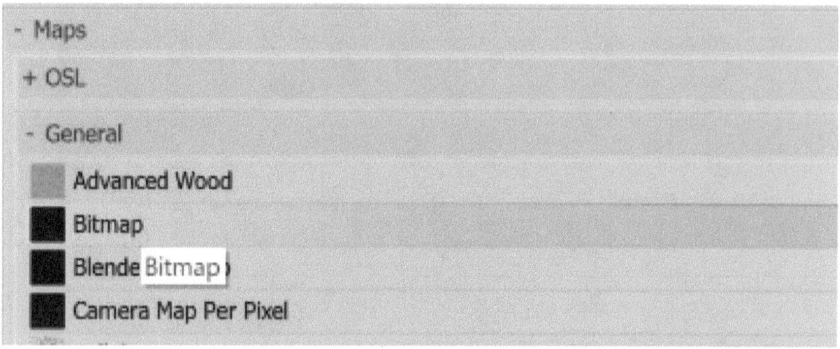

Figure 6–68

12. The *Select Bitmap Image File* dialog box opens. Browse to the ...*Maps* folder in the practice files folder. Select **GuitarDiffuse.jpg** and click **Open**. A new node for Bitmap is added to the *View1* sheet and its output socket is connected to the base_color input socket of the **BODY** material node, as shown in Figure 6–69. The new **Bitmap** node and **Advanced Wood** Map node might overlap. Select the header of one of the nodes to move them apart. Delete the **Advanced Wood** Map node by clicking its title bar heading and pressing <Delete>.

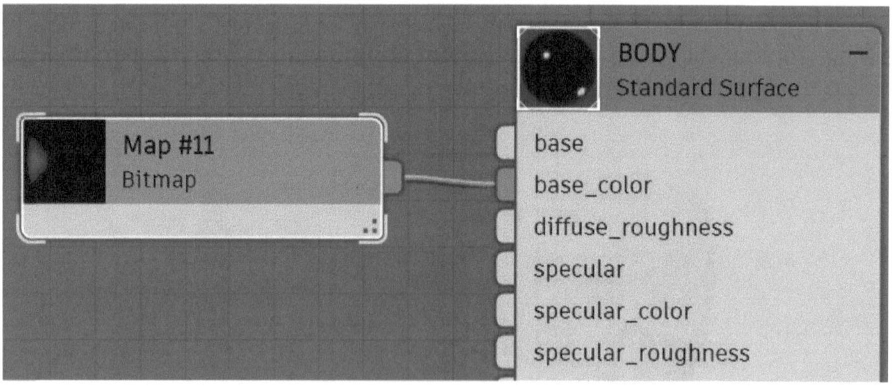

Figure 6–69

13. Click on the new **Bitmap** node title bar to display its Parameter Editor. In the *Coordinates* rollout, ensure that **Use Real-World Scale** is cleared and that the *Tiling* is set to **1.0** in both **U** and **V**, as shown in Figure 6–70.

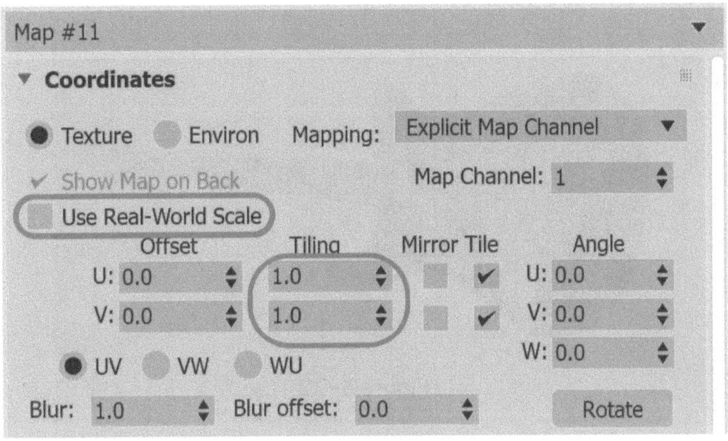

Figure 6–70

- As the Body material with the map is already assigned, the new map on the guitar body should display in the viewport.

14. In the Main Toolbar, click (Render Production) to render. Leave the Arnold RenderView window open.

- Your brightness and shading might look different than that shown in Figure 6–71.

Figure 6–71

Hint: Use Mix Map Type

You could also mix the wood grain with the bitmap by selecting a Mix map type. The mix material on the guitar displays as shown in Figure 6–72.

Figure 6–72

15. To use a Color Correction map along with the Bitmap, in the *Material/Map Browser*, open the **Maps>General** categories. Double-click on the **Color Correction** map. A new node for **Color Correction** is added to *View1*, as shown in Figure 6–73. To relocate a node in the active sheet, hold and drag the title bar heading and place the new **Color Correction** node in between the **Bitmap** node and the **Body** node, as shown in Figure 6–73.

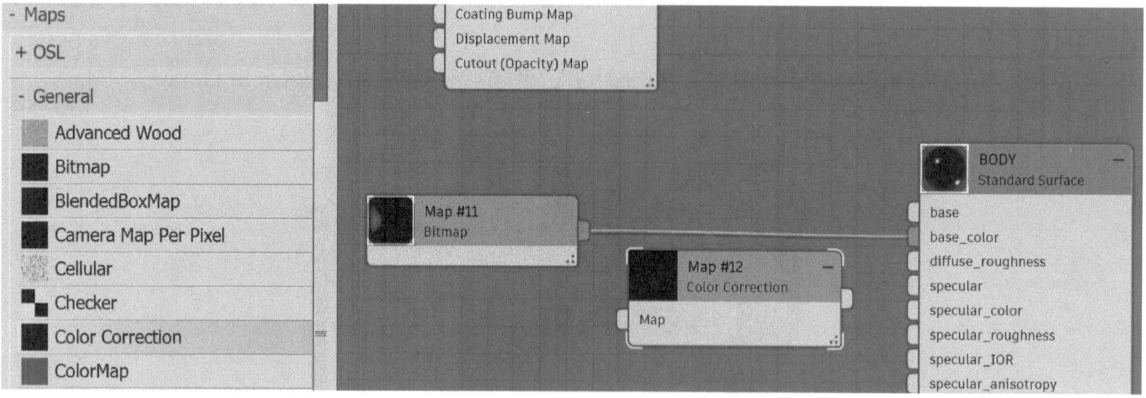

Figure 6–73

16. Select the wire that connects the **Bitmap** node to the *base_color* entry of the **BODY** material and press <Delete>.

17. For the **Bitmap** node (**Map # Bitmap**), select the material output socket (right socket) and drag/drop the wire to the material input socket (left socket) for the **Color Correction** node (**Map # Color Correction**), as shown in Figure 6–74. Note that the wired slots display in green.
    - Note that the input socket of **Color correction** is used for a **Map**.

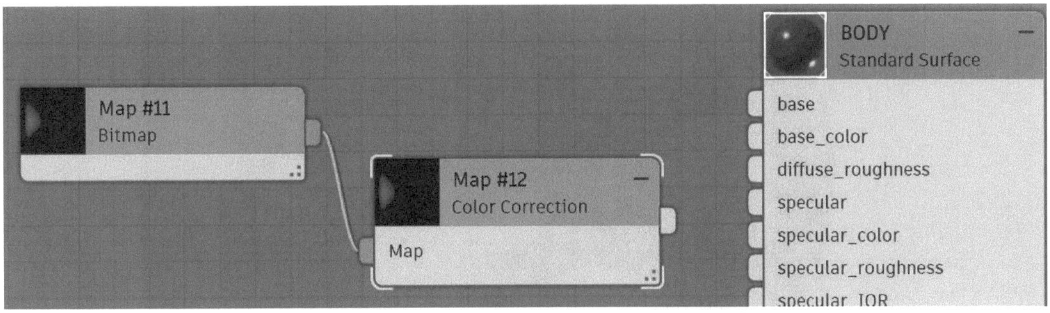

Figure 6–74

18. Select the material output socket (right socket) for the **Color Correction** node and drag the wire to the material input socket for the *Diffuse Color* entry in the **BODY** material node, as shown in Figure 6–75.

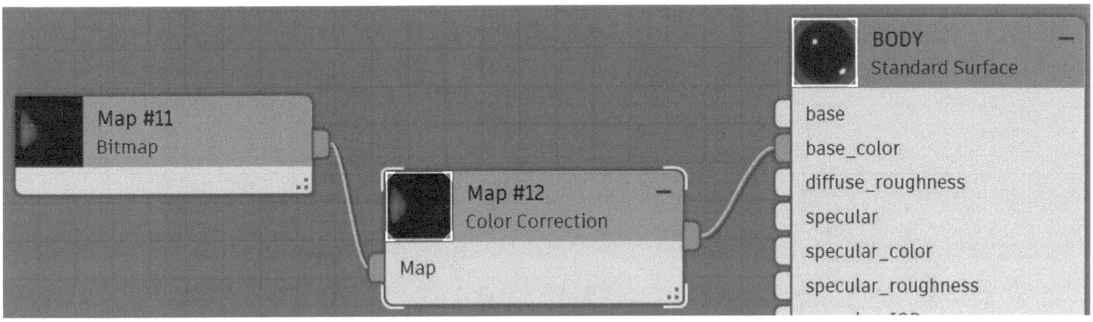

Figure 6–75

19. Click on the Color Correction heading to open its Parameter Editor. In the *Color* rollout, change the *Hue Shift* slider and note that the guitar changes color interactively in the viewport. Set the slider to any color (such as a green color hue).

20. In the Arnold RenderView window, click (Refresh Render) (located in the toolbar near the top right side of the render window) to render the scene. The guitar takes the hue similar to that shown in Figure 6–76. If you closed the Arnold RenderView window, in the Main Toolbar, click (Render Production) to render.

Figure 6–76

21. Save your work as **MyGuitar.max**.

End of practice

6.5 General Materials

General materials are the most basic materials provided with the Autodesk 3ds Max software. They can be accessed by expanding the **Materials>General** categories in the *Material/Map Browser*, as shown in Figure 6–77.

> **Note:** *Depending on the renderer you are using, the list of the materials might differ from the figure shown.*

Figure 6–77

- You can use General materials directly as is or customize them by modifying their parameters to create your own materials, as required.

Physical Material

Physical Material has parameters that create reasonable shading effects and are appropriate for scenes with physically-based lighting. Using Physical Material, you can create materials that are based on the physical properties of a material.

- Physical materials are real world materials that are organized in an easy interface that follows a logical layout.

- Materials are comprised of either a base layer that is assigned a diffuse color with dielectric reflections, or a base color with metallic reflections, as shown in Figure 6–78.
- In addition to the diffuse color, the materials have transparency, sub-surface scattering, self-illumination (emission), and a top clearcoat layer, as shown in Figure 6–78.
- These materials contain both standard and advanced parameters that are designed for physically-based material adjustments.
- A number of presets (as shown in Figure 6–79) are also available with their parameters set for their optimum values. They are provided to be used directly and require minimum modification.
- Physical Material works well with ART (Autodesk® Raytracer) and the Autodesk 3ds Max Arnold renderers.

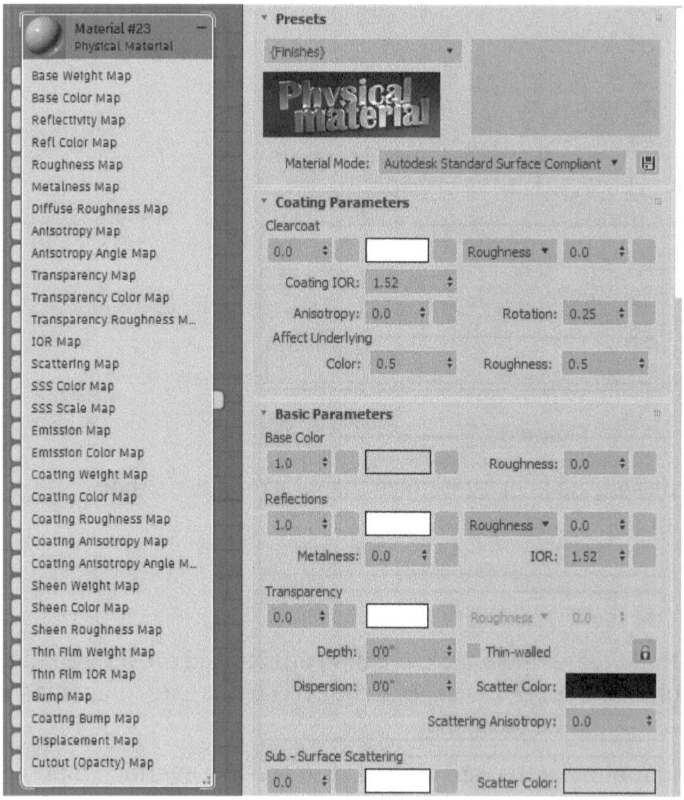

Figure 6–78

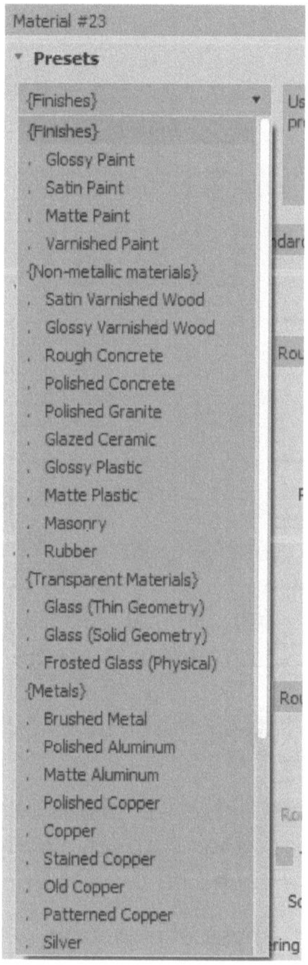

Figure 6–79

Physical Material Parameters

The parameters of the Physical Material are easy and follow a simple workflow. The available parameters are:

- The *Coating Parameters* rollout (shown in Figure 6–80) contains options that are used for applying a clear coat onto the finish of the surface.
  - To create a glossy coating on the material, set the *Clearcoat* weight to **1.0**.
  - *Coating IOR* sets the reflectivity of a clear coat. The higher the value, more reflective the clear coat is.
  - *Roughness* adds a softer sheen and makes a clear coat less glossy.
  - *Affect Underlying* area adds an affect to the base diffuse color.

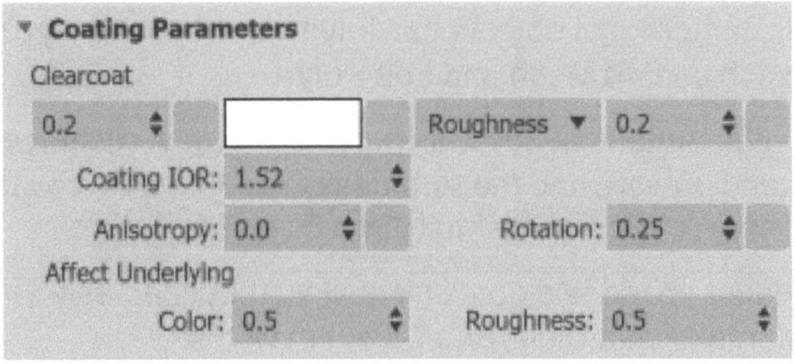

Figure 6–80

- In the *Basic Parameters* rollout (shown previously in Figure 6–78), the *Base Color* and *Reflections* areas enable you to set the base color of the material surface and add the type and amount of reflectivity.
  - A value of **0** has no color, and a value of **1** is full color.
  - *Metalness* determines how the surface reflects. A value of **0.0** creates standard reflections (such as for plastics), and a value of **1.0** creates a metal surface (such as for steel or aluminum).
  - *Roughness* and *IOR* work in a similar fashion as the Clearcoat settings, but alter the base surface of the material. A value of **0.0** is a hard surface, and **1.0** is a soft surface.
- In the *Basic Parameters* rollout, the *Transparency* area enables you to create clear materials, like glass.
  - A value of **0.0** is completely opaque, and **1.0** is fully transparent.
  - *Thin Walled* creates a glass-like appearance to the surface by making the interior hollow.
- In the *Basic Parameters* rollout, *Sub-Surface Scattering* is a feature that causes light to dissipate through the volume of an object.
  - *Scatter Color* sets the color of the scattered light within the volume of the object.
  - *Depth* sets the distance the light scatters through the object in a real-world distance.

- In the *Basic Parameters* rollout, the *Emission* area enables you to create a material that can emit light and illuminate the scene.
    - An *Emission Weight* of **1** sets the material to full emission and defaults to a *Luminance* of 1500 cd/m² (candelas per meter square).

Multi/Sub-Object Materials

Objects might require different materials on each face. For example, a door or window might need different materials for front and back frames, mullions, and glazing. For this, Multi/Sub-Object materials are used, as shown in Figure 6–81.

- They enable you to stack multiple materials into a single *parent* material, each with a material ID number.
- Faces and polygons of individual objects can have a corresponding ID number assigned through modifiers such as **Edit Mesh** and **Edit Poly**.
- Objects brought into the Autodesk 3ds Max software from vertical applications, such as the AutoCAD Architecture software and the Autodesk Civil 3D software are divided into multiple objects by material and do not require Multi/Sub-Object materials.
- The *Slate Material Editor* provides a convenient view that enables you to visually identify all of the materials that make up a Multi/Sub-Object material.
    - Initially, when the material is created, the parent material node opens with 10 default slots. You can wire sub-materials to each slot. Each of the sub-materials can be modified or you can add new materials to the view and rewire into any of the slots.
    - Figure 6–81 shows an example of a Multi/Sub-Object material that is wired to five materials. Slots can be added or deleted using the **Add** or **Delete** options in the *Multi/Sub-Object Basic Parameters* rollout.

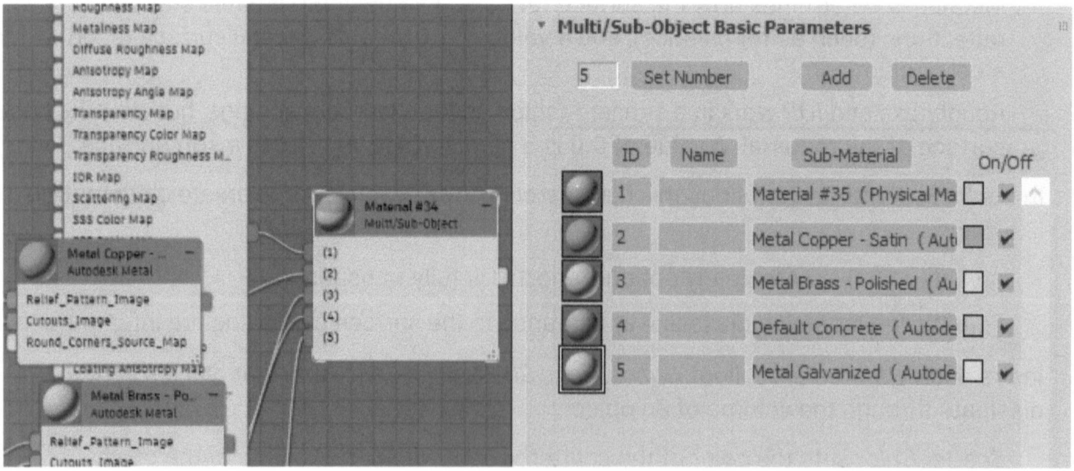

Figure 6–81

Additional General Materials

Depending on the renderer, some of the additional General materials available for use are described as follows:

Blend	Combines two materials to create a third.
Composite	Enables multiple materials to be combined into a single, composite material through additive colors, subtractive colors, or opacity mixing.
DirectX Shader	Enables you to shade objects in the viewport to more accurately display how objects look when exported to real-time viewing.
Double Sided	Enables you to have one material assigned to the outside of objects and another to the inside (the back-facing sides).
Ink 'n' Paint	Creates a flat shaded cartoon rendering with the contours or edges as ink lines.
Shell Material	Used with *texture baking*, which is the process of creating replacement color maps that include the scene illumination (illumination is *baked in*).
Shellac	Superimposes two materials together through additive composition.
Top/Bottom	Assigns different materials to faces with normals pointing *up* and *down*.
XRef Material	Assigns a material applied to an object to another Autodesk 3ds Max scene file. As with XREF scenes and objects, you can only change the material parameters in the original source file.

Practice 6e
Work with Physical Materials

Practice Objective

- Assign a Physical material and modify it.

In this practice, you will assign a Physical material to an object and apply the various presets provided with the material. You will then modify the Physical material to create different-looking materials from it.

You must set the paths to locate the External files and XREFs used in the practice. If you have not done this already, return to Chapter 1 and complete Task 1 to Task 3 in *Practice 1a: Organize Folders and Work with the Interface*. You only have to set the user paths once.

Task 1: Use presets in Physical materials.

1. Open **Physical Material.max.**
2. Ensure that the *Camera-Lamp-Focus* view is the maximized viewport.
3. Click  (Render Production) in the Main Toolbar to display a rendered image and note the flat color on the table lamp. Leave the Arnold RenderView window open, make it smaller and move it to one side of the screen.
4. In the Main Toolbar, click 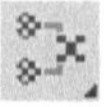 to open the *Slate Material Editor*.
5. In the *Material/Map Browser*, expand the **Materials>General** categories. In the list, double-click on the **Physical Material** material to add it to the *View1* sheet.
6. In the *View1* sheet, click on the **Physical Material** material title bar heading to open its Parameter Editor. Rename the material **Lamp**, as shown in Figure 6–82.

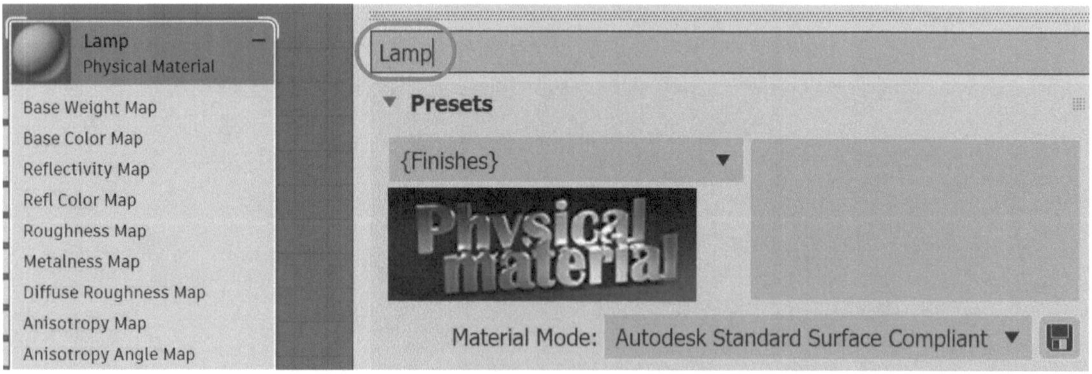

Figure 6–82

7. In the viewport, select the **1-Desk Lamp** object.

8. Assign the **Lamp** Physical material to the selected lamp object by clicking (Assign Material to Selection) in the *Material Editor* toolbar.
   - You can also use any other method of assigning the material.

9. In the **Lamp** Parameter Editor, in the *Presets* rollout, open the *Presets* drop-down list. Scroll down in the list and in the **{Metals}** category, select **Silver**.

10. If the Arnold RenderView window is still open, click (Refresh Render) (located in the toolbar near the top right side of the render window) to display the look of the preset silver material, as shown in Figure 6–83. You can zoom in to the rendered image to see the finish more closely.
    - If you closed the Render Window, open it again from the Main Toolbar by clicking (Render Production).

Figure 6–83

11. Open the *Presets* drop-down list again and in the **{Metals}** category, select **Polished Gold**.

12. Render the scene, as shown in Figure 6–84. ( (Refresh Render) in the Arnold RenderView window or  (Render Production) in the Main Toolbar.)

Figure 6–84

13. Similarly assign other materials from the *Presets* list and render the scene to see the look of the lamp change. Note that a number of presets are available. With their parameters set for optimum values, the presets can be used either directly as provided or with minimum modification.

Task 2: Modify the parameters.

1. Assign the **Copper** metal material from the *Presets* category and render the scene, as shown in Figure 6–85.

Figure 6–85

2. You will modify the parameters of the **Copper** material to get a different-looking material. In the *Basic Parameters* rollout, select the **Base Color and Reflections** swatch, as shown in Figure 6–86. In the *Scene Color Selector*, set that color to a blue color, similar to the one shown in Figure 6–87, then click **OK**.

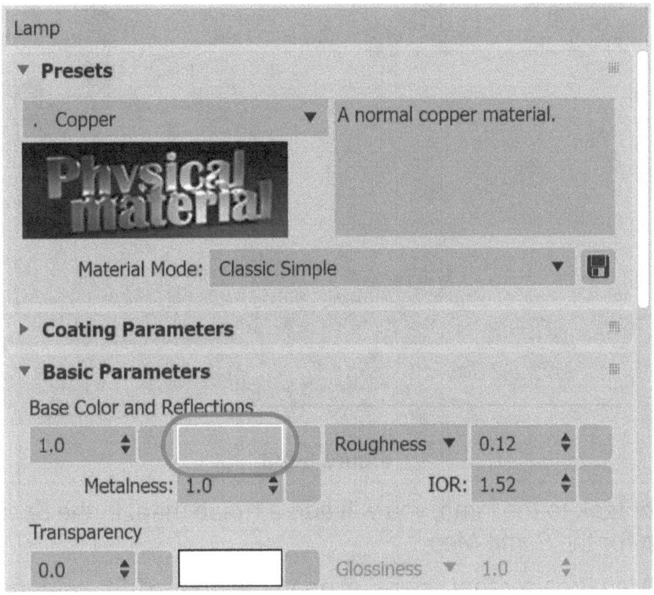

Figure 6–86

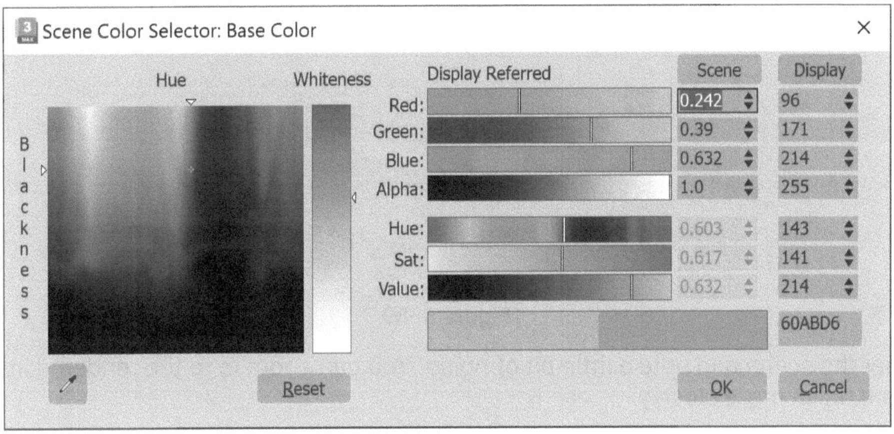

Figure 6–87

3. Render the scene, as shown in Figure 6–88.

Figure 6–88

4. To add a rougher look to the lamp, you will add a **Noise** map. In the *Special Maps* rollout, click on **No Map** for the *Bump Map*.
5. In the *Material/Map Browser* that opens, expand the **Maps>OSL** categories and select **Noise**. Click **OK**. The **Map # (OSL: Noise)** is displayed instead of *No Map*, as shown in Figure 6–89. Also increase the *Bump Map* value to **1.0**, as shown in Figure 6–89.

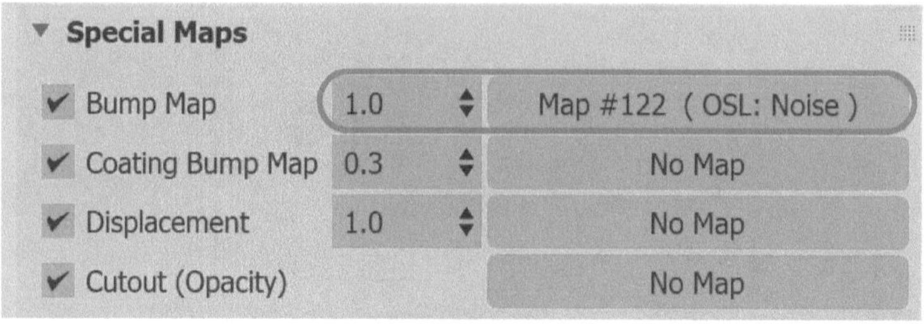

Figure 6–89

6. Render the scene and note a little bit of noise. You can zoom in to the rendered image to see the finish more closely.

7. To add a little more roughness, in the *Basic Parameters* rollout, reduce the *Metalness* to **0.8** and increase the *Roughness* to **0.8**, as shown in Figure 6–90. Render the scene and note that the lamp is not shiny.

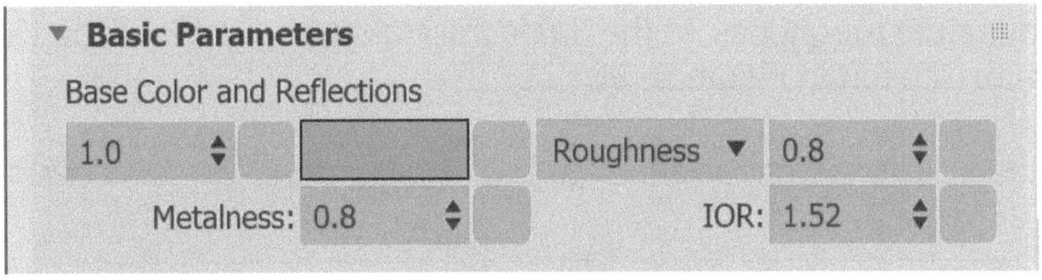

Figure 6–90

8. In the *Coating Parameters* rollout, set *Clearcoat* to **0.6** and change the clearcoat color to a red color (clicking on the swatch). Then, set the *Roughness* to **0.2** and the *Affect Underlying>Color* to **0.5** (as shown in Figure 6–91) to add a subtle red glossy coating with a soft sheen to the material.

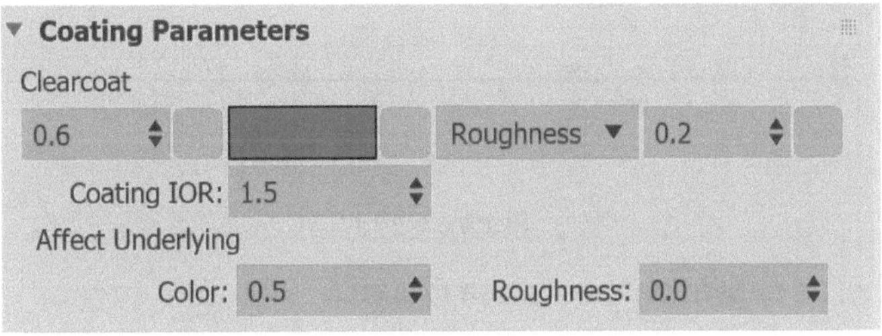

Figure 6–91

9. Render the scene, as shown on the right in Figure 6–92.

Figure 6–92

10. To remove the red hue on the lamp, in the *Coating Parameters* rollout, set *Clearcoat* to **0.0**, as shown in Figure 6–93.
    - The color will not have any effect as long as the value is set to **0.0**.
11. To further reduce the roughness, in the *Basic Parameters* rollout, reduce the *Roughness* to **0.2**, as shown on the left in Figure 6–93.

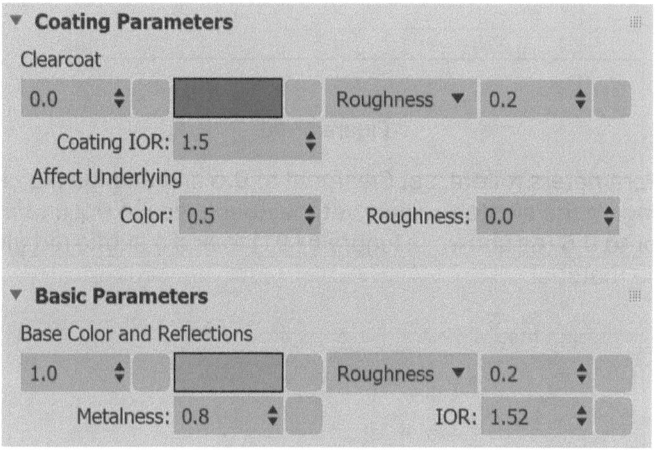

Figure 6–93

12. Render the scene, as shown on the right in Figure 6–94.

Figure 6–94

13. Close the *Slate Material Editor* and the Render Window.
14. Save your work as **MyPhysical_Material.max**.

End of practice

Practice 6f
Work with Multi/Sub-Object Materials

Practice Objective

- Create a Multi/Sub-Object material and assign different materials to specific faces of a single object.

In this practice, you will create a Multi/Sub-Object material with various materials on different material IDs. You will assign an instanced scene material to all the faces of the wall system, a Physical material to some of the outside faces, and an accent paint color to other interior faces using material ID numbers of the Multi/Sub-Object material.

You must set the paths to locate the External files and XREFs used in the practice. If you have not done this already, return to Chapter 1 and complete Task 1 to Task 3 in *Practice 1a: Organize Folders and Work with the Interface*. You only have to set the user paths once.

Task 1: Identify and apply Multi/Sub-Object materials.

1. Open **Interior Model.max**.
2. In the Main Toolbar, click 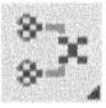 to open the *Slate Material Editor*. (If a warning dialog box opens, **Clear** and **Close** it.)
3. In the *Material/Map Browser*, expand the **Scene Materials** categories and note that six of the materials in the scene are **Multi/Sub-Object** materials.

4. Click, and then drag and drop the **Curtain Wall Doors** material on **PivotDoor07** (door in the front facing wall of the model), as shown in Figure 6–95.

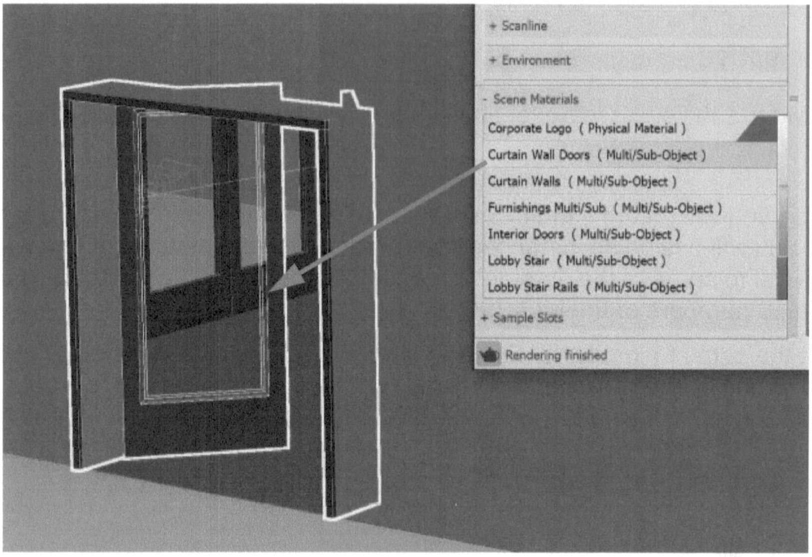

Figure 6–95

5. Select **PivotDoor07** object and click  (Zoom Extents Selected). The doors have glass panels and solid frames, as shown in Figure 6–95. Click  (Orbit) to display the doors similar to that shown in Figure 6–96.

Figure 6–96

Task 2: Create a Multi/Sub-Object material.

1. In the *Material/Map Browser*, expand the **Materials>General** categories. Double-click on **Multi/Sub-Object** or drag an instance of it to add it to the *View1* sheet, as shown in Figure 6–97.

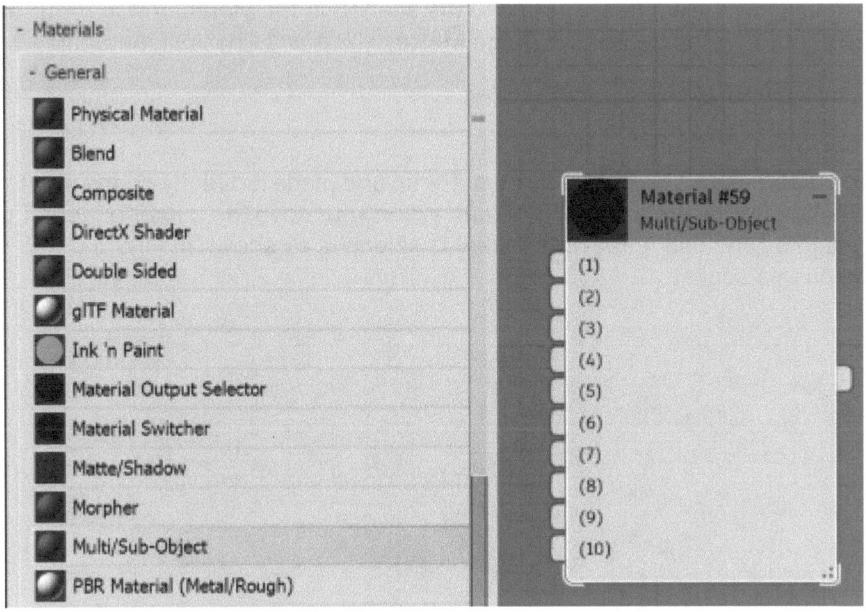

Figure 6–97

2. Right-click on the title bar heading for the new material and select **Rename**, as shown in Figure 6–98.

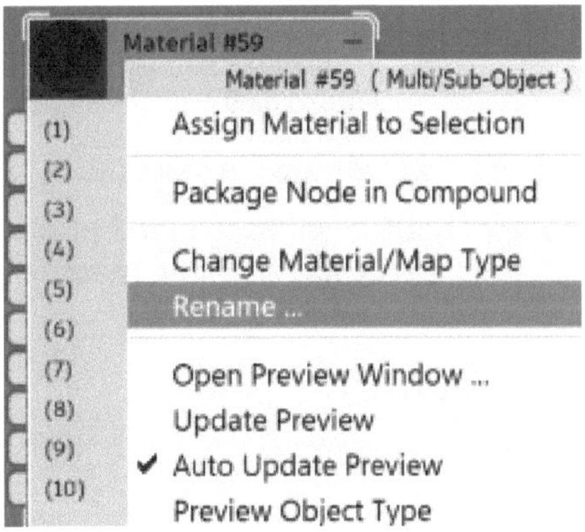

Figure 6–98

3. In the *Rename* dialog box, enter **Wall Multi** and click **OK**.

4. There are ten default slots in a *Multi/Sub-Object* material. This material only requires five slots. To set the number of materials, click on the **Wall Multi** material title bar to open its Parameter Editor. Click **Set Number**, enter **5** in the *Number of Materials* edit box and click **OK**. Note that the material node has only 5 slots now.
5. You will use an instanced copy of the **Paint – Beige Matte** material present in the scene for your sub-material 3. (This material displays dark grey/brown in this practice but will look more like beige when lights are added to the scene.) In the *Material/Map Browser*, in **Scene Materials** category, locate **Paint – Beige Matte,** which is a Physical material.

   Note: *To display all of the materials in the Scene Materials, expand the category, if required, and use its scroll bar.*

6. Click and drag the **Paint – Beige Matte** material and place it directly on the input socket **3** in the **Wall Multi** (Multi/Sub-Object material). When you move the cursor on top of the socket, it is highlighted, indicating that the socket is selected, as shown in Figure 6–99. Drop the material on this socket.

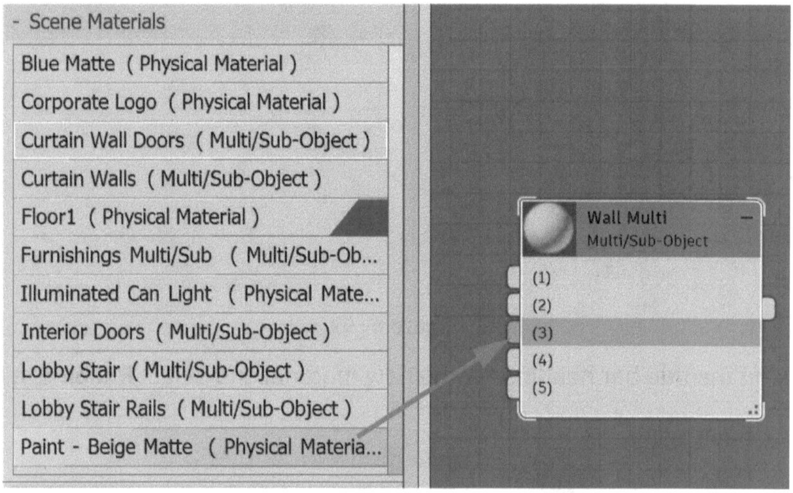

Figure 6–99

7. In the *Instance* dialog box, verify that **Instance** is selected and click **OK**.
8. The *Paint – Beige Matte material* node is wired to slot 3 of **Wall Multi** material. Use the pan and zoom (middle mouse button) to display both the material nodes in the *View1* sheet.

9. Verify that the **Wall Multi** (Multi/Sub-Object material) node has a white dashed boundary indicating that its Parameter Editor displays. Note that the **Paint – Beige Matte** material displays on the *ID3* slot, as shown in Figure 6–100.

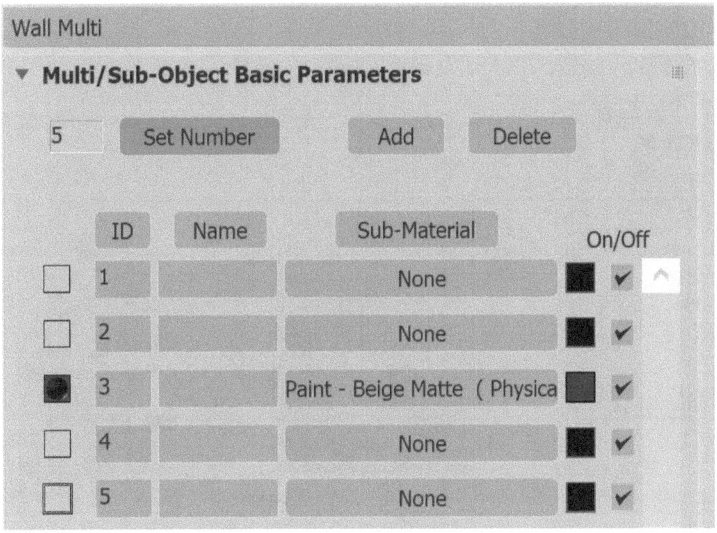

Figure 6–100

10. In the *Material/Map Browser*, in the **Materials>General** categories, double-click on **Physical Material** to display it in the *View1* sheet.
11. Click on the **Physical Material** node to display its Parameter Editor.

12. Rename the material to **Paint Front**, as shown in Figure 6–101.
13. In the *Basic Parameters* rollout, select the **Base Color** swatch. In the *Scene Color Selector*, set that color to cyan, similar to the one shown in Figure 6–102. Click **OK**.

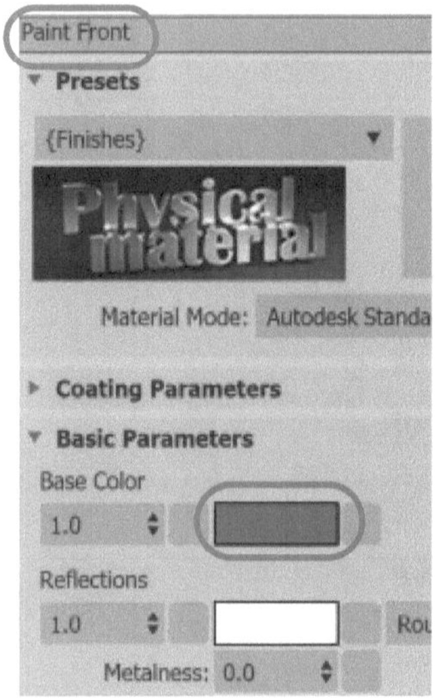

Figure 6–101

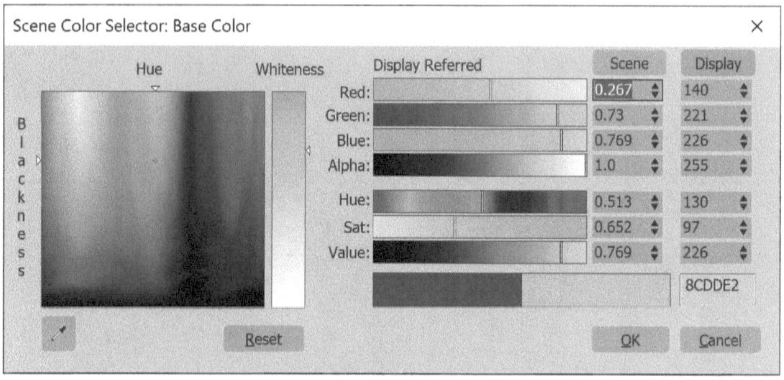

Figure 6–102

14. In the *Coating Parameters* rollout, set *Clearcoat* to **0.2** to add a glossy coating on the material. Then, set the *Roughness* to **0.2** (as shown in Figure 6–103) to add a softer sheen to the material.

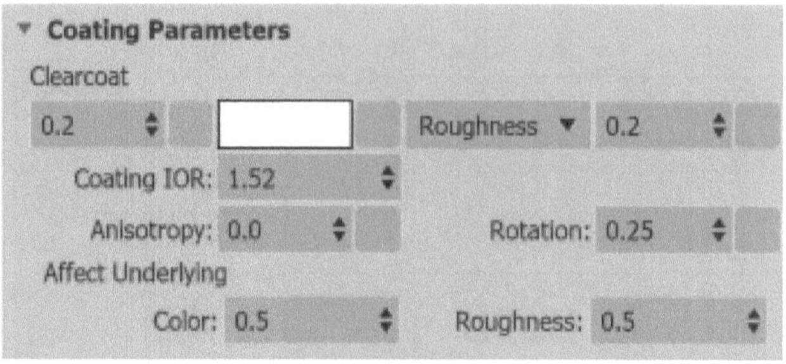

Figure 6–103

15. In the *View 1* sheet, click on the output socket of the **Paint Front** material and drag its wire to connect to the slot 5 of the **Wall Multi** material.

16. The nodes might overlap each other in the active sheet (*View1*). In the *Slate Material Editor* toolbar, click (Lay Out All - Vertical) to arrange the sub-materials vertically, as shown in Figure 6–104. Click on the **Wall-Multi** material title bar to display its Parameter Editor. Note that in the Parameter Editor of the **Wall Multi** material, the *ID5* slot now displays **Paint - Front (Physical Material)**, as shown in Figure 6–104.

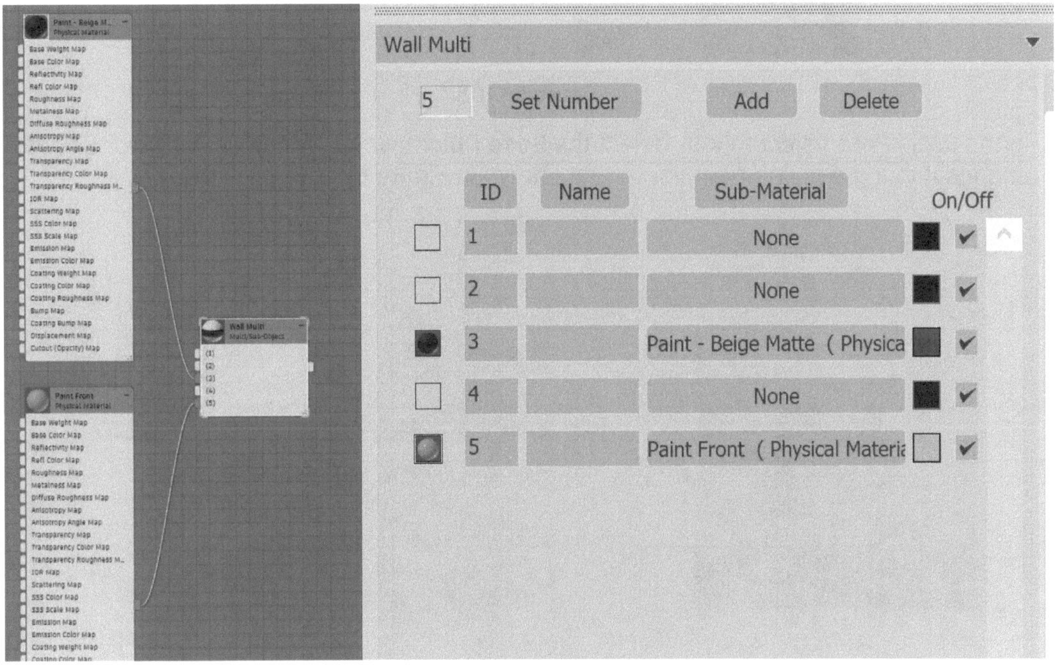

Figure 6–104

17. In the *Material/Map Browser*, in the **Scene Materials** category, click and drag the **Paint - Beige Matte** material and place it on the input socket for sub-material 4 in the **Wall Multi** material.
18. In the *Instance* dialog box, select **Copy** and click **OK**.

Note: *Use (Lay Out All - Vertical), if required.*

19. Click on the title bar heading for the new **Paint - Beige Matte** material (slot 4) to open its Parameter Editor.

20. Change the material name to **Paint - Accent**, as shown in Figure 6–105.

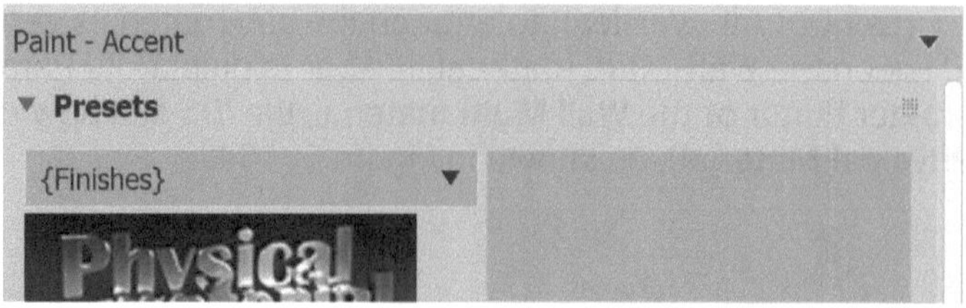

Figure 6–105

21. In the *Basic Parameters* rollout, select the **Base Color** swatch. In the *Scene Color Selector*, change it to a green color, similar to that shown in Figure 6–106. Click **OK**.

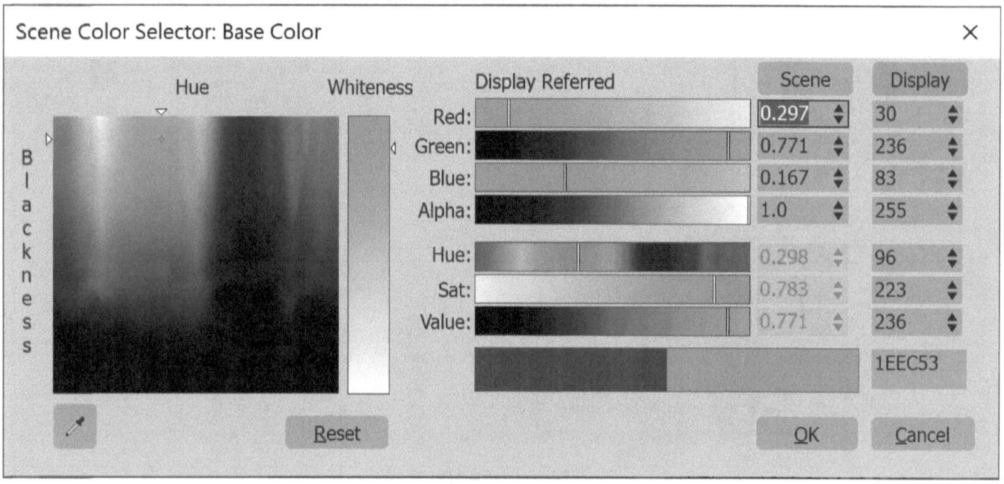

Figure 6–106

22. Close the *Slate Material Editor*.

Task 3: Assign material ID numbers to the wall system.

1. In the **Perspective** viewport, zoom out and pan so that the entire model displays in the viewport.

2. In the Scene Explorer ( (Display None)> (Display Geometry)), select **Layer:VIZ-1-Walls** object, which selects all of the walls in the lower floor in the viewport.

3. In the Command Panel, in the *Modify* panel (), note that it is an Editable Mesh in the *Modifier Stack*. Select the **Polygon** Sub-object mode, as shown in Figure 6–107.

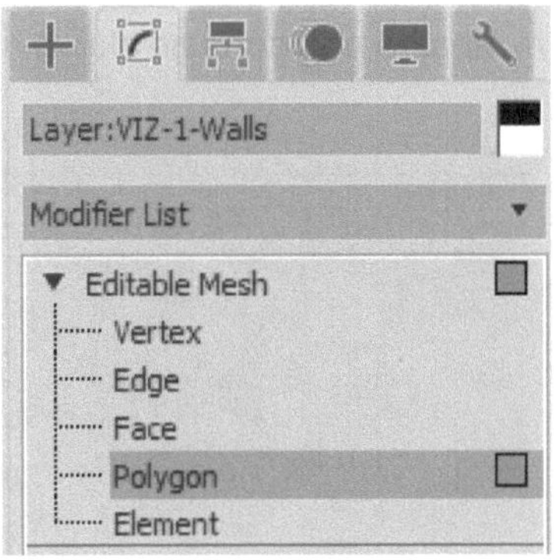

Figure 6–107

4. Press <Ctrl>+<A>. Note that all of the polygons of the walls in the lower floor turn red, indicating that all polygons are selected.
5. In the Command Panel, in the *Surface Properties* rollout, in the *Material* area, set *Set ID* to **3** and press <Enter>. Note that the *Select ID* also changes to **3**, as shown in Figure 6–108. This sets the selected polygons (all polygons) to *ID 3* and will associate the **Paint – Beige Matte** material with all the walls.

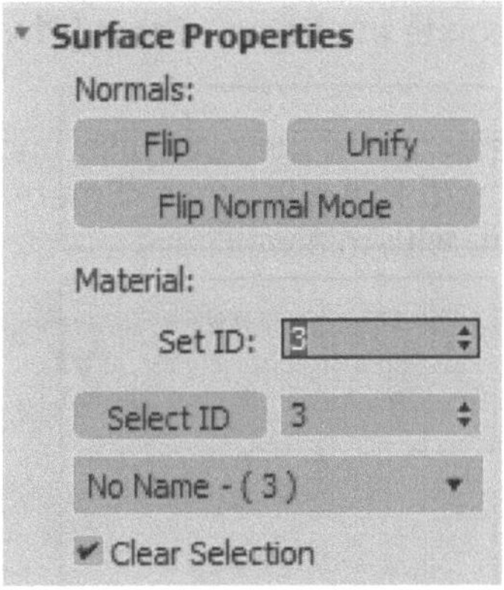

Figure 6–108

6. Clear the selection by clicking anywhere in the empty area.

7. In the viewport, click the **[Edged Face]** *Per-View Preference* label and select **Wireframe Override**. Use (Orbit) until your model displays as shown in Figure 6–109. Right-click in empty space to exit the command and maintain the selection.
8. Using <Ctrl>, select the two front side polygons as shown in Figure 6–109.

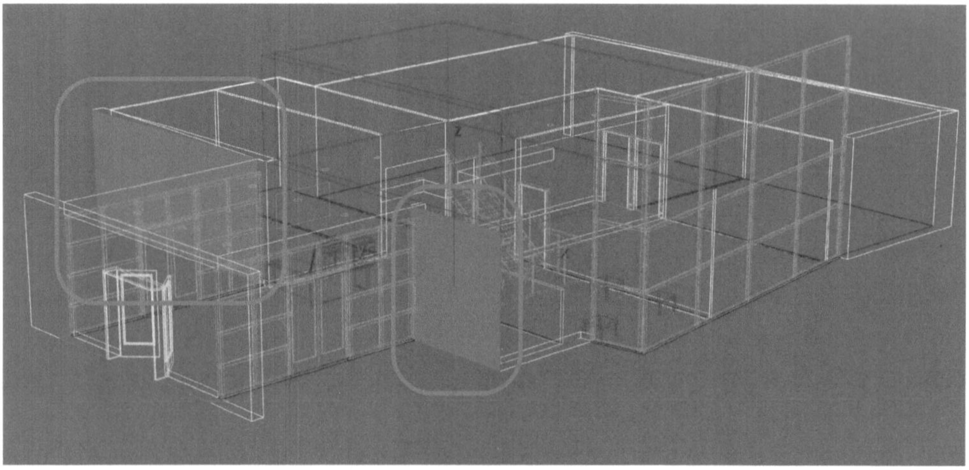

Figure 6–109

9. In the Command Panel, in the *Surface Properties* rollout, in the *Material* area, set *Set ID* to **5,** and press <Enter>. Note that the *Select ID* also changes to **5**. This sets the selected polygons to *ID 5* and will associate the **Paint – Front (Physical Material)** (cyan color) with those two walls.
10. Click anywhere to clear the selection of the two walls, and select the inside polygon, as shown in Figure 6–110. Set *Set ID* to **4** and press <Enter>. This will associate the **Paint - Accent** material (green) with this wall.

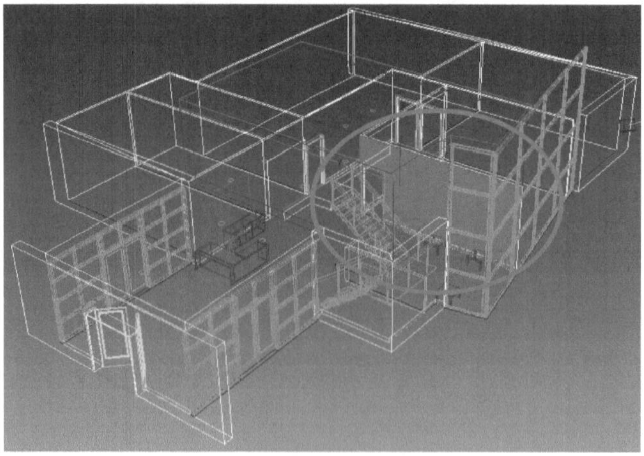

Figure 6–110

11. In the Command Panel, select **Editable Mesh** to exit the *Sub-object* mode.
12. Change the visual display to **Default Shading** and **Edged Faces** by clicking the **[Wireframe]** *Per-View Preference* label and selecting **Default Shading**. There is no change in the model because the material has not yet been assigned.
13. With the wall object (**Layer:VIZ-1-Walls**) still selected (if not, select it), open the *Slate Material Editor*, select the **Wall Multi** material title bar heading in the *View1* sheet. In the *Slate Material Editor* toolbar, click  (Assign material to Selection).
14. Note that the interior wall displays as green (**Paint – Accent**) and the two exterior front facing side walls display in cyan (**Paint – Front**), as shown in Figure 6–111. The rest of the walls display the **Paint – Beige Matte** (dark grey) color.
    - Use  (Orbit) to properly display the color of the walls.

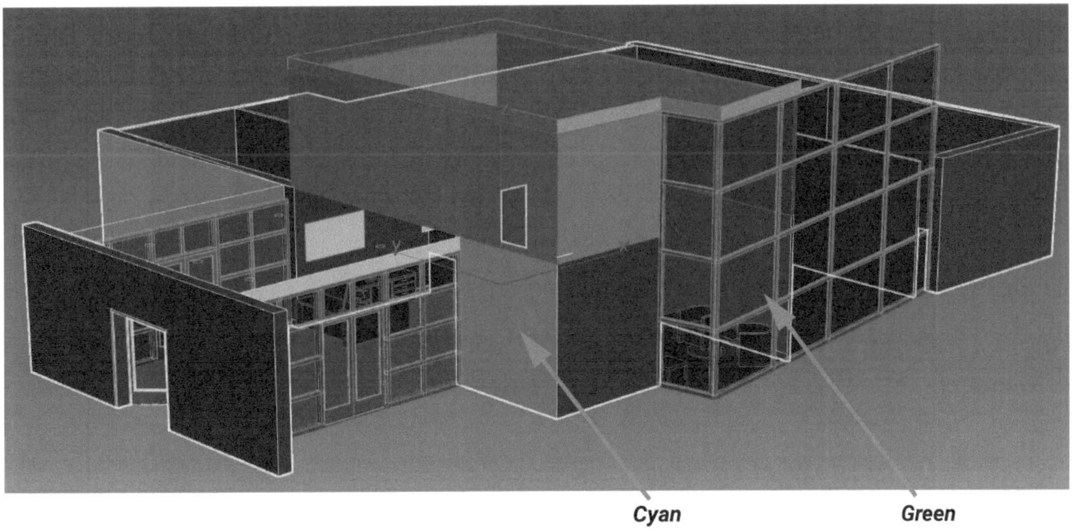

Figure 6–111

15. In the *Slate Material Editor*, click on the **Paint - Front (Physical Material)** title node to open its Parameter Editor.

16. In the *Basic Parameters* rollout, select the **Base Color** color swatch (currently cyan) to open the *Scene Color Selector*. Change the color to a different one, such as red. In the viewport, note that only the color of the two walls that have *ID 5* changes, as shown in Figure 6–112. This indicates that your **Multi/Sub-Object** materials have been applied.
17. Similarly, change the color of the **Paint - Accent** material to a blue color. The inner wall connected to *ID 4* changes to blue, as shown in Figure 6–112.

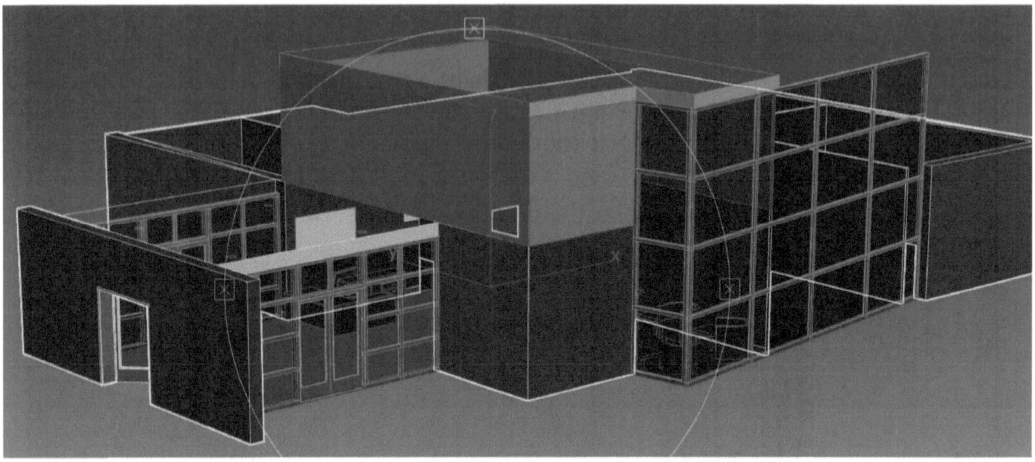

Figure 6–112

18. Save the file as **MyInterior Model MultiMaterials.max**.

End of practice

6.6 Opacity, Bump, and Reflection Mapping

You can use simple objects with materials and textures applied to them to add detailed effects without adding complex geometry to a scene. For example, leaves on trees or a chain link fence can be generated using a simple model with mapped textures and materials rather that creating it with complex geometry.

Opacity Mapping

Opacity mapping controls the transparency of objects, as shown with the lace curtains in Figure 6–113.

Figure 6–113

To create an Opacity map, add a map to the *Cutout map* channel, under the *Maps* rollout of the material.

- The black to white values are mapped to the transparent state, where black creates a hole (completely invisible), white makes a surface (100% opaque), and grays create a semi-transparent effect, good for clouds and fabrics.
- If a color image is used as an Opacity map, the RGB color is ignored and only the Luminance value is used. Opacity maps are usually created by taking digital photos and manipulating them in other programs.

Hint: Two-Sided Opacity Mapped Material

When you create an opacity mapped material, it is recommended to make the material two-sided to see the backsides of faces if looking inside/through an object.

Bump Mapping

Bump mapping gives the illusion of an embossed or pitted surface without geometry being present on the model, as shown for a braided carpet in Figure 6–114. As with Opacity mapping, it uses black to white values to generate the appearance of a raised surface.

- When combined with texture mapping, it helps the scene lighting integrate with the textures to place shadows in cracks, and generally add a veneer of three-dimensionality to the surfaces.
- The white value raises the surface fully while the black value does not raise it at all.

Figure 6–114

Reflection Mapping

Reflection mapping gives a surface the ability to mirror the world surrounding the object, as shown on the glass in Figure 6–115.

- Using Standard materials, you can place a bitmap or a reflection map type in the *Reflection map* channel.
- If you add a bitmap to the *Reflection map* channel, the faces reflect the bitmap based on shininess and scene lighting.
- If you add a Reflect/Refract or Raytrace map, the objects in the scene reflect along with the environment.

Figure 6–115

Practice 6g
Texture Mapping with Physical Material

Practice Objective

- Assign a BaseColor map, Cutout map, and Bump map to an object.

In this practice, you will create a chain link fence using cutout and bump mapping to display the cutouts in a solid piece of geometry.

You must set the paths to locate the External files and XREFs used in the practice. If you have not done this already, return to Chapter 1 and complete Task 1 to Task 3 in *Practice 1a: Organize Folders and Work with the Interface*. You only have to set the user paths once.

Task 1: Assign the texture map.

1. Open **start_chainlink.max**.
2. Click the *Shading Viewport* label and select **High Quality**.
3. In the viewport, select the object **Line01** (yellow fence object). You can also select **Line01** from the Scene Explorer (using (Display Shapes)).
4. In the Main Toolbar, click to open the *Slate Material Editor*.
5. In the *Material/Map Browser*, expand the **Materials>General** categories. In the list, double-click on the **Physical Material** material to add it to the *View1* sheet.
6. Assign the **Physical Material** material to the selected fence object by clicking (Assign Material to Selection) in the *Material Editor* toolbar.
7. In the *View1* sheet, click on the **Physical Material** material title bar heading to open its Parameter Editor. To open a separate *Material/Map Browser*, in the *Basic Parameters* rollout, next to *Base Color* color swatch, click (None), as shown in Figure 6–116.
   - Ensure that you select **None** for the *Color* Map and not the *Metalness* Map.

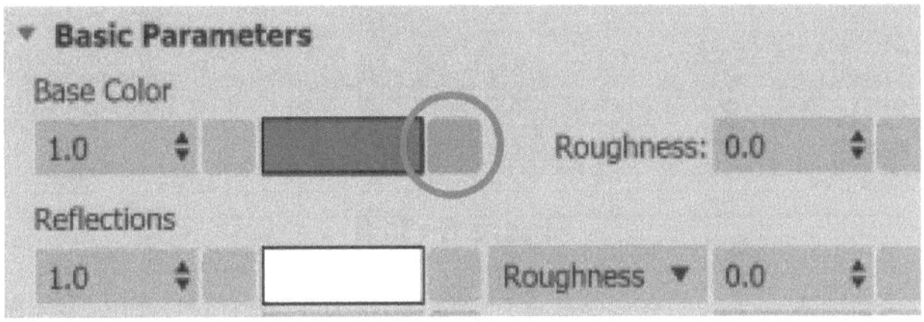

Figure 6–116

8. Expand the **Maps>General** categories and double-click on **Bitmap**, as shown in Figure 6–117.
9. In the *Select Bitmap Image File* dialog box, in the practice files ...*Maps* folder, open **Chain-link.bump.jpg**.
   - Note that in the Parameter Editor the icon changes to , as shown in Figure 6–117. Also note that in *View1* sheet, the output socket of the **Bitmap** node is wired to the *Base Color Map* input socket of the **Physical Material** material, as shown in Figure 6–117.

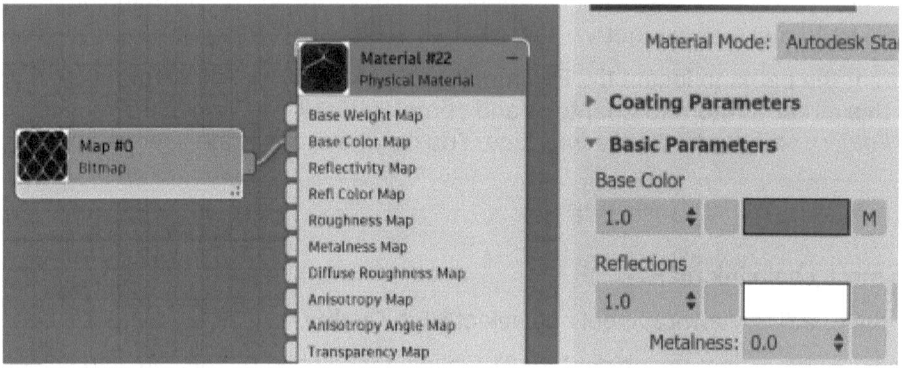

Figure 6–117

10. In the *View 1* sheet, select the **Map # Bitmap** and then click  (Show Shaded Material in Viewport).
11. In the *View1* sheet, verify that the **Map # Bitmap** is selected and its Parameter Editor is open.
12. In the *Coordinates* rollout, clear **Use Real-World Scale** and set *Tiling* as **U: 1.0** and **V: 2.0**, as shown in Figure 6–118. Press <Enter> for the values to take effect. The **Chainlink** texture should display in the viewport.

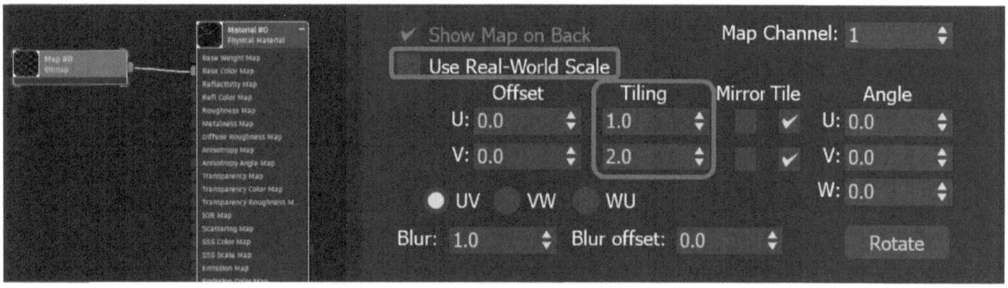

Figure 6–118

13. In the Main Toolbar, click  (Render Production). The map displays in the Arnold RenderView window. Leave it open.
   - You can minimize the Render Window such that it does not block the view of other objects on the screen. You can maximize it when required.

14. In the Arnold RenderView window, click  (Refresh Render). The rendered view should display as shown in Figure 6–119. Leave the window open.

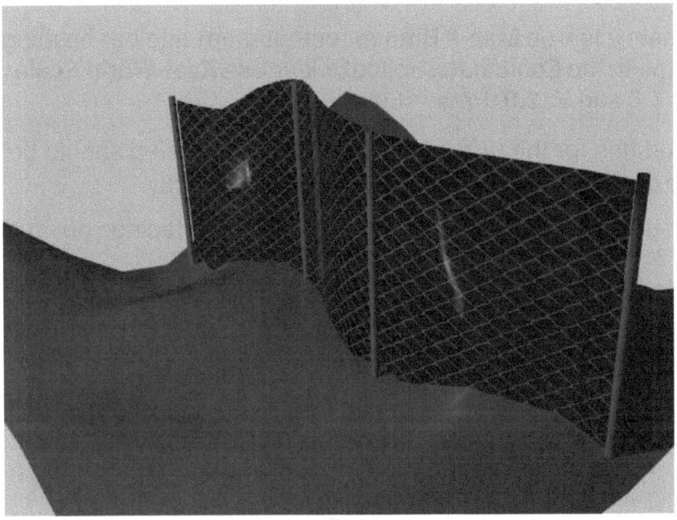

Figure 6–119

Task 2: Assign the Opacity map.

1. In the *Slate Material Editor*, in the *View1* sheet, click on the **Physical Material** material title bar heading to open its Parameter Editor.
2. Expand the *Generic Maps* rollout and note that the **Chain-link.bump** map is already applied to the *Base Color* channel.
3. To control the transparency, apply the map as a **Cutout** map. Expand the *Special Maps* rollout and click **No Map** for *Cutout (Opacity)*, as shown in Figure 6–120.

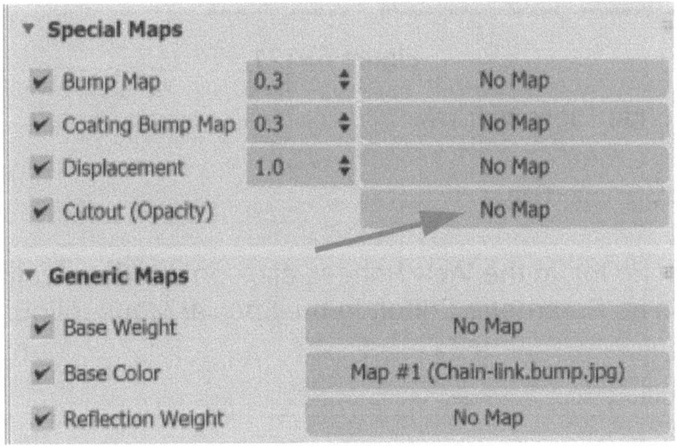

Figure 6–120

4. In the *Material/Map Browser*, expand the **Maps>General** categories. Double-click on **Bitmap** to open the *Select Bitmap Image File* dialog box. Open **Chain-link.cutout.jpg** (from the ...\ *Maps* folder). Note that this bitmap is wired to *Cutout (Opacity) Map* for Physical Material. It also replaces **No Map** in the *Special Maps* rollout of the Parameter Editor.
5. In the *View1* sheet, click on **Map # Bitmap** (cutout map) title bar heading to open its Parameter Editor. In the *Coordinates* rollout, clear **Use Real-World Scale**, if required, and set the *Tiling* to **U: 1.0** and **V: 2.0**. Press <Enter>.
   - The *Tiling* settings for the *Diffuse* map and the *Cutout* map should be the same so that they overlap each other for the cutout to display correctly.
6. Orbit around in the **Perspective** view so that the fence is facing you. In the Arnold RenderView window, click  (Refresh Render). Note that the background displays through the fence, as shown in Figure 6–121. This is caused by the map on the *Cutout* channel. The colors in your rendering might be slightly different than that shown in Figure 6–121.

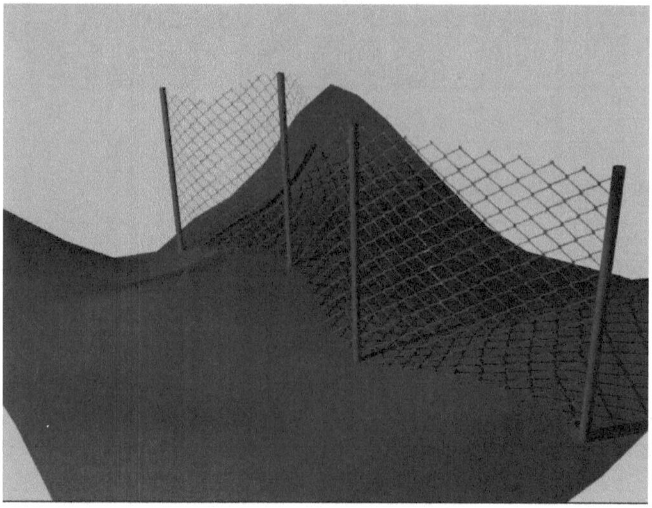

Figure 6–121

7. Close the Arnold RenderView window.

Task 3: Assign the Bump map.

1. In the *Slate Material Editor*, in the *View1* sheet, click on the **Physical Material** material title bar heading to open its Parameter Editor. In the *Special Maps* rollout, for *Bump Map,* click **No Map**.

   Note: *You can also drag and drop the map from the Base Color onto the Bump Map and select* ***Copy*** *in the dialog box.*

2. In the *Material/Map Browser*, in the **Maps>General** categories, double-click on **Bitmap** to open the *Select Bitmap Image File* dialog box. Open **Chain-link.bump.jpg** (from the ...*Maps* folder). Note that this bitmap displays on **Bump Map**, as shown in Figure 6–122 (the same map was used on the *Base Color* channel). Note that in the *View1* sheet, it is wired to **Bump Map** in the **Physical Material** material, as shown in Figure 6–122.

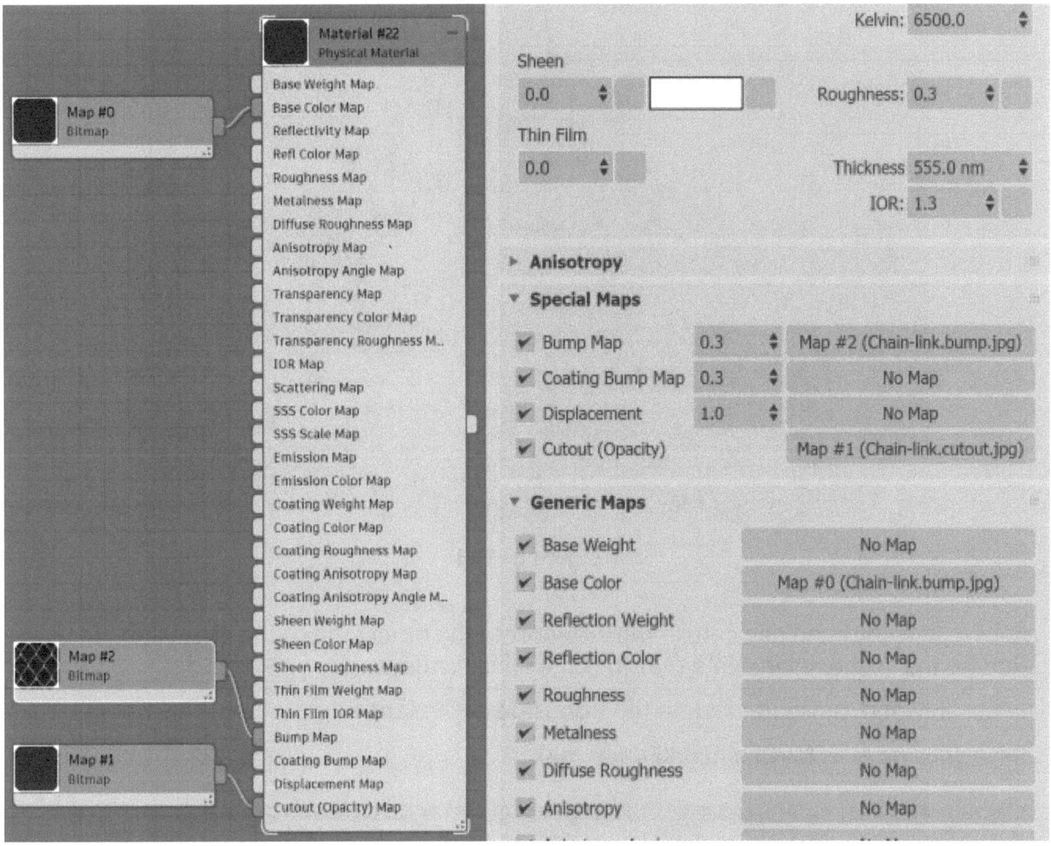

Figure 6–122

3. In the *View1* sheet, click on the **Map # Bitmap** (*Bump* channel) title bar heading to open its Parameter Editor. In the *Coordinates* rollout, clear **Use Real-World Scale**, if required, and set the *Tiling* to **U: 1.0** and **V: 2.0**.

   Note: *You can also copy the map. The settings are also copied and you are not required to enter the Tiling values.*

4. Click  (Render Production) to render the scene.

5. To make the chain link more realistic (smaller cutouts), set the *Tiling* values for all the three map channels to **U: 2.0** and **V: 4.0**. Click on each map title bar heading to open its Parameter Editor and change the values.

6. Render the scene again. The rendered scene should be similar to the one shown in Figure 6–123.

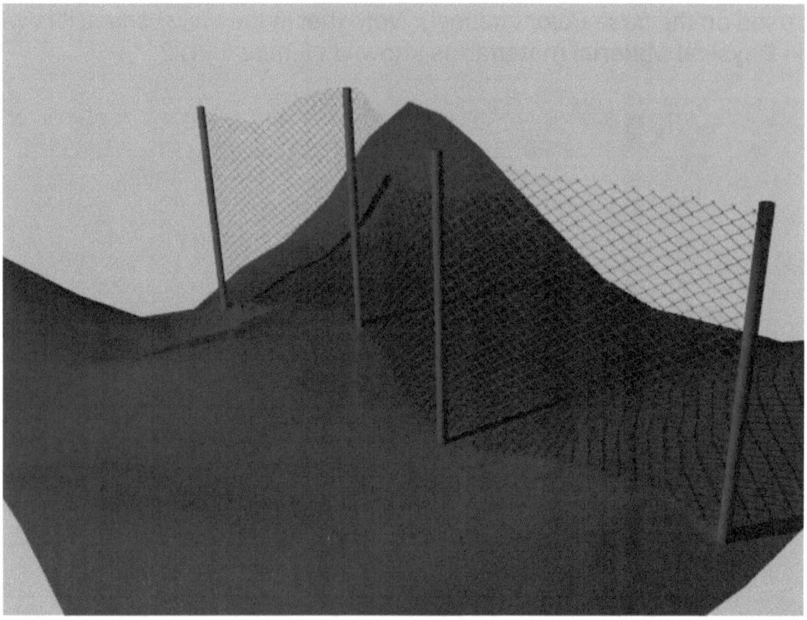

Figure 6–123

7. Click  (Orbit) and navigate in the viewport to the other side of the chain link fence. Render the scene again. Note that the chain link displays.
8. In the viewport, navigate back to the front side of the fence.
9. Save your work as **MyChainLinkFence.max**.

End of practice

6.7 Scanline Materials

Scanline materials are another set of basic materials included in the Autodesk 3ds Max software and are best used with the **Scanline** renderer. These materials can be accessed by expanding the **Materials>Scanline** category in the *Material/Map Browser*, as shown in Figure 6–124.

> ***Note:*** *Depending on the current renderer used, the list of the materials might differ. Scanline materials are not available with the* ***Arnold*** *renderer.*

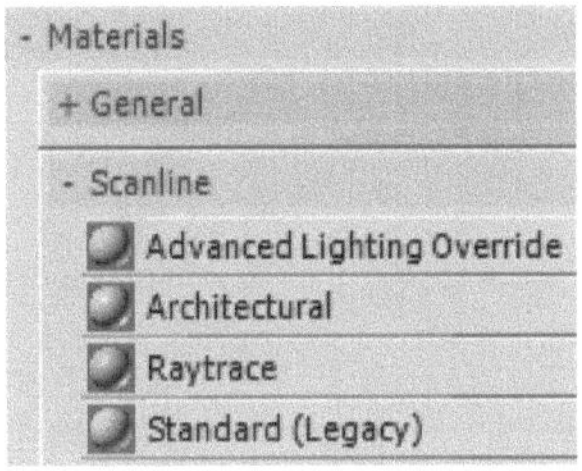

Figure 6–124

Architectural Materials

Architectural materials are a type of Scanline material (as shown above in Figure 6–124) that are appropriate for scenes with physically-based lighting.

- Architectural materials use a streamlined interface that highlights the parameters and maps that are most likely to change.
- Controls that are not directly available to Standard materials are also available, such as refraction, luminance, and advanced lighting overrides.

Raytrace Material

The Raytrace material is used to create highly configurable, realistic reflections and refractions. These materials support fog, color density, translucency, fluorescence, and other effects. Some Architectural materials (such as the ones with the mirror template) automatically generate raytraced results.

Standard (Legacy) Materials

Standard materials are the basic materials and consist of four color components: Ambient color, Diffuse color, Specular color, and Filter color. These materials can be used in most models and can be easily customized.

Advanced Lighting Override Material

The Advanced Lighting Override material is not a regularly used material and is used only to supplement any renderable base material. It is used when there is a need to directly control the radiosity properties of a material.

6.8 Autodesk Materials

The Autodesk 3ds Max software offers a number of **Autodesk** base materials, as shown in Figure 6–125. These can be used as templates to build materials as per your requirements. Their default parameters are already set to produce the optimum effect.

Additionally, there are categories of precreated Autodesk materials present in the *Autodesk Material Library* (as shown in Figure 6–126), which can be used directly in your scene.

Figure 6–125

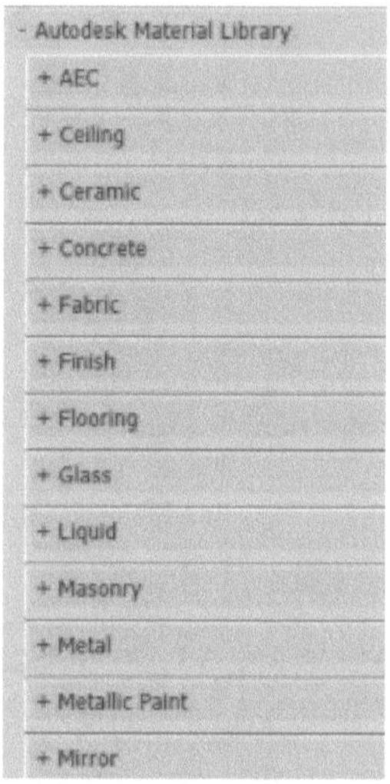

Figure 6–126

- The Autodesk Materials are only available for use with the **ART** renderer and the **Quicksilver Hardware** renderer.
- The Autodesk materials should be used with physically accurate (photometric) lights.
- The Autodesk materials have a much simpler interface and contain presets that enable faster selection of specific material parameters and preassigned bitmaps.
- You can adjust the reflection, refraction, and transparency of the material.
- It enables you to round corners through a post-production pixel shader and an Ambient Occlusion setting that adds subtle detail enhancement to surface corners, cracks, and crevices.
- The Autodesk Material Library was designed specifically for architectural visualization and includes material categories for *Ceramic, Concrete, Fabric, Finish, Flooring, Glass, Liquid, Masonry, Metal*, etc.
- These materials are aligned with the latest release of the Autodesk Revit software, which means that the materials applied in the Autodesk® Revit® Architecture software display as Autodesk Material Library materials inside the Autodesk 3ds Max software.

6.9 The Material Explorer

The Material Explorer enables you to manage all of the materials used in a scene. It displays the material's *Name*, *Type*, *Show in Viewport* setting, and *Material ID*, as shown in Figure 6–127.

- You can open the *Material Explorer* dialog box by selecting **Rendering>Material Explorer**.

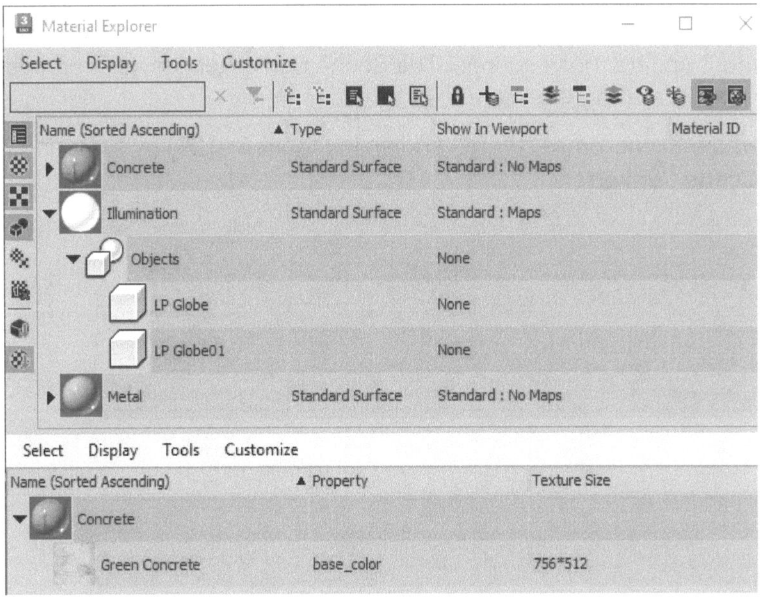

Figure 6–127

- Selecting the various headings sorts the materials in various ways. For example, if you select the *Type* heading, materials of the same type are listed alphabetically according to the material type (such as Architectural, Standard Surface, etc.).
- The bottom panel of the interface displays information on the maps or other properties of the material. This panel has its own menu that enables you to manipulate each material's properties.
- From the *Material Explorer*, you can save directly to a new material library (as shown in Figure 6–128) or perform a variety of tasks depending on the type of the material.

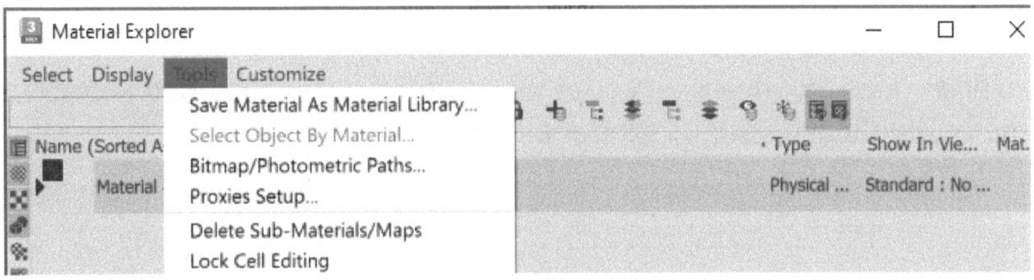

Figure 6–128

6.10 Scene Converter

With many feature changes in the Autodesk 3ds Max 2019 software, the Scene Converter has become a valuable tool for enabling legacy scenes to work with the modern renderers (**ART** and **Arnold**) provided with the software. Since the scenes are based on the renderer used, the materials, lights, cameras and other objects used therein are specific to that renderer. These legacy components are not physically accurate and they are not compatible with the latest renderers. To take advantage of the newer realistic and physically accurate components and renderers, you must update those scenes. The Scene Converter provides an easy and an efficient method of converting the scenes.

- You can open the Scene Converter (as shown in Figure 6–129) by selecting **Rendering>Scene Converter**.

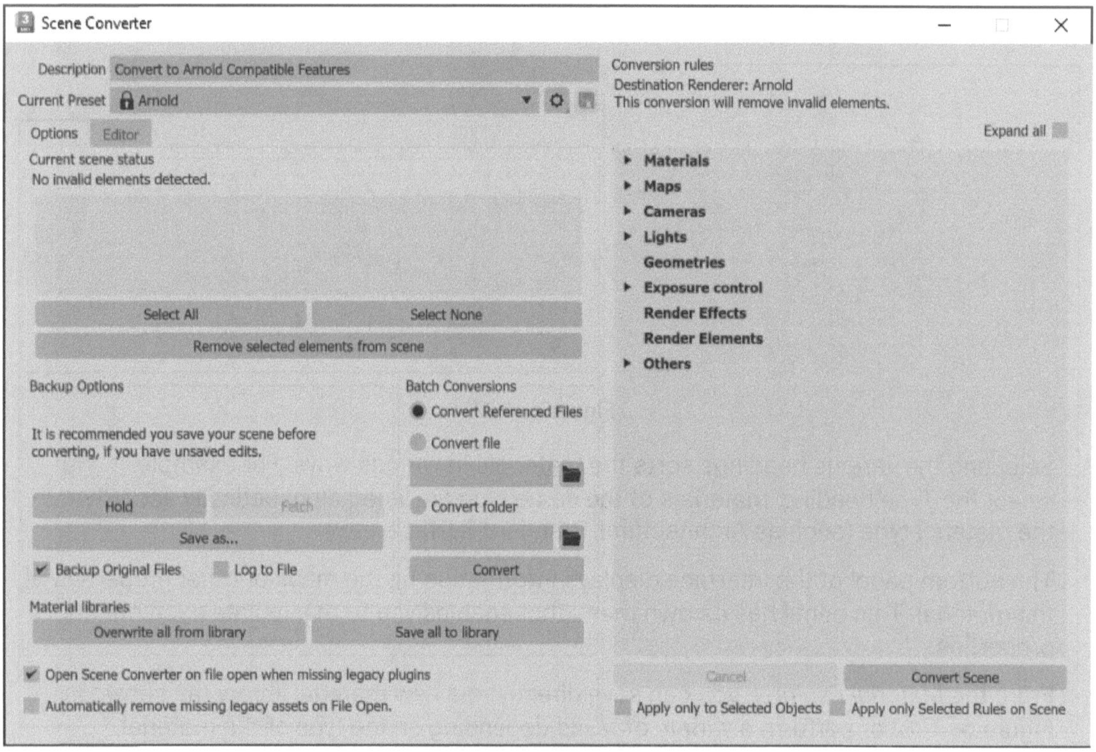

Figure 6–129

- Scene Converter uses a conversion script file to convert the specified legacy materials maps, cameras, lights and various render elements.

- In the *Conversion rules* area, you can expand the various categories to check the conversion details. For example, in the **Materials** category, this script is designed to convert all the *mental ray Arch and Design* materials, *Autodesk Materials,* and *Standard Materials* to the physically based modern **Physical Material**, as shown in Figure 6–130.

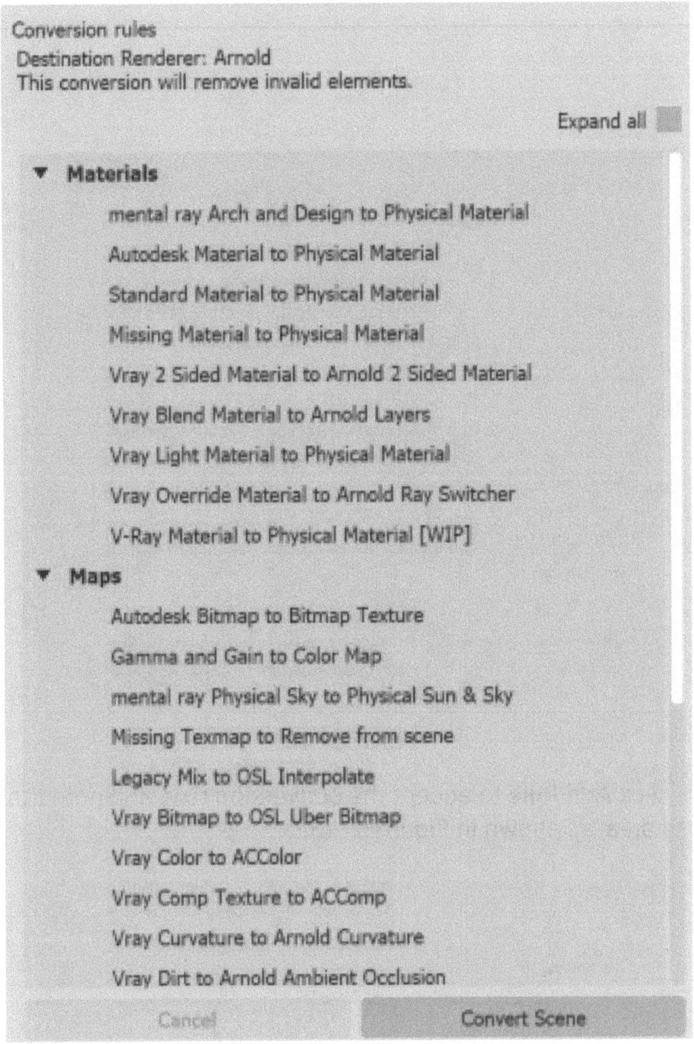

Figure 6–130

- The *Editor* tab enables you to create a new script file and set all the conversion details as per your requirements. In the *Source* area, you can select the elements that you want to convert and then select what you want that element converted into in the *Destination* area. For example, you can convert the *Autodesk Generic* material into a **Physical Material**, as shown in Figure 6–131.

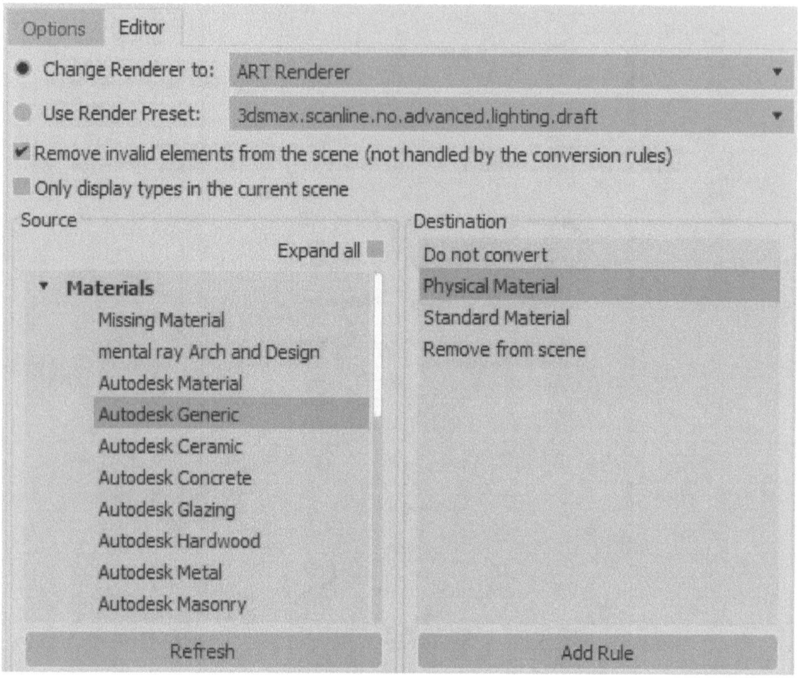

Figure 6–131

- After selection, click **Add Rule** to accept the conversion rule, and note that it is added to the *Conversion rules* area, as shown in Figure 6–132.

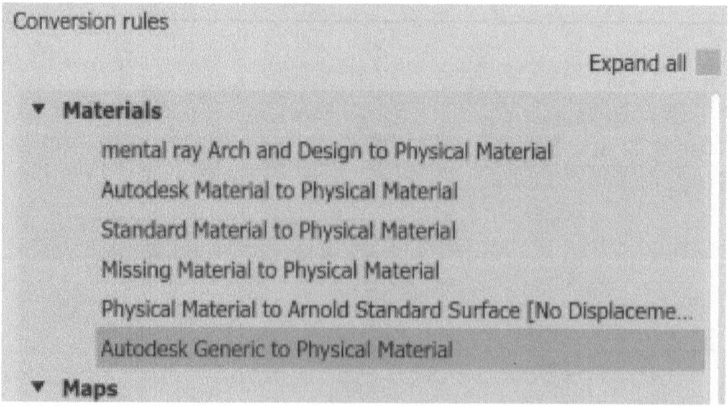

Figure 6–132

- You can also remove the rules that are not relevant for your scene by selecting the rule in the *Destination* area of the Editor and clicking **Remove Rule**.
- After all of the conversion rules are set, click (Save Preset File) or use one of the Preset commands (click (Preset Command list) as shown in Figure 6–133) to save the preset file. When you use the **Save** command, it opens the *Save Preset* dialog box. The new preset file is saved to the path where the scene converter files are saved (*users\<username>\Autodesk\3ds Max 2025\User Tools\Scene Converter\ConversionPresets*). Enter a new name for your created preset. The script files are saved as .MS (3ds Max maxscript) files.

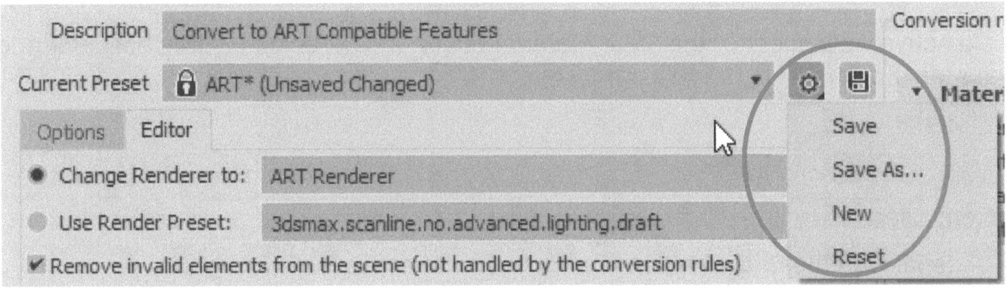

Figure 6–133

- You can also start creating a script file from scratch by using the **New** preset option.
- In the *Options* tab, you can use the **Batch Conversions** options to convert more than one scene file at the same time.
- You can save a temporary file that can be fetched later by clicking **Hold** in the *Options* tab.

Chapter Review Questions

1. The materials and maps listed in the *Material/Map Browser* are dependent on...
   a. The active scene.
   b. The active renderer.
   c. The active viewport.
   d. The active material editor.

2. In the active view sheet of the *Slate Material Editor*, the green color (title bar) of a node indicates that it is a...
   a. Material
   b. Map
   c. Controller
   d. Material with the **Show Map In Viewport** option applied.

3. In the active view sheet of the *Slate Material Editor*, a white border around a material node indicates that the...
   a. material is being used in the scene.
   b. map is assigned to one of the channels (socket) of the material.
   c. parameters of the material display in the Parameter Editor.
   d. material is a customized material.

4. Which one of the following parameters should you increase to create a brushed metal look in the **Standard Surface** Arnold material?
   a. Emission
   b. Roughness
   c. Transmission
   d. Indirect Diffuse

5. Which type of general material enables you to stack multiple materials into a single parent material, each with a material ID number?
   a. Multi/Sub-Object material
   b. Architectural material
   c. Physical material
   d. Shell material

6. Which type of mapping gives the illusion of an embossed or pitted surface without actual geometry having to be present on the model?
   a. Opacity mapping
   b. Bump mapping
   c. Reflection mapping
   d. Cutout mapping

Command Summary

Button	Command	Location
	**Compact Material Editor**	• **Main Toolbar** • **Rendering:** Material Editor>*Compact Material Editor*
N/A	**Material Explorer**	• **Rendering:** Material Explorer
	**Render Production**	• **Main Toolbar**: Render flyout • **Rendering:** Render
	**Render Setup**	• **Main Toolbar** • **Rendering:** Render Setup
	**Slate Material Editor**	• **Main Toolbar** • **Rendering:** Material Editor>*Slate Material Editor*

Chapter 7

Mapping Coordinates and Scale

When creating a realistic representation of a model, both materials and image texture maps can be used. They can be incorporated in a material or you can use specific map modifiers and scaling controls to further control how these elements look in a model.

Learning Objectives

- Work with mapping coordinates required for objects with texture maps.
- Assign mapping coordinates using various tools.
- Adjust the size of the image maps using the various map scaling options.
- Assign spline mapping to a curved object.

7.1 Mapping Coordinates

Most of the sample materials provided with the Autodesk® 3ds Max® software are assigned image texture maps, especially the Diffuse Color and Bump maps. Objects that are assigned materials with maps require mapping coordinates to control how the map is projected onto the object. For example, a rectangular sign can use planar or box mapping and a cylindrical can uses cylindrical mapping.

- Mapping is referenced by its own local coordinate system, described by UVW coordinates.
- Many objects (including primitives) are automatically assigned mapping coordinates. This is controlled by **Generate Mapping Coords** in the Command Panel, in the object's *Parameters* rollout, as shown in Figure 7–1.
- Linked or imported objects with materials assigned in AutoCAD® automatically have mapping coordinates if the **Generate coordinates for all objects** is selected in the import or link preset options, as shown in Figure 7–2.

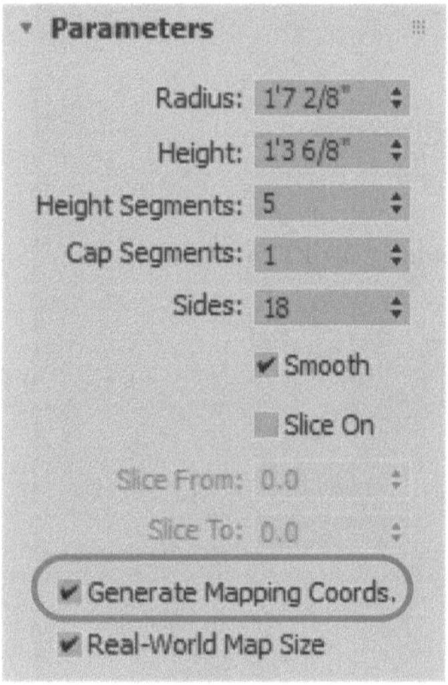

Figure 7–1

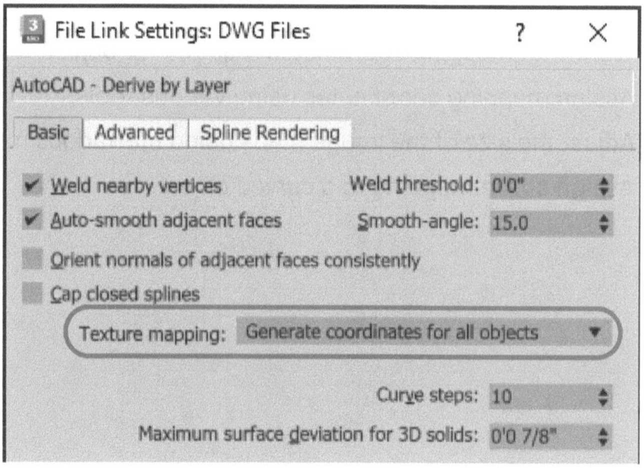

Figure 7–2

- The Autodesk 3ds Max software provides a number of different modifiers (such as **UVW Map, Unwrap UVW**, and **MapScaler**) that can be used to reassign mapping manually.
- Mapping is often disturbed by editing (as through an Edit Mesh modifier) and by Boolean operations. The Edit Poly modifier has a Preserve UVW's feature that can be toggled on to prevent the need for remapping.
- If you select to render an object without mapping coordinates, you receive a warning message that the maps might not render correctly.

Mapping Controls in Slate Material Editor

At the map level of the *Slate Material Editor*, in the Parameter Editor of the map (shown in Figure 7–3), the **Use Real-World Scale** option manipulates the positioning of a map with mapping coordinates.

Use Real-World Scale On

The **Use Real-World Scale** attempts to simplify the correct scaling of textures by specifying the actual height and width (as shown in Figure 7–3) as represented by the 2D texture map. This option requires that the object use UV texture mapping set to **Real World Map Size** and that the Material also have **Use Real-World Scale** selected. It replaces the *Tiling* fields with a Size value for **Width** and **Height**.

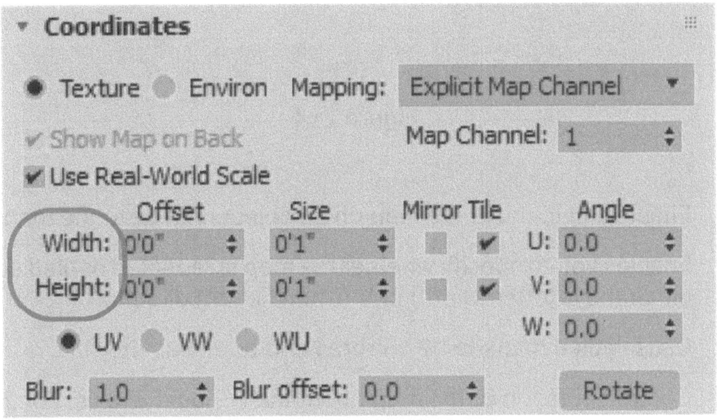

Figure 7–3

Hint: Importing with Use Real-World Scale

Using the **Use Real-World Scale** option when importing from earlier versions of the Autodesk 3ds Max software might cause textures to display incorrectly. It can be due to **Real World Map Size** and **Use Real-World Scale** trying to create an extreme texture. If you leave these on, you need to reset *Tiling* to a different value. You can use **0.01** or a similar small value before you can see the bitmap texture, or go larger and use **10** or **20**. If the texture does not display correctly, it might be easier to toggle off **Use Real-World Scale** and set *Tiling* to **1.0** x **1.0**.

Use Real-World Scale Off

When the **Use Real-World Scale** is toggled off, the map texture is placed with respect to the UV values, as shown in Figure 7–4.

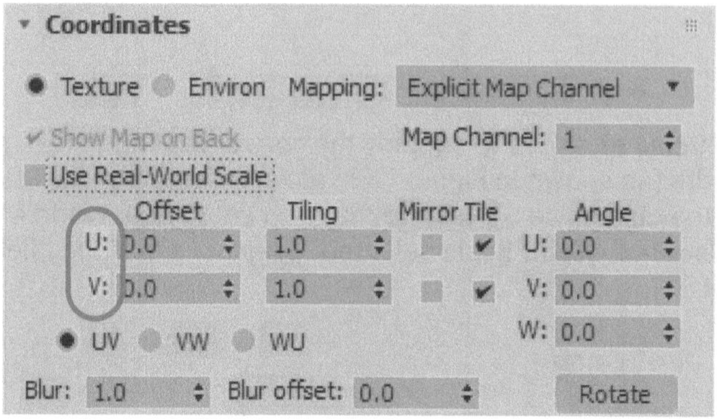

Figure 7–4

Offset	Enable you to move the map on an object relative to the mapping coordinates.
Tiling	Enables you to specify whether the map is repeated or tiled across the surface, in either the U (often width) or V (often height) direction.
Mirror	Causes tiled maps to be mirrored end-to-end as they tile.
Angle (W-rotation field)	Controls rotation of the map about the W (local Z) axis. For 2D maps (such as with an image file) this value typically is used to rotate the map on the surface of an object.

MapScaler Modifier

You can use the **MapScaler** modifier (*Modifier List* in the *Modify* panel ()) to project a map perpendicular to each face of an object. There are two MapScalers:

- **MapScaler World Space Modifier (WSM)** (shown in Figure 7–5) keeps the map scale constant if the object size changes with the Scale transform.

- **MapScaler Object Space Modifier (OSM)** (shown in Figure 7–6) scales the map proportionally.

Figure 7–5

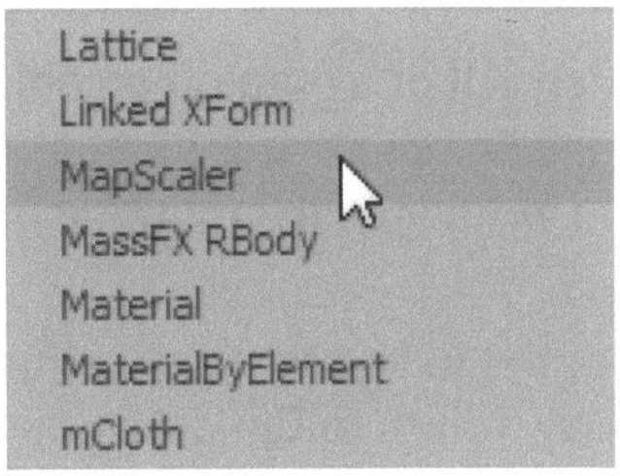

Figure 7–6

- MapScalers enable automatically generated, continuous tiling across complex geometry that might be difficult with UVW Maps. They tend to work well with geometry imported from the AutoCAD Architecture and the Autodesk Revit software.
- One method of repositioning a map on an object assigned a MapScaler is to adjust the U- and V-offset settings in the *Bitmap Parameters* rollout in the Material Editor. Otherwise, apply a UVW XForm modifier to the object and apply the offsets there instead.
- MapScaler modifiers are generally used on objects that have tiling material maps but do not have a defined beginning or end point, such as concrete pads, metals, asphalt, grass, and sometimes brick. MapScalers do not always project well on curved surfaces.

UVW Map Modifier

The **UVW Map** modifier (*Modify* panel ()>*Modifier List*) enables you to apply a map to an object, where you select a specific shape and location to project the map onto.

- The **UVW Map** modifier has a gizmo for transforming in Sub-object mode.
- UVW Maps might not project as well as MapScalers on geometry that does not lend itself to the standard projection shapes (planar, box, cylinder, etc.).

Hint: Unwrap UVW

The Unwrap UVW modifier is another commonly used mapping method. For more information on ***Unwrap UVW***, see the Autodesk 3ds Max Help files.

Practice 7a
Apply Mapping Coordinates

Practice Objective

- Adjust the placement of a map on an object.

In this practice, you will adjust the material mapping using the UVW Map and MapScaler (WSM) modifiers.

You must set the paths to locate the External files and XREFs used in the practice. If you have not done this already, return to Chapter 1 and complete Task 1 to Task 3 in *Practice 1a: Organize Folders and Work with the Interface*. You only have to set the user paths once.

1. Open **Light Pole Mapping.max**.
2. In the viewport or in the Scene Explorer ( (Display None) and  (Display Geometry)), select the **LP Base** object and then click  (Zoom Extents Selected) to zoom in to the concrete base object, as shown in Figure 7–7. When this cylinder was created, the mapping coordinates were generated automatically.

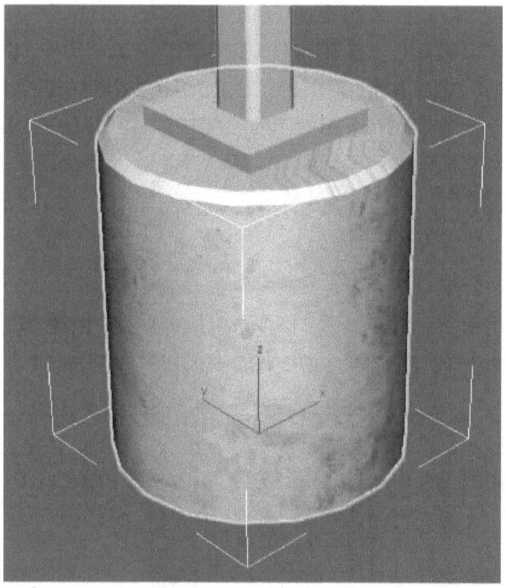

Figure 7–7

3. With the **LP Base** object selected, in the Command Panel>*Modify* panel (), expand the **Modifier List**. In the *OBJECT-SPACE MODIFIERS* group, select **UVW Map**, as shown in Figure 7–8.

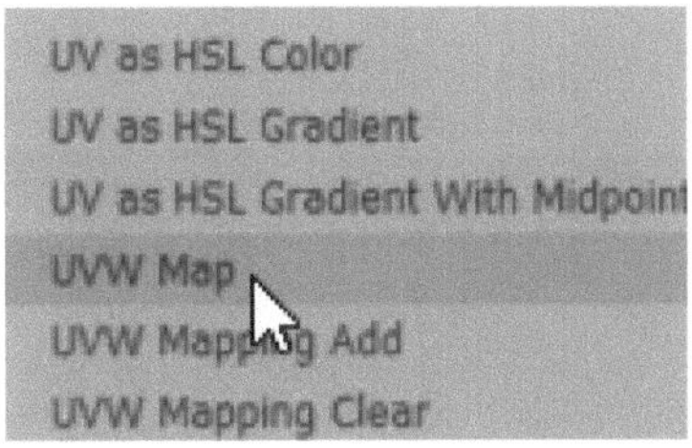

Figure 7–8

4. In the *Parameters* rollout, in the *Mapping* area, select **Box,** as shown in Figure 7–9. Scroll down and select **Real World Map Size** to display the map in the viewport. Note that the Box mapping projects the concrete map onto the object from all six sides of an imaginary box, causing a seam to form in places, as shown in Figure 7–10.

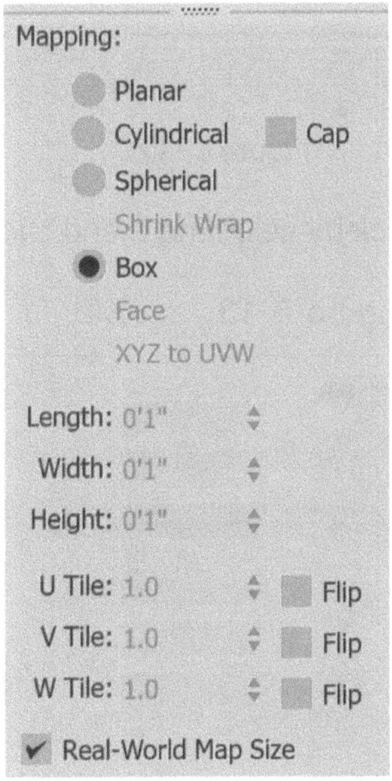

Figure 7–9

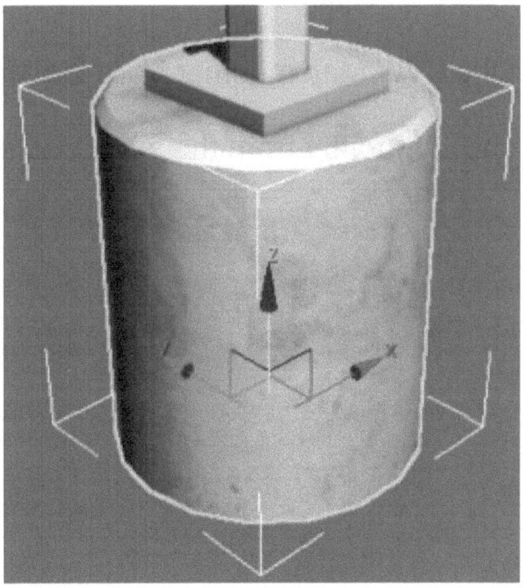

Figure 7–10

5. Change the projection to *Cylindrical* and then *Planar*, noting the differences of how map will be projected.
    - The Cylindrical projection does not display the top very well, as shown in Figure 7–11.
    - The Planar projection does not display the cylindrical base correctly, as shown in Figure 7–12.

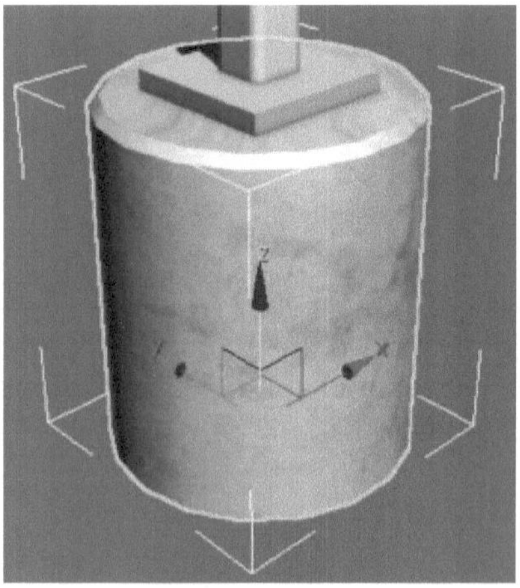

Figure 7–11

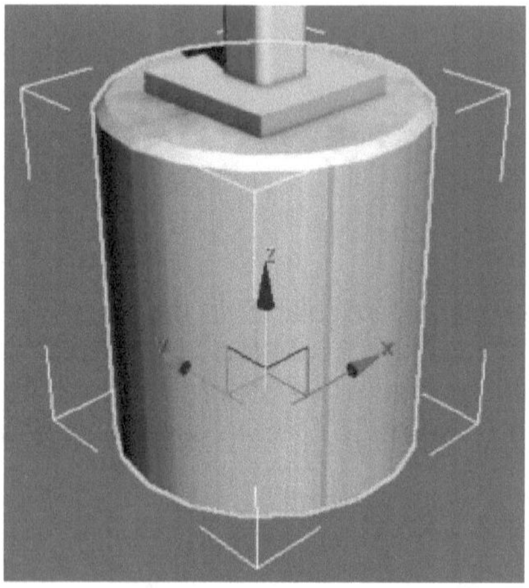

Figure 7–12

6. Remove the UVW Map modifier from the *Modifier Stack* by selecting it and clicking  (Remove modifier from the stack), as shown in Figure 7–13.

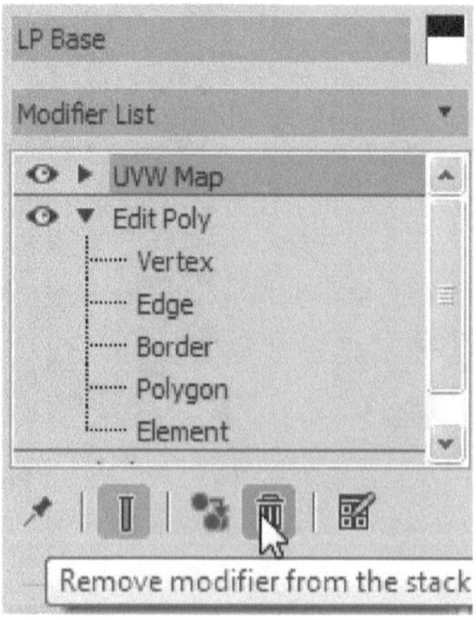

Figure 7–13

7. In the *Modifier* drop-down list, in the WORLD-SPACE MODIFIERS, select **MapScaler (WSM)**. This MapScaler automatically projects the texture perpendicular to each face of an object.

8. Change the *Shading Viewport* to **High Quality**.
9. Note that the map is stretched out and does not display on the base object. In the *Parameters* rollout, adjust the *Scale* spinner up/down and note the changing map. Leave the Scale spinner where the look of the map displays correctly on the top, as well as on the cylindrical base, such as at **0'1"**, as shown in Figure 7–14.

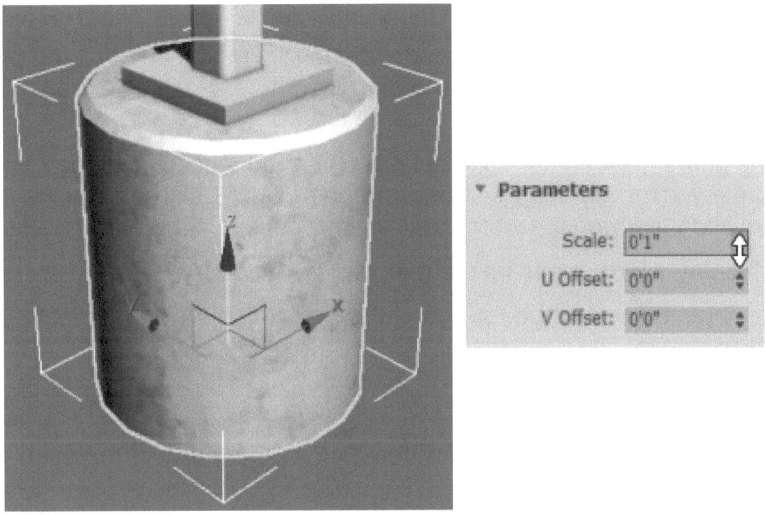

Figure 7–14

10. Save your work as **MyLight Pole Mapping.max**.

End of practice

Practice 7b
Map a Large Scale Image

Practice Objective

- Assign a map to a model and apply mapping coordinates.

In this practice, you will apply a scanned image to a terrain model and map it accurately. You will use the *Slate Material Editor* and the **UVW Map** modifiers to assign a map to a model, apply mapping coordinates, and adjust the map.

You must set the paths to locate the External files and XREFs used in the practice. If you have not done this already, return to Chapter 1 and complete Task 1 to Task 3 in *Practice 1a: Organize Folders and Work with the Interface*. You only have to set the user paths once.

1. Open the **Mapping a large scale image.max** file.
2. If your Units setup is maintained for Imperial, a *Units Mismatch* dialog box opens. Click **OK** to accept the defaults. The units for this file are set to **Meters** and the *System Unit Scale* is **1 Unit=1 Meter**. This is required because the map that will be used is set for Metric units.
3. Note that a large scale square terrain object displays in the viewport. A vertex coloring has been applied to paint the landscape in different colors. The colors represent the different terrain areas.
4. In the Main Toolbar, click 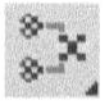 (Material Editor) to open the *Slate Material Editor*. (If a *Render Message* dialog box opens, click **Clear** and click **Close**.) In the *Material/Map Browser*, expand the **Materials>General** category. Double-click on **Physical Material** to add it to the *View1* sheet. Click on the title bar heading for this new material to open in the Parameter Editor. Change the material name to **Quad Map**.
5. In the *Generic Maps rollout*, click **No Map** for *Base Color*. A separate *Material/Map Browser* opens.
6. In the *Material/Map Browser,* expand the **Maps>General** categories. Double-click on **Bitmap** to open the *Select Bitmap Image File* dialog box. Navigate to the ...*Maps* folder in the practice files folder and open the image **q257938.tif**.
7. In the *View1* sheet, note that the **Map # Bitmap** is wired to the Input socket of *Base Color* Map of the Quad Map material. (Depending on the number of maps opened so far, the current number for the map might vary.) Click on the Bitmap title bar heading to open its Parameter Editor. In the *Bitmap Parameters* rollout, in the *Cropping/Placement* area, click **View Image** to open the bitmap to inspect it. Close the *Specify Cropping/Placement* window.

8. In the *Coordinates* rollout, clear **Use Real-World Scale**, if required. Clear *Tile* for both **U** and **V** (as shown in Figure 7–15) because you want this map to display only once and in a specific location.

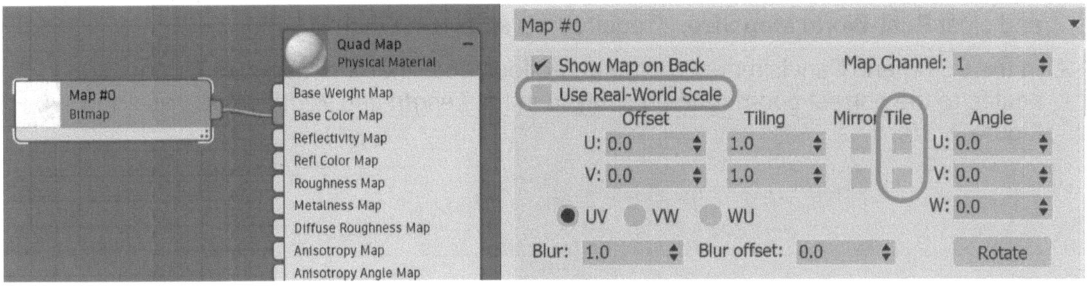

Figure 7–15

9. In the viewport or the Scene Explorer, select the **Terrain01** object. In the *View1* sheet, select the **Quad Map** material and in the *Material Editor* toolbar, click  (Assign Material to Selection). The material does not preview in the viewport.
10. In the viewport, right-click on the **Terrain01** object and select **Object Properties**. In the *Display Properties* area, clear **Vertex Channel Display** and click **OK**. The terrain displays as blank.
11. In the Main Toolbar, click  (Render Production) to render the scene. If a *Missing Map Coordinates* dialog box displays, click **Cancel** in the *Missing Map Coordinates* dialog box and close the Render frame window.

12. In the viewport or the Scene Explorer, select the **Terrain01** object, if required. In the Command Panel, select the *Modify* panel ( ), and in the *Modifier List*, select **UVW Map**. Since the map is not meant to tile, in the *Parameters* rollout, verify that **Planar** is selected and clear **Real-World Map Size**, if required, as shown in Figure 7–16.
13. In the Command Panel, in the *Parameters* rollout, note that the map was automatically scaled to the correct coordinates displayed in the *Length* and *Width* values, as shown in Figure 7–16.

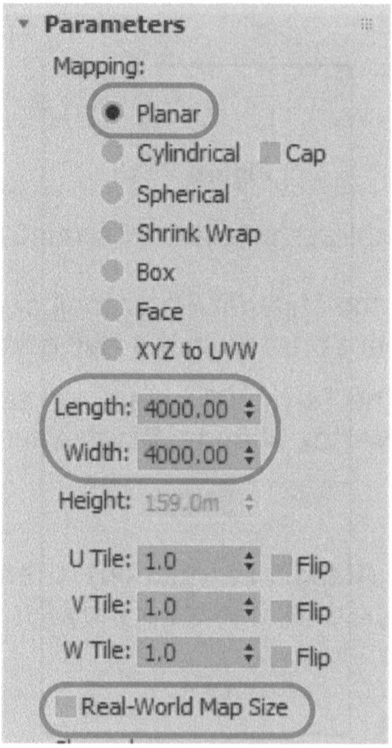

Figure 7–16

14. In the Main Toolbar, click (Render Production) to render the scene. The terrain model should now resemble a 3D map, as shown in Figure 7–17.
    - A white background has been added for printing clarity.

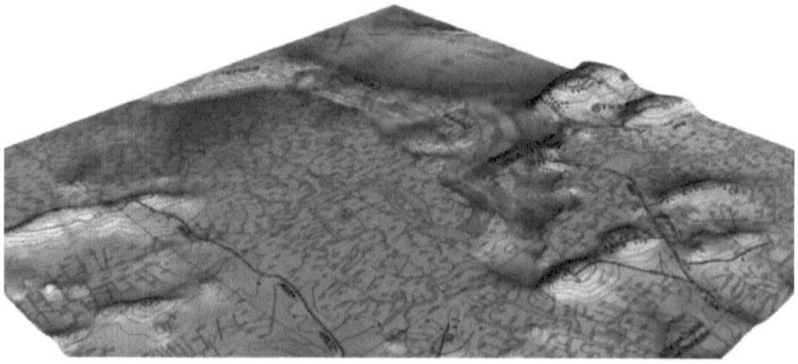

Figure 7–17

- Without any direct manipulation, it appears that this texture map is being applied correctly. This is because the contours that were used to create the surface were trimmed very close to the geographic boundary of the image file.

15. Close the Render frame window.
16. If the map does not display in the viewport, in the *Slate Material Editor* toolbar, click (Show Shaded Material in Viewport) to display the map in the viewport.
17. In the *Modifier Stack*, expand *UVW Map* and select **Gizmo** to enter Sub-object mode, as shown in Figure 7–18.

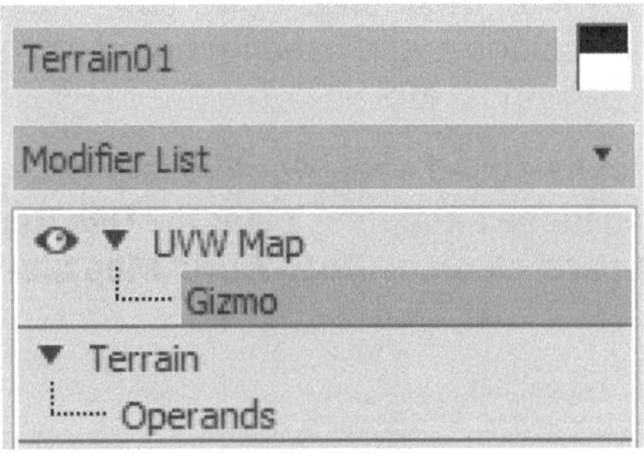

Figure 7–18

18. In the Main Toolbar, click (Select and Move) and move the image map on the terrain object. You can adjust the map more precisely using the *UVW Map* gizmo.
19. In the Command Panel, select **UVW Map** to exit the sub-object level mode. Clear the selection in the viewport.
20. Save your work as **MyLargeScaleProjectMapped**.

End of practice

7.2 Mapping Scale

Mapping Scale is directly related to mapping coordinates and both are often addressed at the same time. Objects that use materials with image maps need to have them sized appropriately.

- Procedural maps also need to be scaled, but they are normally controlled by scale parameters at the Map level of the Material Editor.

Explicit Map Scaling

The size parameters of the UVW Map modifier enables you to control the number of times a map displays. Examples of this include maps used in materials for 3D models of signs, billboards, computer screens, paintings, etc.

- These kinds of maps are not assigned a real-world scale since they often require to be sized manually for each object. In these situations, clear the **Use Real-World Map Scale** option in the *Map Coordinates* rollout and clear the **Real-World Map Size** in the **UVW Map** parameters, as shown in Figure 7–19.

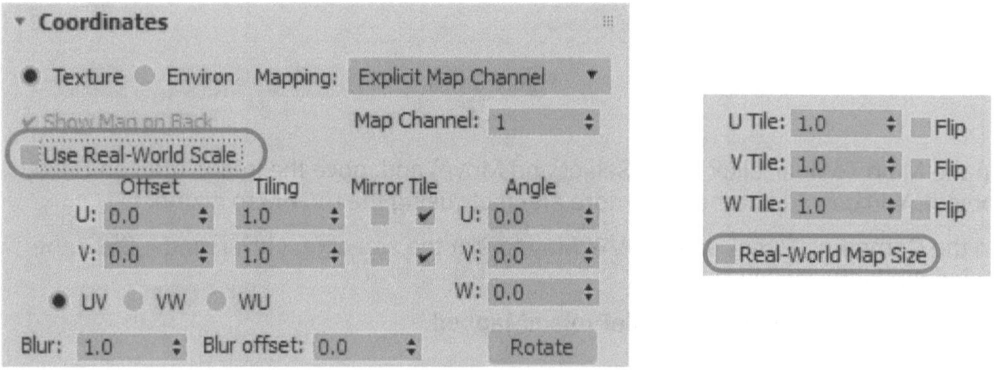

Figure 7–19

- To display the map once, the U and V tile values should be set to **1.0** in both the *Map Coordinates* rollout of the Material Editor and the **UVW Map** modifier parameters.
- To display the map in the V-direction twice, for example (the map's local Y-direction), set the V tile value to **2** in one of these locations, but not both.

Continuous Map Scaling

When material maps are meant to tile continuously across an object, a continuous approach can be used. The size of these maps can be controlled by a Real World scale that affects all objects using the map, or they can be sized directly using **UVW Map** or **MapScaler** size parameters for each object. Setting a Real World scale makes it easier to affect a global map scale change to multiple objects. You might need to determine the physical size you want to display an image file map in your scene.

Calculating Real World Scales

The **Brick** material uses an image file for a diffuse color map, as shown in Figure 7–20. This image map represents a section of wall that is five bricks wide (measured along the long edges) and 16 courses tall. If you want to use this material to represent bricks that are 11" on center laid in 4" courses, this brick map should be scaled to exactly **4'7" (11" x 5)** in the U-direction and **5'4" (4" x 16)** in the V-direction.

Figure 7–20

You can set this scale in various ways:

- At a global scale, enable **Use Real-World Scale** and assign appropriate size values in the map's *Coordinates* rollout, as shown in Figure 7–21.

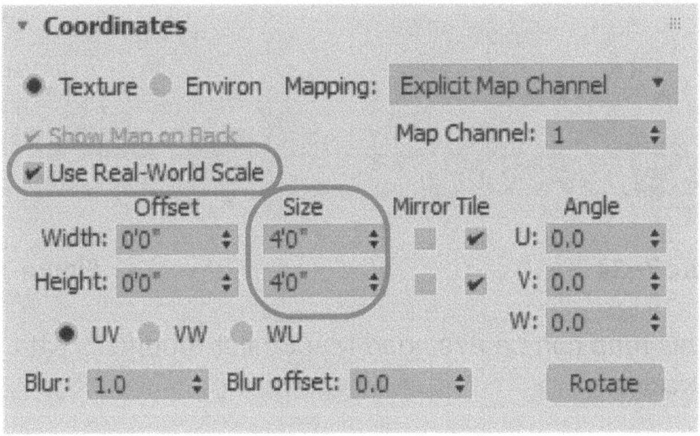

Figure 7–21

- If mapping coordinates are required, apply UVW Maps or Map Scalers to objects displaying this map. UVW Maps should have the **Real World Map Size** option enabled as shown in Figure 7–22. The Map Scalers should be set to a size of one scene unit (such as 1"), as shown in Figure 7–23, in the *Parameters* rollout of WSM modifier.

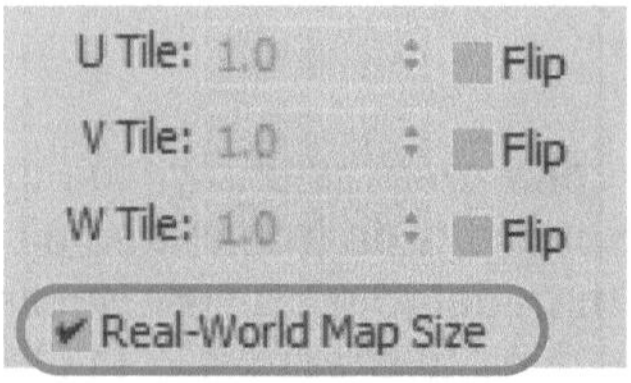

Figure 7–22

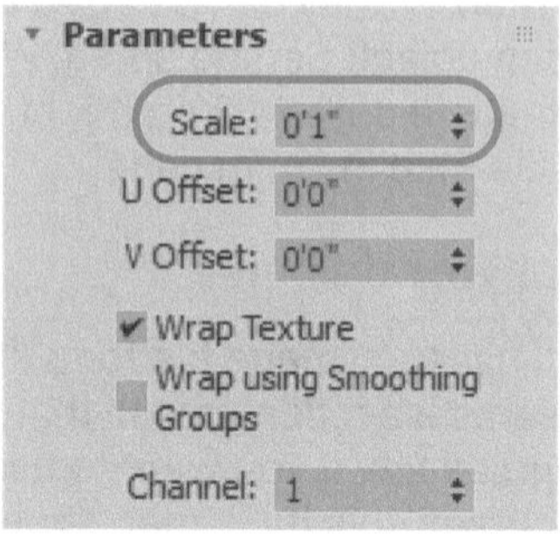

Figure 7–23

- If you want to control map scaling of individual objects through a UVW Map, clear the **Use Real-World Scale** option in the *Coordinates* rollout and set the *Tiling* values to **1.0**, as shown in Figure 7–24.
- Objects showing map can be assigned sizes directly through the UVW Map modifier's **Length**, **Width** and **Height** parameter values. Clear **Real-World Map Size** in the **UVW Map** parameters.
- If you want to control map scaling on individual objects with a Map Scaler, clear the **Use Real-World Scale** option, set the *U-Tiling* value to **1.0** and the *V-Tiling* value equal to the ratio of the U-scale divided by the V scale, as shown in Figure 7–25.

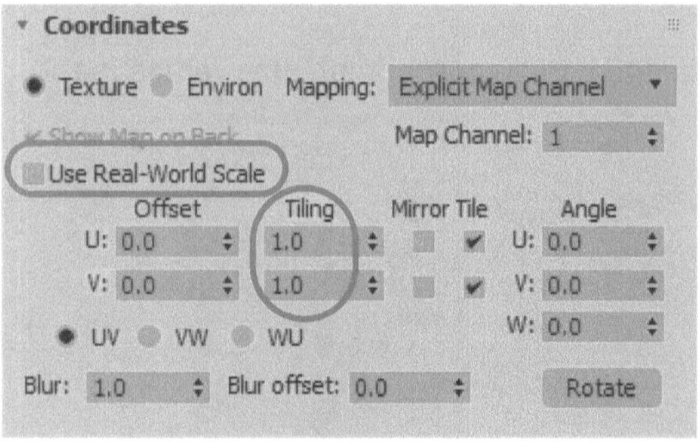

Figure 7–24

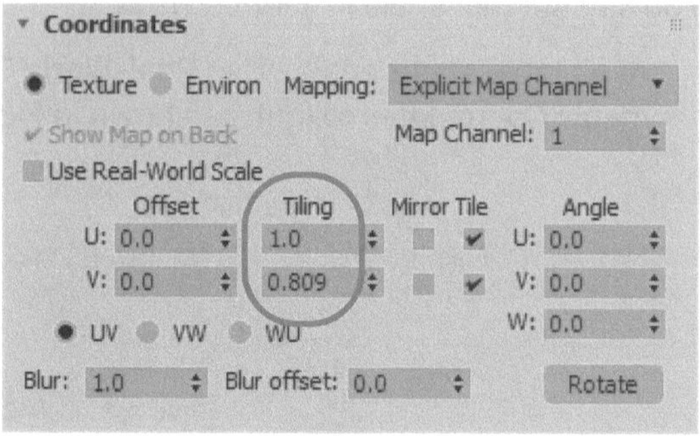

Figure 7–25

- Objects showing this map can be assigned MapScaler modifiers with the **Scale** parameter value set to the U scale.

Practice 7c
Assign Map Scales

Practice Objectives

- Assign a material that contains an image map.
- Adjust the size of the image maps.

In this practice, you will assign a material containing an image map to an object in a scene. You will then use the **MapScaler (WSM)** modifier to adjust the image map and the scaling options to position it correctly in the scene.

You must set the paths to locate the External files and XREFs used in the practice. If you have not done this already, return to Chapter 1 and complete Task 1 to Task 3 in *Practice 1a: Organize Folders and Work with the Interface*. You only have to set the user paths once.

Task 1: Position and scale the brick maps.

1. Open the **Interior Mapping.max** file. If you completed the Terrain Mapping practice, the *Units* were changed to **Metric**, and a *Units Scale Mismatch* dialog box opens. Click **OK** to accept the defaults and adopt the file's units (Imperial).
2. In the Scene Explorer, (Display None) and (Display Geometry). Select **Layer:VIZ-1- Walls** to select all of the walls in the lower floor in the viewport.
3. In the Main Toolbar, click (Material Editor) to open the *Slate Material Editor*.
4. In the *Scene Materials*, double-click on the **Wall Multi (Multi/Sub-Object)** material to open it on the *View1* sheet. Locate the **Masonry** material, wired to input socket number (5) of the **Wall Multi** material, as shown in Figure 7–26. Note that this material has bitmaps wired to the *Diffuse* and *Bump Map* channels.

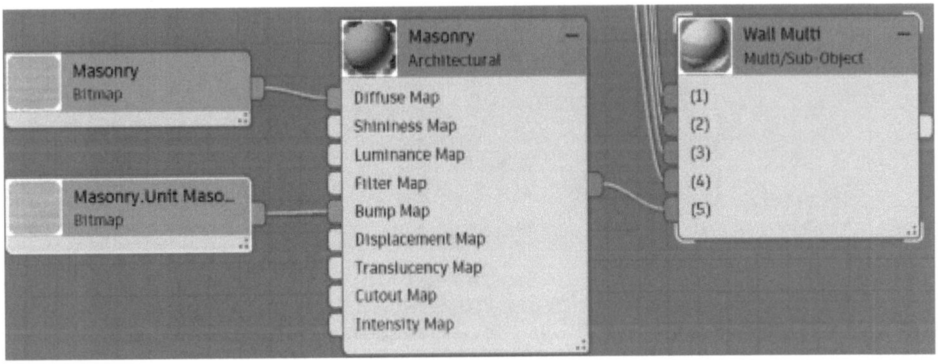

Figure 7–26

5. Verify that **Layer:VIZ-1-Walls** is still selected. In the *View1* sheet, select the **Masonry** material, click (Assign Material to Selection). The **brick** material is assigned to the walls but it does not display in the viewport.
6. Minimize the *Slate Material Editor*. With the **Layer:VIZ-1-Walls** still selected, in the *Modify* panel ( ), select **MapScaler (WSM)** from the *Modifier List*. If the brick texture is not visible, click the *Shading Viewport* label and select **Materials>Shaded Materials with Maps**. In the *Parameters* rollout, use the spinner to get the *Scale* value close to **0'1"**, as shown in Figure 7–27, and then enter the value of **0'1"**. In the viewport, note that the bricks become visible.

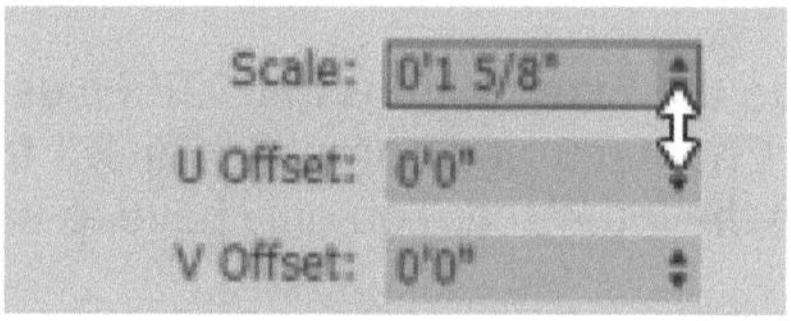

Figure 7–27

7. In the **Perspective** viewport, use the various navigation tools, such as (Zoom), (Pan), and (Orbit), to zoom in to and obtain the required orientation (corner of the two walls) of the brick walls. The brick texture displays as shown in Figure 7–28.

Figure 7–28

8. Maximize the *Slate Material Editor*. Click on the **Masonry Bitmap**, which is wired to the **Masonry** material's *Diffuse Map*, to open its Parameter Editor.

9. In the *Coordinates* rollout, verify that **Use Real-World Scale** is selected and set the following, as shown in Figure 7–29:

   - *Width, Size:* **4'7"**
   - *Height, Size:* **5'4"**

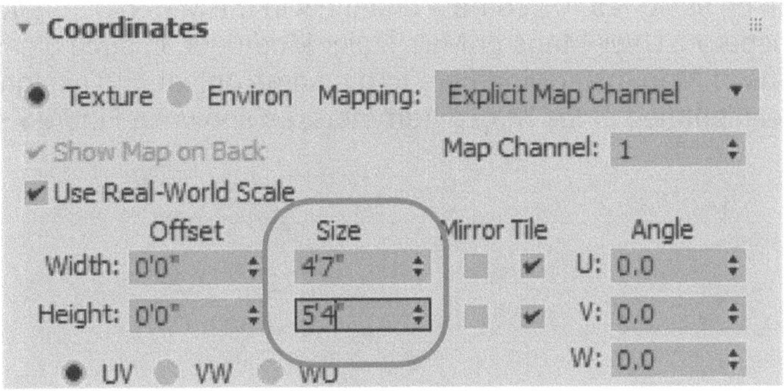

Figure 7–29

   - Note that the brick size becomes bigger and the brick texture terminates in acceptable positions along the top and wall edges, as shown in Figure 7–30.

Figure 7–30

10. For images in a material to be aligned, all of their mapping coordinates' parameters should also match. In the *Slate Material Editor*, double-click on the title bar heading for the **Masonry.Unit** bitmap, wired to the *Bump Map* of the **Masonry** material. In the *Coordinates* rollout, set the *Width* and *Height Size* values that were used for the Diffuse Map. This makes the bitmap texture display more realistic.
11. Save your work as **MyInterior Mapping.max**.

Hint: Multiple Sets of Mapping Coordinates

In the example, you scaled a Multi/Sub-Object material map with a single MapScaler Modifier. What if another material's map in Wall Multi required a **UVW Map** or different **MapScaler Scale** parameter?

Material maps can be assigned to separate channels in the *Material Editor*, so that each can be controlled by separate UVW Maps or MapScaler Modifiers. In such a case, you can apply multiple UVW Maps or MapScaler Modifiers to the same object and assign each of the applicable channel identified in the **Map** parameters, as shown in Figure 7–31.

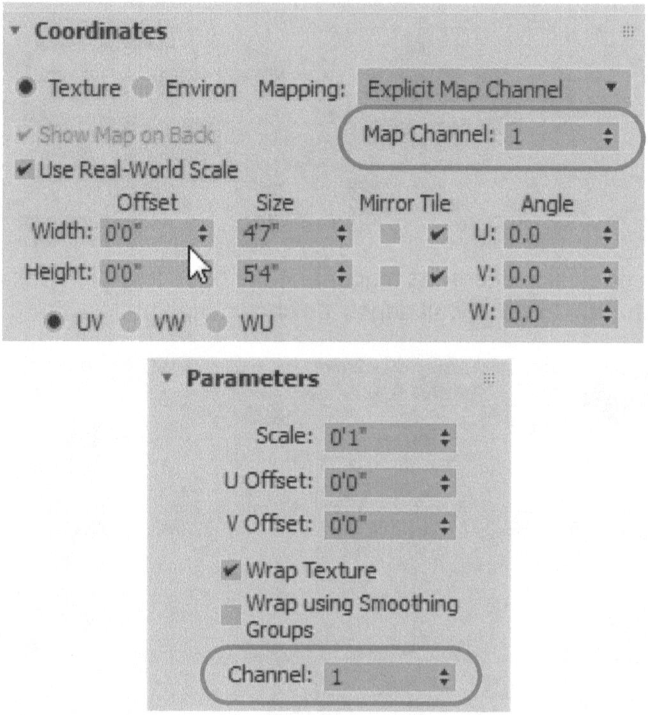

Figure 7–31

End of practice

7.3 Spline Mapping

Generating mapping coordinates that follow the path of extrusion is useful when a texture needs to follow the curvature of the lofted object. The **Unwrap UVW** modifier enables you to apply spline mapping and to select a spline for the basis of the mapping coordinates. You can use the Mapping gizmo to modify the mapping along the cross-section.

- It is applied at a sub-object level (Polygon or Face), as shown in Figure 7–32.
- It is present in the *Wrap* rollout of the **Unwrap UVW** parameters, as shown in Figure 7–33.

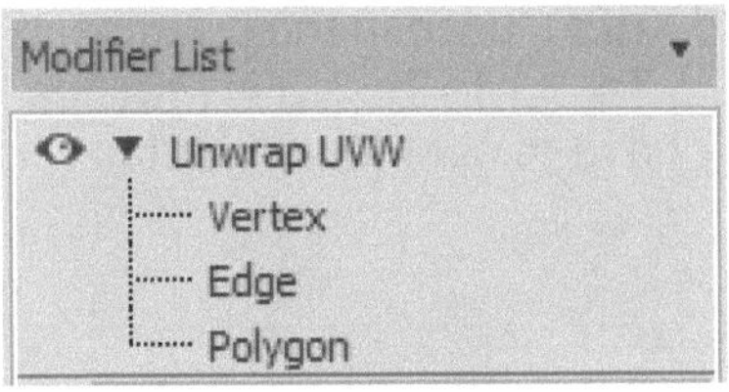

Figure 7–32

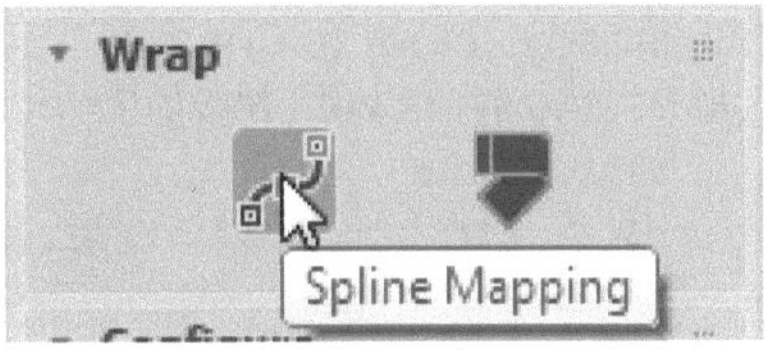

Figure 7–33

- In the *Spline Map Parameters* dialog box (shown in Figure 7–34), you can set the mapping.
  - Use **Planar** mapping for roads and planar surfaces with a line cross-section.
  - Use **Circular Mapping** for objects with a circular cross-section.

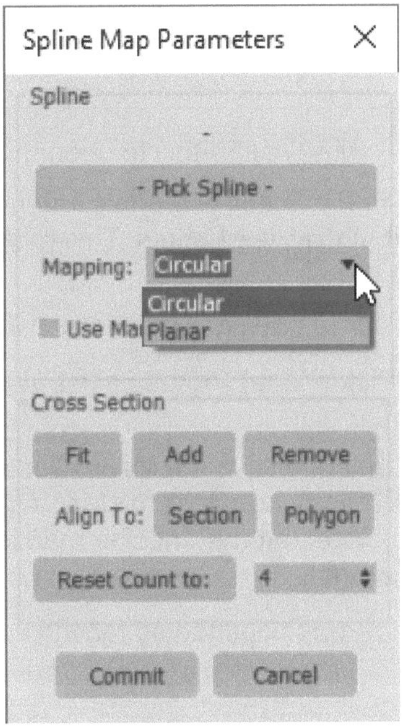

Figure 7–34

Practice 7d
Spline Mapping

Practice Objective

- Apply spline mapping to a curved object.

In this practice, you will apply spline mapping to a curved object using the **Unwrap UVW** modifier and adjust the scale and position to place it appropriately.

You must set the paths to locate the External files and XREFs used in the practice. If you have not done this already, return to Chapter 1 and complete Task 1 to Task 3 in *Practice 1a: Organize Folders and Work with the Interface*. You only have to set the user paths once.

Task 1: Position and scale the checker map.

1. Open **Spline Mapping.max**. There is a curved object that needs to be mapped to display the correct road texture.
2. Select the object **Roadshape01**. A spline has already been prepared in this file and it runs (yellow line) through the center of the curved **Roadshape01** object. You can change the *Per-View Preference* to **Wireframe Override** to display the spline more clearly and then change it back to **Default Shading**.
3. Expand the *Modify* panel () and, in the *Modifier Stack*, verify that a Line object and an **Extrude** modifier are listed.
4. In the Main Toolbar, click  (Material Editor) to open the *Slate Material Editor*.
5. In the *Material/Map Browser*, in the **Scene Materials** category, double-click on **02 - Default (Physical Material)** to place it in the *View1* sheet. This material has already been assigned to the **Roadshape01 o**bject.
6. Click on the **02 - Default** title bar to open its *Parameter Editor*, if required. In the *Basic Parameters* rollout, click  (Pick a Map) for the *Base Color* channel, as shown in Figure 7–35.
7. In the *Material/Map Browser* that opens, in the **Maps>General** categories, double-click on **Checker**. In the *Generic Maps* rollout, note that the **Map # (Checker)** displays for the **Base Color** slot. In the *View1* sheet, note that the Checker map is also wired to the *Base Color Map* slot of the **02-Default** material.
   - Depending on the number of maps opened so far, the current number for the checker map might vary.

8. In the Parameter Editor, in the *Generic Maps* rollout, click to put a checkmark next to the **Base Color**, as shown in Figure 7–36. In the *View1* sheet, note that the **Checker** node is wired to the input socket of *Base Color Map* of the **02- Default** material. Minimize the *Slate Material Editor.*

Figure 7–35

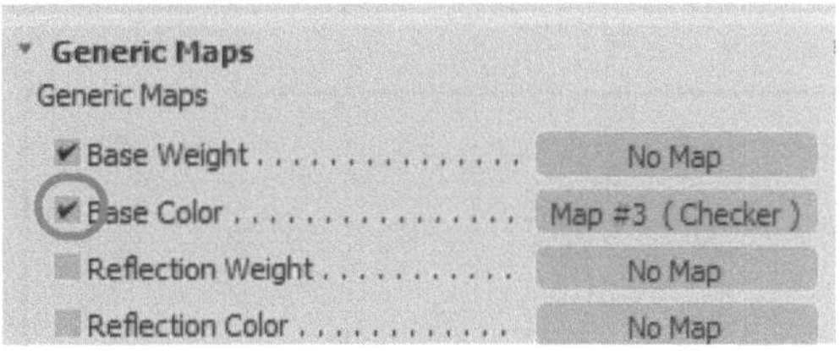

Figure 7–36

9. Click the *Shading Viewport* label and select **Materials>Shaded Materials with Maps**. The checker map displays on the object in the viewport, but does not show correctly. In the *View1* sheet, click on the **Map # Checker** title bar to open its Parameter Editor. Verify that the **Use Real-World Scale** option is cleared. For the *Tiling* values, enter **0.03** in both *U* and *V* edit boxes, as shown in Figure 7–37. Note that the checker texture displays on the road shape in the viewport, as shown in Figure 7–38.

   - Note that the checker map is projected as a single sheet on top of the rectangular object and not generated to follow the curvature of the spline.

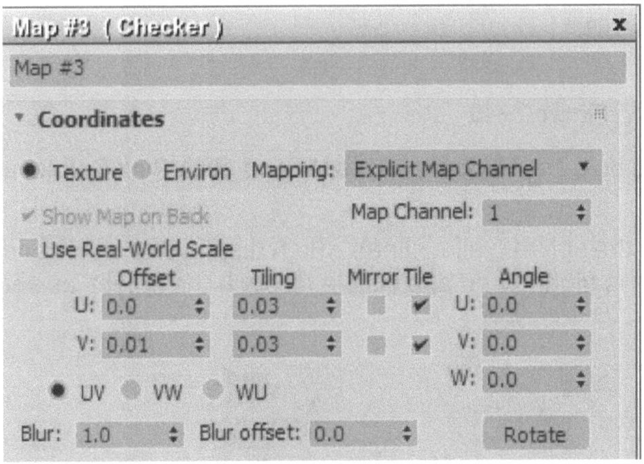

Figure 7–37

Figure 7–38

Note: A checkerboard mapping material is useful for identifying map scaling and orientation issues. These issues can then be corrected before applying the final texture map.

10. In the Command Panel>*Modify* panel (), in the *Modifier List*, select **Unwrap UVW**. Note that the **Unwrap UVW** is listed above **Extrude** in the *Modifier Stack.*

11. In the *Modifier Stack*, expand **Unwrap UVW** and select **Polygon**, as shown in Figure 7–39.

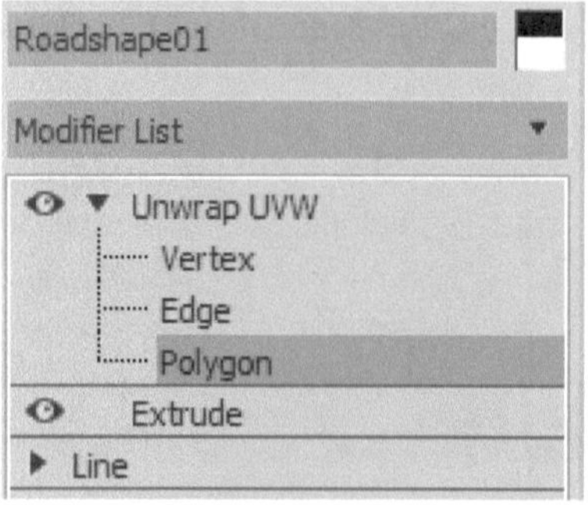

Figure 7–39

12. In the viewport, select the top face along the curve of the **Roadshape01** object. Note that the top checker face displays in a red hue indicating that the face is selected.

13. In the Command Panel, pan down to the *Wrap* rollout. Click  (Spline Mapping), as shown in Figure 7–40.

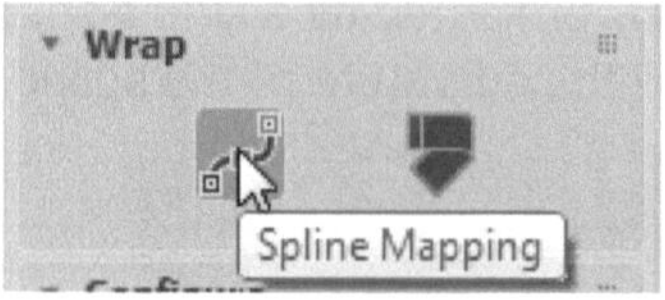

Figure 7–40

14. In the *Spline Map Parameters* dialog box, set *Mapping* to **Planar** and click **Pick Spline**, as shown in Figure 7–41.

15. In the viewport, hover the cursor on the spline (yellow line), which displays at either end of the **Roadshape01** object. The spline is highlighted and visible through the object, as shown in Figure 7–41. Select this spline.

Figure 7–41

16. In the *Spline Map Parameters* dialog box, click **Commit**.
17. In the *Modifier Stack*, select **Unwrap UVW** to clear the selection and exit Sub-object mode. The checker texture is lost, indicating that the position and scale need to be corrected.
18. Maximize the *Slate Material Editor*. In the *View1* sheet, click on the **Map # Checker** title bar to display its Parameter Editor, if required. In the *Coordinates* rollout, select **Use Real-World Scale** and set the following, as shown in Figure 7–42:
    - *Size Width*: **0'0.75"**
    - *Size Height*: **0'0.1"**
19. Press <Enter> and verify that the *Offset* values are **0'0.0"** for both *Width* and *Height*.
    - It is recommended to use the spinners to increase and decrease the *Size Width* while checking the interactive display of checker in the viewport. The checker line should pass through the center, following the curve path line.

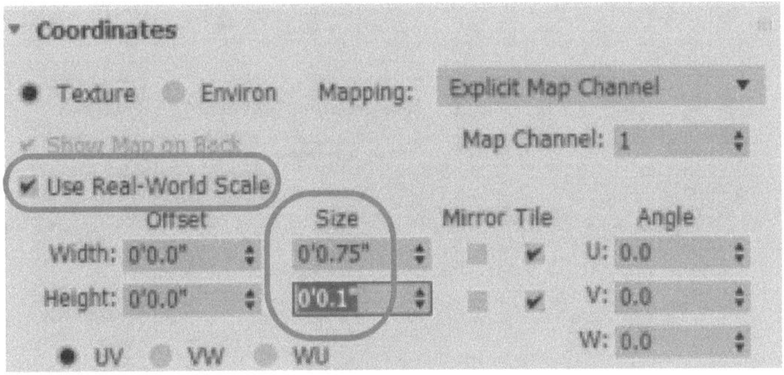

Figure 7–42

- The checker map displays as shown in the Figure 7–43. This is the correct position and scale of the **checker** material as it follows the spline path.

Figure 7–43

Task 2: Assign the road material.

1. In the *Material/Map Browser*, expand the **Maps>General** categories. Double-click on **Bitmap** to open the *Select Bitmap Image File* dialog box. Open **TextureForRoad.jpg** (from the ...\ *Maps* folder in the practice files).
   - Note that a new node for this bitmap is added in the *View1* sheet but is not associated with any material.
2. Delete the wire that currently exists between the **Checker** Map and the *Base Color Map* of **02 Default** material by selecting the wire and pressing <Delete>.
3. Draw a new wire linking the input socket of the Base Color Map for **02 Default** material to the output socket of the road texture bitmap (**Map #4 Bitmap**), as shown in Figure 7–44.

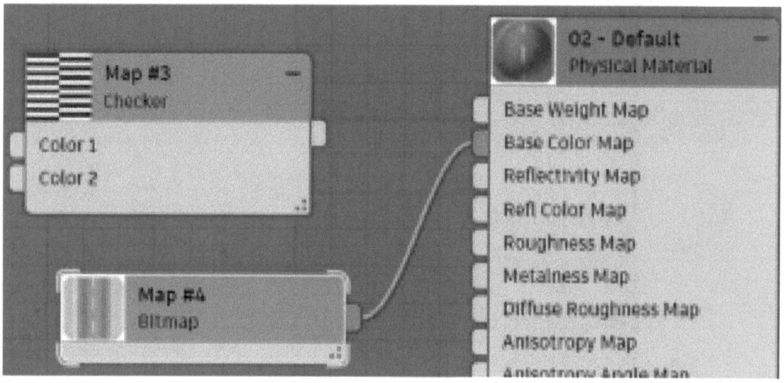

Figure 7–44

4. In the viewport, the road texture should display on the face of the **Roadshape01** object. If it does not display, click the *Shading Viewport* label and select **Materials>Shaded Materials with Maps**.
5. The road texture displays following the curve of the road, but needs to be modified for the texture to display correctly. The Parameter Editor for the road bitmap node **Map # Bitmap (TextureForRoad)** should be displayed. (If not, click on its header.) In the *Coordinates* rollout, clear **Use Real-World Scale**, if required.

6. Set *Tiling* for **U: 2** and **V: 8**. Use the spinners for **Offset U** and **V** to center the road. Increasing the **Tiling V** brings the dashes closer to the middle of the road while decreasing it makes the dashes longer and farther apart along the center curve. Use the **Offset U** spinner to increase or decrease the value so that the dashed line is placed along the center of the road, as shown in Figure 7–45.

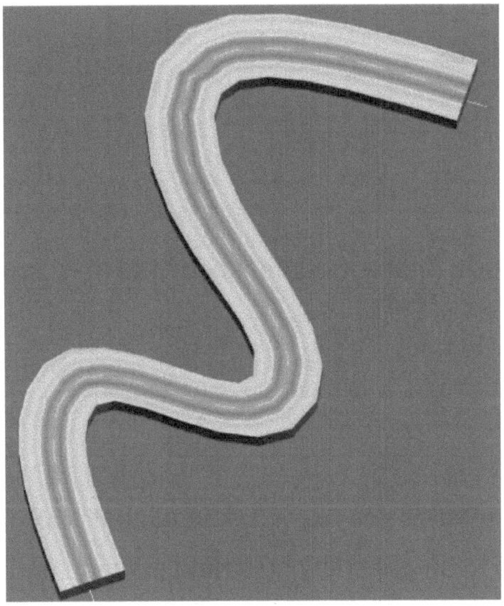

Figure 7–45

7. Save your work as **MyStartSplineMapping.max**.

End of practice

Chapter Review Questions

1. Which option manipulates the positioning of a map with mapping coordinates at the map level of the *Slate Material Editor*?
   a. Generate coordinates for all objects.
   b. Generate Mapping Coords
   c. Unwrap UVW
   d. Use Real-World Scale

2. The **MapScaler in the World Space** modifier keeps the map scale constant if the object size changes with the Scale transform.
   a. True
   b. False

3. The **UVW Map** modifier enables you to.... (Select all that apply.)
   a. Explicitly apply a map to an object by selecting a shape and location.
   b. Use a gizmo for transforming in Sub-object mode.
   c. Perfectly project on geometry with non-standard projection shapes.
   d. All of the above.

4. Which of the following is the correct method for controlling map scaling of individual objects using a UVW Map? These options are accessed in the Parameter Editor of the map in the *Slate Material Editor*.
   a. Select **Use Real-World Scale** and assign the appropriate size (*Width* and *Height*) values.
   b. Select **Use Real-World Scale** and assign both the *Width* and *Height Size* values to the U-scale value.
   c. Clear **Use Real-World Scale** and set the *Tiling U* and *V* values to **1.0**.
   d. Clear **Use Real-World Scale** and set the *U-Tiling* value to **1.0** and the *V-Tiling* value equal to the ratio of the U-scale divided by the V scale.

5. Which mapping modifier is used to generate a map to follow the curvature of the spline along which the object was extruded (Spline mapping)?
   a. UVW Map
   b. Unwrap UVW
   c. MapScaler (WSM)
   d. MapScaler (OSM)

Chapter

8

Photometric Lighting and Cameras

Photometric lights are generally used to accurately represent real-world lighting. Once the lights are added, their parameters can be modified to create realism in a design. You can include cameras to set up physically-based photorealistic scenes. To further enhance realism in the scenes, add background images to the viewports and renderings.

Learning Objectives

- Learn the various lighting strategies, such as default lighting, global illumination, and local illumination.
- Create photometric lights and modify them by changing their parameters.
- Cast realistic shadows from opaque objects using the shadow-casting methods available with photometric lights.
- Create different types of cameras and control their parameters.
- Use image files as viewport and rendering backgrounds.

8.1 Lights

Once you add materials to an Autodesk® 3ds Max® project, lighting can be used to further enhance and create a realistic representation of the model. Projects automatically include default illumination that can be further enhanced or modified to create local or global illumination. Illumination can be accomplished using photometric, Arnold, or standard lights.

The Autodesk 3ds Max software provides different kinds of scene lighting and enables you to add lighting objects that simulate real lights. Commonly used lighting methods provide either local or global illumination.

Default Illumination

By default, the Autodesk 3ds Max software automatically adds light to unlit scenes with invisible, unselectable light objects referred to as default lighting.

- A key light is located in the front and to the left of a scene and a fill light is located behind as well as to the right. These lights act as omni lights that illuminate in all directions. When user-defined light objects are added to a scene, the default lighting is automatically disabled for rendering.

Global Illumination

Global Illumination (GI) algorithms describe how light interacts with multiple surfaces. The illumination and rendering methods, which take GI into account, include radiosity and raytracing.

- Radiosity is a lighting/rendering strategy that calculates diffuse inter-reflections of light. It automatically generates ambient illumination and light mixing, producing realistic results especially when daylight is involved.
- Radiosity is designed to work with physically based (photometric) lights that have parameters derived from real-world lighting properties.
- Exposure control is a method of balancing illumination levels in rendered output. It is essential to work with global illumination, using radiosity.
- Ray tracing is not used as a stand-alone rendering method but rather to compliment the other rendering methods.
- Although it takes a bit longer to generate, the results of Global Illumination (GI) approaches are often more realistic. GI approaches are very popular in architecture, interior design, and related fields.

- Figure 8–1 was created with global illumination, showing an interior scene with night time lighting. Figure 8–2 was created with global illumination, showing an interior scene with daytime lighting.

Figure 8–1

Figure 8–2

Local Illumination

With a traditional local illumination approach, light sources only affect those objects that they can directly illuminate. They do not account for the diffuse light that bounces off of one surface to illuminate another nor do the effects of this reflected light become mixed together.

- Using a local illumination strategy (also referred to as Standard Lighting) requires arbitrary fill or ambient lights to simulate indirect lighting.
- When a scene is illuminated with standard lighting (local illumination), without ambient or indirect light, the ceiling and shadows are dark as there are no lights pointed directly at those areas, as shown in Figure 8–3. When the ambient lights are added with standard lighting, the ceiling and shadows become softer, as shown in Figure 8–4.

Figure 8–3

Figure 8–4

Types of Lights

Three types of lights are provided with the software:

- **Photometric** lights: Best used with the ART and Arnold renderers.
- **Arnold** lights: Similar to Photometric lights and are meant to be used with the Arnold renderer.
- **Standard** lights: Work best with the Scanline renderer.

There are many parameters available when you create these types of lights. They can be created using the Command Panel. In the *Create* panel (+), click (Lights), and select the type of light in the drop-down list, as shown in Figure 8–5. Alternatively, you can select **Create>Lights** and then select the type you want to create, either **Photometric, Arnold**, or **Standard**. The Photometric lights are the default type available.

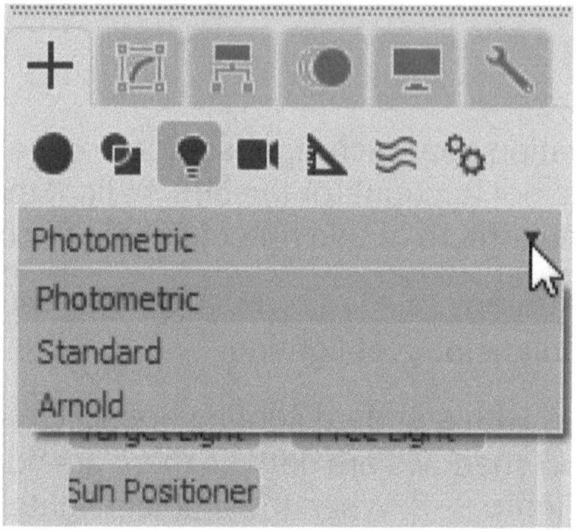

Figure 8–5

Note: *Photometric lights are the preferred lighting technique when working with the ART and Arnold renderers.*

8.2 Photometric Light Objects

Photometric light objects are based on quantitative measurements of light levels and distribution. They provide a real-world lighting and accurate scene illumination when used with ART renderer, Arnold renderer, and other global illumination solutions. In the Autodesk® 3ds Max® software, photometric lights are the default choice for creating lights.

- Photometric lights take advantage of physically-based color, intensity, and distribution properties. They can be defined with real-world lighting parameters in engineering units.
- Since photometric lights are based on real-world calculations of light energy, they are **scale-specific**. Scenes using photometric lights and radiosity should have an appropriate system unit scale.
- All photometric lights automatically decay (attenuate) with an inverse-square relationship. Far attenuation can be controlled manually, to save calculation time and energy.
- Photometric lights work for Scanline, ART, and Arnold renderers.
- Exposure control should be used with Photometric lights objects to adjust the brightness of the scene, the Shadow/Midtones, and the Highlight areas of the image.

Photometric Light Types

In the Command Panel's *Create* panel (+), when you select (Lights), **Photometric** is the default light type, as shown in Figure 8–6. The object types for photometric lights are:

- **Target Light**
- **Free Light**

Figure 8–6

While creating a Target Light or a Free Light, you can set different parameters to illuminate the scene accurately and effectively. Once the lights have been created, you can modify the parameters using the *Modify* panel in the Command Panel.

Templates Rollout

With the Target or Free photometric lights, there are templates to select from, as shown in Figure 8–7. Selecting a template controls the intensity and color temperature of the light.

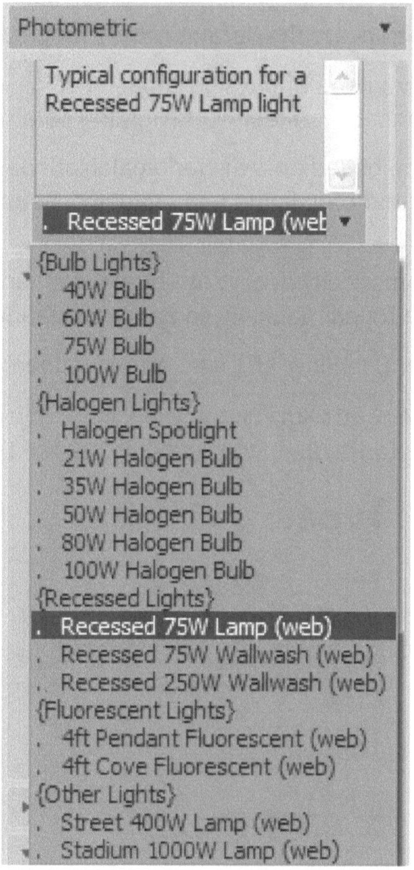

Figure 8–7

General Parameters Rollout

The *General Parameters* rollout controls some of the basic settings for toggling the light on/off in the scene and the different shadow casting methods (**Ray Traced**, **Adv. Ray Traced**, **Area shadows**, and **Shadow Map**). The options found in the *Light Properties* area and *Shadows* area are similar to the options found in Standard Lights (discussed previously), and can be used in the same manner.

Any Free Light can be changed into a Targeted Light (and vice-versa) using the **Targeted** option in the *Light Properties* area. When the **Targeted** option is enabled, a tooltip displays as you move the target indicating the illumination, as shown in Figure 8–8.

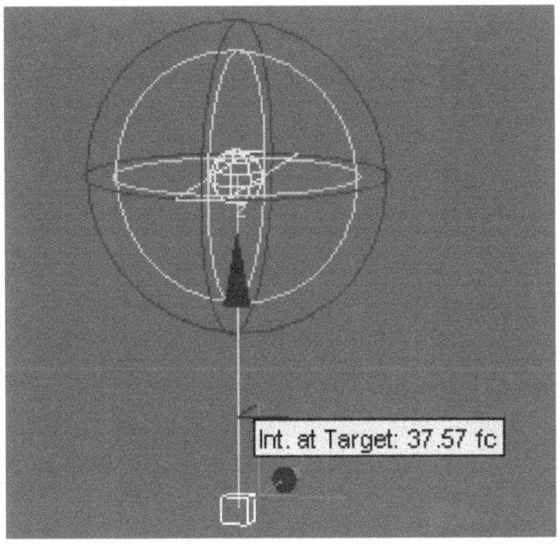

Figure 8–8

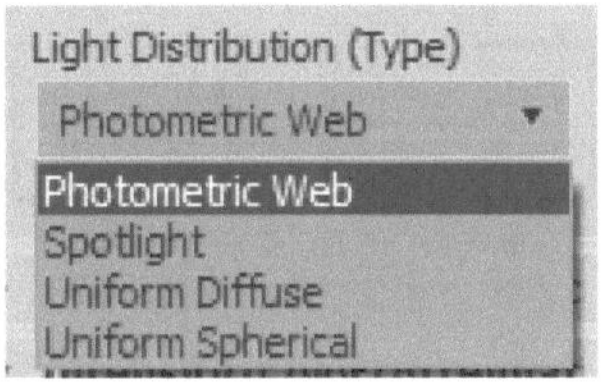

Figure 8–9

The *Light Distribution* area (shown above in Figure 8–9) contains a list of the photometric light distribution types available in the software. These control the way the light illuminates the surrounding space. The options are described as follows:

Uniform Spherical	Casts light in all directions, like a standard Omni light.
Uniform Diffuse	Casts light in one hemisphere only and mimics the way light emits from a surface.
Spotlight	Provides hotspot and falloff parameters identical to standard spotlights.
Photometric Web	Casts light according to a 3D representation of light intensity as determined by a lighting file format, such as IES, LTLI, or CIBSE. These are files provided by lighting manufacturers, usually available via the Internet.

Distribution (Photometric Web) Rollout

If you select Photometric Web in the Light Distribution type list, the *Distribution (Photometric Web)* rollout displays, as shown in Figure 8–10. Real-world luminaries (lighting fixtures) nearly always cast light in varying amounts in different directions. The Web distribution method enables the Autodesk 3ds Max software to simulate the laboratory-determined light distribution of specific lighting fixtures.

- Photometric lights can make use of web distribution information from IES, LTLI, or CIBSE photometric web data files that can be obtained from lighting manufacturers for specific light fixture models. They are often available directly from manufacturers' web sites.
- Lights with Web distributions are indicated with photometric web icons (as shown in Figure 8–11) that graphically represent the 3D distribution of light cast from the light fixture.

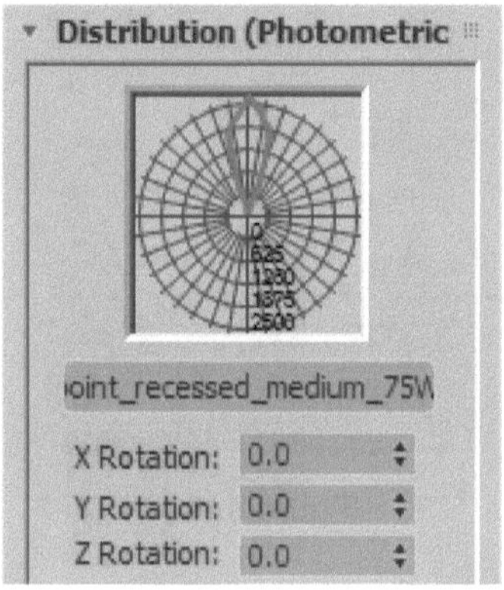

Figure 8–10

Figure 8–11

Web Distribution in Viewports

You can see the web distribution in the viewport. Click the *Shading Viewport* label (such as **[High Quality]**) and select **Lighting and Shadows>Illuminate with Scene Lights** (as shown in Figure 8–12) to see the lights in the viewport. You can add shadows by selecting **Shadows** and toggle on **Ambient Occlusion** in the viewport to add subtle detail enhancement. These options only take effect in viewport and have no effect on the actual renderings.

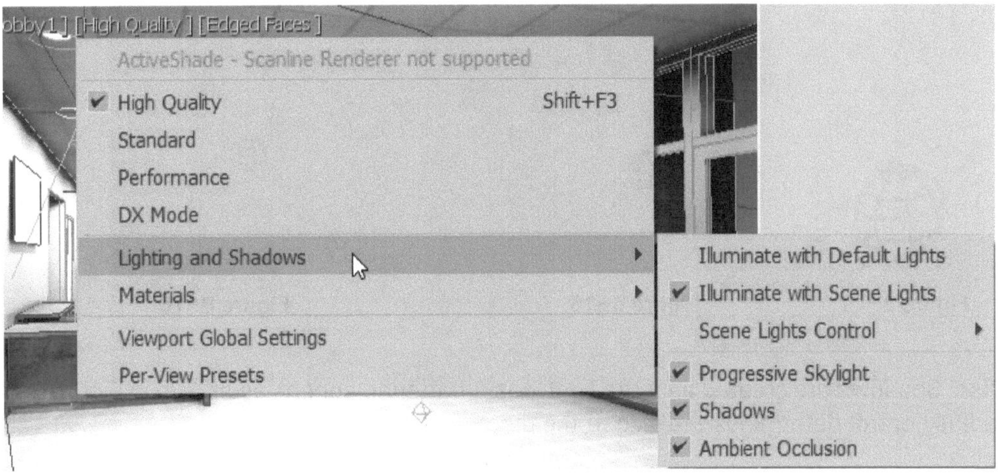

Figure 8–12

Shape/Area Shadows Rollout

The Shape/Area Shadow controls are used to generate a shadow casting shape and to calculate shadows based on a particular shape. The various shapes have different parametric controls and the shapes can be selected in the *Shape/Area Shadows* rollout, as shown in Figure 8–13.

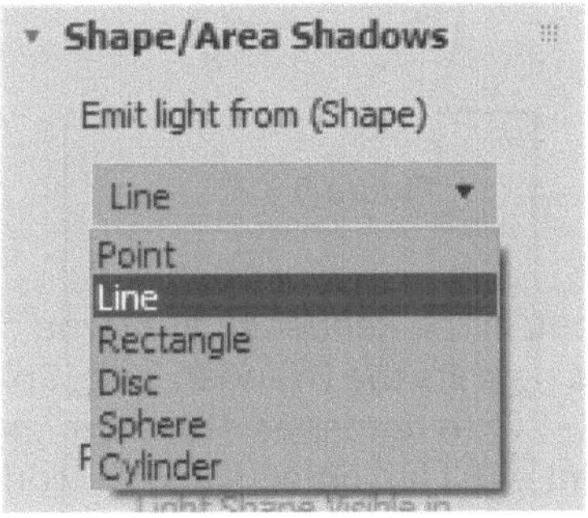

Figure 8–13

- **Point:** Shadows are created as if the light was one single point, as shown in Figure 8–14.
- **Line:** Shadows are created as if the light was one single line, as shown in Figure 8–15. The size of the line is controlled with the **Length** parameter.
- **Rectangle:** Shadows are created as if the light was a rectangular area (as shown in Figure 8–16) governed by **Length** and **Width** parameters. This can be used for fluorescent tubes or rectangular ceiling lights.

Figure 8–14

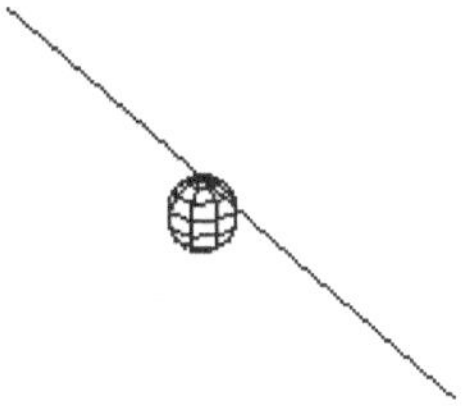
Figure 8–15

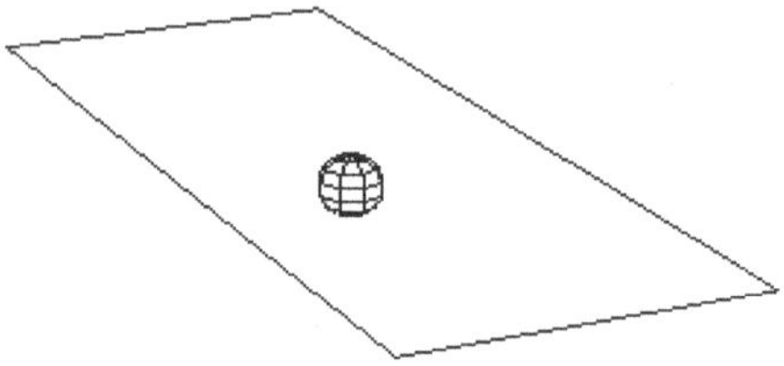
Figure 8–16

- **Disc:** Shadows are created as if the light was a flattened sphere, as shown in Figure 8–17. A radius control determines the size of the disc.
- **Sphere:** Shadows are created as if the light was a round ball or globe, as shown in Figure 8–18. Again a radius control determines the size of the sphere.
- **Cylinder:** Shadows are created as if the light emitter is cylindrical, as shown in Figure 8–19. **Radius** and **Length** are the two parameters to control the cylinder proportions.

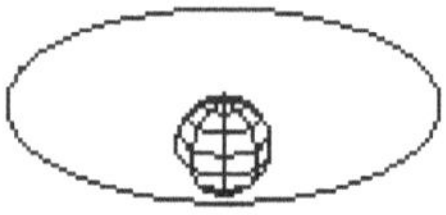
Figure 8–17

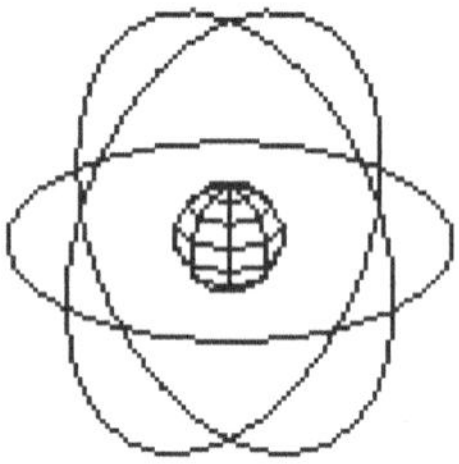
Figure 8–18

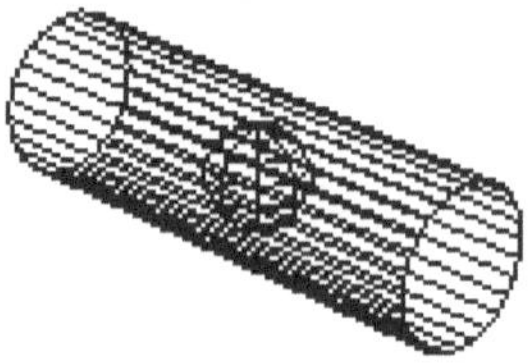
Figure 8–19

In the *Shape/Area Shadows* rollout, in the *Rendering* area, you can also select the **Light Shape Visible in Rendering** option. This permits the Cylinder, Disc, Sphere, and Rectangle light shapes (as shown on the top in Figure 8–20) to render as objects in the viewport (as shown on the bottom in Figure 8–20). The Point and Line objects do not work with this feature.

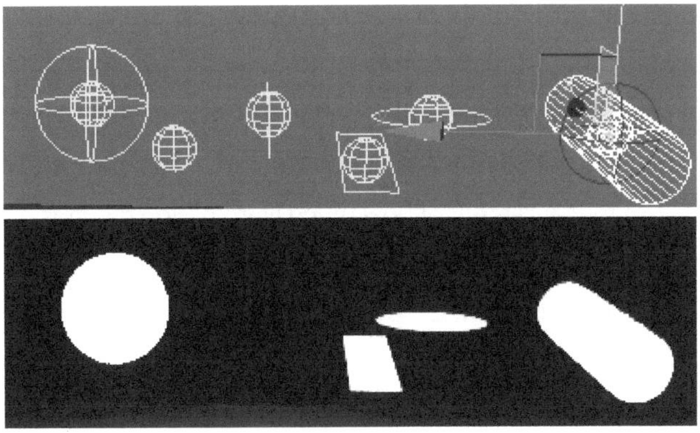

Figure 8–20

Intensity/Color/Attenuation Rollout

Photometric light color can be assigned through a lamp specification (such as fluorescent, halogen, incandescent, etc.) or through a temperature specified in degrees Kelvin. This color can also be filtered (tinted) through a color swatch. All of these options can be selected in the *Color* area of the *Intensity/Color/Attenuation* rollout, as shown in Figure 8–21.

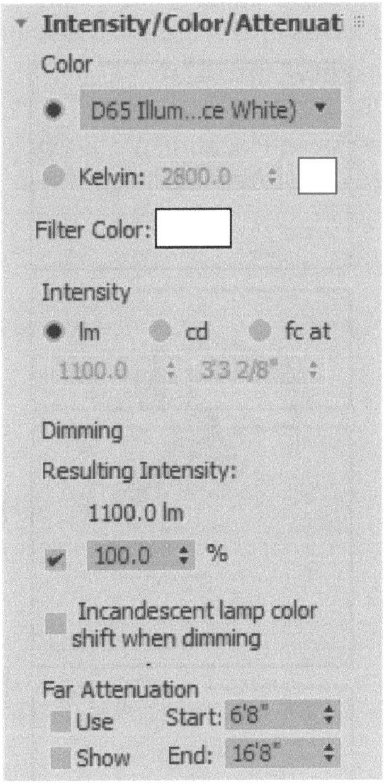

Figure 8–21

The overall brightness of Photometric lights can be specified as one of three intensity values (*Intensity* area):

Luminous flux	The overall output strength of the lamp, measured in lumens (lm).
Luminous intensity	The light energy that is released over time, measured in candelas (cd).
Illuminance	A measurement of how much illumination reaches a surface a set distance away from a lamp with a certain facing. Illuminance is measured in foot-candles (fc, lumens/ft2) or lux (lumens/m2). When using this option, specify both the Luminous flux (lumens) and the distance at which that brightness occurs

Hint: Photometric Lights Data

The Autodesk 3ds Max software ships with a host of sample lighting templates that you can use out-of-the-box.

The Autodesk 3ds Max Help lists a number of sample fixtures in the **Common Lamp Values for Photometric Lights** section.

Lights that combine the geometry of a light fixture with the correct photometric light distribution model are referred to as luminaries. These are assemblies with a hierarchy created so that the photometric light is linked to the geometry. You can obtain luminaries from manufacturer websites (such as ERCO). You can also import lighting fixtures from the Autodesk® Revit® software using FBX import.

The *Far Attenuation* area controls the end location of the Photometric light and the area that is graduated as the end of the range is approached, as shown in Figure 8–22.

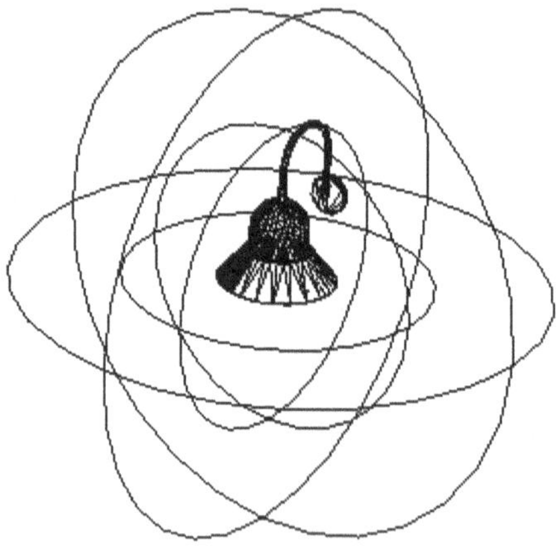

Figure 8–22

8.3 Shadow Types

Autodesk 3ds Max Photometric lights are able to cast realistic shadows from opaque objects. There are several shadow-casting methods available, such as Shadow Mapped, Ray Traced, Area, etc. While creating light objects, you can set the type and aspect of shadow by selecting it in the drop-down list (as shown in Figure 8–23), in the *Shadows* area of *General Parameters* rollout. Alternatively, after creating the light objects, you can control or change them using the Modify panel () parameters of light objects. Individual lights might cast different kinds of shadows in the same scene and shadow casting can be disabled for specific lights.

Figure 8–23

Figure 8–24 shows the shadow-casting methods available.

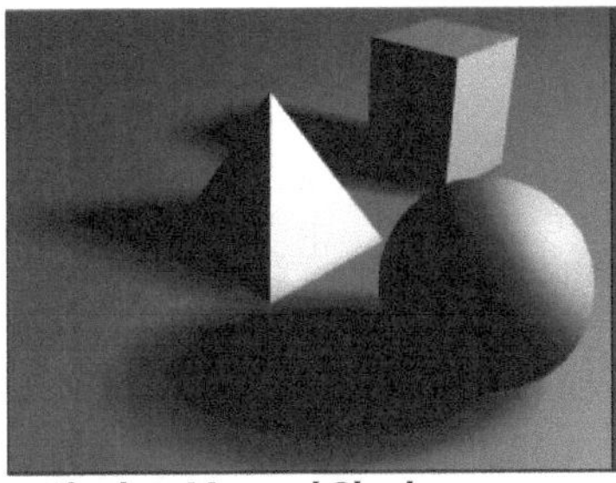

Shadow Mapped Shadows

Ray Traced Shadows

Advanced Ray Traced Shadows

Area Shadows

Figure 8–24

Shadow Type	Description, Advantages	Disadvantages
Shadow Map	Traditional approach, shadow mapping is relatively fast and creates soft-edged shadows. **Animation:** Shadows only need to be calculated once when scene geometry is not animated.	Not as accurate as other methods; might not be appropriate for shadow studies. Uses a lot of RAM. Does not support materials with transparency or opacity maps.
Ray Traced Shadows	More accurate than shadow maps, supports transparency and opacity mapping. **Animation:** Shadows only need to be calculated once when scene geometry is not animated. In these cases, RT might be best for animations (including animated shadow studies) in terms of rendering time.	Slower than shadow maps, and shadows have sharp edges.
Advanced Ray Traced	A good, general-purpose shadow type that is an improvement on RT shadows. It is more accurate than Shadow Maps, supports transparency and opacity mapping. Uses less RAM than standard raytraced shadows, therefore is generally faster for producing still renderings. Offers several parameters that can help soften and smooth shadows.	Slower than shadow maps. **Animation:** Shadows must be calculated at every frame, regardless of whether scene geometry is animated or not. Avoid omni lights with Advanced Ray Traced shadows whenever possible, as they require 6x the processing time of spot and directional lights.
Area Shadows	Enables a simulation of shadows cast from an area light (the other methods assume point light sources). Supports transparency and opacity mapping, uses relatively little RAM.	Generally slower than shadow maps, Ray Traced and Advanced Ray Traced. **Animation:** Shadows must be calculated at every frame, regardless of whether scene geometry is animated or not.

Common Shadow Parameters

The most commonly used shadow parameters in the Autodesk 3ds Max software are:

General Shadow Parameters

All lights have certain general parameters (*Shadows* area in *General Parameters* area) common to all shadow types, as shown in Figure 8–25.

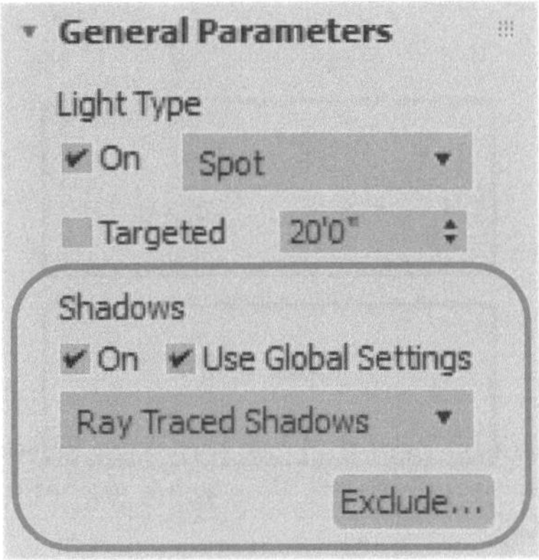

Figure 8–25

On	Enables you to select whether to cast shadows from this light or not and the type of shadows to use.
Use Global Settings	Controls whether the scene's global shadow generator or the light's own individual shadow generator is used.
Drop-down list	Contains all the types of shadows available in the software. Selecting the type provides a shadow specific rollout that can be used to control the advanced settings in the selected shadow type.

Shadow Map Parameters

In the *General Parameters* rollout, in the *Shadows* area, selecting **Shadow Map** in the drop-down list provides a *Shadow Map Params* rollout, as shown in Figure 8–26. Lights set to cast shadow mapped-shadows have additional controls that are specific to the Shadow Map type of shadow.

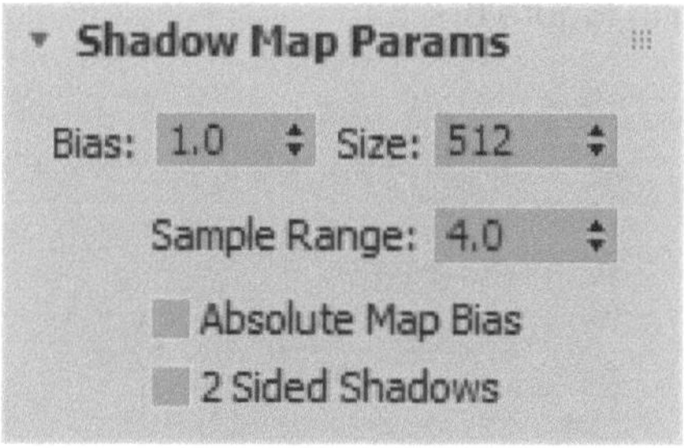

Figure 8–26

Bias	A relative adjustment that can move the shadow closer to or further away from the objects casting them. This value sometimes needs to be adjusted with large scenes.
Size	The height and width (in pixels) of the image map used to create the shadows. Shadow detail and computation time increase as the size increases.
Sample Range	Controls the amount of blending and smoothing. If shadow mapped-shadows appear grainy, increase this value.
Absolute Map Bias	Enables the Bias to be fixed to a value measured absolutely in scene units rather than a relative, normalized value. This option should normally not be used unless shadows flicker and disappear during an animation.
2 Sided Shadows	Enables both sides of a face to cast shadows. Double-sided mode is discussed in the rendering information.

Ray Traced Shadows

In the *General Parameters* rollout, in the *Shadows* area, selecting **Ray Traced Shadow** in the drop-down list provides a *Ray Traced Shadow Params* rollout, as shown in Figure 8–27. This rollout contains additional settings for lights set to cast (standard) ray traced shadows.

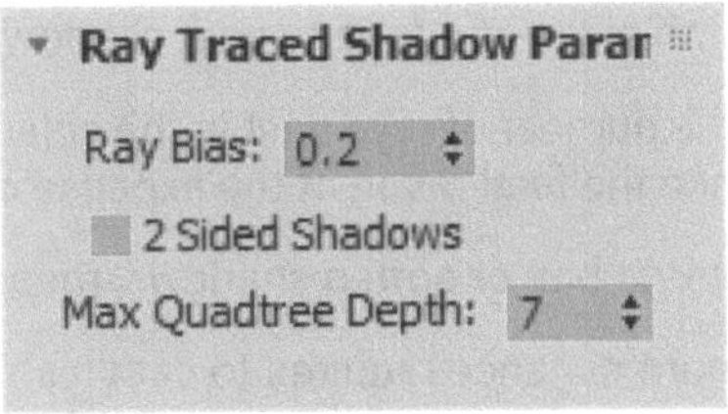

Figure 8–27

Ray Bias	Similar to shadow map bias, ray bias is a relative adjustment to move a shadow closer or further away from an object casting them. This value might need to be adjusted for large scenes.
2 Sided Shadows	Enables both sides of a face to cast shadows.
Max Quadtree Depth	Controls ray-tracing performance. Increasing the quadtree depth can speed up ray-tracing time but requires more RAM. You need to experiment to determine the most efficient quadtree settings for individual scenes (default = 7).

Advanced Ray-Traced Shadows

In the *General Parameters* rollout, in the *Shadows* area, selecting **Adv. Ray Traced** in the drop-down list provides an *Adv. Ray Traced Params* rollout (as shown in Figure 8–28) and the *Optimizations* rollouts (as shown in Figure 8–29). Both rollouts contain additional settings for lights set to cast advanced ray-traced shadows.

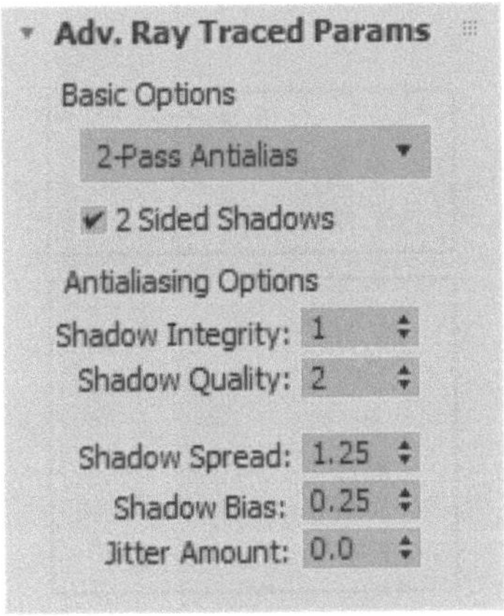

Figure 8–28

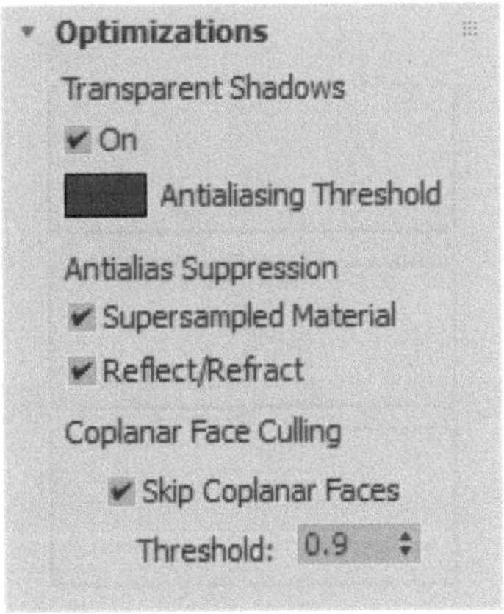

Figure 8–29

Adv. Ray Traced Params Options

Basic Options	The menu assigns either a mode without antialiasing (simple), or a single or double-pass antialiasing mode. Antialiasing is an additional calculation made to smooth pixelated edges of shadows.
2 Sided Shadows	Enables both sides of a face to cast shadows.
Shadow Integrity and Quality	Controls the number of rays cast in the calculation. Increasing these values can enhance the final result at the expense of longer calculation time.
Shadow Spread	A parameter to blur or soften shadows, measured in pixels.
Shadow Bias	The minimum distance required to cast a shadow. This parameter should be increased as shadow spread is increased.
Jitter Amount	Blurred shadows sometimes cause artifacts to form. Increasing jitter can help break up the patterns of these artifacts and make them less noticeable.

Optimizations Options

Transparent Shadows	When enabled, transparent objects cast colored shadows based on their transparency and diffuse color.
Antialias Suppression	When using supersampling, reflections, or refractions, this option disables the second pass in two-pass antialiased mode. This is a good idea to save time since the second pass often adds little in these situations. (Supersampling is discussed in the rendering and animation material.)
Skip Coplanar Faces	Prevents coplanar faces from shading each other (those that lie overlapped in the same plane).

Practice 8a
Work with Photometric Lights

Practice Objectives

- Create photometric lights and modify their parameters.
- Use preset lamps and their provided data.

In this practice, you will create and adjust photometric lights. You will use different lamp presets to apply realistic lighting to the lobby model.

You must set the paths to locate the External files and XREFs used in the practice. If you have not done this already, return to Chapter 1 and complete Task 1 to Task 3 in *Practice 1a: Organize Folders and Work with the Interface*. You only have to set the user paths once.

Task 1: Create free photometric lights.

1. Open **Photometric Lighting start.max**.
2. Maximize the **Top** viewport and click  (Zoom Extents) to display the floorplan. Verify that the scene displays in *Wireframe* mode.
3. Zoom in to the foyer area (leftmost area). Note the small yellow circles that represent the opening for recessed lighting.
4. In the *Create* panel (), click  (Lights) and verify that **Photometric** displays in the drop-down list. In the *Object Type* rollout, select **Free Light**, as shown in Figure 8–30.

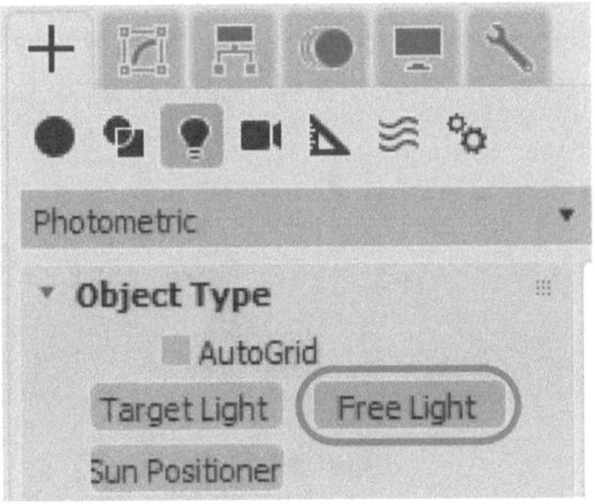

Figure 8–30

5. Click near the approximate center of the upper left yellow circle to place a light, as shown in Figure 8–31. You will position it accurately in the next step. Note that there are 13 additional yellow circles provided as the location of the recessed lighting. You will be placing the lights in all of them.

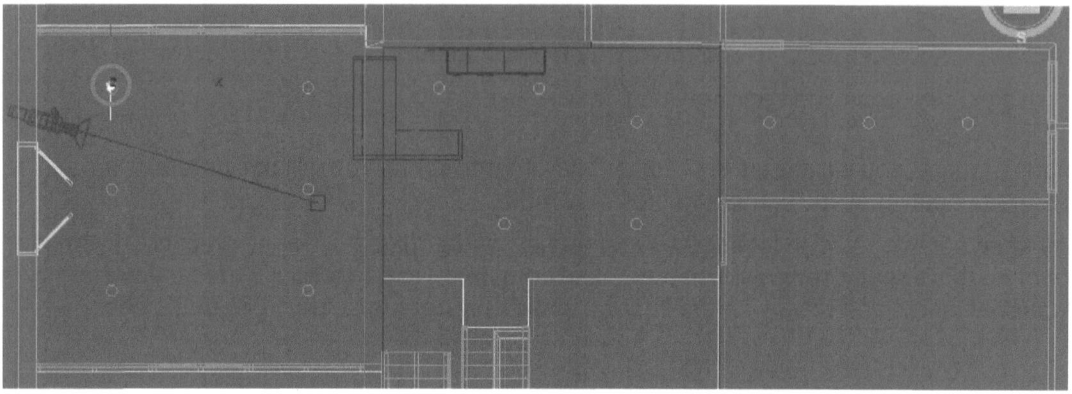

Figure 8–31

6. In the Main Toolbar, right-click on  (Select and Move) to open the *Move Transform Type-In* dialog box. In the *Absolute:World* area, set the following, as shown in Figure 8–32. (You can also enter the values in the *Transform Type-In* area in the Status Bar.)
   - *X*: **84'7"**
   - *Y*: **126'10"**
   - *Z*: **9'11"** (elevation)

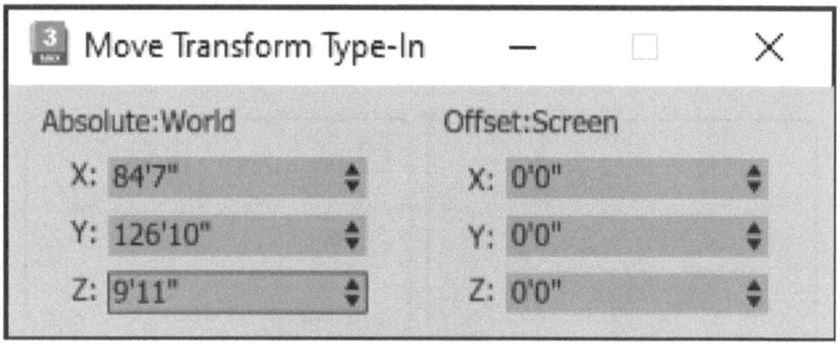

Figure 8–32

In addition to placing the light at the exact center of the recessed fixture, it places the light at a height of 9'11", which is 1" below the ceiling height.

7. Close the dialog box. With the light object selected, in the *Modify* panel (), rename the light object as **Light – Downlight A 00**.

8. In the *General Parameters* rollout, set *Light Distribution (Type)* to **Spotlight**, as shown in Figure 8–33. Note that the shape of the light object changes in the viewport.

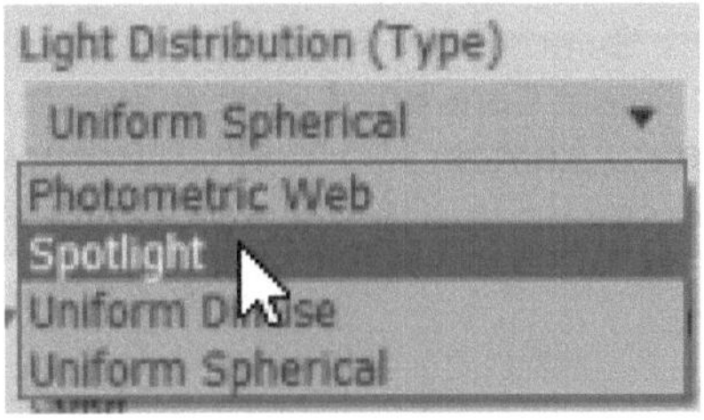

Figure 8–33

9. In the *Intensity/Color/Attenuation* rollout, set *Color* to **HID Quartz Metal Halide**, as shown in Figure 8–34.

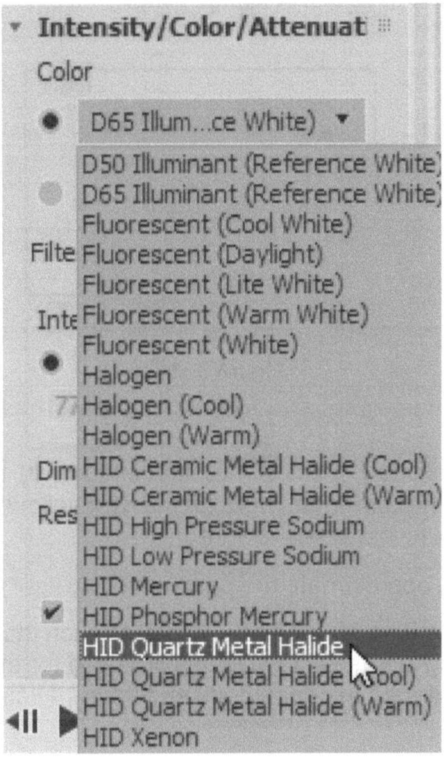

Figure 8–34

Hint: Accessing Photometric Lights Data

When using metal halide lamps, you can find suggestions for their photometric light parameters in the Help system. Select **Help>Autodesk 3ds Max Help**. In the *Search* box, enter **Common Lamp Values**. Select **Common Lamp Values for Photometric Lights** and scroll down to **Par38 Line Voltage Lamps**. The **Medium Beam** has intensities between 1700-4000 candelas, as shown in Figure 8–35. The values for *Beam* and *Field* angles are also displayed.

Par38 Line Voltage Lamps

Class.	Watts	Type	Intensity	Beam	Field
Narrow Beam	45	Spot	4700	14	28
Narrow Beam	75	Spot	5200	12	25
Narrow Beam	150	Spot	10500	14	28
Medium Beam	45	Spot	1700	28	60
Medium Beam	75	Spot	1860	30	60
Medium Beam	150	Spot	4000	30	60

Figure 8–35

10. With the new light still selected, click  (Select and Move), if required, and then use <Shift> + click and drag the light to the right on the next yellow circle. Select **Instance** in the *Clone Options* dialog box to instance the light.
    - In the interest of time, approximate the position of the light over the yellow circle.
11. Using the method used in Step 10, instance the lights such that they correspond to the rest of the symbols for Ceiling Lights (yellow circles provided for the locations of the recessed lighting). You can approximate their positions and have 14 lights with the last one named **Light - Downlight A 013**.
12. Click the **[Top]** *Point of View* label and select **Cameras>Camera - Lobby1** (any one) to display the **Camera - Lobby1** viewport. Verify that the *Shading Viewport* label is set to **Standard** and change the **[Wireframe]** *Per-View Preference* label to **Default Shading** and **Edged Faces** to display the 14 spotlights, as shown in Figure 8–36.

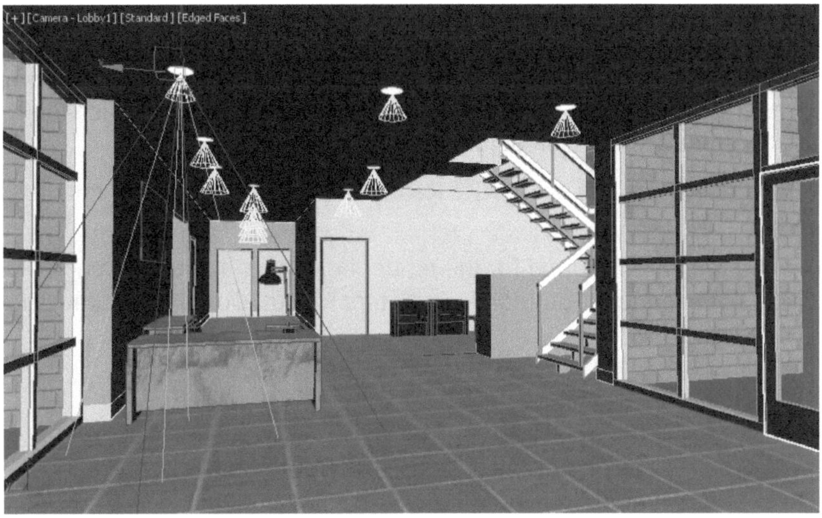

Figure 8–36

13. Select **Rendering>Exposure Control** to open the *Environment and Effects* dialog box. Note that the **Logarithmic Exposure Control** option is selected in the *Exposure Control* rollout.
14. In the *Exposure Control* rollout, select **Active**, if required. Click **Render Preview** and note that the render preview is dark.
15. In the *Logarithmic Exposure Control Parameters* rollout, increase the *Brightness* to **100**, press <Enter>, and watch the render preview update. It looks too bright. Change the *Brightness* to **70**, press <Enter>, and note the render preview update as shown in Figure 8–37. Close the dialog box.

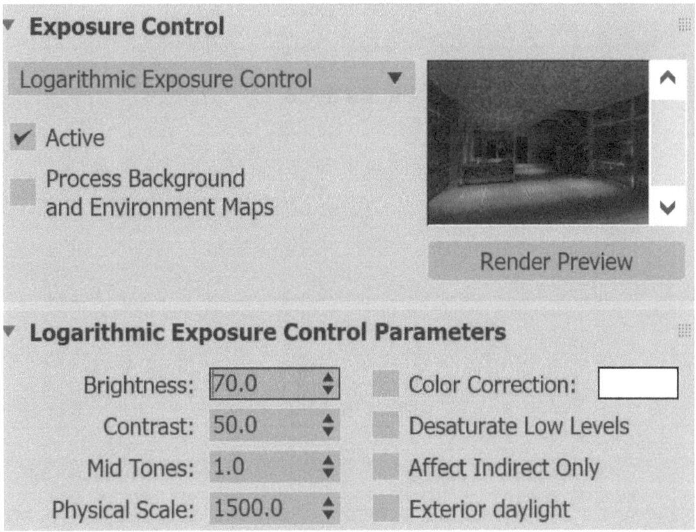

Figure 8–37

16. In the Main Toolbar, click (Render Production) to render the viewport. In the *Rendering* dialog box, note the progress of the rendering. When the *Rendering* dialog box closes, indicating that the rendering is complete, note the rendered scene, which looks dark, and that the light parameters need an adjustment.
    - The *Production Renderer* is set to **ART Renderer**. It might take a few minutes to complete the render.
    - If you want a faster turnaround for the rendering, render a smaller image (*Render Setup* dialog box>*Common* tab>*Common Parameters* rollout>*Output Size* area, click **320x240**.)

Task 2: Adjust the light parameters.

1. In the viewport, select any one of the lights. In the Command Panel, *Modify* panel ( ), in the *Distribution (Spotlight)* rollout, note that *Hotspot/Beam* and *Falloff/Field* have default values of **30°** and **60°**.
2. If you have access to a photometric data file for a light fixture, you can use it for this light. In the *General Parameters* rollout, set *Light Distribution (Type)* to **Photometric Web**, as shown in Figure 8–38. Note that changing the *Light Distribution Type* changes the shape of the light object (in the viewport) accordingly.

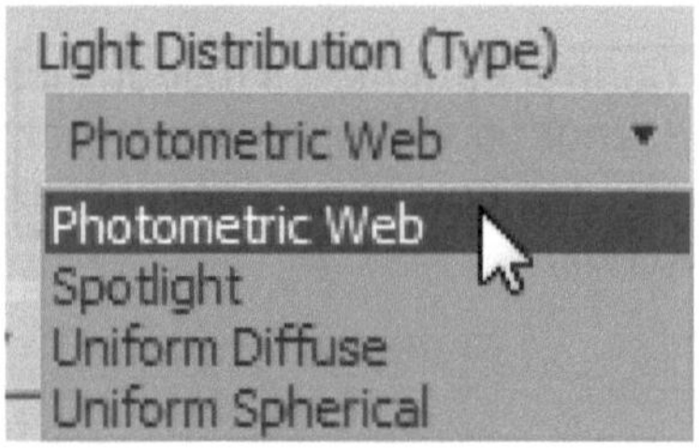

Figure 8–38

3. In the *Distribution (Photometric Web) Parameters* rollout, click **< Choose Photometric File >** and in the Practice Files folder, in the ...*\sceneassets\photometric* folder, open **sample_downlight.ies**. The thumbnail diagram of the selected web file with a red shape displays as shown in Figure 8–39.

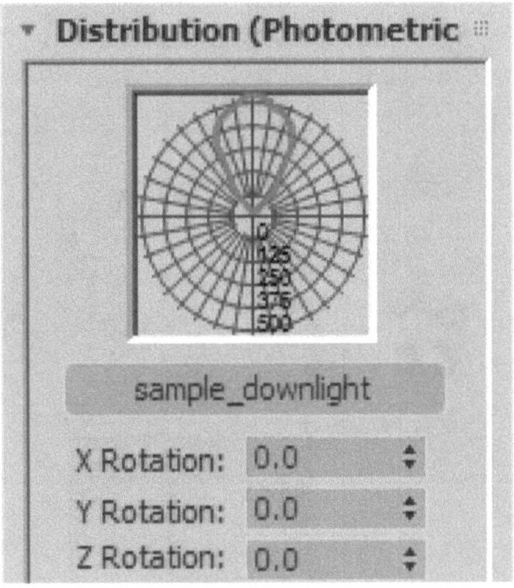

Figure 8–39

4. Note that in the *Intensity/Color/Attenuation* rollout, in the *Intensity* area, the intensity of the light has been updated to **3298.0 cd**.
5. In the *General Parameters* rollout, in the *Shadows* area, select **On** and **Use Global Settings**. Select **Shadow Map** in the drop-down list, as shown in Figure 8–40.

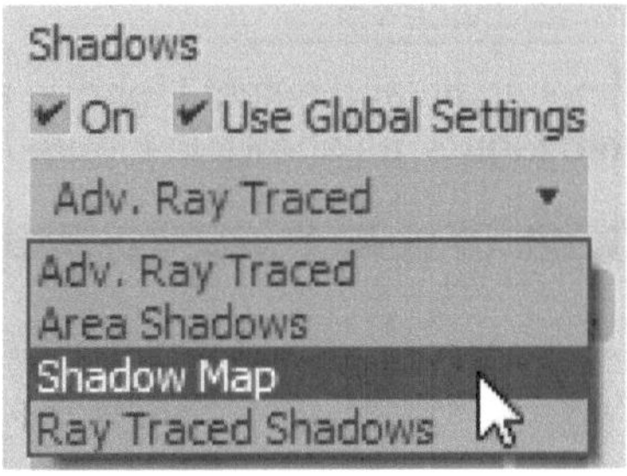

Figure 8–40

6. Click **Render** in the Rendered Frame Window. Note that the dark areas have been removed but the scene is washed out.

7. In the *Intensity/Color/Attenuation* rollout, in the *Intensity* area, set the intensity to **1100** cd. Render the scene again and note that the rendering has slightly improved, as shown in Figure 8–41. Close the Rendered Frame Window.

Figure 8–41

8. The photometric lights representation displays in the viewport and you can control their effects individually. Click the *Shading Viewport* label and select **Lighting and Shadows> Illuminate with Scene Lights**. Selecting **Illuminate with Scene Lights** automatically clears **Illuminate with Default Lights** and vice-versa.

9. Click the *Shading Viewport* label again and select **Lighting and Shadows>Scene Lights Control>Auto Display Selected Lights**, as shown in Figure 8–42.

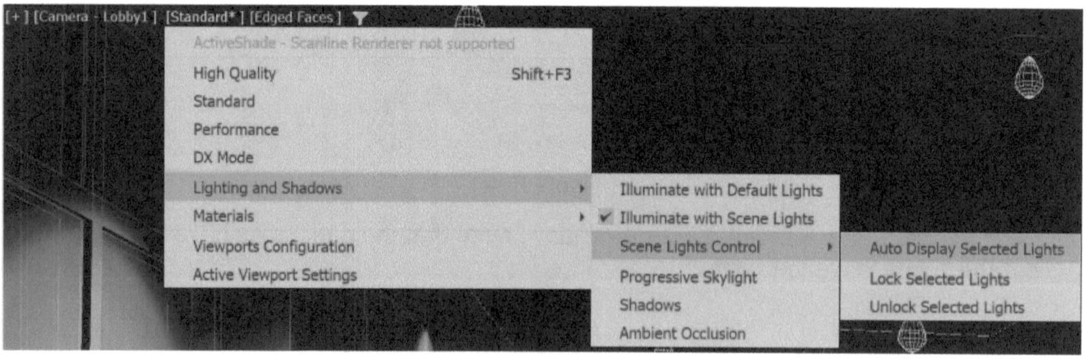

Figure 8–42

10. In the viewport, select one of the lights to enable it. You will see the effect of that light individually in the viewport (the area below the light brightens). Select another light and see its effect in the viewport. Using <Ctrl>, select a few more lights to activate them together and visually see the effects.
11. Click the *Shading Viewport* label and select **Lighting and Shadows>Shadows** to display the shadows that are cast along with the lighting effect of the light selected.

    Note: *The display of shadows in the viewport is dependent on the driver you are using. The shadows are previewed in the viewport if you are using Nitrous or the Direct 3D drivers.*

12. With one of the lights selected, in the Command Panel, *Modify* panel ( ), in the *Templates* rollout, select **75 W Bulb** as shown on the left in Figure 8–43. Note the changes in the viewport, as shown on the right in Figure 8–43.

Figure 8–43

13. With one of the lights selected, in the Command Panel, *Modify* panel ( ), in the *Templates* rollout, select **Recessed 75W Lamp (web)**. This uses a different IES file.

14. Click (Render Production) to render the scene. Once the rendering is complete, note that the lighting is dark and moody, as shown in Figure 8–44.

Figure 8–44

15. (Optional) This might take longer to render the scene: With one of the lights selected, in the Command Panel, *Modify* panel ( ), in the *Templates* rollout, select **75 W Bulb** and render the scene. Once the rendering is complete, note that the lighting now illuminates differently and the reflections and shadows add realism, as shown in Figure 8–45.

Figure 8–45

16. Save your work as **MyPhotometricLighting.max**.

Hint: Using Light Lister

The Autodesk 3ds Max software includes a **Light Lister** utility (as shown in Figure 8–46) (**Tools>Light Lister**) that enables you to view and change light properties without having to select them first. You can change the settings for all lights together or for the selected lights.

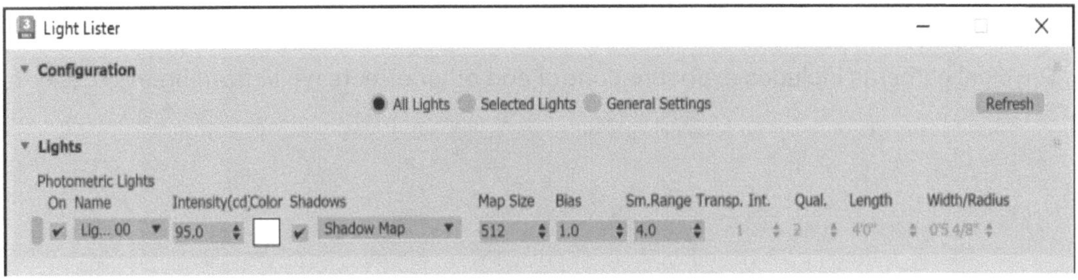

Figure 8–46

End of practice

8.4 Cameras

Cameras are created using (Cameras) in the Command Panel's *Create* panel ( ), as shown in Figure 8–47. Alternatively, you can create a camera by selecting **Create>Cameras**.

- Target cameras have a target object that can be selected and transformed separately from the camera itself.
- Free cameras do not have a target object.
- Physical cameras includes exposure control and other effects while framing the scene.

Figure 8–47

- Cameras can also be created on the fly to match a **Perspective** viewport using **Views>Create Standard Camera From View** or **Views>Create Physical Camera From View.**

Physical Camera

The **Physical Camera** (shown in Figure 8–48) is the best option for setting up photorealistic, physically based scenes. The Physical Camera integrates framing the scene with per-camera exposure control, perspective control, distortion, depth of field, and motion blur. The options that can be incorporated while using the Physical camera is dependent on the active renderer. The Physical Camera works well with both ART and Arnold renderers.

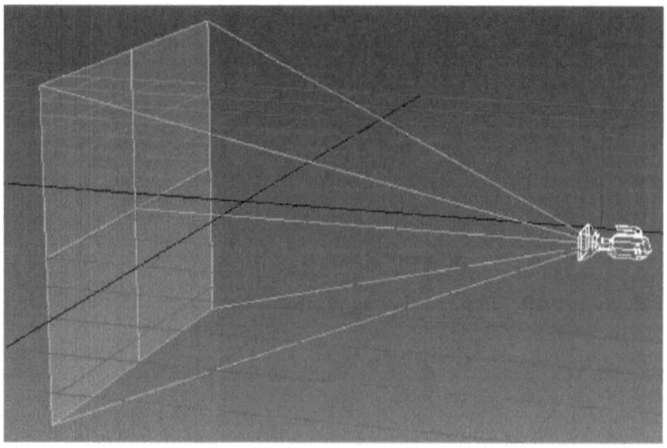

Figure 8–48

The **Physical Camera** parameters (shown in Figure 8–49) are described in the following table.

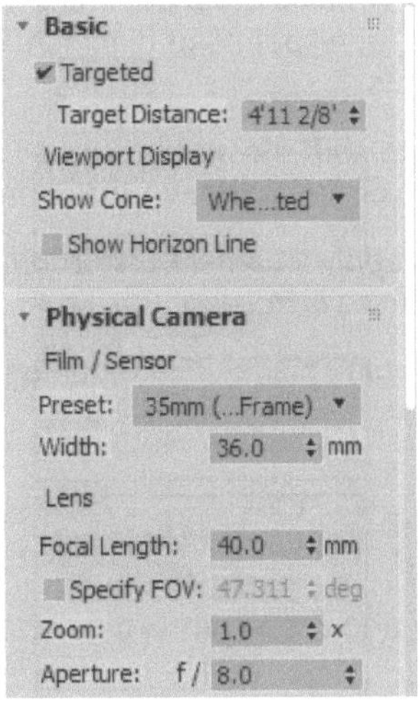

Figure 8–49

Basic **rollout**	When **Targeted** is selected, it defines properties for a target camera, and viewport display options.
Physical Camera **rollout**	Contains properties to define the scene view using real world camera values for accurate reproduction of a camera shot scene. Presets are available for common camera types which define *Lens* properties, focus, and shutter speed.
Exposure **rollout**	Defines exposure properties to be used with the physical camera. These properties do not affect the *Global Exposure* settings in the Physical Camera Exposure Control in the Environment settings. 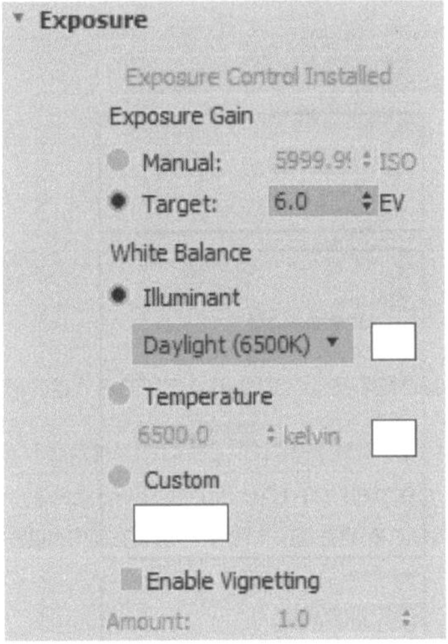

***Bokeh (Depth of Field)* rollout**	Properties to create a blurring effect in areas of the image that are out of focus. This effect is most apparent when the out-of-focus areas of the scene have small points of high contrast, typically from light sources or bright objects.
***Perspective Control* rollout**	Properties to shift the perspective of the camera scene without changing the location or orientation of the camera.
***Lens Distortion* rollout**	Settings to apply a camera distortion effect to the rendered image using cubic or texture distortion.
***Miscellaneous* rollout**	Enables clipping planes and modifies near and far environment ranges.

Target and Free Camera Parameters

As with any other object, the **Target** and **Free Camera** parameters are available in the Command Panel, in the *Modify* panel (), as shown in Figure 8–50.

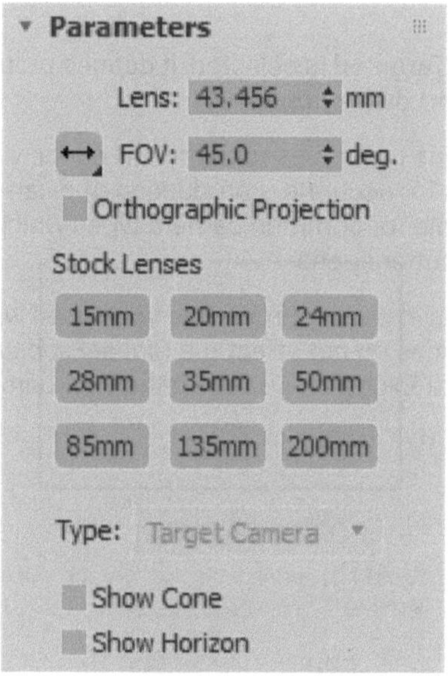

Figure 8–50

The Camera parameters found in the *Parameters* rollout for the Target and Free camera are:

- The focal length of real-world cameras is the distance between the focus point (the film or light-sensitive media) and the optical center of the lens. The *Lens* option available governs how much of the scene is visible to the camera. This corresponds to the focal length of real-world cameras.

- The camera focal lengths are directly related to that camera's field of view (*FOV*), which is an angular measurement of how much of the horizon can be seen by the camera. The field of view can be measured horizontally, vertically, or diagonally using the different field of view options, as shown in Figure 8–51.

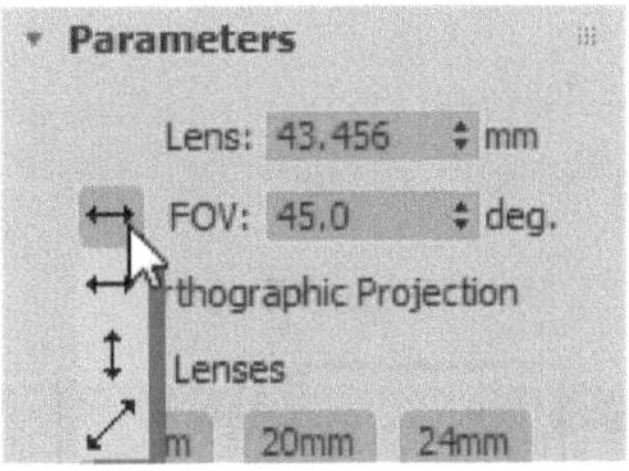

Figure 8–51

- Human vision is often approximated with a 45° field of view and it varies from 60 degrees above to 75 degrees below the horizontal meridian. A focal length of 50mm is very commonly used in real-world cameras, which relates to about a 40° field of view in the Autodesk 3ds Max software.
- Other stock focal lengths are provided in the Autodesk 3ds Max software as button presets. Focal lengths below 50mm are considered short or wide-angle lenses, while those above 50mm are called telephoto lenses.
- The **Orthographic Projection** option (shown in Figure 8–52) causes a camera view to display as an orthographic or user view (axonometric rotated) rather than a three-point perspective.

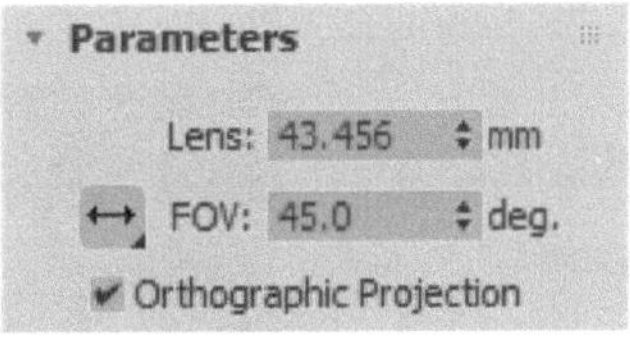

Figure 8–52

- The camera's cone of vision is visible when the camera is selected, as shown in Figure 8–53. The **Show Cone** option causes it to remain visible even after the camera is no longer selected.

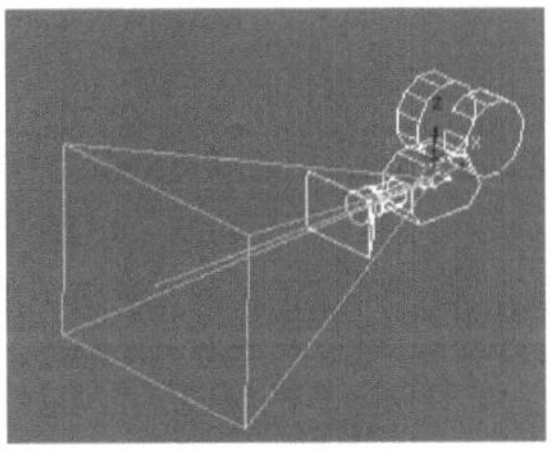

Figure 8–53

- The **Show Horizon** option (shown in Figure 8–54) displays a dark gray line in the camera viewport, representing the horizon in the camera view. It is helpful when aligning a camera to a background image.

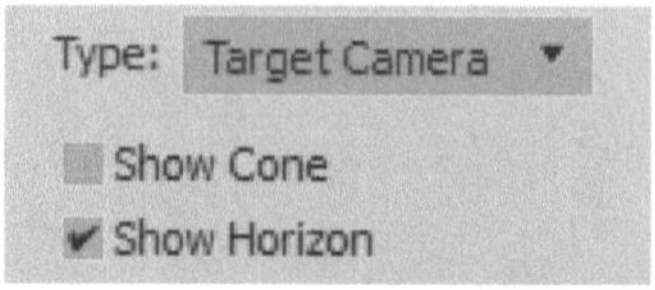

Figure 8–54

Hint: Two-Point Perspectives Through Cameras

By default, camera and perspective viewports show three-point perspective views. You can display a two-point perspective by adding a Camera Correction modifier to the camera object. To do so, select **Camera Correction** in **Modifiers>Cameras**, as shown in Figure 8–55. Two-point perspective causes vertical lines to remain vertical rather than converge over distance.

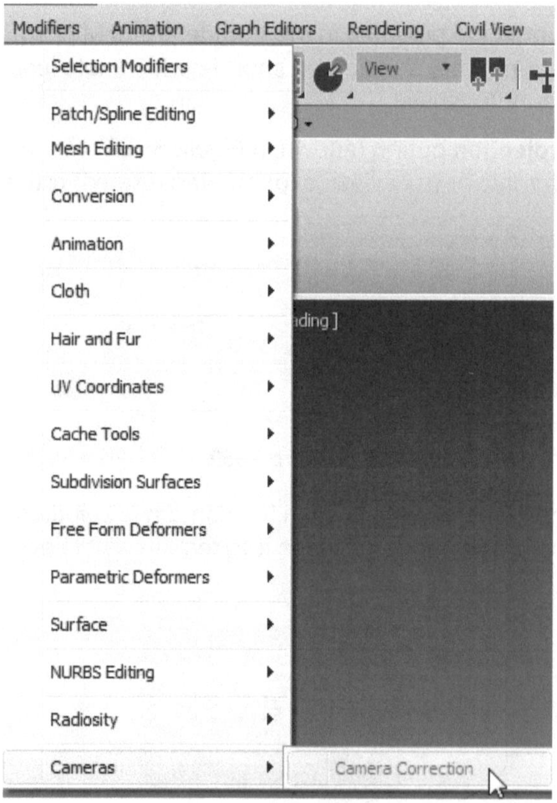

Figure 8–55

Some additional **Target** and **Free Camera** parameters are shown in Figure 8–56.

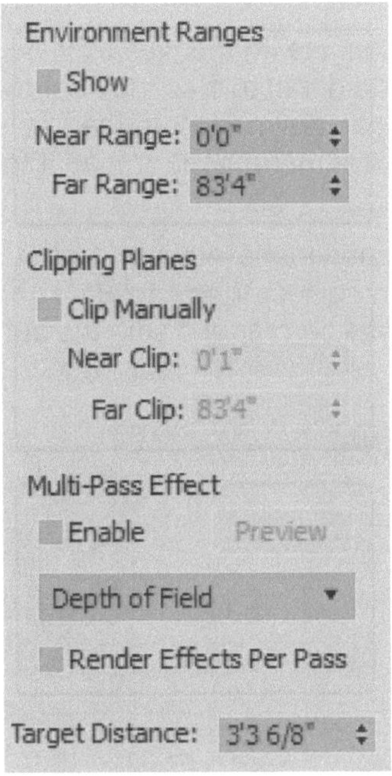

Figure 8–56

- The *Environment Ranges* are contains the near and far range distances measured from the camera for the atmospheric effects. You can set the atmospheric effects in the *Atmosphere* rollout in the *Environment* tab in the *Environment and Effects* dialog box (**Rendering> Environment**).
- The *Clipping Planes* area contains the cutoff distances for the geometry that displays in the camera. When enabled, only the geometry between the clip distances is visible.
- The *Multi-Pass Effect* area (default option is **Depth of Field**) is a camera-specific rendering effect that causes distance blurring, where only a certain point is in focus. This effect simulates how areas away from the focal point display blurred in human vision and photography. You can select **Depth of Field** or **Motion Blur** (as shown in Figure 8–57). Depending on the selected effect, a Parameters rollout specific to that effect (Depth of Field Parameters or Motion Blur Parameters) opens below the Cameras Parameters rollout.

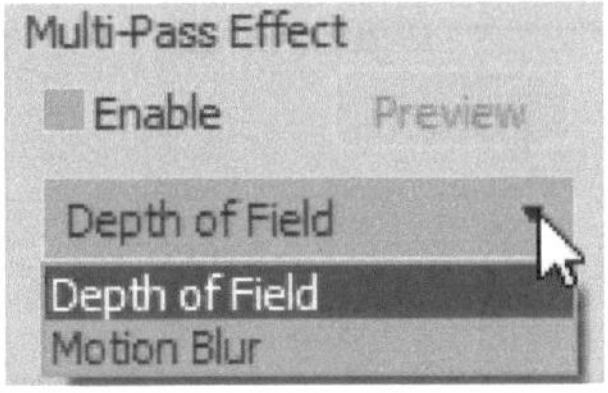

Figure 8–57

8.5 Background Images

The Autodesk 3ds Max software can use image files as viewport and rendering backgrounds. Background images are used to add detail to a scene or show a proposed construction project in its real-world context. You can load an image into the viewport background, independent of the rendering background (the environment map) or load it to both the viewport and rendering backgrounds.

You can set the different backgrounds in the viewport from the *Shading Viewport* label menu. Click the *Shading Viewport* label and select **Viewport Background** and the required option, as shown in Figure 8–58. These options correspond with the options in the *Viewport Configuration* dialog box.

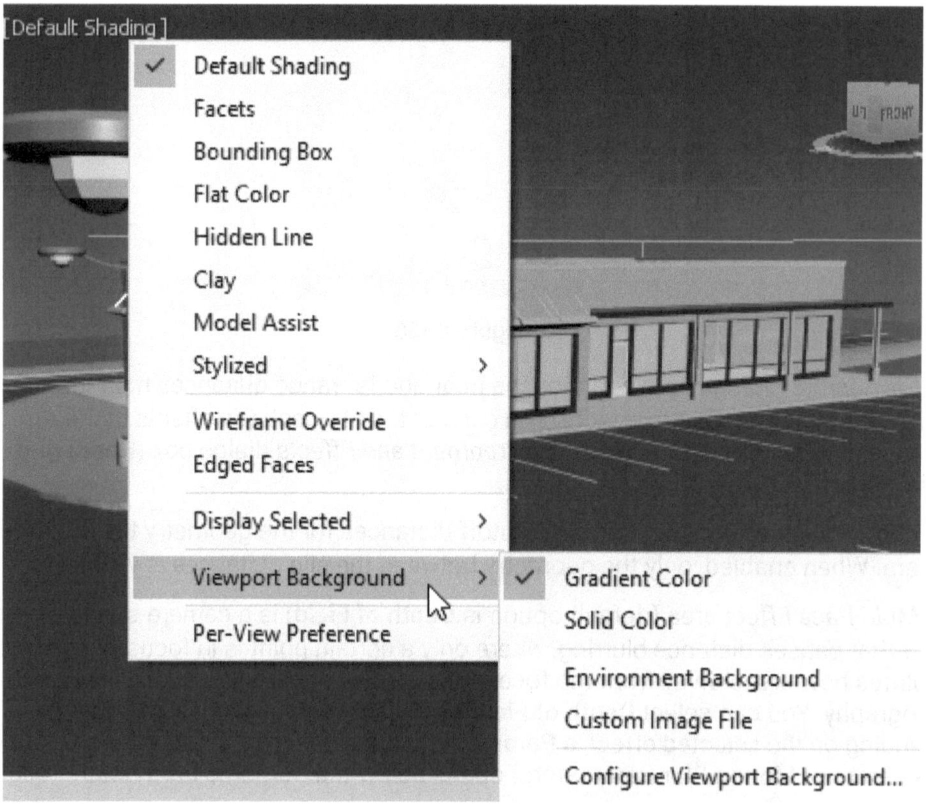

Figure 8–58

How To: Enable a Background Image to Viewports

1. Select **Views>Viewport Configuration>***Background* tab (<Alt>+<B>). The *Background* tab options display as shown in Figure 8–59.

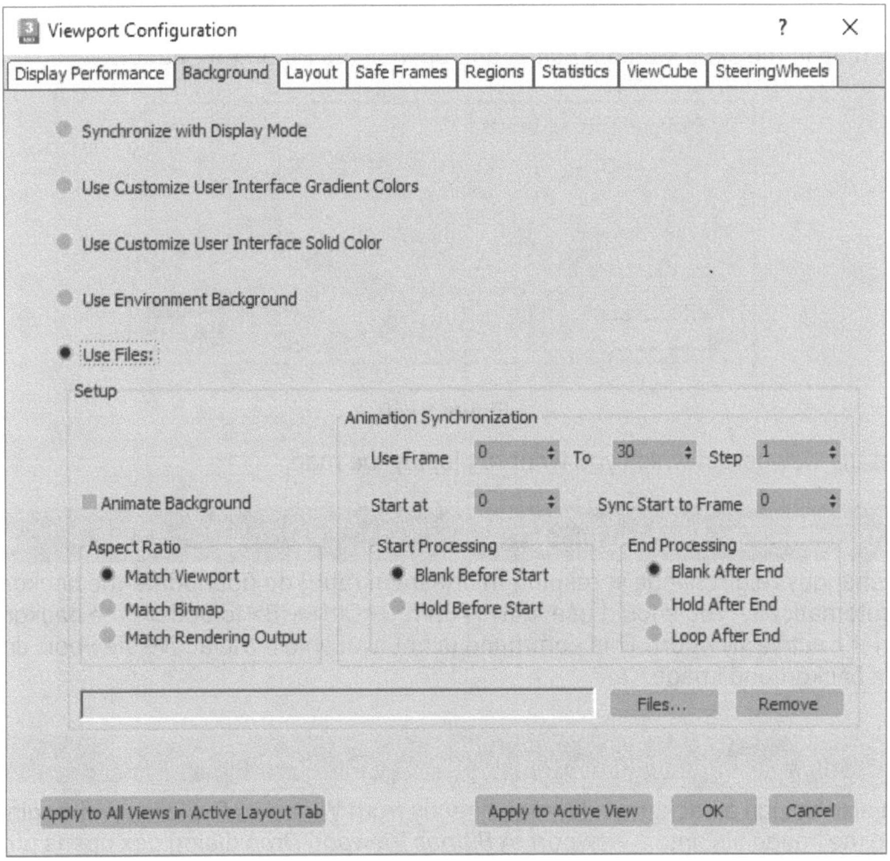

Figure 8–59

2. Select **Use Files** to make the *Setup* area available for use.

   Note: *If any option other than the* ***Use Files*** *option is selected, the Setup area will be grayed out.*

3. In the *Aspect Ratio* area, select **Match Bitmap** to keep the aspect ratio of the image file constant.
4. Click **Files...** to browse for the image file and open it.
5. Click **Apply to Active View** to only display the image in the active viewport or click **Apply to All Views in Active Layout Tab** to display it in all of the viewports.
6. Click **OK**.

How To: Assign an Environment Map

1. To enable an Environment map to display in a viewport, you need to select the **Use Map** option and load a map using the *Environment Map* slot in the *Environment and Effects* dialog box, as shown in Figure 8–60. (Select **Rendering>Environment** to open the *Environment and Effects* dialog box.) You can adjust the map parameters using an instance of the map in the *Slate Material Editor*, and opening its Parameter Editor.

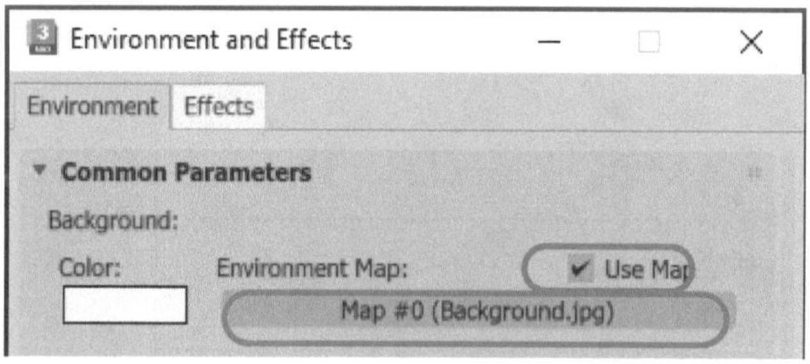

Figure 8–60

2. Select the viewport in which you want to display the map.

Hint: Updating a Background Image

Certain changes (e.g., change in resolution or aspect ratio) do not update the background image automatically. You should use <Alt>+<Shift>+<Ctrl>+<B> to update the background image in the active viewport. This command is not available if the active viewport does not display a background image.

Hint: Assign Background Image from Windows Explorer

You can also assign a background image directly from Windows Explorer by dragging and dropping the image file onto a viewport. A *Bitmap Viewport Drop* dialog box opens prompting you to select it as a viewport background, an environment map, or as both, as shown in Figure 8–61.

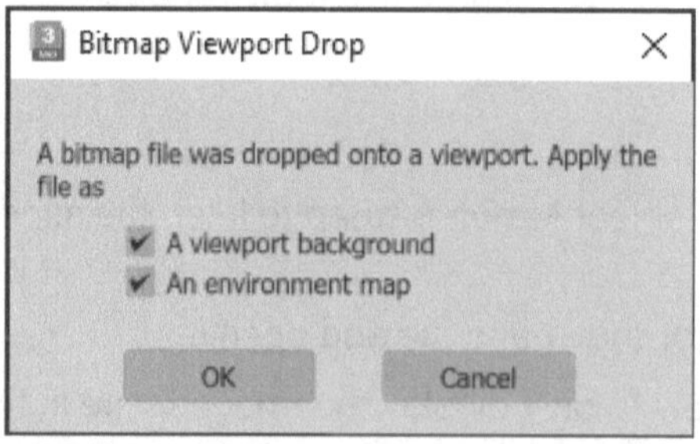

Figure 8–61

Aspect Ratio

The Autodesk 3ds Max software uses an aspect ratio to describe image proportions, which is the relationship between length and width of images, renderings, and viewports. For example, an HDTV video can be created at a resolution of 1920 x 1080 pixels (1080p), which has an aspect ratio of 1.78 (1920 / 1080 = 1.78).

It is recommended to match the aspect ratio of a background image to the aspect ratio of a viewport and the rendered output. This enables you to see a more accurate representation of the final output in the viewports. The composition of a massing study displays different in the viewport (as shown in Figure 8–62) than it does in the rendered output (as shown in Figure 8–63), when their aspect ratios do not match.

Figure 8–62

Figure 8–63

You can maintain the aspect ratio of the viewport background using the options in the *Aspect Ratio* area in the *Viewport Configuration* dialog box, in the *Background* tab, as shown in Figure 8–64.

Figure 8–64

Match Viewport	Enables you to match the aspect ratio of the image to the aspect ratio of the viewport.
Match Bitmap	Enables you to lock the original aspect ratio of the image.
Match Rendering Output	Enables you to match the aspect ratio of the image to the active rendering output device.

Safe Frames

Safe Frames is a viewport display option that defines the portions of the viewport for rendered display. To enable this option, click the **[+]** *General Viewport* label and select **Configure Viewports** or select **Views>Viewport Configuration**. When the *Viewports Configuration* dialog box opens, select the *Safe Frames* tab, as shown in Figure 8–65.

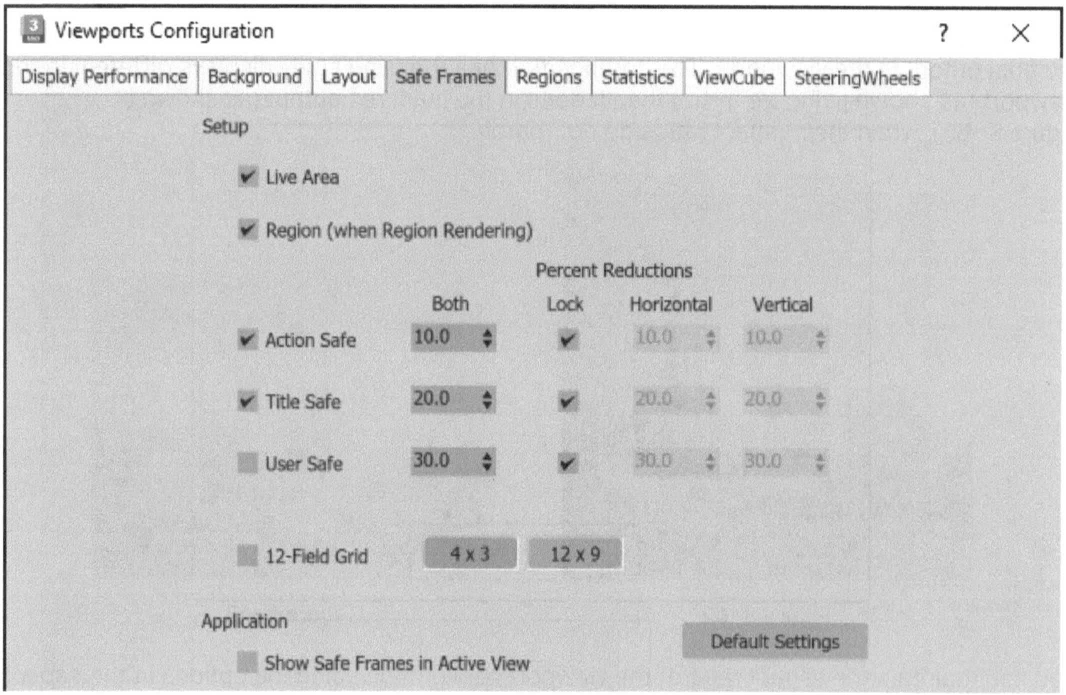

Figure 8–65

The *Safe Frames* tab offers setup options that relate to safe areas for animated action and titles when creating graphics for television. When set, these display as rectangles in the active view, as shown in Figure 8–66:

- The outer rectangle is the *Live* area, the limits of what is rendered.
- The middle rectangle is the *Action safe* area, the recommended area for any animated action when creating graphics for television.
- The inner rectangle is the *Title safe* area, the recommended area for titles when creating graphics for television.

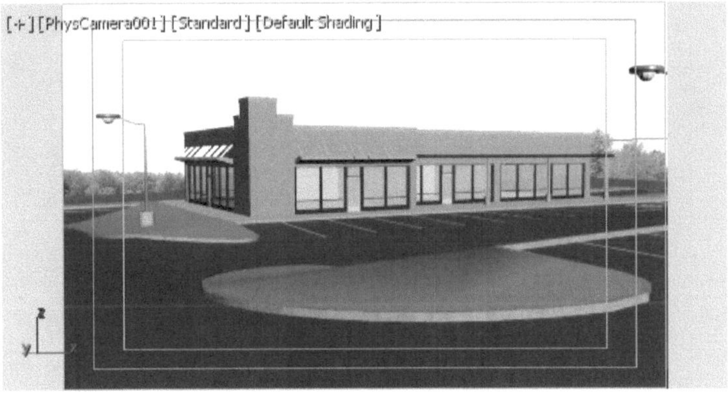

Figure 8–66

- The *User Safe* frame can be enabled, if required. It can be toggled on and customized to any proportion.
- The *12-Field Grid* frame displays a grid of cells (or fields) in the viewport. The 12-field grid yields either 12 (4x3) or 108 (12x9) cells and is used mainly by directors to reference specific areas of the screen.

Assigning Size and Aspect Ratio for Rendered Output

The rendering size (in pixels) and the aspect ratio of rendered output can be assigned in the *Output Size* area of the *Render Setup* dialog box, as shown in Figure 8–67 (**Rendering> Render Setup>***Common* tab). There are several different presets available for output size.

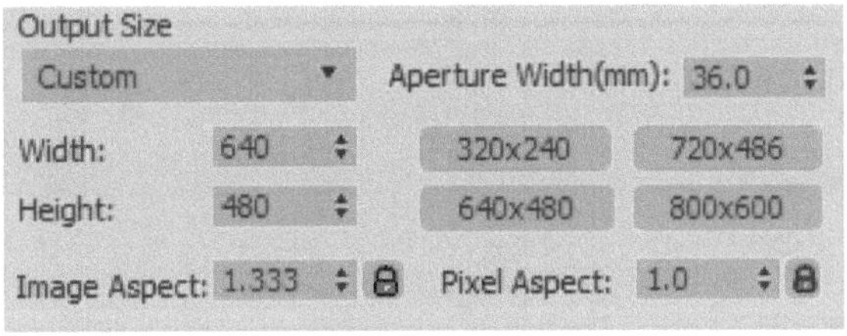

Figure 8–67

Do not confuse the *Image Aspect* ratio with the *Pixel Aspect* ratio. You can define the proportions of the pixel rectangle independent from the image. Consider the pixels to be individual tiles in a mosaic, where the tiles can be narrow, long, or short and wide.

Hint: Use Standard Aspect Ratios

Be cautious about selecting random width and height values. Most outputs have a required width and height value for a particular media type. Problems occur when non-standard choices are made for the rendering aspect ratio.

Practice 8b
Cameras and Background Images

Practice Objectives

- Apply a bitmap image as a background for the scene.
- Create a Physical Target Camera and modify the parameters.

In this practice, you will apply a bitmap image as an Environment map in a rendered scene and as a background image in a viewport. You will then create a Physical Camera and modify its parameters to correctly display scene objects on top of the background image.

You must set the paths to locate the External files and XREFs used in the practice. If you have not done this already, return to Chapter 1 and complete Task 1 to Task 3 in *Practice 1a: Organize Folders and Work with the Interface*. You only have to set the user paths once.

Task 1: Apply an Environment map.

You will first configure an Environment map to serve as a viewport and rendering background.

1. Open **Camera Background.max**.
   - This is the retail exterior scene with standard exterior lighting.
2. Activate the **Perspective** viewport. Click the *Shading Viewport* label and select **Viewport Background** and **Gradient Color**. Note the gradient color background behind the building.
3. In the menu bar, select **Rendering>Environment**. The *Environment and Effects* dialog box opens.
4. In the *Environment* tab, in the *Common Parameters* rollout, in the *Background* area, click **None** for *Environment Map*.
5. In the *Material/Map Browser,* open the **Maps>General** categories and double-click on **Bitmap**.
6. In the *Select Bitmap Image File* dialog box, open **Background.jpg** (from the ...*Maps* folder of the practice files folder).
   - Note that *None* is replaced with **Map # (Background.jpg)** and **Use Map** is automatically enabled, as shown in Figure 8–68.

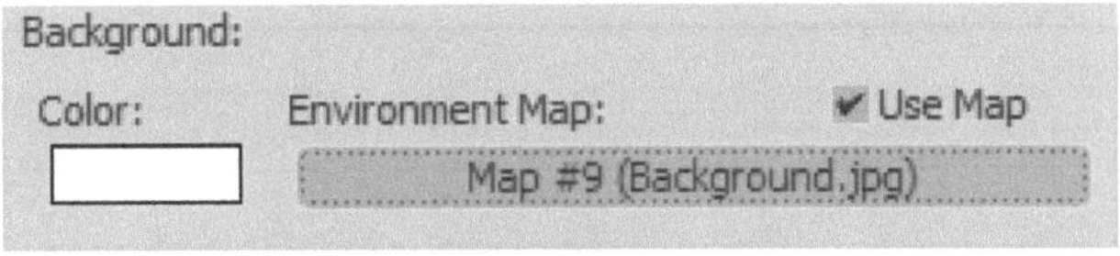

Figure 8–68

7. Close the *Environment and Effects* dialog box.

8. Activate the **Perspective** viewport, if required, and click  (Render Production). The background image of trees displays behind the model, as shown in Figure 8–69.
    - The Production renderer has been set to Arnold for this practice.

Figure 8–69

    - Note that the image file only displays in the rendering as a background and not in the viewport because the viewport background is set to *Gradient Color*.
    - The position of the background image needs to be adjusted.
9. Close the Rendered Frame Window.
10. In the **Perspective** viewport, click the *Shading Viewport* label and select **Viewport Background>Environment Background**. Note how the background image displays behind the scene in the **Perspective** viewport as well.

- Open the *Viewports Configuration* dialog box in the *Background* tab (*Shading Viewport* label>**Viewport Background>Configure Viewport Background**). Note that **Use Environment Background** has been automatically selected, as shown in Figure 8–70. Click **OK**.

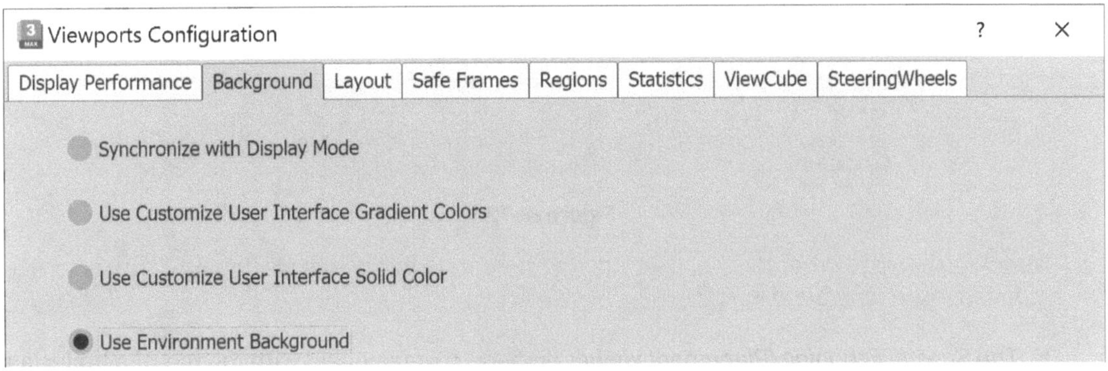

Figure 8–70

11. To modify the image, open the *Slate Material Editor*.
12. In the *Material/Map Browser*, in the *Scene Materials* category, scroll down to locate **Map # (Background.jpg)**. Double-click on it to place its node on the *View1* sheet, as shown in Figure 8–71.

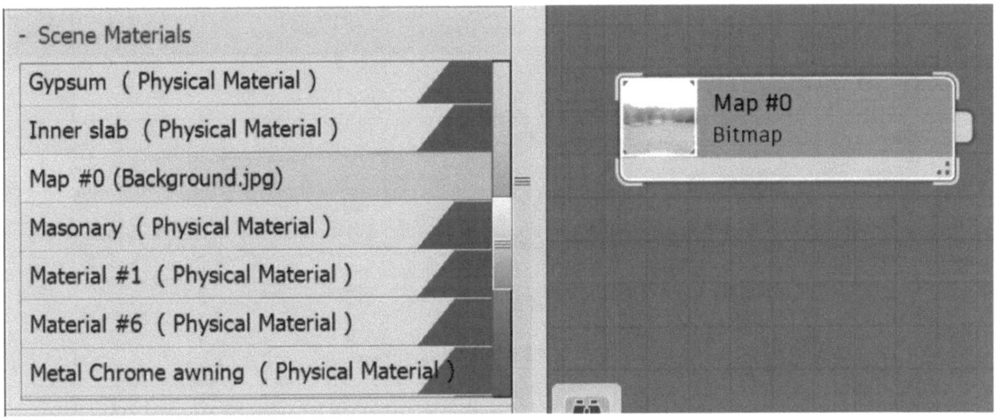

Figure 8–71

13. Verify that the **Map # Bitmap** is selected and its Parameter Editor is open. In the *Bitmap Parameters* rollout, click **View Image**, as shown in Figure 8–72.

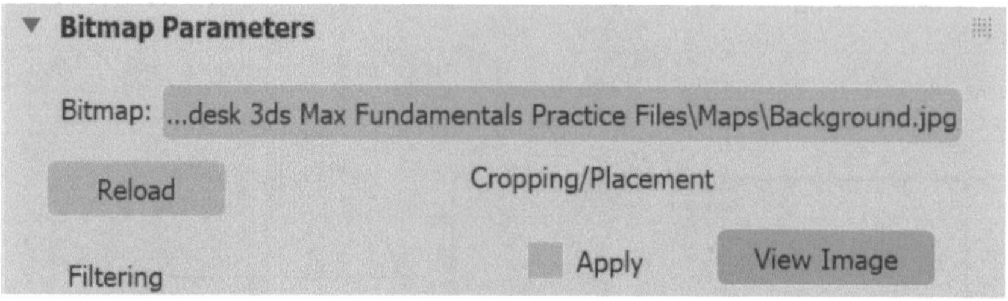

Figure 8–72

Note: *You can use programs such as Adobe Photoshop to remove features that are not required in a background image.*

- The *Specify Cropping/Placement* viewer displays a grassy field with the top of a trailer, as shown in Figure 8–73.

Figure 8–73

- In the viewer, you can specify the image cropping (the limit of the area to be displayed) by re-sizing the red rectangle around the image. When required, cropping is enabled in the *Bitmap Parameters* rollout, in the *Cropping Placement* area, using the **Apply** option.

14. Right-click and hold over the image to access the color and other image data information, as shown in Figure 8–74. The image is currently 1200 pixels wide by 750 pixels high. An *Aspect* value of **1.00** means that this image is displaying normally. Close the *Specify Cropping/Placement* viewer.

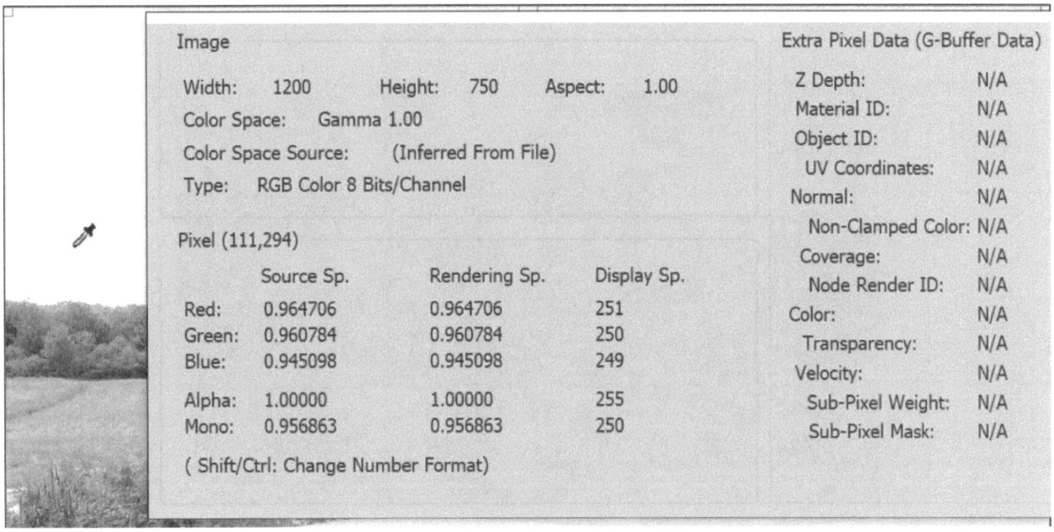

Figure 8–74

15. In the *Map* Parameter Editor (*Slate Material Editor*), in the *Coordinates* rollout, verify that the **Environ** is selected. This indicates that the map is used as a 2D backdrop. In the *Mapping* drop-down list, select **Screen**, as shown in Figure 8–75. Close the *Slate Material Editor*.

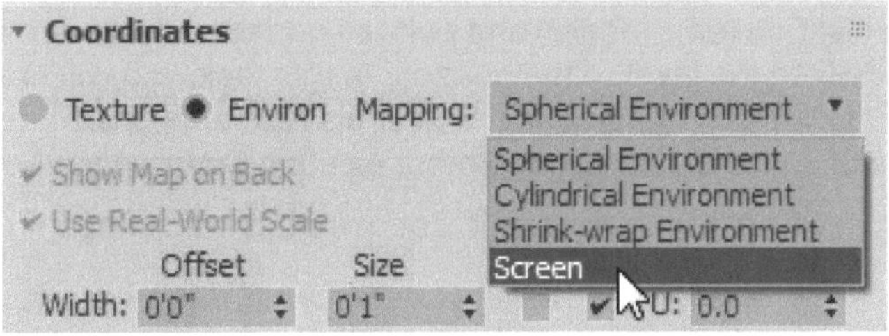

Figure 8–75

- In the **Perspective** viewport, note that the background image is updated and that a small portion of the tree line displays behind the building and is visible along the right and left sides.

16. Render the **Perspective** viewport. The tree line in the image displays partially behind the model, as shown in Figure 8–76. Note that the position of the image needs to be adjusted further. Close the Rendered Frame Window.

Figure 8–76

Task 2: Create a camera.

The background photograph was taken from about the center of the westerly end of the proposed parking lot curb island location. The camera was approximately eleven feet above the proposed first floor elevation (on a ladder) and pointed horizontally towards a proposed interior wall corner and vertically to the level of the horizon. In this task, you will create a camera approximately lined up with the background image. This type of approximation is required when exact measurements of camera position and other existing features are not available.

1. Activate the *Top* viewport and maximize it. Zoom in to the building and parking lot area.

2. In the Command Panel>*Create* panel ( ), click (Cameras), and click **Physical**. Start with the approximate camera location, near the left of the middle double parking lot, click and hold to place the camera. Still holding the mouse button, drag the cursor to locate the target approximately over the midpoint of the building's back wall and release to place the target, as shown in Figure 8–77.

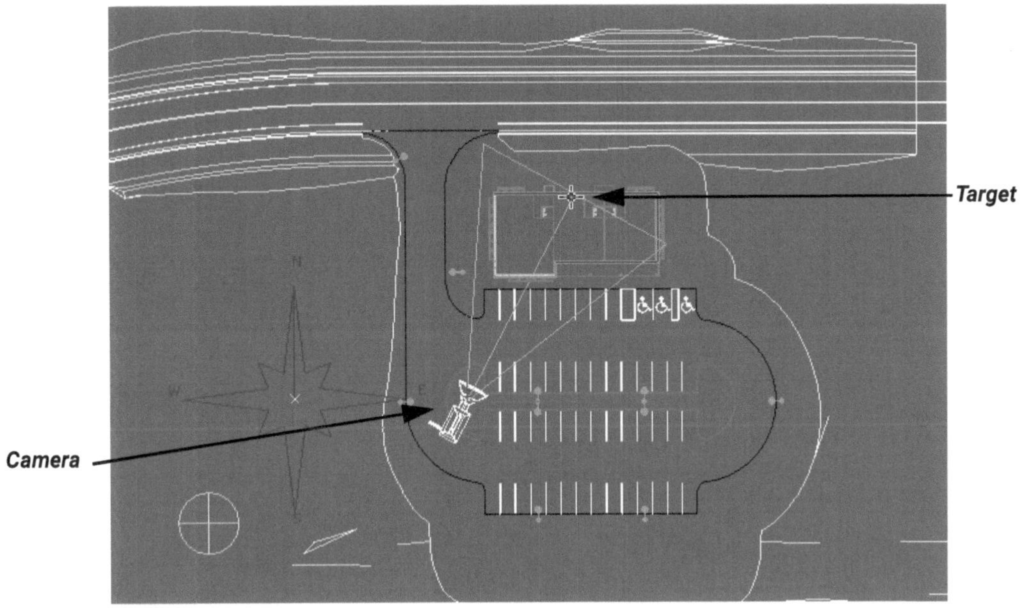

Figure 8–77

3. Maximize to the four viewports. Press <Esc> to exit the **Cameras** command and then activate the **Perspective** viewport.
4. Click the **[Perspective]** *Point of View* label and select **Cameras>PhysCamera001** (the camera view that was created in Step 2). Note that the background image is visible in the viewport with the building being viewed at an angle from the bottom up, and that the top of the trailer might be visible in the front.
   - Depending on the camera location and the target location that you selected, your camera view might differ.
5. In the Scene Explorer, select the camera object by selecting **PhysCamera001**. In the Main Toolbar, click (Select and Move). In the Status Bar, note that the *Z* elevation is **0'0"**. Set *Z* to **11'0"** to raise the camera object. Note that the building is visible at eye level, the tree lining is visible behind the building on the left side, and the trailer top is not visible.

6. You can now further adjust the camera. In the *Top* Viewport, move the Camera object back and keep looking in the **PhysCamera001** viewport until you get the scene similar to that shown in Figure 8–78.

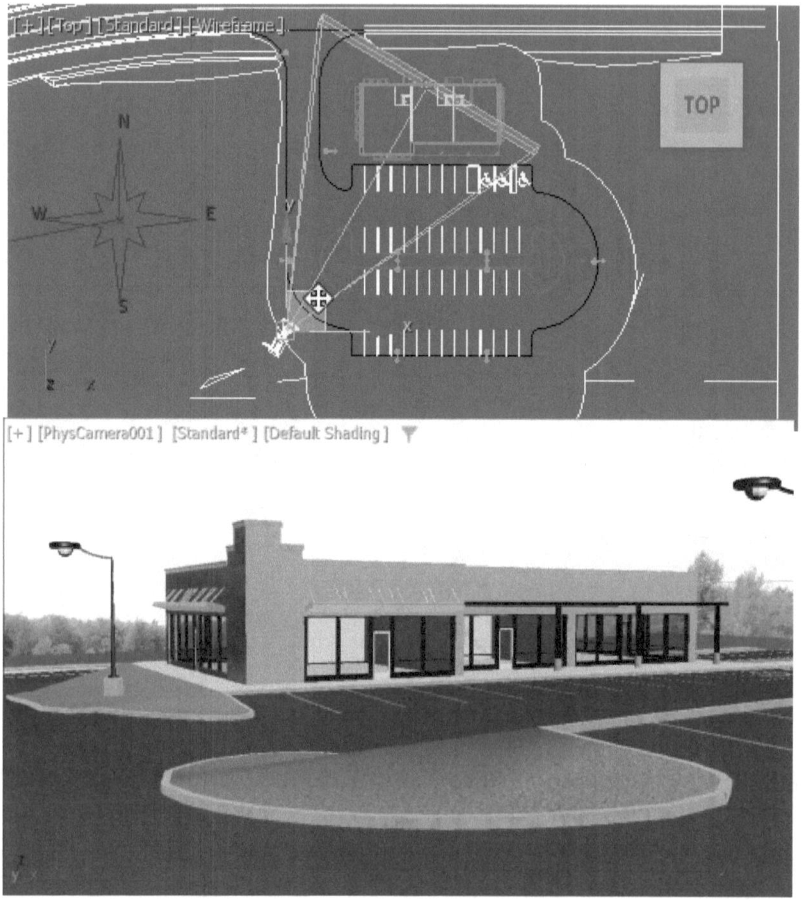

Figure 8–78

Task 3: Adjust the camera settings.

The background image has an aspect ratio of 1.6 (1200 pixels wide/750 pixels high). You will match the viewport and rendering to this aspect ratio.

1. In the Main Toolbar, click  (Render Setup) or select **Rendering>Render Setup**.

2. In the *Render Setup* dialog box, in the *Common Parameters* rollout, in the *Output Size* area, set *Image Aspect* to **1.6.** Click  next to it to activate it (lock it). Set the *Width* to **600** pixels and press <Enter>, as shown in Figure 8–79. Note that the *Height* is automatically adjusted to **375** because the *Image Aspect* is locked at **1.6**.

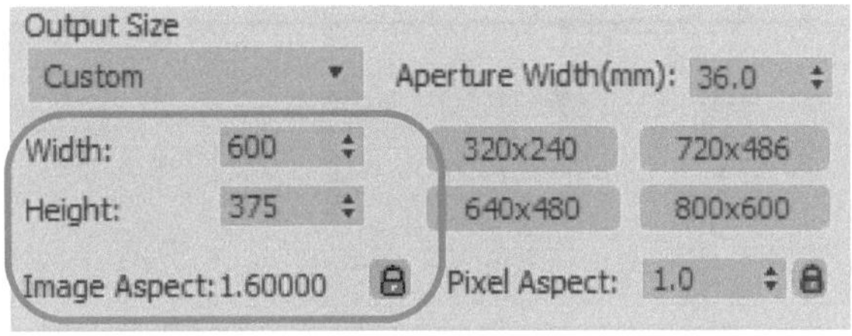

Figure 8–79

3. Close the dialog box.
4. Click the **[PhysCamera001]** *Point of View* label and select **Show Safe Frames**. Note that the safe frames are added in the viewport, as shown in Figure 8–80.

Figure 8–80

5. Select the camera object in any viewport or Scene Explorer, and in the Command Panel, select the *Modify* panel (). In the *Physical Camera* rollout, note that in the *Film/Sensor* area, the *Preset* is set to **35mm (Full Frame)**. This indicates that the photo was taken with a 35mm camera that had an adjustable lens.
   - Real-world 35mm cameras indicate the diagonal measurement of their film.
6. In the *Exposure* rollout, verify that the **Exposure Control** has been installed (grayed out). If it is not installed, click **Install Exposure Control** to install it manually.

7. Render the **PhysCamera001** viewport and note that the rendering is washed out.
8. For the Physical Camera, in the *Exposure* rollout, change the *Target* to a value between **8.5** to **9.0** EV, as shown in Figure 8–81. Verify that the *Illuminant* is set to **Daylight (6500K)**. Render the scene and note that the rendering is no longer washed out.

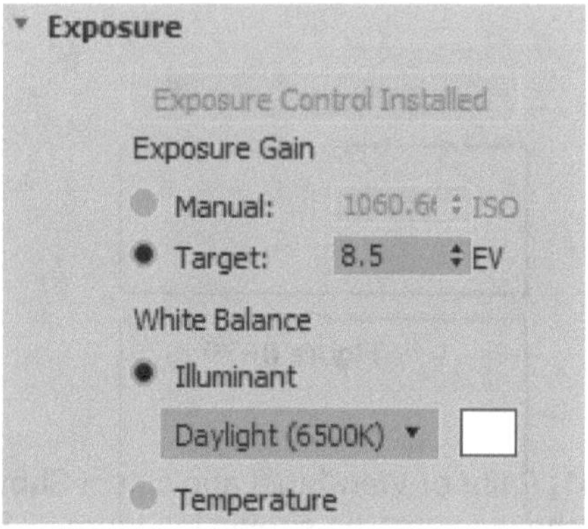

Figure 8–81

9. In the *Basic* rollout, in the *Viewport Display* area, select **Show Horizon Line**, as shown in Figure 8–82. In the **PhysCamera001** viewport, note that a horizontal line displays across the viewport. It represents the horizon of the 3D model as seen by the camera.

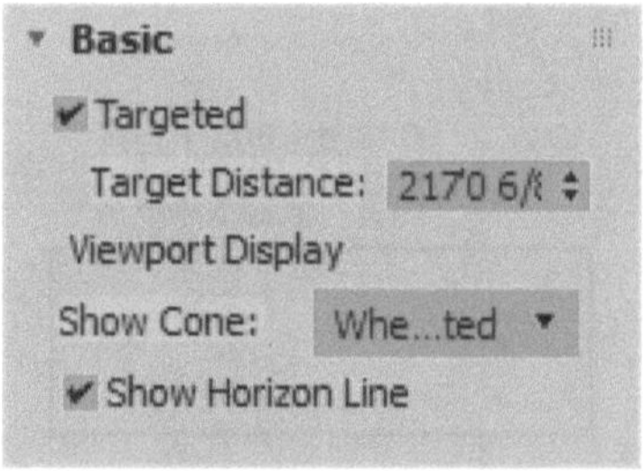

Figure 8–82

10. To adjust the position of the horizon, in the *Perspective Control* rollout, in the *Lens Shift* area, set the *Vertical* value to **-10.0**%, as shown in Figure 8–83. Note that the horizon line moves down and the tree line is now visible behind the building.

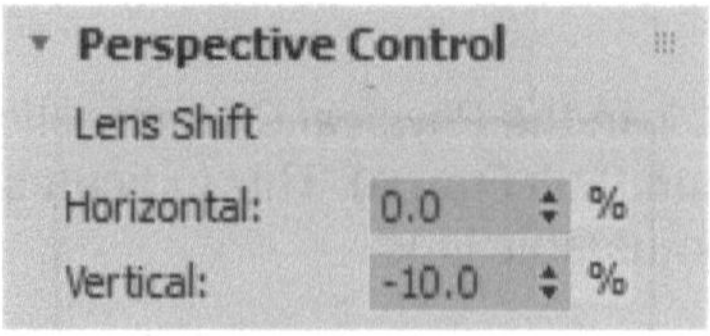

Figure 8–83

11. Verify that the **PhysCamera001** viewport is active and render the scene. Note that, with the help of some assumptions, you have reasonably located the model over an existing photograph, as shown in Figure 8–84.

Figure 8–84

12. Save your work as **MyCamera Background.max**.

End of practice

Chapter Review Questions

1. Which photometric light distribution type only casts light in one hemisphere and mimics the way light emits from a surface?
   a. Uniform Spherical
   b. Uniform Diffuse
   c. Spotlight
   d. Photometric Web

2. Since photometric lights are based on real-world calculations of light energy, they are not scale-specific.
   a. True
   b. False

3. For photometric lights, which of the following shadow casting methods does not support materials with transparency or opacity maps?
   a. Shadow Map
   b. Ray Traced Shadows
   c. Advanced Ray Traced
   d. Area Shadows

4. What is the most commonly used focal length in real-world cameras?
   a. 30mm
   b. 50mm
   c. 70mm
   d. 90mm

5. For background images, which keys do you press to update the active viewport with the specific changes made to the image (the changes that do not update automatically)?

   a. <Alt>+<B>

   b. <Alt>+<Ctrl>+<B>

   c. <Alt>+<Shift>+<B>

   d. <Alt>+<Ctrl>+<Shift>+<B>

Command Summary

Button	Command	Location
	**Cameras**	• **Command Panel:** *Create* panel • **Create:** Cameras
	**Lights**	• **Command Panel:** *Create* panel • **Create:** Lights
	**Render Production**	• **Main Toolbar** • **Rendering:** Render
	**Render Setup**	• **Main Toolbar** • **Rendering**: Render Setup
	**Systems**	• **Command Panel:** *Create* panel

Chapter 9

Arnold Lighting

Once materials have been added to an Autodesk® 3ds Max® project, lighting can be used to further enhance and create a realistic representation of the model. Although the Photometric lights work well with the Arnold renderer, the 3ds Max software provides you with Arnold lights that are specifically meant to be used with the Arnold renderer.

Learning Objectives

- Work with Arnold Lights and control the various parameter settings.
- Learn the shape types available for Arnold lights and control their specific settings.

9.1 Arnold Lights

The 3ds Max software provides you with Arnold lights that are specifically meant to be used with this renderer. It has parameters that are geared towards rendering using Arnold.

The Command Panel shows the various light parameters for Arnold Lights, as shown in Figure 9–1.

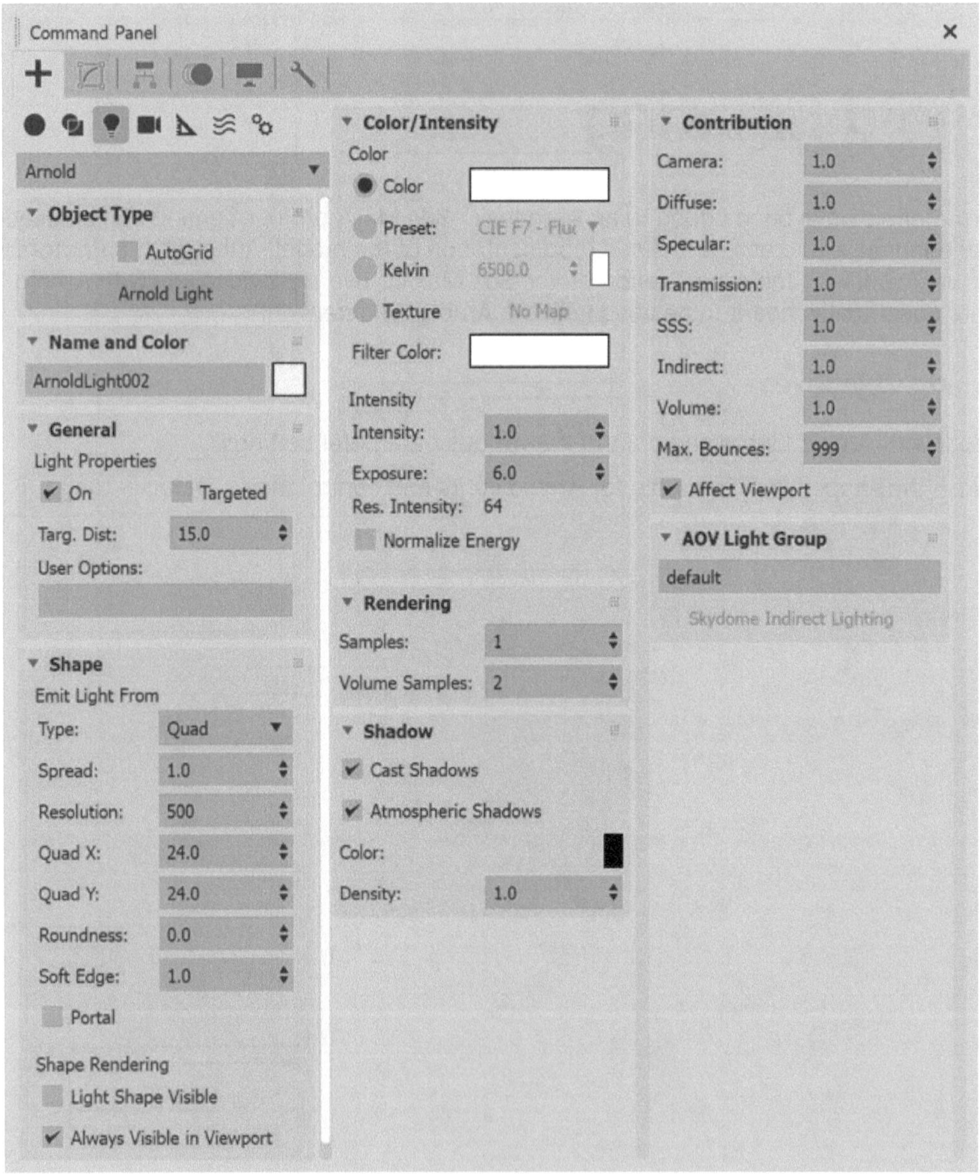

Figure 9–1

You can open the Arnold lights from the Command Panel's *Create* panel (+) by selecting (Lights) and selecting **Arnold** from the list, as shown in Figure 9–2.

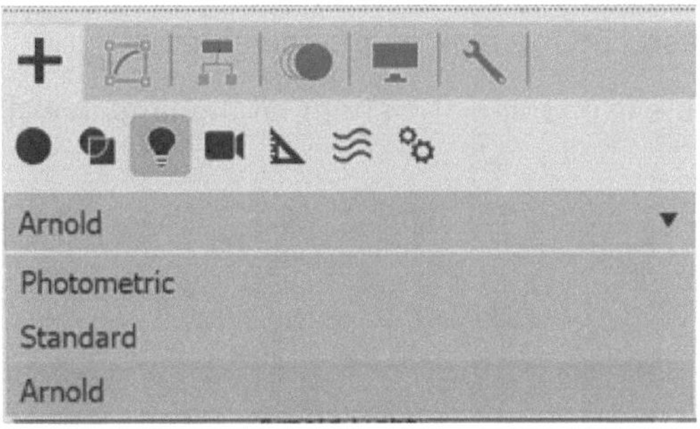

Figure 9–2

Object Type rollout

To create an Arnold light, in the *Object Type* rollout, click **Arnold Light**, as shown in Figure 9–3.

General rollout

- In the *General* rollout, you can toggle the **Light Properties** on or off, as shown in Figure 9–3. You can also set the light either as *targeted* or *free* by selecting or clearing the **Targeted** checkbox. By default, **Targeted** is cleared, which automatically creates the light as a free light.

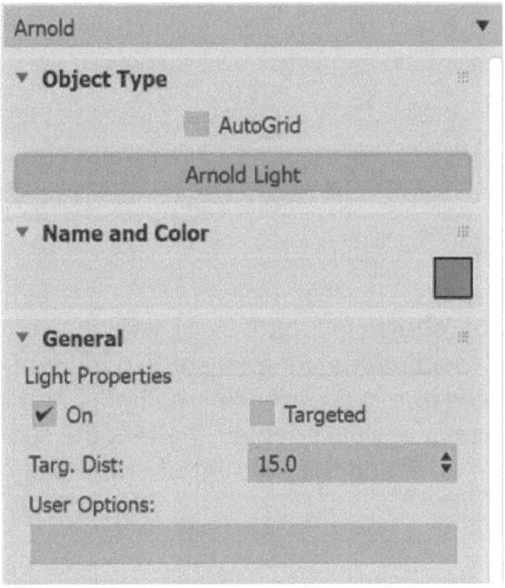

Figure 9–3

Shape rollout

- In the *Shape* rollout, you can select the shape of the light, as shown in Figure 9–4. The shape you select controls how the light is emitted. By default, the **Quad** option is selected, which illuminates a rectangular area and emits the light only in one direction. The parameters in the *Shape* rollout are based on the type of light selected.
- When **Light Shape Visible** is enabled, the shape of the light is visible in the render as a self-illuminated object.

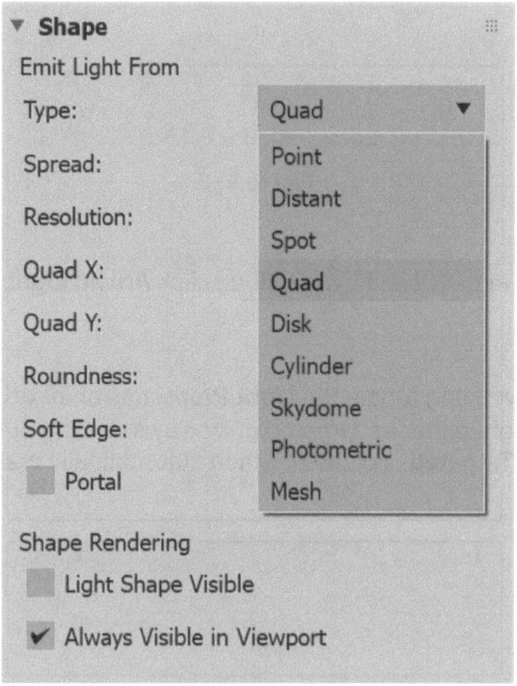

Figure 9–4

Color/Intensity rollout

- In the *Color/Intensity* rollout (shown in Figure 9–5), you can set the color of the light source. Typically, you are required to adjust the *Intensity* or *Exposure* of the light source to get a good render of a scene. *Exposure* is an intensity multiplier and increases the intensity in multiple jumps. If **Normalize Energy** is enabled, it alters the shadow softness by changing the size of the light without affecting the amount of emitted light.

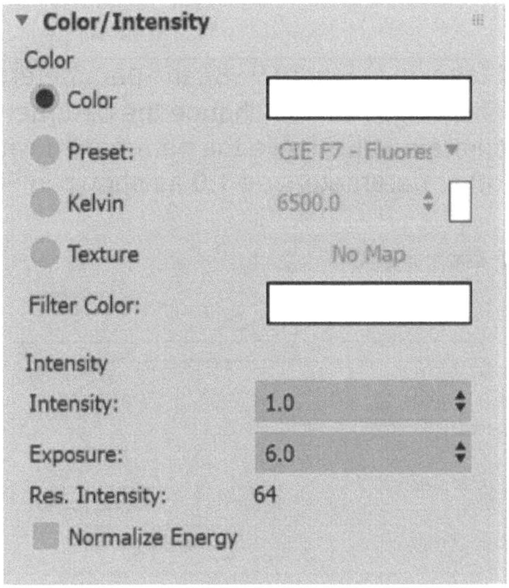

Figure 9–5

Rendering rollout

- In the *Rendering* rollout (shown in Figure 9–6), you can adjust the quality of specular highlight and shadows. Increasing the *Samples* value reduces the noise in shadow areas, but increases the render time.

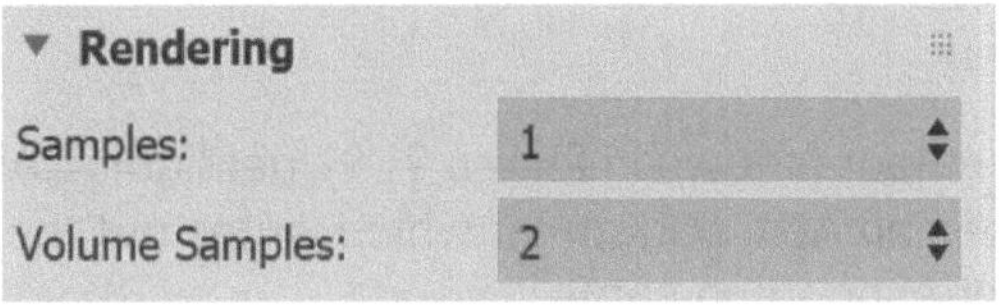

Figure 9–6

Shadow rollout

- In the *Shadow* rollout (shown in Figure 9–7), you can toggle the casting of shadows from the light on or off. The **Atmospheric Shadows** option controls the calculations of volumetric shadows.

Figure 9–7

Contribution rollout

- In the *Contribution* rollout (shown in Figure 9–8), the parameters control the aspects of light contribution in the final rendering. You can change the parameter values for artistic control. To achieve physically accurate results, leave the parameters with their default values (*Max. Bounces* as **999** and the other parameters as **1.0** as shown in Figure 9–8).

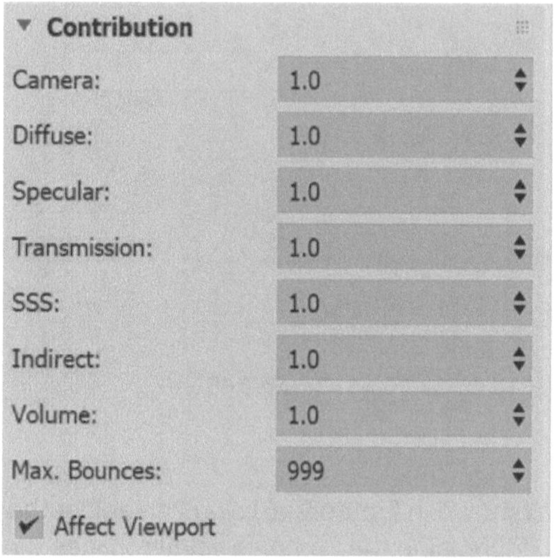

Figure 9–8

AOV Light Group rollout

- In the *AOV Light Group* rollout (shown in Figure 9–9), per-light AOVs are available via a string parameter. Each light has an AOV parameter which writes out the light contribution to a separate AOV with a corresponding name.

  Note: *Light Groups can be created and deleted in Render Setup: Arnold, AOVs>AOV Light Group Manager.*

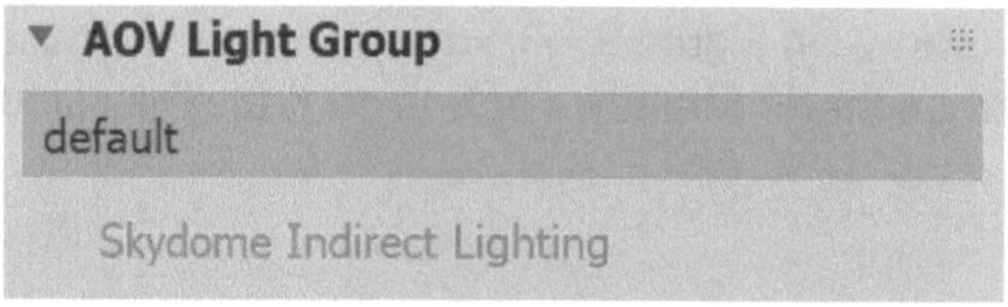

Figure 9–9

Arnold Shape Types

The various Arnold light types are **Point**, **Distant**, **Spot**, **Quad**, **Disk**, **Cylinder**, **Skydome**, **Photometric**, and **Mesh** as shown in Figure 9–10.

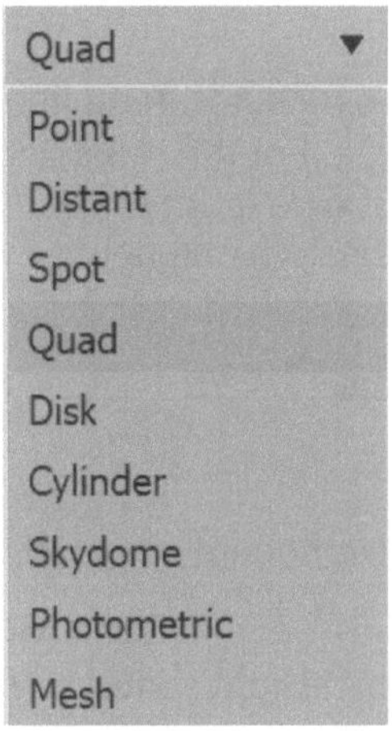

Figure 9–10

Quad Light

Creates light from an area source (a quadrilateral, specified by four vertices). It can be used to model light from an extended source or in some cases from a window.

General rollout

You can set the light as either **Free** or **Targeted**.

When **Targeted** is selected, the rendered image displays as shown on the right in Figure 9–11. When **Targeted** is cleared (free), the rendered image displays as shown on the right in Figure 9–12.

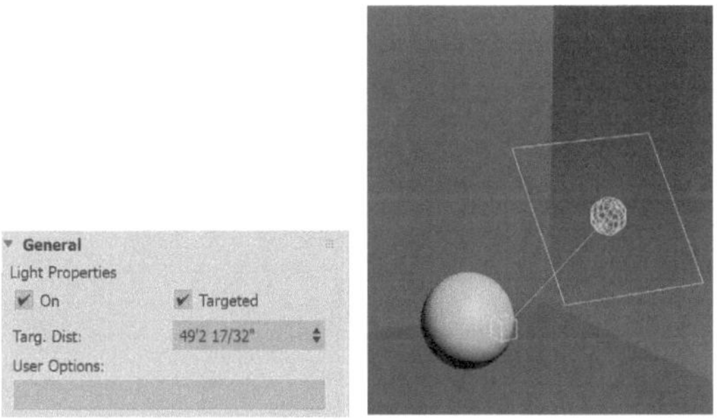

Figure 9–11

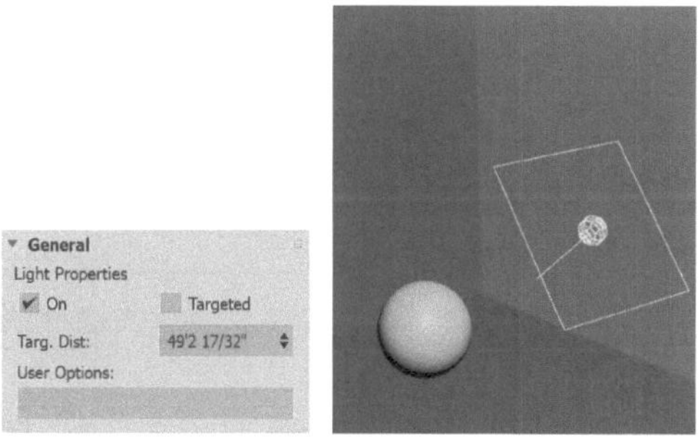

Figure 9–12

Shape rollout (Quad light)

The parameters in the *Shape* rollout (as shown in Figure 9–13) are as follows:

- **Spread:** Radiates light in the direction along normal. The default value of **1** creates diffuse emission, while lower values focus the light more until it becomes a laser like beam at value **0**.
- **Resolution:** The resolution of the importance sampling table used to accurately examine the color texture, especially of HDRI type. For the most accurate results, the resolution must be set to match the image resolution, however, in many instances it can be set lower without a noticeable loss of detail in reflections. The higher the value, the longer the light will take to determine the importance tables.
- **Quad X:** Quad size in the X direction.
- **Quad Y:** Quad size in the Y direction.
- **Roundness:** Adjust the shape, from a square shape at **0**, to rounded corners, to a disk shape at **1**.
- **Soft Edge:** Specifies an area where the light's intensity smoothly falls off to zero at the edge.

When Portal is selected, it disables anything related to the illumination generated by the light (a portal does not generate light), and the object now becomes a light portal.

Figure 9–13 shows the *Shape* and *Color/Intensity* parameters, and the rendered scene for a free **Quad** light.

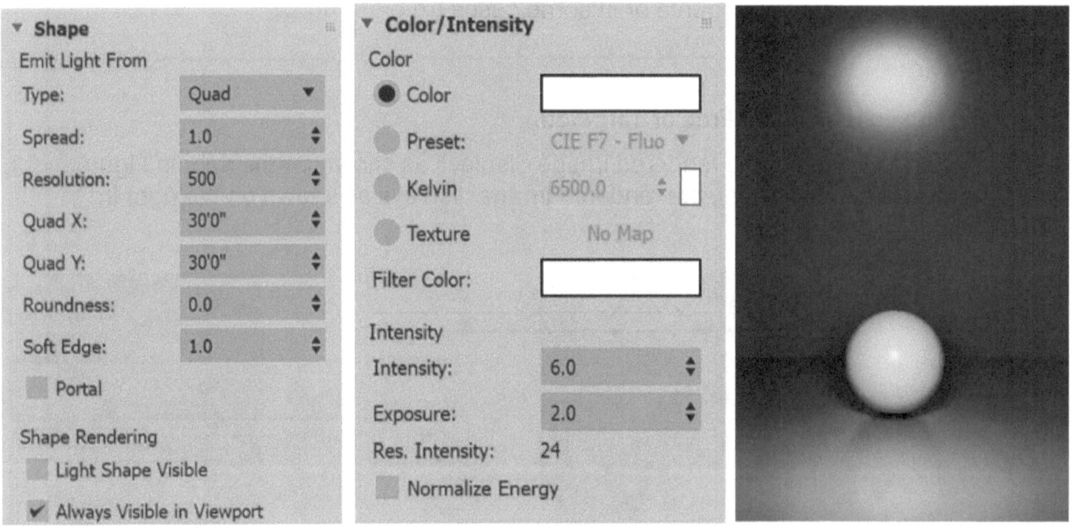

Figure 9–13

Point Light

This light source can model light either from a point source or from a sphere, producing less sharp shadows. The light is cast evenly in all directions.

General rollout

You can set the light only as a free light and the rendered image displays as shown in Figure 9–14.

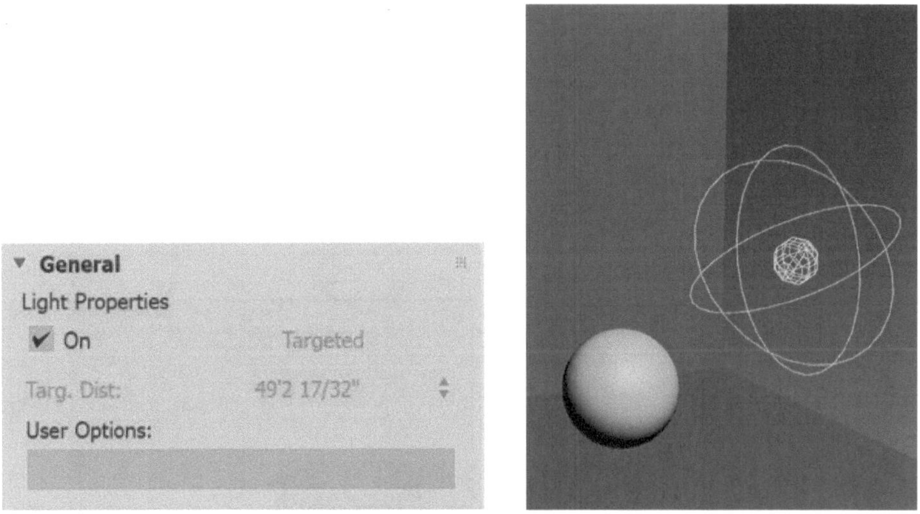

Figure 9–14

Shape Rollout (Point light)

- **Radius:** The radius of the light's surface.

Figure 9–15 shows the *Shape* and *Color/Intensity* parameters, and the rendered scene for a free **Point** light.

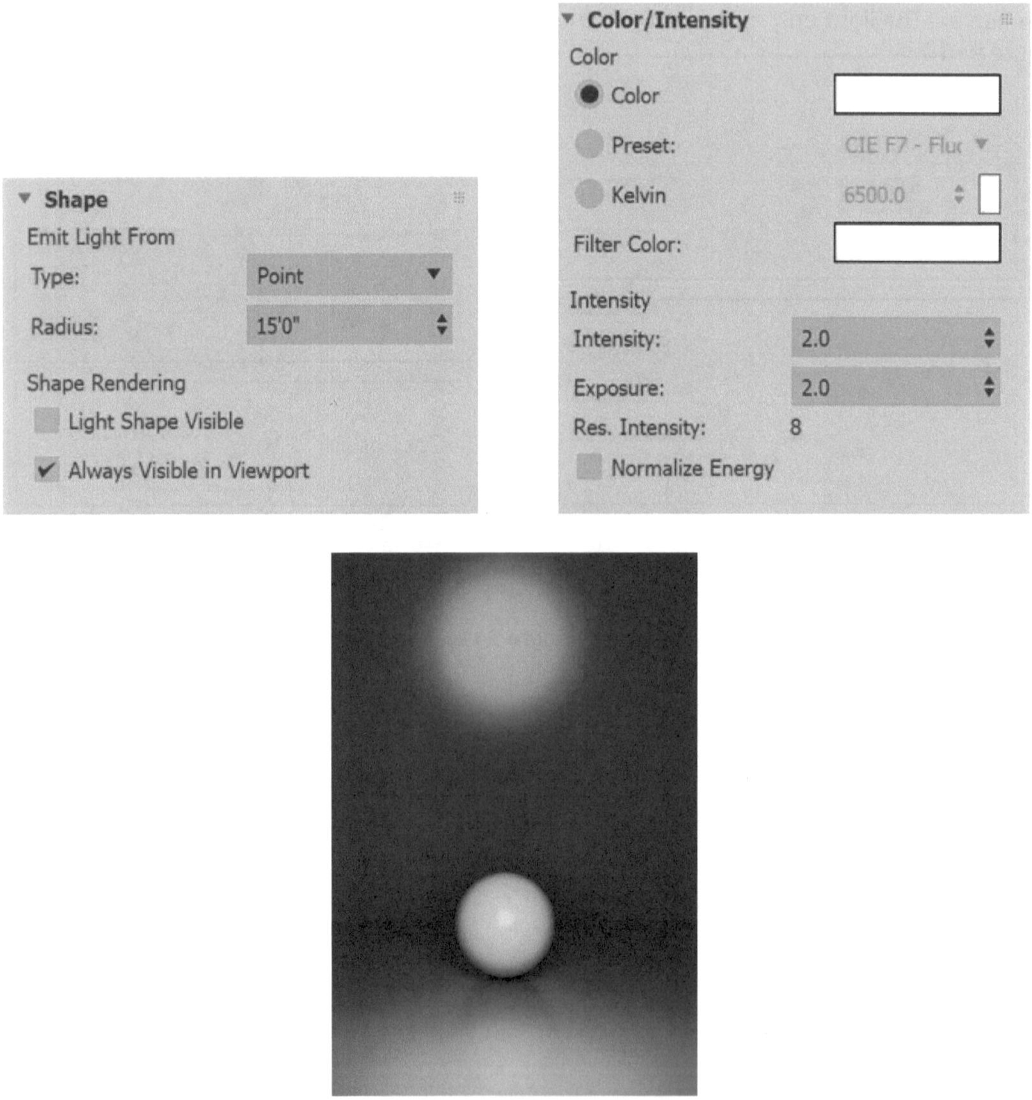

Figure 9–15

Distant Light

This is a parallel light from a distant source, specified in terms of a direction vector. This light can be used to simulate sunlight.

General rollout

In the *General* rollout, you can set the light as either **Free** or **Targeted**. When **Targeted** is selected, the rendered image displays as shown in Figure 9–16. When **Targeted** is cleared, the rendered image displays as shown in Figure 9–17.

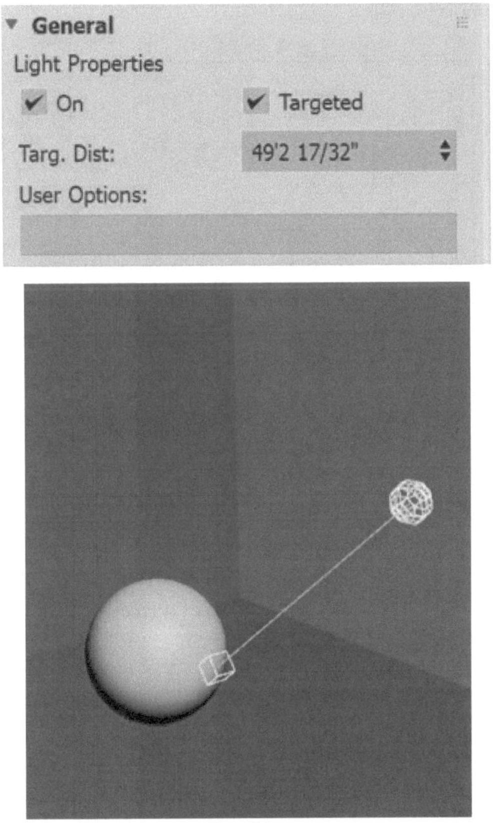

Figure 9–16

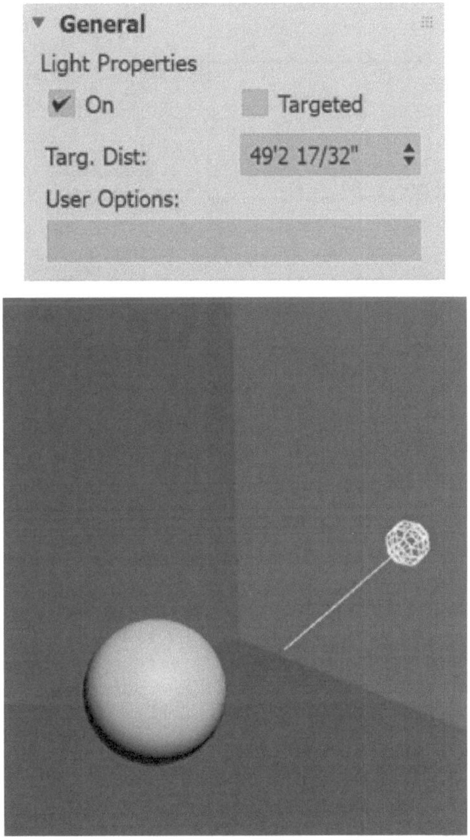

Figure 9–17

Shape rollout (Distant light)

Angle: The size of the light, in degrees. Non-zero values provide realistic soft shadows.

Figure 9–18 shows the *Shape* and *Color/Intensity* parameters, and the rendered scene for a free **Distant** light.

> ***Note:*** *If the* ***Normalize Energy*** *checkbox in the* ***Color/Intensity*** *panel is selected, you will be able to alter the shadow softness by altering the size of the light, without affecting the amount of emitted light.*

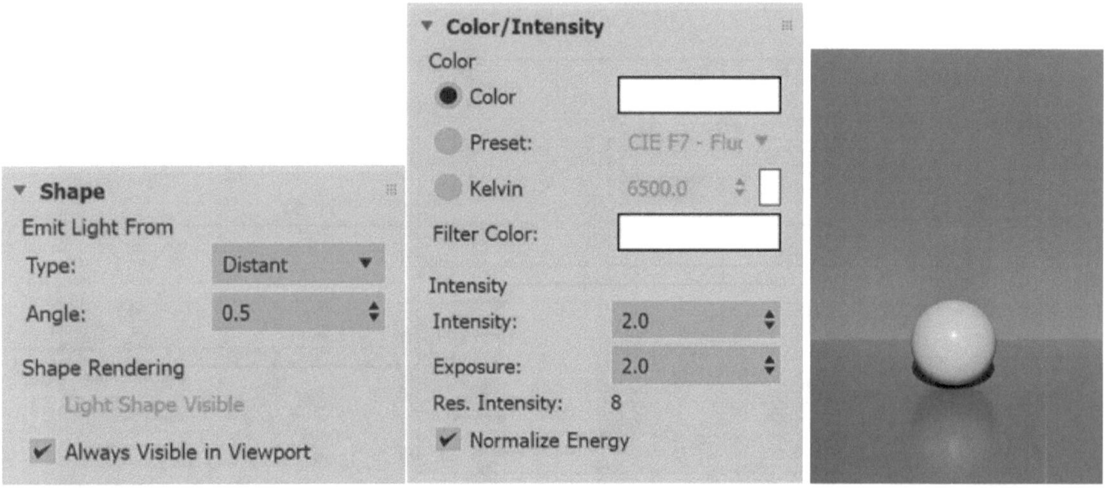

Figure 9–18

Spot Light

This creates a cone of light by starting at the current position of the light and extending to the point it is pointed at.

General rollout

In the *General* rollout, you can set the light as either **Free** or **Targeted**.

When **Targeted** is selected, the rendered image displays as shown in Figure 9–19. When **Targeted** is cleared, the rendered image displays as shown in Figure 9–20.

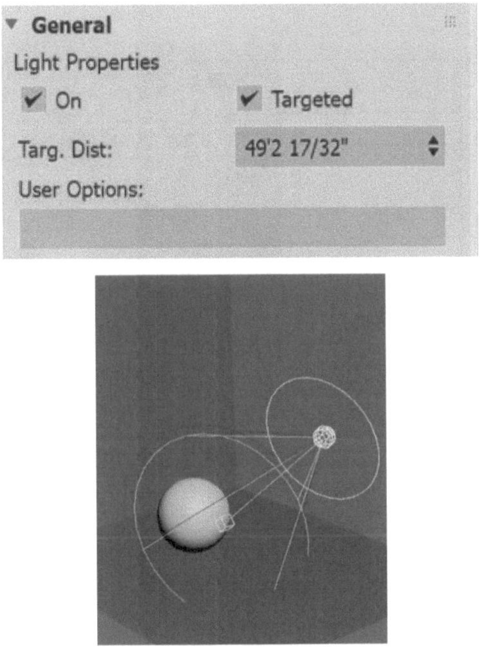

Figure 9–19

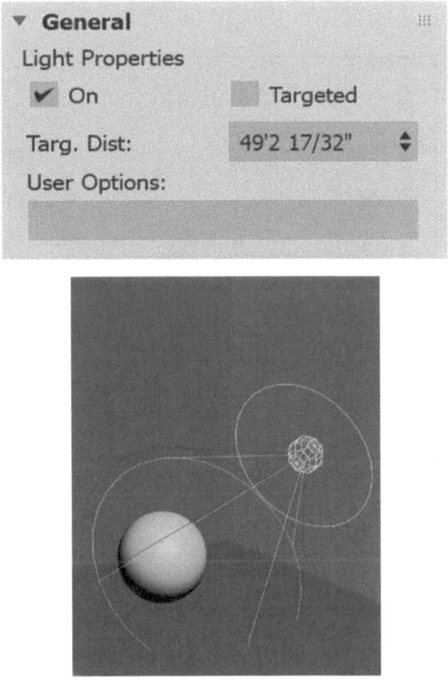

Figure 9–20

Shape rollout (Spot light)

The parameters in the *Shape* rollout are as follows:

- **Radius:** The radius of the Light' surface.
- **Cone Angle:** The cone angle in degrees. Light will not be emitted outside of the cone.
- **Lens Radius:** When set to **0'0"**, the spot light vertex cone coincides with the light's specified position. If non-zero, the cone becomes truncated, the light is assumed to be from a virtual position that is behind the light's specified position. This simulated the effects of real-world luminaires that combine a light bulb and a parabolic reflector inside a small, closed fixture.
- **Penumbra Angle:** Set this to **1.0** for a cone with a circular cross section; for an elliptical cross section, set it to another value. Elliptical cross sections produce theatre lights such as PAR cans.
- **Aspect Ratio:** Measured in degrees, this angle, from the outer edge of the cone towards the spotlight smoothly falls off to **0.0** at the cone edge.
- **Roundness:** Adjust the shape, from a square shape at **0**, to rounded corners, and to a disk shape at **1**.

Figure 9–21 shows the *Shape* and *Color/Intensity* parameters, and the rendered scene for a free **Spot** light.

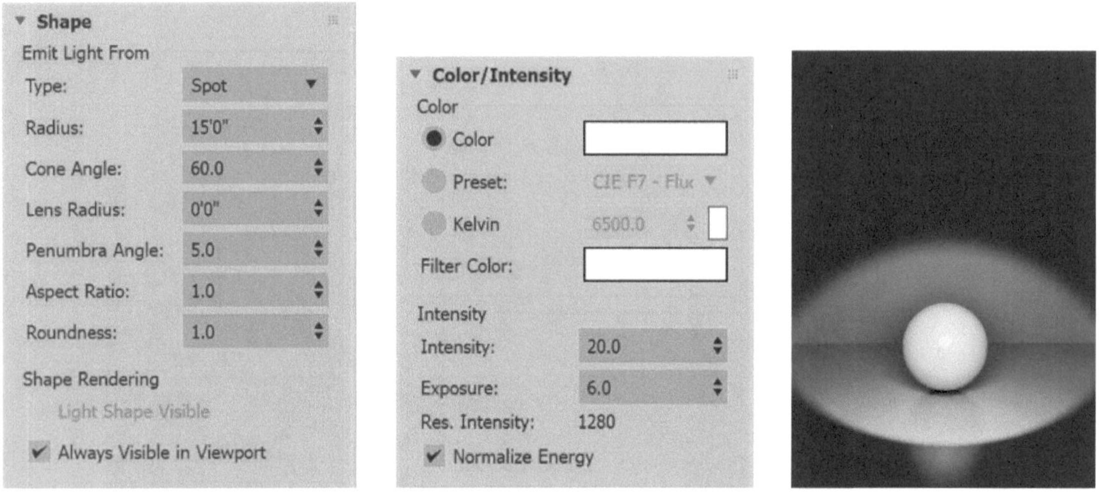

Figure 9–21

Disk Light

This creates light from a circular area source (flat disk).

General rollout

In the *General* rollout, you can set the light as either **Free** or **Targeted**. When **Targeted** is selected, the rendered image displays as shown in Figure 9–22. When **Targeted** is cleared, the rendered image displays as shown in Figure 9–23.

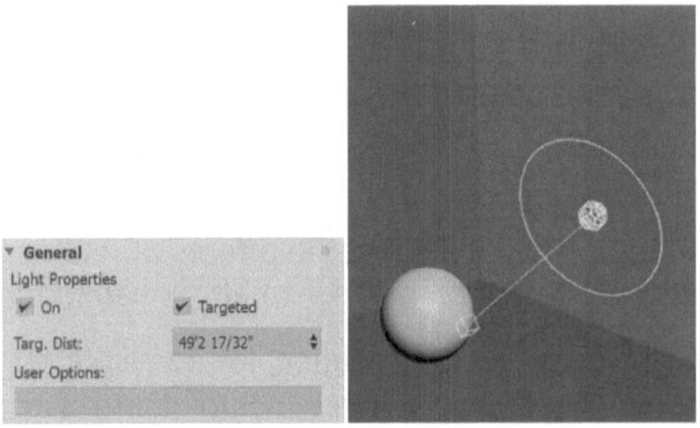

Figure 9–22

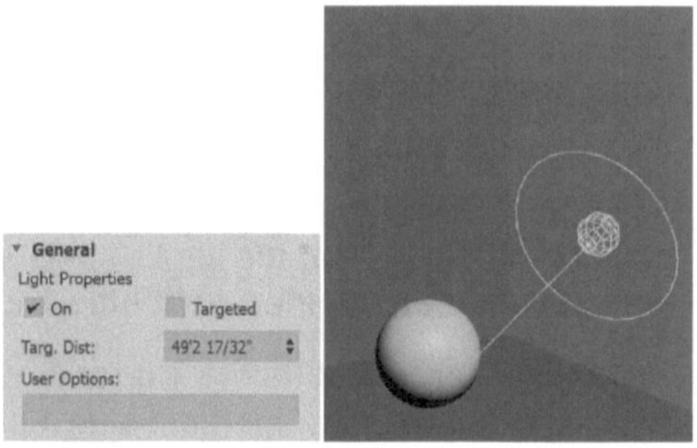

Figure 9–23

Shape rollout (Disk light)

- **Radius:** The radius of the Light' surface.
- **Spread:** Radiates light in the direction along normal. The default value of **1** creates diffuse emission, while lower values focus the light more until it becomes a laser like beam at value **0**.

Figure 9–24 shows the *Shape* and *Color/Intensity* parameters, and the rendered scene for a free **Disk** light.

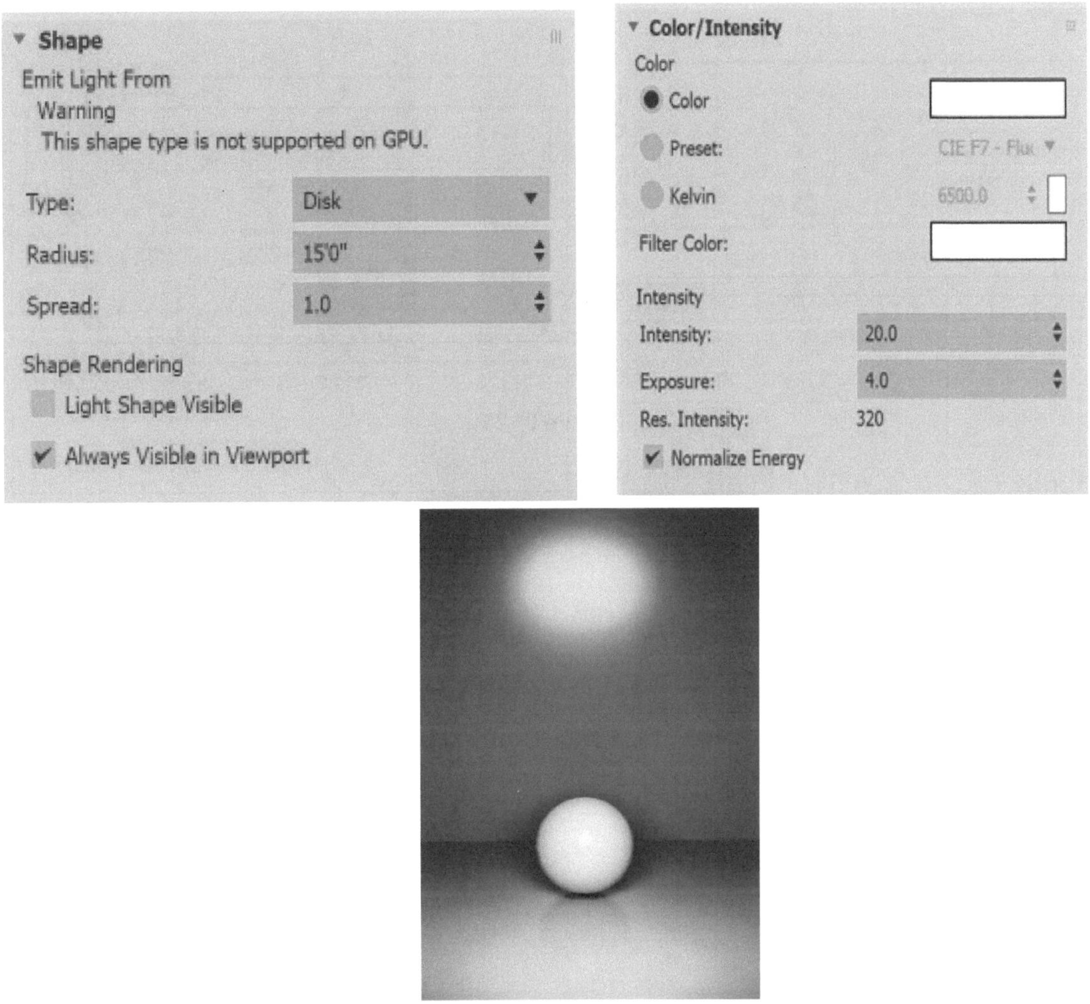

Figure 9–24

Cylinder Light

This creates light from a cylindrical area source (tube shape). Could be used for florescent Lights.

General rollout

You can set the light only as a free light, as shown in Figure 9–25.

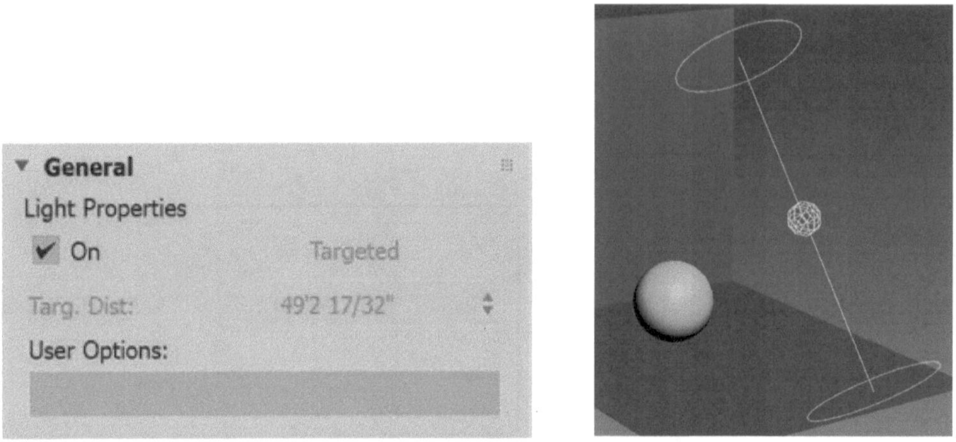

Figure 9–25

Shape rollout (Cylinder light)

- **Radius:** Light' radius surface.
- **Height:** Cylinder's height shape.

Figure 9–26 shows the *Shape* and *Color/Intensity* parameters, and the rendered scene for a free **Cylinder** light.

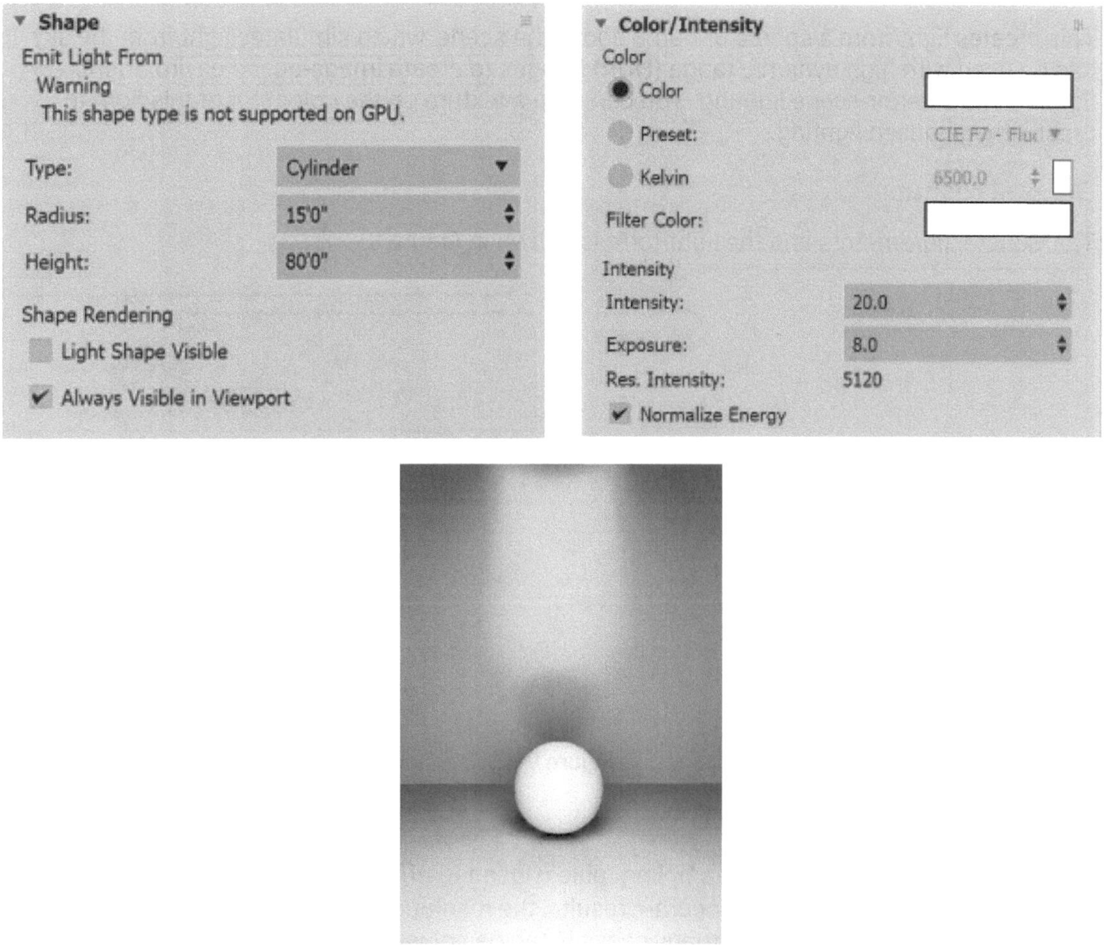
Shape
Emit Light From
Warning
This shape type is not supported on GPU.
Type:
Cylinder
Radius:
15'0"
Height:
80'0"
Shape Rendering
Light Shape Visible
Always Visible in Viewport
Color/Intensity
Color
Color
Preset:
CIE F7 - Fluc
Kelvin
6500.0
Filter Color:
Intensity
Intensity:
20.0
Exposure:
8.0
Res. Intensity:
5120
Normalize Energy

Figure 9–26

Skydome Light

This creates light from a sphere or dome above the scene, which simulates light from the sky. It can be used with high dynamic range (HDR) images to create image-based environment lighting and exterior-scene lighting. You can map a texture on the color slot of this light to create image-based lighting.

General rollout

The General parameters and the light form is shown in Figure 9–27.

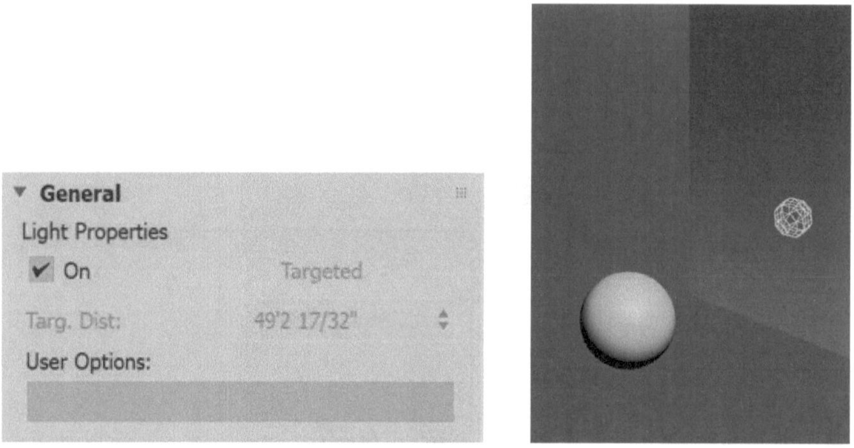

Figure 9–27

Shape rollout (Skydome light)

- **Resolution:** The importance sampling table is used to efficiently look up the texture, especially of HDRI type. For accurate results, the resolution must be adjusted to match the image resolution, however, in many cases it can be adjusted lower without a noticeable loss of detail in reflection. The higher the value, the longer the light will talk to recompute the importance table.
- **Format:** Indicates the format of the map being connected. The maps types available in the drop-down are **LatLong**, **Mirrored Ball**, and **Angular**.
- **Portal Mode:** Identifies how the skydome light interacts with quad lights flagged as portals, from the dropdown.
    - **Off:** Turns off portals.
    - **Interior Only: B**locks any light outside portals for interior only scenes.
    - **Interior/Exterior:** Allows light outside portals through for mixed interior and exterior scenes.

Figure 9–28 shows the *Shape* and *Color/Intensity* parameters, and the rendered scene for a free **Skydome** light.

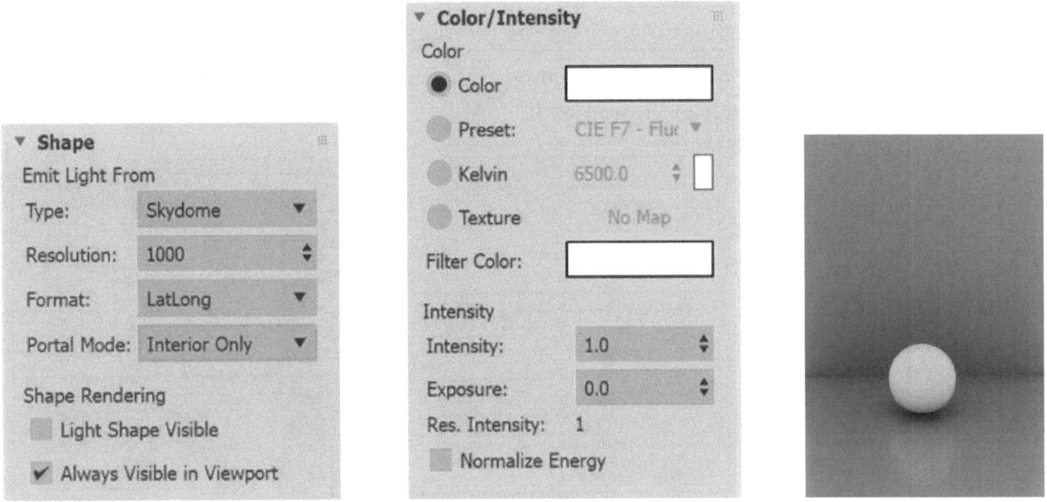

Figure 9–28

Photometric Light

This light uses data measured from real-world lights, often directly from bulb and enclosure manufacturers themselves. You can import IES files from light companies to provide accurate intensity and spread data for a given light model.

General rollout

You can set the light as either **Free** or **Targeted**.

When **Targeted** is selected, the rendered image displays as shown in Figure 9–29. When **Targeted** is cleared, the rendered image displays as shown in Figure 9–30.

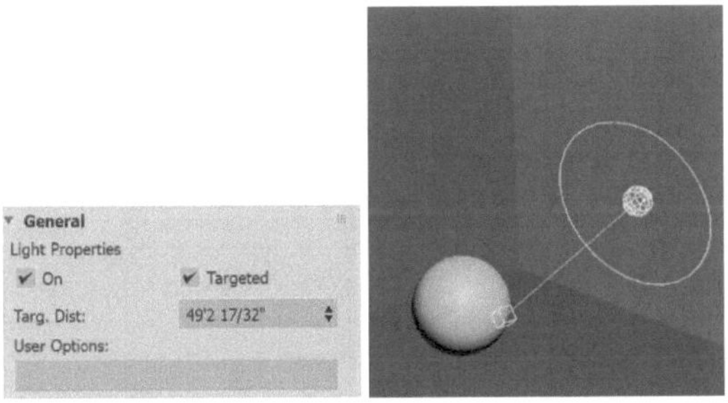

Figure 9–29

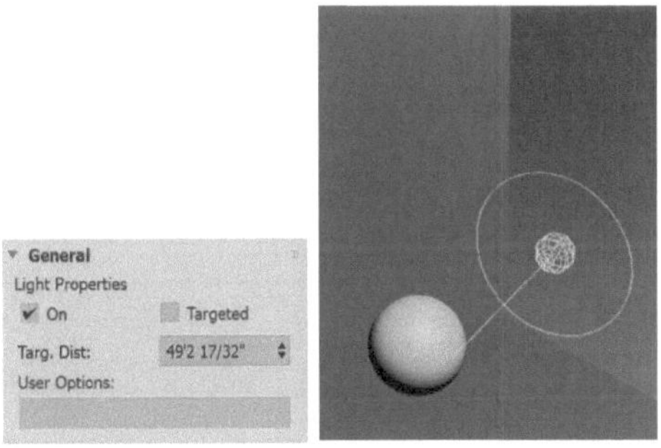

Figure 9–30

Shape rollout (Photometric light)

- **Radius:** The Light' surface radius.
- **File:** The IES light profile that determines the distribution of light.

Figure 9–31 shows the *Shape* and *Color/Intensity* parameters (with **Normalize Energy** enabled), and the rendered scene for a free **Photometric** light.

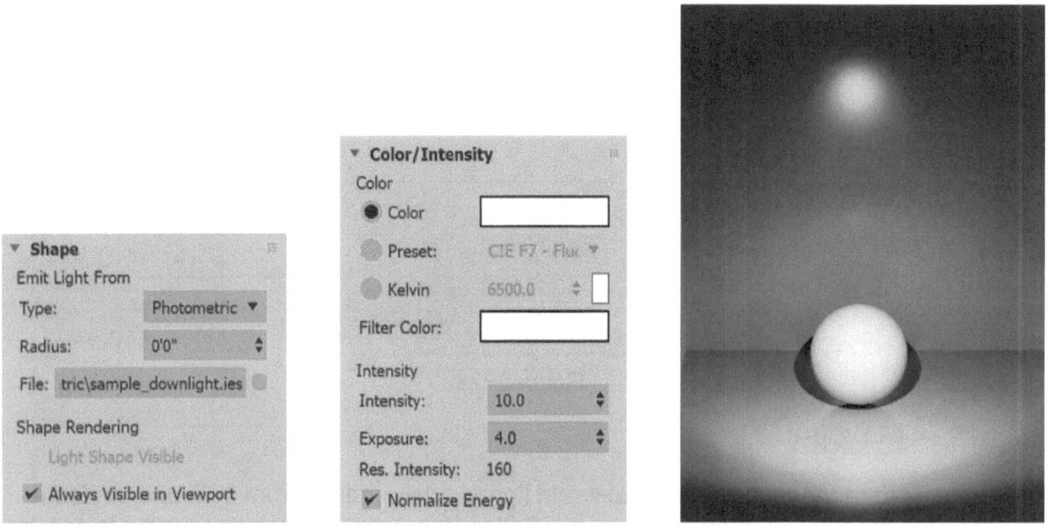

Figure 9–31

Mesh Light

You can use the **Mesh** light type when conventional light types are not sufficient to create the required lighting effects.

Mesh lights can create complex lighting effects that are difficult to create using any other light type. For example, effects such as neon lighting or a car light motion trail effect can be achieved more easily with mesh lights.

> ***Note:*** *NURBS surfaces do not work with mesh lights.*

General rollout

You can set the light only as a free light, as shown in Figure 9–32.

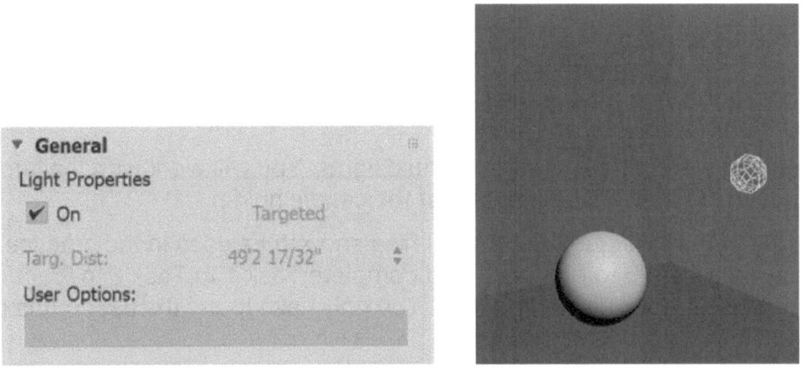

Figure 9–32

Shape rollout (Mesh light)

- **Mesh:** The polygon mesh defining the light's appearance.

Figure 9–33 shows the *Shape* and *Color/Intensity* parameters, and the rendered scene (without selecting a Surface) for a free **Mesh** light.

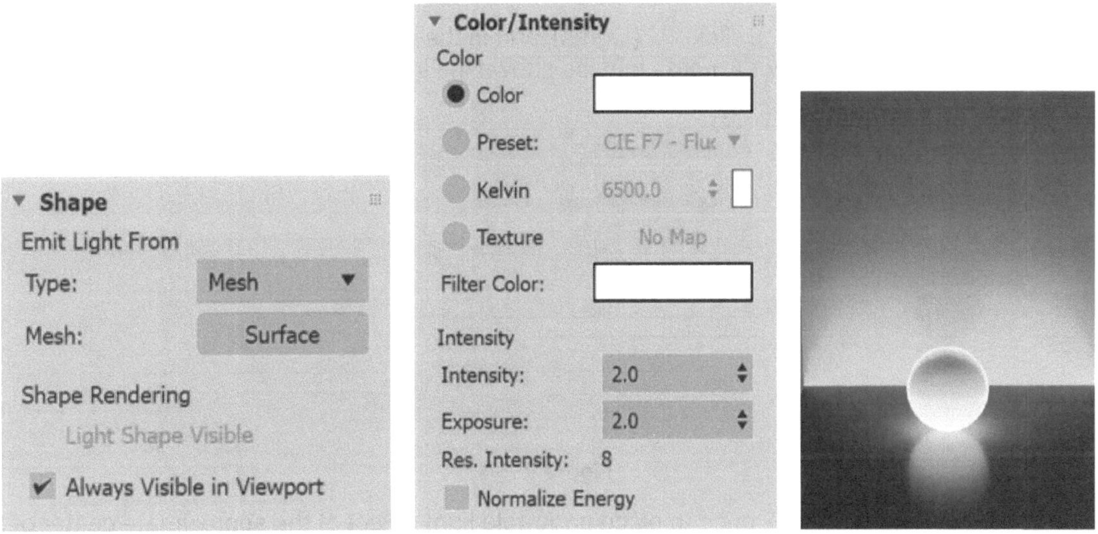

Figure 9–33

Practice 9a
Work with Arnold Lights

Practice Objective

- Create Arnold lights and modify their parameters.

In this practice, you will create and adjust Arnold lights. You will work with the intensity and exposure values to create a crisp rendering of the candle holder.

You must set the paths to locate the External files and XREFs used in the practice. If you have not done this already, return to Chapter 1 and complete Task 1 to Task 3 in *Practice 1a: Organize Folders and Work with the Interface*. You only have to set the user paths once.

Task 1: Create Arnold lights.

1. Open **Arnold Lights.max**.
2. Verify that the **Camera01** viewport is active. In the Main Toolbar, click (Render Production) to render the viewport. Note that the rendered scene has no shadows as the scene is illuminated by default lights. Leave the Rendered Frame Window open.
   - The Production Renderer is set to **Arnold**.
3. In the *Create* panel (+), click (Lights), and in the drop-down list, select **Arnold**. In the *Object Type* rollout, select **Arnold Light**, as shown in Figure 9–34.

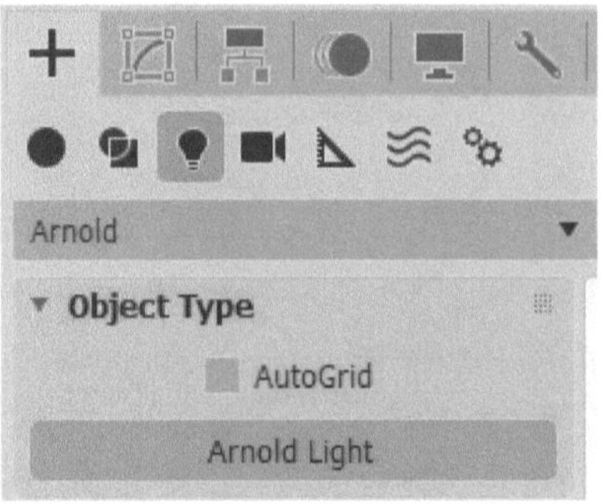

Figure 9–34

4. In the *Top* viewport, click once to place an Arnold light object at the approximate center of the candle holder. Note that you might not be able to see the light because it is placed at the bottom of the candle holder, which is not visible in the **Top** view. Do not click again as another light will be created.
5. In the Command Panel, name the light as **Light Top**.

6. Verify that in the Command Panel, **Arnold Light** is still highlighted in blue. In the **Top** viewport, click under the bottom horizontal line, as shown in Figure 9–35. Another light object is created.

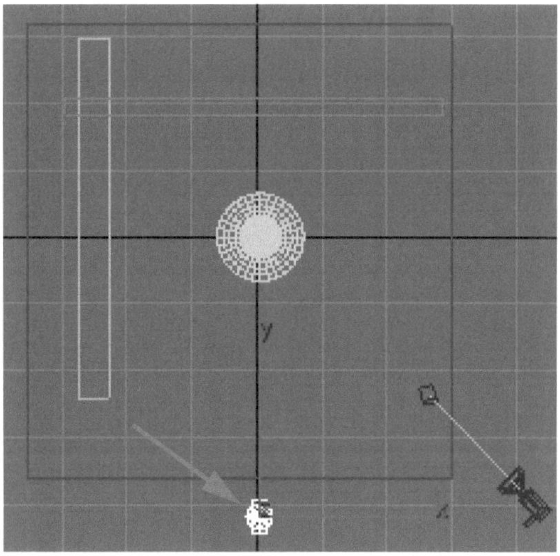

Figure 9–35

7. In the Command Panel, name this light as **Light Front**. Press <Esc> to exit the light creation tool (verify that Arnold Light is not highlighted in blue).
8. Activate the **Camera** viewport and render it. Note that the rendering is completely dark (black).
9. In the Scene Explorer, select **Light Top**. In the *Left* viewport, note that it is located at the bottom of the candle holder and there is a small vertical line below the light object (as shown in Figure 9–36), which indicates that the direction of the light is pointing below the countertop.

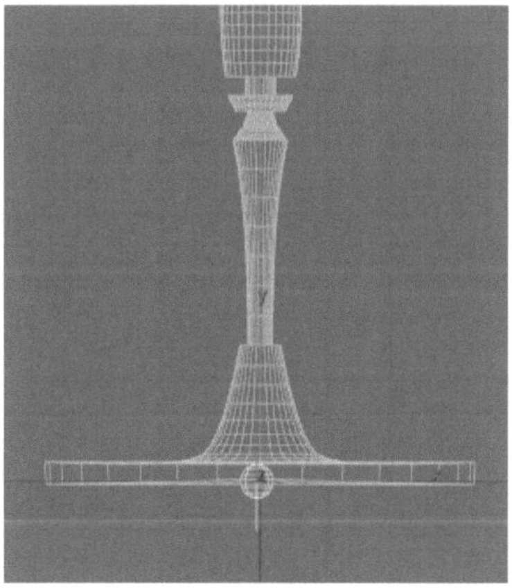

Figure 9–36

10. With the **Light Top** selected, select  (Select and Move). In the Status Bar, enter **500.0** in the *Z Transform Type* to move the light up.
11. In the Render Frame Window, expand the *Viewport* drop-down list and select **Quad4 - Camera 01**. Select  such that it is highlighted in blue, as shown in Figure 9–37. This will render the Camera viewport even if some other viewport is active. Click **Render** and note that the rendering is still all dark.

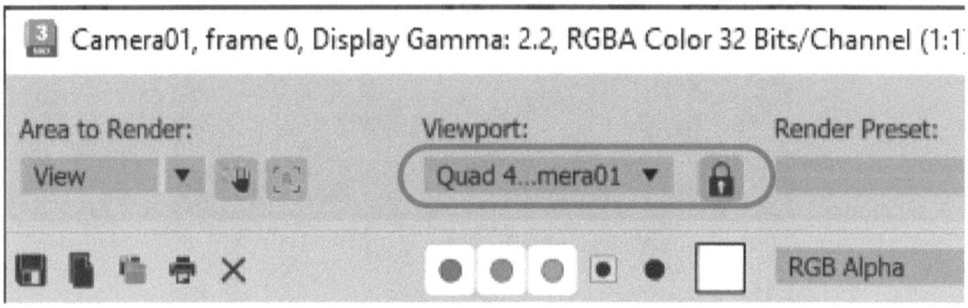

Figure 9–37

Task 2: Modify the light parameters.

1. Select the **Light Top** if required, and in the *Modify* panel (), in the *Color/Intensity* rollout, in the *Intensity* area, note the **Res. Intensity** value. Increase the *Intensity* to **3.0** and the *Exposure* to **10.0**, as shown in Figure 9–38. Note that the **Res. Intensity** value increases.

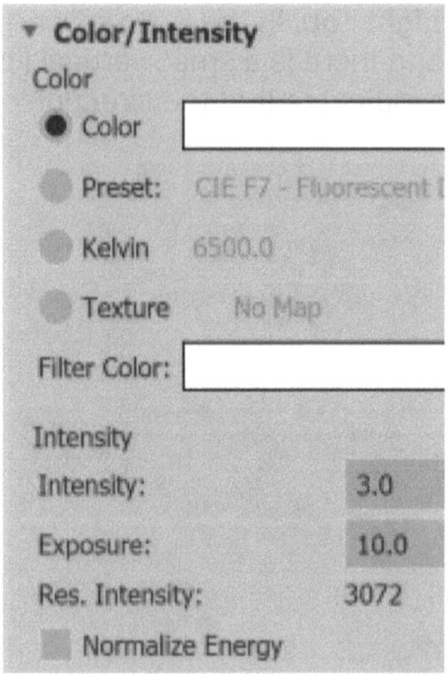

Figure 9–38

2. Render the *Camera* viewport and note that the scene has light, but the candle holder is not very crisp, as shown in Figure 9–39.

Figure 9–39

3. In the Scene Explorer, select **Light Front**. Using  (Select and Move), in the Status Bar, enter **500.0** in the *Z Transform Type* to move the light up. In the *Color/Intensity* rollout, increase both the *Intensity* and the *Exposure* to **10.0**.
4. Render the **Camera** viewport and note that the scene has become brighter and the shadows are being cast on the wall and on the tiles, as shown Figure 9–40.

Figure 9–40

5. Verify that the **Light Front** is still selected (or select it if not). In the *Shadow* rollout, clear the **Cast Shadows** option. Render the **Camera** viewport and note that the shadow on the wall has been removed. Select **Cast Shadows** again.

6. With the **Light Front** still selected, in the *Shape* rollout, note that **Quad** is listed as it is the default type of light created. Open the *Type* drop-down list and select **Point**. In the *Color/ Intensity* rollout, in the *Color* area, select **Kelvin** and note the default value is 6500. Enter a value of **4500.0**. Render the **Camera** viewport and note that a warmth (more yellow) has been added but the shadow is removed.

   - Kelvin changes the color temperature of the light. Reducing the value adds a warm tone, whereas increasing the value adds a cool tone.

7. Change the Type back to **Quad**. Verify that **Cast Shadows** is selected and **Kelvin** is set at **4500.0.** In the *Rendering* rollout, increase the *Samples* to **3**. Render the **Camera** viewport and note that the candle stand and the shadow has become sharper, as shown in Figure 9–41, but the rendering time has increased.

Figure 9–41

8. Save your work as **MyArnold Lights.max**.

End of practice

Practice 9b
Arnold Lighting for an Interior Scene

Practice Objective

- Create Arnold lights and adjust their parameters.
- Add a Skydome Arnold Light to add realism to the scene.

In this practice, you will work with Arnold lighting to be used with the Arnold renderer. You will model interior lighting conditions by creating an Arnold Spot light and array it to position it at various locations around the room. You will adjust the parameters to make the scene realistic. You will add an Arnold Skydome light that simulates light from a sphere or dome above the scene, representing the sky.

You must set the paths to locate the External files and XREFs used in the practice. If you have not done this already, return to Chapter 1 and complete Task 1 to Task 3 in *Practice 1a: Organize Folders and Work with the Interface*. You only have to set the user paths once.

Task 1: Create, array, and instance light objects.

1. Open **Arnold Lighting–Interior.max**.
2. You will add lights in the **Top** viewport such that they point toward the floor. Maximize the **Top** viewport.
3. Zoom into the foyer area (leftmost area). Verify that the **Wireframe Override** is selected in the *Per-View Preference* label.

4. In the *Create* panel (), click  (Lights). In the drop-down list, select **Arnold**. In the *Object Type* rollout, click **Arnold Light**. In the *General* rollout, verify that **Light Properties** is selected and in the *Shape* rollout, expand the *Type* drop-down list and select **Spot**, as shown in Figure 9–42.

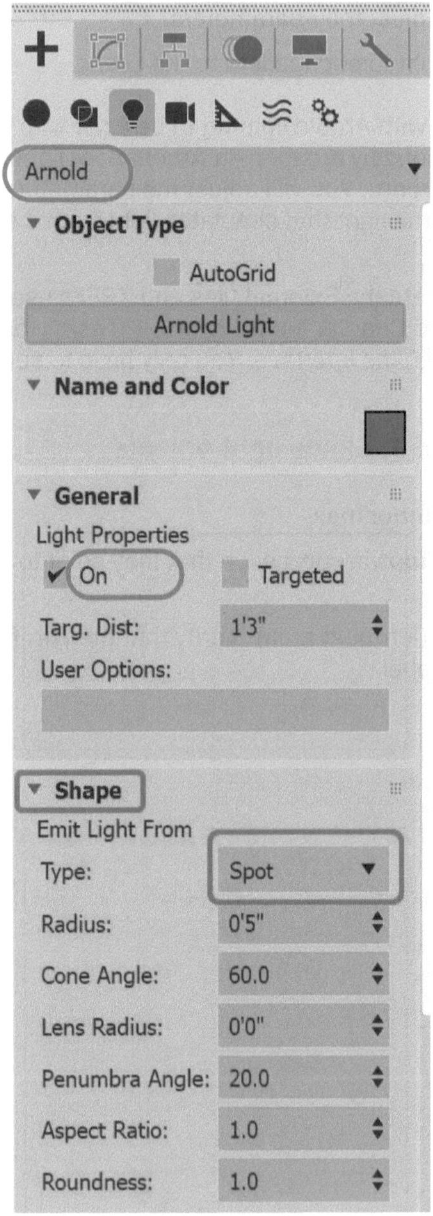

Figure 9–42

5. Note the small yellow circles that represent the openings for recessed lighting. Click near the approximate center of the upper left yellow circle. A free spotlight is added at that location, as shown in Figure 9–43. You will position it accurately in the next step.

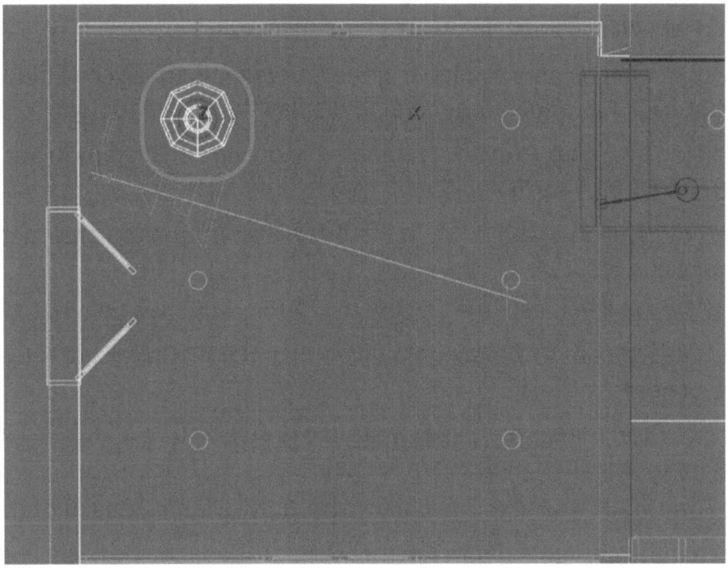

Figure 9–43

6. With the light object still selected, click (Select and Move).

7. In the Status Bar, set the (Absolute Mode Transform Type-In). Set the following, as shown in Figure 9–44, and press <Enter>:

   - *X*: **84'7"**
   - *Y*: **126'10"**
   - *Z*: **9'11"**

Figure 9–44

In addition to placing the light at the exact center of the recessed fixture, it places the light at a height of 9'11", which is 1" below the ceiling height.

8. With the light object selected, in the Command Panel, select the *Modify* panel ( ) and name the light **Ceiling Downlight 00**.

9. Note that there are six light openings in the foyer area. They are 12' apart along the world X-direction and 6' apart along the world Y-direction. The exact coordinates were determined using the **Measure** tool in the **Utilities** Command Panel. You will use the **Array** command to locate these light objects at the center of the circles representing the recessed fixtures. With the light selected, click **Tools>Array** in the menu bar.
   - The **Array** command is also available in the *Extras* toolbar, which is hidden by default. Use the right-click Interface Item menu to display the *Extras* toolbar.
10. In the *Array* dialog box, click **Preview** to enable the previewed display in the scene and enter the following values, as shown in Figure 9–45:
    - For the first dimension of the array, in the *Array Transformation* area, set the *X Incremental* value to **12'0"**.
    - In the *Array Dimensions* area, set *1D Count* to **2** to create two columns of lights.
    - Select **2D**, set *2D Count* to **3,** and in the *Incremental Row Offset, set Y* to **-6'0"** to create three rows of lights.
    - In the *Type of Object* area, verify that **Instance** is selected so that the parameters of all the lights can be adjusted at the same time.
    - Note that *Total in Array* is automatically set to **6** (two lights in each of the three rows).
    - Also note that the six lights display in the viewport because **Preview** is selected.

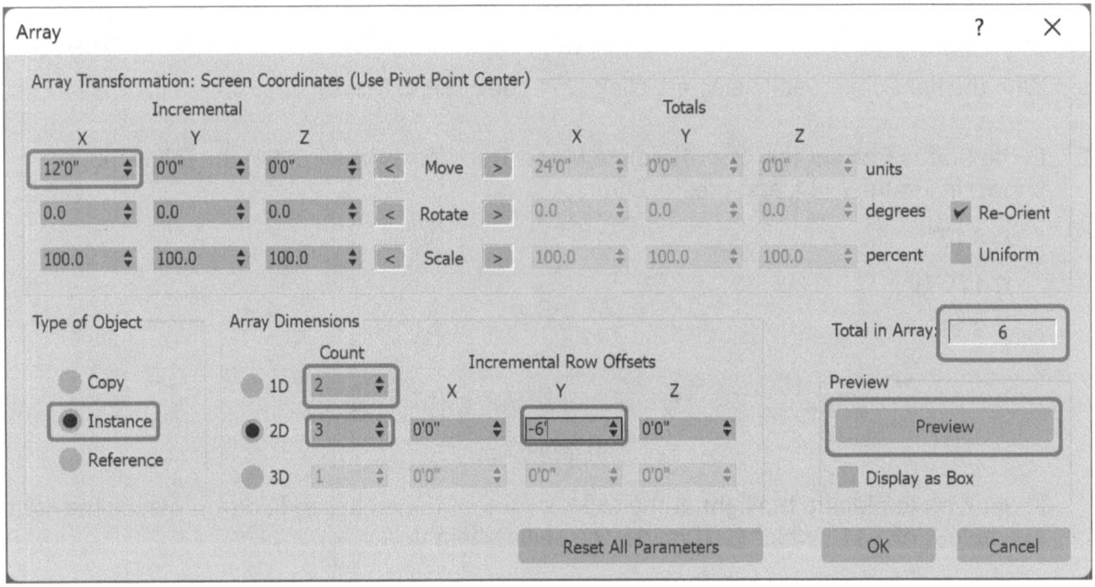

Figure 9–45

11. Verify that the lights preview in the correct positions (as shown in Figure 9–46) and click **OK** in the dialog box.

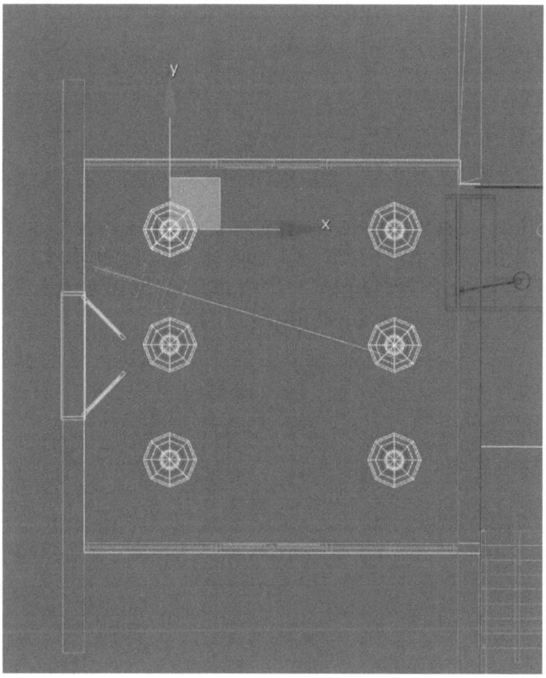

Figure 9–46

12. In the Scene Explorer, click  (Display None) and  (Display Lights). Note that the software has automatically incremented the name by 1.
13. Select **Ceiling Downlight 001** and note that in the viewport, the light in the upper right corner in foyer is selected. Using  (Select and Move) and holding <Shift>, drag along the Transform gizmo's X-axis to locate the light over the desk area, in the approximate center of the yellow circle provided, as shown in Figure 9–47. In the *Clone Options* dialog box, select **Instance** and click **OK**.

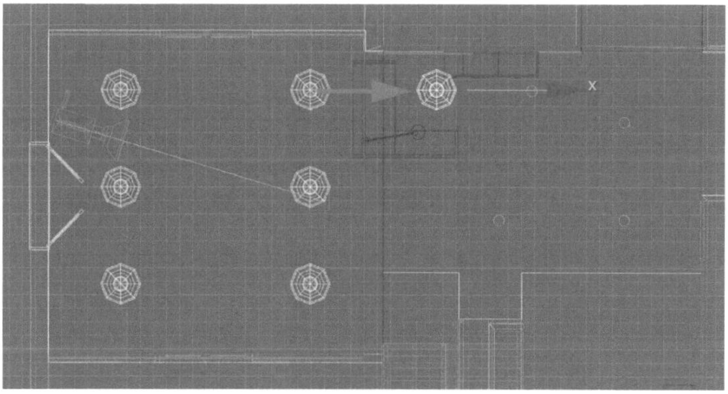

Figure 9–47

14. With the light still selected, in the Status Bar, set the *X* value to **104'7"** and ensure that the *Y* value is set to **126'10"** and the *Z* value is set to **9'11"**, as shown in Figure 9–48.

Figure 9–48

15. Continue to <Shift> + click and drag to instance the remainder of the Ceiling Downlights, to the yellow circles provided for the locations of the recessed lighting, as shown in Figure 9–49. In the interest of time, approximate their positions. You should have 14 lights with the last one named as **Ceiling Downlight 013**.

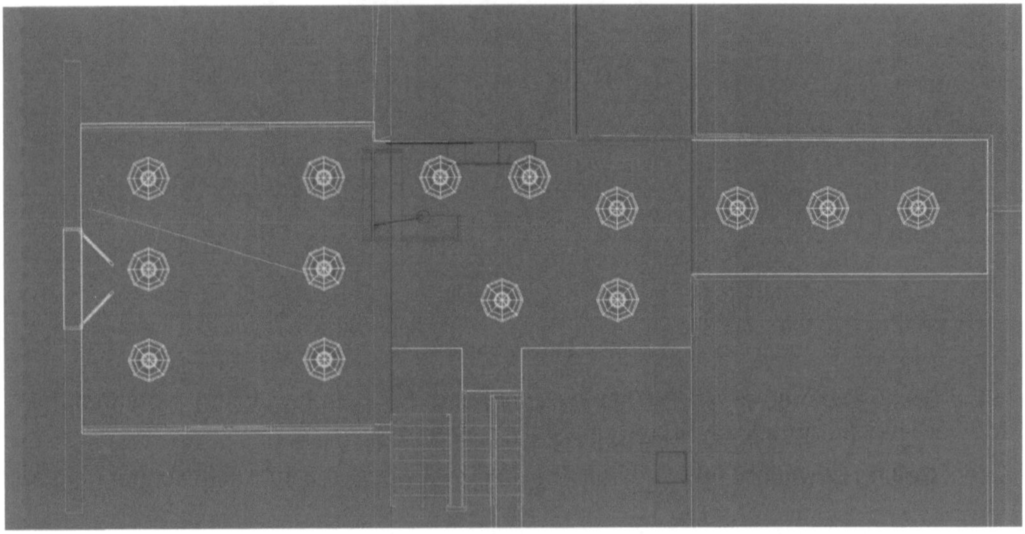

Figure 9–49

Task 2: Adjust Arnold light parameters.

In Task 1, you made instances of each of the lights so that their parameters can be adjusted together. You will now adjust lighting levels through the light object parameters.

1. Select **Rendering>Exposure Control**. In the *Environment and Effects* dialog box, in the *Exposure Control* rollout, select **Physical Camera Exposure Control**. In the *Physical Camera Exposure Control* rollout, change the *EV Compensation for Physical Cameras*: to **-2.0 EV**, as shown in Figure 9–50. Close the *Environments and Effects* dialog box.

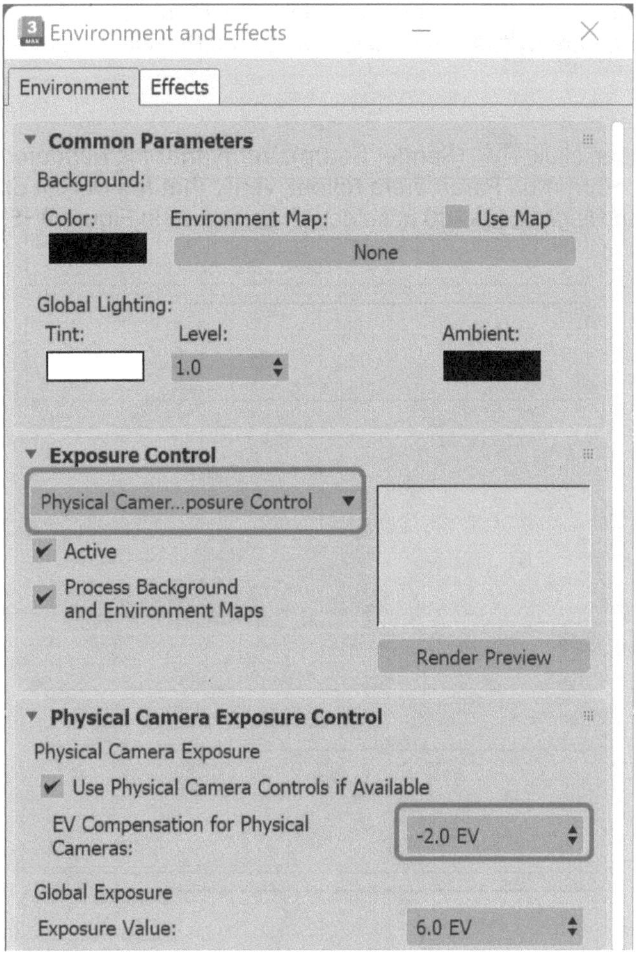

Figure 9–50

2. Select any of the instanced lights. In the Command Panel, verify that the *Modify* panel () is open and that the **Ceiling Downlight** (any number) name displays (i.e., selected). In the General rollout>*Light Properties Parameters* area, set the *Targ. Dist* to **9'11"**, and press <Enter>, as shown in Figure 9–51.

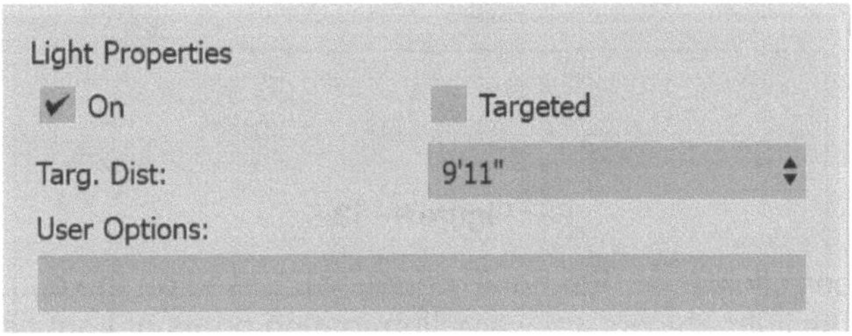

Figure 9–51

3. Change to the **Camera - Lobby1** view by clicking the **[Top]** *Point of View* label and selecting **Cameras>Camera - Lobby1**. Additionally, change the *Per-View Preference* label to **Default Shading**.

4. In the Main Toolbar, click  (Render Setup). Verify that the *Renderer* is set to **Arnold**. In the *Common* tab>*Common Parameters* rollout, verify that the *Output Size* is set to **Custom**, and for *Width and Height* **640x480** is selected, as shown in Figure 9–52. Close the dialog box.

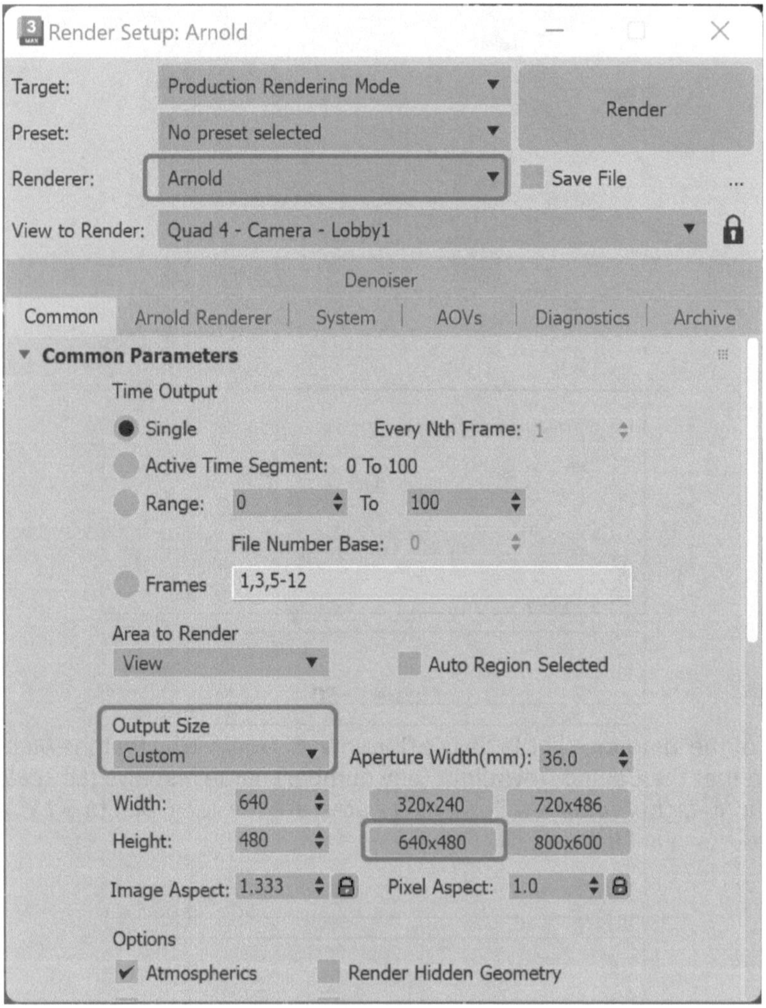

Figure 9–52

5. In the Main Toolbar, click  (Render Production). Based on the current hotspot and falloff values of the light objects, they are illuminating pools of light on the floor, as shown in Figure 9–53.

Figure 9–53

- The **Layer:VIZ-1-Ceiling Lights** object is formed from extruded circles representing the openings for your recessed lighting. They have been assigned a self-illuminated material to make the openings display brightly lit. The light objects that you added to the scene do not render.
- The brightness of your rendering might vary as it is dependent on your computer settings.

6. In the viewport, select one of the instanced lights, if not already selected (Any Ceiling Downlight name should be displayed in the *Modify* panel). In the *Shape* parameters rollout, set the *Penumbra Angle* to **20.0** (as shown in Figure 9–54) and press <Enter>.

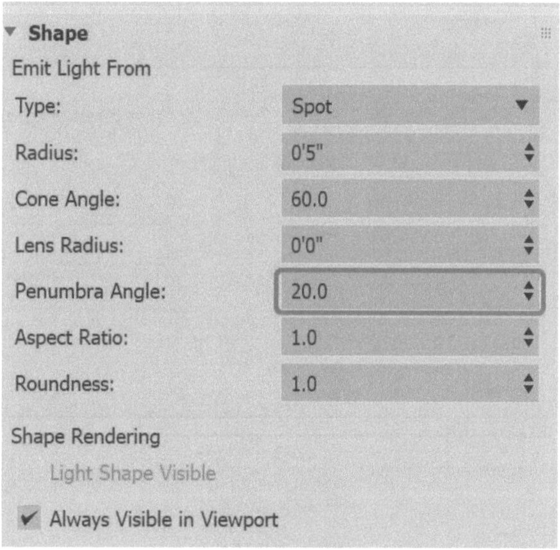

Figure 9–54

7. Render the scene. The illumination now spreads out but the ceiling is still dark, as shown in Figure 9–55. Leave the Rendered Frame Window open.

   - As you need to change some of the parameters and render again, you can leave the Rendered Frame Window open because it is a modeless dialog box. After changing a parameter, render the viewport again from the window itself.

Figure 9–55

8. In the viewport, select one of the instanced lights, if not already selected (Any Ceiling Downlight name should be displayed in the *Modify* panel). In the *Color/Intensity* parameters rollout, set the *Exposure* to **10**, as shown in Figure 9–56.

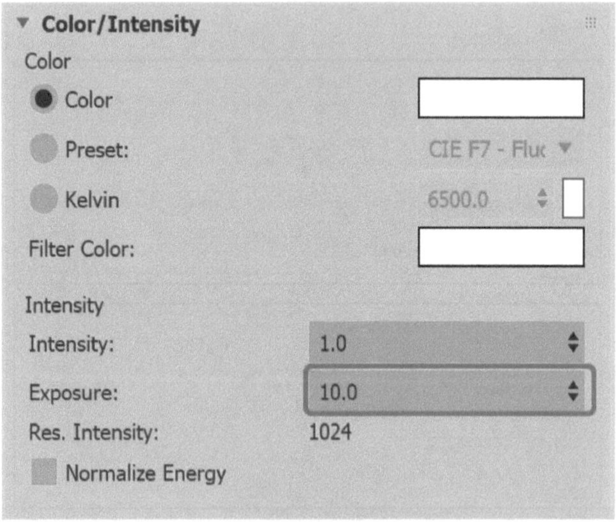

Figure 9–56

9. Click **Render**. The ceiling area is lighter, as shown in Figure 9–57.

Figure 9–57

Task 3: Add Interior/Exterior lighting.

Change the Background color to brighten the area.

1. To add a background color, use the *Environment and Effects* dialog box by selecting *Rendering>Environment* in the menu bar.
2. In the *Environment* tab>*Common Parameters* rollout>*Global Lighting* area, select the **Background** color swatch, as shown in Figure 9–58.

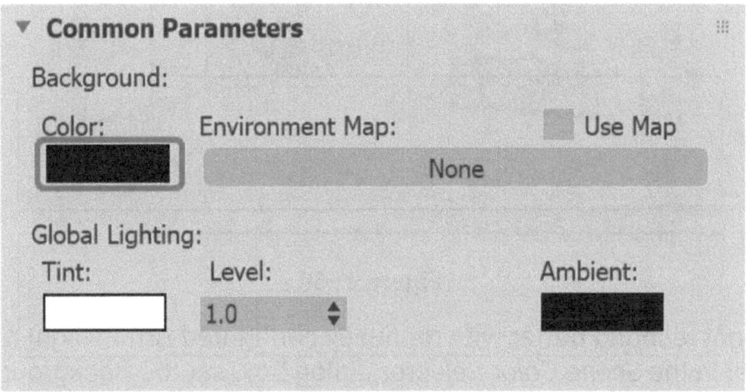

Figure 9–58

3. In the *Scene Color Selector* dialog box, change the *Scene Value* to **1**, as shown in Figure 9–59, and press <Enter> (Click the **Scene** button to activate the *Value* edit box.). Leave both the *Environment and Effects* dialog box and *Scene Color Selector* dialog box open.

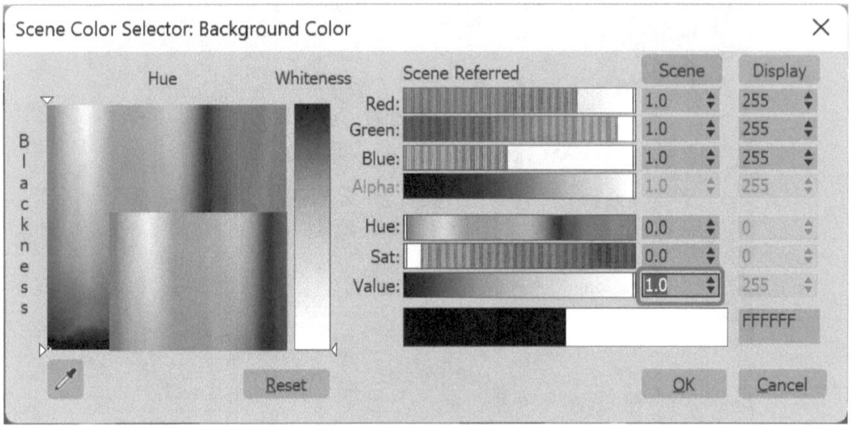

Figure 9–59

4. Render the scene. In this rendering, many areas have become lighter. The scene is overall brighter but the background color passing through the window is too bright, as shown in Figure 9–60.

Figure 9–60

5. This scene might respond better with manually configured Arnold light rather than the global settings. In the *Scene Color Selector* dialog box, set the Background color *Value* to **0** and press <Enter>. Close both the dialog boxes.

6. Change to the **Top** view by clicking the **[Camera - Lobby1]** *Point of View* label and selecting **Camera - Lobby1**.

7. In the *Create* panel (), click  (Lights). In the drop-down list, select **Arnold**, and in the *Object Type* rollout, click **Arnold Light**. In the *Shape* rollout, expand the *Type* drop-down and select **Skydome** as shown in Figure 9–61. Verify that the *Portal Mode* is set to **Interior Only**.

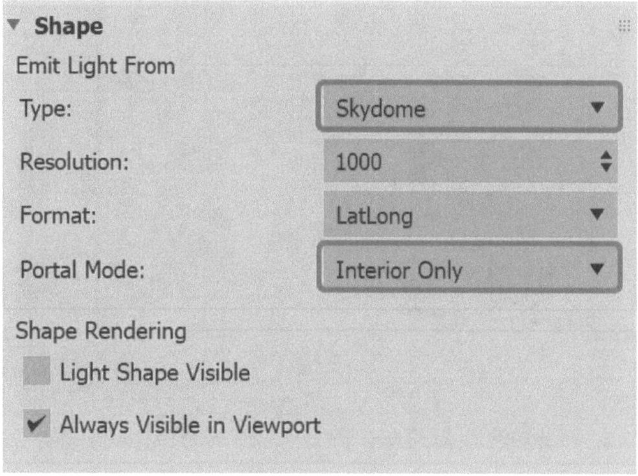

Figure 9–61

8. Place the light in the foyer area as shown in Figure 9–62. The exact location of the light is not needed. Name the light **SkyDome**.
   - Skydome light simulates light from a sphere or dome above the scene, representing the sky. You can also use textures and use high dynamic range (HDR) images to perform image-based environment lighting.

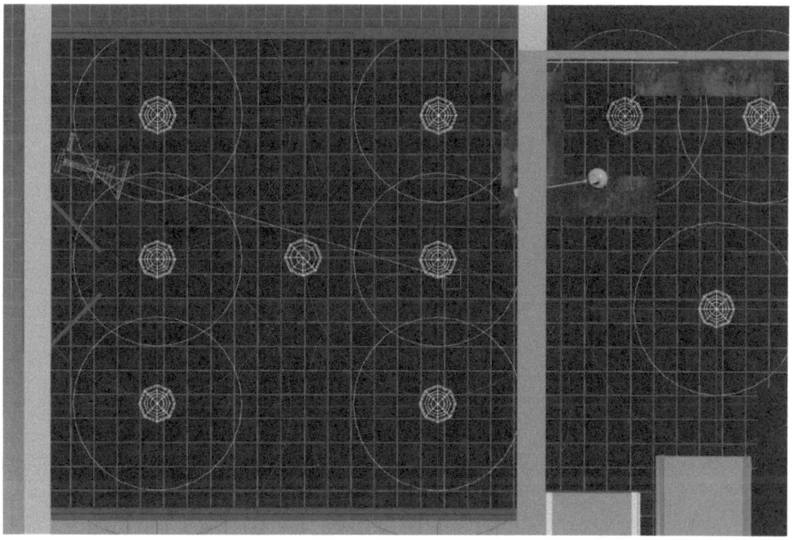

Figure 9–62

9. Change back to the **Camera – Lobby1** view. Click **Render**. The scene now is lighter, and the light passing through the windows looks more natural, as shown in Figure 9–63.

Figure 9–63

10. Save your work as **MyStandard Lighting – Interior.max**.

End of practice

Chapter Review Questions

1. Which is the default shape type for Arnold lights?
    a. Point
    b. Spot
    c. Quad
    d. Photometric

2. In the *Rendering* rollout what does increasing the *Samples* value do?
    a. Increases the noise in shadow areas.
    b. Reduces the noise in shadow areas.
    c. Increases the intensity in multiple jumps.
    d. Reduces the render time.

3. Which Arnold light type can be used to easily create a neon lighting or a car light motion trail effect?
    a. Skydome
    b. Mesh
    c. Distant
    d. Cylinder

4. Which of the following parameters in the Arnold light source is an Intensity multiplier?
    a. Exposure
    b. Samples
    c. Volume Samples
    d. Diffuse

5. Which Arnold light type can be used with high dynamic range (HDR) images to create image-based environment lighting?
   a. Photometric
   b. Disk
   c. Mesh
   d. Skydome

Command Summary

Button	Command	Location
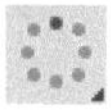	**Array**	• **Extras toolbar** • **Tools:** Array
	**Lights**	• **Command Panel:** *Create* panel • **Create:** Lights
	**Render Production**	• **Main Toolbar** • ***Rendering:*** Render

Chapter

10

Exposure Control, Daylight, and Rendering

The Autodesk® 3ds Max® software is set so that the default rendering options provide excellent rendering results; however, understanding the different rendering options and presets that you can use to customize and save rendering settings will help you further control the results obtained in your renderings. Additionally, the use of Sun Positioner in a daytime scene and the use of exposure controls can help to add realism.

Learning Objectives

- Work with various Exposure Control methods and control the method-specific parameters.
- Create Sun Positioner and modify the parameters to enhance the lighting in a scene.
- Set the common options available in all of the renderers.
- Control specific options for the Arnold renderer, Scanline renderer, and ART renderer.
- Create scene states and render pass states using the State Sets feature.
- Set the print resolution, paper size, and other options for a rendering.

10.1 Exposure Control

Lighting, Materials, and Exposure Control are all used together to produce a real-world rendered image.

- **Exposure Control** parameters are a global adjustment used to modulate the output levels and color range of renderings and viewport displays to expected values. The exposure control methods are optional when using the Scanline renderer.
- The Autodesk 3ds Max software can incorporate exposure control in the viewport but is dependant on the driver used. To display exposure control in the viewport and modify it interactively, use the Nitrous or Direct 3D display drivers.
- The Autodesk 3ds Max software calculates real-world illumination values through ART and Arnold. Computer monitors (and printed media) are only able to show a small fraction of the total brightness range visible to your eyes.
- Exposure control enables you to adapt the often large dynamic range (the variation of lighting levels) into the relatively small dynamic range that can be displayed on a computer screen or printed on paper.

Exposure Control Methods

The various exposure control methods are available in the *Environment* tab in the *Environment and Effects* dialog box (**Rendering>Environment** or **Rendering>Exposure Control**). In the *Exposure Control* rollout, select an exposure control method in the drop-down list, as shown in Figure 10–1.

- Exposure Control is used when the **Active** option is enabled.

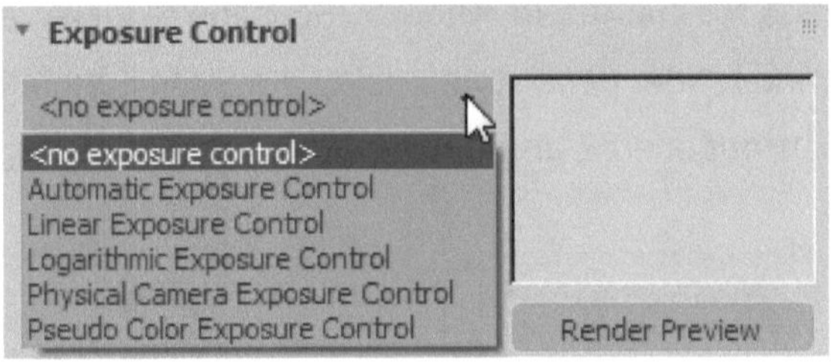

Figure 10–1

- **Automatic Exposure Control:** Attempts to automatically adjust the sample range of lighting levels. It is appropriate for still renderings with very large dynamic ranges. This method can cause flashing when animating, because different frames could be modulated differently.
- **Linear Exposure Control:** Interprets and adjusts the lighting levels linearly, which might provide better results when working with low dynamic ranges (small variations in lighting levels).

- **Logarithmic Exposure Control:** Interprets and adjusts the lighting levels with a logarithmic distribution and provides additional controls that can be used effectively for animations. It enables you to control the *Brightness*, *Contrast*, *Midtones*, and *Color Correction.* Presets automatically adjust the settings, but if a rendering is overly bright or too dark, you can adjust the *Physical scale* setting.
- **Physical Camera Exposure Control:** Interprets and adjusts the exposure value and uses color-response curve to set exposure for physical cameras. This is the recommended exposure control to use with ART and Arnold renderers.
- **Pseudo Color Exposure Control:** Generates a lighting analysis rendering colorized by luminance (light source brightness) or illuminance (the amount of illumination that arrives at a surface). The different colors in the render (shown in Figure 10–2) give a representation of lighting levels, red for overlit areas, blue for underlit areas, and green for good lighting level areas.

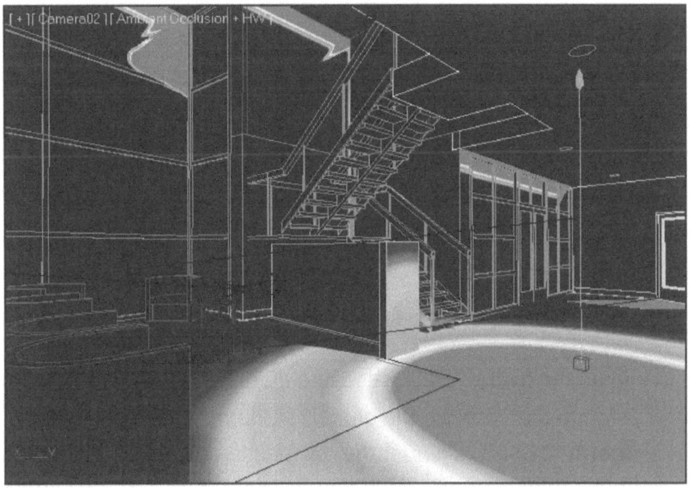

Figure 10–2

Logarithmic Exposure Control Parameters

When **Logarithmic Exposure Control** is selected as the *Exposure Control* method, a corresponding rollout with parameters specific to this method displays, as shown in Figure 10–3.

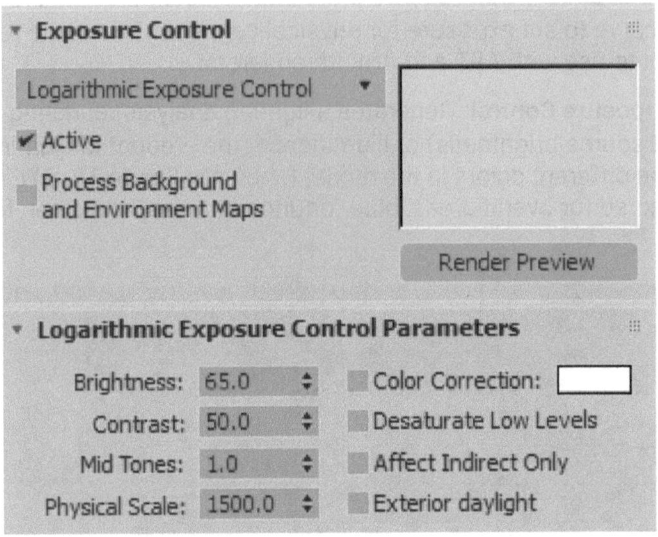

Figure 10–3

Brightness/ Contrast	Adjusts the overall brightness and contrast of the rendered image. • Brightness: Controls the perceived illumination of surfaces. • Contrast: Used to adjust the difference between light and dark portions of the image. Images that look washed out (with only a small difference in brightness levels) often benefit from increasing contrast.
Mid Tones	Enables you to shift the brightness levels of the middle portion of the color range. Increasing the midtones value brightens the middle tones of an image, while lowering the value darkens them.
Physical Scale	Sets the real-world luminous intensity value of standard lights measured in candelas. This value has no effect on scenes that only have Photometric or IES lights.
Color Correction	Enables you to adjust the color caste of an image so that the color in the swatch displays as white in the final rendering. This adjustment takes place automatically in human vision and is manually adjusted in some real-world cameras using balancing.
Desaturate Low Levels	Converts dark colors to shades of gray, simulating what happens to human vision under dim lighting.

Affect Indirect Only	Enables you to apply exposure control only to indirect lighting, not the direct lighting of your light objects. When working with standard lights this is a helpful option that enables you to manipulate the light object's direct illumination separate from the calculated ambient light.
Exterior daylight	Indicates that you are working with outdoor illumination values, which are much higher than is normally used indoors. When rendering with a camera outside in daylight this option is essential to avoid over exposure.

Physical Camera Exposure Control

When working with ART and Arnold rendering workflow, it is recommended to use the **Physical Camera Exposure Control**. When it is selected as the Exposure Control method, a corresponding rollout with parameters specific to this method displays, as shown in Figure 10–4.

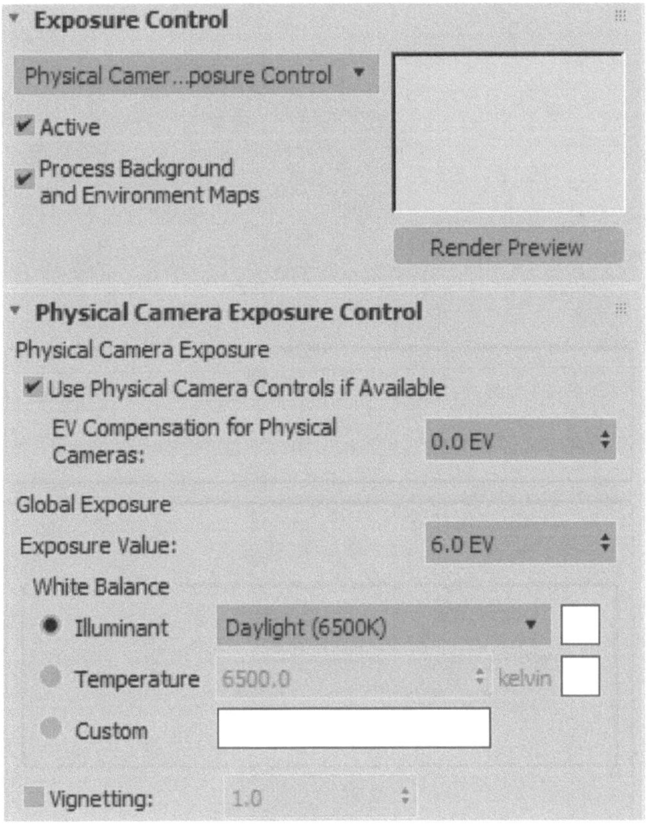

Figure 10–4

Physical Camera Exposure	Controls the settings of a specific physical camera rendering.The *EV Compensation for Physical Cameras* sets the exposure value for the physical camera.
Global Exposure	Controls the settings of all the physical camera renderings. The *Exposure Value* has a default value of 6.0.
Image Control	Enables you to adjust the color response curve for *Highlights*, *Midtones* and *Shadows* which have default values of 0.25, 1.0 and 0.2 respectively.
Physical Scale	Sets the real-world luminous intensity value of non-photometric lights (standard lights). This value has no effect on scenes that have only Photometric or IES lights.

10.2 Daytime Lighting

Lights can be used to illuminate a nighttime interior scene or a scene that does not have openings to allow in daylight. Nighttime exterior scenes can be lit similarly, with outside light sources such as light fixtures and dim fill lights. Both interior and exterior scenes can be lit with specialized light objects during daytime.

Sunlight represents the direct illumination of the sun, as shown in Figure 10–5 (thick parallel arrows). The light that reflects off of the earth's surface and back down from the atmosphere (and the light that diffuses through the atmosphere on overcast days) is represented as skylight. Skylight illuminates a scene as if it were cast down from a hemispherical dome, as shown in Figure 10–5 (smaller, solid white arrows).

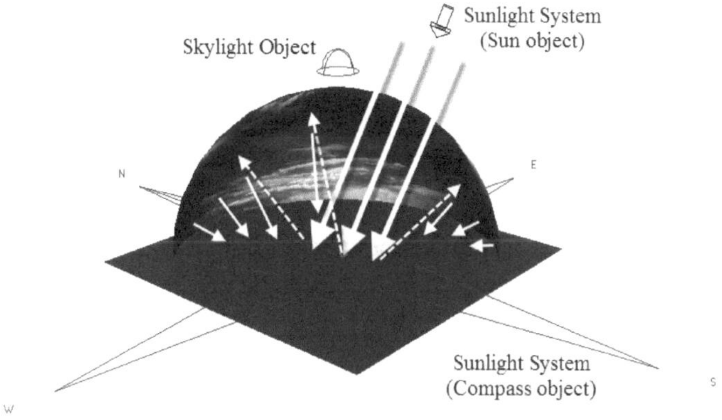

Figure 10–5

In Autodesk 3ds Max, you can create a **Daylight System** using either of the following methods:

- Sun Positioner and Physical Sky
- Sunlight and Skylight systems (legacy system)

Sun Positioner Daylight System

A Sun Positioner enables you to create a light system that provides realistic sunlight with a full sky environment. This system uses a simple and intuitive workflow to create a geographically correct positioning and movement of the sun.

How To: Create a Sun Positioner Object

1. In the *Create* panel (), click  (Lights).
2. In the drop-down list, ensure that the **Photometric** option is selected.

3. Click **Sun Positioner**, as shown in Figure 10–6.

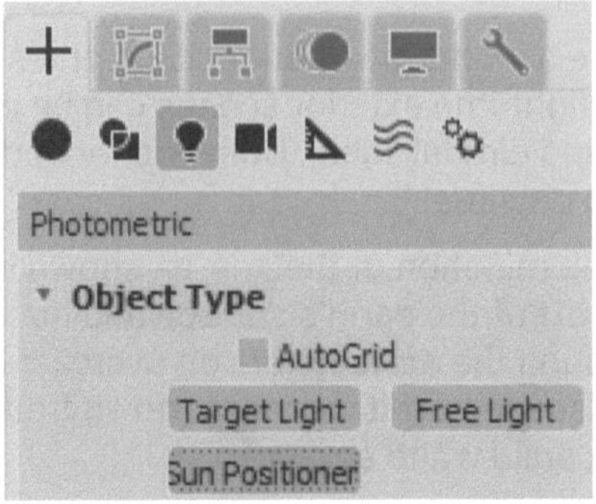

Figure 10–6

- The **Sun Positioner** option enables you to create a compass rose and a light source that mimics the sun. Creating a sun positioner is a three-click process. The first click sets the location and size of the compass rose, as shown on the left in Figure 10–7. The second click sets the orientation of the sun by specifying the cardinal directions (N, S, E, W), as shown on the left in Figure 10–7. The third click sets the distance of the sun, as shown on the right in Figure 10–7. You can modify the settings of the sunlight system using the sun positioner parameters.

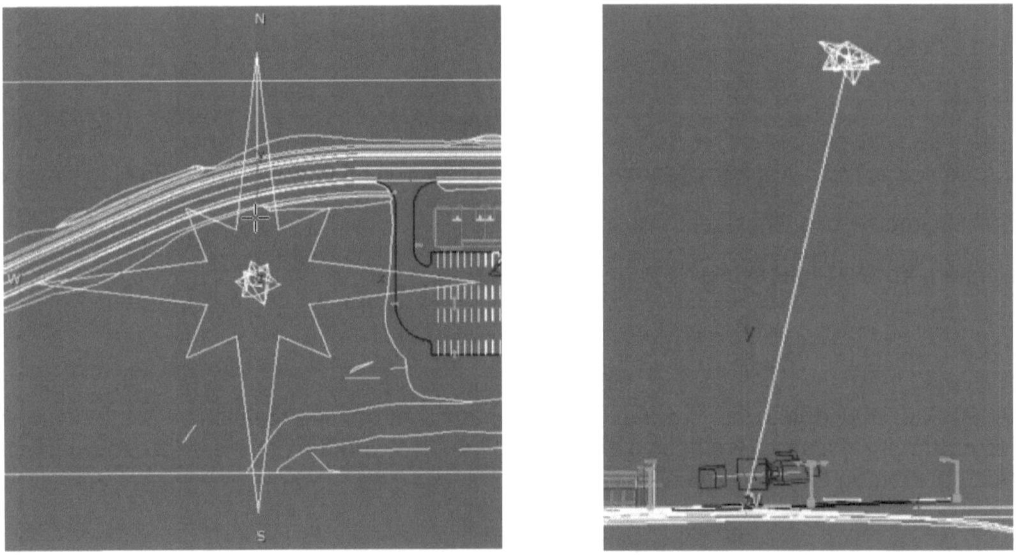

Figure 10–7

- The *Display* rollout (shown in Figure 10–8) enables you to control the display of the *Compass Rose* and set its radius. Using the *North Offset* option, you can set the cardinal direction and place the sun based on the date and time. In the *Sun* area, you can set the distance of the sun from the compass rose.

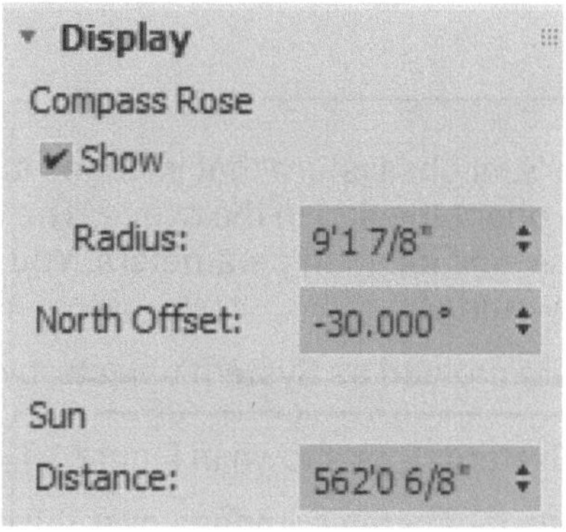

Figure 10–8

- The *Sun Position* rollout (shown in Figure 10–9) enables you to set the position of the sun. The *Date & Time* area enables you to set the time, day, month, and year. You also have the option of using daylight savings time and setting the range of days to be used. The *Location on Earth* area (shown in Figure 10–10) enables you to set the location using a database file, or set the *Latitude* and *Longitude* coordinates.

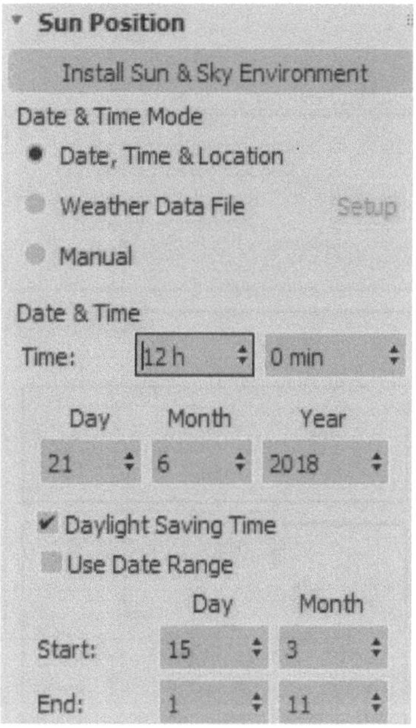

Figure 10–9

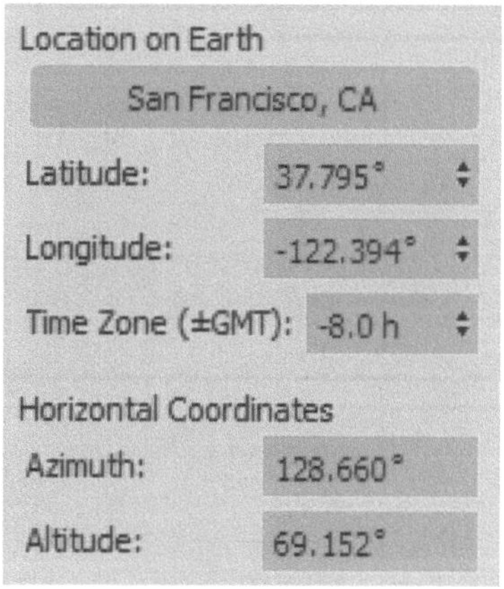

Figure 10–10

Sunlight and Skylight System

The Daylight system can also be created by combining both Sunlight and Skylight systems. This is a legacy system, and the workflow uses five different components to create the Daylight system.

Sunlight System

Sunlight can be modeled with a Sunlight system that includes a sun object (a direct light) and a compass object that is used to orient the sun in the scene. The angle of the sun's light can be controlled through the date, time, and location parameters. You can also animate the position of the sun over time for shadow studies.

Sunlight and **Daylight** objects are created as System objects, by selecting the *Create* panel (+) and clicking (Systems), as shown in Figure 10–11.

When creating a Sunlight system, locate the compass over the center of your site at an approximate ground elevation and control the sun's position using the Control Parameters, as shown in Figure 10–12. Once a sun object has been created, these Control Parameters become available in the Command Panel's *Motion* panel ( ).

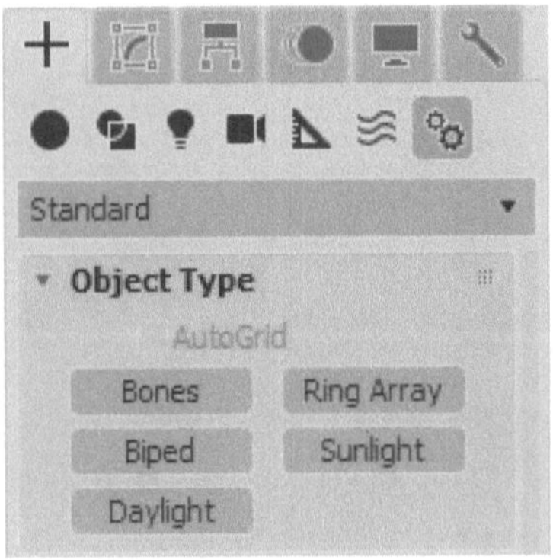

Figure 10–11

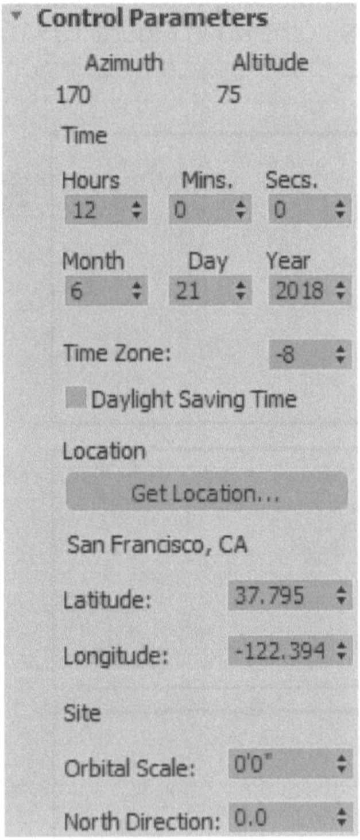

Figure 10–12

- Parameters in the *Time* and *Location* areas enable you to interactively position the sun in the correct location.
- The angle that indicates north in the current coordinate system can be entered in the *North Direction* field. This is used to orient the sunlight to your project geometry.
- The *Orbital Scale* value is the distance from the sun object to the compass (and the ground). The orbital scale should be large enough so that there are no objects behind the sun.

Sun objects are directional lights. Their *Modify* panel () parameters are similar to those for directional lights. To generate shadows correctly, it is sometimes required to clear the **Overshoot** option in *Directional Parameters* rollout and increase the *Hotspot/Beam* value until it encompasses the entire site.

Skylight System

A Skylight object is not part of the Sunlight system, and is an entirely separate object. With a standard lighting approach, the illumination of a skylight object is not controlled by the date, time, or location settings of the sunlight system. The skylight's brightness (multiplier) parameter can be set manually and animated to change over time.

To create a **Skylight** object as a standard light object, in the *Create* panel (), click  (Lights), and then click **Standard**, as shown in Figure 10–13. Skylight objects have special controls available in the *Skylight Parameters* rollout, as shown in Figure 10–14.

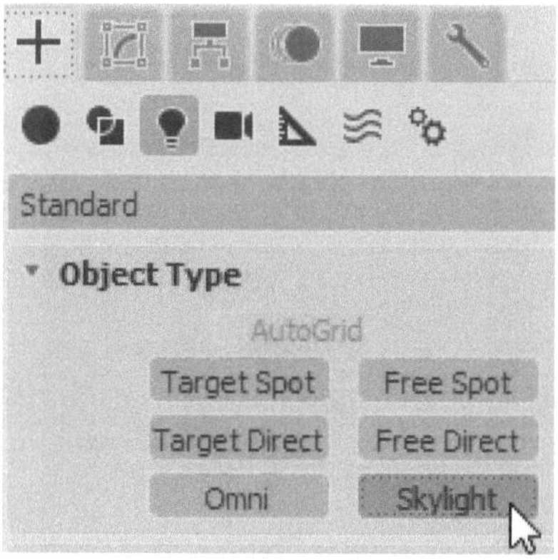

Figure 10–13

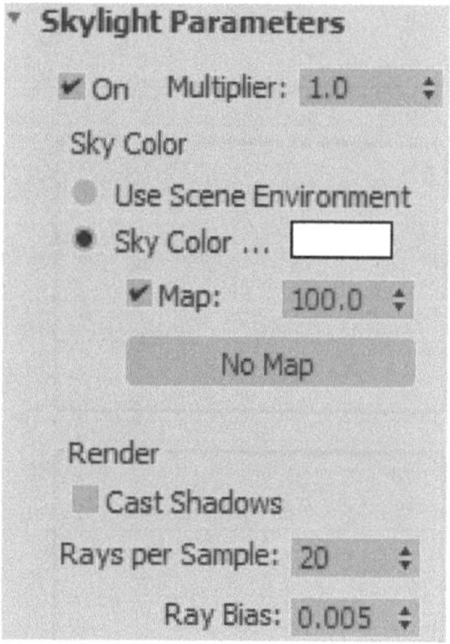

Figure 10–14

- The light cast from skylights can be colored based on the scene environment map. The **Use Scene Environment** option uses the environment that has been set up in the *Environment* tab in the *Environment and Effects* dialog box (**Rendering>Environment**).

- The **Sky Color** option enables you to use a single color or a map and it comes with the illumination capabilities in all renderers.

Skylight creates complex shadows that can be realistic and enhance scenes lit with natural lighting. The following settings help control the overall quality (and calculation time) of sky shadows:

Rays per Sample	The number of illuminated rays collected at each sampling point. Lower values result in faster renderings but grainier shadows. Set this value low for test renderings but increase it for the final product (use 15 for still images, but animations might need as much as 20 or 30 to avoid flickering).
Ray Bias	This is the minimum distance between two points for one to cast sky shadows on the other. Increasing this value in scenes with a lot of small detail might speed up rendering time without significantly lowering rendering quality.

Practice 10a
Lighting with Sun Positioner

Practice Objective

- Create a Daylight system using Sun Positioner for Arnold renderer.

In this practice, you will create an Sun Positioner daylight system and modify the parameters to get a realistic rendering of the scene.

You must set the paths to locate the External files and XREFs used in the practice. If you have not done this already, return to Chapter 1 and complete Task 1 to Task 3 in *Practice 1a: Organize Folders and Work with the Interface*. You only have to set the user paths once.

1. Open **Retail Exterior-Daylight.max**.

2. In the Main Toolbar, click  (Render Setup) or select **Rendering>Render Setup** to open the *Render Setup* dialog box. In the upper area of the dialog box, in the *Renderer* drop-down list, verify that **Arnold** is set as the renderer, as shown in Figure 10–15. In the *Common* tab>*Common Parameters* rollout>*Output Size* area, select **640x480**. Close the *Render Setup* dialog box.

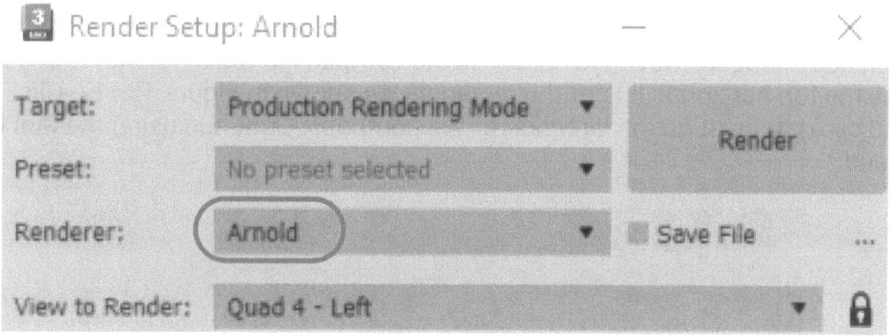

Figure 10–15

3. Maximize the **Top** viewport (the upper right viewport) and zoom to the extents of the scene. Note that the scene should display a white layout rectangle around the scene objects.

4. In the *Create* panel (), click  (Lights). In the *Object Type* rollout, click **Sun Positioner**, as shown in Figure 10–16.

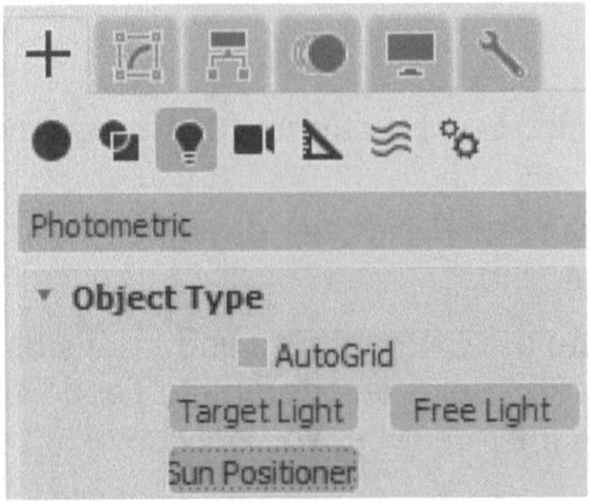

Figure 10–16

5. Creating a sun positioner is a three-click process. The first click sets the location and size of the compass rose. Near the center of the **Top** viewport, click, hold, and drag out to create a compass rose similar to the size shown in Figure 10–17. The north and south points of the compass should approximately touch the top and bottom horizontal lines of the white layout area rectangle. Release the mouse button to complete the creation. You are still in the **Sun Positioner** command.
6. The second click sets the direction of the compass rose. Verify that the North (N) (if the direction has changed, move the cursor till the compass is North facing) is still pointing towards the top horizontal line of the rectangle, as shown in Figure 10–17. Click again (second click) to position the direction of the compass. Continue using the **Sun Positioner** command.

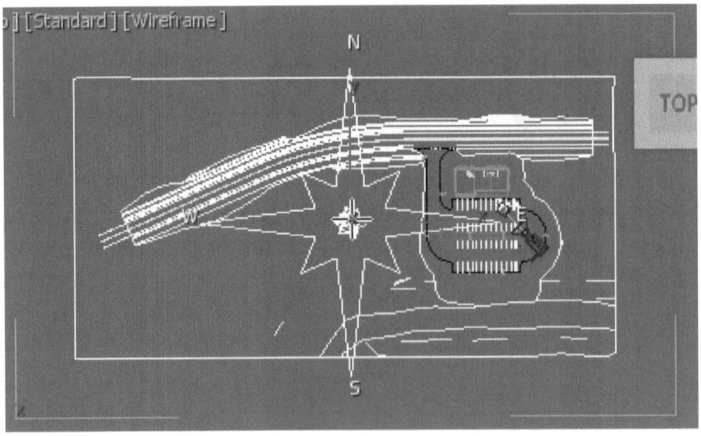

Figure 10–17

7. The third click sets the distance of the sun. Move the cursor and note that the sun object is attached to it and you are still in the **Sun Positioner** command (do not click). Press <L> to change to a **Left** view. Move the cursor up and down to graphically set the initial orbital scale of the sun object. Click (third click) when the sun is at a position similar to that shown in Figure 10–18.
   - You will set the exact distance in the *Parameters* area of the Command Panel.

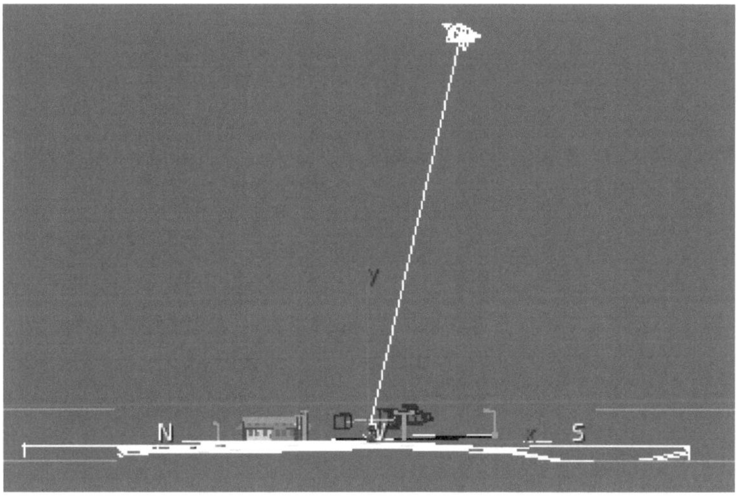

Figure 10–18

8. Sun objects should be placed back from the scene for the shadows to be generated correctly. With the Sun positioner object still selected, in the *Modify* panel (), in the *Display* rollout, in the *Compass Rose* area, do the following as shown in Figure 10–19:
   - Set the *Radius* to **7'0".**
   - Verify that the *North Offset* is set at **0.0.**
   - In the *Sun* area, set the *Distance* to **300'0".**

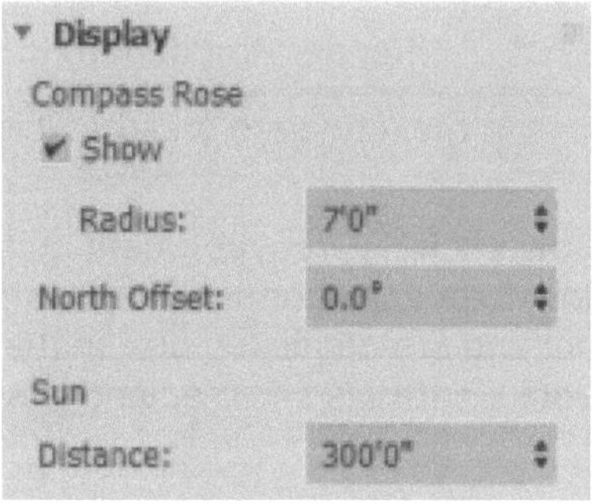

Figure 10–19

9. In the *Sun Position* rollout, in the *Location on Earth* area, click the default **San Francisco, CA** location. In the *Geographic Location* dialog box, select **Portland, ME** and click **OK**. Note the changes in *Latitude* and *Longitude*. The *Time Zone* is set to **-5.0 h**, as shown in Figure 10–20.
10. In the *Date & Time* area, set the following, as shown in Figure 10–21:
    - *Time:* **7 h** and **0 min**
    - *Day:* **21**
    - *Month:* **3**
    - *Year:* **2024**

    Note in the viewport, the location of the sun object changes as it is based on the time and date.

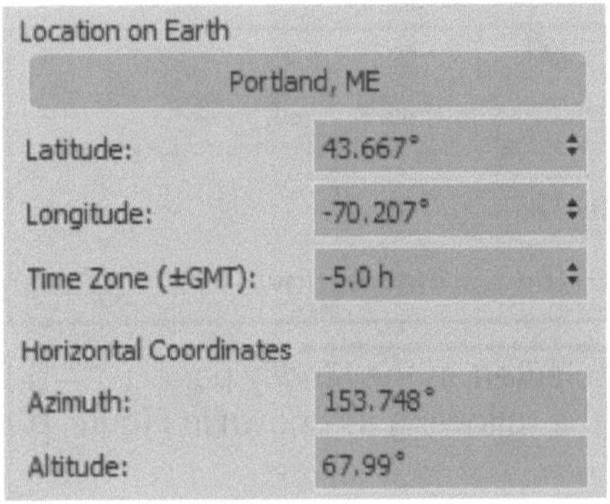

Figure 10–20

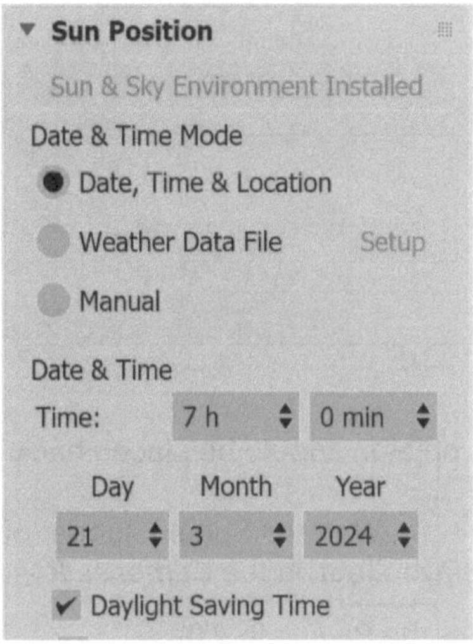

Figure 10–21

11. Change to the four viewports display and activate the **Camera - Southeast View** viewport (the upper left viewport). Click  (Render Production) to render the view.
    - Note that not much displays in the rendering and that it is completely washed out.
12. In the Rendered Frame Window, click  (Environment and Effects (Exposure Controls)). Alternatively, select **Rendering>Exposure Control** to open the *Environment and Effects* dialog box. In the *Environment and Effects* dialog box, in the *Exposure Control* rollout, note that **Physical Camera Exposure Control** is selected and is set to **Active**.

13. In the *Physical Camera Exposure Control* rollout, in the *Physical Camera Exposure* area, set the *EV Compensation for Physical Camera* to **-5.0**. In the *Exposure Control* rollout, click **Render Preview** and note the dim light and an early morning sky, as shown in Figure 10–22. Close the dialog box.

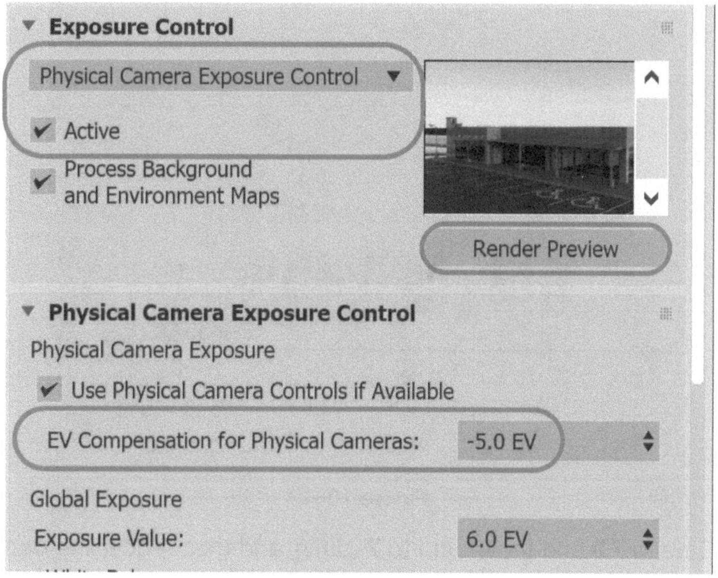

Figure 10–22

14. In the Rendered Frame Window, click **Render**. Note the lighting is based on **7 a.m** in the month of **March**, as shown Figure 10–23.

Figure 10–23

15. In the Scene Explorer, select the **Sun Positioner**. In the *Modify* panel, *Sun Position* rollout> *Date & Time* area, change the *Time* to **12 h** and render the **Camera** viewport again. Note the bright light of a mid-day sky as the rendering is set for 12 noon in the month of March. Note the bright sunlight and note where the shadows are at this time, shown Figure 10–24.

Figure 10–24

16. Change the *Time* to **7 h** and the *Month* to **7** (July), and then render the **Camera** viewport again. Note the bright morning sky and long shadows in the month of July, as shown Figure 10–25.

Figure 10–25

17. Save your work as **MyDaylight.max**.

End of practice

10.3 Rendering Options

You can set, modify, and change the different options in the *Render Setup* dialog box, as shown in Figure 10–26. The various ways to open the *Render Setup* dialog box are as follows:

- Select **Rendering>Render Setup**.
- Press <F10>.
- In the Main Toolbar, click  (Render Setup).
- In the Rendered Frame Window, click  (Render Setup).

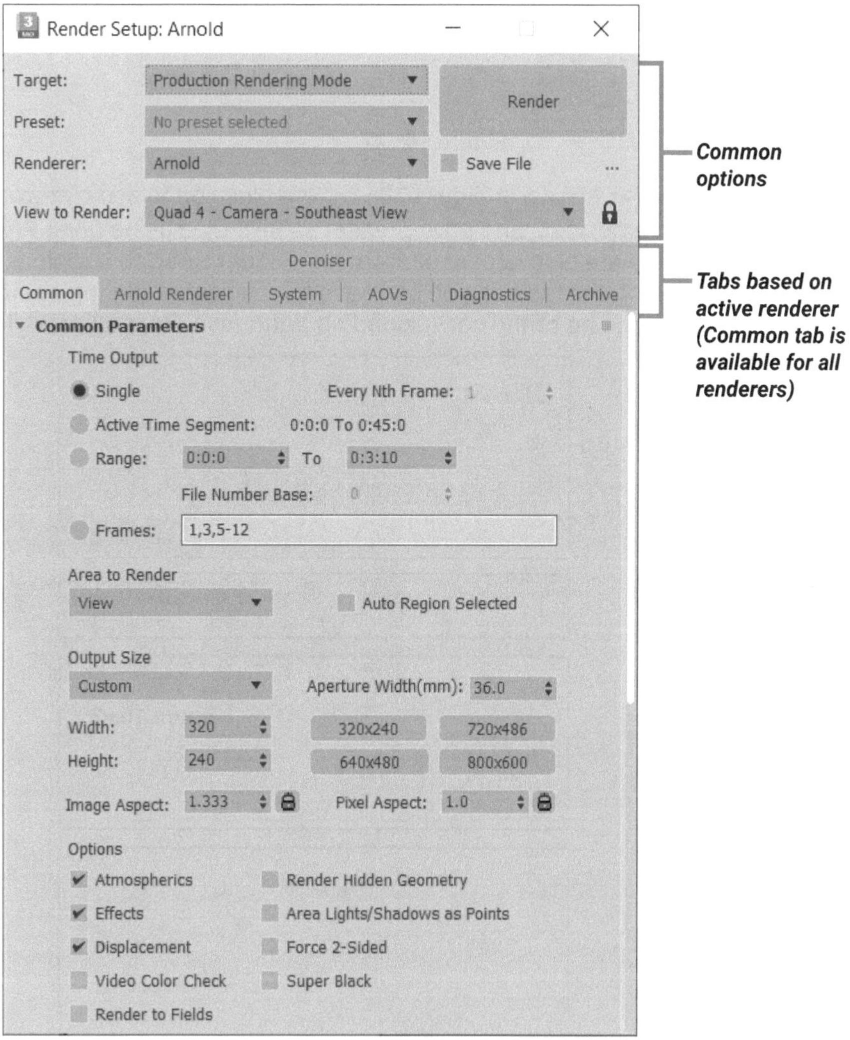

Figure 10–26

Common Options

Common options are available for all the renderers and are located at the top of the dialog box. These include:

- The *Target* drop-down list enables you to select the rendering options, such as Production, Iterative, A360 Cloud, etc., as shown in Figure 10–27.

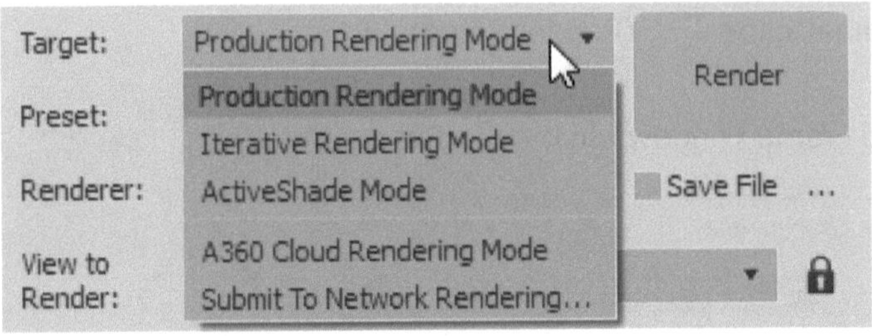

Figure 10–27

- The *Preset* drop-down list (as shown in Figure 10–28) enables you to swap between the available preset files or create, load, and save presets as RPS files using **Load Preset** and **Save Preset**. These presets are also accessed from the Render Shortcuts toolbar, as shown in Figure 10–29. When using the toolbar, you can save the current rendering settings as preset A, B, or C by selecting one of the corresponding buttons in the toolbar while holding <Shift>.

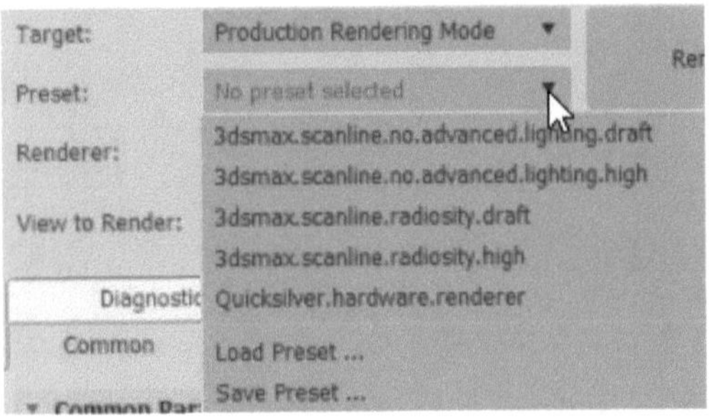

Figure 10–28

Figure 10–29

- The *Renderer* drop-down list enables you to select the required rendering system, as shown in Figure 10–30.

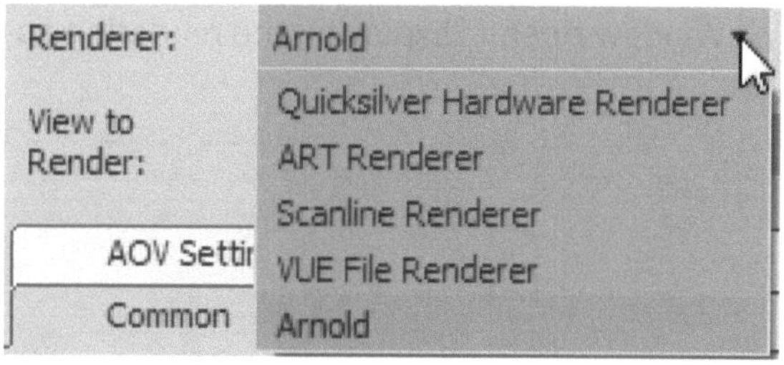

Figure 10–30

- You can also select the rendering system in the *Assign Renderer* rollout in the *Common* tab of the dialog box.
- The tabs in the *Render Setup* dialog box change according to the active renderer.

The various rendering systems are listed below:

Quicksilver Hardware Renderer	Uses the system's graphics hardware (GPU) to quickly produce high-quality images. In order to use this renderer your graphics hardware must support Shader Model 3.0 (SM3.0) or a later version.
ART Renderer	A physically based renderer that uses the CPU only and renders the scene quickly.
Scanline Renderer	Intended to be used with both standard lighting (local illumination) and radiosity-based lighting.
VUE File Renderer	A legacy functionality that is not a graphical renderer. It uses ASCII text files to describe the position and transformation of objects, lighting, etc.
Arnold Renderer	A separate lighting and rendering system that accurately renders ray tracing light paths to create physically based renderings.

- Clicking **Render** in the *Render Setup* dialog box or clicking  (Render Production) in the Main Toolbar, renders the active viewport based on the settings in the *Render Setup* dialog box. A Rendered Frame Window opens, displaying the rendering as it is being calculated, as shown in Figure 10–31.

Figure 10–31

- A *Rendering* dialog box also opens displaying the status of the rendering along with other information, as shown in Figure 10–32. Once the *Rendering* dialog box closes, it indicates that the rendering is complete. You can also abort the rendering process by clicking **Cancel**.

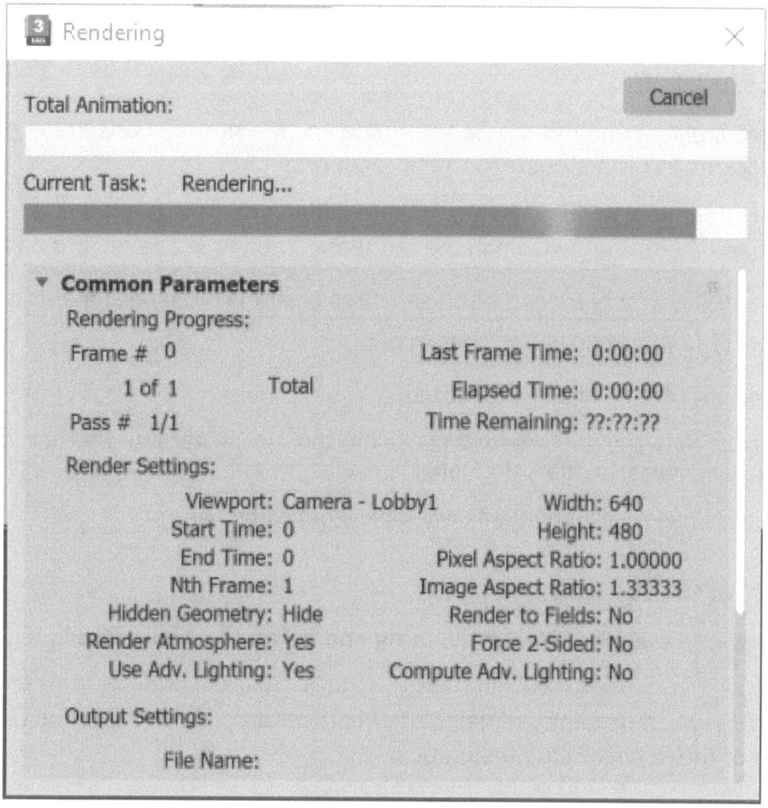

Figure 10–32

- Press <F9> to re-render the last rendered viewport without using the *Render Setup* dialog box.

Common Tab

The *Common* tab contains settings applicable to all rendering systems. Some of the options are described in the following sections.

Common Parameters rollout

- The *Time Output* area designates whether you are rendering a still frame (Single) or an animation. When rendering an animation you can specify to render the entire animation (Active Time Segment), a certain range (Range) or specify individual frames (Frames).
- The *Area to Render* area enables you to define what portion of the scene is rendered, such as View, Selected, Region, Crop, or Blowup.
- The *Output Size* area contains the render size options.

- The *Options* area enables you to select the objects and effects to render (**Atmospherics, Render Hidden Geometry**, etc.). You can also select the overrides (**Area Lights/Shadows as Points, Force 2-Sided**).
- The *Advanced Lighting* and *Bitmap Performance and Memory Options* areas provide additional options to further customize the rendering.
- The *Render Output* area enables you to specify a filename before rendering. Some of the commonly used file formats in which the rendering images are saved are as follows:

JPEG	The JPEG is a lossy format, which sacrifices quality in exchange for a smaller file size.
BMP	Windows Bitmap (24 bit, 16.7 Million Colors).
TGA	Targa (as 24 or 32 bit uncompressed).
PNG	Portable Network Graphics (as 24 or 48 bit color, no interlacing). This has the best file size to quality ratio as it offers the highest color depth with a smaller compression.
TIFF	Tagged Image File Format (24 bit color without compression).

Assign Renderer Rollout

In this rollout, you can switch rendering systems and select the **ActiveShade** renderer that you want to use.

- Alternatively, they can be changed using the *Renderer* drop-down list in the *Common* area near the top of the *Render Setup* dialog box.

Email Notifications Rollout

In this rollout, you can set the option of having an email notification sent to you or another user whose email address has been specified. This is useful when the render is run without being monitored, in the case of lengthy renders.

Scripts Rollout

In this rollout, you can enable the software to run a selected script before a rendering process has begun or after the process has been completed. The valid scripts that can be run are MAXScript file (.MS), macro script (.MCR), batch file (.BAT), and executable file (.EXE).

Renderer Tab

The *Renderer* tab displays renderer-specific options. It is provided for all of the renderers with render-specific options.

10.4 Arnold Renderer

The Arnold renderer is a physically accurate renderer that renders by tracing the light paths and by progressively refining the image until it has completed the rendering process. It is a CPU based render that does not take into consideration the graphics or video card of the computer. Setup is minimal and simple, similar to a point and shoot camera.

- It supports both physical materials and advanced Arnold materials. In physical material, the custom reflection curve feature is not supported by Arnold. In addition to the above materials, other materials supported by Arnold are Multi/Sub-object, Double Sided, Direct X, and Shell.
- It supports Photometric lights and Sun Positioner Daylight system.
- When Arnold is selected as the active renderer, the *Common* tab, *Arnold Renderer* tab, *System* tab, *AOV Settings* tab, *Diagnostics* tab, and *Archive* tab become available in the *Render Setup* dialog box.

Arnold Renderer Tab

The *Arnold Renderer* tab contains options that are easy to set and quite intuitive to work with.

- In the *Samples and Ray Depth* rollout (shown in Figure 10–33), you can control the quality of the rendered image and the noise in the rendering. In the *General* area, increasing the number of **Samples** improves the render quality but it also increases the rendering time. **Camera (AA)** is a multiplier for all other values. Increasing its value extends the rendering time.

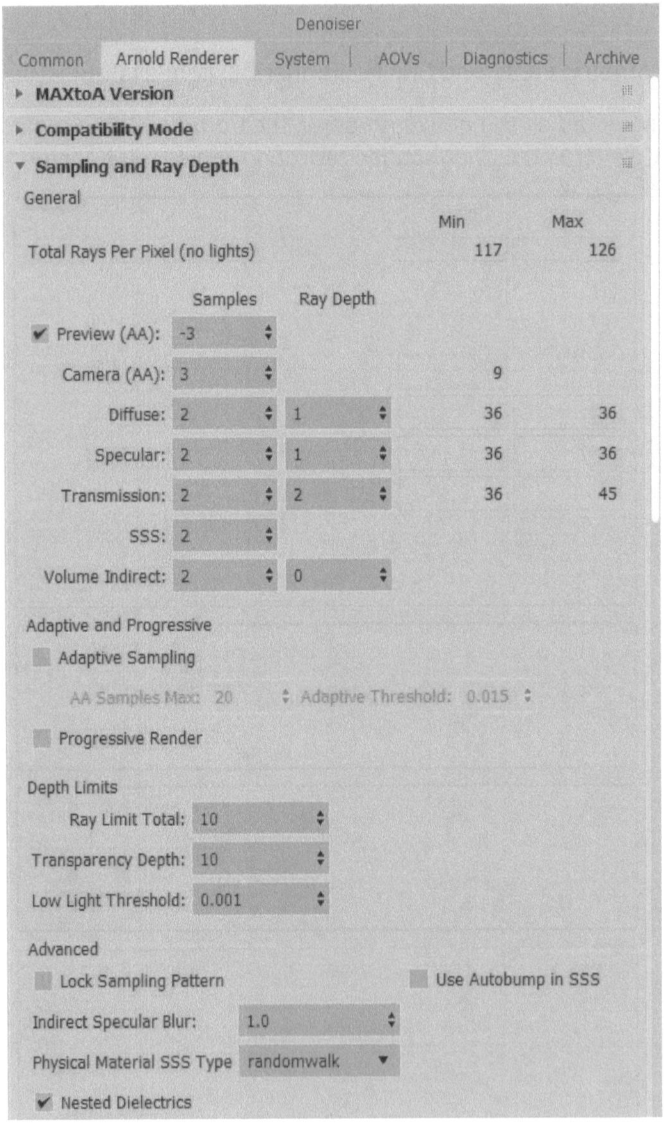

Figure 10–33

- The *Filtering* rollout (shown in Figure 10–34) contains filters that are used for legacy purposes. It is recommended to use the **Gaussian** (default) or the **Blackman-Harris** filter types. While the type of filter used has no effect on the render time, the filter width can affect it slightly.

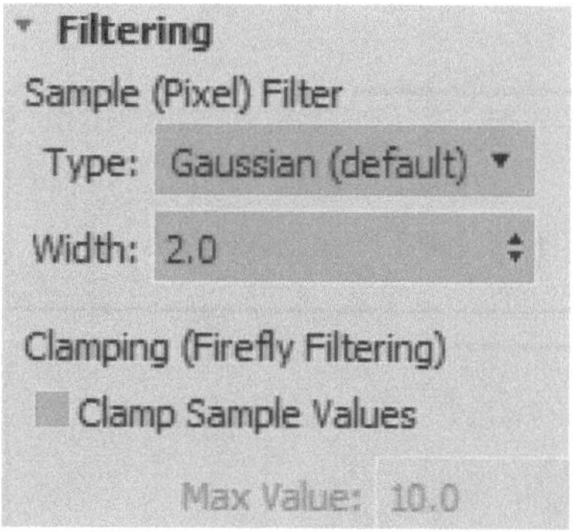

Figure 10–34

- In the *Environment, Background & Atmosphere* rollout (shown in Figure 10–35), you can control how the image based lighting is being used. The **Physically-Based** setting provides automatic and optimized image-based lighting. In this case, the software automatically uses a hidden Skydome to provide IBL. To manually control the settings, use the **Advanced** mode.

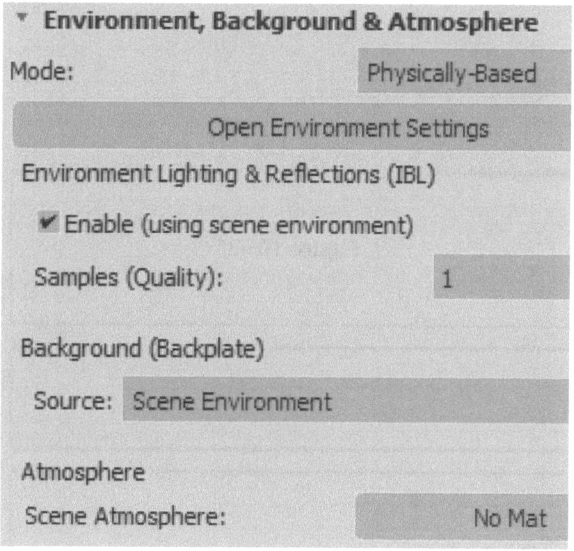

Figure 10–35

- In the *Motion Blur* rollout (shown in Figure 10–36), you can control the **Motion Blur** option to apply it to objects in a scene. You can respect the settings that were defined in the Physical Camera. You can also control the motion blur shape as a **Box** (default), **Triangle**, or a **Curve** that can be adjusted manually.

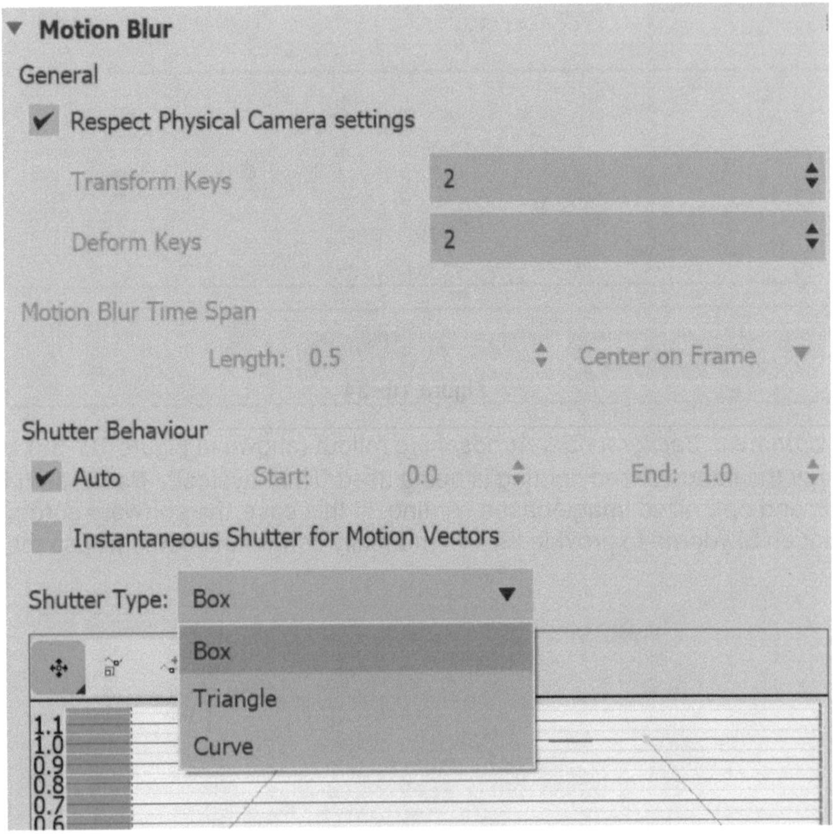

Figure 10–36

- The *Geometry, Subdivision & Hair* rollout (shown in Figure 10–37) contains global settings for tessellation of subdivision surfaces. The *Displacement Default Subdivision* area enables you to set the subdivision rule that is used for the polymesh at the time of rendering. You can use **None** (ignores any subdivision), **Linear** (places vertices in the middle of each face), or **Catmull-Clark** (creates a mesh of quadrilateral faces). The *Hair (Curves) and Points* area controls how the curves are rendered. To create hair, fur, or grass, set the *Type* to **Ribbon**. To create spaghetti like hair, select **Thick.**

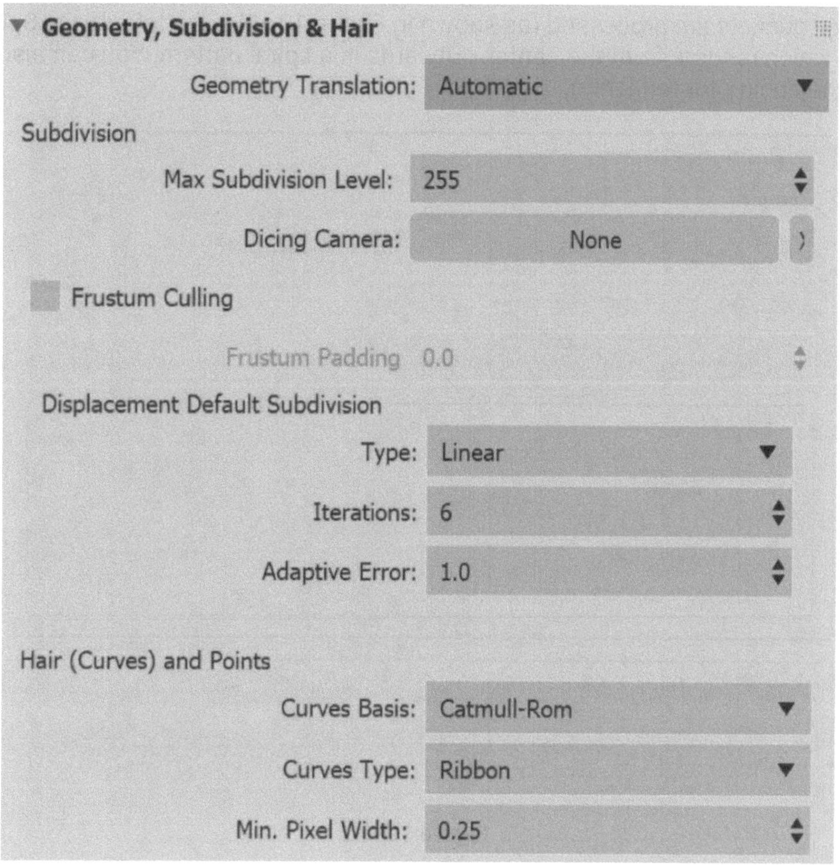

Figure 10–37

System Tab

The *System* tab (as shown in Figure 10–38) contains options to control the Arnold rendering settings.

- Arnold uses Bucket rendering that enables you to see different portions being rendered. If they are not rendered correctly, you can cancel the process, make the required modifications, and start the rendering again. The *General* area enables you to control how the image buckets are processed (as shown in Figure 10–38). By default, the **Spiral** method in used, which renders from the center, outwards in a spiral pattern. You can also set the size of the bucket for rendering.

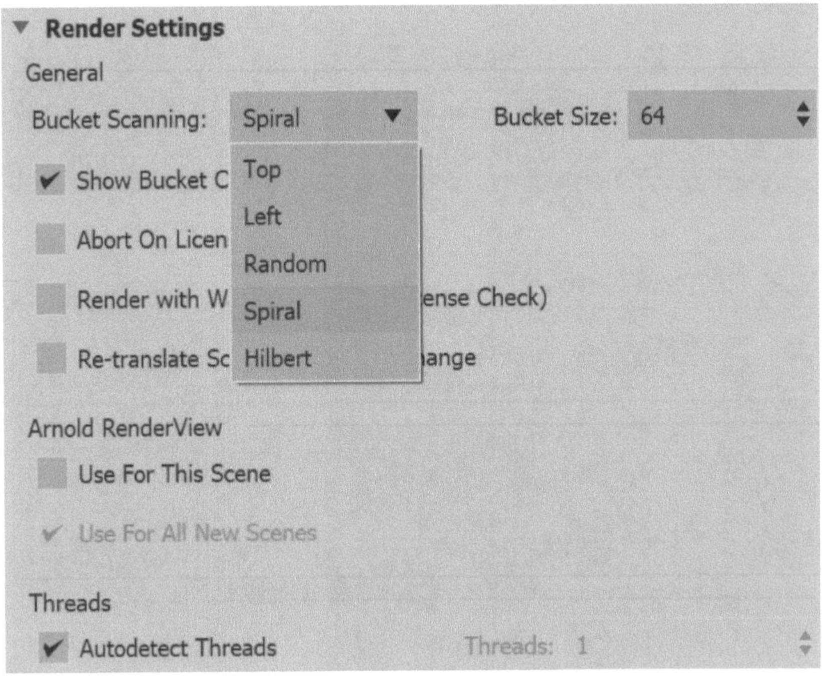

Figure 10–38

Archive Tab

The 3ds Max scenes can be stored as .ASS (Arnold Scene Source) files that are saved and rendered outside of the 3ds Max software. From the *Archive* tab (shown in Figure 10–39), you can export the scene as an .ASS file. You can also select the node types that are included in this type of file.

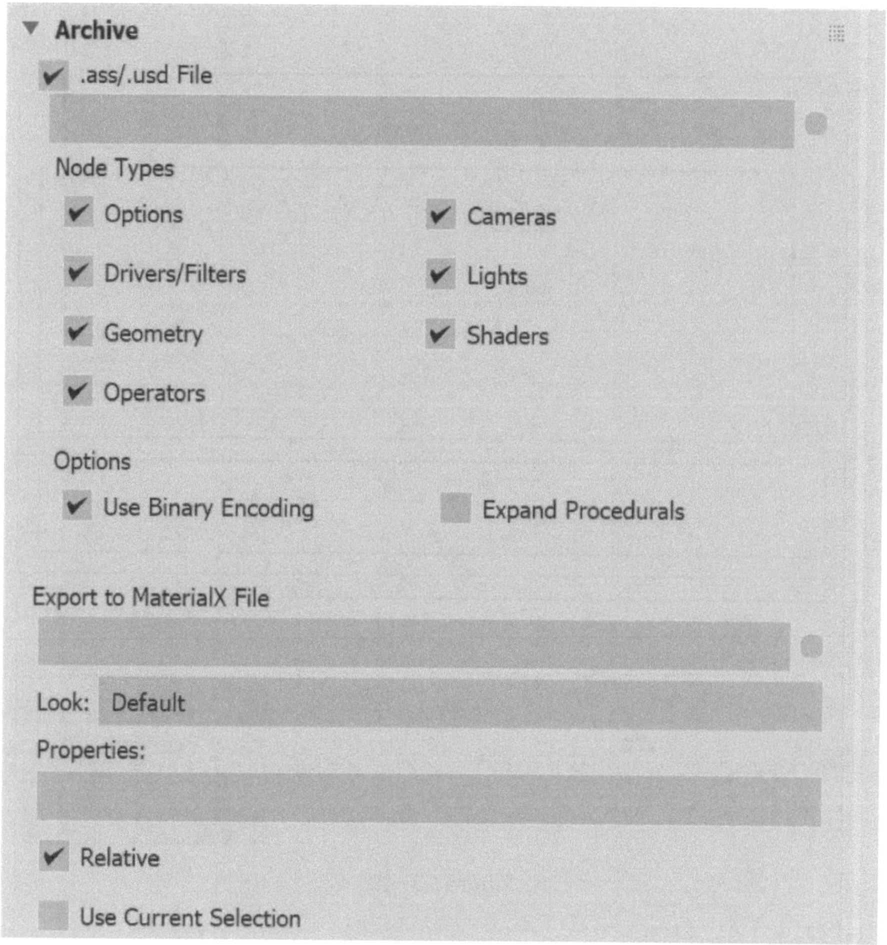

Figure 10–39

Diagnostics Tab

In the *Diagnostics* tab (as shown in Figure 10–40), Arnold generates a log file providing you with errors encountered, other information, and warnings. This file is a great tool for debugging and improving the render. In the *Error Handling* rollout, you can set how the information is provided when an error is encountered.

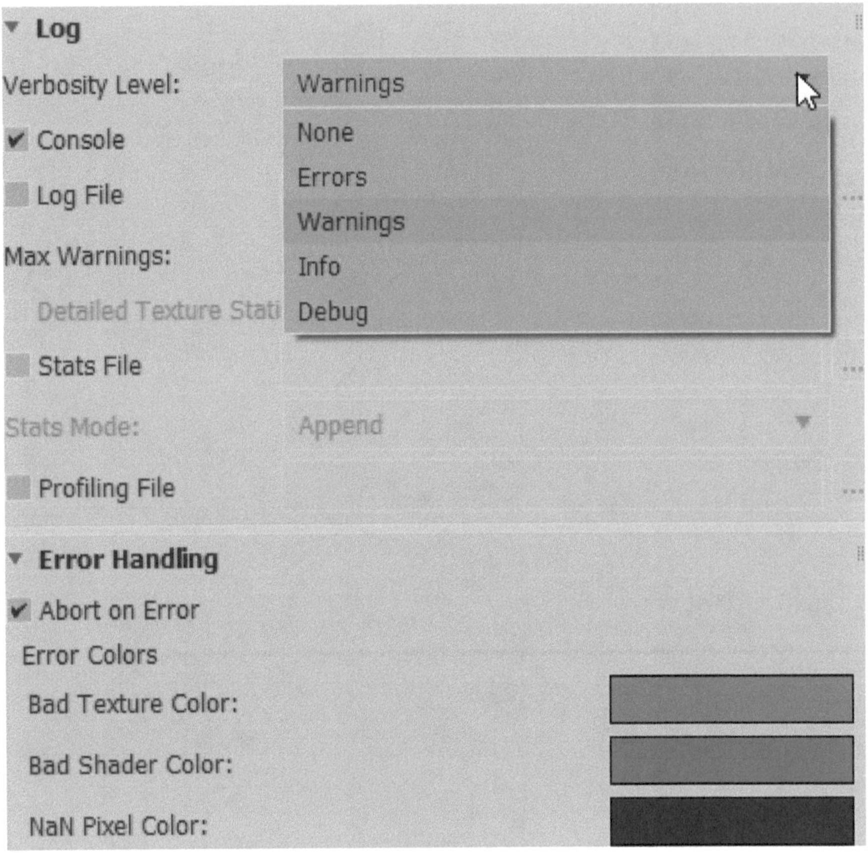

Figure 10–40

AOVs Settings Tab

In the *AOVs Settings* tab, you can set the various Arbitrary Output Variables (AOVs) for a scene. AOVs are separate image files for various elements of the rendered image, such as a separate image for a diffuse pass or an image for the Specular pass. You can check the AOV files for issues and make modifications to that element only to improve the final renders. You can also use these AOV files for creating compositing workflows which can reduce the need to re-render the complete scenes multiple times.

Image Based Lighting

Image Based Lighting (IBL) is a rendering technique that involves a scene representation of real-world light information as a photographic image. The image used is typically in a high dynamic range file format, such as, .HDR or .EXR. In the Autodesk 3ds Max software, this image displays as an environment map and is used to simulate the lighting for the objects in the scene. This enables detailed real-world lighting to be used to light the scene.

Image Based Lighting is available when **ART** or **Arnold** are the active Production renderers. When using **Arnold** as the active renderer, you can control the IBL settings in the *Arnold Renderer* tab, in the *Environment, Background & Atmosphere* area, as shown in Figure 10–41. The *Environment Lighting & Reflections (IBL)* should be set to **Enable**. Increasing the *Samples (Quality)* creates sharper images but increases render times. In the *Background (Backplate)* area, you can set the *Source* to use the default **Scene Environment** or you can use the **Custom Color** or **Custom Map** options.

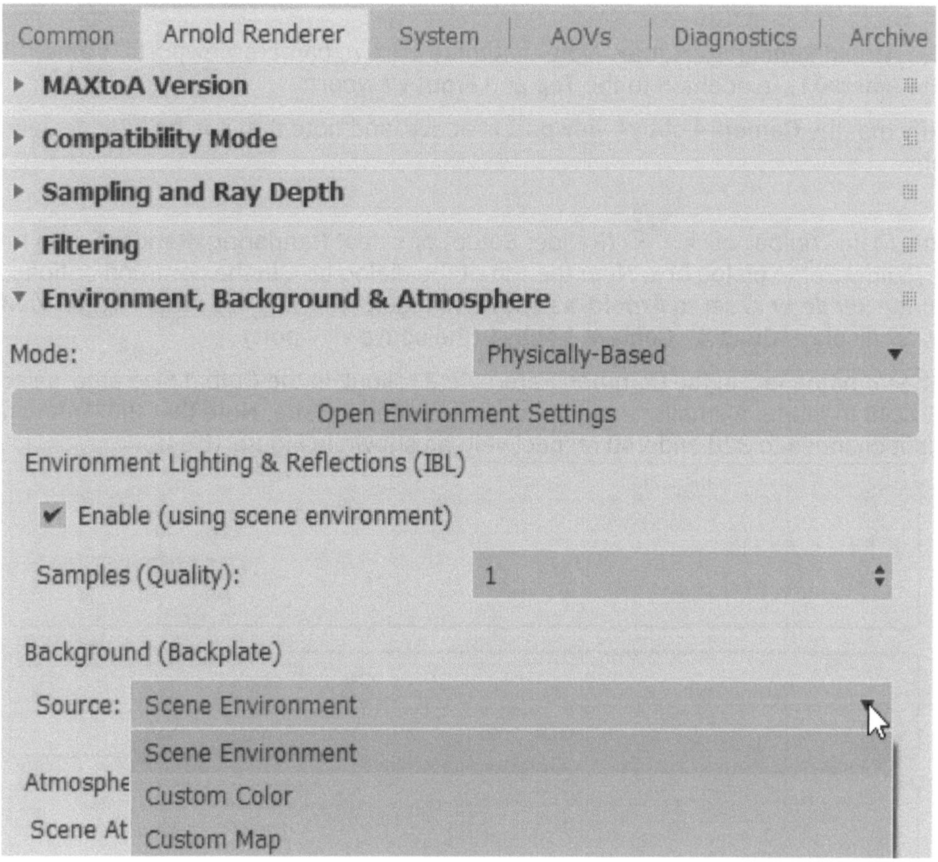

Figure 10–41

Practice 10b
Work with the Arnold Renderer

Practice Objective

- Set various rendering options to improve the rendering of a scene.

This practice uses the Arnold renderer as the active renderer. In this practice, you will set some of the Arnold rendering parameters to enhance the rendered image.

You must set the paths to locate the External files and XREFs used in the practice. If you have not done this already, return to Chapter 1 and complete Task 1 to Task 3 in *Practice 1a: Organize Folders and Work with the Interface*. You only have to set the user paths once.

Task 1: Set exposure control.

1. Open **Arnold Render Start.max.** Note that there are two camera viewports (**Camera-Lobby1** and **Camera01**), in addition to the **Top** and **Front** viewports.
2. Verify that the **Camera-Lobby1** viewport is active, and note that it is an interior view of the lobby.
3. In the Main Toolbar, click  (Render Setup) or select **Rendering>Render Setup** to open the *Render Setup* dialog box. Near the top of the dialog box, in the common options, note that the *Renderer* is set to **Arnold**, as shown in Figure 10–42. Also note that the *View to Render* displays **Quad 4 - Camera-Lobby1** (the active viewport).
4. In the *Common* tab, in the *Common Parameters* rollout, in the *Output Size* area, select **320x240** to render a smaller image to reduce rendering time. Note that the *Width* and the *Height* changes to **320** and **240** respectively, as shown in Figure 10–42.

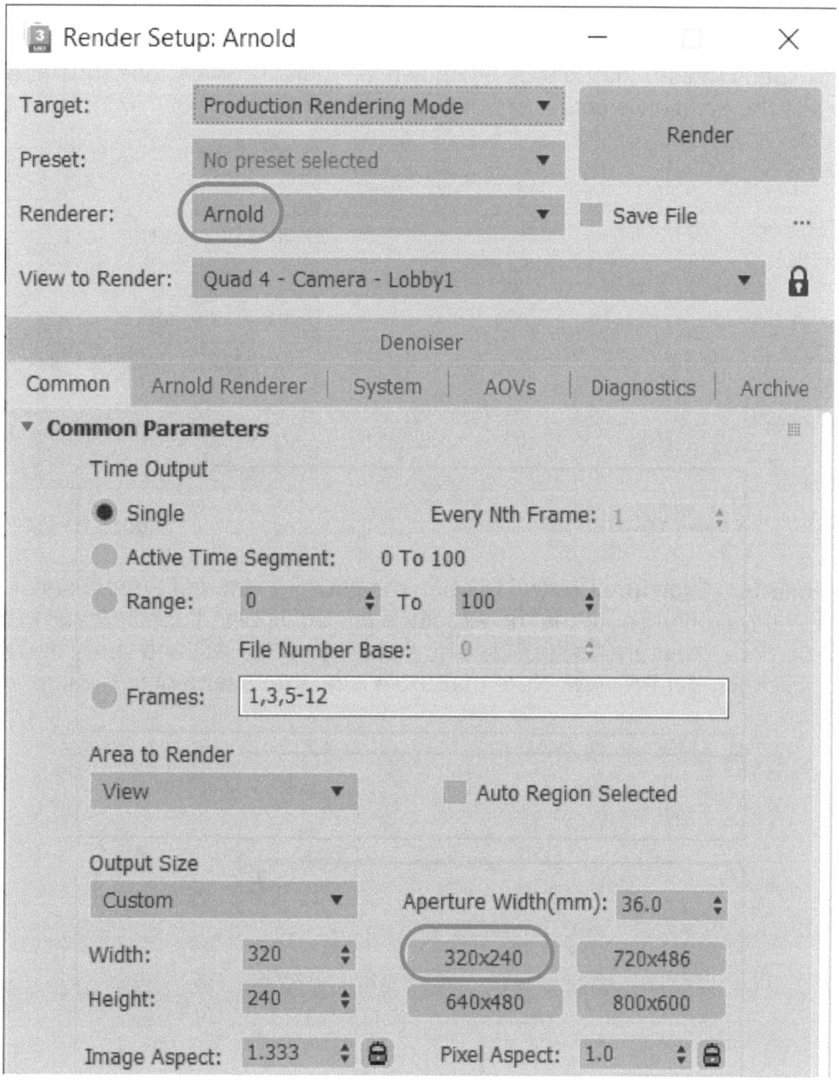

Figure 10–42

5. In the *Common* tab, in the *Common Parameters* rollout, in the *Advanced Lighting* area, verify that the **Use Advanced Lighting** option is enabled and clear the **Compute Advanced Lighting when Required** option, if required.

6. Click **Render**. A *Rendering* dialog box displays the status of the rendering, as shown in Figure 10–43. Note that the rendering is fast, but that the rendered image is washed out with black specs (noise) throughout, as shown in Figure 10–44. Close the Rendered Frame Window and the *Render Setup: Arnold* dialog box.

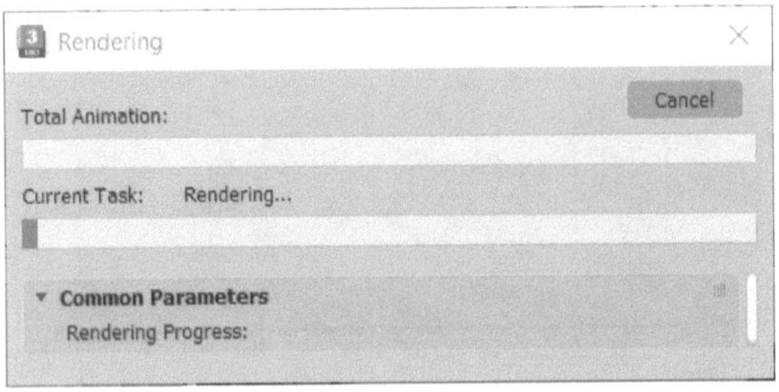

Figure 10–43

Figure 10–44

7. Select **Rendering>Exposure Control** to open the *Environment and Effects* dialog box. In the *Exposure Control* rollout, note that no exposure control is being used. Change this to **Physical Camera Exposure Control** (as shown in Figure 10–45) and verify that **Active** is selected. Click **Render Preview**. Note that there is no improvement in the image.

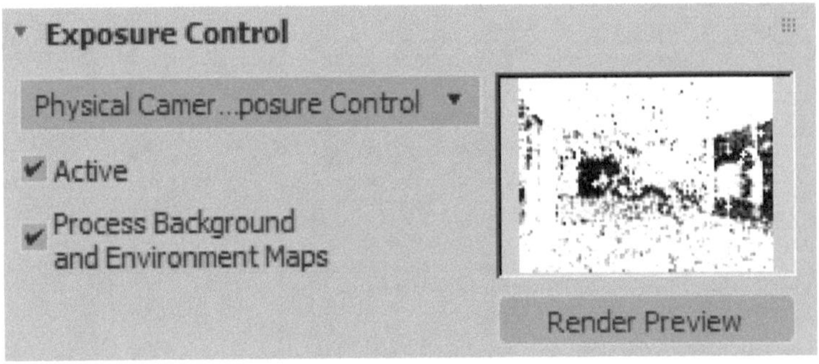

Figure 10–45

8. In the *Physical Camera Exposure Control* rollout, set the *EV Compensation for Physical Cameras* to **-5.0** and press <Enter>. Note that the washing out effect has been removed, as shown in Figure 10–46. Close the dialog box.

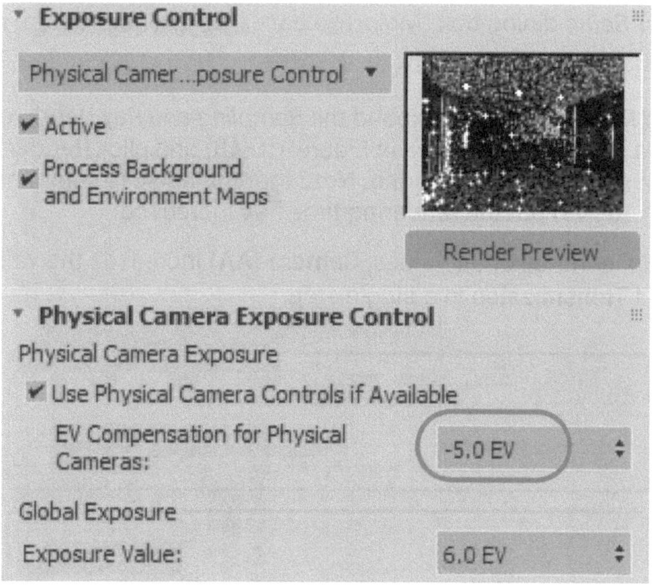

Figure 10–46

9. In the Main Toolbar, click  (Render Production) to render the **Camera-Lobby1** view. The rendered image is not washed out but has a lot of noise and is overall dark (although the sun light is coming through the windows on the left), as shown in Figure 10–47. Leave the Rendered Frame Window open.

Figure 10–47

Task 2: Set Arnold render parameters.

1. Open the *Render Setup* dialog box (Main Toolbar>  (Render Setup) or Rendered Frame Window> ).
2. Open the *Arnold Renderer* tab and expand the *Sampling and Ray Depth* rollout. In the *General* area, set *Camera (AA)* to **4** (as shown in Figure 10–48) and click **Render**. A *Rendering* dialog box displays the status of the rendering. Note that the noise is substantially removed (as shown in Figure 10–49) but the rendering time has increased.
   - Being a multiplier for all other values, **Camera (AA)** increases the values of **Diffuse**, **Specular**, and **Transmission** in a single step.

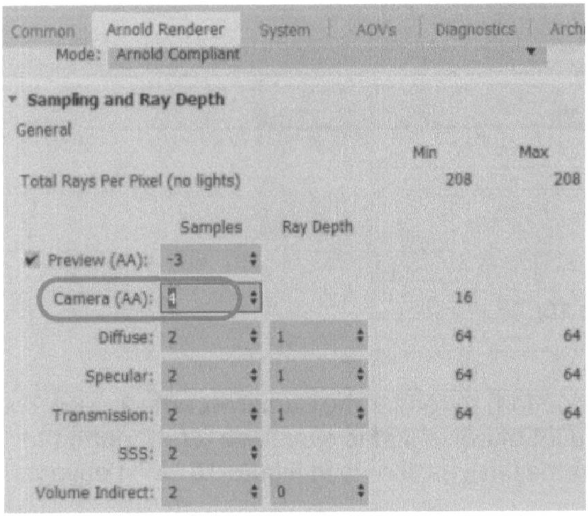

Figure 10–48

Figure 10–49

3. In the *Render Setup* dialog box, set the *Diffuse Samples* to **4** (as shown in Figure 10–50) and render the scene again. The noise is further reduced, but it is still dark inside. Note that the doors at the back of the room are not visible.

   Note: *Note that with each increase in number, the rendering takes longer to render.*

4. Set the *Diffuse Ray Depth* to **4** and render again. Note that the doors at the back have become slightly visible as more light is reflected around the space, as shown in Figure 10–50.

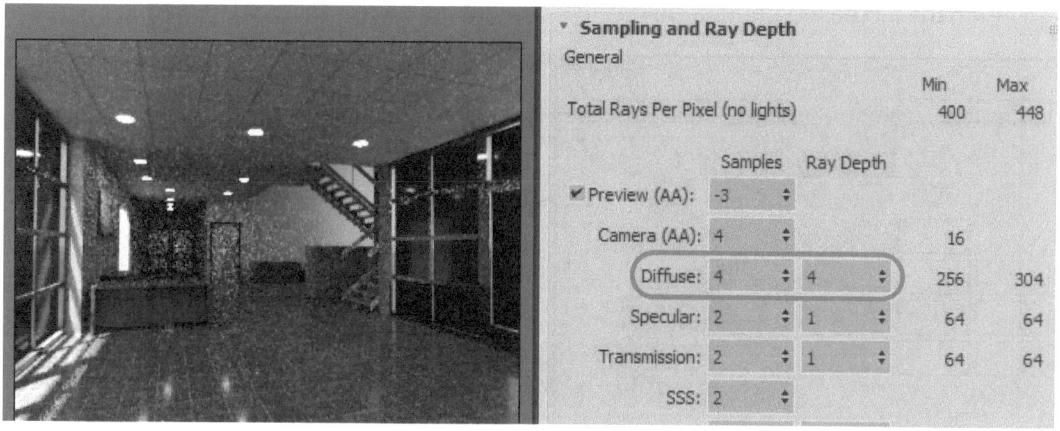

Figure 10–50

5. Note that you cannot see out of the curtain wall windows. Set the *Transmission Ray Depth* to **4** and render again. Note that it takes longer to render but the outside is visible through the curtain wall windows, as shown in Figure 10–51.

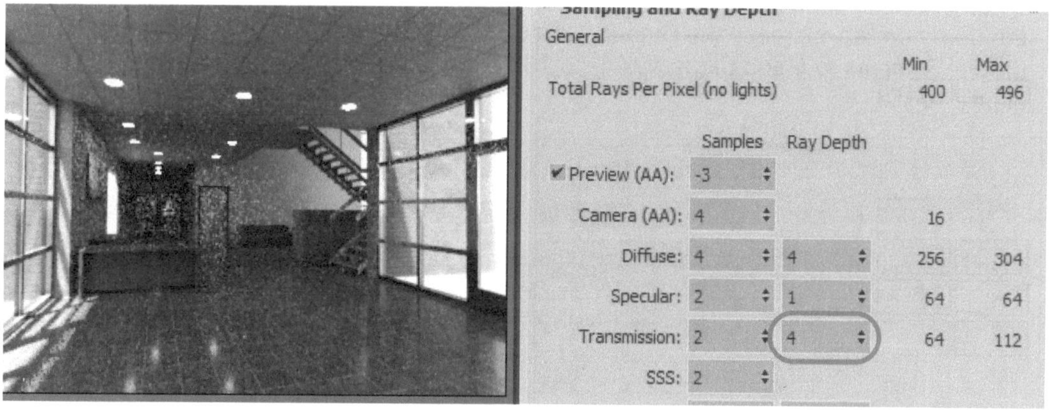

Figure 10–51

6. Increasing the **Camera (AA)** value removes the noise but significantly increases the render time. Set the *Camera (AA)* to **7** and render the viewport. Note the significant noise reduction and brightening of the interior areas, as shown in Figure 10–52.
   - With the increased **Camera (AA)** value, it might take a few minutes to render.

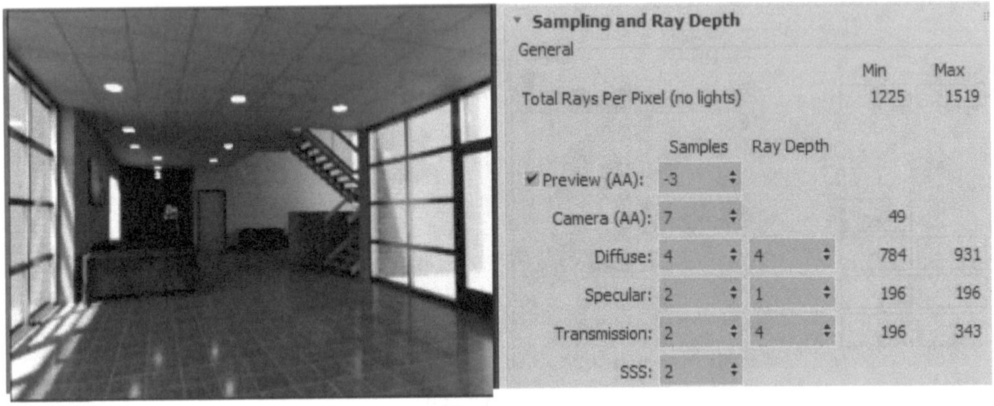

Figure 10–52

7. Save your scene as **MyArnold_Render.max**.
8. (Optional – note that this render might take a significant amount of time to complete.) When possible, open the **MyArnold_Render.max** and open the *Render Setup* dialog box. In the *Common* tab, increase the *Output Size* to **640X480**. In the *Arnold Renderer* tab, set *Diffuse Samples* to **6** and *Camera (AA)* to **10** and render the scene, as shown in Figure 10–53.

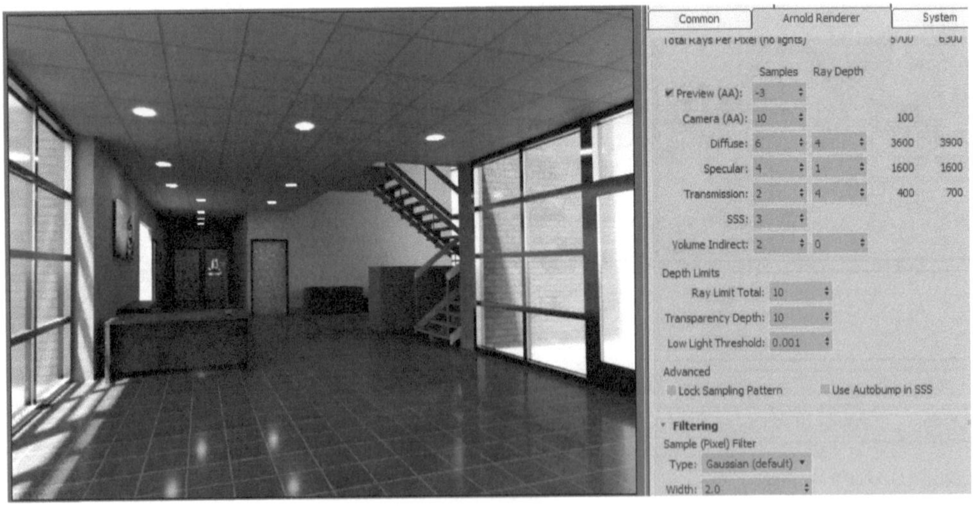

Figure 10–53

End of practice

Practice 10c
Image Based Lighting in the Arnold Renderer

Practice Objective

- Light a scene using the light in an environment map image.

In this practice, you will learn to light an exterior scene using an HDR image using the Image Based Lighting (IBL) technique in the Arnold renderer.

You must set the paths to locate the External files and XREFs used in the practice. If you have not done this already, return to Chapter 1 and complete Task 1 to Task 3 in *Practice 1a: Organize Folders and Work with the Interface*. You only have to set the user paths once.

1. Open **Retail Exterior.max.**
2. In the Main Toolbar, click  (Render Setup) or select **Rendering>Render Setup**. In the *Renderer* drop-down list, verify that **Arnold** is set as the renderer. Close the *Render Setup* dialog box.
3. Select **Rendering>Environment** or press <8> to open the *Environment and Effects* dialog box.
4. In the *Environment* tab>*Common Parameters* rollout>*Background* area, click **None** that displays for *Environment Map*.
5. In the *Material/Map Browser* that opens, expand the **Maps>General** categories and double-click on **Bitmap**.
6. In the *Select Bitmap Image File* dialog box, open **CountryRoad.hdr** in the ...\sceneassets\images folder of the practice files folder. This image will provide the lights for the scene.

7. In the *HDRI Load Settings* dialog box, in the *Internal Storage* area, verify that **Real Pixels** and **Def. Exposure** are selected, as shown in Figure 10–54. Click **OK**.

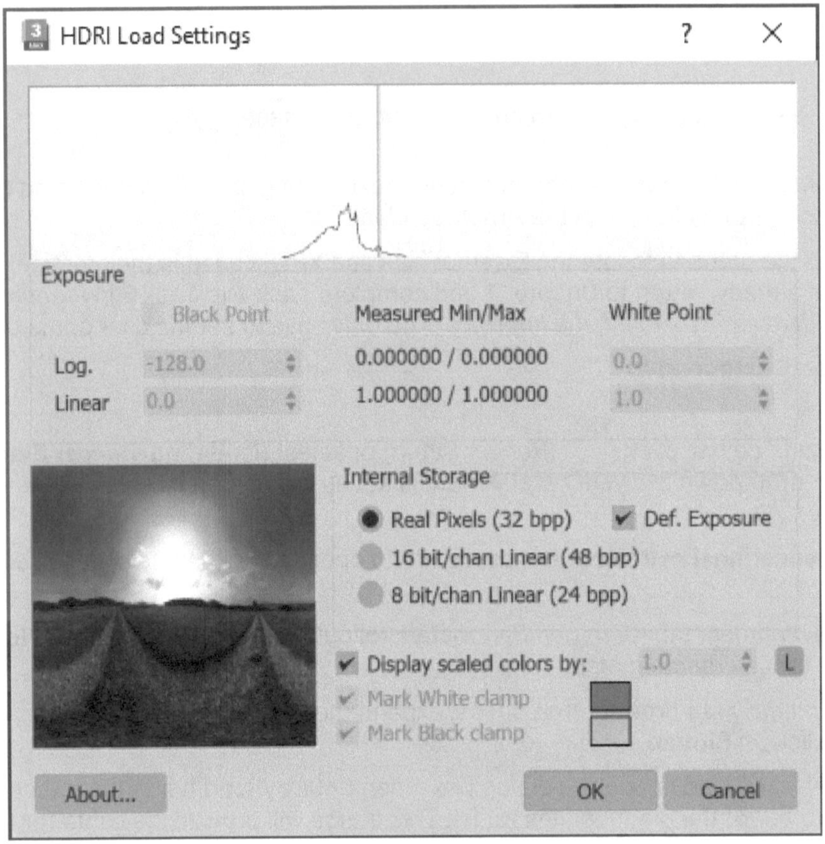

Figure 10–54

8. In the *Environments and Effects* dialog box, note that **None** has been replaced with **Map #9 (CountryRoad.hdr)**. Do not close the dialog box.

9. In the Main Toolbar, click  (Material Editor) to open the *Slate Material Editor*.

10. From the *Environments and Effects* dialog box, drag and drop **Map #9 (CountryRoad.hdr)** onto the *View1* sheet in the *Slate Material Editor*.

11. In the *Instance (Copy) Map* dialog box, verify that **Instance** is selected and click **OK**. The **Map # Bitmap** node is placed on the *View1* sheet.

12. In the *View1* sheet, click the **Map # Bitmap** title bar, if required to open its Parameter Editor.

13. In the Parameter Editor, in the *Coordinates* rollout, note that **Spherical Environment** is selected for *Mapping*, as shown in Figure 10–55. This indicates that the light from the image illuminates the scene from all directions.

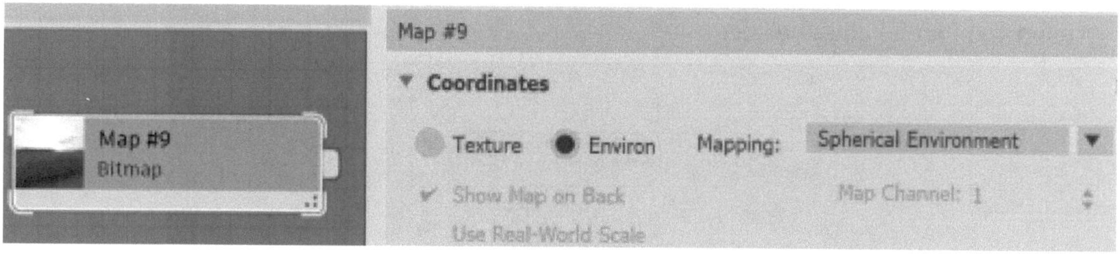

Figure 10–55

14. Close the *Slate Material Editor* and the *Environments and Effects* dialog box.

15. Open the *Render Setup* dialog box ( (Render Setup)). In the *Render Setup* dialog box, open the *Arnold Renderer* tab. Expand the *Environment, Background & Atmosphere* rollout. Verify that **Enable (using scene environment)** is selected in the *Environment Lighting & Reflections (IBL)* area and that *Source* is set as **Scene Environment** in the *Background (Backplate)* area, as shown in Figure 10–56. Do not close the *Render Setup* dialog box.

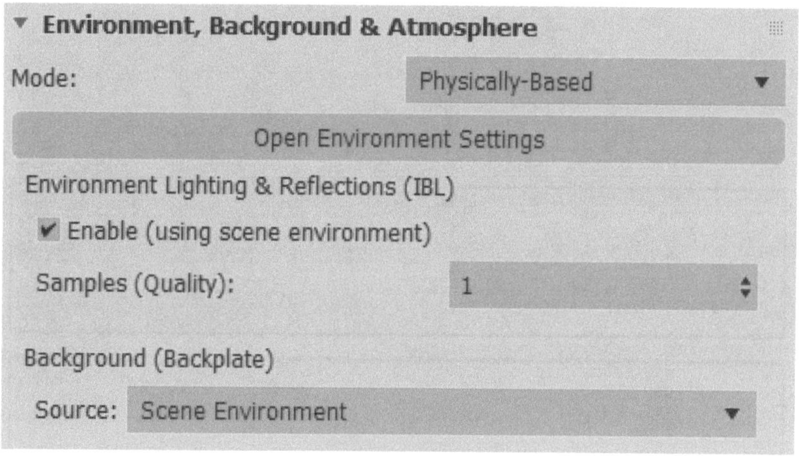

Figure 10–56

16. Verify that Camera - Southeast View is active. Click **Render** in the *Render Setup* dialog box to render the scene, as shown in Figure 10–57 (you can also use  (Render Production)). Once the rendering is complete, note that the environment background is used and that it lights the scene.

Figure 10–57

17. In the Rendered Frame Window, using the mouse wheel, zoom in to the portion of one of the door and window front, as shown in Figure 10–58. Note that the image is not sharp. Leave the Render Frame Window open.

Figure 10–58

18. In the *Render Setup* dialog box, in the *Arnold Renderer* tab, in the *Environment, Background & Atmosphere* rollout, set the *Samples (Quality)* to **2** and click **Render**. Note the image has improved slightly. Close the *Render Setup* dialog box.
19. In the Render Frame Window, zoom out to see the complete view and leave the Rendered Frame Window open.
20. Select **Rendering>Environment** or **Rendering>Exposure Control** to open the *Environment and Effects* dialog box. In the *Environment* tab, in the *Exposure Control* rollout, note that the **Logarithmic Exposure Control** is already set, but it is not currently used because **Active** is not checked. Keep the dialog box open.
21. In the Scene Explorer, select **Camera - Southeast View** (the camera object). In the *Modify* panel (), in the *Exposure* rollout, click **Install Exposure Control** and click **OK** to replace the existing exposure control and install the Physical Camera Exposure Control. In the *Environment and Effects* dialog box, note that the **Physical Camera Exposure Control** is used and is set as **Active**. Close the dialog box.
22. In the Render Frame Window, click **Render**. Note that the scene brightens up as it permits more light into the camera.

23. In the *Exposure* rollout, in the *Exposure Gain* area, increase the *Target* to **6.5 EV**, as shown. Render the **Camera - Southeast View** again and note how the brightness is slightly lowered, as shown in Figure 10–59.

Figure 10–59

24. Close the Rendered Frame Window and save the file as **MyIBL.max**.

End of practice

10.5 ART Renderer

The Autodesk Ray Trace (ART) renderer is a path tracing renderer which generates fast and accurate renderings using few settings. ART is a physically based renderer and uses only the CPU of a computer. It supports photometric lights, the Sun Positioner, and physical material.

ART is compatible with the Autodesk® Revit® software and is capable of creating highly accurate renderings of architectural scenes due to ART's support of the photometric and day lighting features in the Autodesk Revit software.

When you select **ART Renderer** as the active renderer, the *Common* tab, *ART Renderer* tab, and *Render Elements* tab are available in the *Render Setup* dialog box, as shown in Figure 10–60.

ART Renderer Tab

The *ART Renderer* tab displays the renderer-specific options, as shown in Figure 10–60.

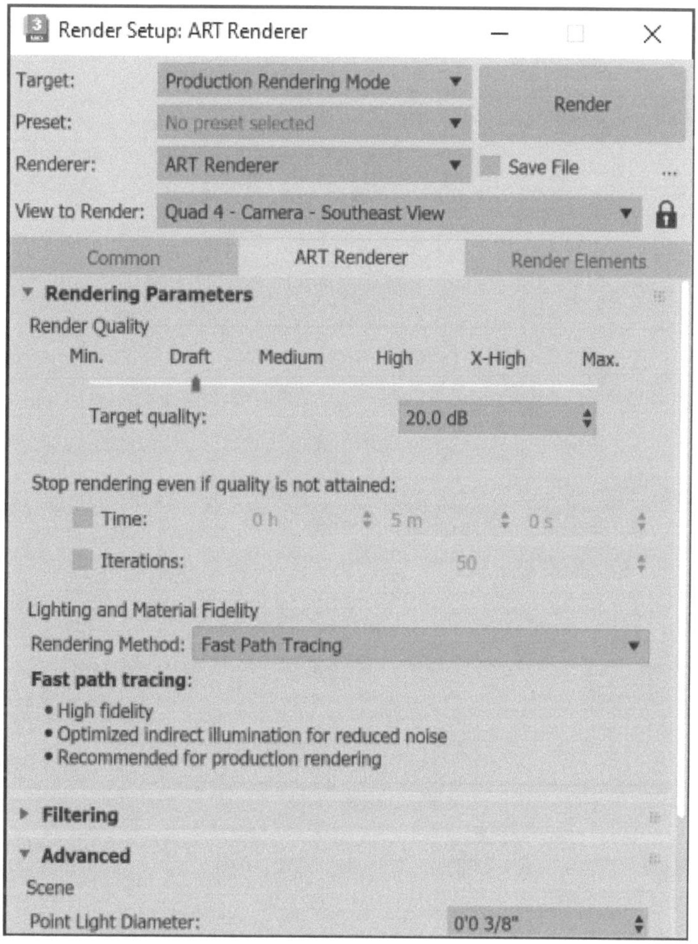

Figure 10–60

- The *Rendering Parameter* rollout enables you to set the *Target Quality,* which is measured in decibels (dB). A lower value is lower quality with more noise in the final image. A higher quality reduces the amount of noise in the final image, but the image takes longer to render.
- You can limit the time or number of iterations for a rendering in the *Stop rendering even if quality is not attained* area. This saves time during image rendering, but the resulting image might not have the desired quality.
- The *Lighting and Material Fidelity* area options are used to create image renderings. You can use the **Fast Path Tracing** method to render high fidelity, indirect illumination, or use the **Advanced Path Method** to generate final renders for true high fidelity images.
- The *Filtering* rollout enables you to activate **Noise Filtering** on final renderings. The **Anti-Aliasing** option sets the *Filter Diameter* in pixels and determines how the ART renderer anti-aliases the edges in the image.
- The *Advanced* rollout has options to set the size of point lights in scene lighting using the **Point Light Diameter** value. You can also use the **Animate Noise Pattern** option to keep the noise pattern from being static in the final rendering.

10.6 Scanline Renderer

The Scanline renderer generates a render by calculating a series of lines starting at the top and moving down. It is intended to be used with both standard lighting and radiosity based lighting.

Renderer Tab

The *Renderer* tab for the Scanline renderer displays its specific options, as shown in Figure 10–61.

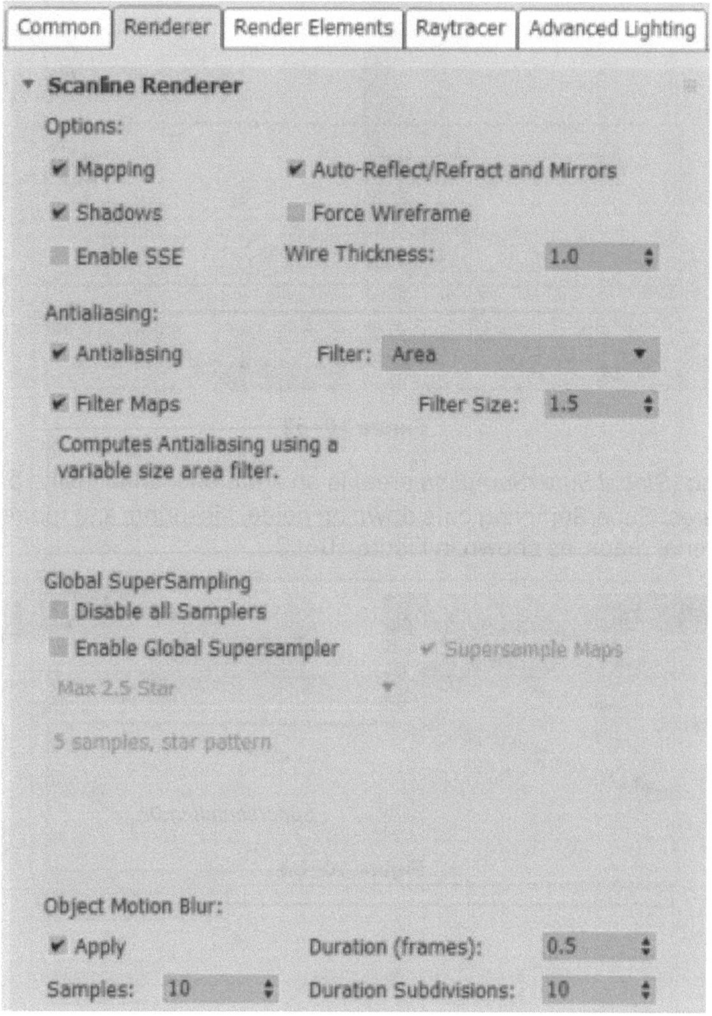

Figure 10–61

- The *Options* area enables you to globally enable or disable the use of all image maps (**Mapping**) or the calculation of all shadows (**Shadows**). The **Force Wireframe** option causes the scene geometry to render as wireframe objects with the **Wire Thickness** parameter listed below.
- The *Antialiasing* area contains options for antialiasing that smooths the jagged diagonal lines and curves in renderings but at a reduced quality, as shown on the left in Figure 10–62.

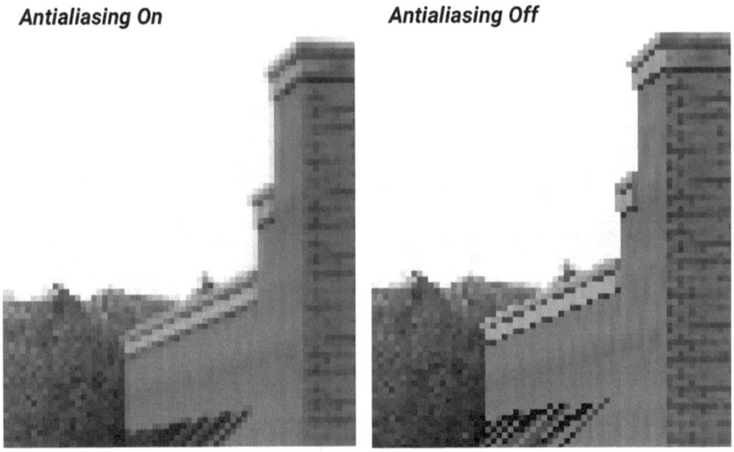

Figure 10–62

- SuperSampling (*Global SuperSampling* area) is an additional antialiasing pass applied to material textures. SuperSampling cuts down on noise, flickering, and moire patterns caused by dense material maps, as shown in Figure 10–63.

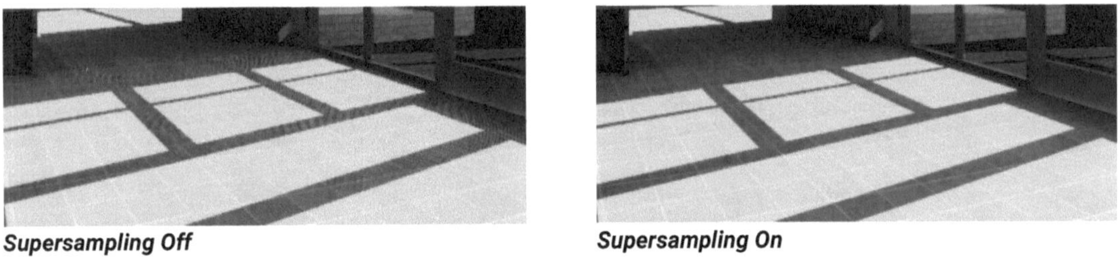

Figure 10–63

Raytracer Tab

Raytracing is a rendering method used to calculate accurate reflections, refractions, and shadows. Raytracing is used for raytrace materials and some Architectural materials with shiny, transparent, or mirrored templates (e.g., glass, mirrors, etc.). Raytraced and area shadows cause raytracing to take place and for Scanline renderer these are managed by the options in *Raytracer* tab, (as shown in Figure 10–64).

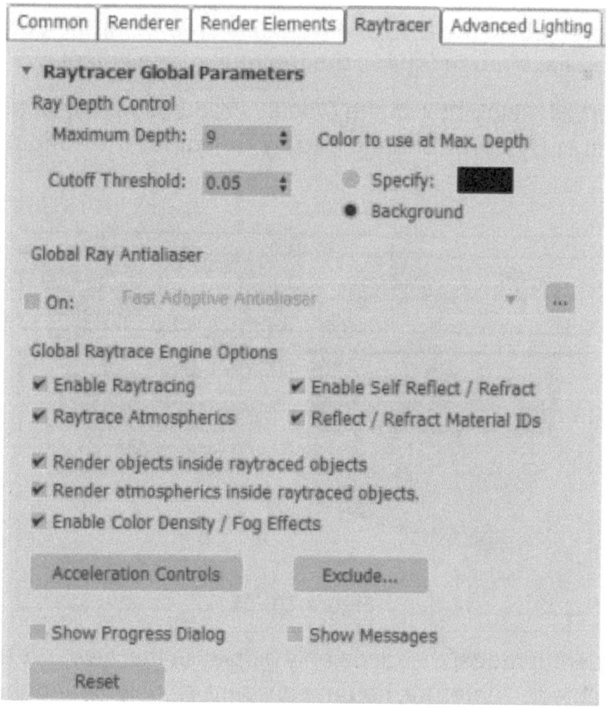

Figure 10–64

- The **Maximum Depth** option is a measurement of how many reflections of reflections you want to permit. The default value of **9** might be excessive, while **3** might be as effective and requires much less rendering time.
- The **Cutoff Threshold** option is a percent value that causes the software to ignore rays that only contribute that percent or less of a pixel's color in the final rendering. Increasing this value reduces rendering time at a cost of lower accuracy.
- If you find that your raytraced reflections or shadows have jagged diagonal lines or curves, you can enable **Global Ray Antialiasing** to add smoothness.
- When cleared, the **Enable Raytracing** option disables all raytracing in the scene.

Note: *Several of these options relate to rendering performance. In many ways, these are black box parameters that need to be adjusted through trial and error for individual scenes.*

Single vs. Double-Sided in Scanline Rendering

When using the Scanline renderer, Autodesk 3ds Max 3D objects are treated as surface models rather than solids, to make calculations faster. 3D geometry is resolved into triangular faces when rendered.

Figure 10–65 displays two identical Box objects, with the one on the right displaying all of its edges as triangular faces. To display triangular faces, right-click on the object and select **Object Properties**. In the *General* tab, in the *Display Properties* area, clear the **Edges Only** option. If the viewport is set to **Edged Face** mode (<F4>), the triangular faces display.

- In the *Object Properties* dialog box, in the *Display Properties* area, all of the options are grayed out if it is set to **By Layer** Change it to **By Object** for the options to be available.

Figure 10–65

- In single-sided rendering mode, the faces only display in the viewport and in renderings from the outside of the object. Therefore, no time is spent on calculating the inner faces of the object. Working in single-sided mode is a more efficient way to render. It is recommended to use single-sided mode whenever possible.
- When using the scanline renderer, rendering in double-sided mode forces the Autodesk 3ds Max software to determine what the inside and the outside of each face looks like, adding significant rendering time.

- In single-sided mode, the Scanline renders faces whose vectors point towards the camera even if at very oblique angles, as shown in Figure 10–66.

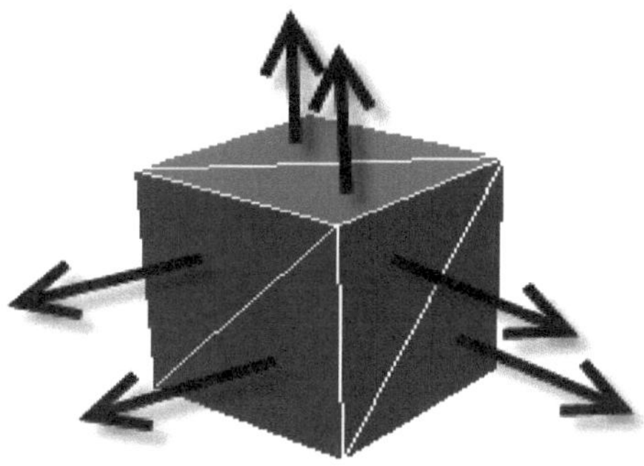

Figure 10–66

- 3D objects such as primitives like these boxes automatically have their face normals pointing to the outside.
- Single-sided rendering mode can cause problems when object normals are inconsistent (inverted). In Figure 10–67, the box on the right has its top face normals pointing down instead of up. This can cause the box to have missing faces. (The back-facing edge lines are shown here for clarity but normally, they would not be visible.)

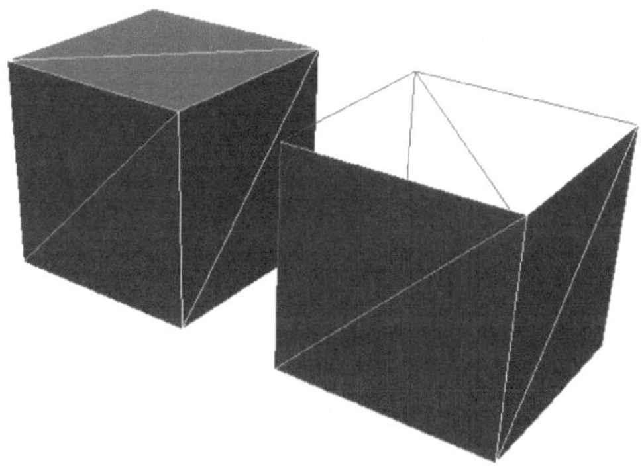

Figure 10–67

- Faces with inverted face normals display in black in the viewport, but are invisible in the scanline rendering. To see through the faces that point away, right-click on the object, select **Object Properties** and in the *Display Properties* area, select **Backface Cull**.
- CAD software packages generally do not assign surface normals to 3D geometry. When you import this data into the Autodesk 3ds Max software, surface normals are automatically assigned to faces based on the order in which the vertices were created, which can result in inconsistent facings.

- When linking or importing 3D blocks and drawing from other software, there might still be inconsistent or inverted face normals, which need to be corrected.
- If the data was imported or linked (.DWG or .DXF file), delete, re-import or reload the linked file, and in the *Import Options* dialog box, select **Orient normals of adjacent faces consistently**, as shown in Figure 10–68. This option should not be selected unless face-normal issues are present.

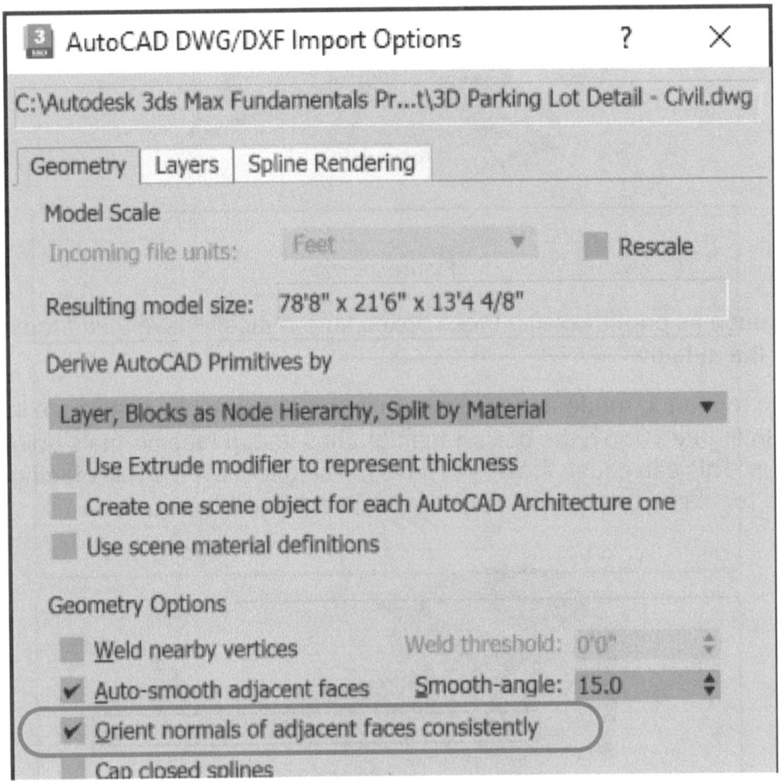

Figure 10–68

- If reimporting or reloading data is not feasible (or the data was not imported/linked), the Normal modifier can be used to unify faces. This object-space modifier has the ability to flip all of the face normals when an object is completely inside out.

- If you have a small number of faces with normals pointing the wrong way (or a large number and some time to spare) you can manually flip and unify face normals. Using the **Edit Mesh** and **Edit Poly** modifiers, select the inverted polygon and then in the *Surface Properties* rollout, use the **Flip** and **Unify** options, as shown in Figure 10–69.

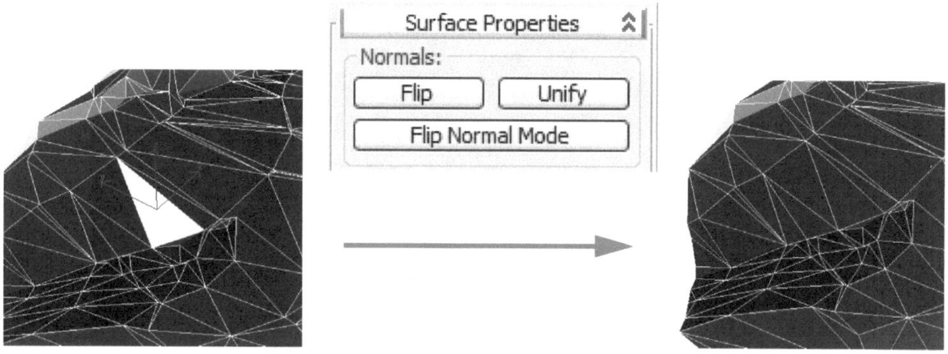

Figure 10–69

Note: *The viewport behavior might vary depending on your video driver.*

Enabling Double-Sided Mode

If you only have certain objects with face-normal issues that cannot be easily fixed, use **2-sided** materials. This renders the objects as double-sided, while rendering the rest of the scene geometry as single-sided. Different scanline materials have the 2-sided options in different rollouts in the Parameter Editor.

- **Scanline>Standard** materials have the **2-Sided** option in the *Shader Basic Parameters* rollout, as shown in Figure 10–70.

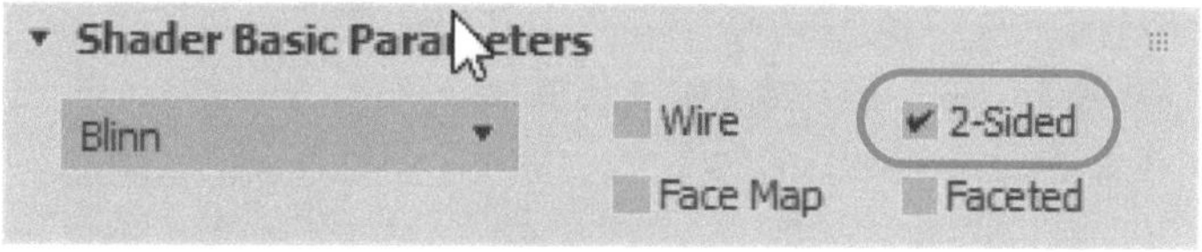

Figure 10–70

- **Scanline>Architectural** materials have the **2-Sided** option in the *Physical Qualities* rollout, as shown in Figure 10–71.

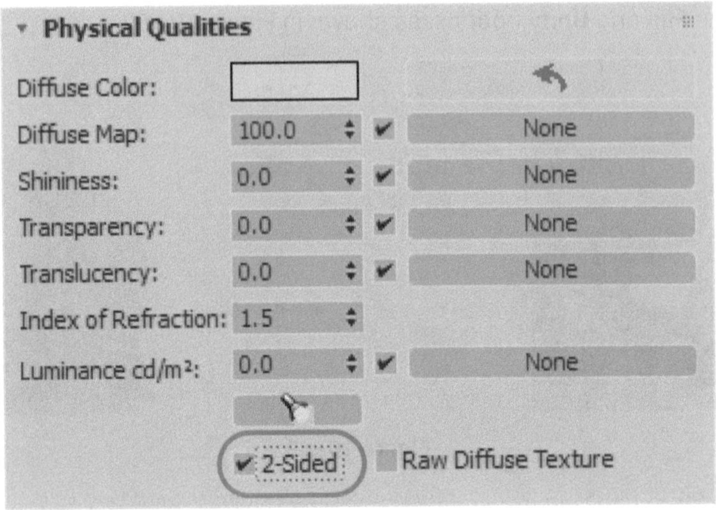

Figure 10–71

- To render a scene double-sided, in the *Render Setup* dialog box, in the *Common* tab, in the *Options* area, enable the **Force 2-Sided** option, as shown in Figure 10–72.

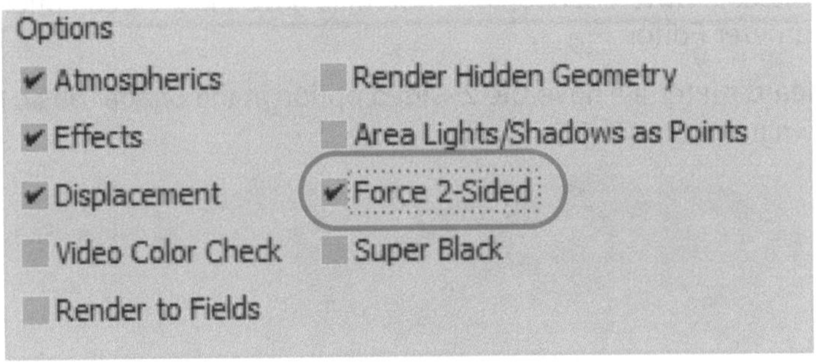

Figure 10–72

Practice 10d
Work with Scanline Rendering Options

Practice Objectives

- Set various rendering options to improve the rendering of the scene.
- Render an object as double-sided using a double-sided and single-sided material.

This practice uses the Scanline renderer as the active renderer. In this practice, you will set various rendering options and render an object as double-sided using a double-sided and single-sided material.

You must set the paths to locate the External files and XREFs used in the practice. If you have not done this already, return to Chapter 1 and complete Task 1 to Task 3 in *Practice 1a: Organize Folders and Work with the Interface*. You only have to set the user paths once.

Task 1: Set rendering options.

1. Open **Rendering Options.max.**

2. In the Main Toolbar, click  (Render Setup) or select **Rendering>Render Setup** to open the *Render Setup* dialog box.
   - Note that the *Renderer* is set as **Scanline Renderer**, as shown in Figure 10–73.

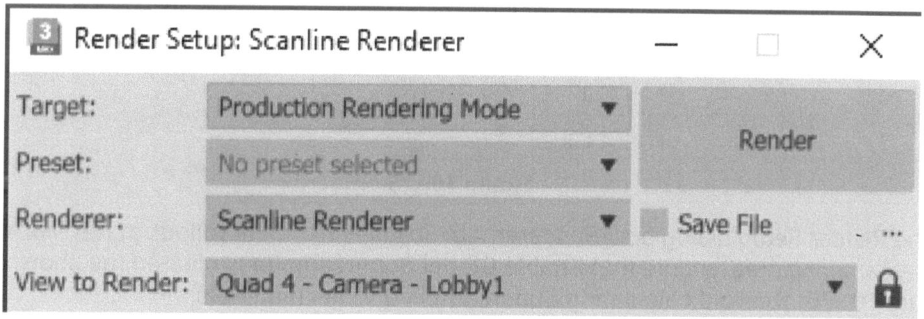

Figure 10–73

3. In the *Common* tab, in the *Common Parameters* rollout, in the *Advanced Lighting* area, verify that **Use Advanced Lighting** is enabled and **Compute Advanced Lighting when Required** is clear, as shown in Figure 10–74.
   - The **Compute Advanced Lighting when Required** option enables the software to recalculate radiosity for the material adjustments you make. They are very subtle, so you can ignore the recalculations for this practice.

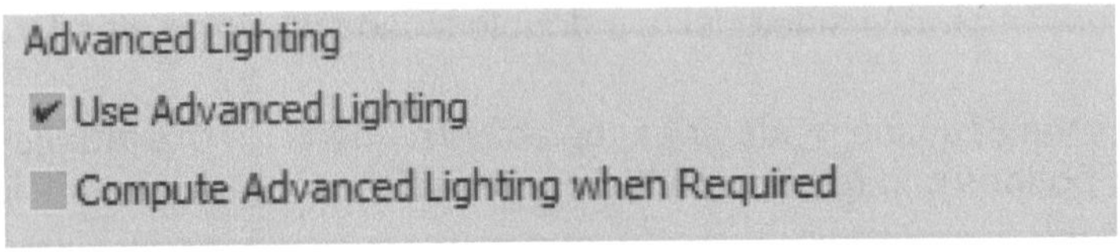

Figure 10–74

4. In the *Render Setup* dialog box, in the *View to Render* edit box, ensure that **Quad 4 - Camera - Lobby1** is selected, indicating that it is the active viewport. Click **Render** in the *Render Setup* dialog box.
5. In the Rendered Frame Window, use the mouse wheel to zoom in to the floor. Note the moire pattern on the tile floor and on the windows, as shown in Figure 10–75.

Figure 10–75

6. In the *Render Setup* dialog box>*Renderer* tab>*Scanline Renderer* rollout, in the *Global SuperSampling* area, ensure that **Enable Global Supersampler** is cleared (as shown in Figure 10–76) to avoid calculating Supersampling for all materials.

Figure 10–76

7. Open the *Slate Material Editor*. In the *Material/Map Browser*, expand *Scene Materials* and double-click on **Finishes.Flooring.Tile.Square.Terra Cotta** to display it in *View1* sheet, as shown in Figure 10–77.

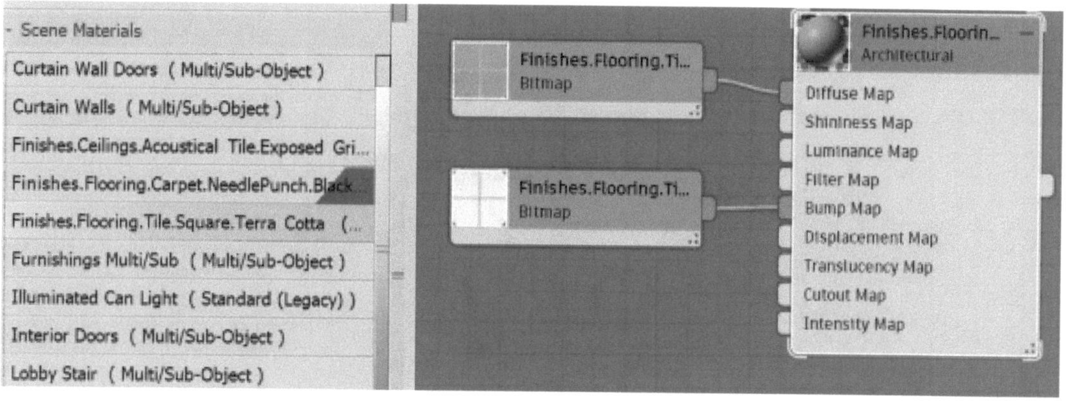

Figure 10–77

8. If required, click on the title bar of the **Finishes.Flooring.Tile.Square.Terra Cotta** material to open its Parameter Editor.

9. Expand the *SuperSampling* rollout and clear **Use Global Settings** to use the **Enable Local Supersampler**, as shown in Figure 10–78. This will calculate supersampling for only the tiled flooring material. Use the default parameters including **Adaptive Halton** as the local supersampler.

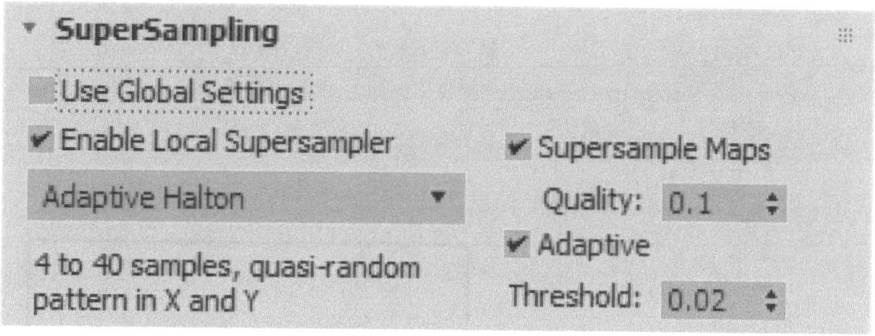

Figure 10–78

10. Render the **Camera – Lobby1** viewport and note that the moire pattern is somewhat reduced, but that the rendering time has increased. The visible edges of the sun's highlight area are also much better defined and antialiased. Some jaggedness displays along the rails in the curtain wall, as shown in Figure 10–79.

Figure 10–79

11. The jaggedness is partially caused by reflections of the shadows being cast near the glass. In the *Render Setup* dialog box, in the *Raytracer* tab, clear **Enable Self Reflect / Refract**, as shown in Figure 10–80.

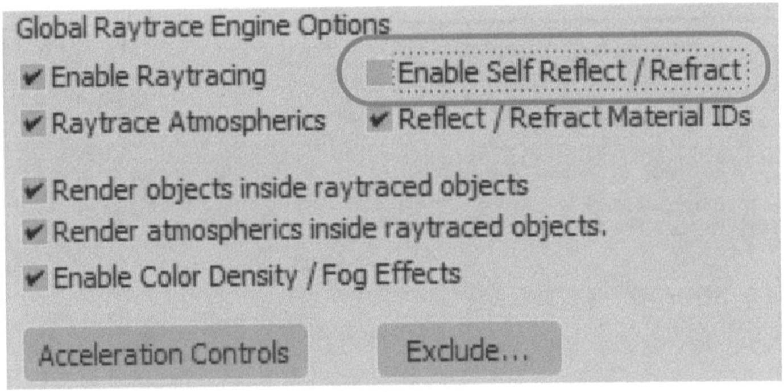

Figure 10–80

12. Render the scene. Note that the outside wall is still jagged and the floor shadows are reflected to the outside.
13. In the *Slate Material Editor*, in the *Material/Map Browser*, in the *Scene Materials*, double-click on **Curtain Walls** and **Curtain Wall Doors** to display both of those materials in the *View1* sheet. Click (Lay Out All - Vertical) to arrange the materials vertically, as shown in Figure 10–81.

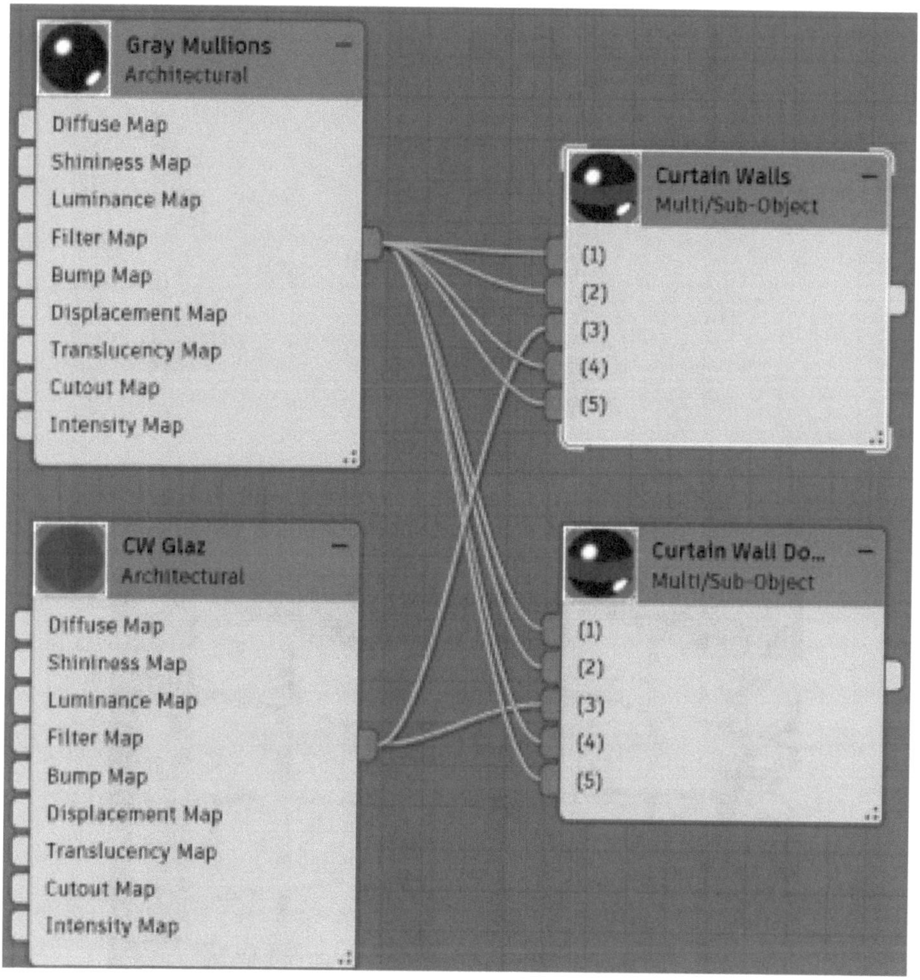

Figure 10–81

14. Click on the title **CW Glaz** (Architectural material) to open its Parameter Editor. In the *Physical Qualities* rollout, note that the default *Index of Refraction* is **1.5**, which causes a significant refraction through the glass, as shown on the left in Figure 10–83. Set the *Index of Refraction* to **1.0** (as shown in Figure 10–82), which results in no refraction.

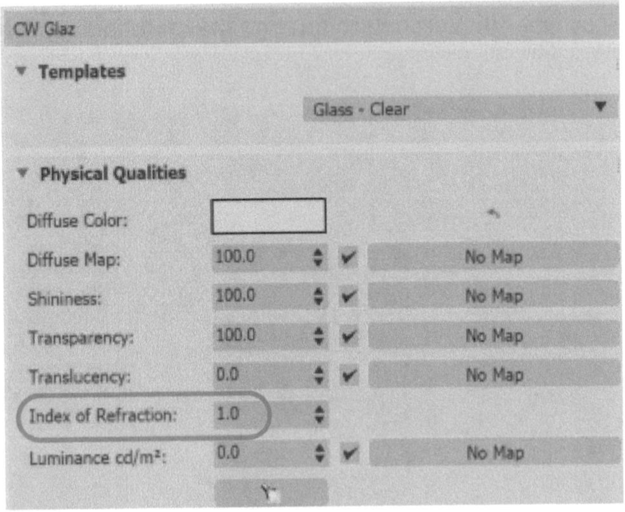

Figure 10–82

15. Render the scene again, as shown on the right in Figure 10–83. The outside wall and rails are less jagged and the glass is less shiny with no floor shadows reflected to the outside.

Index of Refraction: 1.5 ***Index of Refraction: 1.0***

Figure 10–83

16. Close the *Slate Material Editor* and all the dialog boxes.
17. Save your scene file as **MyRendering Options.max**.

Task 2: Assign a double-sided material.

1. Reset the scene.
2. In the Command Panel>*Create* panel ( ), click (Geometry), and in the *Object Type* rollout, click **Teapot**. In the **Perspective** viewport, click and drag to create the teapot object of any size.
   - At the University of Utah in 1975, Professor Martin Newell developed the teapot object. It was used for testing rendering algorithms. Today, the (Newell) teapot still exists in many 3D applications, including the Autodesk 3ds Max software.
3. With the teapot selected, select the *Modify* panel ( ) and in the *Teapot Parts* area in the *Parameters* rollout, clear the **Lid** option, as shown in Figure 10–84.
4. In the **Perspective** viewport, use (Orbit) to change the orientation of the teapot so that the inside displays. Change the *Viewport Shading* to **High Quality** to clearly display the inside of the teapot, as shown in Figure 10–85. Note that the faces on the inside of the teapot are visible.

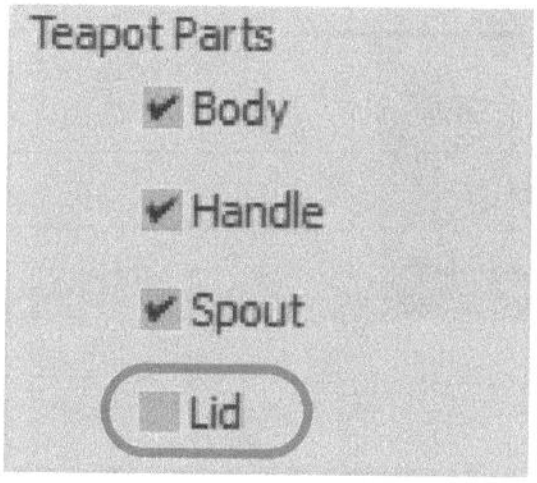

Figure 10–84

Figure 10–85

5. Select the teapot, if required, right-click, and select **Object Properties**. In the *General* tab, in the *Display Properties* area, verify that **By Object** is displayed. If **By Layer** is displayed, click it to change it to **By Object**. Select **Backface Cull** (as shown in Figure 10–86) and click **OK**. Note that the inside faces of the teapot become invisible.

Figure 10–86

6. Click  to open the *Render Setup* dialog box and set the *Renderer* to **Scanline Renderer**. Click **Render** to render the **Perspective** view. Note that the inside of the teapot is black, due to the black background (as shown in Figure 10–87) indicating that the inside faces of the teapot are missing. Leave the Rendered Frame Window open.

Figure 10–87

7. Open the *Slate Material Editor*. In **Materials>General** categories, double-click on the material **Double Sided**. Both the **Facing** and the **Back** materials are gray. Click on the material node wired to the *Facing* slot and assign a blue color to the **Base Color** swatch in the *Basic Parameters* rollout of the Physical material. Similarly, click on the material node wired to the *Back* slot and assign a red color to the **Base Color** swatch. Drag and drop (or use ) to assign the **Double Sided** material to the teapot.

8. Render the scene. The inside faces are now visible in the rendering, as shown in Figure 10–88. The Object properties are overridden by the double-sided material.

Figure 10–88

Task 3: Use the double-sided rendering option.

1. In the *Slate Material Editor,* open the **Materials>Scanline** categories and double-click on the **Standard (Legacy)** material. The **Standard** material is not double-sided. Click to open the Parameter Editor and assign the color red to its **Diffuse** channel in the *Blinn Basic Parameters* rollout. Assign this material to the teapot. Close the *Slate Material Editor.*
2. Render the scene. The faces inside the teapot are missing and display as black because of the background color.
3. Open the *Render Setup* dialog box ( (Render Setup) in the Main Toolbar). In the *Common* tab, in the *Common Parameters* rollout, in the *Options* area, select **Force 2-Sided,** as shown in Figure 10–89.

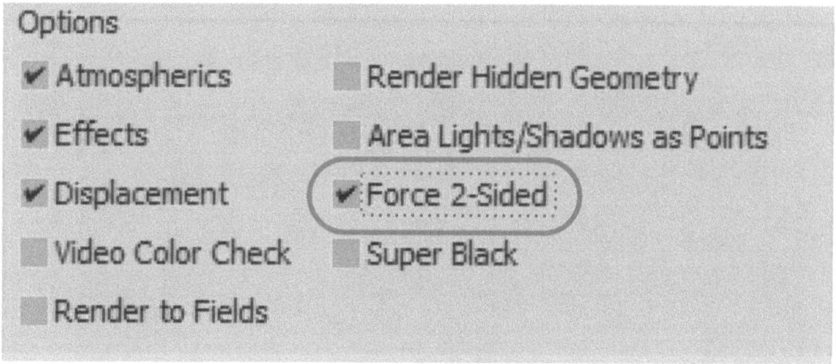

Figure 10–89

4. Render the scene. The teapot renders double-sided, as shown in Figure 10–90.

Figure 10–90

5. Save your work as **MyTeapot.max**.

End of practice

10.7 State Sets

State Sets is a scene management/render pass manager in the Autodesk 3ds Max software. The *State Sets* dialog box enables you to record the changes made to the scene at different intervals and saves them in an hierarchical form. Select **Rendering>State Sets** or click in the State Sets toolbar to open the State Sets Explorer, as shown in Figure 10–91. It opens in the tree view called *States* in which the states are recorded and managed.

- The tree view opens with the master state at the top, which displays as State Sets, and contains the **State01** state.
- You can add a new state by clicking next to the master state or by selecting **States>Add State**. A new state with the name **State02** is added in the tree view, as shown in Figure 10–91.

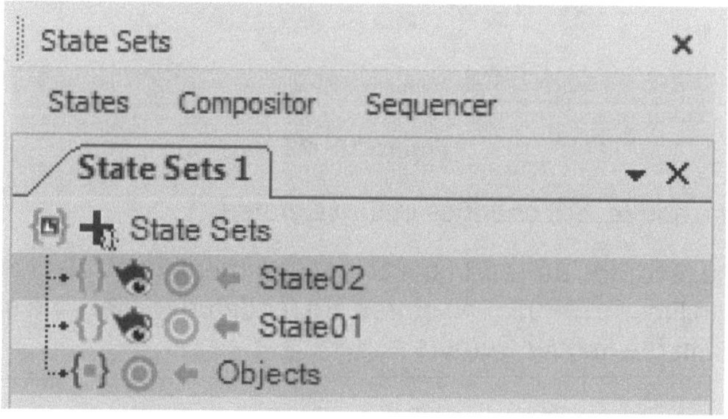

Figure 10–91

- To make a state current, click on the gray arrow. An active state is indicated by a green arrow.

- To record changes to a state, click (gray circle) next to the state. The (gray circle) changes to (black circle), indicating that the state is being recorded, and that you can start making changes to the scene. Once you have made your changes, click (black circle) to stop recording. The recorded changes display as a children for this state, as shown in Figure 10–92.

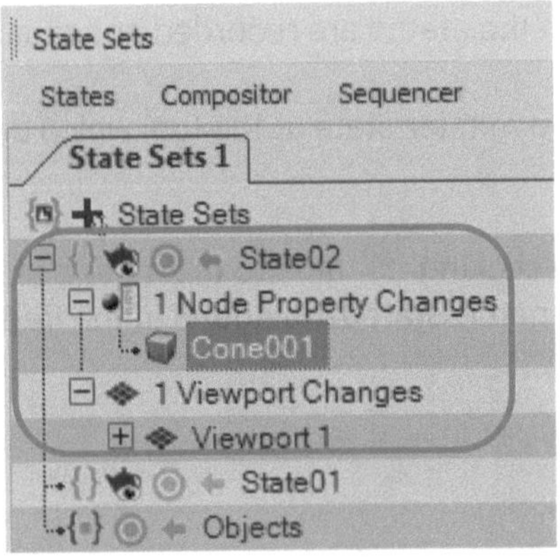

Figure 10–92

- You can add states and record changes in those states.
- To render all of the recorded states, in the State Sets menu bar, select **States>Render All States**, as shown in Figure 10–93. The states are rendered to files and saved in the path and filename specified in the *Render Outputs* panel.

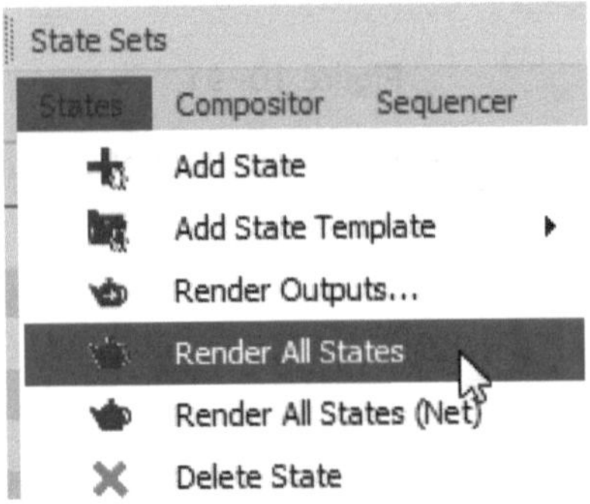

Figure 10–93

- To set a name and path for the output files, select **States>Render Outputs** to display the render outputs panel where you can browse and set the path for the files.

  Note: *Some of the changes, such as using transforms, are not recordable by State Sets. See the Autodesk 3ds Max Help for a list of properties that can be used with the State Sets.*

Compositer View

You can display the Compositor View by selecting **Compositor> Compositor View** in the dialog box menu bar with similar functionality to the View sheet in the *Slate Material Editor*, as shown in Figure 10–94.

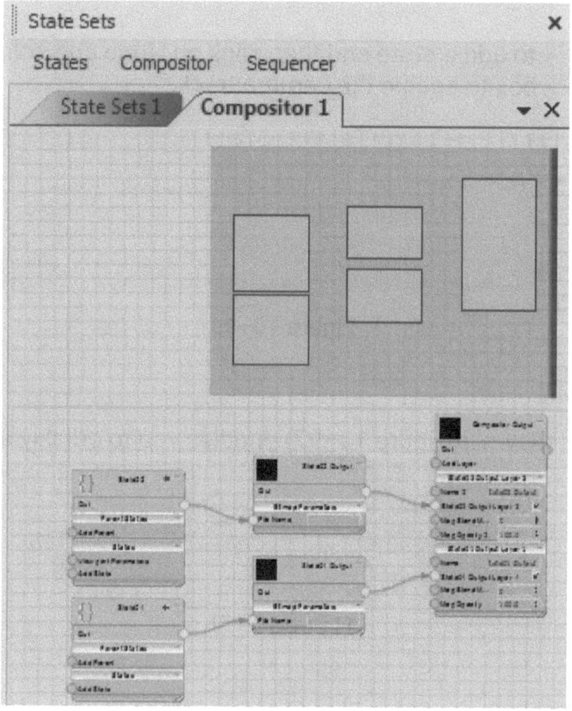

Figure 10–94

Note that in the Compositor View, all of the wired states display. You can modify the composition by modifying the nodes. You can select **Compositor>Compositor Link** to output the composition to the After Effects software or select **Compositor>Create PSD** to output the composition to an Adobe Photoshop .PSD file, as shown in Figure 10–95.

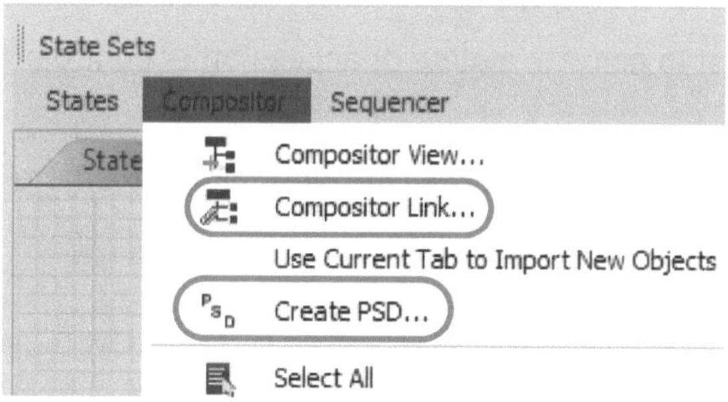

Figure 10–95

Camera Sequencer

You can use the Sequencer mode to set up an animation using multiple camera views. Select **Sequencer>Sequencer Mode** to activate a window along the bottom of the viewports with a track window indicating the cameras that are in use along with the range of frames for active cameras, as shown in Figure 10–96.

To add a camera, use  to add a state and then click on **None** and select camera from the menu. Click on the check box to enable the camera track.

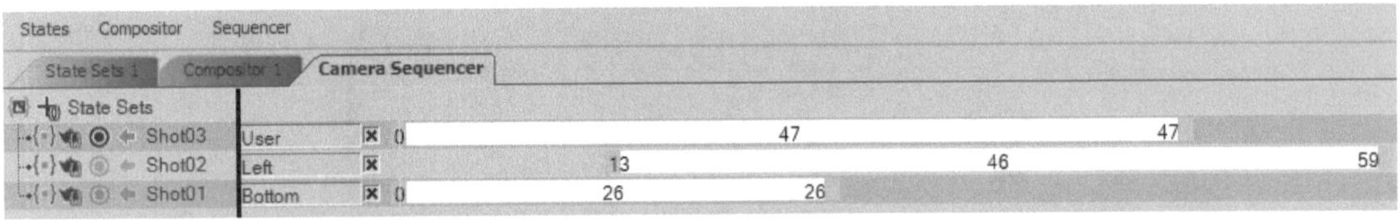

Figure 10–96

State Sets Toolbar

The State Sets toolbar (shown in Figure 10–97) enables you to quickly access the State Sets features.

Figure 10–97

- Click  to open or close the State Sets Explorer. When you toggle it on and then select **Render All States** from the **States** menu in the *State Sets* dialog box, the state is rendered with the changed properties.
- Click  to toggle the render output for the state on or off. When you toggle it on and then select **Render All States** from the **States** menu in the State Sets Explorer, the state is rendered.
- Use the drop-down list to activate a state or access other controls.
- Click  to open the *Select Composite Link File* dialog box where you can browse and use the selected .SOF (state output file).

10.8 The Print Size Wizard

When you create renderings for print, the *Print Size Wizard* (shown in Figure 10–98) can help you select an appropriate rendering based on a required output resolution. To access the wizard, select **Rendering>Print Size Assistant**.

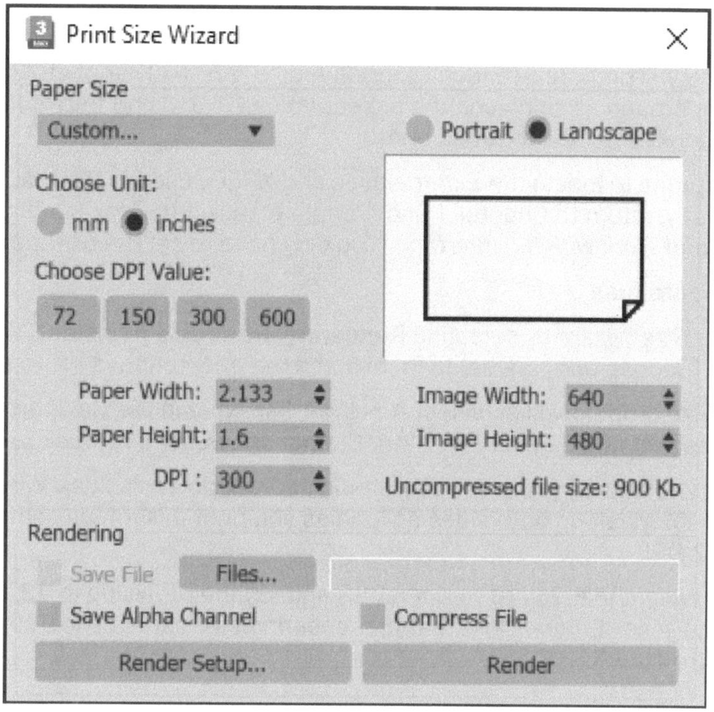

Figure 10–98

- A rendering's print resolution describes how many pixels show per printed inch, often referred to as pixels-per-inch on screen (ppi) or dots-per-inch on paper (DPI). Select the required dpi in the *Choose DPI Value* options.
- Rendering time increases exponentially with size, so select the lowest resolution that provides an acceptable result.
- Many laser printers and plotters output between 300-600 DPI, however, when rendering values such as 72-150 DPI you can also get good results. High-end equipment plotting at 1200 DPI or better creates outstanding prints at 200-300 dpi and on high-quality paper.
- Higher quality paper can get better results than increasing resolution.

Note: *Trial and error might be required to determine an appropriate resolution.*

Practice 10e
Use the Print Size Wizard

Practice Objective

- Set the print resolution, paper size, and other options for a rendering.

In this practice, you will prepare a rendering for an A-size, 8.5" x 11" print at 72 DPI. You want at least a 1/2" border around all sides and the aspect ratio of 1.6. Using the *Print Size Wizard*, you will set all the options to get the required print.

You must set the paths to locate the External files and XREFs used in the practice. If you have not done this already, return to Chapter 1 and complete Task 1 to Task 3 in *Practice 1a: Organize Folders and Work with the Interface*. You only have to set the user paths once.

1. Open **Print Wizard.max**.
2. Open the *Print Size Wizard* by selecting **Rendering>Print Size Assistant**. Verify that the printing units (*Choose Unit*) are set to **inches** and the orientation is set to **Landscape**.
3. In the *Paper Size* drop-down list, select **A – 11x8.5in**. Note in the viewport that this setting changes the aspect ratio (11"/8.5" = 1.29). Change the *Paper Size* back to **Custom**.
4. Set the *Paper Width* to **10** (11" minus a half-inch border on each side). When printing, the 1/2" border displays along both sides as long as you print this image centered on an 8.5" x 11" page at 72 DPI.
5. Set the *Paper Height* to **6.25** (10"/1.6 = 6.25") and set the *DPI* value to **72**, as shown in Figure 10–99. Press <Enter>. Note that the rendering size changes to 720 x 450 pixels, as shown in Figure 10–99.

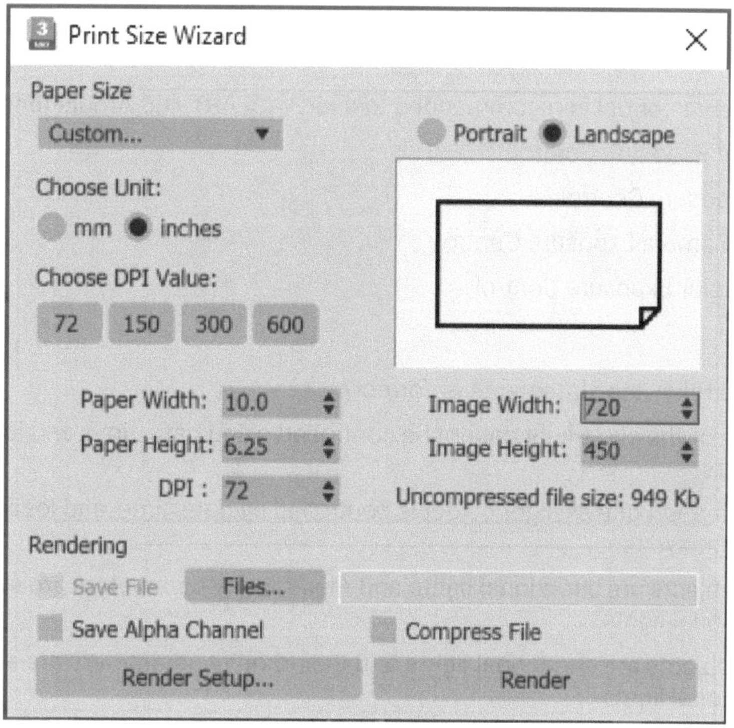

Figure 10–99

6. Click **Render**.

   - Once rendered, you can save the image by clicking (Save Image) in the Rendered Frame Window and then open it in an image editor or layout program to add your company logo, titles, labels, and other additional details.
   - You can also print directly to the current system printer by clicking (Print Image) in the Rendered Frame Window.

7. Save the file as **MyPrint Wizard.max**.

End of practice

Chapter Review Questions

1. Which exposure control is recommended to used with ART and Arnold renderers?
   a. Automatic Exposure Control
   b. Linear Exposure Control
   c. Physical Camera Exposure Control
   d. Pseudo Color Exposure Control

2. Which of the following statements is correct?
   a. The angle of the sun's light cannot be controlled using date, time, and location parameters.
   b. The illumination of a skylight object is controlled by date, time, and location settings of the sunlight system.
   c. Skylight objects are directional lights and their modify parameters are similar to those for directional lights.
   d. Sunlight objects are directional lights and their modify parameters are similar to those for directional lights.

3. Which of the following is not supported by Arnold renderer?
   a. Standard lights
   b. Photometric lights
   c. Physical materials
   d. Sun Positioner

4. Which Production renderer must be active for the Image Based Lighting (IBL) rendering technique to become available?
   a. Scanline Renderer
   b. Arnold Renderer
   c. VUE File Renderer
   d. Quicksilver Hardware Renderer

5. Which renderer in the Autodesk 3ds Max software is not a graphical renderer and uses ASCII text files to describe the position and transformation of objects, lighting, etc.?
   a. Scanline Renderer
   b. VUE File Renderer
   c. Quicksilver Hardware Renderer
   d. ART Renderer

6. When saving a rendering as an image file, which of the following format offers highest color depth with a smaller compression? In other words, this image file format is the best choice regarding file size to quality ratio.
   a. .JPEG
   b. .BMP (Bitmap)
   c. .TGA (Targa)
   d. .PNG (Portable Network Graphics)
   e. .TIFF (Tagged Image File Format)

7. In rendering, which of the following is used to calculate accurate reflections, refractions, and shadows?
   a. Antialiasing
   b. SuperSampling
   c. Motion Blur
   d. Raytracing

Command Summary

Button	Command	Location
	**Effects and Environment dialog box**	• **Rendered Frame Window** • **Rendering:** Environment
	**Render Setup**	• **Main Toolbar** • **Rendering:** Render Setup
	**State Sets**	• **State Sets Toolbar** • **Rendering:** State Sets
N/A	**Viewport Configuration dialog box>*Background* tab**	• **Views:** Viewport Background>Configure Viewport Background • **Keyboard**: <Alt>+<B>

Chapter 11

Animation

Animations created in the Autodesk® 3ds Max® software involve the use of Animation and Time Controls. These enable you to animate and keyframe a camera to create a walkthrough animation or to create single-frame images and then assemble them to create a movie.

Learning Objectives

- Work with Animation and Time Controls and set various options.
- Create animation output using the various approaches available.

11.1 Animation and Time Controls

Animations in the Autodesk 3ds Max software are created by playing back a number of still frames in rapid succession using desktop animation files such as .AVIs and .MOVs.

- Traditional movies play back a sequence of still images in rapid succession.
- Computer movie formats compile a sequence of still images into a compressed format, keeping track of the changes from frame to frame at the pixel level.
- Animations are based on keyframes (or keys), which are time indexes at which objects change their position, rotation, scale, and/or a limited number of object parameters.
- The Autodesk 3ds Max software generates animations by interpolating between a small number of user-defined keyframes – smoothly or otherwise.
- The Autodesk 3ds Max animation system offers powerful controls to create animations, ranging from simple camera movements to extremely complex sequences.
- The animation controls enable you to create and play back a preview animation in one or more viewports.

Time Slider and Track Bar

The time slider and the track bar (shown in Figure 11–1) are found below the viewports and enable you to advance and reverse along an animation forward or backwards in time.

- The numbers below the time slider indicate the current time or frame number. Use the greater than (>) and lesser than (<) keys as shortcuts for moving the time slider a frame at a time.
- The shortcut menu in the Track bar contains the key properties and the controller properties. Selecting a key and then right-clicking displays all of the values for that key. Using the shortcut menu, you can also delete keys and use filter options for the display of the track bar.

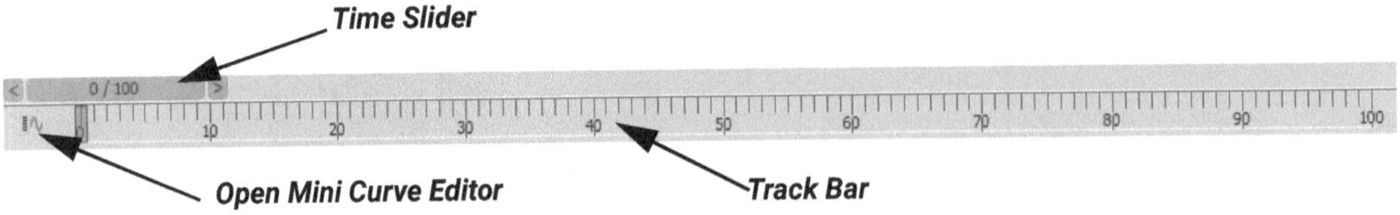

Figure 11–1

- On the left side of the track bar, clicking  (Open Mini Curve Editor) opens the *Mini Curve Editor* (as shown in Figure 11–2), which replaces the track bar and the time slider. The Curve Editor contains a menu bar, toolbar, controller window, and the key window. You can collapse the Curve Editor by clicking **Close** at the left end of the Curve Editor toolbar.

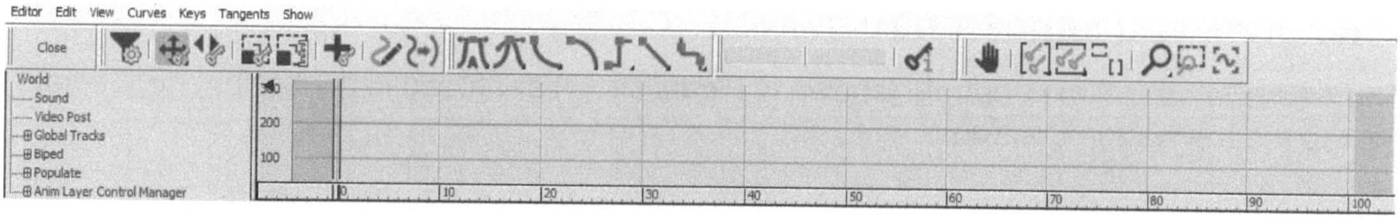

Figure 11–2

Hint: Track View: Using the Curve Editor and Dope Sheet

The Curve Editor and Dope Sheet are two animation data editors which graphically display and enable you to modify the animation controllers that are used to interpolate the objects in a scene.

- To open the *Track View - Curve Editor*, in the Main Toolbar, click , or in the Menu Bar, select **Graph Editors>Track View- Curve Editor**.
- In the Curve Editor, the animation displays in the form of function curves, as shown in Figure 11–3. You can visualize and modify the motion by controlling the curves (i.e., tangent handles) at various keys.

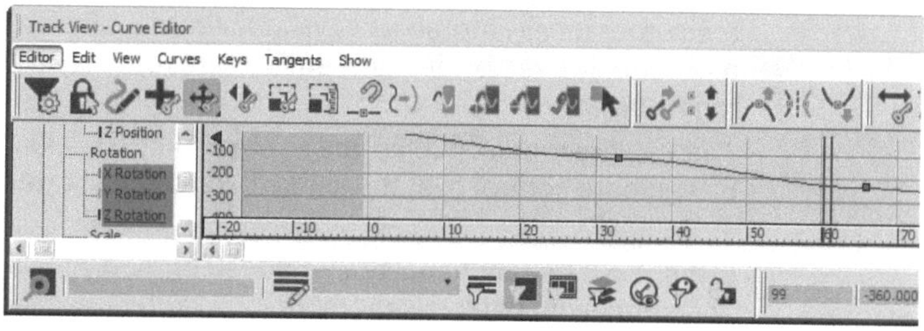

Figure 11–3

- To open the *Track View - Dope Sheet*, in the Menu Bar, select **Graph Editors>Track View- Dope Sheet**.
- In the Dope sheet, the animation displays in the form of a spread sheet displaying keys and ranges, as shown in Figure 11–4. You can visualize and modify the motion by controlling the keys directly.

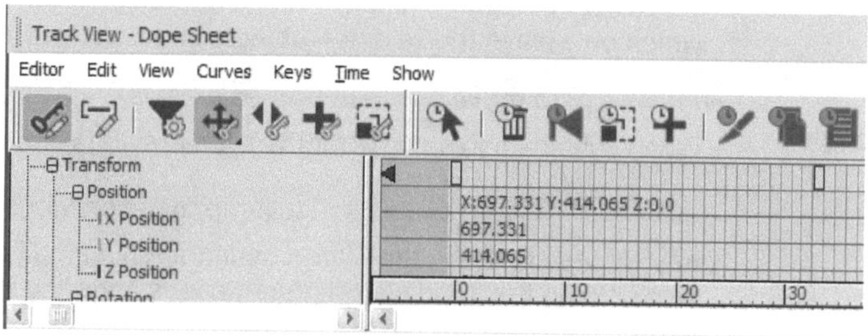

Figure 11–4

Animation and Time Controls

The Animation and Time Controls (shown in Figure 11–5) are found in the bottom right corner next to the Navigation Controls.

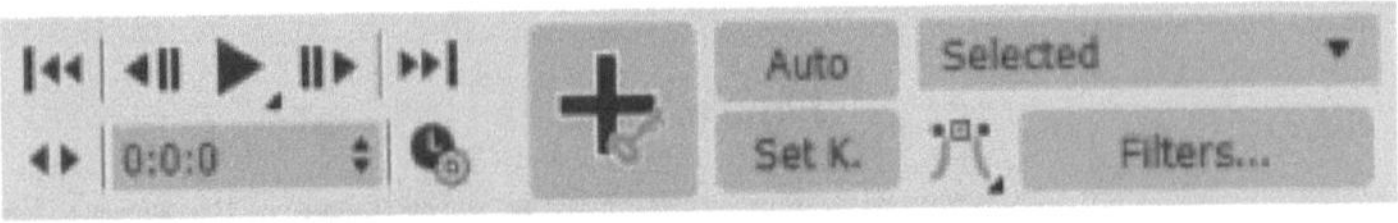

Figure 11–5

The various Animation and Time controls are as follows:

	Enables you to manually add an animation key at the time shown in the time slider.
Auto/Set Key	Activates either **Auto** or **Set Key** animation modes. When either **Auto** mode or **Set Key** mode is active, their corresponding buttons display in red, indicating that you are in the animation mode. • When **Auto** mode is active all movement, rotation, and scale changes are automatically stored as keys at the current frame. This method is more widely used by design visualizers. Press <N> as a shortcut to toggle on the mode. • The **Set Key** mode enables you to create keys, set key information, and offers more control over the kinds of keys you create through filters by using . Its functionality was added primarily for character animators who used this methodology in other packages. Press <'> (single apostrophe) as a shortcut to toggle on the mode.
Previous/Play/ Next 	Enable you to play an animation in your viewport(s) and advance to the next or previous frame/key. • When you click  (Play Animation), the software plays the animation in the active viewport and replaces this icon with  (Stop Animation). •  (Play Animation) is a flyout and contains  (Play Selected), which only plays the selected objects in the active viewport.
 (Key Mode Toggle)	Enables you to move between frames or keys. • When you are in Key mode (active), the Previous and Next icons display as  and enable you to jump to the previous or next keyframe. • Keyframes are set in the *Time Configuration* dialog box (Key Steps area). When Key mode is off, the Previous and Next icons display as  and you can jump to the previous and next frame.

(Go to Start)/ (Go to End)	Enable you to move directly to the beginning or end of an animation. The time slider jumps to the selected location.
86 (Current Frame)	Enables you to advance to a specific frame or time in the animation.
Key Filters...	Opens the *Set Key Filters* dialog box, which enables you to select the tracks on which the keys can be created. The track sets are created with the **Set Key** mode. The *Selected* drop-down list contains the created track sets and selection sets and enables you to select the required one quickly.
(Default In/Out Tangents for New Keys)	Contains a list of tangent types. 
(Time Configuration)	Opens the *Time Configuration* dialog box.

Time Configuration

Clicking  (Time Configuration) opens the *Time Configuration* dialog box (as shown in Figure 11–6) where you assign an animation, its length, playback rate, and other critical parameters. It is recommended to adjust these parameters before you start configuring an animation.

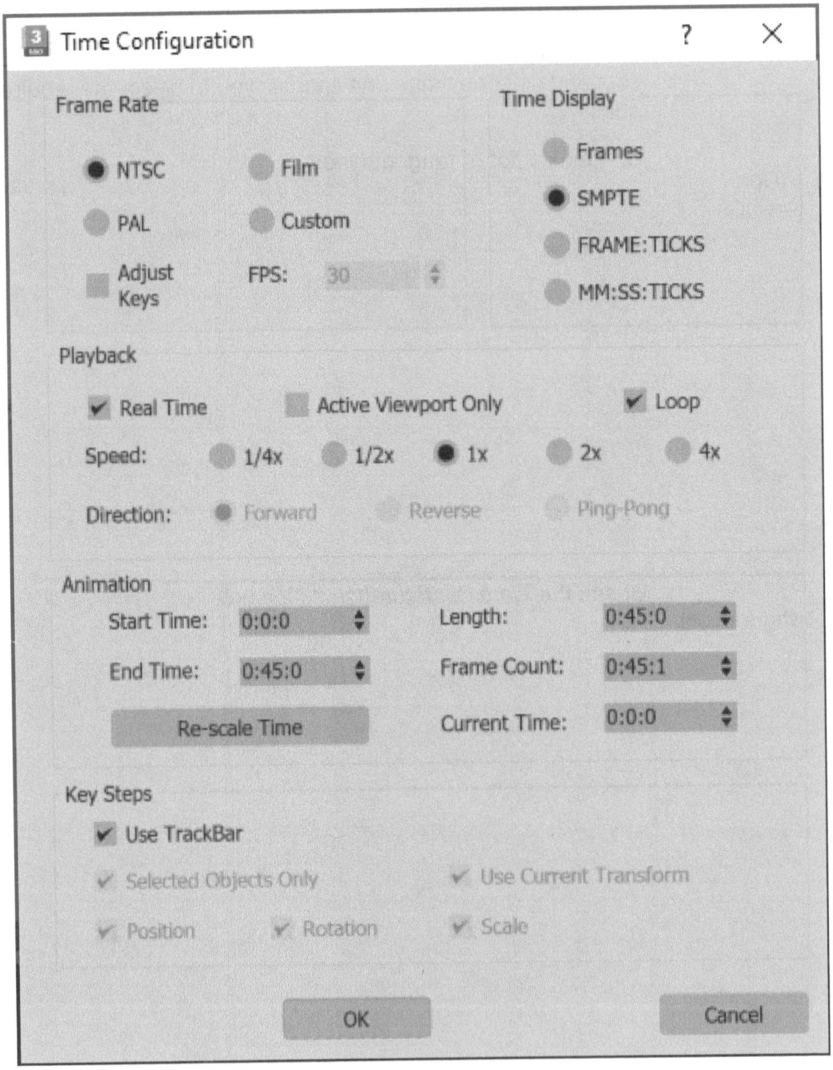

Figure 11–6

The *Frame Rate* area provides options to define how many still frames to show per second (FPS). When setting a frame rate, the goal is to create an animation that flows smoothly without rendering additional frames. The best choice for frame rate depends on the medium where you intend to play your animation.

NTSC	**National Television Standards Committee:** the standard television frame rate used across most of the Americas and Japan: 30 FPS.
PAL	**Phase Alternate Line:** the standard used across Europe: 25 FPS.
Film	Assigns the frame rate used in film production: 24 FPS.
Custom	Enables you to select a specific frame rate. Animations created for desktop and web-based presentations are often set 12-25 FPS.

The *Time Display* area provides options to select how you want to measure time during your animation.

Frames	Measures time in the number of frames that have elapsed since the beginning of the animation.
SMPTE	The time measurement standard used by the Society of Motion Picture Technical Engineers for video and television productions. This standard measures time in minutes, seconds, and frames separated by colons (such as 1:22:43).
FRAME:TICKS	Measures time in frames and ticks only. A tick is a unit of animated time that equals 1/4800 of a second.
MM:SS:TICKS	Measures time in minutes, seconds and ticks.

The *Playback* area provides options to control how the animation is played back in the viewports.

Real Time	Plays the animation at the real world playback rate, skipping frames, if required. Clearing this option displays all frames in sequence, even if it slows down the animation preview. This is used by most animators to inspect every frame for problems.
Speed	When **Real Time** is enabled, speed up or slow down the animation using this option or continually play using the **Loop** option.
Direction	When not using **Real Time** you can select to play the animation forwards, backwards, or ping-pong (forwards and backwards again) using the **Direction** option.
Active Viewport Only	Limits the animation preview to the active viewport, which might be required if system resources are taxed by the animation playback.

The options in the *Animation* area define the active time segment (the current animation length) between the starting and ending time.

Start Time	Can be equal to 0, a positive, or negative time value as required.

End Time	Can be equal to 0, a positive, or negative time value as required.
Length	The calculated time between the starting and ending points.
Frame Count	A value equal to the animation length + 1 frame, to account for the rendering of frame 0.
Current Time	Provides the frame you are on in the animation. Use this field to change to a different frame without exiting the dialog box.

When animation times are changed in this dialog box, the existing keys do not automatically scale to the new time. For example, if you lengthen an existing animation by increasing the end time, the current animation still stops at the old end time (unless you then manually adjust the keys).

To expand or contract an animation's overall length, click **Re-scale Time**, to open the *Rescale Time* dialog box, as shown in Figure 11–7. Changing the animation times spaces the existing keys along the new animation length.

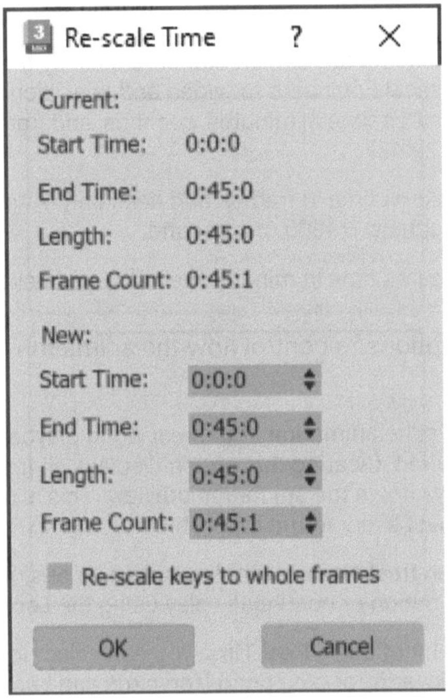

Figure 11–7

The *Key Steps* area provides options to limit how and which animation keys are created in Key mode. Leave the **Use TrackBar** option enabled to not limit key creation.

Progressive Display and Adaptive Degradation

The Progressive Display (only for Nitrous drivers) and Adaptive Degradation is a display option that can be very useful when playing animations in the viewport or when navigating large files in the viewport. When enabled (in the Status Bar, click , or use <O> to toggle it on/off) it degrades an animation preview to a simpler display method to display the correct playback rate. It enables you to play a complex animation in a viewport at the correct speed, even if it means simplifying the display to a less detailed display mode, such as wireframe.

In the Status Bar, right-click on (Adaptive Degradation) to open the *Viewport Configuration* dialog box in the *Display Performance* tab, as shown in Figure 11–8. You can also open this dialog box by selecting **Views>Viewports Configuration** and then selecting the *Display Performance* tab. Alternatively, click the **[+]** *General Viewport* label and select **Configure Viewports**. Using the menu bar or the *Viewport* label menu opens the dialog box in the *Visual Style & Appearance* tab. Select the *Display Performance* tab.

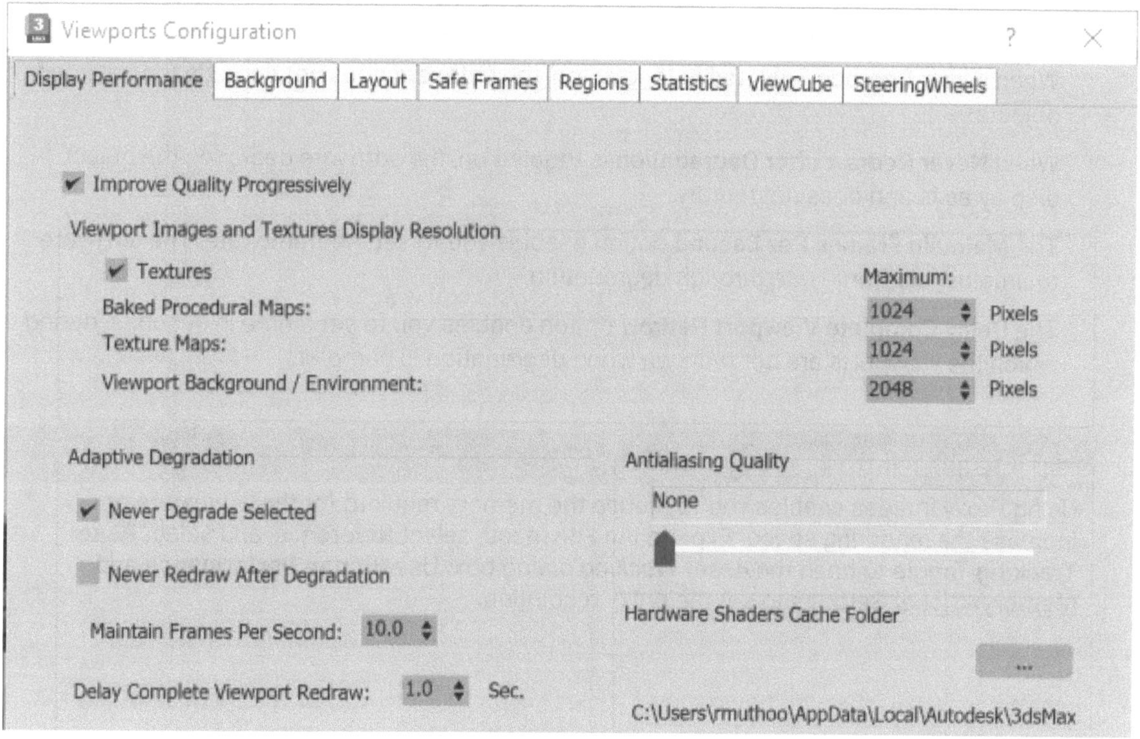

Figure 11–8

Note: *If you are using one of the legacy display drivers (Direct3D or Open GL), the Adaptive Degradation tab replaces the Display Performance tab in the Viewport Configuration dialog box.*

Improve Quality Progressively

This option (only available for Nitrous display drivers) enables you to improve the viewport quality through successive iterations. Once the iterations have been completed, a high quality rendered image displays in the viewport. You can also activate or clear this option in the menu bar (**Views>Progressive Display**).

The *Viewport Images and Textures Display Resolution* area contains the following options:

Baked Procedural Maps	Enables you to set the resolution, in pixels, that is used to display the procedural maps in the viewports.
Texture Maps	Enables you to set the resolution in pixels, that is used to display the texture maps in the viewports.
Viewport Background/ Environment	Enables you to set the resolution in pixels, that is used to display the environment and background maps.

Adaptive Degradation

The *Adaptive Degradation* area has the following options:

- When **Never Degrade Selected** is toggled on, the software does not degrade the selected objects.
- When **Never Redraw after Degradation** is toggled on, the software degrades the object display as is and does not redraw.
- The **Maintain Frames Per Second** option enables you to set the frame rate. The software maintains this frame rate through degradation.
- The **Delay Complete Viewport Redraw** option enables you to set a time in seconds, during which the viewports are not redrawn when degradation is complete.

Hint: Bitmap Proxy Images

Using Proxy images enables you to reduce the memory required for the 2D texture and increase the rendering speed. Expand the **File** menu, select **Reference**, and select **Asset Tracking Toggle** to open the *Asset Tracking* dialog box. Use **Bitmap Performance and Memory>Global Settings** to set the proxy resolution.

Antialiasing Quality

Enables antialiasing in the viewport, which attempts to soften the rough edges in 3D Geometry. Note that higher quality settings can reduce system performance.

Hardware Shaders Cache Folder

The folder, along with the complete path where the hardware shaders are saved, displays. Click **...** (as shown in Figure 11–9) to open the *Configure User and System Paths* dialog box, which enables you to modify the location for saving the hardware shaders.

Figure 11–9

11.2 Walkthrough Animation

When animating cameras, it is often easier to have a camera follow a linear path than to configure the camera's position manually. For example, in Figure 11–10, you can animate a camera following a path going up a street to the house.

Figure 11–10

- To animate a target camera following a path, you create a helper object called a dummy object, as shown in Figure 11–11. While a dummy object is not required, it provides more control.
- The path can be a spline (shown in Figure 11–11) created in the Autodesk 3ds Max software or a linked/imported object. You then create a target camera and dummy object and align them so they share a similar orientation. Multiple paths can be assigned and weighted during an animation.

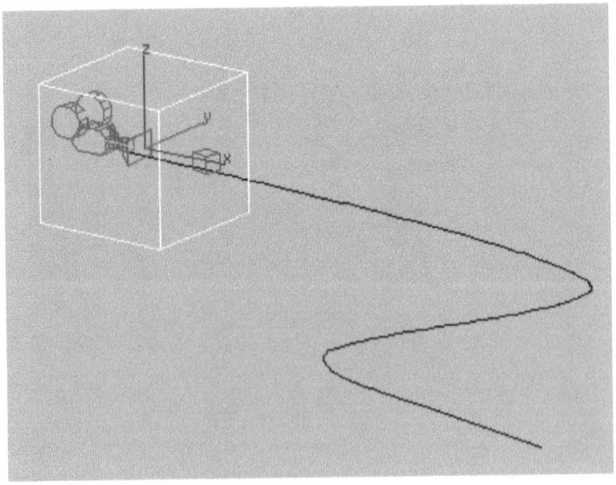

Figure 11–11

- To create a dummy object, in the Command Panel>*Create* panel (), click  (Helpers). In the *Object Type* rollout, click **Dummy**, as shown in Figure 11–12.
- A dummy object (white square object) is usually drawn in the **Top** viewport to ensure orientation with world space, as shown on the right in Figure 11–12. Dummies have no parameters in the *Modify* panel and do not render in your final animation.

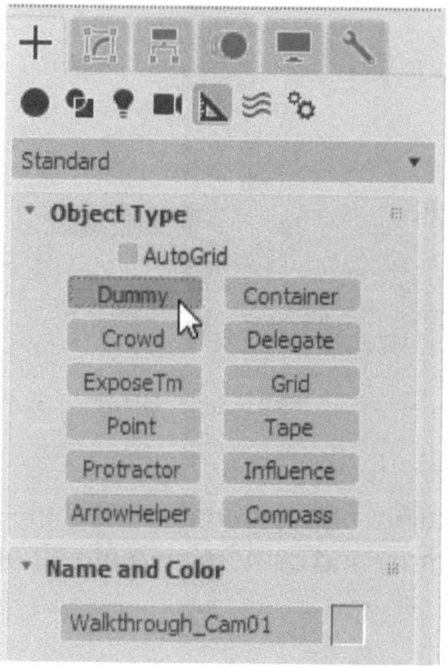

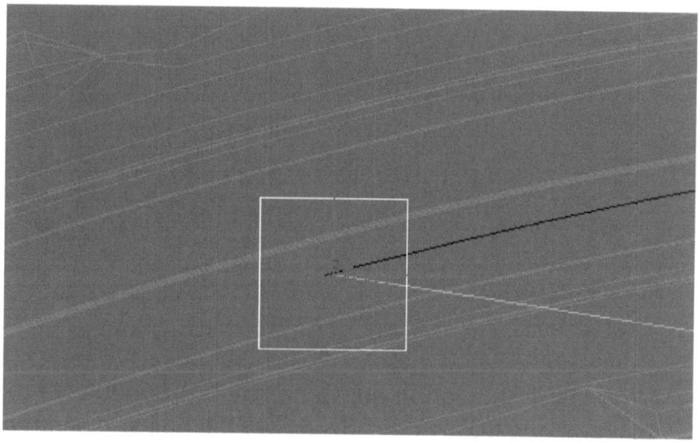

Dummy object drawn in Top viewport

Figure 11–12

- In the Main Toolbar, use  (Select and Link) to link the camera and dummy.

- To animate the dummy object and camera, define a Path Constraint. Select **Animation>Constraints>Path Constraint**, as shown on the left in Figure 11–13. A dotted line displays in the viewport, as shown in Figure 11–13. Select the spline to be used as the path. If you cannot see the path, you can press <H> to select the path by name from the *Select From Scene* dialog box.

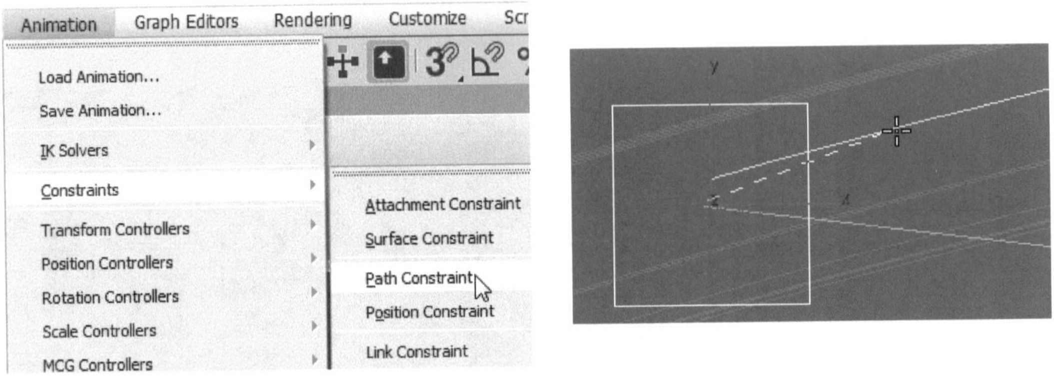

Figure 11–13

- Alternatively, the target object can be positioned over the subject and left unanimated. In this case, the target stays fixed over the building and the dummy and camera animate along the path.

Practice 11a
Create a Turntable Animation

Practice Objective

- Animate a building by rotating a camera around it at keyframe intervals.

In this practice, you will animate a camera rotating around the retail exterior building. You will add a dummy object on the building and set the keyframes, then apply rotation at the keyframes. You will then add interpolation to the keys using the dialog box and the Curve Editor. This creates the illusion that the viewer is standing still and the building is revolving as if on a turntable.

You must set the paths to locate the External files and XREFs used in the practice. If you have not done this already, return to Chapter 1 and complete Task 1 to Task 3 in *Practice 1a: Organize Folders and Work with the Interface*. You only have to set the user paths once.

Task 1: Add a dummy object and keyframe it.

1. Open **Turntable_Animation_Start.max**.
2. Activate and maximize the **Top** viewport.
3. In the Scene Explorer or in the viewport, select the camera (**Turntable camera** is the only camera object). Click  (Zoom Extents All Selected) to display the camera and its target, which includes the entire building and a part of the parking lot, as shown in Figure 11–14.

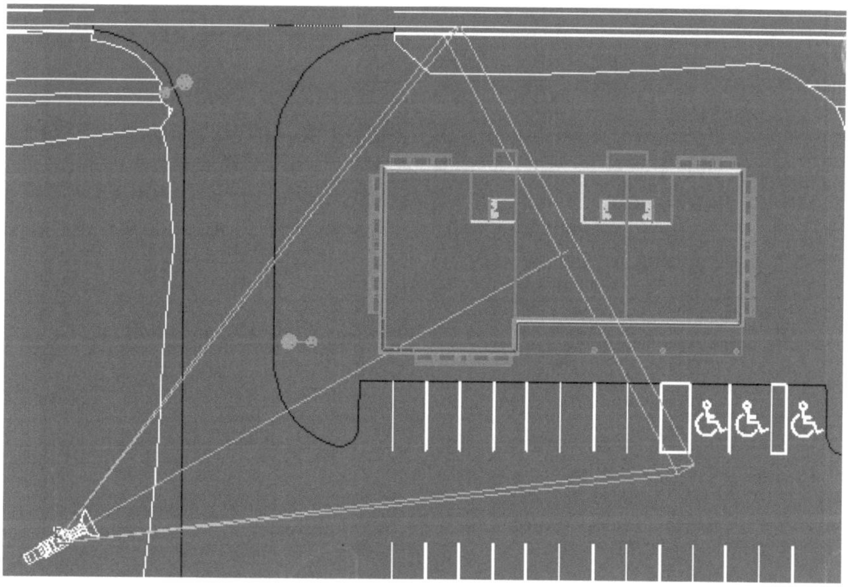

Figure 11–14

4. In the Command Panel>*Create* panel ( ), click (Helpers).
5. In the *Object Type* rollout, click **Dummy**. Starting from the camera target, click and hold on the target (the small blue square in the center of the building, as shown in Figure 11–15). Then, drag to create a dummy object (a square box) large enough to approximately extend beyond the two side (vertical) walls of the building, as shown in Figure 11–15.

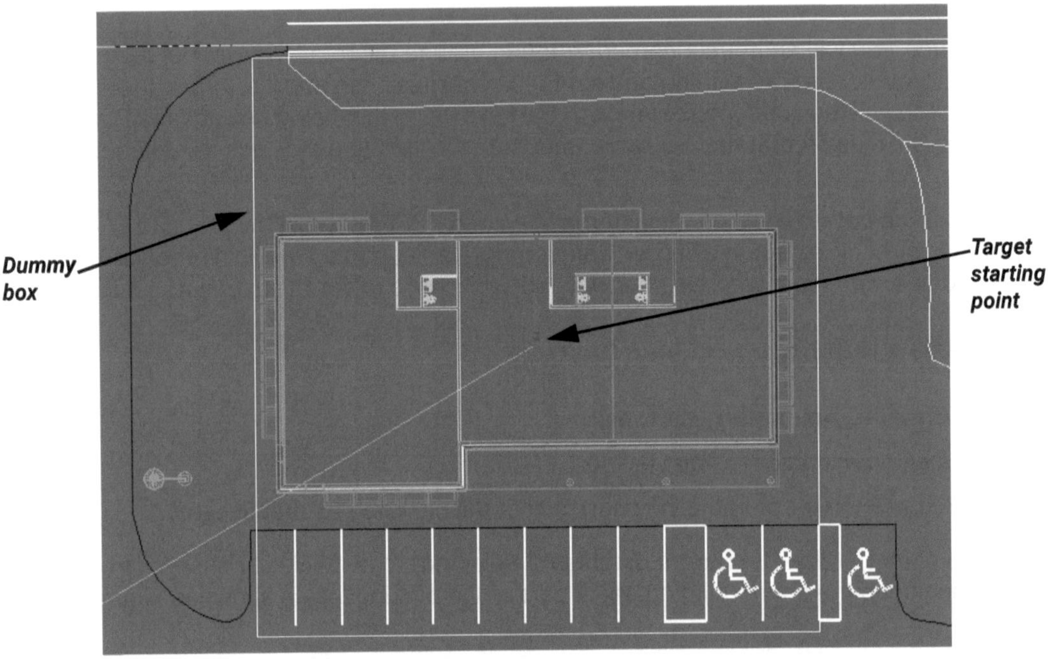

Figure 11–15

6. In the Main Toolbar, click (Select and Link). In the viewport, select **Turntable camera** (camera object). Note that the cursor displays as two linked squares when you hover it over the selected camera. Starting from the camera object, click and drag the cursor to the dummy object (box). A white dotted line displays between the camera and the dummy, and the dummy box turns yellow, as shown in Figure 11–16. Release the mouse to link the camera to the dummy.

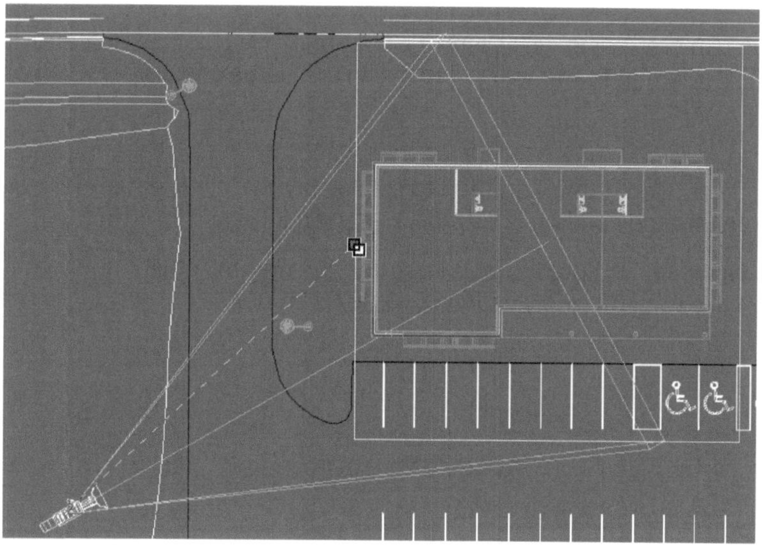

Figure 11–16

7. To test it, click  (Select and Move) and move the dummy object (the square box). The camera object should move with it. Undo the move after the test and click  (Select Object) to exit the **Move** command.

8. In the Animation playback controls, click  (Time Configuration) to open the dialog box. Set the following:

   - *Time Display* area: **Frames**
   - *Animation* area - *End Time*: **99**

9. Click **OK**. Near the bottom of the viewport, note that the Time Slider displays as **0/99**.

10. Using the layout overlay (holding <win> and pressing <Shift>), maximize the **Turntable camera** viewport.

11. In the Animation controls, click the **Auto** button, which displays a red background indicating that the scene is in the **Auto Key** animation mode. Drag the Time Slider to **frame 33**. The Track Bar displays a blue rectangular bar at frame 33, as shown in Figure 11–17.

   - In addition to the **Auto** button displaying in red, the slider bar area also displays in red and a red border surrounds the current viewport.

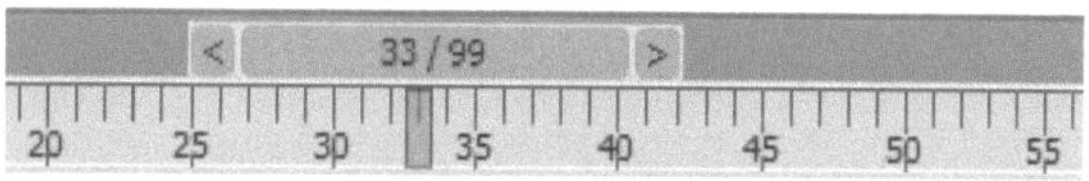

Figure 11–17

12. In the Scene Explorer, using (Display None) and (Display Helpers), select **Dummy001**. Verify that **Dummy001** displays in the *Name and Color* rollout of the Command Panel.

13. Click (Select and Rotate). In the Status Bar, in the *Z* field, enter **-120,** and press <Enter>. Note that the building is rotated as shown in Figure 11–18.
    - You can also use the Rotate gizmo to rotate the dummy object horizontally until the values on the screen display as [**0.00**, **-0.00**, **-120.00**].

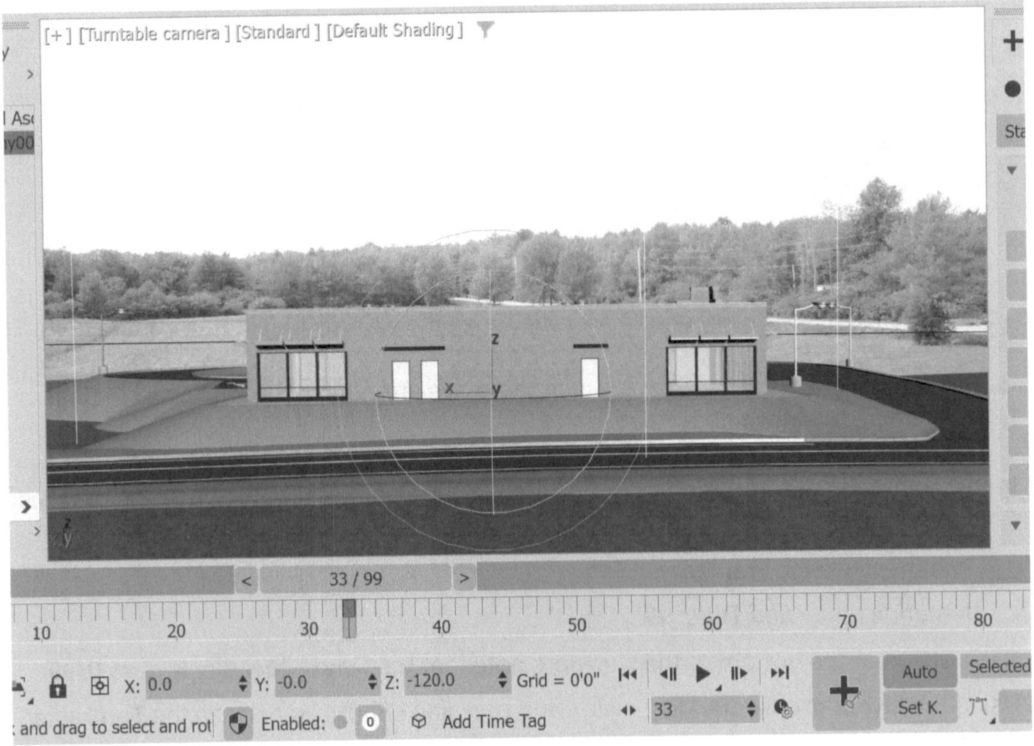

Figure 11–18

14. Drag the Time Slider to frame **66** and rotate the dummy object (along with the building) another 120°, by entering **-240** in the *Z* field of the Status Bar and press <Enter>, as shown in Figure 11–19.

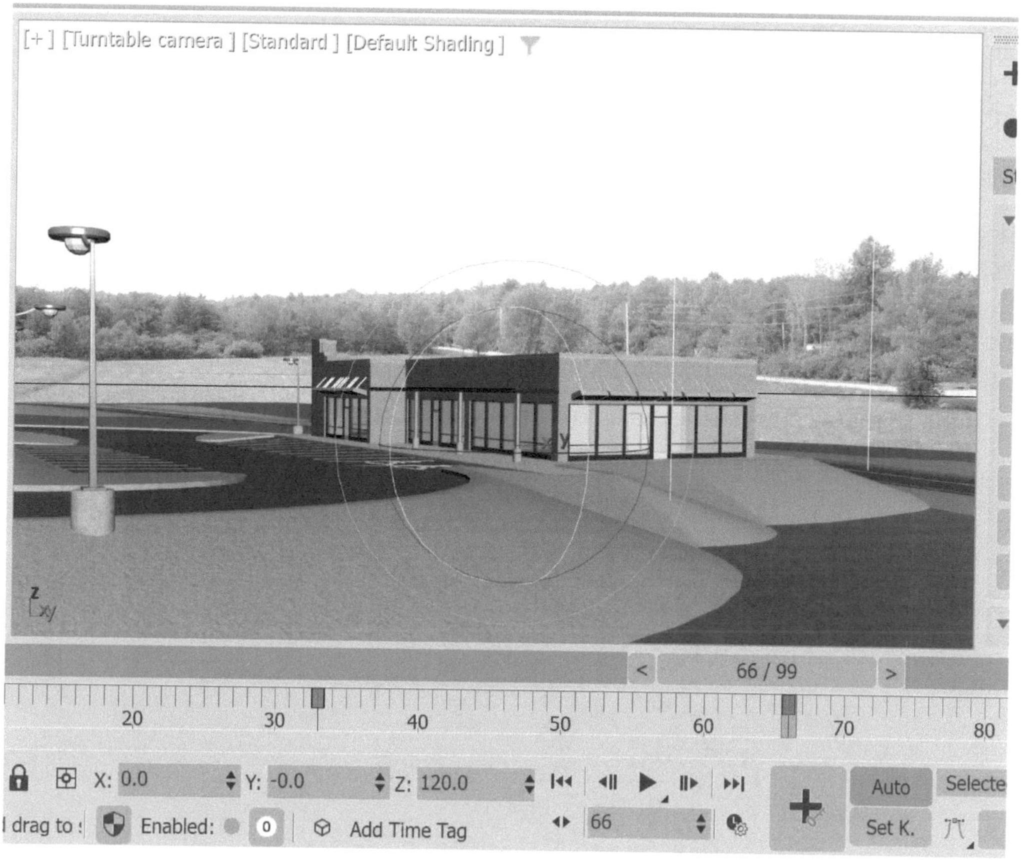

Figure 11–19

15. Drag the Time Slider to frame **99** (the end of the time slider bar) and rotate the dummy object another 120 degrees, by entering **-360** in the *Z* field. Press <Enter>.

16. In the Animation controls, click to play the animation. Note that the turntable animation of the building is created by the camera's revolution around it. Additionally note that there is a pause with each revolution of the camera. Pause the animation by clicking .

17. If your animation has a lag, in the Status Bar, click (Adaptive Degradation). If your animation plays without a lag, move to Step 21.

18. In the Animation controls, click . Note that over time, the objects change into a wireframe model and animate smoothly. (The working of the Adaptive degradation depends on your system configuration. You might not see the wireframe model while using Adaptive Degradation). Pause the animation by clicking . Note that the model is redrawn as shaded almost immediately.

19. Right-click on (Adaptive Degradation) to open the *Viewport Configuration* dialog box in the *Display Performance* tab. In the *Adaptive Degradation* area, set *Delay Complete Viewport Redraw in* to **5.0** seconds. Click **OK** to close the dialog box

20. Click . Let the animation play in the viewport until the complete model has been degraded to a wireframe model and then click . Note that the model remains a wireframe for 5 seconds before it is redrawn as a shaded model.

21. Verify that the dummy object is still selected. To fix the pause at each revolution, right-click on the green key in the timeline at frame 99 and select **Dummy001: Z Rotation**, as shown in Figure 11–20. You can pause the animation, if it is still running.
    - If the animated object is not selected, the modified keys (green keys) are not displayed in the timeline.

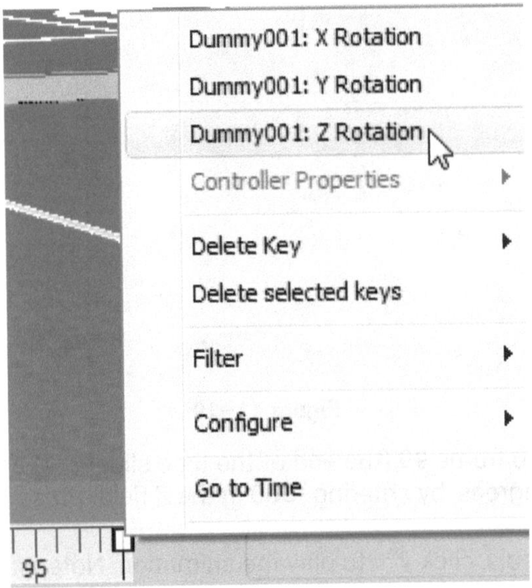

Figure 11–20

22. In the dialog box that opens, expand the *In* interpolation to display the interpolation tools flyout, as shown in Figure 11–21. Click  (Linear interpolation).

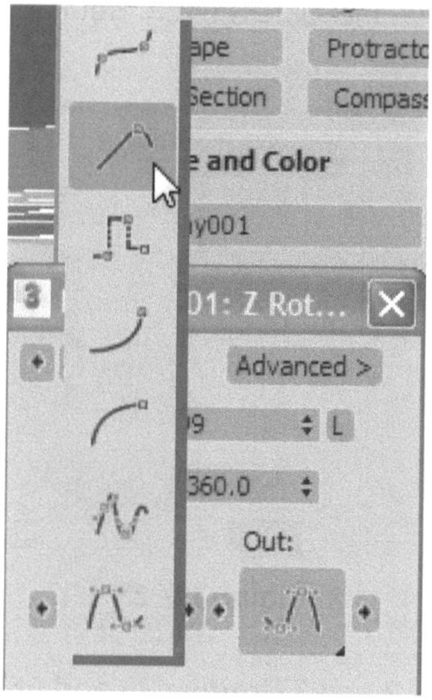

Figure 11–21

23. Similarly, change the *Out* interpolation to  (Linear interpolation), as shown in Figure 11–22.
    - This sets the interpolation to **Linear** at frame 4 (99).

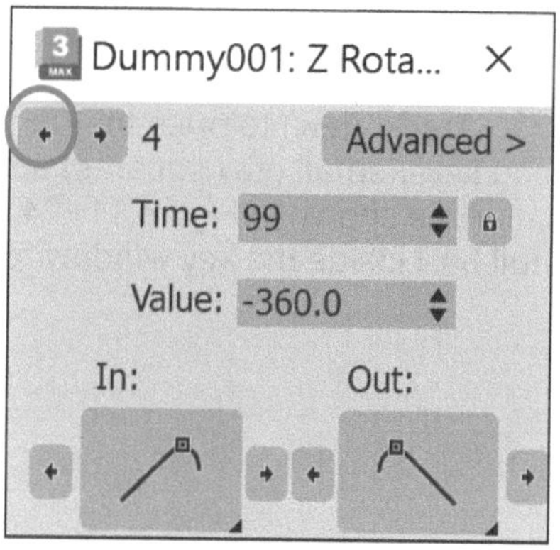

Figure 11–22

24. You will set the interpolation to **Linear** for the other three frames (0, 33, 66). In the upper left corner of the dialog box, click (left arrow) (as shown above in Figure 11–22) three times such that you advance to key **1**, which is the key number. The *Time* displays as **0** and the *Value* displays as **0.0**, as shown in Figure 11–23. Set the *In* and *Out* Interpolation to **Linear** for key 1.

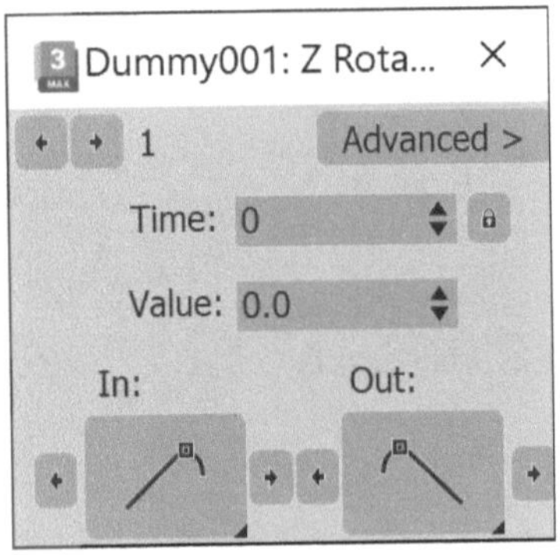

Figure 11–23

25. Repeat for the remaining keys **2** and **3** (frames 33 and 66), using (right arrow) to move to the required key. Close the dialog box.

26. Click to play the animation. It should rotate in a loop without any pause.

27. Click to pause the animation.

Task 2: Use the Curve Editor.

1. In the Main Toolbar, click (Track View) to open the Curve Editor. It displays the key window (right side) containing keys (small gray squares) and the linear slanting line (blue line) that displays the animation, as shown in Figure 11–24. You might have to zoom/pan and scroll up/down (use scroll bar) inside the key window for the keys and the animation line to display.

2. Hover the cursor over the Controller window (left side). It displays as a **Hand** icon. If required, hold and drag it until the dummy object is listed with its applied Transforms, as shown in Figure 11–24.

3. In the *Rotation* node of the dummy object, select **X Rotation**, **Y Rotation**, and **Z Rotation**, if not already selected, as shown in Figure 11–24.

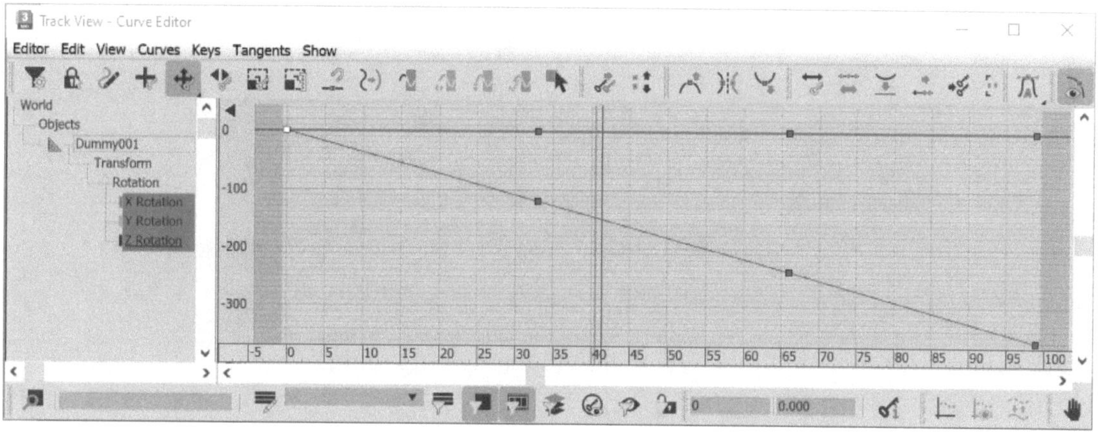

Figure 11–24

4. In the Key window, on the blue animation line, select the key (small gray square) at frame 33. It changes to white, indicating that it has been selected. In the Curve Editor toolbar, click  (Set Tangents to Slow), as shown in Figure 11–25.
   - Note that a curve is added at this frame 33.

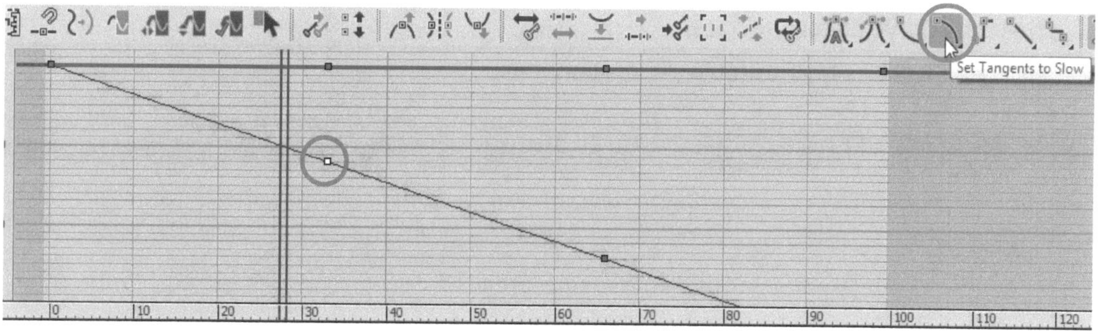

Figure 11–25

Note: *The selected key in the Curve Editor is represented as white in color.*

5. Click to play the animation and note that the animation slows down slightly when it reaches frame 33. Click to pause the animation.
6. Add **Set Tangents to Slow** to the keys at frame 0, 66, and 99. Slight curves are added to these frames, as shown in Figure 11–26.

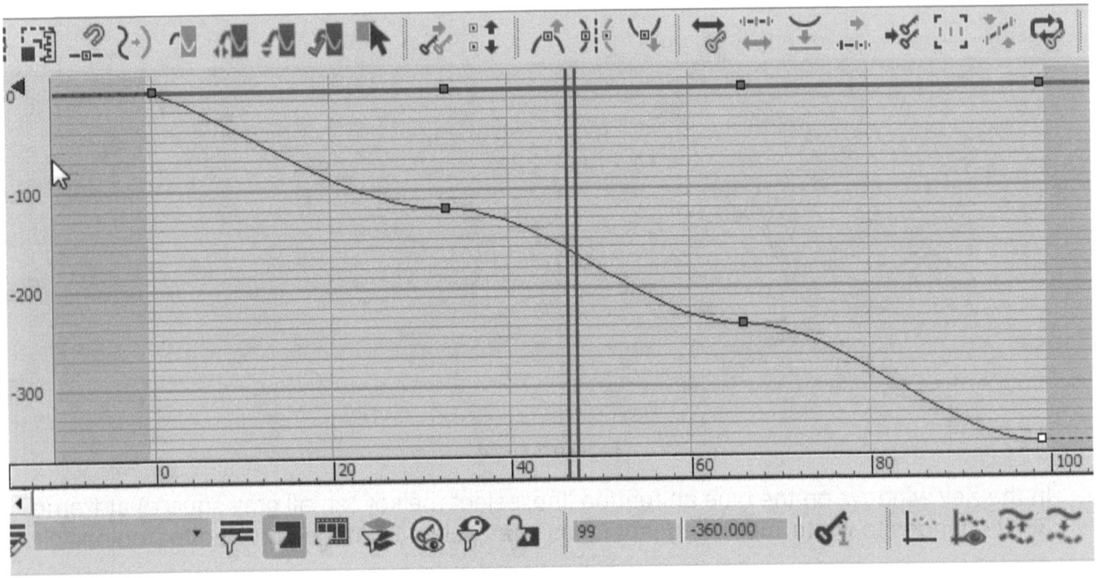

Figure 11–26

7. Click to play the animation and click to pause.
8. Close the Curve Editor.
9. Save your work as **MyTurntable_Animation.max**.

End of practice

Practice 11b
Keyframe a Camera Animation

Practice Objective

- Animate a camera to fly over the site.

In this practice, you will add a camera to the scene and set the animation for the camera. You will then modify the animation by creating a new key and modifying the camera position at this key. This approach is similar to manually configuring a walkthrough or drive-by animation.

You must set the paths to locate the External files and XREFs used in the practice. If you have not done this already, return to Chapter 1 and complete Task 1 to Task 3 in *Practice 1a: Organize Folders and Work with the Interface*. You only have to set the user paths once.

Task 1: Configure the camera animation.

1. Open **Presets.max**.
2. Maximize the **Top** viewport and zoom and pan until the building, parking lot, and the end of the road on both sides of the building display.
3. In the Command Panel>*Create* panel (+), click (Cameras). In the *Object Type* rollout, click **Physical**. Create a camera and the target in the approximate positions, similar to that shown in Figure 11–27.

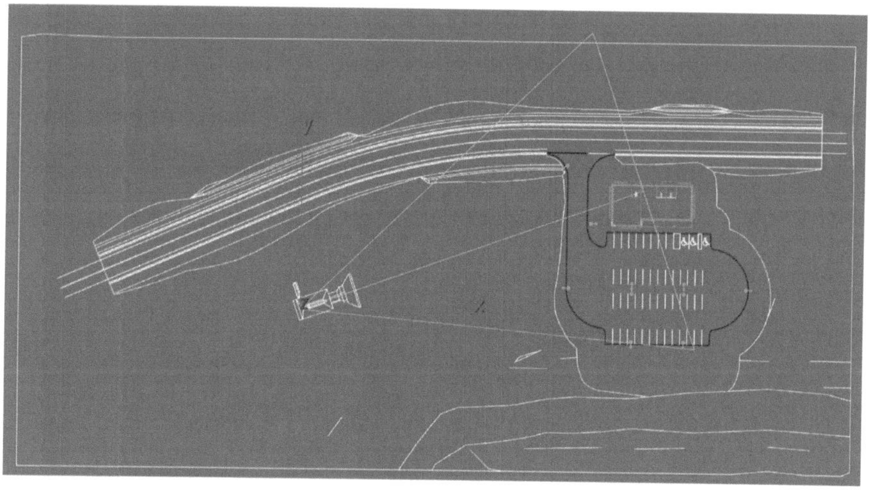

Figure 11–27

4. Click (Render Setup) to open the *Render Setup* dialog box and verify that **Arnold** is the current renderer used. Close the dialog box.

5. In the Scene Explorer, select the new camera (PhysCamera001), if required. Select the *Modify* panel ( ) and change its name to **Camera Flyover**.
6. With **Camera Flyover** selected, in the *Exposure* rollout, change the *Exposure Target* parameter to **10.0 EV**, as shown in Figure 11–28.

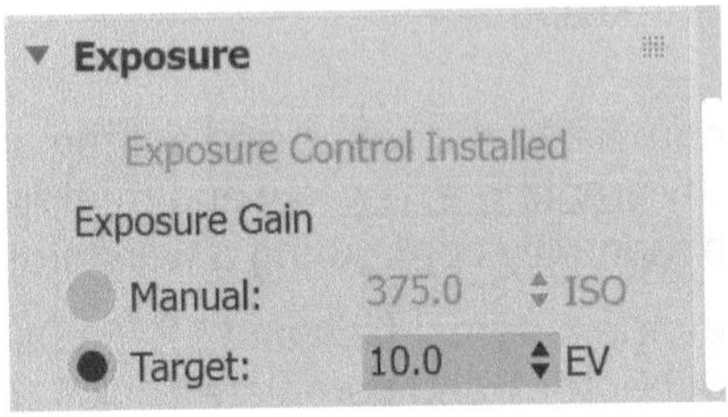

Figure 11–28

7. In the *Rendering* menu, click **Exposure Control t**o open the *Environment and Effects* dialog box.
8. Under *Physical Camera Exposure Control* area, verify that the *EV Compensation for Physical Cameras* is **-5.0 EV**, as shown in Figure 11–29.

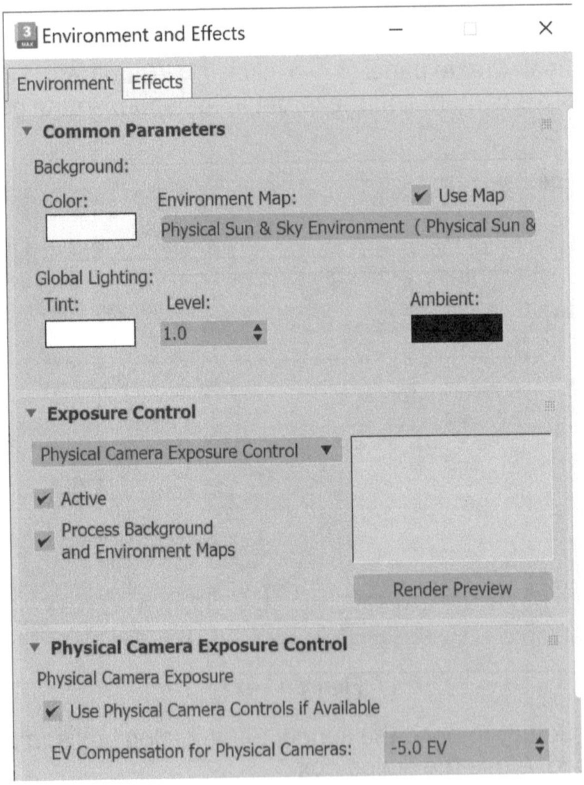

Figure 11–29

9. Maximize to display all four viewports. Change shading to Default Shading. Right-click in the **Front** viewport to activate it. Change shading to Default Shading. Change that view to show the **Camera Flyover** view (as shown in Figure 11–30) by clicking the **[Front]** *Point of View* label and selecting **Cameras>Camera Flyover**. Maximize the **Camera Flyover** view.

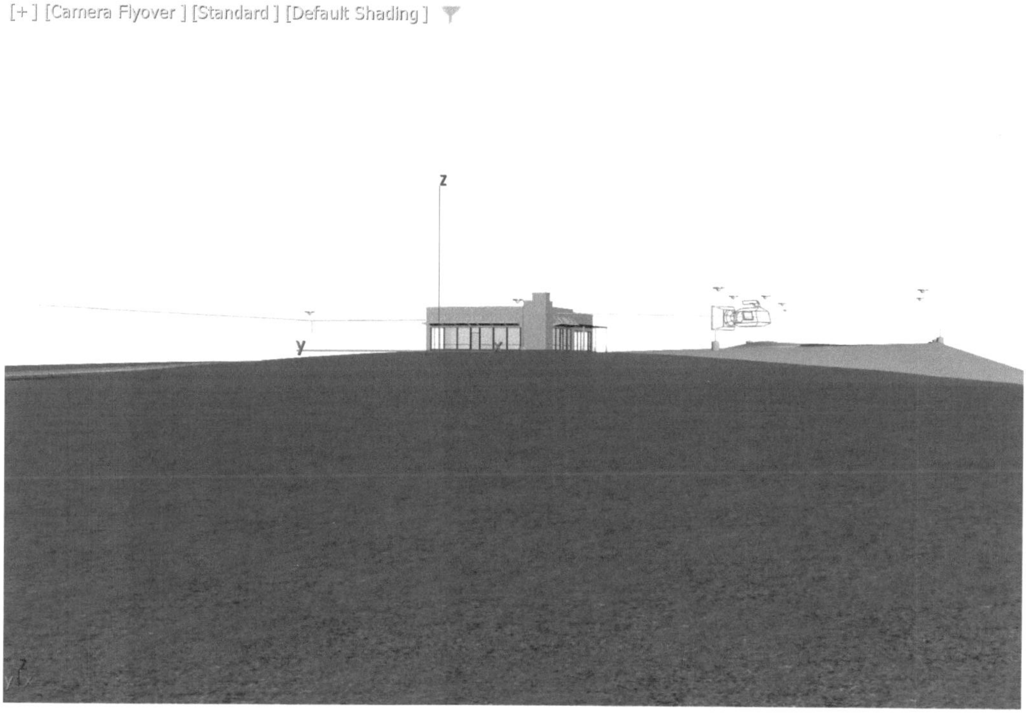

Figure 11–30

10. In the *Animation* controls, click  (Time Configuration). In the *Frame Rate* area, select **Custom**, set *FPS* to **20**, and in the *Animation* area, set *End Time* to **0:30:0**, as shown in Figure 11–31. Verify that all of the other values match the values in Figure 11–31. Your animation is 30 seconds long and intended for desktop playback at 20 FPS. Click **OK**.

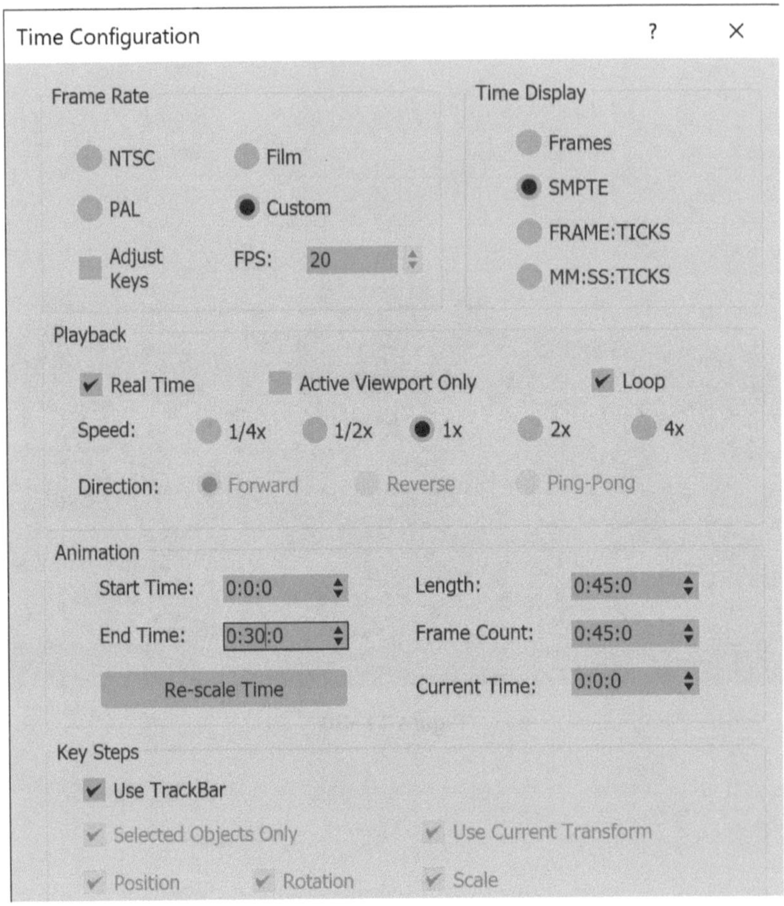

Figure 11–31

11. Verify that the Time Slider is currently located at time **0:0:0**, as shown in Figure 11–32.

Figure 11–32

12. Click the **Auto** button, which displays with a red background. Note that the Time Slider and outline of **Camera Flyover** viewport also display in red.

13. Drag the Time Slider all of the way to the *end time* of **0:30:0**, as shown in Figure 11–33. Note the blue marker on the scale.

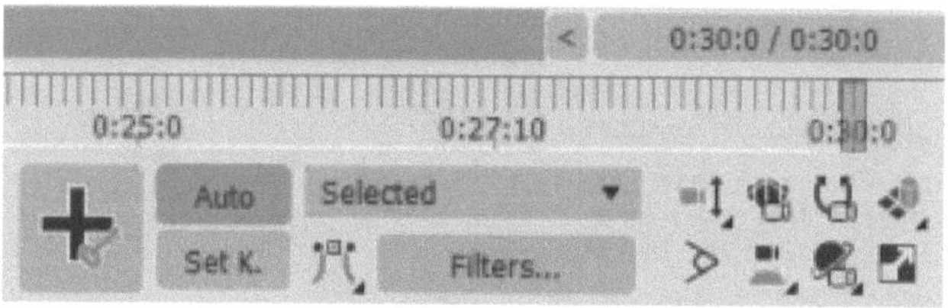

Figure 11–33

14. In the Scene Explorer, select the **Camera Flyover** camera object (note the name in the *Modifier Stack*). Click  (Select and Move) and in the Status Bar, in the *Transform Type-In* area enter **X = 300'0"**, **Y = 0'0"**, and **Z = 0'0"**, as shown in Figure 11–34. The roundoff error might change your X-coordinate to a value just below 300' (this occurs sometimes, but does not significantly affect this animation).

Figure 11–34

15. Click the **Auto** button again to toggle off Auto mode.
    - If you do not click the **Auto** button again to toggle the mode off, you can create an unintended animation.
16. Slide (scrub) the Time Slider left and right and watch the camera move. With the **Camera Flyover** viewport active, click  to see a preview of the animation. Note that the camera is low and there are times in the animation when the camera views through the ground.
17. Pause the animation by clicking . Move to the beginning by clicking  (Go to Start) or by dragging the Time Slider to the start position.

Task 2: Modify the animation by adding a new key.

You are currently skimming at elevation 0, which makes you fly directly through some slopes of the terrain. To make the animation look more like a flyover, you will add another key in the middle of the animation and raise the camera up in the Z-direction at that point.

1. Verify that the **Camera Flyover** camera object is selected.
2. Move the Time Slider to exactly **0:15:0** (the midpoint of the animation) and click  (Set Keys). A new key is created at this point.

3. In the Time Slider, right-click on this new key and select **Camera Flyover: Z Position** (as shown in Figure 11–35). Set the *Value* to **30'0"** (as shown Figure 11–36), press <Enter>, and close the dialog box. This raises the camera higher at the midpoint of the animation.

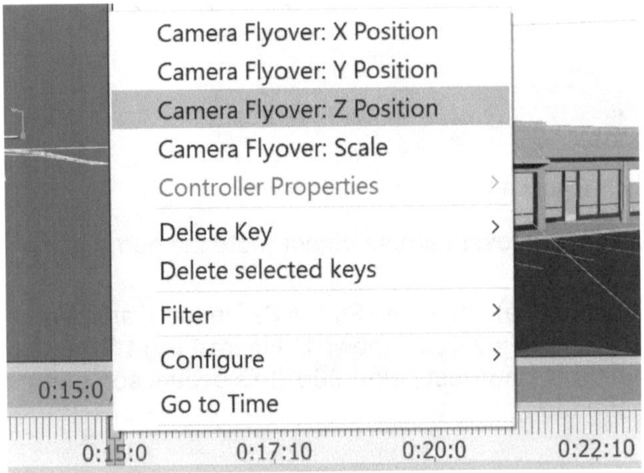

Figure 11–35

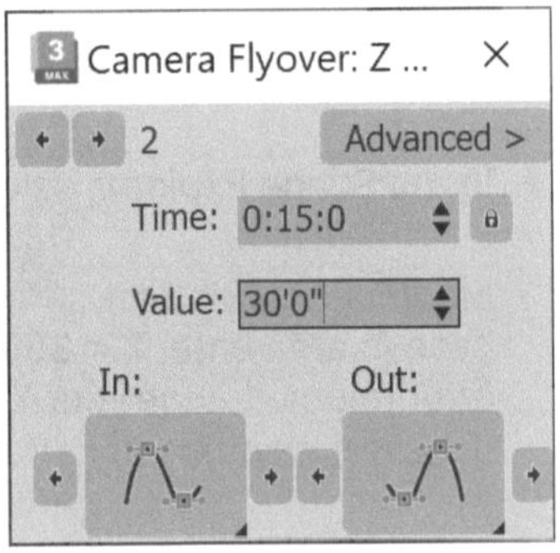

Figure 11–36

4. Click  (Go to Start) to return to the beginning and click  (Play) to preview the animation. Note the vertical change has been adjusted but now at around the midpoint the camera is too close to the building. You will pull the camera back from the building at the midpoint. Pause the animation by clicking .
5. Drag the Time Slider to exactly **0:15:0** and click the **Auto** button.
6. Maximize to display all four viewports. Right-click in the **Top** viewport to activate it, and verify that the **Camera Flyover** camera is still selected (if not, then select it). Click  (Select and Move) and in the Status Bar, in the *Transform Type-In* area, set the following, as shown in Figure 11–37:
   - *X:* **15'0"**
   - *Y:* **-120'0"**
   - *Z:* **30'0"**

   This moves the **Camera Flyover** camera away from the building. Since this is done in **Auto** mode, the camera's existing key at 0:15:0 is updated with this new position.

Figure 11–37

7. Click the **Auto** button to toggle it off.

8. Maximize the **Camera Flyover** view. Click to return to the beginning and click to preview the animation. Note how the camera has been moved away from the building.

   Pause the animation by clicking .

9. Click (Render Setup) to open the *Render Setup* dialog box. In the *Common* tab, in the *Common Parameters* rollout, in the *Time Output* area, select **Active Time Segment** (which is the entire animation), as shown in Figure 11–38.
10. In the *Common Parameters* rollout, in the *Output Size* area, set the *Width* to **300** and press <Enter>, as shown in Figure 11–38. With the aspect ratio locked at 1.6, a rendering *Height* of **188** is automatically calculated. Normally, you select a filename and location to save the render to. Close the dialog box.

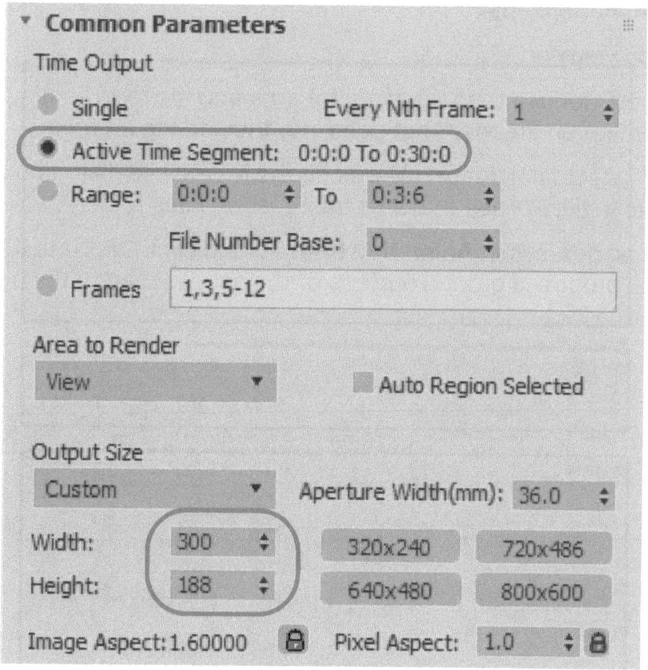

Figure 11–38

11. Save the file as **MyCameraAnimationFlyover.max**.

End of practice

Practice 11c
Create a Walkthrough Animation

Practice Objective

- Animate a camera object along a path in a scene.

In this practice, you will merge a Max file in which the path has been created and then animate the camera along that path to create a walkthrough animation.

You must set the paths to locate the External files and XREFs used in the practice. If you have not done this already, return to Chapter 1 and complete Task 1 to Task 3 in *Practice 1a: Organize Folders and Work with the Interface*. You only have to set the user paths once.

1. Open **Camera Animations.max**.
2. Maximize the **Top** viewport.
3. In the **Top** viewport, zoom into the parking lot area and the road leading into it. Note that there is no path (line) on the road that goes into the parking lot area.
4. In the Menu Bar, select **File>Import>Merge**. In the Merge File dialog box, select **Animation Path.max** located in the *Scenes* folder of the Practice Files folder. Click **Open**.
5. In the *Merge* dialog box, select **Animation Path 3D** and click **OK**. Note that the spline path is located along the proposed ground surface of the access road to the parking lot area, as shown in Figure 11–39.

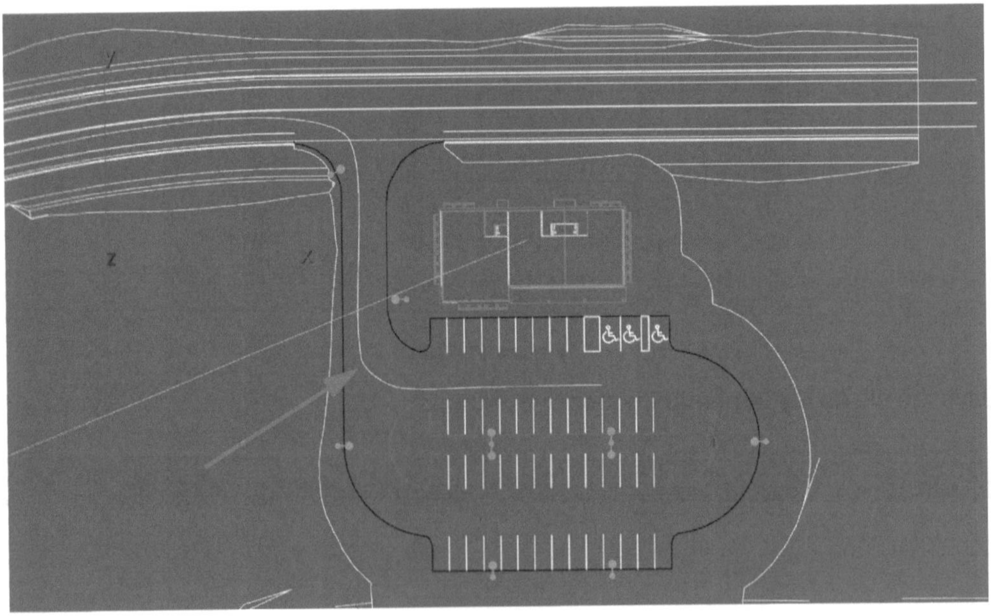

Figure 11–39

6. Using the Scene Explorer, select the object group ( )_**Site Model**. Right-click and select **Child Nodes**.
7. Right-click in the viewport and select **Freeze Selection** in the quad menu. The Site model geometry displays in a dull gray color and you can easily see the blue path that travels along the street. If required, use **Zoom** and **Pan** to display the complete path in the viewport.
8. In the Command Panel>*Create* panel (+), click (Cameras). In the *Object Type* rollout, click **Physical**. Click and hold near the left end of the path to place the camera, and then drag to the center of the building. Release to set the target, as shown in Figure 11–40. In the *Name and Color* edit box, enter the name of the camera as **Walkthrough_Cam01**.

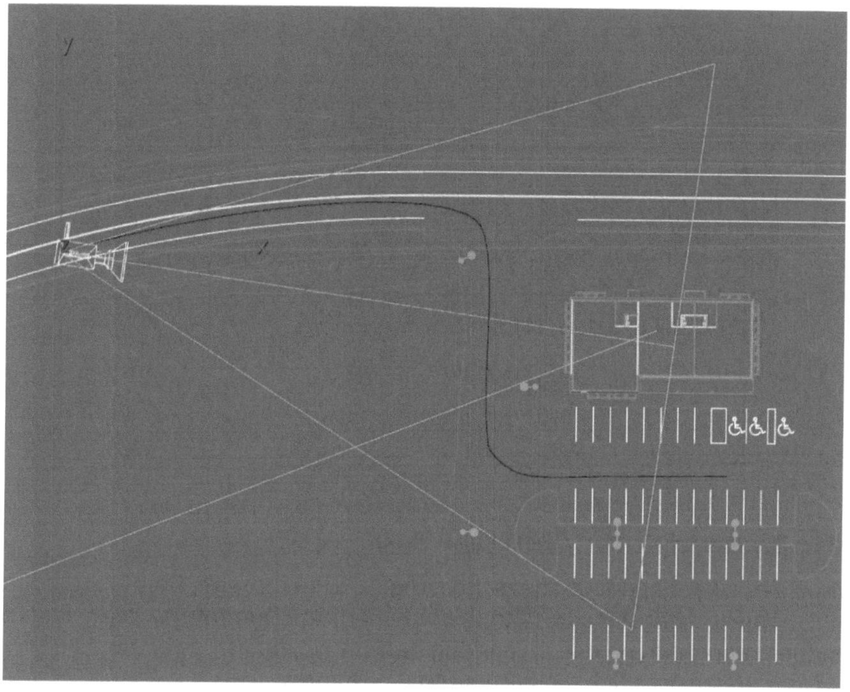

Figure 11–40

9. In the *Exposure* rollout, set *Target:* to **10.0 EV**, as shown in Figure 11–41.

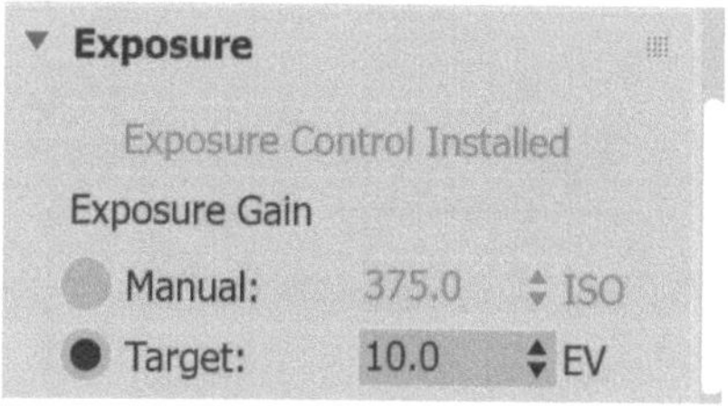

Figure 11–41

10. Click in the viewport to clear any selection. In the viewport, zoom into the camera object and the beginning of the path.If required, move the camera object close to the start point of the path.

11. In the Command Panel>*Create* panel (), click  (Helpers). Click **Dummy**.

12. Click and drag to create the dummy object around the camera by starting at the beginning of the animation path spline, as shown in Figure 11–42.

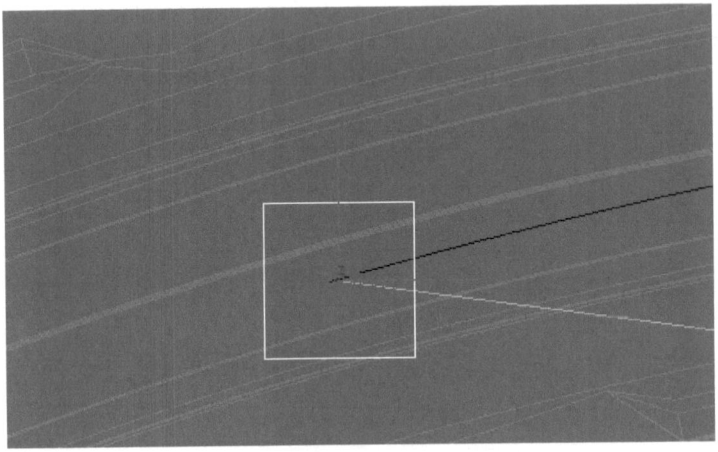

Figure 11–42

Note: *If you were flying a camera through the interior of a design, you would align the camera to the dummy at this point. In this animation, it is not required for this type of exterior flyby.*

13. In the Main Toolbar, click  (Select and Link).

14. In the viewport, select and hold the newly created **Walkthrough_Cam01** object to define it as the child object. Drag the cursor to the outline of the **Dummy**. A dotted line displays between the cursor and the object, and the dummy object turns yellow, as shown in Figure 11–43. Release to link the camera to the **Dummy**.

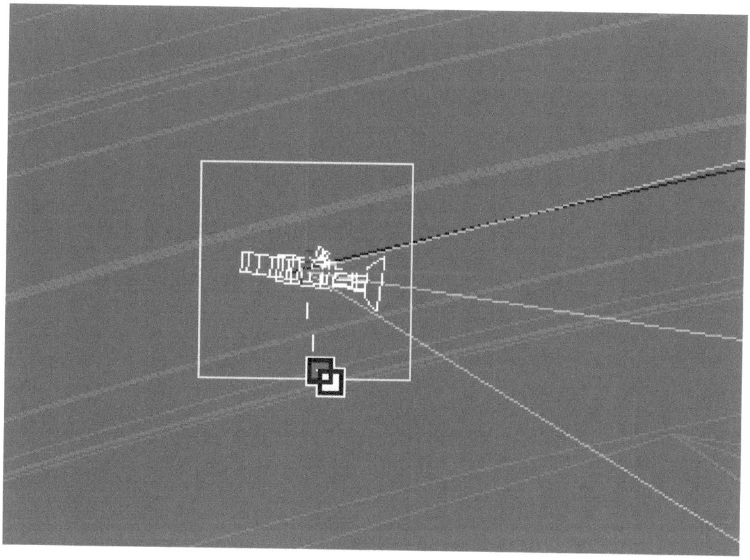

Figure 11–43

15. To check it, in the Main Toolbar, click  and move the dummy object. You should see the camera move with it. This confirms that the linkage is correct. Undo the move.
16. To constrain the dummy object to the path, select the dummy object (square) in the viewport and in the Menu bar, select **Animation>Constraints>Path Constraint**. The cursor is connected with a dotted line to the pivot point of the dummy object. Click anywhere over the blue path (Animation Path 3D) to select it as the animation path, as shown in Figure 11–44. The pivot point of the dummy automatically shifts to coincide with the start point of the path.
    - When you hover the cursor over the path, it should turn yellow to show that it is going to be selected. Once it turns yellow, click to select it.

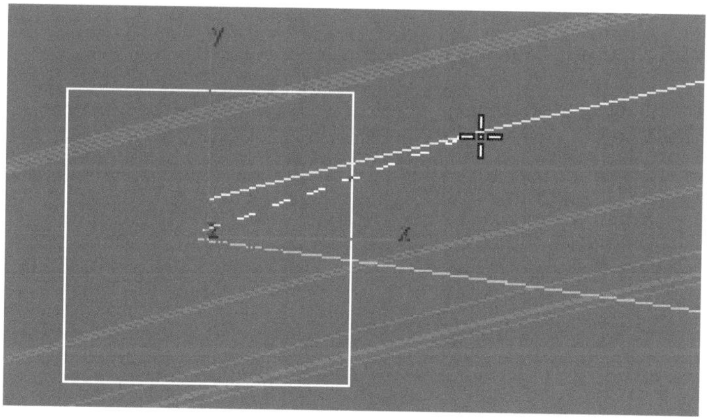

Figure 11–44

17. Zoom out till the entire blue path displays. Click  to play the animation. The dummy and the camera animate along the path, as shown in Figure 11–45. Click  to pause the animation.

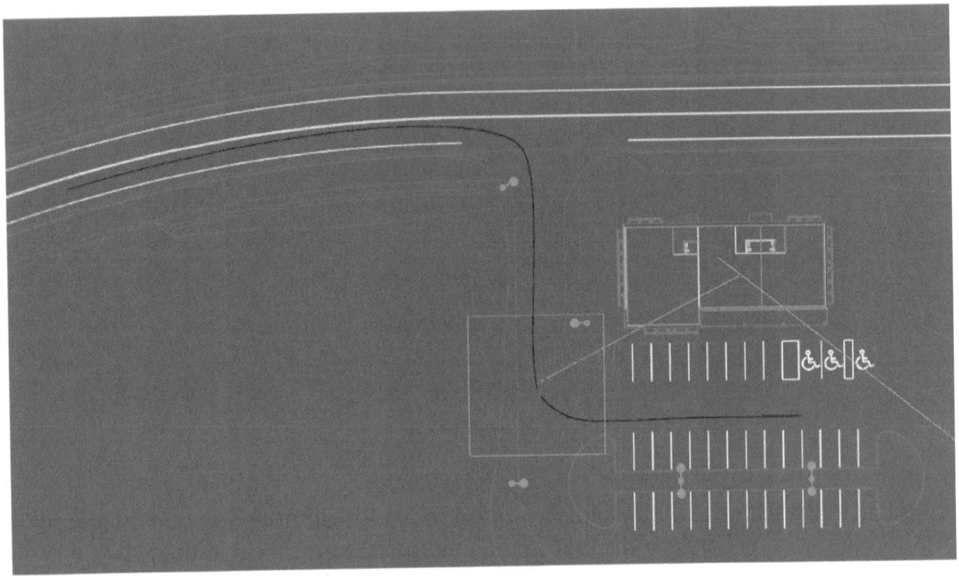

Figure 11–45

18. Maximize to display all four viewports. Activate the **Exterior** Camera viewport and change it to the **Walkthrough_Cam01** viewport (click the *Point of View* label and select **Cameras> Walkthrough_Cam01**).
19. Right-click in the viewport and select **Unfreeze All**. The site model displays with full color. Click  to play the animation. To improve the animation, the camera should be raised higher off the ground.
20. Click  to go to the start of the animation, at frame zero.

21. Since the camera is a child of the dummy, you can add transforms to the camera without affecting the dummy's animation. In the Scene Explorer, use (Display Cameras) and select **Walkthrough_Cam01**, child of **Dummy001** (as shown in Figure 11–46), and rename it as **Camera_Flyby**.

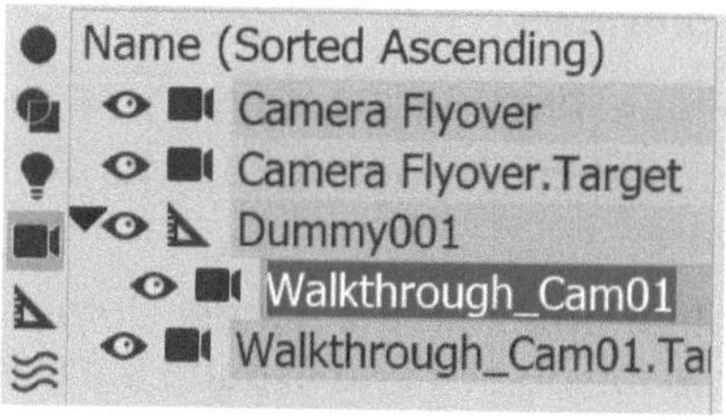

Figure 11–46

22. With the **Camera_Flyby** object selected, in the Main Toolbar, right-click on (Select and Move) to open the *Move Transform Type-In* dialog box.
23. In the *Absolute:World*, change the *Z* value to **6'0"** and press <Enter>. Close the dialog box. Since the **Auto** button is off, this lifts the camera for the entire animation.
24. Play the animation in the **Camera_Flyby** viewport. Stop the animation.
25. Save your work as **MyCameraAnimationFlyby.max**.

End of practice

11.3 Animation Output

There are two strategies for creating animation output:

- Render directly to a single, composite animation file such as a .MOV or .AVI. This is generally recommended for previews.
- Render each still image (such as .PNG, .JPEG, .BMP, .TIFF, etc.) and later combine the stills into a composite animation using the Autodesk 3ds Max RAM Player, Video Post, or 3rd party post-production software.

You can select an animation output option in the *Render Output File* dialog box. To open this dialog box, open the *Render Setup* dialog box and expand the *Common Parameters* rollout in the *Common* tab. In the *Render Output* area, click **Files...**, as shown in Figure 11–47.

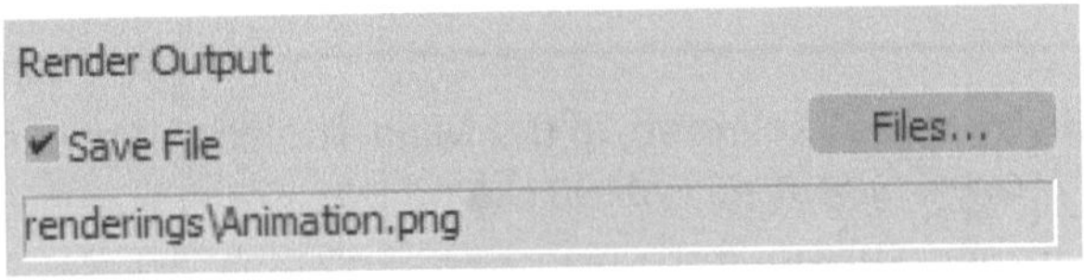

Figure 11–47

The *Render Output File* dialog box opens. In the *Save as type* drop-down list (shown in Figure 11–48), you can select to render to a single, compressed animation file (.MOV or .AVI) or to individual frames (such as .PNG, .JPEG, .BMP, .TIFF, etc.). If you select to render as individual frames, you need to provide the name once and the software automatically creates individual files for each frame, which are numbered sequentially.

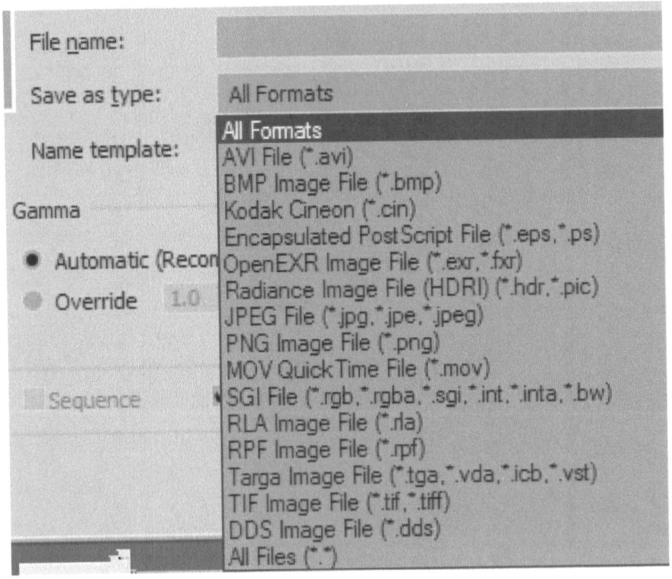

Figure 11–48

Assembling Animations

It is recommended to render files individually and then combine them into an animation. The Autodesk 3ds Max RAM player is a utility used for comparing two images side-by-side, or for previewing and compiling animations. It is called a RAM player because it loads these images into RAM.

The RAM player (shown in Figure 11–49) can be opened in the menu bar by selecting **Rendering>Compare Media in RAM Player**.

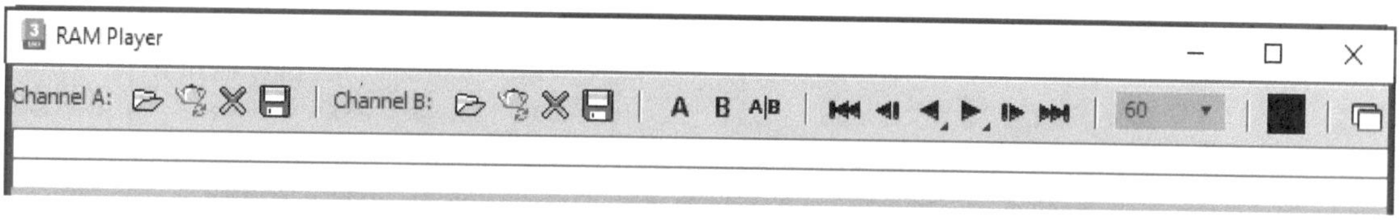

Figure 11–49

Click (Open Channel A) to open the *Open File* dialog box, shown in Figure 11–50. Enter the path and the first filename of the sequentially numbered image files. Selecting the **Load as sequence** option opens all of the files, which are named as specified in the *File name* field.

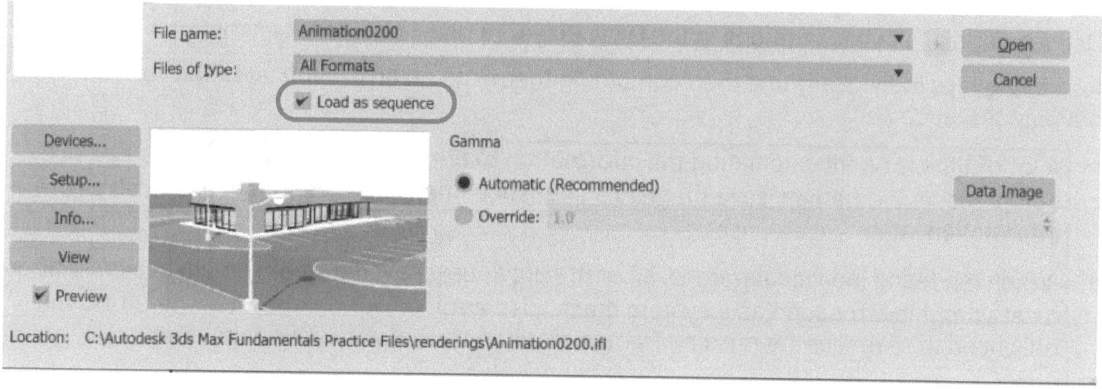

Figure 11–50

Once you open the specified image file, the *Image File List Control* dialog box opens (as shown in Figure 11–51), which displays the folder where the image file list (.IFL) is being created. (The image file list is an ASCII list of the files that were used, in the order used.) The dialog box also provides you with options to limit the animation to certain frames.

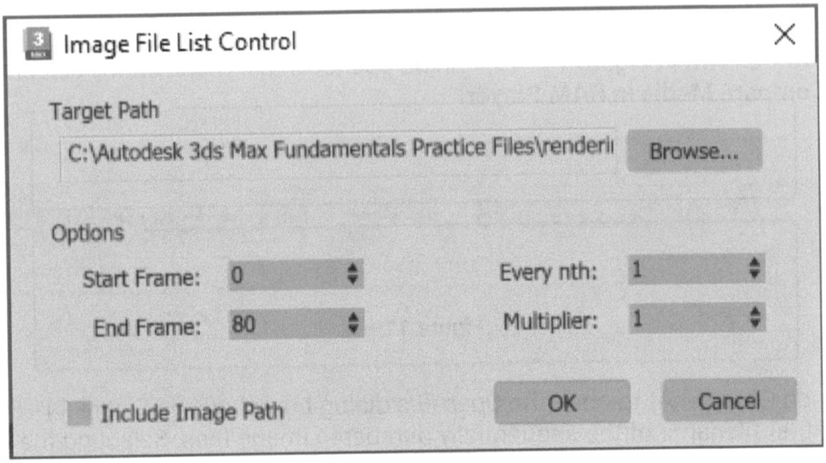

Figure 11–51

Use the various playback options in the RAM Player to play the created animation.

Rendering files individually and then combining them into an animation later has various advantages, such as:

- A lot of time is spent calculating the information to create a rendered frame. Instead of compressing the frames, save them as a sequence of still images for access to all of the information later.
- When rendering individual frames, all of the previously saved frames remain available after a catastrophic error such as a system crash, disc error, power outage, etc. Therefore, you only need to re-render the missing frames required to complete your animation.
- When rendering animations, material, lighting or geometry, errors might occur in certain frames. Unlike compressed animation files, rendering to frames enables you to easily adjust, fix errors, and re-render the affected frames.
- When rendering to an animation file you need to first select the compression or video quality settings. If you do not like the results, select another value and re-render the entire animation.
- When rendering to stills, select a quality value after rendering is complete to try different settings and save out another composite file from the same still renderings.
- Rendering to a still image file format that supports an alpha channel (transparency) enables you to use a compositing package such as Combustion or Adobe After Effects for post-production processing and assembly.

Practice 11d
Create an Animation Output

Practice Objective

- Create an animation preview and create single-frame file images.

In this practice, you create single-frame file images at 5 frame intervals and save them as .PNG file format. You will then assemble the individual frame images to create a movie using the RAM Player.

You must set the paths to locate the External files and XREFs used in the practice. If you have not done this already, return to Chapter 1 and complete Task 1 to Task 3 in *Practice 1a: Organize Folders and Work with the Interface*. You only have to set the user paths once.

Task 1: Create still frames.

1. Open **Camera_Animation_Start_Render.max.**
2. Make the **Camera - Flyover** viewport active.
3. Click  (Time Configuration) to open the *Time Configuration* dialog box. Change the *Time Display* to **Frames, if required**.
4. In the *Animation* area, change the *End Time* to **600** indicating that you have a 600 frame animation. Click **OK**. Note that the *Time slider* displays as **0/600.**

5. Rendering 600 frames might take a long time. Therefore, selecting a shorter range and setting *Every Nth Frame* will make it manageable. Click  (Render Setup) to open the *Render Setup* dialog box. In the *Common* tab, verify that the *Common Parameters* rollout is expanded. In the *Time Output* area, set the following, as shown in Figure 11–52:
   - Select **Range**.
   - Set a *Range* of **200** to **600**.
   - Set *Every Nth Frame* to **5**.

   This renders every fifth frame between 200 and 600, which is a total of 81 frames of animation.

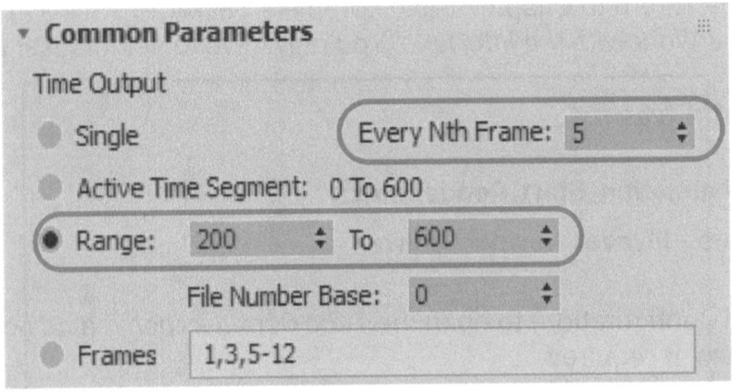

Figure 11–52

6. In the *Output Size* area, note that the *Width* and *Height* is set to **300** and **188** respectively. This will create small images but rendering will be faster.
   - Optional: If you have time, you can change the *Width* to **600**. which automatically changes the *Height* to **376** to create bigger renderings.
7. In the *Render Output* area, click **Files...**.
8. The *Render Output File* dialog box opens. Locate the ...*\renderings* folder in the practice files folder. Set the *Save as type* to **PNG Image File (*.png)**, and in the *File name* enter the name **Animation**. Click **Save**.
9. In the *PNG Configuration* dialog box, select **RGB 24 bit** and leave **Alpha channel** enabled. Click **OK**. Note that the folder location is set and the **Save File** option is checked in the *Render Output* area of the *Render Setup* dialog box, as shown in Figure 11–53.

Figure 11–53

10. In the *Render Setup* dialog box, verify that the **Quad 4 - Camera - Flyover** is displayed as the *View to Render*. Click **Render** to begin creating individual renderings for every fifth frame between the 200 and 600 frame range.

11. The Rendered Frame Window opens with each fifth frame being rendered and the *Rendering* dialog box opens (as shown in Figure 11–54), displaying information about the renderings, number of files to be rendered, estimate of the remaining rendering time, render settings, etc.

    - It might take some time to complete the 81 frames of animation. Depending on the time you have, you can stop the process with some frames completed, or let it continue until all of the frames have been created.

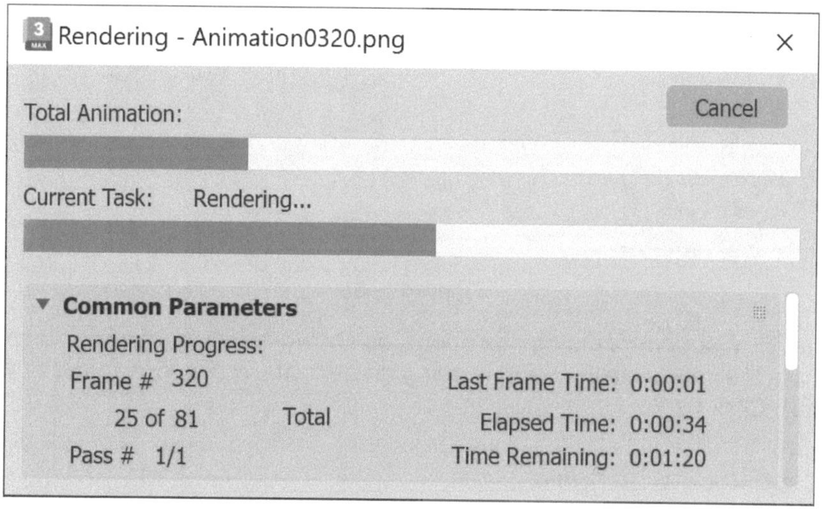

Figure 11–54

12. Once completed, close the Rendered Frame Window and the *Render Setup* dialog box.

Task 2: Assemble the final animation.

1. In the menu bar, select **Rendering>Compare Media in RAM Player** to open the RAM player. The RAM player is a utility used for comparing two images side-by-side or previewing and compiling animations.

2. In the *Channel A* area, click (Open Channel A), as shown in Figure 11–55.

Figure 11–55

3. In the *Open File, Channel A* dialog box, in the practice files folder, browse to the *renderings* folder. Note that there are 81 still images, starting at Animation0200.png, and then every fifth frame (i.e., Animation0205.png, Animation0210.png, Animation0215.png, etc.). Select **Animation0200.png** and verify that **Load as sequence** is enabled, as shown in Figure 11–56. Click **Open**.
   - The **Load as sequence** option enables the system to open all of the .PNGs named **Animation*.png**.

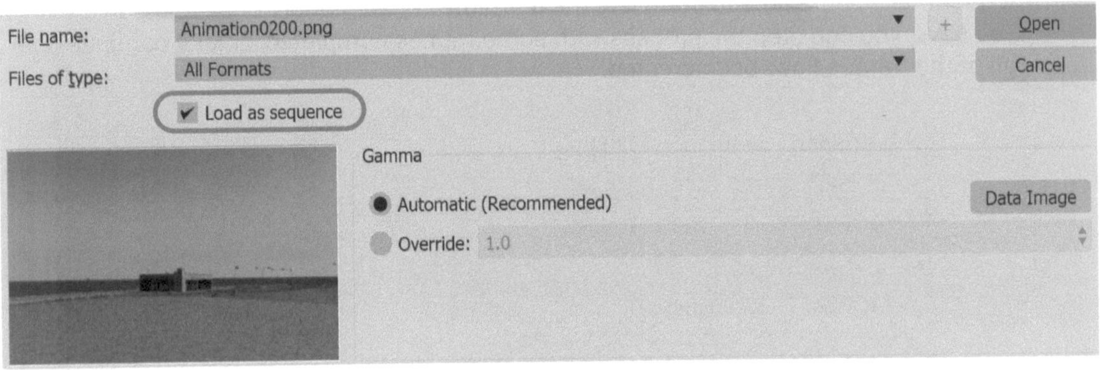

Figure 11–56

4. The *Image File List Control* dialog box opens, as shown in Figure 11–57. It displays the folder where the image file list (.IFL) is being created (the *renderings* folder of your practice files folder). Click **OK**.

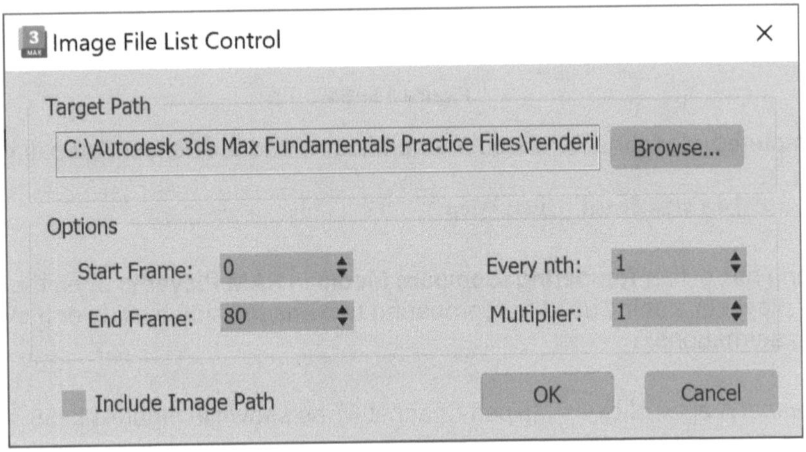

Figure 11–57

5. The *RAM Player Configuration* dialog box opens. It enables you to change the image size or aspect ratio on import, to limit the number of frames to use, and the maximum amount of RAM you want to dedicate to the process. Click **OK**.

6. After the animation has loaded into the RAM player you can play back the animation at different frame rates by selecting a number in the drop-down list, as shown in Figure 11–58. Click (Playback Forward) to play the animation. Select different frame rates and play the animation to see the effect. Stop the animation.

   - The lesser frame rate slows down the animation, while the higher frame rate plays it faster.

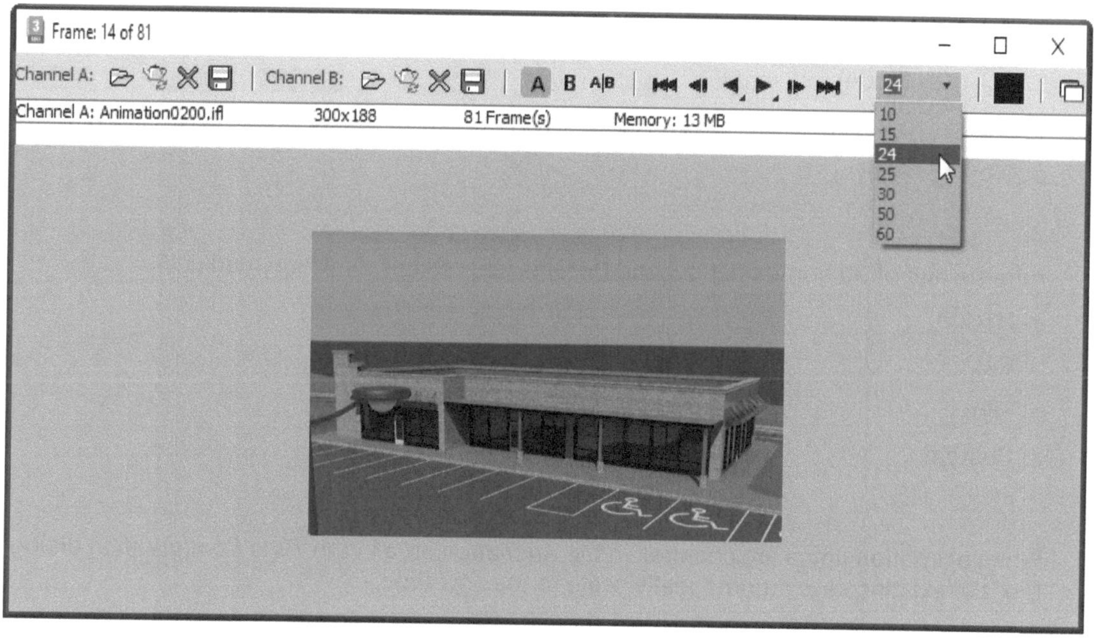

Figure 11–58

7. To save a desktop animation file, click (Save Channel A).
8. In the *Save File, Channel A* dialog box, browse to the ...*\renderings* folder. Set *Save as type* to **AVI File (*.avi)**. Save the animation as **FlybyAnimation**.
9. In the *AVI File Compression Setup* dialog box, for the *Compressor*, select **MJPEG Compressor**, set the *Quality* to **60**, and click **OK**.
10. Exit the RAM Player and save your work as **MyCameraAnimation.max**.
11. In your Windows Explorer, navigate to your renderings folder and play **Flyby Animation.avi** file to watch the animation.

Note: *If the quality of the animation is not good enough, you can try other methods or qualities until you have an acceptable result.*

End of practice

Chapter Review Questions

1. Activating (toggling on) which option in the Animation Controls changes **Previous, Play,** and **Next Frame** ( ) to **Previous**, **Play**, and **Next Keyframe** ( )?
   a. **Auto** animation mode
   b. **Set Key** animation mode
   c. (Key Mode)
   d. (Set Keys)

2. A frame rate of 30 frames per second (FPS) is best suited for which medium?
   a. NTSC
   b. PAL
   c. Film
   d. Custom

3. When animation times are changed in the *Animation* area in the *Time Configuration* dialog box, the existing keys automatically scale to the new time.
   a. True
   b. False

4. Which category in the *Create* panel ( ) contains **Dummy** as its Object Type?
   a. (Geometry)
   b. (Shapes)
   c. (Cameras)
   d. (Helpers)

5. If you render each still image (such as .PNG, .JPEG, etc.), which utility can you use to combine the stills into a composite animation?
    a. Media Player
    b. RAM Player
    c. Batch Render
    d. Panorama Exporter

Command Summary

Button	Command	Location
Auto Key	**Auto Key animation mode**	• **Animation Controls Toolbar**
	**Cameras**	• **Command Panel:** *Create* panel • **Create:** Cameras
	**Curve Editor**	• **Main Toolbar** • **Graph Editors:** Track View - Curve Editor
	**Default In/Out Tangents for New Keys**	• **Animation Controls Toolbar**
N/A	**Dope Sheet**	• **Graph Editors:** Track View - Dope Sheet
	**Go to End**	• **Animation Controls Toolbar**
	**Go to Start**	• **Animation Controls Toolbar**
	**Helpers**	• **Command Panel:** *Create* panel
	**Key Mode**	• **Animation Controls Toolbar**
	**Mini Curve Editor**	• **Track bar**
	**Previous, Play, Next Frame**	• **Animation Controls Toolbar**
	**Progressive Display**	• **Status Bar**
	**Render Setup**	• **Main Toolbar** • **Rendering:** Render Setup
	**Select and Link**	• **Main Toolbar**
Set Key	**Set Key animation mode**	• **Animation Controls Toolbar**
	**Set Keys**	• **Animation Controls Toolbar**
	**Time Configuration**	• **Animation Controls Toolbar**

Appendix A

Optional Topics

There are some additional tools available in the Autodesk® 3ds Max® software that you can use when creating and animating models. This appendix provides details about several additional tools and commands.

Learning Objectives

- Access Autodesk 3ds Max Help and use the various Help tools.
- Work with architectural materials and the *Compact Material Editor*.
- Replace a 2D symbol of an instanced object and it with a 3D object.
- Create hierarchies by collecting objects together with parent/child relationships.
- Customize the user interface elements.

A.1 Getting Help with Autodesk 3ds Max

The Help menu contains an extensive list of help options, which are organized as submenus so that finding information is easy. Some of the available help options are described as follows:

- The **Autodesk 3ds Max Help** is robust, well illustrated, and often the fastest way to find what an option or parameter controls and how to use it. This help is in the form of HTML files at autodesk.com website and you are required to have a working internet connection to access Help. To access help, in the menu bar, select **Help>Autodesk 3ds Max Help**. You can also press <F1> to access the help. The 3ds Max Help screen opens with all the help topics listed in a tree structure along the left side of the page, as shown in Figure A–1. The topics are in the form of links. Click on the topic to display the related help along the right side of the Help screen, as shown in Figure A–1.

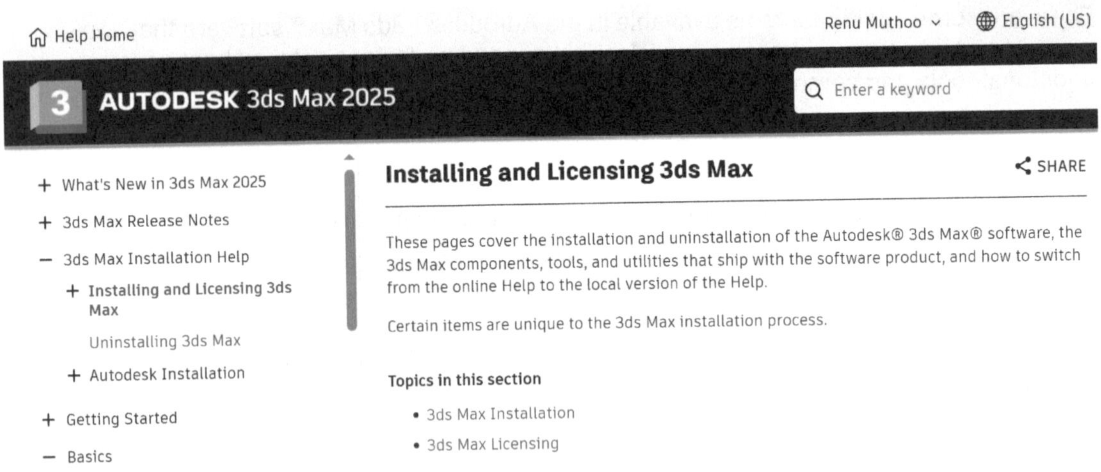

Figure A–1

- You can also search for a specific help topic by entering a keyword and selecting from the list of available related topics, as shown in Figure A–2.

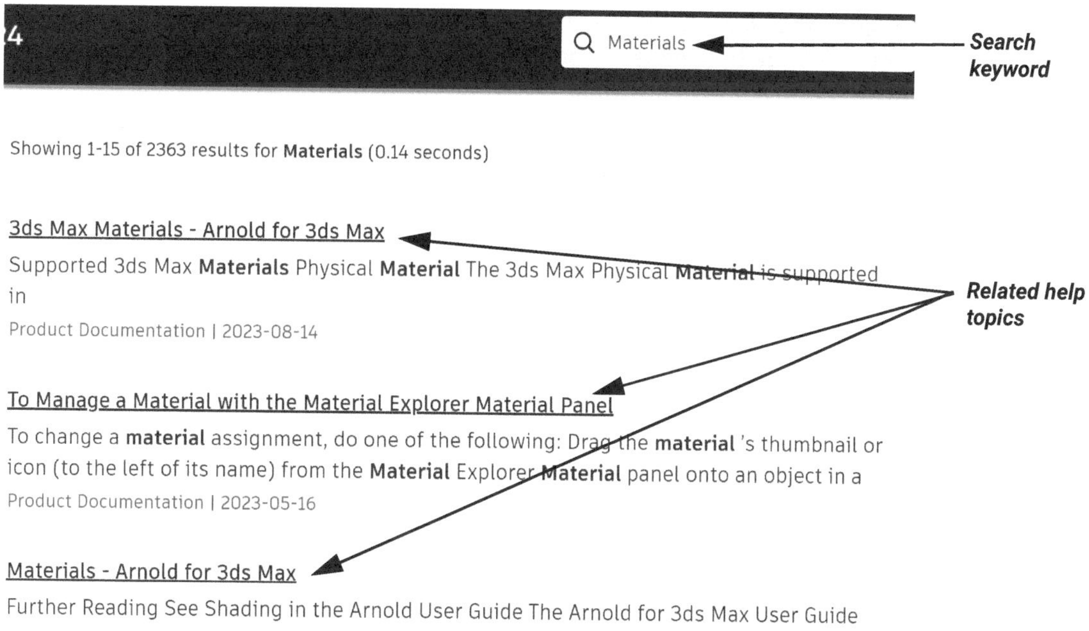

Figure A–2

- The **Autodesk 3ds Max Tutorials** (select **Help>Tutorials**) offer thorough and comprehensive learning materials to get you started with almost all of the features in the Autodesk 3ds Max software. The tutorials are in various formats (as shown in Figure A–3), and selecting an option from the list connects you to the related pages on the Autodesk website.

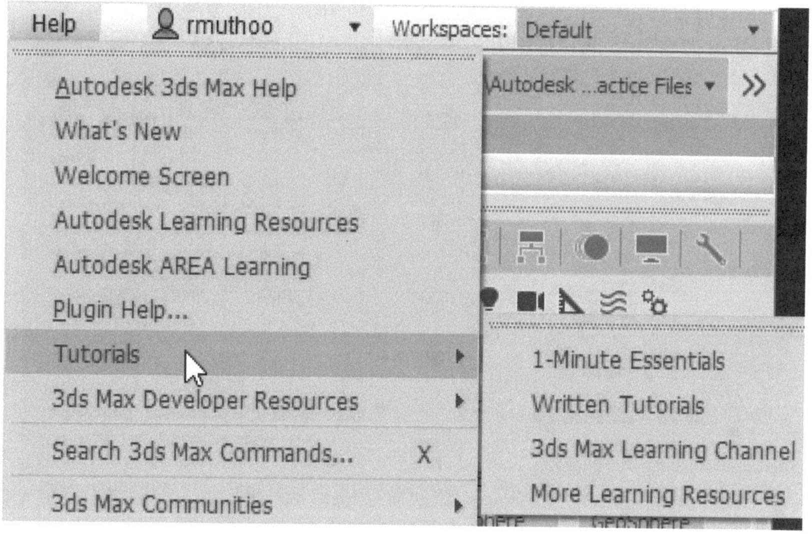

Figure A–3

- **3ds Max Communities:** Select **Help>3ds Max Communities>Autodesk AREA, Student Community,** and **Facebook** to access the community, which provides a single location for users to interact with each other. In addition to the Autodesk 3ds Max forum, the AREA contains forums for other Autodesk products. You can also connect with other Autodesk 3ds Max users and share information using the Autodesk 3ds Max Facebook page.
- **3ds Max Resources and Tools:** Select **Help>3ds Max Resources and Tools** (as shown in Figure A–4) to link you to the following:
  - **Autodesk App Store:** Enables you to download various applications for 3ds Max.
  - **Keyboard Shortcut Map:** Enables you to download a printable PDF of the keyboard shortcuts, etc.

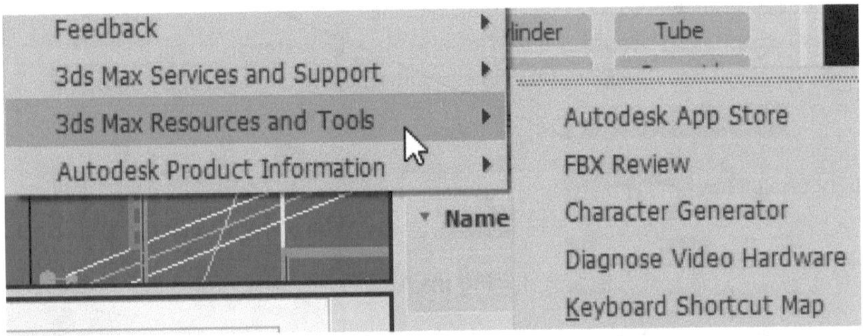

Figure A–4

- **Feedback:** The Autodesk 3ds Max software provides various **Speak Back** options, as shown in Figure A–5. Selecting an option connects you to web pages for reporting a bug in the software or making a request for small enhancements and new features, as shown in Figure A–5. It also enables you to activate the **Desktop Analytics Program**.

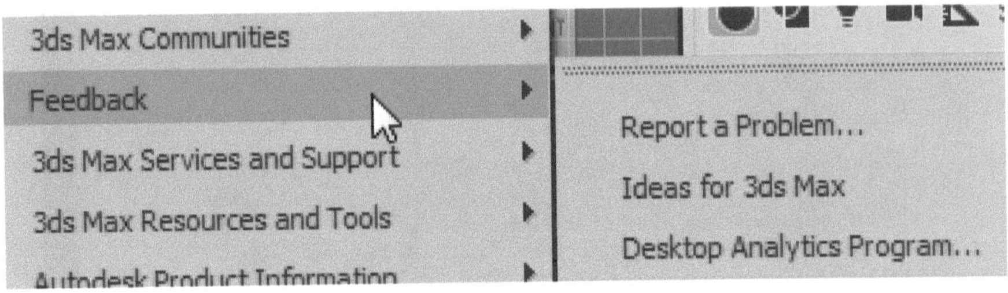

Figure A–5

- **3ds Max Services and Support:** Select **Help>3ds Max Services and Support>Support Center** (as shown in Figure A–6) to connect to the support site. It has many frequently updated technical support articles available. There might also be documents describing how to fix commonly occurring problem. Autodesk Subscription customers also have access to email support directly from Autodesk.

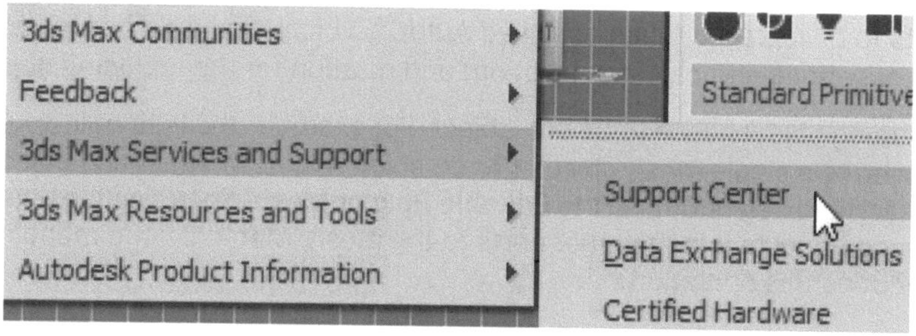

Figure A–6

- **Arnold Help:** You can access separate and detailed help about the Arnold renderer. For example, the Arnold for 3ds Max User Guide can be opened by selecting **Arnold>Help>User Guide**, as shown in Figure A–7. Information about the Arnold renderer for 3ds Max has been provided to guide you through the various features of the Arnold renderer.

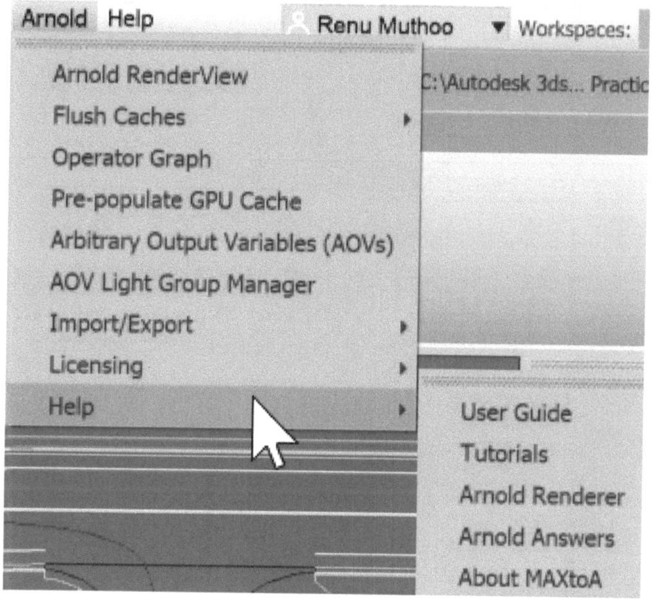

Figure A–7

A.2 Object Substitution

Linked or imported AutoCAD Blocks can be automatically replaced with 3D objects using the **Substitute** modifier. The **Substitute** modifier enables you to take a 2D symbol of an instanced object and replace it with a 3D object at multiple locations in a scene.

- The Objects to be replaced (such as linked AutoCAD blocks) should be located with the correct 3D coordinates (including elevation) and rotation for the replacing object.
- The substituting object needs to be one object. For example, the light pole could be used if it was collapsed to a single mesh object. (To do so, right-click on the base object in the Modifier Stack and select **Convert to Editable Poly or Mesh**. Then use the object's **Attach** in the Command Panel to join the other parts to the mesh. Materials and mapping can be preserved during this operation).
- The substitute object can be present in the same scene as the object to be replaced or it can be XREFed in from another scene.
- Although this is commonly used for AutoCAD blocks, other Autodesk 3ds Max objects can be substituted as well with this modifier.

Practice A1
Substitute the Parking Lot Light Poles

Practice Objective

- Replace 2D symbol based objects with 3D photorealistic object blocks.

In this practice, you will substitute completed 3D light pole objects for 2D blocks in a scene using the **Substitute** modifier.

You must set the paths to locate the External files and XREFs used in the practice. If you have not done this already, return to Chapter 1 and complete Task 1 to Task 3 in *Practice 1a: Organize Folders and Work with the Interface*. You only have to set the user paths once.

1. Open **Substitution_Start.max.**
2. Switch the viewport to **Wireframe override** by pressing <F3>.
3. If required, zoom out on the area of the parking lot to display the green 2D circular and square symbols joined by a line, as shown in Figure A–8. These objects in the parking area are 2D light pole blocks. The parking lot and the grading surfaces have been hidden so that you can see the lamp symbols.

Figure A–8

4. In the Scene Explorer, use  (Display None)>  (Display Shapes) and expand any one of **Block:Light Pole - Single**. Select the **Layer:LIGHTPOLE_SINGLE**, as shown in Figure A–9.

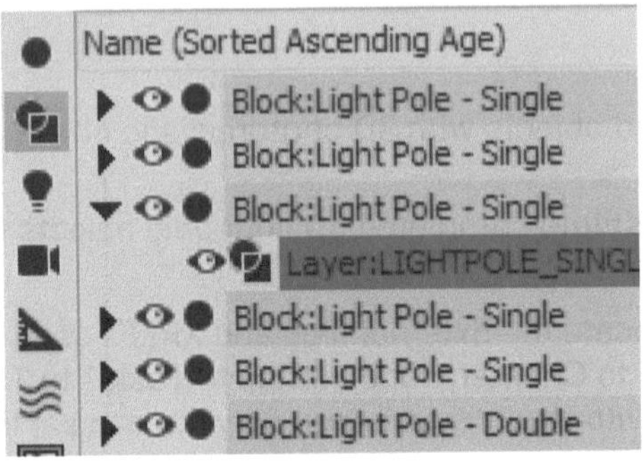

Figure A–9

5. Only one 2D object is required to be selected because AutoCAD blocks are linked as instances of each other, as indicated by the bold **Linked Geometry** in the Modifier Stack, as shown in Figure A–10. In the Command Panel, select the *Modify* panel () and then select **Substitute** in the Modifier List.
6. Verify that the **Substitute** parameters match the parameters, as shown in Figure A–11 (default). Click **Select XRef Object...**.

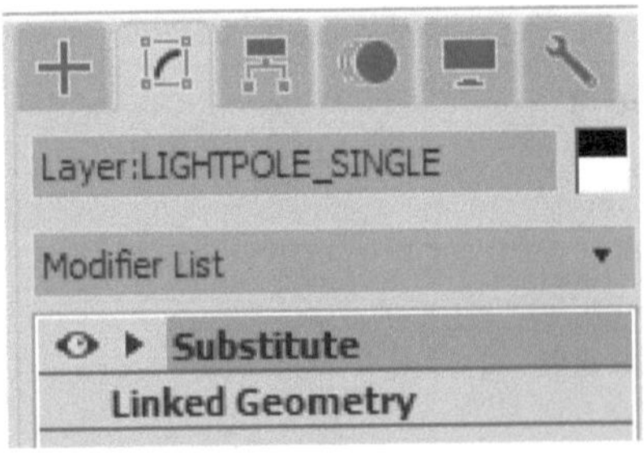

Figure A–10

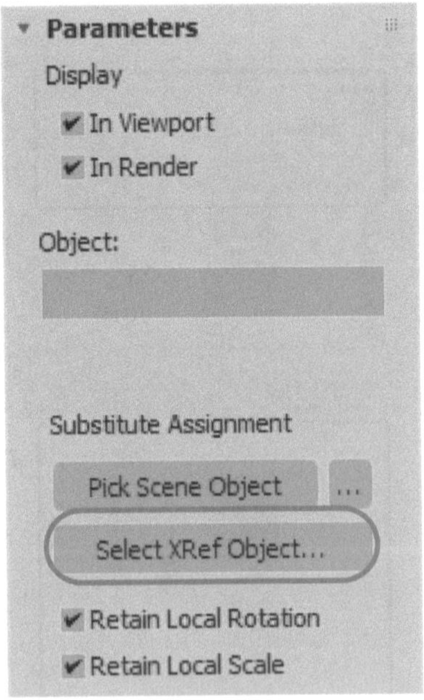

Figure A–11

7. In the *Open File* dialog box, open **Light Poles for Substitution.max** from the practice files folder.
8. In the *XRef Merge* dialog box, select the object named **LP_Single** and click **OK**.
9. In the *Duplicate warning message* dialog box, select **Apply to All Duplicates** to keep both materials, and click **Auto-Rename Merged Material**.
10. In the *Substitution Question* dialog box, click **Yes** to enable the substitute object's material to be used in this scene. Note that the 2D light pole blocks are replaced by the 3D single light pole models.
11. Repeat this process for one of the **Layer:LIGHTPOLE_DOUBLE** objects (expand **Block:Light Pole - Double**), substituting **LP_Double** from **Light Poles for Substitution.max**.
12. In the viewport, click the *Per-View Preference* label and select **Default Shading**. The 3D models of both the single light poles and the double light poles display as shown in Figure A–12.

Figure A–12

13. Save your work as **MyCivilBaseSubstitution.max**.

End of practice

A.3 Creating Hierarchies

Autodesk 3ds Max Hierarchies are collections of objects linked together with parent/child relationships. When used, transforms applied to a parent are automatically passed to its children. Once you have created linkages between objects, you can animate them using forward kinematics where you move/rotate the parent, which in turn moves/rotates the children. Connecting multiple objects in a hierarchical chain can enable sophisticated animations such as the motion of jointed robotic arms.

In the case of the hierarchy file link options, incoming AutoCAD blocks are brought in as multiple objects so that they can maintain multiple material assignments from AutoCAD. They display together with a Block/Style Parent object, enabling you to transform the block as a unit by selecting the parent. The parent object itself does not have any geometry and does not render. Most modifiers are applied to the objects in the hierarchy rather than the parent.

Practice A2
Create Hierarchies

Practice Objective

- Create hierarchical relationships between objects.

In this practice, you will want to create hierarchical relationships so that objects move together when moved. You will create linkages and animate them using forward kinematics to move the parent and rotate the children.

You must set the paths to locate the External files and XREFs used in the practice. If you have not done this already, return to Chapter 1 and complete Task 1 to Task 3 in *Practice 1a: Organize Folders and Work with the Interface*. You only have to set the user paths once.

1. Open **Lamp Start Linking.max**. This is a model of a desk lamp, as shown in Figure A–13.

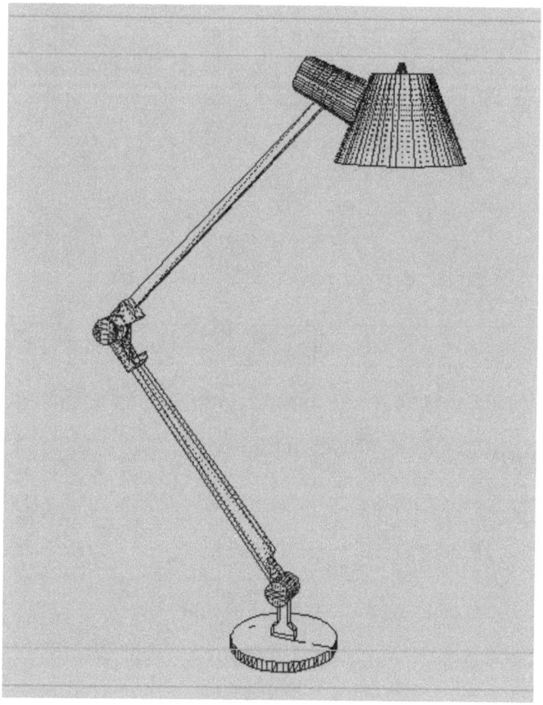

Figure A–13

2. In the Scene Explorer, use (Display None) and (Display Geometry) and note the six geometry objects in the scene. The names are not indented and are located at the same level, indicating that there are no linkages.

3. In the viewport, move the Base object that is at the bottom of the lamp. Note that it moves by itself and the other objects are unaffected. Undo the move and clear the selection.
4. Similarly, move any other object (such as the lamp shade) and note that it also moves separately. Undo the move.
5. In the Main Toolbar, click  (Select and Link). Starting at the top, select and hold each object and drag a dotted line to its parent. You will repeat the process five times as follows:
   - Select **Lampshade** and link it to **Upper Arm - Lamp**, as shown in Figure A–14.
   - Select **Upper Arm - Lamp** and link it to **Lower Arm**.
   - Select **Lower Arm** and link it to **Lower Hub**.
   - Select **Lower Hub** and link it to **Stand**.
   - Select **Stand** and link it to **Base**.

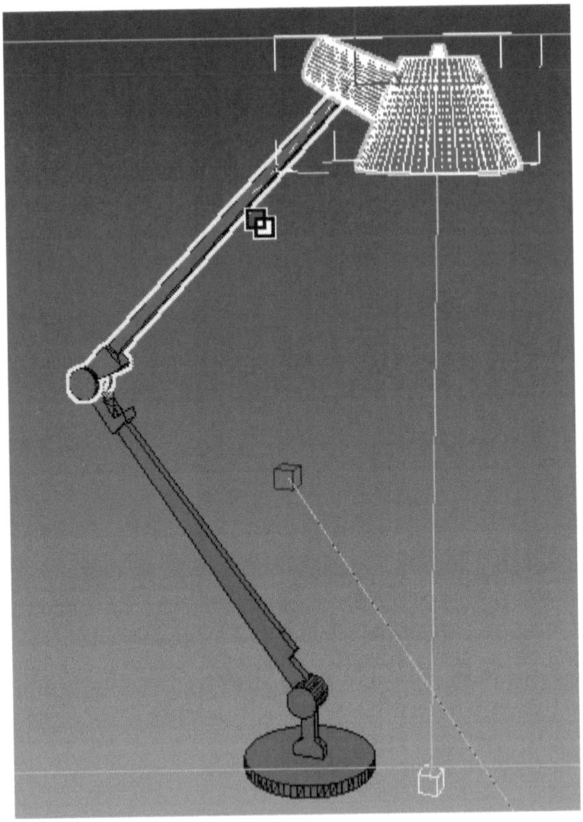

Figure A–14

6. In the Main Toolbar, click  (Select Object) to end the linking process.

7. In the Scene Explorer, note that only **Base** is visible. Expand Base to display its dependent, **Stand**. Expand **Stand** to display its dependent and similarly expand each child to display the dependencies, as shown in Figure A–15.

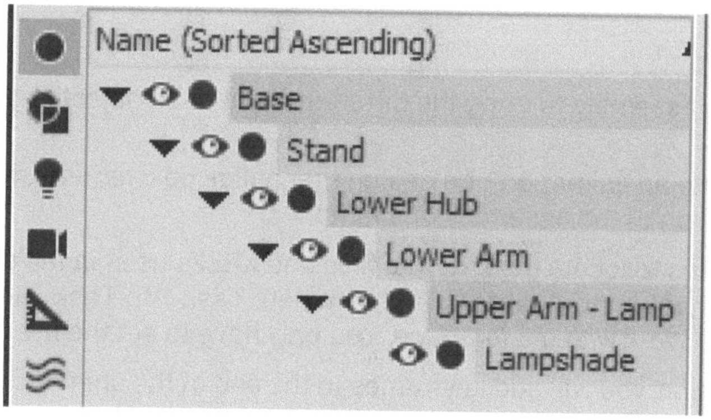

Figure A–15

8. Move the **Base** and note that the entire lamp moves with it. The base is the parent object and other objects are children and descendants. Undo the move.
9. Rotate the **Lower Arm** and note that the **Upper Arm - Lamp** and **Lampshade**, also rotates along with it. The Lower Hub, Stand, and Base are not part of the rotation. Undo the rotations.
10. Save your scene file as **MyLampStartLinking.max**.

End of practice

Practice A3
Create an Assembly Animation

Practice Objective

- Create animation assembly to bring the different parts of an object together.

It is common to create an animation of a design that builds up over time. In this practice, you will create an animation of the assembly of a lamp.

You must set the paths to locate the External files and XREFs used in the practice. If you have not done this already, return to Chapter 1 and complete Task 1 to Task 3 in *Practice 1a: Organize Folders and Work with the Interface*. You only have to set the user paths once.

In this kind of animation, you will add keyframes to the end of the animation and then adjust the start and end ranges for each component.

1. Open **Lamp Start Linking Animation.max.**
2. In the Animation Controls, click  (Time Configuration). In the *Time Configuration* dialog box, in the *Animation* area, set the *End Time* to **200** and click **OK**.
3. Press <Ctrl>+<A> to select all objects in the viewport at once.
4. In the Time Slider, right-click on the **0/200** slider bar to open the *Create Key* dialog box. Clear **Rotation** and **Scale** leaving **Position** selected and set the *Destination Time* to **160**, as shown in Figure A–16. Click **OK**.

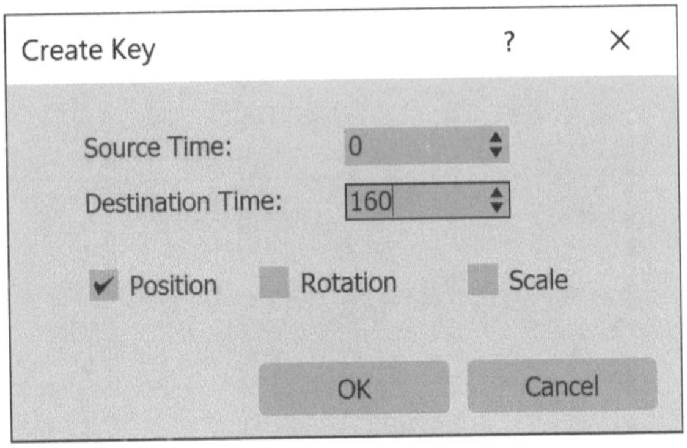

Figure A–16

- A Position key for all objects is placed at frame 160. Note that in the Track Bar, a red box is set at 160, as shown in Figure A–17.

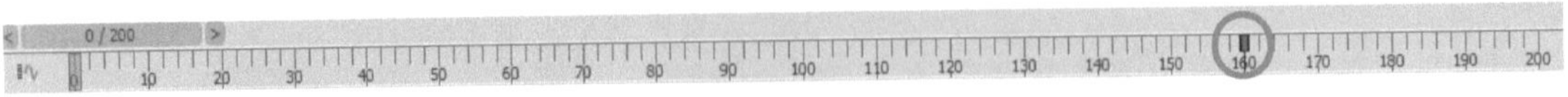

Figure A–17

5. Click **Auto** to activate it. Note that Auto key, the slider bar, and the viewport border display in red.

6. Verify that your slider bar is located at **0** (0/200). Clear the object selection, and move each individual part of the lamp randomly on the screen, similar to that shown in Figure A–18. (The placement of the objects can be different to that shown in the image.)

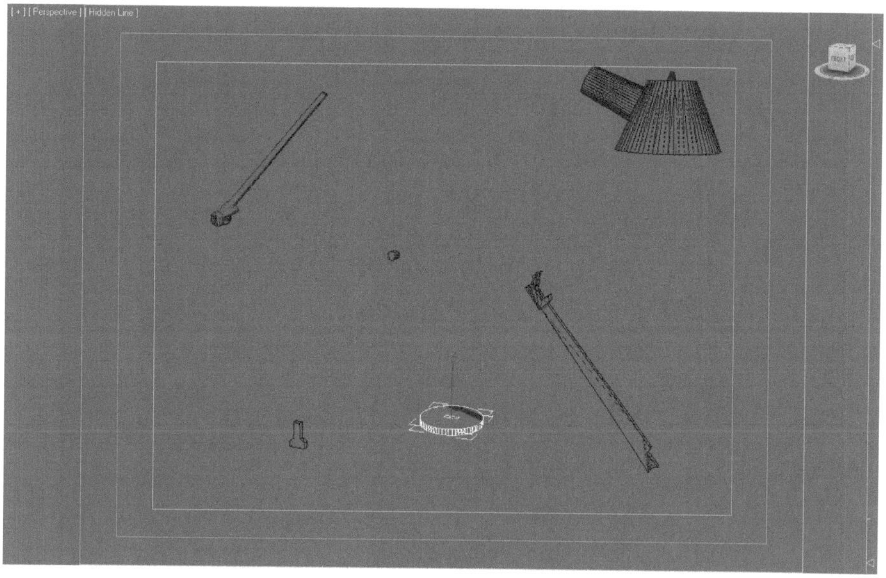

Figure A–18

7. Click ▶ (Play) and note that starting from frame 0, the components start drifting towards their original position and complete their original position at frame 160. Stop the animation.

8. Save your scene file as **MyLampAnimation.max**.

Hint: Set the Selection Range

To have the components assemble one after another, using <Ctrl> select both keys in the Time Slider. Right-click and select **Configure>Show Selection Range**. A bar is added below the track bar indicating the duration of movement for the selected component. You can now move the ends of the range to control when the object starts to move and when it finishes. The shorter the line, the quicker the movement of the object.

End of practice

A.4 Customizing the User Interface

The Autodesk 3ds Max software has a flexible and highly customizable user interface that can be modified using the *Customize User Interface* dialog box, as shown in Figure A–19. Select **Customize>Customize User Interface**.

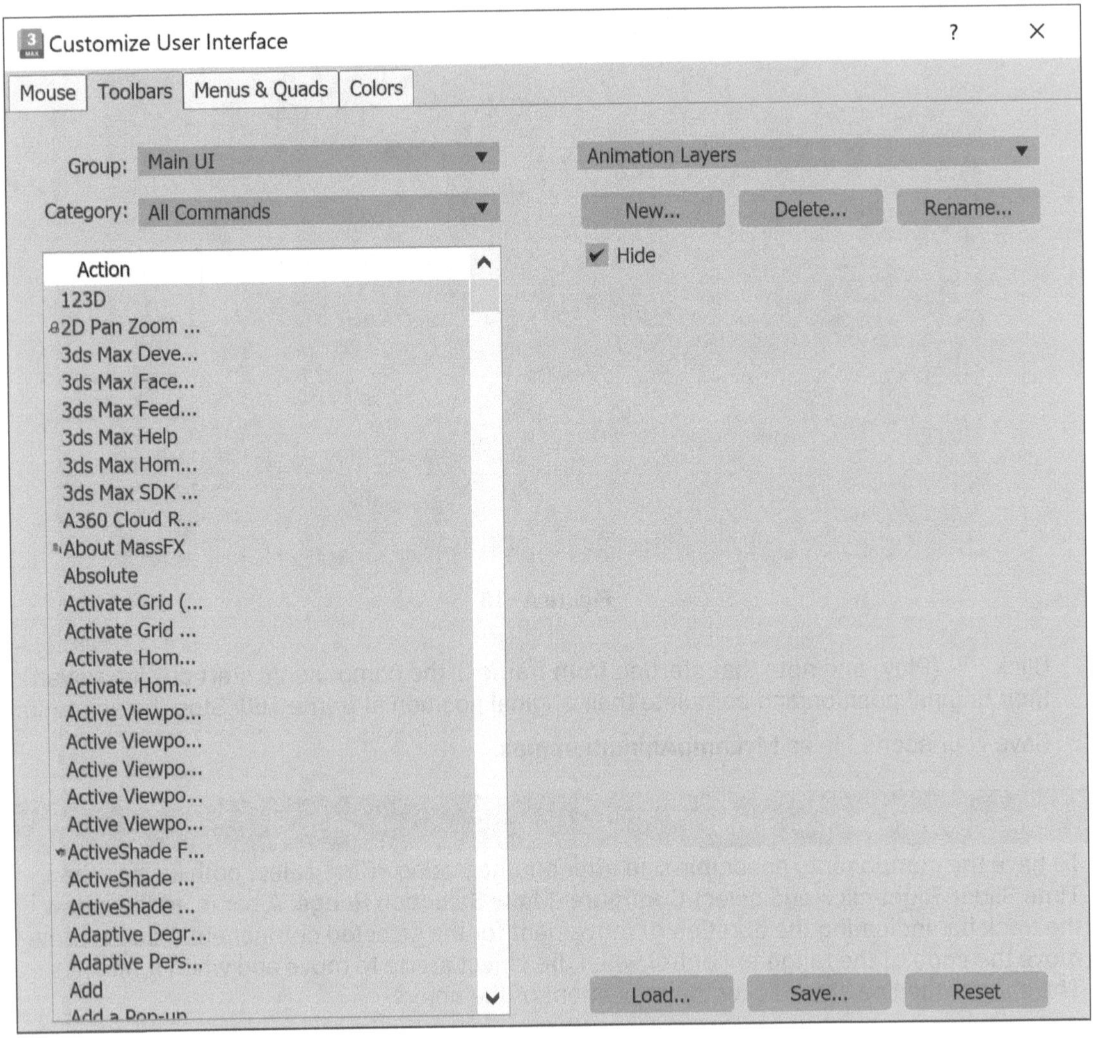

Figure A–19

- The settings located in each tab can be saved or swapped out independently with **Load...** and **Save...**.

- All of the interface settings can be loaded and saved at once using **Customize>Load/Save Custom UI Scheme**.

Mouse tab	Enables you to load and save the mouse settings. The mouse settings are dependent on the interaction mode set in the *Preferences* dialog box, in which you can set the Autodesk 3ds Max mode or Autodesk Maya mode.
Toolbars tab	Enables you to create custom toolbars and modify the existing one based on your requirements.
Colors tab	Enables you to set color options for the interface elements.

- The menus and quads are customized using the *Menu Editor* dialog box. Select **Customize>Menu Edtor** to open the *Menu Editor* dialog box.
- All of the toolbar and menu custom settings are saved in an upgraded file format (.MUSX for mouse settings, .CUIX for toolbar settings, .MNUX for quad menus and menu settings, and .CLRX for color settings).

Practice A4
Customize the User Interface

Practice Objective

- Customize the user interface.

In this practice, you will learn to customize the user interface by adding different commands in the quad menu. You will then add different icons for a command to the Main Toolbar.

1. Reset the file so that you have a blank file open.
2. Right-click in any viewport to open the quad menu. Note that the **Clone** option displays after **Snap Pivot**, as shown in Figure A–20.

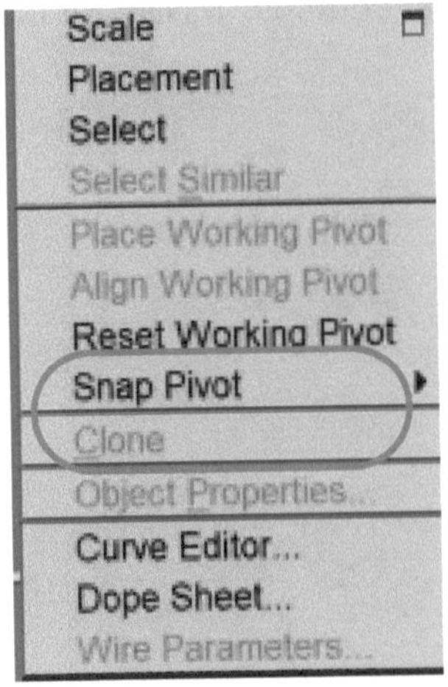

Figure A–20

3. Select **Customize>Menu Editor** to open the *Menu Editor* dialog box.
4. Select the *Quads* tab. Click on any item in the *Action* list and press <O> to jump to commands starting with letter O.

5. Locate **Orbit View Mode**. Click and drag it to the quad list on the right, placing it just above **Clone**, under the line, as shown in Figure A–21. This enables you to select **Orbit View Mode** through the right-click quad menu. Also note that its position is between **Snap Pivot** and **Clone**.

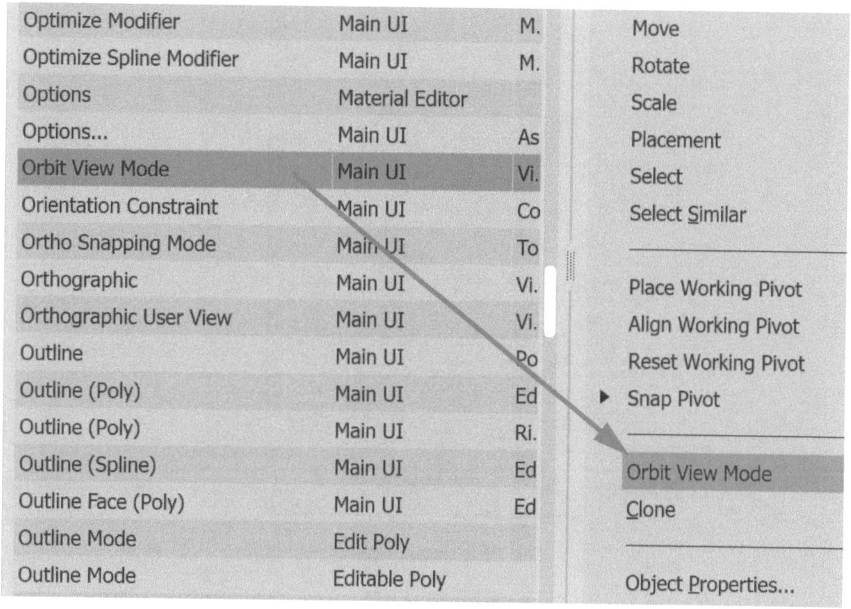

Figure A–21

6. In the *Action* list, select **Toggle ViewCube Visibility**, drag it to the quad list on the right, and place it just below **Orbit View Mode**, as shown in Figure A–22.

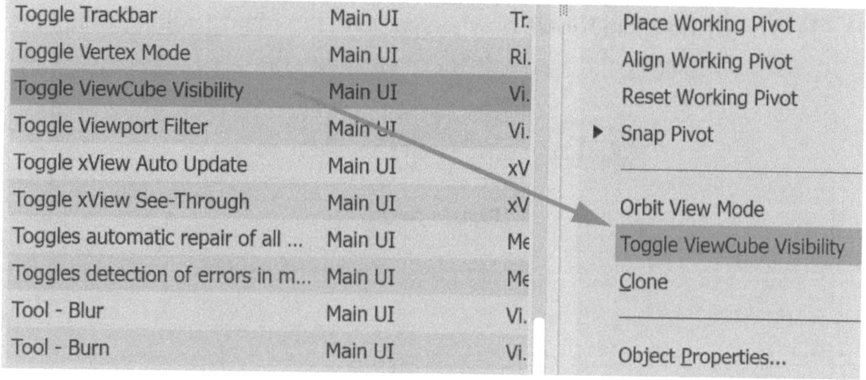

Figure A–22

- You can delete or edit the names of the listed commands by right-clicking on the command in the newly created quad list and selecting **Delete Item** or **Rename**.

7. Click **Done** in the dialog box.

8. Right-click on any viewport and note the two new commands between **Snap Pivot** and **Clone**, as shown in Figure A–23.

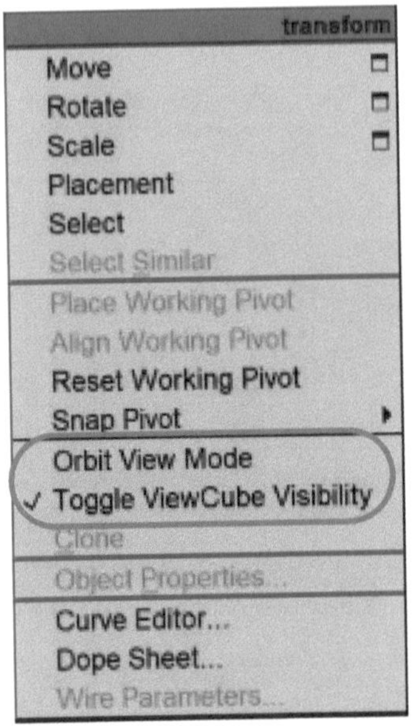

Figure A–23

9. Select **Toggle ViewCube Visibility** to toggle it off. Note that the ViewCube is not visible in the viewports anymore. Toggle it back on.
10. Select **Customize>Customize User Interface**.
11. In the dialog box, select the *Toolbars* tab. In the *Action* list, click **Ortho Snapping Mode**. Drag this entry to the Main Toolbar, and drop it before the **3D Snaps** icon, as shown in Figure A–24. The **Ortho Snap** tool is now available in the Main Toolbar. Close the dialog box.

Figure A–24

12. In the Main Toolbar, right-click on the newly placed **Ortho Snap** tool and select **Delete Button**, as shown in the Figure A–25. In the *Confirm* dialog box, click **Yes**. The button is removed.

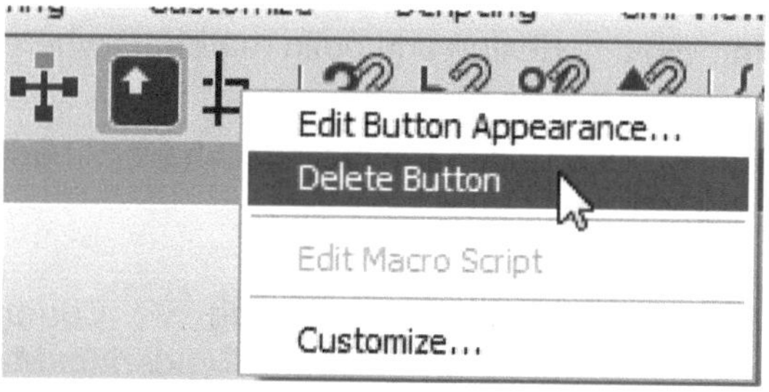

Figure A–25

13. In the Main Toolbar, right-click on **Select Object** or **Render Setup**. No shortcut menu displays, indicating that you cannot delete or modify them. Only the added buttons and some of the toggle buttons can be deleted.

End of practice

A.5 Compact Material Editor

The Autodesk 3ds Max software contains two editors for working with materials:

- **Slate Material Editor**: Used to design and build materials where the material components display graphically.
- **Compact Material Editor**: Used when the materials have already been created and you just need to apply them.

- The *Compact Material Editor* can be opened by clicking  (Compact Material Editor) in the Main Toolbar (*Material Editor* flyout), or by selecting **Rendering>Material Editor> Compact Material Editor**.
- The *Compact Material Editor* (shown in Figure A–26) opens with sample slots for materials and various tools in the toolbars.
- A material shown in a sample slot is previewed as applied to a 3D object. A map previewed in a sample slot is shown as a flat 2D rectangle.
- The *Compact Material Editor* toolbars (shown in Figure A–26) work in the same way as the tools present in the *Slate Material Editor*.

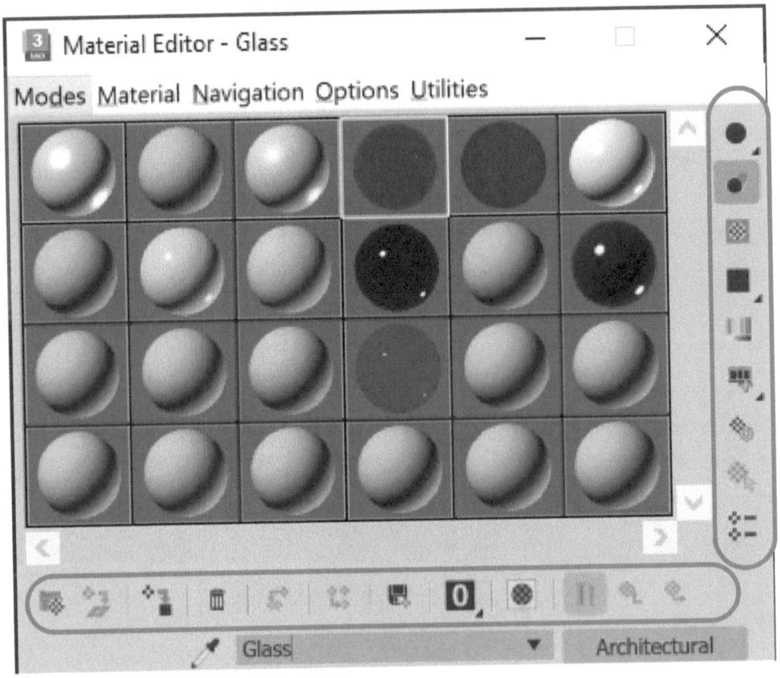

Figure A–26

- The *Material/Map Browser* (shown in Figure A–27) can be accessed by clicking (Get Material) in the toolbar. Once you have located a required material in the browser, drag it from the browser to a scene object or to a sample slot in the *Material Editor*.

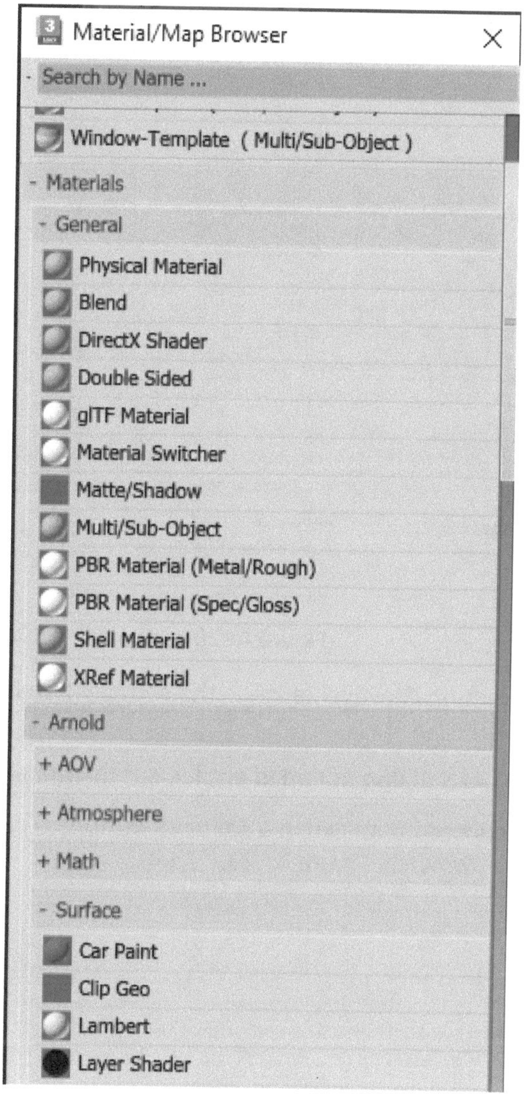

Figure A–27

- It is possible to have a material in the scene that has not been loaded into the editor.
- You can use (Pick Material from Object) in the *Material Editor* and select the object in the viewport to get the material from the object into the *Compact Material Editor*.

- **Options>Options...** in the *Material Editor* opens the *Material Editor Options* dialog box, that offers controls that can help speed up performance when several large or complex materials are present in the editor.
- Right-clicking on a material slot opens a shortcut menu. Figure A–28 shows the various options available in the shortcut menu. The options enable you to copy the materials from one slot to another, rotating and resetting the rotation of the material sample, and set the number of slots.

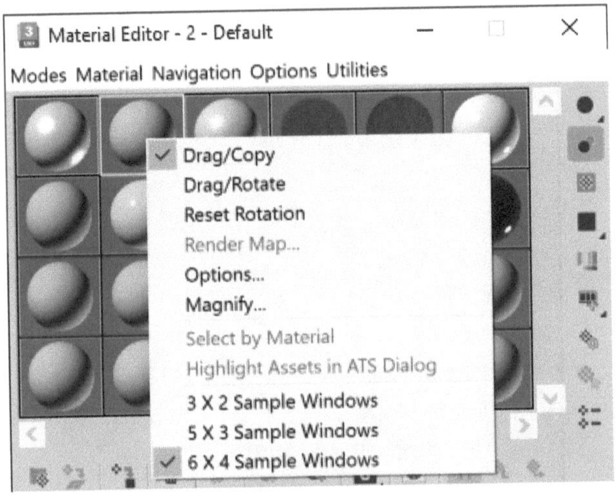

Figure A–28

- The **Select by Material** option is available when the sample material contains a scene material.
- The **Highlight Assets in ATS dialog** option is available if the material contains a map.
- Previews of the materials can be shown in a list or as buttons. The display can be changed in the shortcut menu, as shown in Figure A–29.

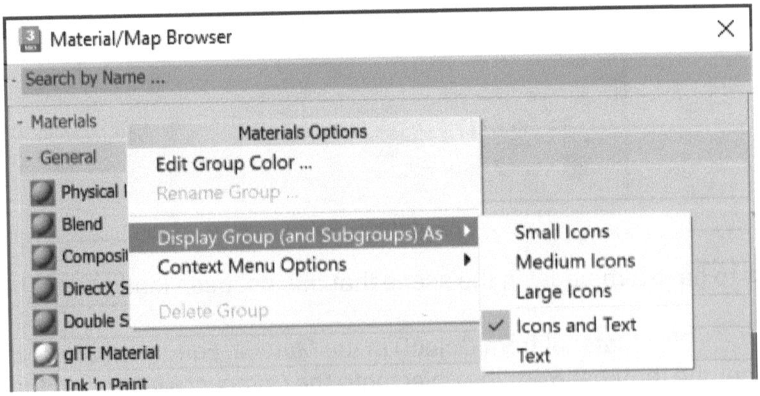

Figure A–29

A.6 Material Shaders

Material Shaders are complex algorithms that describe how light interacts with surfaces. The material color, highlights, self-illumination, and many other features are dependent on the material shaders.

- In Standard materials, the shader type is selected through the *Shader Basic Parameters* rollout, as shown in Figure A–30.

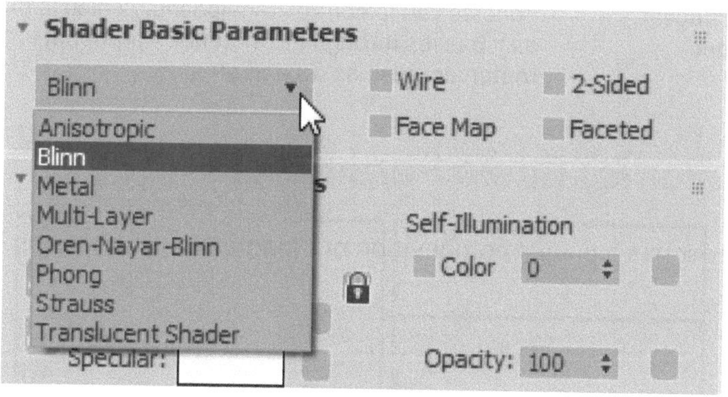

Figure A–30

The standard shader types are described as follows:

	**Anisotropic**	Shader for materials with elliptical highlights, such as hair, glass, or brushed metal.
	**Blinn**	General purpose shader for shiny, smooth objects with soft, circular highlights. Blinn is the default shader for Standard materials.
	**Metal**	Shader for luminous metallic surfaces.
	**Multi-Layer**	Enables two sets of anisotropic controls for complex or highly polished surfaces.
	**Oren-Nayar-Blinn**	A variation of the Blinn shader that provides additional controls for matte surfaces, such as fabric or terra cotta.

	**Phong**	Related to the Blinn shader, also used for shiny, smooth surfaces with circular highlights. The Phong shader generates harder, sharper (often less realistic) highlights than Blinn.
	**Strauss**	For metallic and similar surfaces, Strauss offers a simpler interface than the Metal shader.
	**Translucent Shader**	Enables you to control translucency, which is the scattering of light as it passes through the material. Appropriate for semi-transparent materials, such as frosted glass.

Shader (Specific) Basic Parameters

Each material shader has a unique combination of parameters (as shown in Figure A–31) that can be controlled.

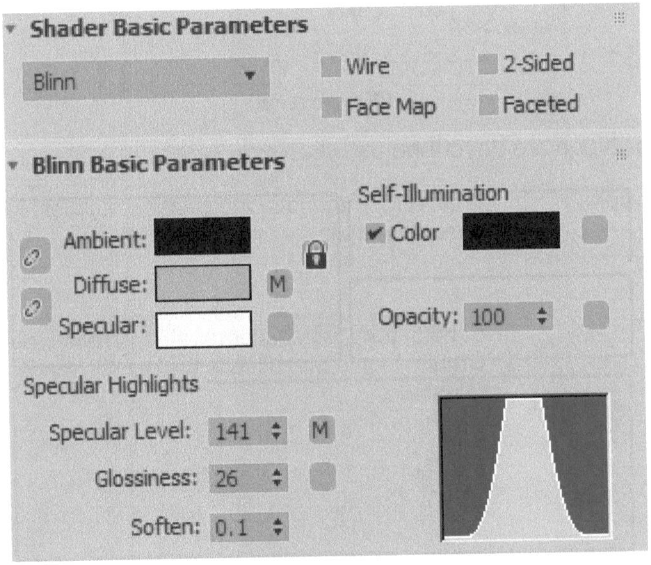

Figure A–31

- Most of these parameters can be replaced by a map when their values are not constant across the surface. For example, a Diffuse Color Map can be used to replace a single diffuse color for a brick material.

- Colors can be selected by picking on the color swatch next to a color parameter, which opens the interactive Scene Color Selector.

Ambient Color	The color of a material under ambient (background) lighting. It can be assigned globally and through standard lights set to cast ambient light. Ambient and diffuse colors can be locked at the same values, if required.
Diffuse Color	The color of a material under direct lighting. This is the base color of a material (outside of highlights).
Specular Color	The highlight color of a material. It is calculated automatically for the Metal and Multilayer shaders.
Self-Illumination	Values greater than 0 cause materials to appear to be illuminated, but surfaces with this material do not illuminate other objects. This parameter is useful for materials used in light fixtures. Self-illuminated objects do not automatically glow. Glows must be assigned as a special effect (**Rendering>Effects**).
Opacity	The percentage measurement of opacity, the opposite of transparency. Materials that have 0% opacity are completely see-through. For example, a typical clear glass material could have an Opacity between 0-10%.

- Many shader properties relate to highlights, the bright areas caused by the specular reflection of a light source on the surface of an object.
- Parameters relating to *Specular Highlights* are listed next to a highlight curve that shows a graphical representation of these settings. Not all of the parameters are available for each shader type. The *Specular Highlights* parameters for Blinn are shown in Figure A–32.

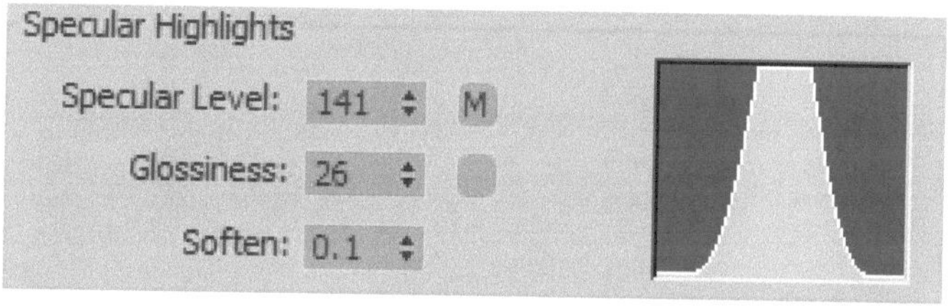

Figure A–32

- The *Specular Highlights* parameters for Anisotropic shaders are shown in Figure A–33.

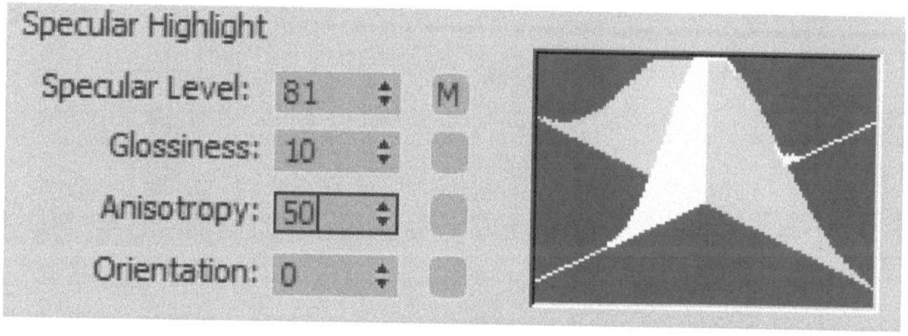

Figure A–33

Specular Level	A relative measurement of the overall highlight intensity.
Glossiness	A relative measurement of the overall size of highlights. The more glossy an object, the smaller and more intense the highlights.
Soften	A relative measurement used to soften the edges of highlights.
Anisotropy	Defines the elliptical shape of Anisotropic highlights, where 0 = round and 100 = a very tight ellipse.
Orientation	Defines the degrees of rotation for an Anisotropic highlight.

A.7 Architectural Materials

Architectural materials are used with the Scanline renderer and are available only when the Scanline renderer is the current one. These materials offer a simplified interface over Standard materials because they have limited control (directly selecting a shader, some specular parameters, etc.). Architectural materials offer additional, built-in controls for translucency, refraction, and global illumination renderers.

Architectural Material Parameters

Architectural materials use Templates to assign shaders, which are predefined with many common material types (such as metals, paint, plastic, masonry, etc.). Selecting a template automatically populates other values in the *Physical Qualities* rollout, as shown in Figure A–34.

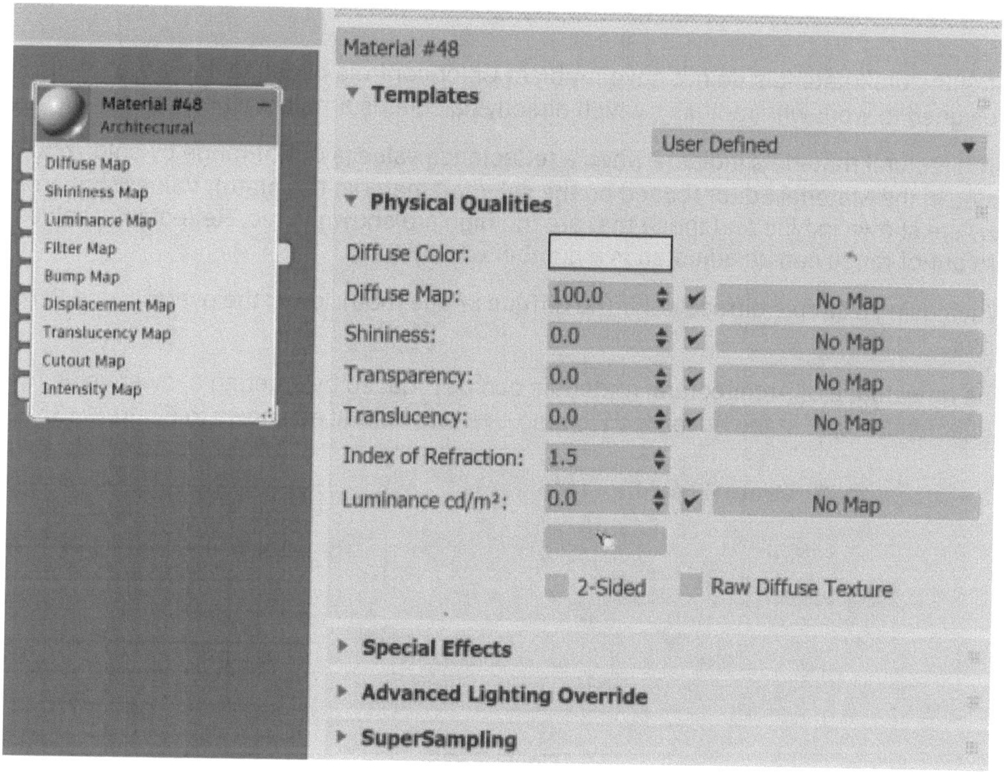

Figure A–34

Diffuse Color/ Diffuse Map	Located at the top of the *Physical Qualities* rollout, which are identical to those for Standard materials.
Shininess	Similar controls to the Specular Level of Standard materials. Architectural material highlights are generated through the **Shininess** and **Index of Refraction** parameters.

Transparency	The overall percentage that a material is transparent. For example, clear glass materials could be assigned transparencies between 90 and 100%.
Translucency	A measure of how much light is scattered as it passes through the object.
Index of Refraction (IOR)	Controls refraction and reflection. Typical values include 1.0 for air (effectively no refractive distortion), 1.33 for water, 1.5-1.7 for thick glass, and 2.5 for diamond.
Luminance	The amount of physically-based light the material emits. Unlike the Self-Illumination parameter of Standard materials, objects assigned Architectural materials can actually add light to scenes through this parameter as if they were light objects. (For example, illuminated materials are often used to represent neon tubes.)
Bump Maps	Can be assigned in the *Special Effects* rollout.

- Architectural materials do not have Ambient Color controls because these materials are designed to work with radiosity, which directly calculates ambient illumination.
- Architectural materials indicate when a reflectance value is out-of-range by colorizing the value in the Material Editor (based on the selected material template). Values that are too low are shown in blue and those that are too high are shown in red. Reflectance values that are out-of-range can be adjusted in a number of ways:
- When using a simple diffuse color (no diffuse image map), lower the overall value (V) of the color.
- The reflectance of Architectural materials can be reduced by entering a lower value for the *Reflectance Scale* in the *Advanced Lighting Override* rollout, as shown in Figure A–35.

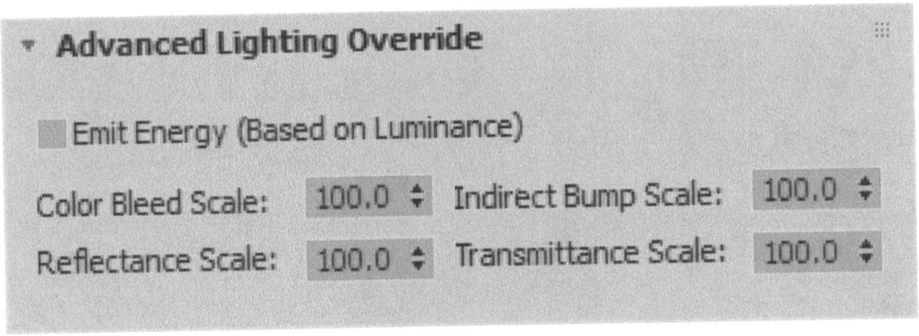

Figure A–35

Command Summary

Button	Command	Location
N/A	**3ds Max Help**	• **Help**: Autodesk 3ds Max Help
	**Compact Material Editor**	• **Main Toolbar:** *Material Editor* flyout • **Rendering:** *Material Editor>Compact Material Editor*
N/A	**Customize User Interface**	• **Customize:** Customize User Interface

Appendix B

Optional Practices

This appendix contains additional practices that can be worked on to provide further practice using the Autodesk® 3ds Max® software.

Practice B1
Create Additional Extrusions

Practice Objective

- Create 3D objects from 2D shapes.

In this practice, you will create extrusions that define a lobby area using the **Extrude** modifier and its various options, as shown in Figure B–1. You will extrude a part of the second floor that connects to the lobby area.

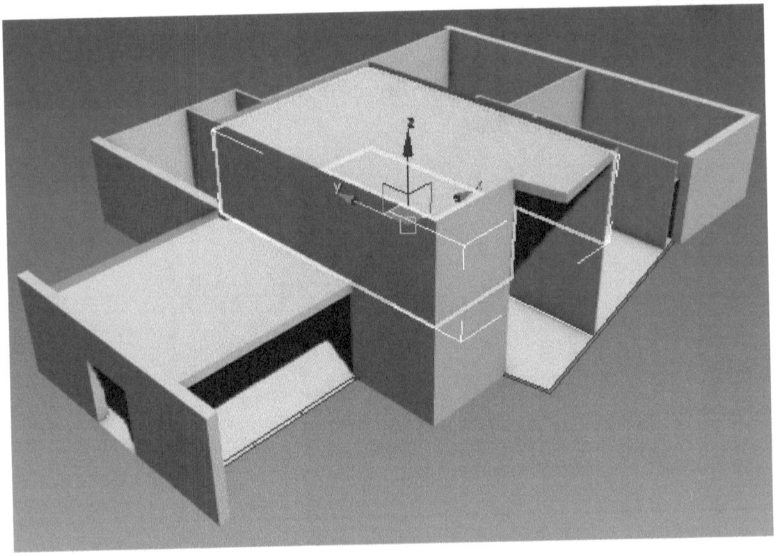

Figure B–1

1. Open **Extruded Walls with Openings.max.**
2. Click the *Shading Viewport* label and select **High Quality**.
3. Select each of the 2D shapes listed in the following table individually (use the Scene Explorer with (Display Shapes)). All of these shapes are **Editable Splines** (which displays in the Modifier stack). For each selected object, use the **Extrude** modifier (*Modify* panel ()>*Modifier List*) and extrude them as described in the table. For each object, set the rest of the parameters (Select **Generate Mapping Coords.**, **Real-World Map Size** and clear **Generate Material IDs**) as shown for **Layer:VIZ-1-Ceiling**, in Figure B–2. Press <Enter> after entering a value in the edit box for it to take affect. For the objects that are required to be moved up (elevation), click (Select and Move) and then, in the Status Bar, enter the *Z* value for elevation, as specified in the table.

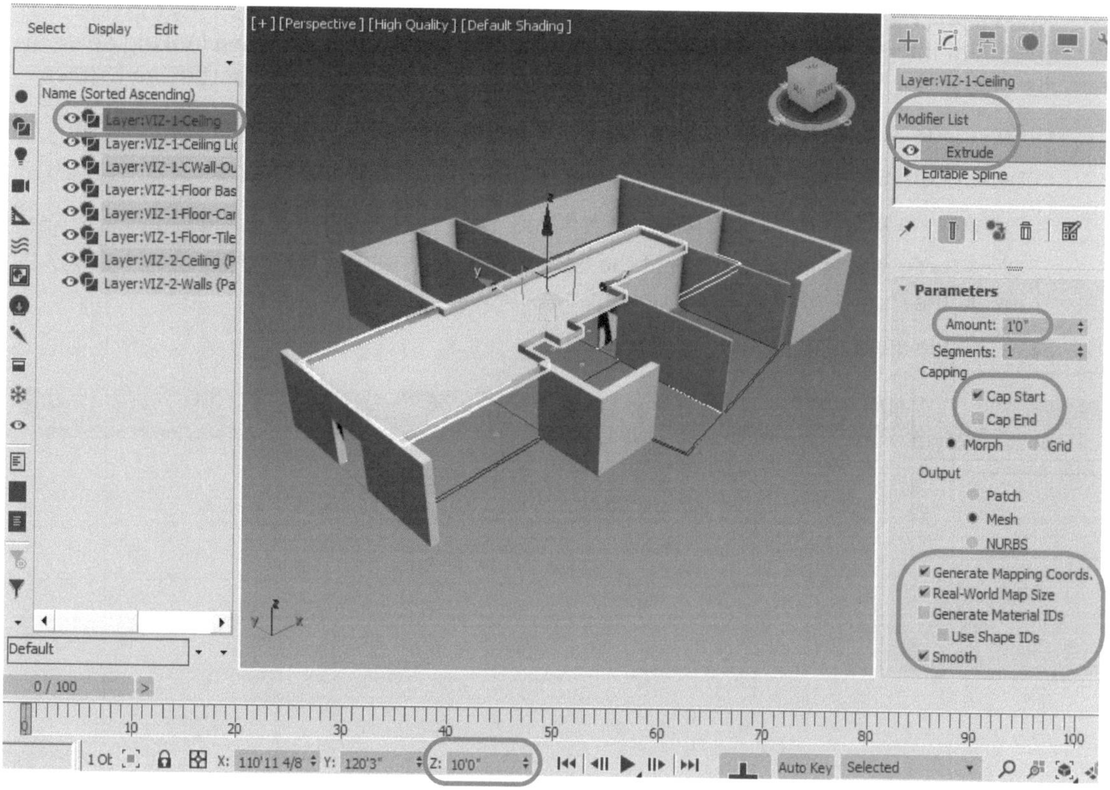

Figure B–2

Autodesk 3ds Max Shape	Extrusion Amount	Notes
Layer:VIZ-1-Ceiling	1'0"	Cap only the start (clear Cap End) Move up to elevation 10'0"
Layer:VIZ-1-Ceiling Lights	0'0"	Cap only the start (clear **Cap End**) Move up to elevation **9'11 7/8"**
Layer:VIZ-1-Floor-Carpet	0'0"	Cap only the end (clear **Cap Start**)
Layer:VIZ-1-Floor-Tile	0'0"	Cap only the end (clear **Cap Start**)
Layer:VIZ-2-Ceiling (Partial)	1'0"	Cap only the start (clear **Cap End**) Move up to elevation **20'0"**
Layer:VIZ-2-Walls (Partial)	9'0"	Cap only the end (clear **Cap Start**) Move up to elevation **11'0"**

4. When using **Cap Start** and **Cap End**, note that the ceilings are visible from the top and bottom of the model. To change the view so that the lobby displays when looking down at the model, but the ceilings display when looking up, set the **Object Properties** as follows:
   - Select the two ceiling layers: **Layer:VIZ-1-Ceiling** and **Layer: VIZ-2-Ceiling (Partial)**.
   - Select **Edit>Object Properties**. The *Object Properties* dialog box opens.
   - In the *General* tab, in the *Display Properties* area, click **By Layer** to change it to **By Object**.
   - Once **By Object** is enabled, select the **Backface Cull** option. This enables you to see inside the model when looking down from the top.
5. Save the file as **MyAdditional Extrude.max**.

End of practice

Practice B2
Make a Chair Base by Lofting Objects

Practice Objective

- Loft 2D shapes along a 2D path to create a 3D object and apply deformations to the shapes.

In this practice, you will create a loft object to represent the base of a chair. The extrude and sweep modifiers both use a single shape that sweeps along a path to create a 3D object. The Loft Compound Object modifier places multiple shapes along a spline path. It also gives you additional deformations to twist, tweeter, scale, and otherwise fit to shape on a graph

1. Open the file **airport_chair_startLoft.max**. The chair seat 3D model and four 2D shapes (in blue) display in the viewport, as shown in Figure B–3.

Figure B–3

2. In the viewport, select the straight line 2D shape directly under the chair. This shape is used as a path for the loft.
   - In the viewport, there are three more shapes: a **Circle**, a **Star** with three points, and a six sided **NGon**. You will blend from shape to shape along the path.
3. In the Command Panel>*Create* panel ( ), click (Geometry), expand the drop-down list, and select **Compound Objects**.
4. In the *Object Type* rollout, click **Loft**.

5. In the *Creation Method* rollout, click **Get Shape**. In the viewport, hover the cursor over the large circle object named **Circle01**. Note the cursor changes to a **Get Shape** cursor. Select this large circle. The circle is lofted along the selected straight line, as shown in Figure B–4.

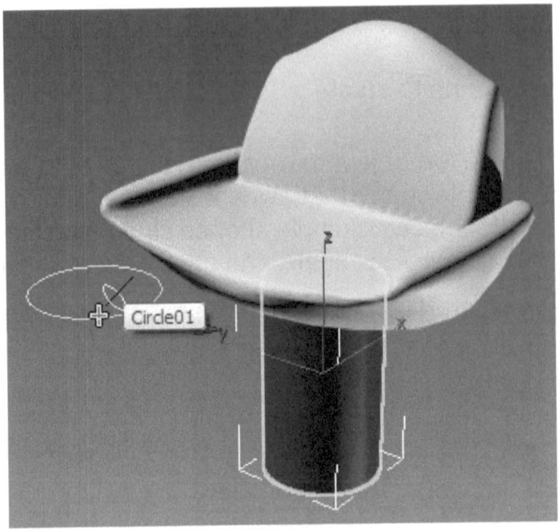

Figure B–4

6. Press <F3> to toggle to wireframe shading or click the *Per-View Preference* label and select **Wireframe Override**.

7. With the **Loft** object selected, in the Command Panel, select the *Modify* panel (). In the *Path Parameters* rollout, set *Path* to **40**. In the viewport, a small yellow **X** indicator moves up the path, as shown in Figure B–5.

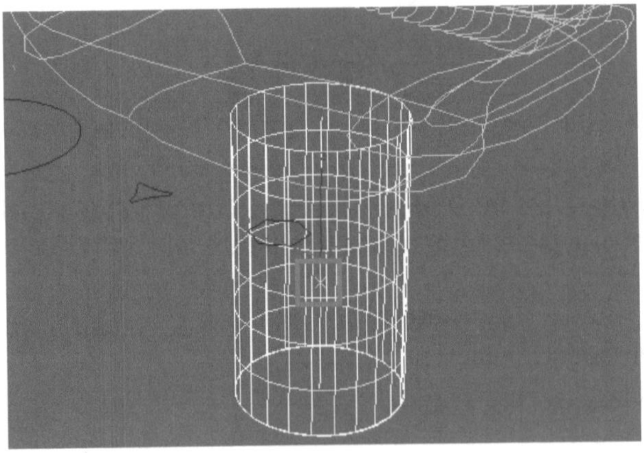

Figure B–5

8. In the *Creation Method* rollout, click **Get Shape**. In the viewport, select **NGon01** (blue **Ngon** inside the loft object). Click the *Per-View Preference* label and select **Default Shading**, then click the *Shading Viewport* label and select **High Quality**. The circular base shape now tapers to a post, as shown in Figure B–6.
   - The **Zoom** and **Orbit** commands were used to display the complete loft object.
   - If shadows are visible over the loft object, click the *Shading Viewport* label, select **Lighting and Shadows**, and clear **Shadows**.

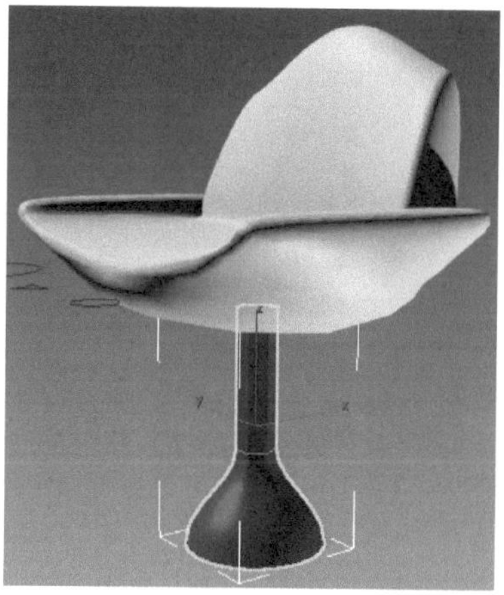

Figure B–6

9. In the *Path Parameters* rollout, set the *Path* value to **60**.
10. Verify that **Get Shape** is still selected (blue background) otherwise select it. Select the **NGon01** again. The NGON is placed at the new location.

11. In the *Path Parameters* rollout, set the *Path* value to **100**. With the **Get Shape** still selected, select the **Circle01**. In the viewport, note that the loft flares up before touching the seat, as shown in Figure B–7.

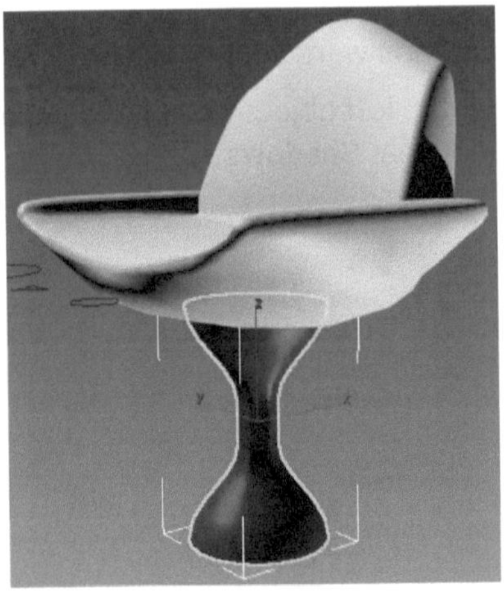

Figure B–7

12. In the *Path Parameters* rollout, set the *Path* value to **50**.
13. Verify that **Get Shape** is still selected (or select it) and select the **Star01** shape. Note that in the center of the loft, the geometry does not look very good. You need to add more points to the star. Click **Get Shape** again to clear its selection.
14. In the Scene Explorer, ((Display Shapes)), select **Star01**. In the *Modify* panel ( ), in the *Parameters* rollout, set the following values for the Star (*Radius 1*: **9'0"**, *Radius 2*: **7'0"**, *Points*: **9**), as shown in Figure B–8. In the viewport, note that both the loft object and the star shape have been modified, as shown in Figure B–9.

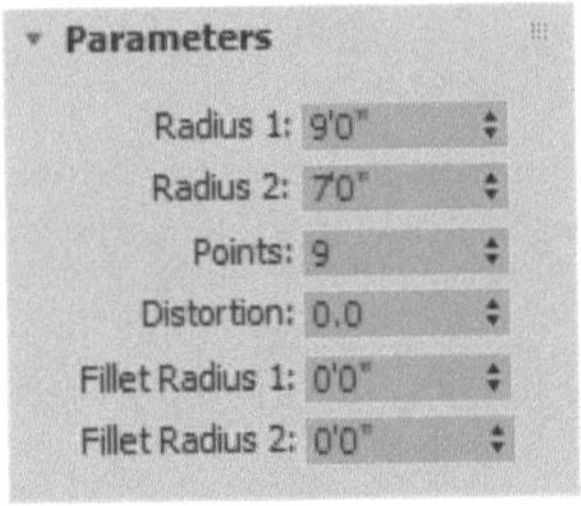

Figure B–8

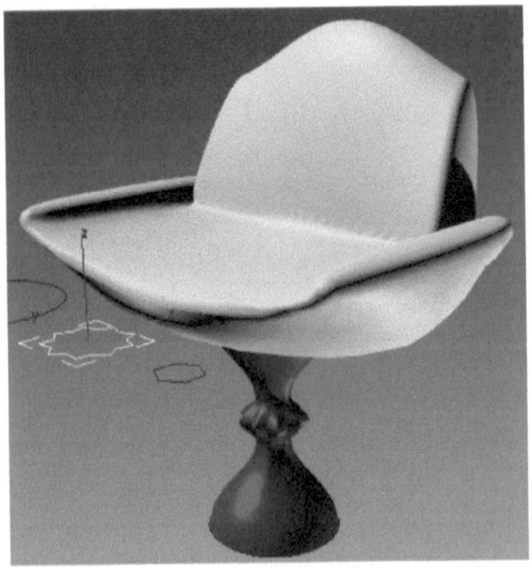

Figure B–9

15. Select the loft object and press <F4> to display in *Edged Faces* mode, as shown in Figure B–10. Note that the mesh looks pretty dense.

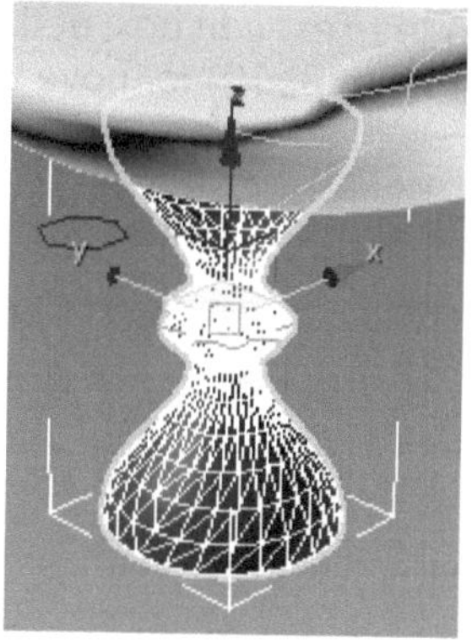

Figure B–10

16. With the base selected (Loft001), verify that the *Modify* panel () is open in the Command Panel.

17. Expand the *Skin Parameters* rollout, and in the *Options* area, set both the *Shape Steps* and *Path Steps* to **2**. The base loses its smoothness. Increase the *Path Steps* to **4** and leave the *Shape Steps as* **2**, as shown in Figure B–11.

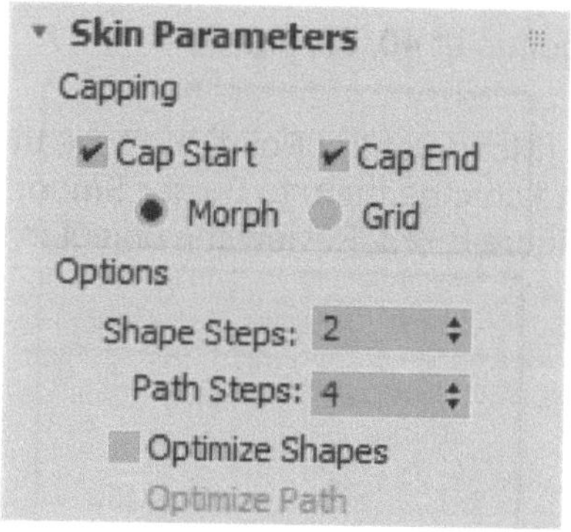

Figure B–11

18. For sculpting the final shape of the Loft object, expand the *Deformations* rollout and click **Scale**. The Scale Deformation graph displays.

19. In the *Scale Deformation* toolbar, click  (Insert Corner Point). When you hover the cursor over the red line, note that it displays as a plus sign. Click on the red line approximately under 20 to set a control point. In the *Text* edit box, at the bottom of the dialog box, enter **20** and press <Enter> (as shown in Figure B–12) to move the control point to the exact position.

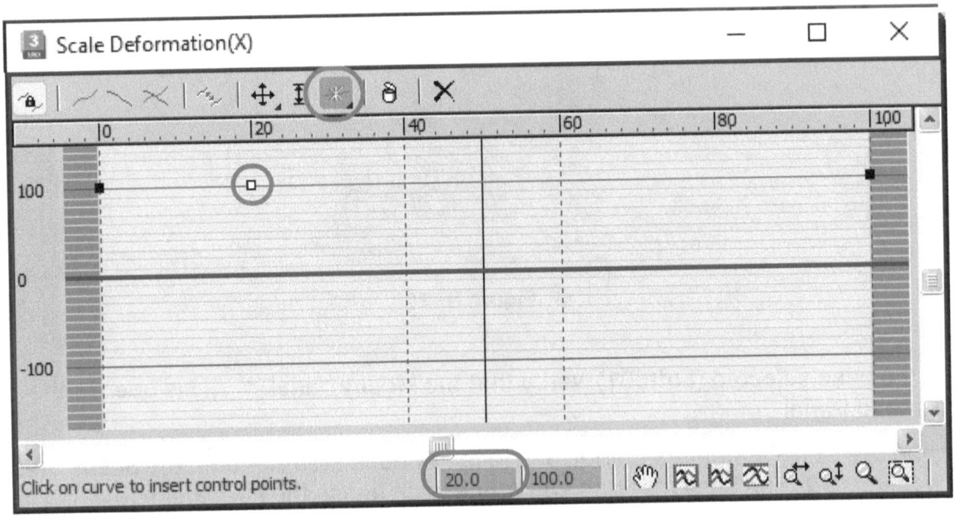

Figure B–12

20. Similarly add new control points at **40**, **50**, and **60**.

21. In the dialog box, click  (Move Control Point) to move the points on the graph. Right-click on the points and change them to **Bezier Smooth** or **Bezier Corner**, then adjust the handles, as shown in Figure B–13. Review the object in the viewport as the points are moved and modified.

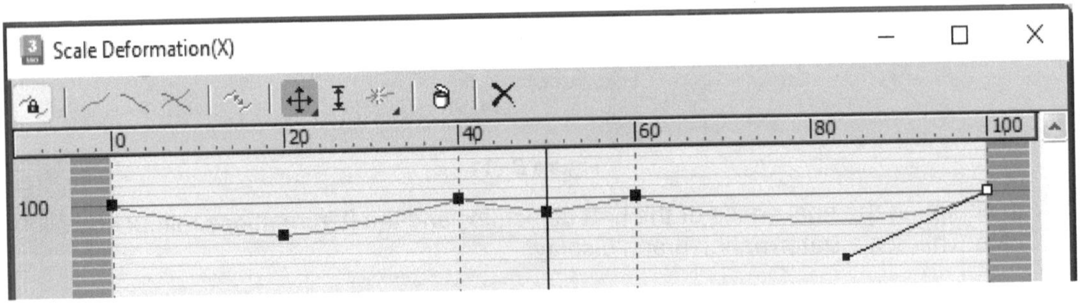

Figure B–13

22. Play with the handles and scale points while watching the interactive results in the viewport.
23. You can use other deformation tools, such as **Twist**, **Teeter**, **Bevel**, and **Fit** and note how they effect the base of the chair.
24. Save the file as **Myarmchair_withBase.max**.

End of practice

Practice B3
Create a Shadow Study Animation

Practice Objective

- Animate the Daylight System to create a shadow study.

In this practice, you will animate the movement of the daylight throughout a day in the exterior scene to create an animated shadow study. This study will provide an accurate representation of how daylight will cast shadows in the scene.

1. Open **Shadow Study.max.**
2. Activate the **Camera01** viewport. This is the non-animated camera view.
3. In the Animation controls, click  (Time Configuration). Set the settings as *Frame Rate*: **Custom**, *FPS*: **20**, *End Time*: **0:30:0**, as shown in Figure B–14. Click **OK**.

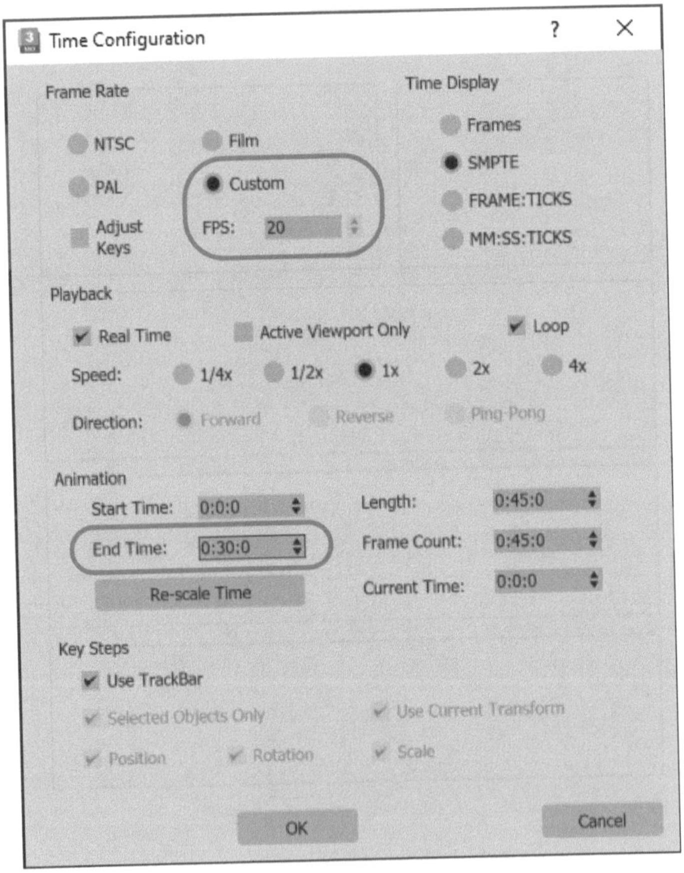

Figure B–14

4. In this shadow study you will animate the **SunPositioner001** object using keyframing. Select the **SunPositioner001** object in the Scene Explorer, using **Display Lights** tool.
5. Verify that the Time Slider is located at a time of **0:0:0** (frame 0), as shown in Figure B–15.

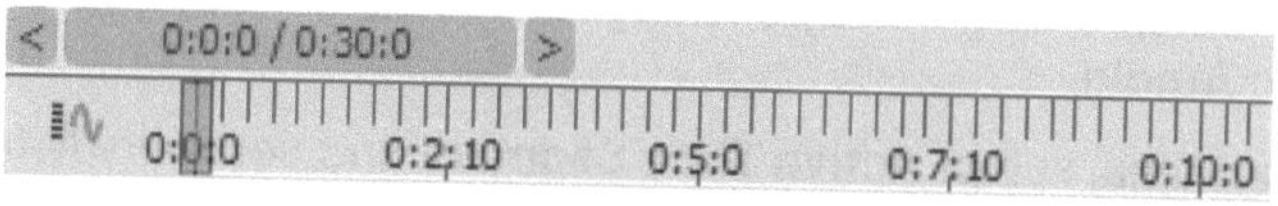

Figure B–15

6. In the Command Panel, select the *Modify* panel (). Start the shadow study animation at frame 0, representing **6:00 AM**. In the *Sun Position* rollout, set the current time to **6h**, as shown in Figure B–16. The date has already been saved with the drawing file.

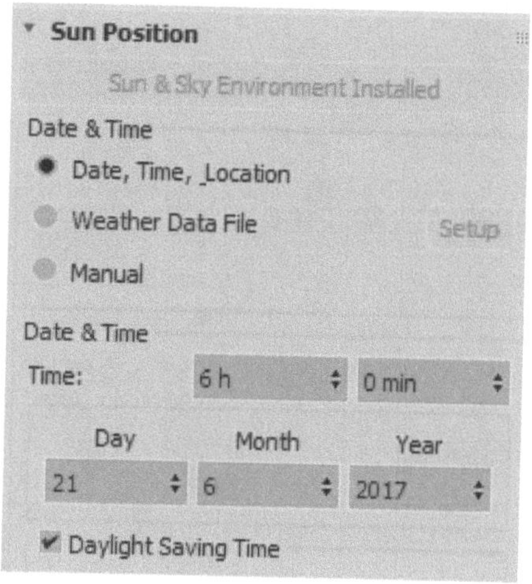

Figure B–16

7. In the Animation Controls, click **Auto** (which then displays in red). While in **Auto** mode, drag the time slider to the end time of **0:30:0**, as shown in Figure B–17.

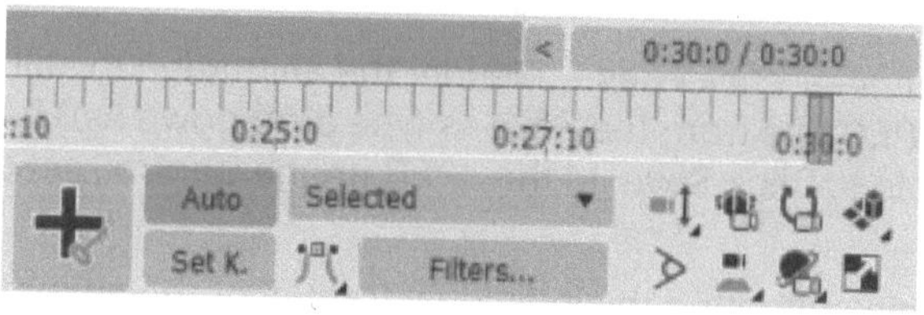

Figure B–17

8. At this time (**0:30:0**) change the sun's position to 7:00 PM by entering **19h** in the *Hours* edit box in the Command Panel.
9. Click **Auto** key again to clear it and end Auto mode.

10. Slide the Time Slider left and right (scrub) and in the viewports (Left and Top), watch the **SunPositioner001** object progress across the sky during the animation.
11. Open the *Render Setup* dialog box by clicking ( (Render Setup)). Verify that the active renderer is set to **Arnold**.
12. In the *Time Output* area, select **Active Time Segment** and set *Every Nth Frame* to **20**, as shown in Figure B–18.
13. In the *View to Render* drop-down list, set the current viewport to **Quad 4 - Camera01**, if required, and click , as shown in Figure B–18. This enables you to always render **Camera01** even if another viewport is active.

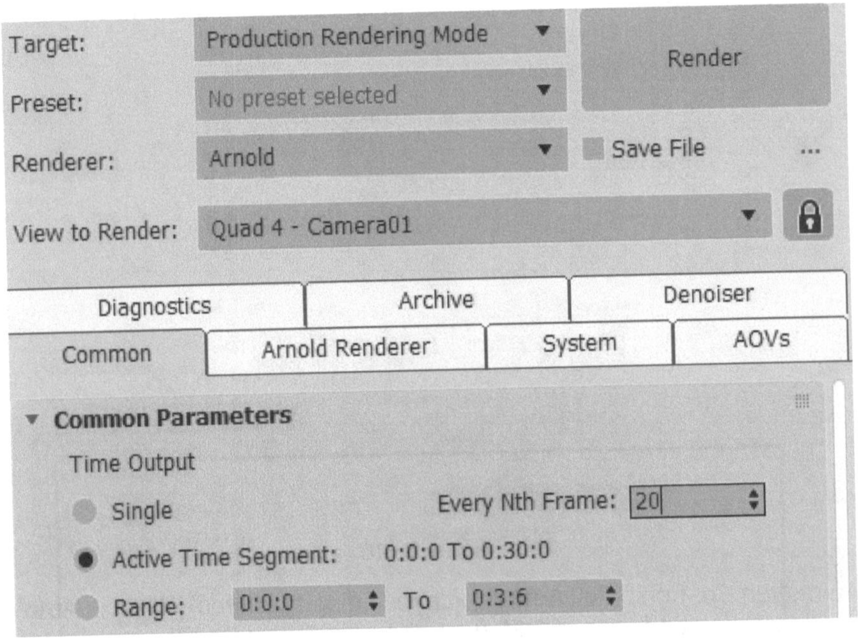

Figure B–18

14. In the *Render Output* area, click **Files...**. Render the animation to still frames named **Shadow Study.jpg** (select **JPEG File** from the *Save as type* drop-down list) in the *renderings* folder in the practice files folder. Click **Save**. In the JPEG Image Control, set *Quality* to **Best** and then click **OK**.
15. Click **Render** to begin animating the individual frames of the animation through the course of a day from 6:00 AM to 7:00 PM. Note the change in brightness of the daylight and the movement of the shadows from one frame to another.
    - It might take a few minutes to render all 31 frames.

16. In the Windows Explorer, in the *renderings* folder in the practice files folder, note the rendered images for **Shadow Study** at different frames, as shown for frame 1 and frame 21 (out of a total of 31 frames rendered) in Figure B–19.

Shadow study at Frame 1

Shadow study at Frame 21

Figure B–19

17. Save the scene file as **My Shadow Study.max**.

End of practice

Appendix

C

Standard Lighting

Illumination can be accomplished using various types of lights such as, photometric, Arnold, or standard lights. Standard lights are used to illuminate the scene when using the Scanline renderer.

Learning Objectives

- Work with standard lights and control the various parameter settings.
- Control the specific settings of various types of standard lights.

C.1 Standard Lighting

Standard lights (as shown in Figure C–1) are objects based on computer calculations, which imitate lights used in everyday life. The following specifics apply to working with a standard lighting strategy. You can create a standard light from the Command Panel by selecting

Create panel (+)> (Lights)>**Standard**.

Figure C–1

- Standard lighting strategies use standard light objects, such as **Spot**, **Directional**, **Omni**, and **Skylight**. They are highly configurable, but are not based on real-world lighting parameters and require arbitrary adjustments to achieve the required effect.
- Objects illuminated with standard lighting can use any material type.
- Scenes lit by standard lighting almost always require additional ambient (fill) lights, either through a global ambient value or ambient light objects.
- Lighting results are calculated at render time and are not stored on the objects. Processing standard lights does not increase file size and mesh subdivision is not required (as with radiosity).
- Standard lighting does not require exposure control. In standard lighting, ensure exposure control is not toggled on as it might result in differences between the viewport display and the rendering result
- Standard lighting is designed for use with the Scanline renderer.
- All of the standard lights except for directional lights, are considered Point lights, which cast light from a single point rather than along a line or from an area.

Common Parameters

All standard lights share common General Parameters and Intensity/Color/Attenuation settings. These parameters can be set while creating each type of standard light, as shown in Figure C–2. Once the lights have been created, you can access these parameters in the Modify panel () in the Command Panel.

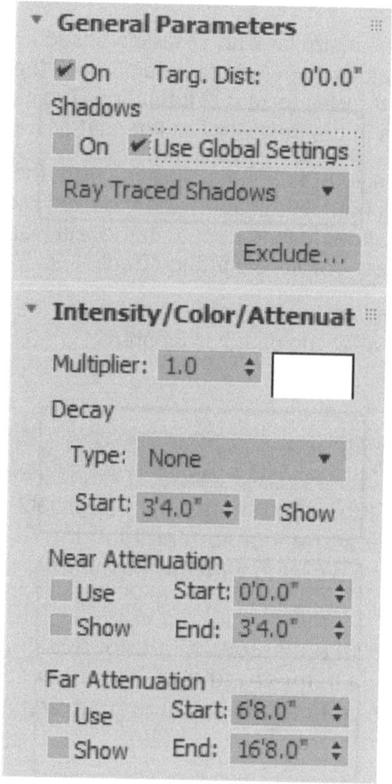

Figure C–2

General Parameters

The *General Parameters* rollout enables you to toggle the light on and off in the scene, select to work with a target, and select shadow settings.

Hint: Target Lights

Several types of lights (and some cameras as well) can have a target object. A light always points directly at its target, enabling you to change the direction of the light by moving the target. Target lights are lights with targets and Free lights are lights without targets.

Intensity/Color/Attenuation Parameters

The *Intensity/Color/Attenuation* rollout provides you with following options:

Multiplier	Controls brightness for standard lights. This is an arbitrary value that needs to be evaluated by trial. Start with a **1.0** value and adjust, as required. Avoid using high Multiplier values, which creates overly bright lighting. The color swatch enables you to select a color to filter the light with.
***Decay* area**	Offers techniques for simulating how light fades over distance.
***Far Attenuation* area**	Provides a similar kind of fading based on explicitly set distances. The *Start* value is where fading begins and the *End* value is the point at which the light fades to zero illumination. Typically you would use either the options in the *Decay* or *Far Attenuation* areas, not both.
***Near Attenuation* area**	Enables you to define a distance from the light where the light starts casting faint illumination and then end with full illumination. Near attenuation does not occur in the real world and is included here as a computer graphics lighting effect
Show (Attenuation option)	Enables a graphical representation of the attenuation distances to remain visible after the object is cleared.

Hint: Global Illumination vs. Standard Lighting

Although longer to generate, Global Illumination (GI) approaches results are often more realistic. Standard lighting is less time consuming than the GI approaches (although there are exceptions), especially when working with simple scenes that contain a small number of objects or surfaces.

GI approaches are very popular in architecture, interior design, and related fields. However, standard lighting still has a place in these industries for conceptual tasks, projects with short timeframes, or projects that do not require extreme photorealism.

C.2 Types of Standard Lights

The type of standard light objects that can be created are **Spot**, **Directional**, **Omni**, and **Skylights**. They can be selected in the *Object Type* rollout, as shown in Figure C–3.

Figure C–3

Omni Lights

Omni lights (shown in Figure C–4) are used to represent point lights that cast light equally in all directions, such as an idealized light bulb. Omni lights are also commonly used for ambient fill lights. A single omni light requires six times the computational effort of a single spotlight, so use spotlights in place of omni lights whenever possible.

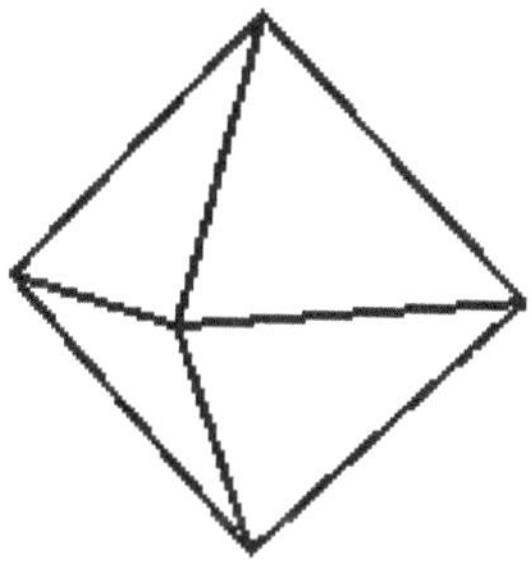

Figure C–4

Spotlights

Spotlights are used to represent point light sources that cast focused beams of light in a cone with a circular or square base. Figure C–5 shows an example of a spotlight with a circular base in 2D, and Figure C–6 shows an example in 3D. Most real world lighting fixtures are more appropriately represented by spotlights rather than omnis or directional lights.

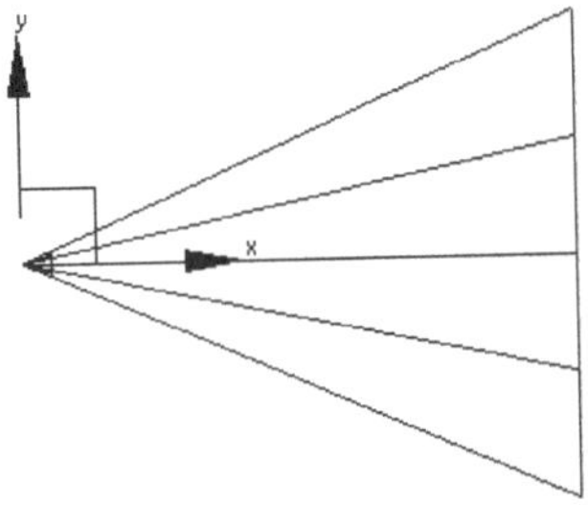

Figure C–5

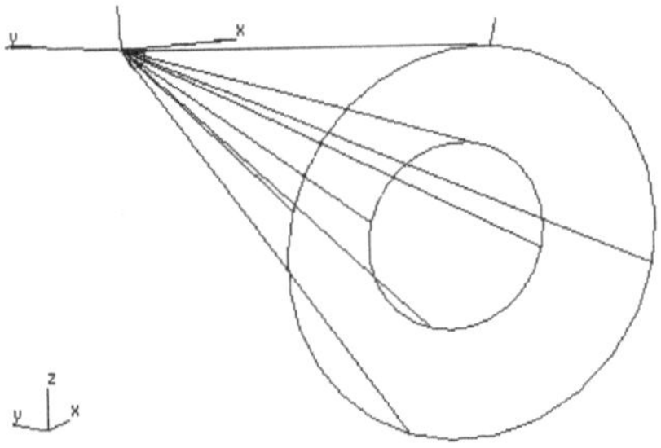

Figure C–6

Two types of spotlight objects are available:

- **Target Spot:** Light objects cast focused beams of light pointing directly at a target.
- **Free Spot:** Light object casts focused beams of light pointing anywhere without a target object.

In addition to the Common Standard Parameters, spotlights have specific parameters (as shown in Figure C–7) to control the distribution of the light they cast.

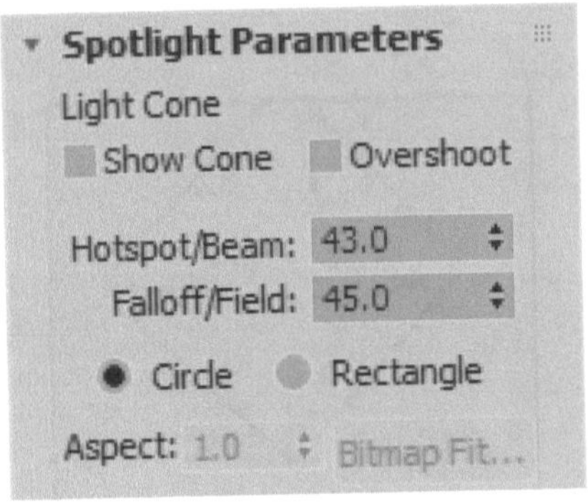

Figure C–7

- The *Hotspot/Beam* value is the angle over which the full lighting intensity is projected. It is represented as the inner cone, as shown in Figure C–6.
- The *Falloff/Field* value is the outer angle that illumination projects. It is represented as the outer cone, as shown in Figure C–6.

- The light fades from full intensity to zero intensity between these two angles. Therefore, when these angles have similar values, the light creates a sharp, defined pool of light. Widely separated angles create a soft, gradual fade.
- The **Overshoot** option enables a spotlight to cast light in all directions (as an omni). However, spotlights only cast shadows within their falloff angle. Overshoot generally looks unnatural and should be used with care.
- The **Aspect** option enables you to define the width and height ratio through a numeric value.
- **Bitmap Fit** enables you to match the rectangular proportions of the lighting area to those of an image bitmap file directly.

Directional Lights

Directional lights are used to represent light sources that cast parallel rays, as shown in Figure C–8. The best example of parallel light would be the light cast from the sun to an Architectural-scale project or smaller. (The sun could be considered an omni light when dealing with massive visualizations at the continental or global scale.)

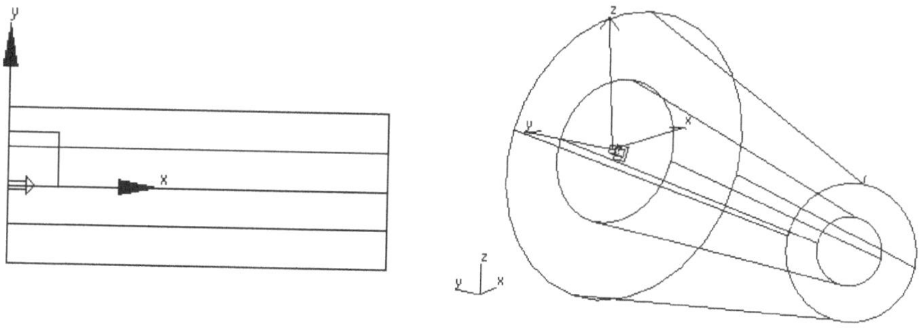

Figure C–8

Two types of directional light objects are available:

- **Target Direct**
- **Free Direct**

In addition to the Common Standard Parameters, directional lights have specific options available through the *Directional Parameters* rollout, as shown in Figure C–9. The *Directional Parameters* options are nearly identical to those in the *Spotlight Parameters* rollout options. The only difference is the *Hotspot/Beam* and *Falloff/Field* values. These are measured in terms of a width parameter rather than an angle.

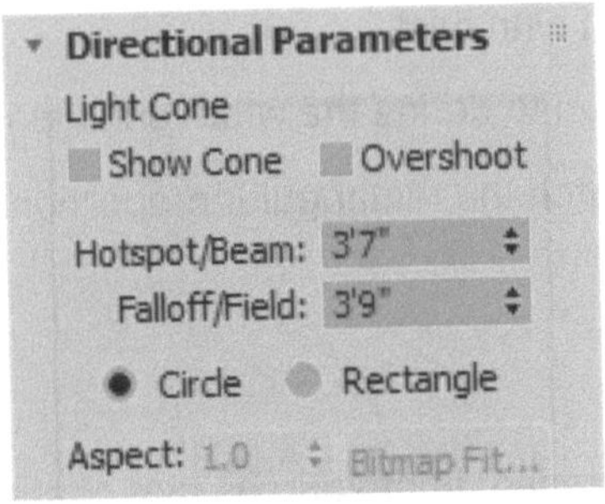

Figure C–9

Fill Lights

Any light can be used to approximate indirect lighting, which is referred to as a fill light. Fill lights can act as normal lights or they can be specifically set to cast ambient light, by selecting the **Ambient Only** option in the *Advanced Effects* rollout in the **Standard lights** parameters, as shown in Figure C–10.

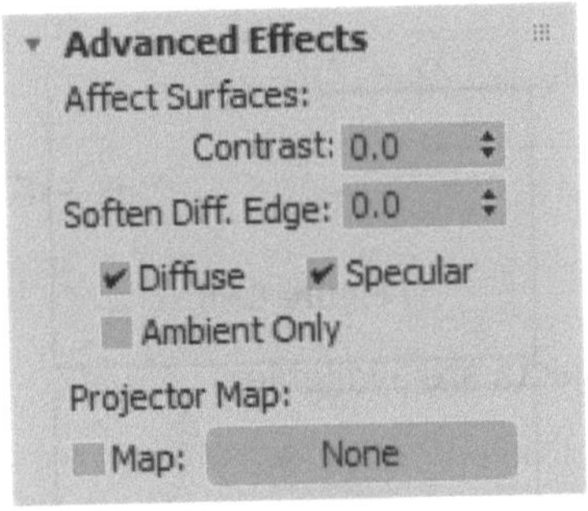

Figure C–10

- Standard materials have an **Ambient color** parameter that can be used when illuminated using ambient lights. This color can be different from the diffuse color produced by normal (non-ambient) lights. The Ambient color is normally locked to the diffuse or it can be set darker than the diffuse color for emphasis.
- Setting a fill light to cast ambient light automatically disables shadow casting because only real-world light sources (the sun and lighting fixtures) are normally permitted to cast shadows.

- If you want your fill lights to cast normal light (which illuminates a material's diffuse color instead of ambient), do not select the **Ambient Only** option, but rather manually disable shadow casting.
- Architectural materials were designed for radiosity and do not have an **Ambient color** parameter. Otherwise, they function similar to Standard materials with standard lighting.

Skylight

The Standard light category also includes a Skylight object, which is used to provide scattered atmospheric light in addition to the direct sunlight.

Hint: Standard Lights Considerations

Standard lights can also be used instead of photometric light objects, but since they are not physically-based, the results achieved are not accurate. For better accuracy, it is not recommended to mix standard and photometric lights in the same scene. The following should be considered:

- The luminous intensity of standard lights is equal to the light's multiplier parameter times the Physical Scale value in Logarithmic Exposure Control. (The default *Physical Scale* value is **1500** candelas in the *Logarithmic Exposure Control Parameters* rollout in the *Environments and Effects* dialog box.) You can make drastic changes to the *Physical Scale* value to compensate for scale problems in lighting a scene. Change this value to **80,000** or **150,000** to brighten a scene.
- To limit the effects of exposure control (i.e., not have the exposure control affect the direct lighting) use the **Affect Indirect Only** option.

Practice C1
Standard Lighting for an Interior Scene

Practice Objectives

- Create standard lights and adjust their parameters.
- Create ambient fill lighting to brighten the dark areas.

In this practice, you will work with Standard lighting to be used with the Scanline renderer. You will model interior lighting conditions by creating a spot light and array it to position it at various locations around the room. You will adjust the parameters to make the scene realistic and add ambient lighting to brighten areas that are not directly illuminated by your standard light objects.

You must set the paths to locate the External files and XREFs used in the practice. If you have not done this already, return to Chapter 1 and complete Task 1 to Task 3 in *Practice 1a: Organize Folders and Work with the Interface*. You only have to set the user paths once.

Task 1: Create, array, and instance light objects.

1. Open **Standard Lighting – Interior.max**.
2. You will add lights in the **Top** viewport such that they point toward the floor. Maximize the **Top** viewport, by selecting it from the overlay (hold <Win> and press <Shift>).
3. Zoom in to the foyer area (leftmost area). Click the *Per-View Preference* label and select **Wireframe Override**.
4. In the Create panel (+), click (Lights). In the drop-down list, select **Standard** and in the *Object Type* rollout, click **Free Spot**, as shown in Figure C–11.

Figure C–11

5. Note the small yellow circles that represent the openings for recessed lighting. Click near the approximate center of the upper left yellow circle. A free spotlight is added at that location, as shown in Figure C–12. You will position it accurately in the next step.

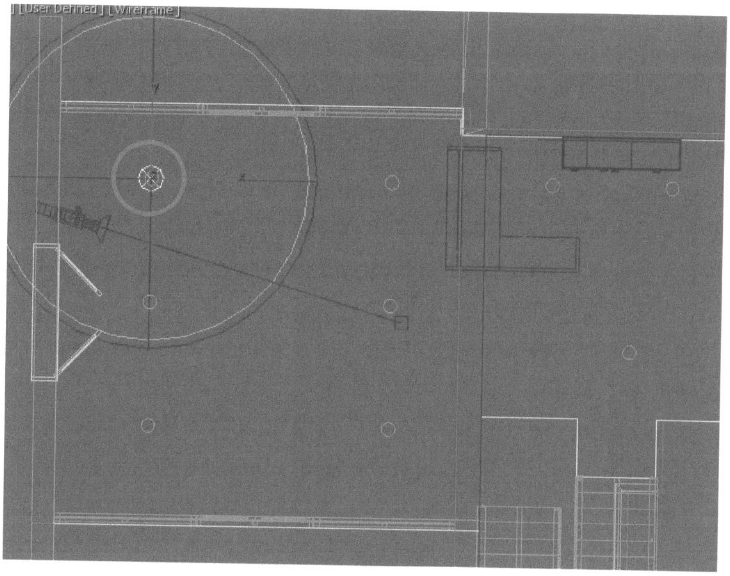

Figure C–12

6. With the light object still selected, click  (Select and Move).

7. In the Status Bar, set the  (Absolute Mode Transform Type-In). Set the following, as shown in Figure C–13, and press <Enter>:

   - *X:* **84'7"**
   - *Y:* **126'10"**
   - *Z:* **9'11"**

Figure C–13

In addition to placing the light at the exact center of the recessed fixture, it places the light at a height of 9'11", which is 1" below the ceiling height.

8. With the light object selected, in the Command Panel, select the Modify panel () and name the light **Ceiling Downlight 00**.

9. There are six lights in the foyer area. They are 12' apart along the world X-direction and 6' apart along the world Y-direction. The exact coordinates were determined using the **Measure** tool in the **Utilities** Command Panel. You will use the **Array** command to locate these light objects at the center of the circles representing the recessed fixtures. With the light selected, click **Tools>Array** in the menu bar.
   - The **Array** command is also available in the Extras toolbar, which is hidden by default. Use the right-click Interface Item menu to display the Extras toolbar.
10. In the Array dialog box, click **Preview** to enable the previewed display in the scene and enter the following values, as shown in Figure C–14:
   - For the first dimension of the array, in the *Array Transformation* area, set the *X Incremental* value to **12'0"**.
   - In the *Array Dimensions* area, set *1D Count* to **2** to create two columns of lights.
   - Select **2D**, set *2D Count* to **3,** and in the *Incremental Row Offset, set Y* to **-6'0"** to create three rows of lights.
   - In *Type of Object* area, verify that **Instance** is selected so that the parameters of all of the lights can be adjusted at the same time.
   - Note that *Total in Array* is automatically set to **6** (two lights in each of the three rows).
   - Also note that the six lights display in the viewport because **Preview** is selected.

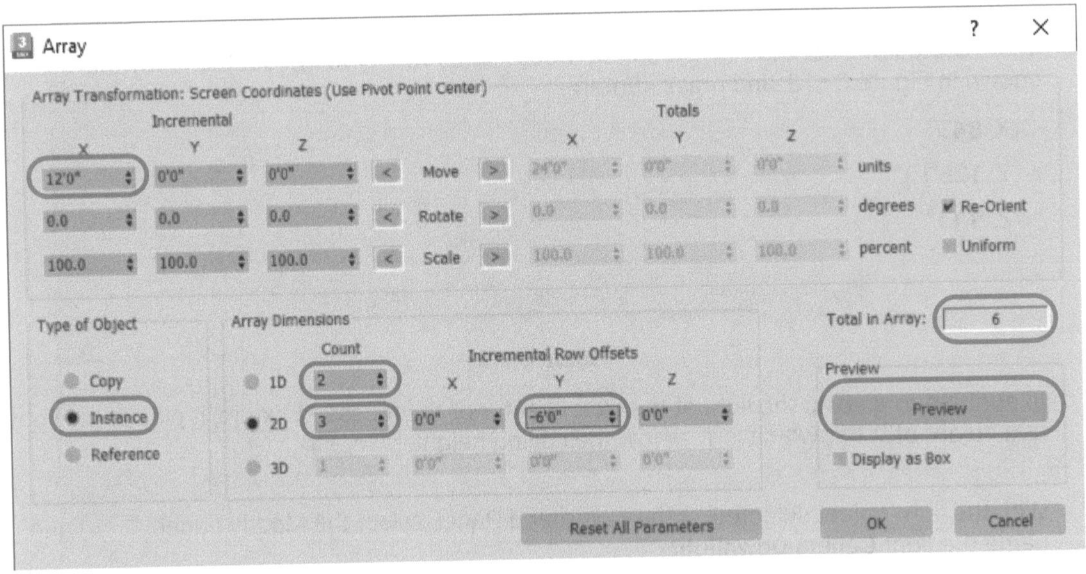

Figure C–14

11. Verify that the lights preview in the correct positions (as shown in Figure C–15) and click **OK** in the dialog box.

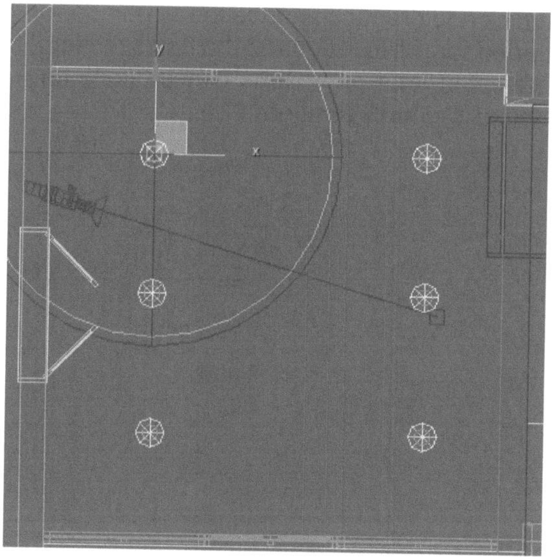

Figure C–15

12. In the Scene Explorer, click (Display None) and (Display Lights). Note that the software has automatically incremented the name by 1.

13. Select **Ceiling Downlight 001** and note that in the viewport, the light in the upper right corner in foyer is selected. Using (Select and Move) and holding <Shift>, drag along the Transform gizmo's X-axis to locate the light over the desk area, in the approximate center of the yellow circle provided, as shown in Figure C–16. In the Clone Options dialog box, select **Instance** and click **OK**.

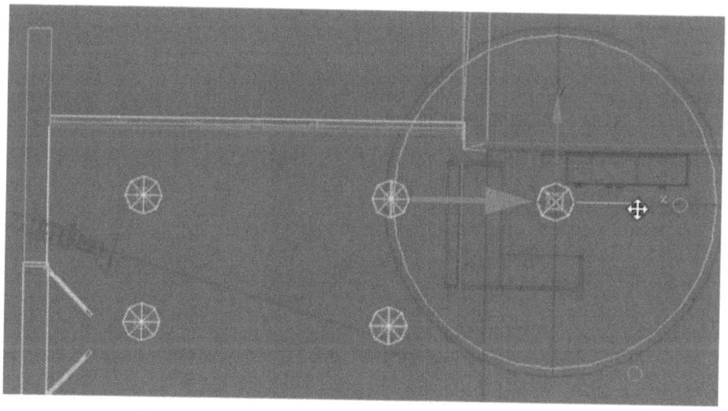

Figure C–16

14. With the light still selected, in the Status Bar, set the *X* value to **104'7"** and ensure that the *Y* value is set to **126'10"** and the *Z* value is set to **9'11"**, as shown in Figure C–17.

Figure C–17

15. Continue to <Shift> + click and drag to instance the remainder of the Ceiling Downlights, to the yellow circles provided for the locations of the recessed lighting, as shown in Figure C–18. In the interest of time, approximate their positions. You should have 14 lights with the last one named as **Ceiling Downlight 013**.

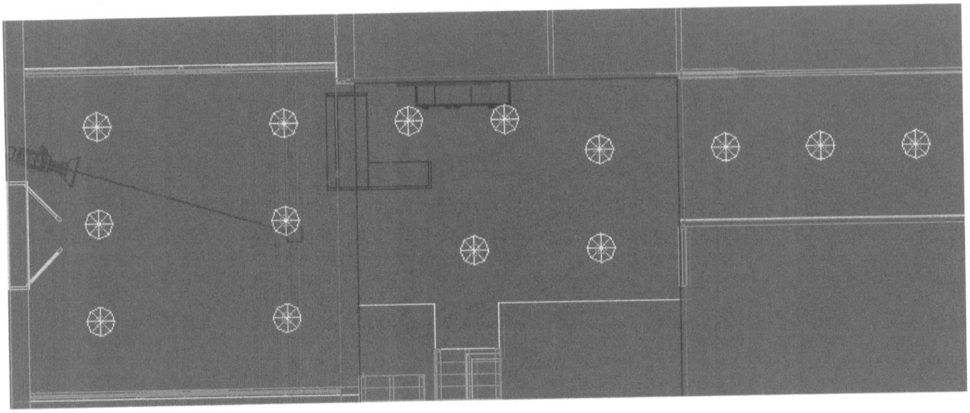

Figure C–18

Task 2: Adjust standard light parameters.

In Task 1, you made instances of each of the lights so that their parameters can be adjusted together. You will now adjust lighting levels through light object parameters, avoiding exposure control.

1. Select **Rendering>Exposure Control**. In the Environment and Effects dialog box, in the *Exposure Control* rollout, clear **Active**, as shown in Figure C–19. Close the Environments and Effects dialog box.

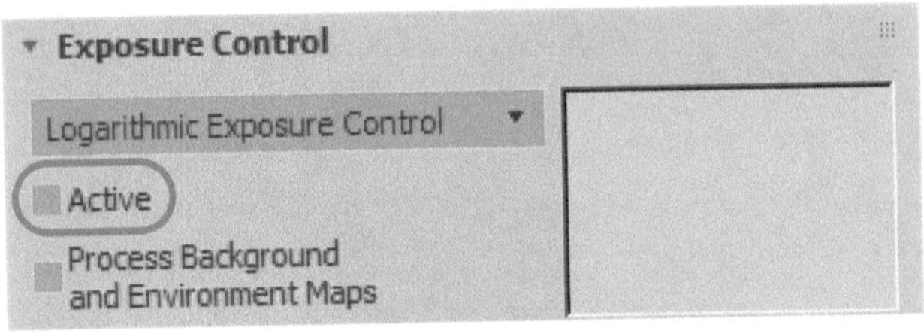

Figure C–19

2. Select any of the instanced lights. In the Command Panel, verify that the Modify panel () is open and that the **Ceiling Downlight** (any number) name displays (i.e., selected). In the *Spotlight Parameters* rollout, set *Hotspot/Beam* to **45**, press <Enter> and verify that **Circle** is selected. Verify that the *Falloff/Field* automatically changes to **47.0**, as shown in Figure C–20.

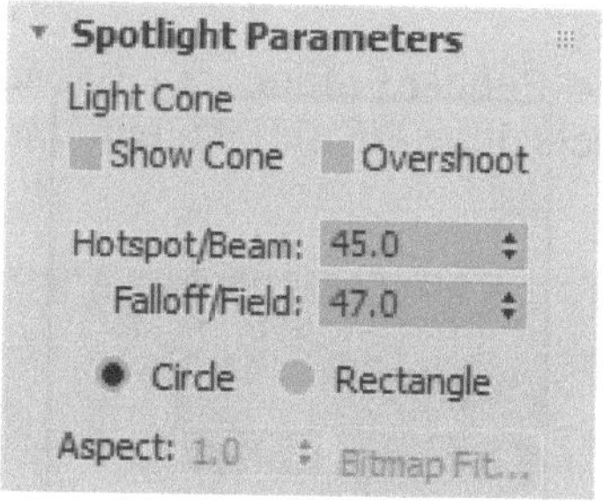

Figure C–20

3. Change to the **Camera - Lobby1** view by clicking the **[Top]** *Point of View* label and selecting **Cameras>Camera - Lobby1**. Additionally, change the *Per-View Preference* label to **Default Shading.**
4. In the Main Toolbar, click (Render Setup). Verify that the *Renderer* is set to **Scanline Renderer**. Open the *Raytracer* tab, and in the *Global Raytrace Engine Options* area, clear the **Enable Raytracing** option, as shown in Figure C–21. Close the dialog box.

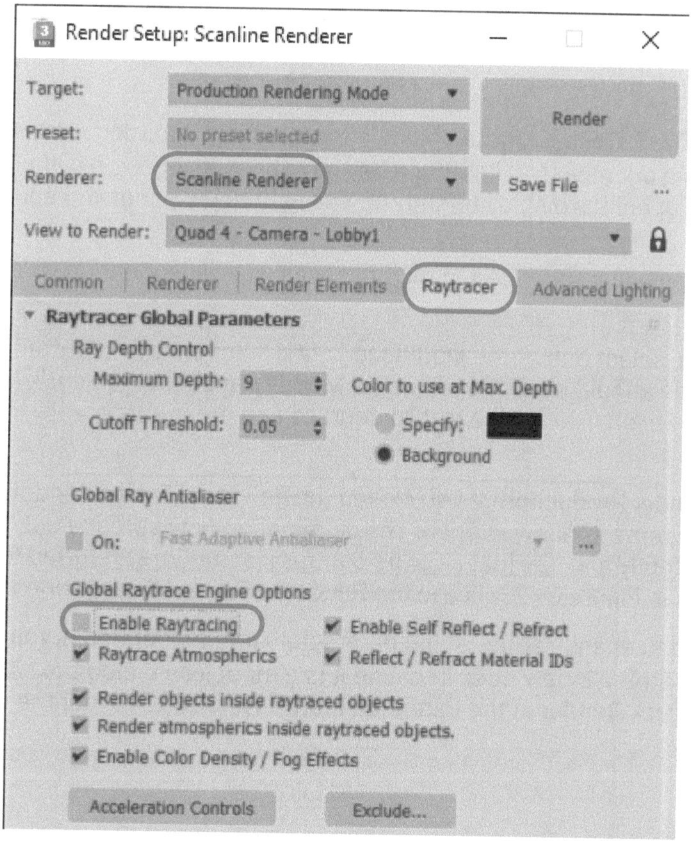

Figure C–21

5. In the Main Toolbar, click  (Render Production). Based on the current hotspot and falloff values of the light objects, they are only illuminating small pools of light on the floor, as shown in Figure C–22.

Figure C–22

- The **Layer:VIZ-1-Ceiling Lights** object is formed from extruded circles representing the openings for your recessed lighting. They have been assigned a self-illuminated material to make the openings display brightly lit. The light objects that you added to the scene do not render.
- The brightness of your rendering might vary as it is dependent on your computer settings.

6. In the viewport, select one of the instanced lights, if not already selected (Any Ceiling Downlight name should be displayed in the Modify panel). In the *Spotlight Parameters* rollout, set the *Falloff/Field* value to **170** degrees and press <Enter>.

7. Click  (Render Production) if you closed the Rendered Frame Window or click **Render** if the Rendered Frame Window is open. The illumination now spreads out, but the floor is being lit too brightly and has lost all of its contrast (sometimes referred to as being washed out), as shown in Figure C–23. Leave the Rendered Frame Window open.
    - As you need to change some of the parameters and render again, you can leave the Rendered Frame Window open because it is a modeless dialog box. After changing a parameter, click **Render** in the Rendered Frame Window to render the viewport again.

Figure C–23

8. In the *Intensity/Color/Attenuation* rollout, in *Far Attenuation* area, select **Use**. Set the following, as shown in Figure C–24:
   - *Start*: **0'0"**
   - *End*: **16'0"**

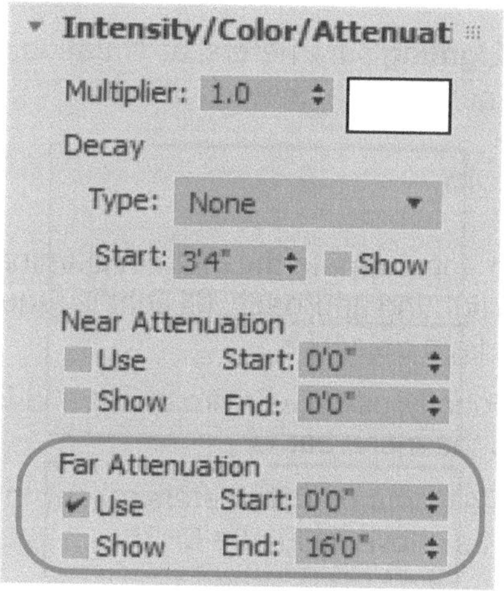

Figure C–24

9. Click **Render**. The washed out effect is removed but the overall render looks dark, as shown in Figure C–25.

Figure C–25

10. Adjust the overall brightness of the lights using the Multiplier. In the *Intensity/Color/Attenuation* rollout, set *Multiplier* to **2.0**. In the *General Parameters* rollout, in the *Shadows* area, click **On**, if required. Click **Render** in the Rendered Frame Window. The surfaces under direct illumination should now become brighter.
    - As with most **Standard Lighting** parameters, attenuation settings are arbitrary and require trial and error to achieve the best result.

Task 3: Add ambient fill light.

Next use ambient fill lighting to approximate the indirect illumination that would be present in the real world. With a standard lighting approach, fill light is required to brighten areas that are not directly illuminated by your light objects.

1. To add the ambient light globally, use the Environment and Effects dialog box by selecting **Rendering>Environment** in the menu bar.
2. In the *Environment* tab, in the *Common Parameters* rollout, in the *Global Lighting* area, select the **Ambient** color swatch, as shown in Figure C–26.

Figure C–26

3. In the Scene Color Selector dialog box, change the *Scene Value* to **25**, as shown in Figure C–27, and press <Enter>. Leave both the Environment and Effects dialog box and Scene Color Selector dialog box open.

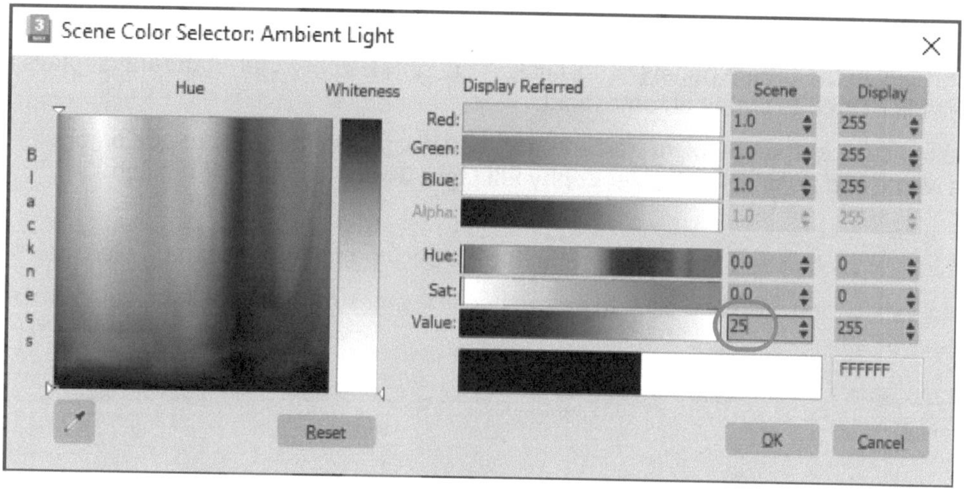

Figure C–27

4. In the Rendered Frame Window, click **Render** to render the scene. In this rendering, many areas have become lighter. In the Scene Color Selector dialog box, change the *Scene Value* to **50** and render again. The ceiling is brighter but objects under direct illumination have lost some contrast, as shown in Figure C–28. The front of the half-wall behind the stairs looks flat because the ambient lighting is so uniform. (This is a pitfall of adding too much global ambient light.)

Figure C–28

5. This scene might respond better with manually configured ambient light rather than the global settings. In the Scene Color Selector dialog box, set the ambient color *Value* to **0** and press <Enter>. Close both the dialog boxes.
6. In the viewport, change to the **Top** viewport by pressing <T> and zoom out to see the floorplan. In the Create panel (+), click (Lights). Verify that **Standard** displays and then click **Omni** to create an omni light.
7. Click once near the approximate center of the six lights in the foyer to add an omni light. In the *Name and Color* rollout, enter **Lobby Fill Light 00** as the name of the light.
8. Click (Select and Move) and in the Status Bar, change its absolute Z-elevation to **2'0"**.
9. Hold <Shift> and drag and click to create two instances of the omni light, as shown in Figure C–29.

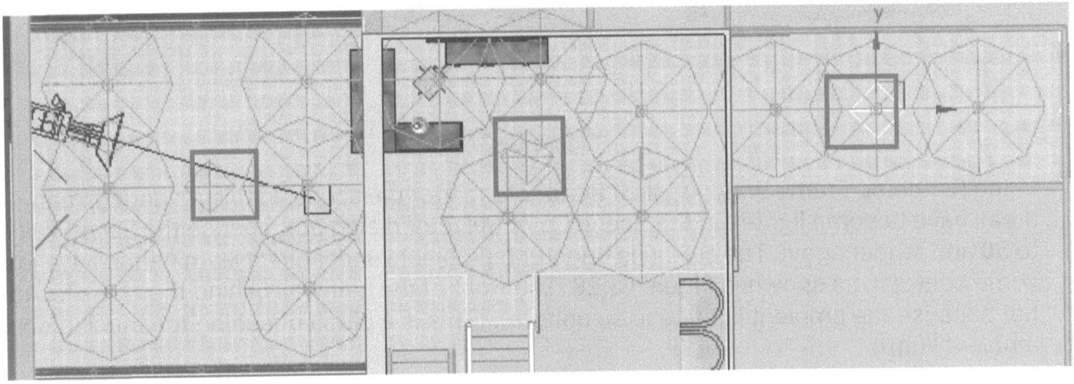

Figure C–29

10. With one of the omni lights selected, in the Modify panel ( ), in the *Advanced Effects* rollout, select **Ambient Only**, as shown in Figure C–30. This setting causes the light to illuminate the ambient color of Standard materials and not to cast shadows.

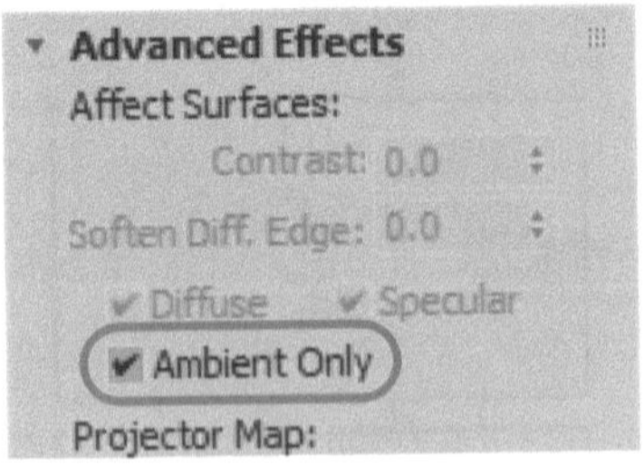

Figure C–30

11. Change to **Camera – Lobby1** viewport and render the scene. Note that everything is washed out. Ambient lights can wash out a scene with their default settings. Leave the Rendered Frame Window open.

12. With any of the omni light still selected, in the *Intensity/Color/Attenuation* rollout, set *Multiplier* as **0.75** and in the *Far Attenuation* area, select **Use**. Additionally, set the following, as shown in Figure C–31:

- *Start:* **0'0"**
- *End*: **16'0"**

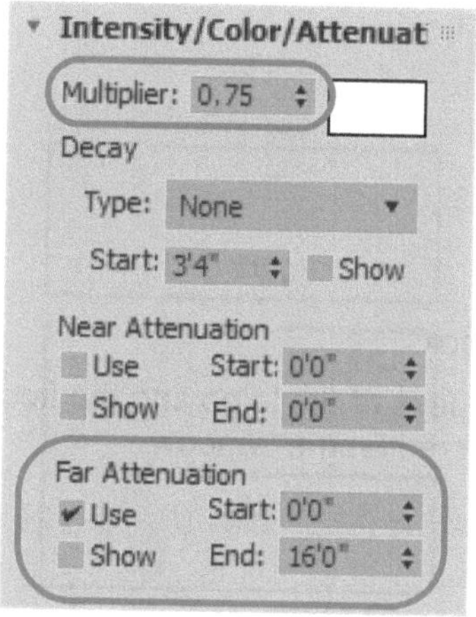

Figure C–31

13. Render the scene. The ambient lighting does not look flat, but the floor and desk lamp are illuminated too brightly, as shown in Figure C–32.

Figure C–32

Note: *Your rendering might not be exactly the same because of your monitor display.*

14. To resolve the brightness issue, you can exclude these objects from the ambient light. With one of the omni lights (Lobby Fill Light) still selected, in the Modify panel (), in the *General Parameters* rollout, click **Exclude**. The Exclude/Include dialog box opens.
15. Verify that **Exclude** is selected. In the list on the left, select **1-Desk Lamp** and **Layer:VIZ-1-Floor-Tile**. Click **>>** to add them to the Exclude list on the right, as shown in Figure C–33.

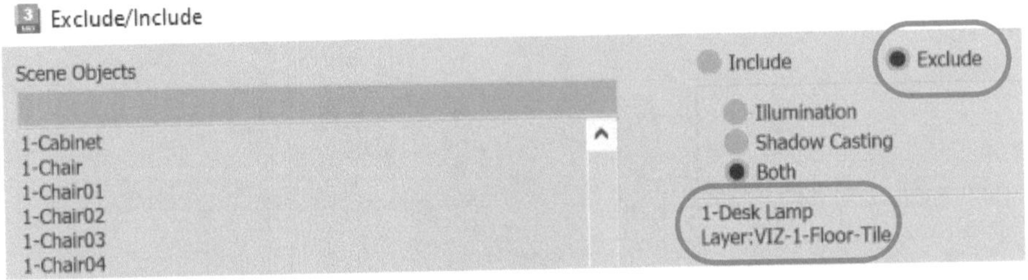

Figure C–33

16. Click **OK** to close the dialog box.
17. Render the scene. The brightness of the lamp and the floor is removed, as shown in Figure C–34. Close the Rendered Frame Window.

Figure C–34

18. Save your work as **MyStandard Lighting – Interior.max**.

End of practice

Practice C2
Work with Shadow Parameters

Practice Objective

- Understand the different types of shadow-casting methods.

In this practice, you will adjust parameters to refine the shadows in a scene.

You must set the paths to locate the External files and XREFs used in the practice. If you have not done this already, return to Chapter 1 and complete Task 1 to Task 3 in *Practice 1a: Organize Folders and Work with the Interface*. You only have to set the user paths once.

1. Open **Shadow Parameters.max**.

2. In the Scene Explorer ((Display None) and (Display Lights)), select one of the Ceiling Downlight objects, such as **Ceiling Downlight 06.**

3. In the Command Panel, select the Modify panel ( ), and examine its parameters. These lights use the default Advanced Ray Traced shadow type (**Adv. Ray Traced** in *General Parameters* rollout), as shown in Figure C–35.

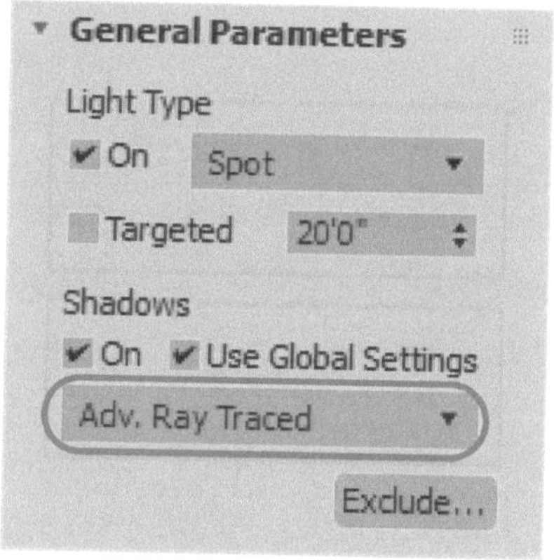

Figure C–35

4. In the Main Toolbar, click (Render Production) to render the scene. In the Rendered Frame Window, zoom and pan to the desk area, as shown in Figure C–36. The edges of the shadow under the desk display jagged. Leave the Rendered Frame Window open.

Figure C–36

5. In the Modify panel ( ), expand the *Adv. Ray Traced Params* rollout and in the *Basic Options* area, select **2-Pass Antialias** in the drop-down list. In the *Antialiasing Options* area, set the following, as shown in Figure C–37:
   - *Shadow Integrity*: **2**
   - *Shadow Quality*: **3**

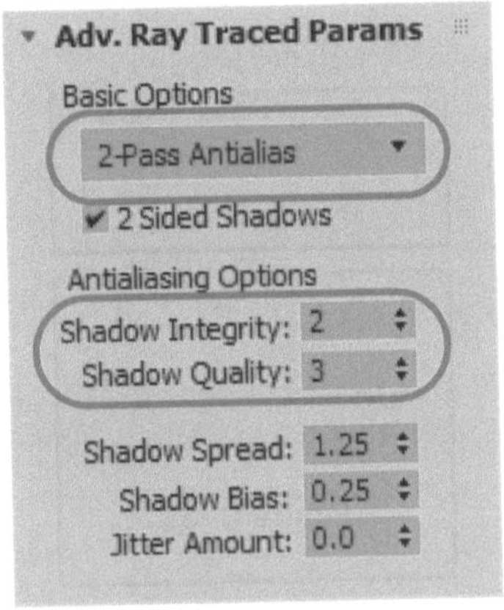

Figure C–37

6. In the Rendered Frame Window, click **Render**. The shadow edges display much less jagged than before, but note that the rendering time has increased.

7. When soft shadows are required or speed is critical, **Shadow maps** make a good alternative. In the *General Parameters* rollout, in the *Shadows* area, change the type from *Adv. Ray Traced* to **Shadow Map** by selecting it in the drop-down list, as shown on the left in Figure C–38.

8. Render the scene. These shadows are fuzzier and less intense (as shown on the right in Figure C–38) but faster to render.

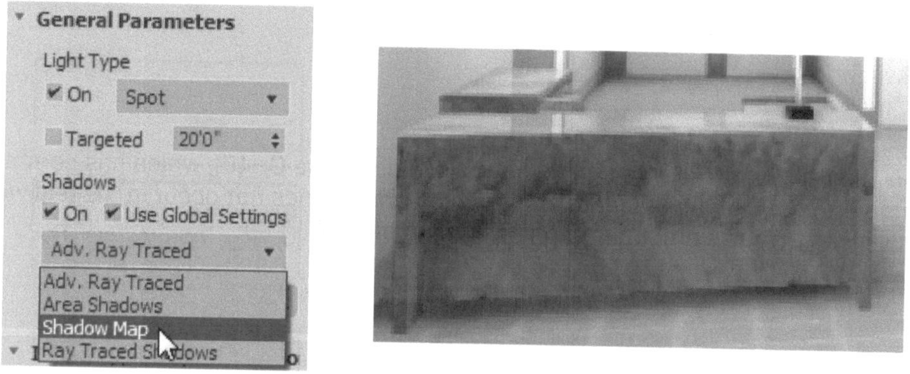

Figure C–38

9. To make the shadow-mapped shadows better defined, increase the map size. In the *Shadow Map Params* rollout, double the *Size* from 512 to **1024**, as shown in Figure C–39.

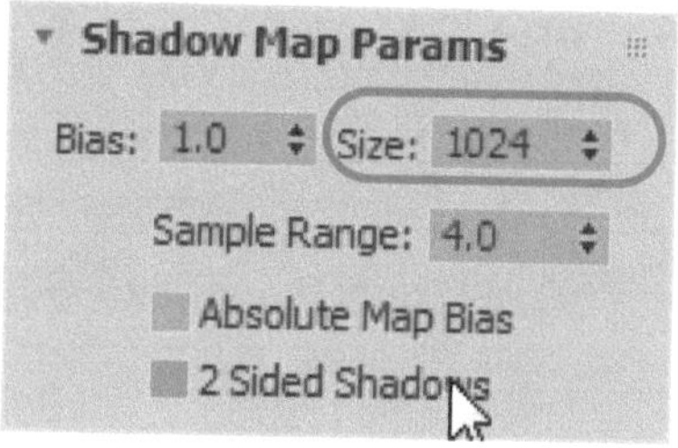

Figure C–39

10. Render the scene. The shadows are now slightly better defined under the desk.

11. Adjust the Shadow map by setting the following:

    - *Size*: **2048**
    - *Bias:* **0.01**

12. Render the scene again. Note that the shadows have become more significant and less jagged under the desk.

13. Save your work as **MyShadow Parameters.max**.

End of practice

Chapter Review Questions

1. Which type of standard lights are used to represent light sources that cast parallel rays?
   a. Omni lights
   b. Spotlights
   c. Directional lights
   d. Skylight

2. In the *Intensity/Color/Attenuation* rollout (shown in Figure C–40), which has common parameters for all of the standard lights, which option does not occur in the real world and is only included as a computer graphics lighting effect?

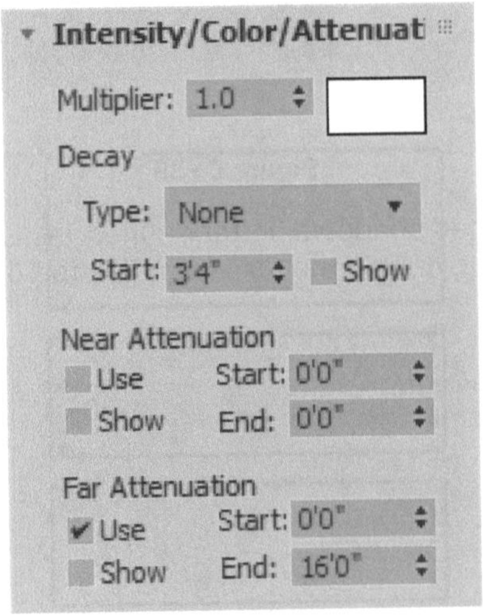

Figure C–40

   a. Multiplier
   b. Decay options
   c. Near Attenuation options
   d. Far Attenuation options

3. In the *Spotlight parameters* rollout (shown in Figure C–41), which option enables a spotlight to cast light in all directions and behave like an omni light? (Hint: Setting this option generally looks unnatural and it should be used with care.)

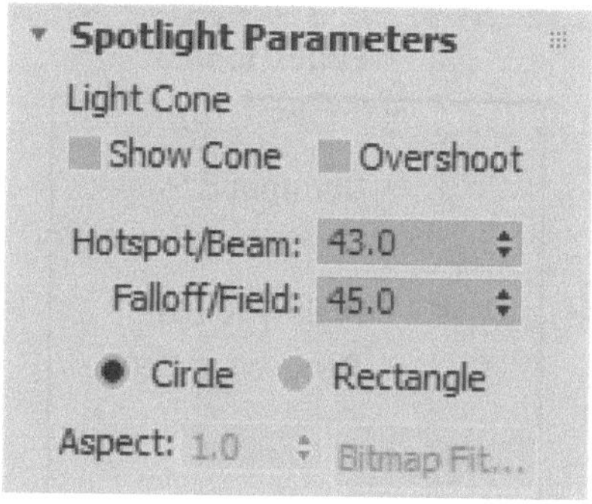

Figure C–41

a. Show Cone
b. Overshoot
c. Hotspot/Beam
d. Falloff/Field

Command Summary

Button	Command	Location
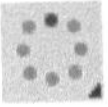	**Array**	• **Extras toolbar** • **Tools:** Array
	**Lights**	• **Command Panel:** *Create* panel • **Create:** Lights
	**Render Production**	• **Main Toolbar** • ***Rendering:*** Render

Index

G

H

I

L

M

Made in United States
Troutdale, OR
10/23/2026

56355284R00412